Understanding FoxPro™ 2.5 for Windows™

Understanding FoxPro™ 2.5 for Windows™

George T. Chou

RANDOM HOUSE
ELECTRONIC PUBLISHING

New York

Understanding FoxPro™ 2.5 for Windows™

Copyright © 1993 by George T. Chou

All rights reserved. No part of the contents of this book may be reproduced in any form or by any means without the written permission of the publisher.

Published in the United States by Random House, Inc., New York, and simultaneously in Canada by Random House of Canada, Limited.

Manufactured in the United States of America

First Edition

0 9 8 7 6 5 4 3 2 1

ISBN 0-679-79160-4

The author and publisher have used their best efforts in preparing this book, and the programs contained herein. However, the author and publisher make no warranties of any kind, express or implied, with regard to the documentation or programs contained in this book, and specifically disclaim without limitation, any implied warranties of merchantability and fitness for a particular purpose with respect to program listings in the book and/or the techniques described in the book. In no event shall the author or publisher be responsible or liable for any loss of profit or any other commerical damages, including but not limited to special, incidental, consequential or any other damages in connection with or arising out of furnishing, performance, or use of this book or the programs.

Trademarks
A number of entered words in which we have reason to believe trademark, service mark, or other proprietary rights may exist have been designated as such by use of initial capitalization. However, no attempt has been made to designate as trademarks or service marks all personal computer words or terms in which proprietary rights might exist. The inclusion, exclusion or definition of a word or term is not intended to affect, or to express any judgment on, the validity or legal status of any proprietary right which may be claimed in that word or term.

New York   Toronto   London   Sydney   Auckland

*Dedicated to my wife, Jane-Wen,
and our children, Doris, Tina, and Tom*

Contents

Preface xix

1 Introduction to Databases 1

An Overview 1
What Is a Data Element? 2
What Is a Database? 2
What Is a Database Management System? 3
Information vs. Data 3
Organizing Data 4
    Data Relations 4
        One-to-One Relations 5   *One-to-Many Relations* 5   *Many-to-Many Relations* 6
Data Models 7
    Hierarchical Data Model 7
    Network Data Model 9
    Relational Data Model 10
        Data Tables 10
Designing a Relational Database 14
    Properties of a Relational Database 15
        Organizing Data in Tables 15   *No Duplicate Rows* 16   *Using Single-Value Data Cells* 16

viii   Contents

    Other Desirable Characteristics   18

        Making Data Structures Flexible 19   *Avoiding Redundant Data* 20
        Indexing Data Logically 20   *Keeping Data Tables Simple* 21

    Relating Data   21

        Handling One-to-One Relations 22   *Handling One-to-Many Relations* 22   *Handling Many-to-Many Relations* 25

Chapter Summary   28

2   An Overview of FoxPro for Windows   29

An Overview   29

What Is FoxPro for Windows?   29

The FoxPro User Interface   30

    The Menu System: Menu Bar And Menu Pads   30
    Dialogs   32

        Dialog Popups 32   *List Boxes* 33   *Push Buttons* 33   *Check Boxes* 33
        Radio Buttons 34   *Nested Dialogs* 34   *Warning Dialogs* 35

    Alerts   36
    Windows   36

        Components of a FoxPro Window 36   *The View Window* 37   *Browse Windows* 38   *The Memo Window* 40   *The RQBE Window* 41   *The Screen Design Window* 41   *The Report Layout Window* 42   *The Label Layout Window* 42   *The Menu Design Window* 43   *Project Windows* 43   *The Command Window* 44   *Text Editing Windows* 44   *Help Windows* 45

The Major Components of FoxPro   46

    The File System   47
    The RQBE Builder   47
    The Screen Builder   49
    The Report Writer   52
    The Label Designer   54
    The Menu Builder   55
    The Project Builder   56
    The Desk Accessories   57

        The Filer 57   *The Calculator* 59   *The Calendar/Diary* 59

    FoxPro Files   60

System Capacities   62

Chapter Summary   62

3 Getting Started 65

An Overview   65

Installing FoxPro for Windows   65

Getting Ready   70
   Creating the Data Directory   70
   File Organization   71
   Installing the Mouse   71

Starting FoxPro for Windows   71
   Mouse Basics   71
      Pointing 71   *Clicking* 72   *Dragging* 73   *Double Clicking* 74
   Keyboard Basics   74
      Function Keys 75   *The Esc Key* 75   *The Enter Key* 76   *Cursor Keys* 76
      The Tab Key 76   *The Ctrl Key* 77   *The Alt Key* 77   *The Shift Key* 77
   Working with Windows   77
      Opening Windows 78   *Moving Windows* 80   *Sizing Windows* 81
      Maximizing Windows 82   *Minimizing Windows* 84   *Arranging Window Icons* 84   *Activating Windows* 85   *Closing Windows* 86
   Setting Screen Colors   87
   Setting Up Printers   90

Setting Default Data Directory   92

Getting Help   93

Exiting FoxPro   94

Chapter Summary   95

4 Creating Databases 97

An Overview   97

Defining the Data Structure   97
   Identifying Data Fields   98
   Defining Data Field Attributes   98
      Naming a Data Field 99   *Specifying Field Type* 100

Creating a Data Table   102
   Creating a New Database File   103
   Specifying Field Attributes   103
   Saving a Data Structure   108
   Entering Data Values   110
      Entering Data in Change Mode 112   *Entering Data in Browse Mode* 113
   Saving Data Records   114

Using FoxPro Commands 114
Chapter Summary 117

5 Displaying Data 119

An Overview 119
Displaying File Directories 119
   Using the Filer 120
      Using FoxPro Commands 121
Viewing Database Files 123
   Invoking the View Window 123
      The Setup Button 124   *The Browse Button* 124   *The Open Button* 125
      The Close Button 125   *The View Panel* 126   *The Set Options On/Off Panel* 126   *The File Selection Push Button* 126   *The Set Miscellaneous Values Panel* 128
   Opening Database Files 128
   Closing Database Files 131
   Displaying Database Structures 131
   Viewing Data Records 131
      Using Change Mode 132   *Switching to Browse Mode* 132   *Using Browse Mode* 133   *Viewing Memo Fields* 142
   Viewing Data Records in Multiple Database Files 143
      Switching between Browse Windows 144   *Setting Type Font* 146
   Viewing Selective Fields 148
      Picking Data Fields 149   *Resetting Data Fields* 151
   Viewing Selective Records 152
      Using Filter Conditions 153
   Printing Data 159
Using FoxPro Commands 159
   Opening a Database File 159
   Closing Database Files 160
   Listing Data Records 160
      Listing Selected Fields 161   *Listing Selected Records* 163
   Listing Memo Fields 163
   Displaying The Data Structure 165
      Using the Display Command 165
   Setting Filter Conditions 167
   Directing Displayed Data to Printers 168

Contents xi

Browsing Data 169
    Browsing Selected Data Fields 170 *Browsing Selected Records* 170
Defining Custom Windows 171
    Browsing Data in a Custom Window 172 *Browsing Memo Fields in a Custom Window* 172 *Browsing Multiple Database Files* 174 *Abbreviating Command Keywords* 175

Chapter Summary 176

6 Sorting and Indexing Data 177

An Overview 177
Ordering Data Records 177
  Sorting vs. Indexing 178
  Sorting Data Records 180
    Defining Sort Order 182 *Saving Selected Data Fields* 191 *Defining Filter Conditions to Save Selected Records* 191
  Sorting with FoxPro Commands 194
    Specifying Sort Order 195 *Sorting Multiple Fields* 196 *Saving Selected Data Fields and Records* 196
  Indexing Data 198
    Index Keys 199 *FoxPro Index Files* 199 *Creating a Structural Compound Index File* 201 *Creating Standard Index Files* 218 *Creating Nonstructural Compound Index Files* 223 *Deleting Index Files* 223
  Indexing with FoxPro Commands 225
    Creating Structural Compound Index Files 225 *Adding Index Tags* 228 *Designating the Master Index* 228 *Removing an Index Tag* 229 *Modifying Index Tags* 229 *Creating Standard Index Files* 229 *Creating Nonstructural Compound Index Files* 230 *Deleting Index Files* 231

Chapter Summary 232

7 Editing Data 233

An Overview 233
Copying Database Files 233
  Using the System's Filer 234
    Copying Associated Files 236 *Copying Multiple Files* 237
  Using the Copy To Menu Option 239
    Copying Selected Data Fields and Records 241
Renaming Database Files 244

Deleting Database Files 245

Modifying the Database Structure 246

    Adding New Data Fields 247

    Rearranging Existing Data Fields 251

    Deleting Existing Data Fields 251

    Redefining Existing Data Fields 252

        Renaming Data Fields 252 *Resetting Field Widths* 253 *Changing Field Types* 253

    Saving Modified Data Structures 254

    Viewing Records in Modified Data Structures 255

    Canceling Structural Changes 257

    Rebuilding Indexes 258

Modifying Data Records 259

    Editing Record Contents 259

        Editing Records in Change Mode 259 *Editing Records in Browse Mode* 260 *Editing Selected Data Fields* 261 *Editing Selected Data Records* 262 *Saving Edited Data Records* 264

    Adding New Data Records 264

    Deleting Existing Data Records 268

        Marking Data Records for Deletion 268 *Marking a Group of Records for Deletion* 269 *Recalling Marked Data Records* 271 *Removing Marked Records* 274

    Replacing Data for Multiple Records 275

    Identifying and Removing Duplicated Records 277

Splitting Database Files 282

Using FoxPro Commands 284

    Copying Database Files 284

    Renaming Database Files 286

    Modifying Data Structures 286

    Editing Data Records 286

    Adding New Data Records 289

    Deleting Data Records 290

    Deleting Database Files 291

    Borrowing Existing Data Structures 291

Chapter Summary 292

Contents   xiii

8 Linking Databases   293

An Overview   293

Relating Database Files   294

   Handling One-to-One Relations   294

      Viewing Related Data Records 299   *Saving Relations to View Files* 301
Using Existing View Files 303

   Handling One-to-Many Relations   304

   Handling Many-to-One Relations   309

   Handling Many-to-Many Relations   311

Chapter Summary   319

9 Querying Data   321

An Overview   321

Locating Data Records   321

   Using the Locate Operation   322

      Defining Search Conditions 323   *Searching for Character Strings* 324
Searching for Numeric Values 328   *Searching for Dates* 328   *Searching for Logical Values* 330   *Using Logical Connectors* 331   *Using LOCATE Commands* 333

   Using Seek Operations   333

      Using SEEK Commands 335

Querying Data with RQBE   337

   Creating RQBE Queries   337

      The RQBE Window 337   *Selecting Output Data Fields* 339   *Identifying Output Destinations* 341   *Ordering Query Results* 342   *Defining Selection Criteria* 343

   Executing RQBE Queries   346

   Saving the Current Query to a File   346

   Repeating an Existing Query   348

   Modifying Existing Queries   348

   More on Selection Criteria   348

      Using the Like Comparison Operator 349   *Using the Not Operator* 355
Using the More Than/Less Than Operator 356   *Using the Between Operator* 358   *Using the In Operator* 359   *Using Formulas in Selection Criteria* 359   *Using Functions in Selection Criteria* 362   *Specifying Compound Selection Criteria* 363   *Using the OR Logical Connector* 363
Using Multiple Database Files in RQBE Queries 366

Displaying Calculated Data Fields   370
Displaying Summary Statistics   371
Producing Group Summary Statistics   375
Using FoxPro Commands   378
Querying Memo Fields   379
Chapter Summary   381

10 Using Memory Variables and Built-In Functions   383

An Overview   383

Memory Variables   384

Types of Memory Variables   385
Naming Memory Variables   386
Storing Data in Memory Variables   387

Using the STORE Command 387   *Using the = Command* 389

Assigning Data Fields to Memory Variables   389
Displaying Memory Variables   390

Using the DISPLAY MEMORY Command 391   *Using the ? Command* 392

Saving Memory Variables to Memory Files   393
Deleting Memory Variables   395
Restoring Memory Variables   396
Deleting Memory Variables from Memory Files   397

Built-In Functions   397

Character String Functions   400

RTRIM(), TRIM() 400   *LTRIM()* 401   *ALLTRIM()* 403   *UPPER()* 403
LOWER() 405   *SPACE()* 406   *STUFF()* 407   *SOUNDEX()* 407
DIFFERENCE() 409   *LEFT(), RIGHT()* 410   *SUBSTR()* 411
PROPER() 412   *AT()* 413   *ASC()* 414   *CHR()* 415   *LEN()* 416

Numeric Functions   417

SQRT() 417   *ABS()* 418   *INT()* 418   *ROUND()* 418   *LOG10()* 418
LOG() 419

Statistical Functions   419

CNT() 419   *SUM()* 420   *AVG()* 421   *STD()* 422   *MAX(), MIN()* 422

Financial Functions   423

PAYMENT() 423   *FV()* 424

Data Conversion Functions   425

CTOD() 426   *DTOC()* 426   *DTOS()* 426   *VAL()* 427   *STR()* 428

Date Manipulation Functions   428
  MDY() 429   *YEAR(), MONTH(), DAY()* 429   *CMONTH()* 430
  CDOW() 430   *DOW()* 430   *GOMONTH()* 430
Chapter Summary   431

11 Producing Reports and Mailing Labels   433

An Overview   433
FoxPro Reports   433
Types of Reports   434
  Column Reports   434
  Form Reports   435
Report Components   436
Creating Reports   439
  The Report Menu   440
    Report Design Tool Palette 442
Creating a Column Report   443
  Report Bands   443
    Title Band 444   *Page Header Band* 444   *Detail Band* 444   *Page Footer Band* 445   *Group Header Band* 445   *Group Footer Band* 446   *Summary Band* 446
  Creating Quick Reports   446
    Selecting Data Fields 447   *Viewing Quick Reports* 448   *Producing Quick Reports* 449   *Saving the Report Environment* 452   *Printing Reports* 453
  Creating Custom Reports   457
    Modifying Existing Reports 457   *Resizing Report Bands* 461   *Adding Pictures* 475
  Using Memory Variables in a Report   487
  Creating Form Reports   488
    Using Quick Report Layouts 490   *Creating a Custom Form Report* 491
Creating Mailing Labels   494
  Designing Mailing Labels   495
    Defining Label Dimensions 497   *Viewing Mailing Labels on the Screen* 498
  Saving Label Forms   499
  Printing Mailing Labels   499
  Producing Reports from Multiple Databases   500
    Extracting Data with RQBE Queries 500

Revising the Report Form 502
Producing Reports 505
Producing Mailing Labels from Multiple Databases 506

Using FoxPro Commands 507

Creating and Modifying Reports 507
Producing Reports 508
Using Memory Variables 509
Creating and Modifying Mailing Labels 510
Producing Mailing Labels 512

Chapter Summary 512

12 Using Custom Data Screens 515

An Overview 515

Creating Custom Data Screens 515
Types of Data Screens 516

Desktop Screens 516 *Window Screens* 517

Screen Layouts 520

Creating Window Screens 520 *Saving the Screen Layout* 527 *Modifying Existing Data Screens* 531 *Adding Graphics Objects* 546 *Adding Radio Buttons* 549 *Adding a Data Maintenance Panel* 554 *Displaying Record Deletion Indicators* 558 *Appending New Records* 560 *Deleting Records* 561 *Adding Popups* 561 *Copying Screen Objects* 564 *Adding Lists* 566 *Adding Spinners* 567 *Adding Screen Background* 569

Working with Multiple Databases 571

Using FoxPro Commands 579

Chapter Summary 580

13 Putting It All Together 581

An Overview 581

A Custom Menu System 581

The File Menu Pad 582
The ViewData Menu Pad 583

Viewing the SALESMAN and OFFICE Databases 583 *Viewing the OFFICE and SALESMAN Databases* 586 *Viewing the REGION and SALESMAN Databases* 590

The EditData Menu Pad   591

Editing the ASSIGN Database 592   *Editing the OFFICE Database* 592
Editing the REGION Database 592   *Editing the SALESMAN Database* 594   *Editing the CUSTOMER Database* 594

The Report Menu Pad   595
The Label Menu Pad   597
The Window Menu Pad   597
The Help Menu Pad   600
The FoxPro Menu Builder   601

Creating a Quick Menu   602

Defining the Menu Pad Prompts   603
Defining the Menu Pad Results   604
Defining Prompt Options   605
Other Features of the Menu Design Window   607
Defining the System Menu Popup   608
Modifying the Quick Menu   610

Deleting Existing Menu Pads 610   *Deleting Existing Menu Options* 611
Adding New Menu Options 612   *Defining the Results of Menu Options* 612   *Rearranging Menu Options* 613

Testing the Menu   614
Adding New Menu Pads   615

Creating Menu Popups 616

Using Nested Submenus   618
Saving the Custom Menu File   624
Generating the Menu Program File   624

Using the Custom Menu 626

Using FoxPro Commands   626
Chapter Summary   627

Appendix A: ASCII Table   629

Index   631

Preface

Welcome to a new horizon in database management: the powerful FoxPro for Windows by Microsoft. The Windows version of the FoxPro software represents another significant milestone in relational database management systems. Not only is the program totally compatible with the Microsoft Windows environment, but the software has incorporated many of Windows powerful and user-friendly features in the new version. FoxPro for Windows is one of the most powerful Windows-based relational database management softwares in the industry.

Just over a decade ago, the power of database management could be enjoyed only by users of large, expensive computer systems. The introduction of microcomputer software drastically changed the way data is organized and manipulated. Because of its sound design and superior performance, FoxPro has been widely recognized as one of the best database management software programs for microcomputers.

This is a book about understanding FoxPro for Windows. It illustrates how to use the software to develop your own database management system. With this system you will be able to effectively manage your data to provide comprehensive information when you need it.

FoxPro for Windows makes it possible to process data in two ways: through interactive processing or batch command processing. Interactive processing enables you to perform all data management functions by choosing the appropriate options from the menu interface or by interactively issuing appropriate FoxPro commands. In the batch command mode, data is manipulated and information is extracted by executing a program that is written in the FoxPro command language. The emphasis of this book is on interactive processing—on learning how to use FoxPro in a powerful way without having to program.

How to Use This Book

A primary function of this book is to demonstrate with a large set of examples how to use the software to develop a database system. For purposes of clarity, the examples have been kept simple and concise to make it easier to understand the underlying principles. And, in order to maintain continuity among the examples, the same databases are used throughout the book to illustrate as many different functions as possible.

To get the most from this setup, it is strongly recommended that you duplicate the examples as you read along in the book. Then, once you fully understand the principles from studying and working with the examples, you can set out to develop your own database system.

Who Should Use This Book

If you own FoxPro for Windows, this is the book for you. But make no mistake—it is not intended to be a user's reference manual. It goes beyond that. Where a user's manual describes the functions of all the tools, this book actually demonstrates how to design and build a database system with the tools.

If you are a beginning user, you will find this book especially beneficial. In addition to learning how to use the software, you will learn the principles behind designing a versatile relational database system. By incorporating the easy-to-follow examples, you can begin developing a simple database after reading the first few chapters.

If you have used earlier versions of FoxPro and FoxBase, you'll no doubt notice that FoxPro for Windows represents a significant improvement over its predecessors. A rich new set of tools and commands have been added to the program, all of which you will learn by studying the examples presented in this book.

Finally, if you are a dBASE user and are planning to expand your productivity by switching to FoxPro for Windows, this book will illustrate how to use the powerful RQBE (Relational Query By Example) to extract information from your databases. In addition, you will learn how to use the versatile Screen Builder and Report Writer to design and develop data entry screens and custom reports.

How This Book Is Organized

Understanding FoxPro for Windows is logically divided into three sections. The first section, comprised of the first three chapters, builds the foundation for understanding the principles of database management and the FoxPro for Windows software. Chapters 4 through 7, the second section, present the basic operations for creating and maintaining a relational database. The final section of the book, Chapters 8 through 13, deals with advanced topics.

Chapter 1, "Introduction to Databases," defines the basic concept of database management. It presents commonly used data models and how they can be used to help you properly organize your data. This chapter also will teach you the principles behind the sound design of a relational database system.

Chapter 2, "An Overview of FoxPro," gives a brief introduction to the design philosophy of the software. In addition, it discusses the powerful and user-friendly FoxPro for Windows menu interface. This chapter also presents an overview of the major components of the program.

Chapter 3, "Getting Started," outlines the steps involved in setting up the program so that you can begin to design and develop your own database management system. It details the procedures for using the keyboard and mouse, setting the screen colors, selecting the printers, and so forth. Working with FoxPro's window environment also is discussed in this chapter.

Chapter 4, "Creating Databases," opens the discussion of the procedures and menu options necessary for performing basic database management functions. It explains in detail the steps for creating a database. You also will learn how to define the structure of a database and enter data into it.

Chapter 5, "Displaying Data," explains how to display the data structure and contents of a database on the screen or output it to a printer. And, along with learning how to display all the data in a database, you also will discover how to define the conditions for displaying selected subsets of the data.

Chapter 6, "Sorting and Indexing Data," deals with ordering data records in a database. This chapter compares and contrasts the Sort and Index operations so that you know the strengths and weaknesses of these two processes, thus enabling you to make the proper choice between the two for your applications.

Chapter 7, "Editing Data," covers the methods used to modify the contents of a database. You will learn how to change the data structure of an existing database and the contents of its data records. You also will learn how to modify the data records in both Browse and Change modes.

Chapter 8, "Linking Databases," discusses the procedures for linking two or more databases so that you can extract more comprehensive information from them. This chapter also illustrates how to join data records from more than one database.

Chapter 9, "Querying Data," explains how to efficiently extract useful information from databases. In addition to an explanation of the Locate and Seek operations, it shows how to use the powerful Relational Query By Example (RQBE) technique for finding the information you need.

Chapter 10, "Using Memory Variables and Built-In Functions," shows you how to create memory variables for storing individual data elements and summary statistics that you can pass to custom reports. You also will learn about the power of FoxPro's built-in functions.

Chapter 11, "Producing Reports and Mailing Labels," teaches you how to use FoxPro's versatile Report Writer and Label Designer to design and create custom reports and mailing labels.

Chapter 12, "Using Custom Data Screens," illustrates the steps required for designing and creating customized screens for viewing data and for data entry. Detailed instructions for using FoxPro's Screen Designer for these purposes also are included in this chapter.

Chapter 13, "Putting It All Together," is the final chapter of the book. It is at this stage that you learn how to integrate all of the components of a database system by using FoxPro's Menu Builder to design and create a custom menu system for performing all data management functions.

I wish to thank my editor, Ron Petrusha, who was instrumental in helping me shape the manuscript. Ron is one of the most knowledgeable and enthusiastic editors I have worked with. I am indebted to him for the many good ideas that he contributed to this book. I also wish to thank Random House, Inc. for giving me the opportunity to write this book. The warm relationship between the authors and the publisher, Mr. Kenzi Sugihara, has made this writing project very enjoyable. Finally, I am grateful for the support and encouragement my wife and children have given me in completing this book.

Understanding FoxPro™ 2.5 for Windows™

1
Introduction to Databases

An Overview

This is a book about understanding FoxPro for Windows, a very powerful database management system software. Its primary purpose is to show you how to use the software to develop your own database management system. With it, you will be able to effectively manage your data so that it provides the information you want when you want it. But before you can design and develop such a system, you need to be familiar with some of the basic concepts and terms of database management systems in general. These are the subjects covered in this chapter.

In simple terms, a database is a collection of interrelated data elements that are arranged and organized in a logical manner. These data elements, when combined in this way, make it possible to access useful information efficiently. However, the type of accessible information and how quickly you can retrieve it from your database is closely related to how you store and organize data elements.

A variety of data models are available for organizing data elements, but because FoxPro for Windows uses the relational model, this chapter discusses only the concepts and structure of that model. As you will see later, the backbone of this structure is the logical relationship between data elements. Understanding how to define and structure these relations within your database is vital to the effectiveness and power of your system. Through the examples in this chapter, you will learn how to design a database with the correct structure that produces the desired information in the least amount of time and with the least amount of effort.

What Is a Data Element?

A data element is a basic unit of information within a database management system. It usually consists of a set of characters that are in the form of alphabetic letters (A–Z, a–z), numeric digits (1–9), or text symbols (hyphens, commas, colons, semicolons, etc.). For example, an employee's last name, say Smith, consisting of a number of alphabetic letters, makes up a data element in a database system. The first name of that employee, say John, makes up another data element. A collection of these data elements makes up various components of a database. Thus, an employee's first and last names make up a database component. In turn, each of these data components can be given a special name, such as data field, data record, or data file. You will learn more about these terms later in this chapter.

What Is a Database?

As already noted, a database is a collection of data elements that are organized in a logical manner and structure. Its actual structure depends on the data model in which you choose to organize those elements; its size is determined by the number of data elements. The relationship between these elements influences the complexity of a database.

A simple database usually has a small number of data elements that can be organized in a very simple structure. For example, a collection of the names and phone numbers of your friends could represent a small yet complete database in which you could organize the data elements in a structure that stores the last name, first name, area code, and phone number as separate items.

On the other hand, a company's sales database that contains a large number of data elements would be organized in a more complex structure. A database such as this would contain all the data elements about its customers, inventory, invoices, and sales transactions. Then, data elements associated only with customers would be stored in one group, and within that group, data belonging to any single customer would be stored in separate data elements; typically, items such as the name, address, and phone number of the selected customer. Data elements associated just with merchandise would be stored in the inventory group; each time a transaction was made, the items about the sale and the invoice would be stored in yet other groups of data elements. Once these data elements are organized and stored in a logical manner, you can easily and quickly collect the appropriate data elements from these groups to generate inventory lists or reports.

What Is a Database Management System?

A database management system (DBMS) offers a systematic approach for managing data elements so that information can be extracted and distributed with a minimum amount of effort. Besides providing information, a correctly designed and structured database management system permits you to efficiently manage data elements. In such a system, you can easily add data elements to your database, modify and change any data elements you already have, or delete data elements you no longer need. The system also is fast, which allows you to quickly find selected elements; and, once that information is located, you can quickly display or present results in an appropriate format.

Although we are talking about a system that is so complicated it requires a computer to handle, a database management system does not have to be complex; neither must it be computerized. A database management system can be a manual system, and a card file that is used to manage information associated with all of your friends is a good example of this. The file, made up of a number of index cards each with a certain number of data elements on it, is a database.

To continue this example, let's say that in this manual database each card lists the name and address of one of your personal friends, and that these cards are arranged in a certain order—alphabetically by last name. As you add a new name, you add a new card in last name alphabetic order in the same way that you find data about an existing friend by searching for his or her last name in the card file. You also can update information or remove a card from your database when you no longer want to maintain data about a particular friend. And, if you need to produce a list of friends who live in the same city, you can sort these cards by city name and then copy the accompanying first and last names to a piece of paper. These are all examples of essential data management functions that you would expect a well-designed database management system to provide.

This book, of course, focuses on computerized database management using FoxPro for Windows. But even though you will be performing all data management functions on a computer, the same principles used in a manual system apply. If you have a good understanding of how to manage a manual system, you have a good foundation for learning the basic functions of a computerized database management system.

Information vs. Data

In database management systems, data elements are ingredients of an information system. These data elements by themselves usually do not provide any meaningful and useful information. It is necessary to link those data elements that are associated with a certain subject in order to make some sense out of it. Therefore, data and information are different things by nature.

The primary purpose of a database management system is to organize data elements so that you can obtain desired information by retrieving all associated data elements. For example, you can save a friend's address in various components that separately hold his or her street address, the city and state, and the zip code. The information about his or her mailing address can be obtained only by retrieving the appropriate data elements from the correct database. The last name of an employee, as another example, is a data element that is made up of several alphabetic characters. All of the last names of the employees in a firm in turn represent a subset of that firm's personnel database. A listing of these last names provides useful information in the form of an employee roster.

Organizing Data

The method you choose to organize data elements is a major consideration in a database management system. The efficiency and usefulness of your database management system is significantly affected by the structure used to store and maintain data elements in the database. If your database is properly structured so that all the data elements are logically organized, you can maintain and manage your data with the least amount of effort.

Because useful information usually requires linking various appropriate data elements in the database, defining the relations among these elements plays a very significant role in determining the efficiency of a database management system. Therefore, before you learn how to design a database management system, you must learn how to relate all of the data elements in your database.

DATA RELATIONS

As already stated, a data element is the basic unit of a database. It describes a single property of a data entity. A data entity is any distinctive object—either a tangible property, such as a person, a table, or a chair; or an intangible object, such as a branch office or a sales region.

When you view the organization of a database, you can see that data entities form the building blocks that bring the structure together. For example, to design a database system that manages the activities and functions of a sales organization, you need to include data entities such as salesmen and saleswomen, sales offices, sales regions, and customer accounts.

Each of these data entities has a number of properties. A salesperson has a set of properties comprised of his or her first and last names, birthdate, salary, home address, etc. A sales office has another set of properties that specifies its address and phone number. Typical database designs allow you to view the links among data entities in one of three basic ways: one-to-one relations, one-to-many relations, and many-to-many relations.

One-to-One Relations

Of these three relations, the one-to-one is the simplest link between any two data entities. To understand such a relationship, assume the following set of rules regarding office assignment in this sales organization: Only one salesperson may be assigned to each sales office and each sales office may have only one salesperson.

As an example, let's assume that there are three branch offices: B1, B2, and B3; and to fill these offices are three salespeople: Anderson, Bell, and Carter. In such a data structure you now have two data entities: sales staff and office. These two data entities are linked in a one-to-one relation as shown in Figure 1.1.

From Figure 1.1 you can see that each sales office has only one salesperson, and that each salesperson belongs to only one sales office; i.e., B1 has only one saleswoman (Anderson), who in turn, belongs to only that one office.

One-to-Many Relations

Of course, the one-to-one relation is no doubt too simple to reflect the actual links between sales staff and office entities in a real world. It is more likely that this organization would have a larger number of sales personnel, and that each office would probably have more than one salesperson. Therefore, the one-to-one relation would not be adequate to describe all the links between the two data entities. A more realistic example relating the sales staff and branch office entities is shown in Figure 1.2.

As you can see, each sales office has more than one salesperson, yet each salesperson belongs to only one sales office. Note that sales office B1 has four salespeople: Anderson, Davidson, Gilbert, and Jones, each of whom belongs to only one sales office—B1.

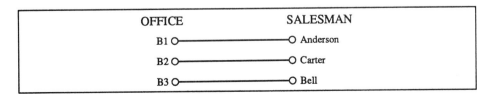

Figure 1.1 One-to-one relations

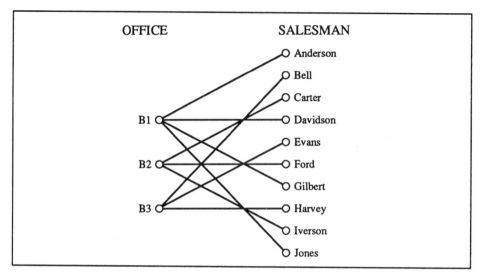

Figure 1.2 One-to-many relations

Of course, by switching the order of the two entities, you can call the relation in Figure 1.2 a many-to-one relation. Therefore, one-to-many relations and many-to-one relations are the same in a database design.

Many-to-Many Relations

A many-to-many relation is the most complex for linking two data entities in a database design. Each object in one data entity is linked to several objects in another entity and vice versa. To show you how these many-to-many relations look, assume that there are 10 salesmen and saleswomen (as in Figure 1.2), each of whom will be assigned to service one or more of the six sales regions. These sales regions are designated as R1, R2, R3, R4, R5, and R6. Figure 1.3 shows how you can link the sales staff and sales regions in many-to-many relations.

In Figure 1.3, you can see that a salesperson can have more than one sales region assigned to him or her, and that each sales region is served by more than one salesperson. For example, saleswoman Harvey has three sales regions (R4, R5, and R6), and sales region R4 is served by two salespeople (Evans and Harvey). Of course, you also can see that not every salesperson has more than one sales region; some have only one sales region assigned to them.

Therefore, a data structure that can accommodate many-to-many relations is always able to handle one-to-many, many-to-one, and one-to-one relations as well. But, the reverse may not be true. If your database design can handle only one-to-one relations, it may not be sufficient to manage one-to-many and many-to-many relations. As a result, you must understand the nature of your data elements and

Introduction to Databases 7

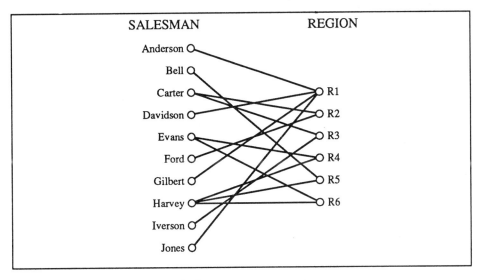

Figure 1.3 Many-to-many relations

anticipate how they are to be used before you can design a sound database structure to accommodate the data and their relations.

Data Models

A number of data models have been developed to manage databases that assume these relations. The three most common are the hierarchical, network, and relational data models. Although this book focuses mainly on the relational data model, a brief description of the others may help you to understand the relational model's simplicity and power. In addition, your knowledge of these models will help you design a better relational database.

HIERARCHICAL DATA MODEL

A hierarchical data model views the relations among data entities as a tree structure with multiple levels of branches. If you were to use a hierarchical data model to view the relations among the three data entities (Office, Salesman, and Region) in our earlier example, it would look like that in Figure 1.4.

As you can see from this figure, the model assumes three levels: a main trunk and two sub-levels of branches. The first level describes Office, and each of its trunks represents an object of the entity and leads to a different number of sub-branches. In turn, each of these sub-branches represents an object in the next data entity, Salesman. As the model continues, each member of the sales staff

8 Understanding FoxPro 2.5 for Windows

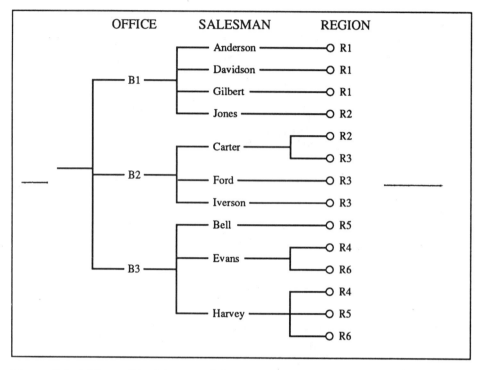

Figure 1.4 A hierarchical data model

sub-branches in turn leads to yet another level of sub-branches—in this case, the third level of branches, which reflects the objects in Region.

When you look at the hierarchical model in Figure 1.4, you can see that all the data elements are organized in a very logical way; i.e., each object of a data entity is logically related to one or more objects in another data entity. You can determine the objects in each data entity and all the relations among them. But study the model a bit further and you will notice that the hierarchical model allows only one-to-one and one-to-many or many-to-one relations. To include many-to-many relations, they must be restructured with duplicated one-to-many relations.

As you saw in Figure 1.3, many-to-many relations exist among the objects in the sales staff and region data entities. That is, a salesperson can have more than one sales region, and a sales region can be assigned to more than one salesperson. For example, Evans has two sales regions, R4 and R6, and each of these regions is assigned to more than one salesperson. Region 4 is assigned to two, Evans and Harvey, and so on.

But return to the hierarchical model in Figure 1.4 and you can see that these many-to-many relations must be structured in repeated one-to-many relations. Note in the tree structure that one branch can lead to several sub-branches, but all sub-branches always lead to only one branch in a higher level. In order to conform

Introduction to Databases 9

to this type of tree structure, you must repeat some objects in the sub-branches to describe many-to-many relations in terms of several one-to-many relations.

Also notice in Figure 1.4 that some objects in Region appear as multiple sub-branches in order to describe their relationship to the objects in Salesman, such as R4 of Region that appears twice as a sub-branch. Each is related to an object in Salesman—one to Evans and the other to Harvey. It is to accommodate this type of repetition that a different data model was developed. It is called a network model.

NETWORK DATA MODEL

A network data model can be viewed as a modified version of the hierarchical model. It too organizes data elements in a tree structure just like the hierarchical model. Unlike a hierarchical model, however, a network model allows you to define many-to-many relations in a tree structure without repeating any object in a data entity. Look at Figure 1.5 to view the relations among the same three data entities in a network model.

Notice that the data model looks very similar to the one in Figure 1.4; they both use a tree structure to relate the objects in the three data entities. Because there is only a one-to-many relationship between the office and sales staff entities, the hierarchical and network models describe these relations in the same manner. But the way in which the network model describes the many-to-many relations between the sales staff and region entities looks quite different from that described by the hierarchical model.

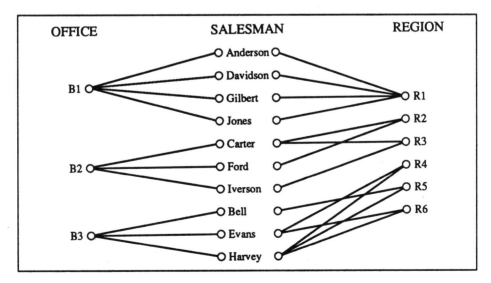

Figure 1.5 A network data model

The important difference is that in the network model each object of the region entity always appears as only one sub-branch, and a sub-branch in the region entity may come from more than one branch at a higher level. For example, the branch describing Evans leads to two sub-branches relating to regions R4 and R6. The sub-branch describing region R4 comes from two branches relating to Evans and Harvey. The branch describing Harvey relates to regions R4, R5, and R6, as represented by three sub-branches in the model.

In both of these models, data elements are organized in a logical way so that you can relate all of your data elements by providing the necessary links. If you were looking for a particular piece of information in your database, you would be able to trace through the appropriate links to retrieve its data elements. In order for you do that, however, the system must have built-in, rather detailed links in the form of pointers, each of which points from one object to another. In addition, in order to speed up the searching process, it is often necessary to arrange the data elements in a certain order. This ordering function is accomplished through operations such as sorting and indexing, but because FoxPro for Windows does not use either one of these models to organize data elements, we will not go beyond this discussion to cover operational details about these two models.

RELATIONAL DATA MODEL

A relational data model is the most popular one that you can use to organize and manage data elements. Most database management software for microcomputers is designed for handling data structures organized according to this model. FoxPro for Windows, FoxBase, Paradox, RBase, and the family of dBASE software products all choose relational data models for structuring their data elements. One of the reasons for the popularity of this model is that it is simple to understand and set up. It can accommodate one-to-one, one-to-many, and many-to-many relations in its structure. When a database structure is correctly set up, you can easily manage data elements. Finding the desired information from the database becomes very quick once you have built in all the links and relations among the data objects.

Data Tables

In a relational data model, all of your data elements and the relations among data objects are organized in data tables. You use a data table to hold data elements that are associated with data objects. Similarly, all the relations among these data objects also are saved as data elements in data tables. As a result, a database in a relational data model contains a set of data tables.

In order to get a better idea of how to organize data elements with a relational data model and store them in data tables, let's continue with the three data entities discussed in the last two models—Salesman, Office, and Region. Each has a

```
Table: Salesman

Salesman ID    Last Name    First Name    Hire Date    Salary

S0             Anderson     Doris         07/01/86     2,800
S1             Bell         George        10/12/88     2,400
S2             Carter       Jack          05/14/87     2,550
S3             Davidson     Edward        06/04/90     1,500
S4             Evans        Henry         03/08/88     2,000
S5             Ford         Ida           11/22/87     2,600
S6             Gilbert      Fred          04/15/87     2,300
S7             Harvey       Candy         12/01/89     2,450
S8             Iverson      Albert        10/25/88     2,200
S9             Jones        Betty         09/26/89     2,500
```

Figure 1.6 A data table in a relational model

number of objects, which in turn have a set of properties. Data elements are then used to describe these properties.

Salesman contains a number of objects, each representing a salesperson—Anderson, Bell, Carter, and so on. Each data object or salesperson has a set of properties that includes his or her identification number, last name, first name, salary, and hire date. The data element used to describe a property consists of a set of characters in the form of alphabetic letters, numeric digits, and symbols. For example, the data elements describing Anderson's first name include a string of alphabetic characters spelling "Doris." A set of numeric digits and symbols—"07/01/86"—specifies her employment date as a data element. All the data elements in Salesman can be organized in a table that looks like the one in Figure 1.6.

Components of a Data Table

In this figure, all the data elements describing the properties of all the objects (salespeople) of the Salesman data entity are stored in a table. You can assign a name—Salesman, in this case—to the table for identification purposes and as a convenient way to refer to it. The table itself is divided into a number of rows and columns; each of the columns also can be named and used to save data elements describing a particular property of the data objects; the rows are used to store data elements associated with a given object—in this case, a salesperson. Rows are identified by the sequence number they are assigned as they are added to the table; you do not have to assign a name to each row in the table.

In the Salesman table, for example, all of the data elements describing the last names of the sales staff are stored in the column labeled "Last Name;" monthly salaries are stored in the Salary column. Each row in the Salesman table holds data

```
Table: Office

Office ID  Address           City         State  Zip    Phone #

B1         100 Park Avenue   New York     NY     10016  800-123-5555
B2         200 Lake Drive    Chicago      IL     60607  800-234-5555
B3         500 Century Blvd. Los Angeles  CA     94005  800-456-5555


Table: Region

Region ID  Region         Manager

R1         Northeast      Alice F. Gibson
R2         Southeast      Bob L. Major
R3         Northcentral   John K. Freed
R4         Southcentral   Cathy M. Wilson
R5         Northwest      Chris C. Hall
R6         Southwest      Helen T. Taylor
```

Figure 1.7 The Office and Region tables

elements describing all the properties (ID #, Last Name, First Name, Hire Date, Salary) for a given salesperson.

Using a similar structure, you can organize all of the data elements associated with the sales office and sales region in two separate tables named Office and Region, respectively, as shown in Figure 1.7.

In this figure, you can see that the Office and Region tables follow the same format as that of the Salesman table. They are both divided into a number of rows and columns, where each row holds the data elements belonging to an object of the data entity, and each column stores data elements associated with a property of that object.

In the Office table, data elements describing the properties of the offices—identification number, addresses, and phone numbers—are stored in the columns. Each row of the table holds data elements associated with a given office. Similarly, in the Region table, properties of the region are stored in the columns. The column named Manager, for example, saves data elements specifying the names of regional managers.

In a relational data model, a database usually contains more than one such data tables, and these data tables are often called database files by relational database software products such as FoxPro for Windows. Each row of the table is called a data record and contains a number of data fields, each of which corresponds to a column in the data table. Therefore, data elements in a relational database are organized in database files (tables). Each database file contains a number of records (rows), and each record (row) has a number of fields (columns).

Using these relational database terms, you can describe the database consisting of Salesman, Office, and Region in the following way:

Table Name:	Salesman
Number of Records:	10
Data Fields:	Salesman ID
	Last Name
	First Name
	Hire Date
	Salary
Table Name:	Office ID
Number of Records:	3
Data Fields:	ID #
	Address
	City
	State
	Zip
	Phone #
Table Name:	Region ID
Number of Records:	6
Data Fields:	ID #
	Region
	Manager

As stated earlier in this chapter, a relational data model not only saves all the data elements describing a data entity in a data table; data tables also are used to hold data elements describing relations among these data entities. Although you will learn more about the way to set up and use this type of data table, Figure 1.8 shows you an example of such a relational table, named Assignment.

If you compare the structure of the Assignment table with that of the Salesman, Office, and Region tables, you will have no trouble noticing their similarities. They all are organized in rows and columns. But there is a significant difference between the Assignment table and the Salesman table: A row in the Salesman table describes the properties of a given salesperson, whereas a row in the Assignment table specifies the *link* between a sales region and a salesperson. For example, the first row in that table contains two data elements, R1 and S1, which are saved in the columns named Region ID and Salesman ID, respectively. The data elements in the first row relate the sales region R1 (Northeast in the Region table) to saleswoman S1 (Anderson in the Salesman table).

```
Table: Assignment

Region ID   Salesman ID

R1          S0
R1          S3
R1          S6
R1          S9
R2          S2
R2          S5
R3          S2
R3          S8
R4          S4
R4          S7
R5          S1
R5          S7
R6          S4
R6          S7
```

Figure 1.8 A relation table

These relational tables play a very significant role in determining the usefulness and power of a relational database. When they are properly structured, you are able to handle any type of relationship that exists among your data entities. You will learn more about these relational data tables later in this chapter.

Designing a Relational Database

The usefulness and power of a database depends primarily on how you set up its data tables to describe data entities and their relations. A correctly structured database gives you rapid and easy access to all information by retrieving the related data elements in the database. But, if you fail to define your database structure correctly, you will find that managing your data becomes very difficult, if not impossible. Therefore, it is always wise to invest some time in planning how to set up your data tables and establish the links that will be necessary for relating the data elements for later use.

When designing a database, begin by studying the nature of your business and thinking about the type of data elements that make up the organization. Looking ahead at the types of information you will need will help you to determine the relevant data elements that you want stored in your database. To elaborate on our example, consider that it might, at some point, be necessary to produce a compensation report detailing the salaries of the sales personnel assigned to a given sales region. For that, you'll need data elements describing their salaries and the sales regions to which they are assigned. To produce invoices, on the other hand, you must have data elements describing each sales transaction: the invoice number; the name and address of the customer to whom you sold the merchandise; and the description, price, and quantity of the merchandise, etc.

Once you have decided which data elements you need, the next step is to organize them in a logical manner. To do that, try to group elements that are associated with an entity in one data table. You would include all the data elements describing the properties of a salesperson in the Salesman table, for example. Each property is, in turn, described by one data element in a data field.

After setting up all the necessary data tables for holding the data elements associated with all of your data entities, then set up the relation table to provide the links among the data elements in various data tables. The number of relational data tables is determined by the complexity of the relations among your data tables. Usually, you do not need to set up relation tables to handle one-to-one and one-to-many relations; they are necessary only for taking care of many-to-many relations. In the forthcoming section you will learn how to structure these types of relations in your database.

PROPERTIES OF A RELATIONAL DATABASE

Designing a database can be a complex process, especially if it has a large number of data tables that include multiple sets of many-to-many relations. But many useful databases have a small number of simple data tables with few relational data tables to handle their links. If you can understand the underlying principles behind a simple relational database, understanding a more complex one will come with experience.

Regardless of the complexity and size of a relational database, it must have a set of properties. Implementing these properties is essential if you want to avoid redundant data elements and correctly link your data elements. These essential properties can be summarized as follows:

- All data elements must be organized in data tables.
- Data elements in a single table must have a one-to-one relationship.
- There may not be duplicate rows in a data table.
- There may not be duplicate columns in a data table.
- Only one data element may be saved in each data cell.

Organizing Data in Tables

The first essential property of a relational database is that data elements associated with a unique data entity must be organized in table form, as seen in earlier examples. A data table is the basic unit of a relational database, and each table may

16   Understanding FoxPro 2.5 for Windows

contain any number of rows (records) and columns (fields). The number and order of the columns are not important; neither is the number of rows.

No Duplicate Rows

In a properly structured relational data table, you must not have two or more rows with identical data elements. Duplicate rows not only are wasteful of valuable storage space, but they slow down processing by making the table unduly large. More important, duplicate rows cause erroneous results (inaccurate row counts) when you include them in summary statistics. If, for instance, you have data elements associated with the same salesperson appearing in more than one row in the Salesman table, you would not get the correct total when you count the number of rows in that table or the accurate total salary for all the sales personnel in the firm when you add up all the salaries in that table.

Using Single-Value Data Cells

The intersection between a row and column in a data table is often called a data cell. Another essential property of a relational database is that only one data element may be stored in a data cell. As an example, let's add the column Phone No to the Salesman table (see Figure 1.9). In that table, the data cell between a row and a column may hold only a single value representing the phone number.

But, suppose the person has more than one phone number. Perhaps saleswoman Anderson has two telephone numbers: 123-4567 and 987-6543. Now you have a problem. Because you cannot save both of them in the cell between the first row

```
Table: Salesman

Salesman ID   Last Name   First Name   Phone No   Hire Date   Salary

S0            Anderson    Doris        123-4567   07/01/86    2,800
S1            Bell        George       234-3456   10/12/88    2,400
S2            Carter      Jack         456-9023   05/14/87    2,550
S3            Davidson    Edward       234-5645   06/04/90    1,500
S4            Evans       Henry        635-2345   03/08/88    2,000
S5            Ford        Ida          345-2345   11/22/87    2,600
S6            Gilbert     Fred         234-4576   04/15/87    2,300
S7            Harvey      Candy        555-2323   12/01/89    2,450
S8            Iverson     Albert       123-3333   10/25/88    2,200
S9            Jones       Betty        342-4567   09/26/89    2,500
```

Figure 1.9 Adding Phone No column to the Salesman table

```
Table: Salesman

Salesman ID   Last Name   First Name   Phone #1    Phone #2    Hire Date   Salary

S0            Anderson    Doris        123-4567    987-6543    07/01/86    2,800
S1            Bell        George       234-3456                10/12/88    2,400
S2            Carter      Jack         456-9023                05/14/87    2,550
S3            Davidson    Edward       234-5645                06/04/90    1,500
S4            Evans       Henry        635-2345                03/08/88    2,000
S5            Ford        Ida          345-2345                11/22/87    2,600
S6            Gilbert     Fred         234-4576                04/15/87    2,300
S7            Harvey      Candy        555-2323                12/01/89    2,450
S8            Iverson     Albert       123-3333                10/25/88    2,200
S9            Jones       Betty        342-4567                09/26/89    2,500
```

Figure 1.10 Adding another column to the Salesman table

and the column labeled Phone No, you must save them in two different cells. There are different solutions to this problem. One is to add another column to accommodate a second phone number. Such a table looks like the one in Figure 1.10.

Look carefully at this revised Salesman table and you will notice an undesirable feature in the new column. It has many blank cells, and unless most of the sales staff have two phone numbers, this will be the case throughout. Further, these blank cells have two major problems associated with them. Because each cell occupies a certain amount of storage space on the disk, blank cells are wasteful. In addition, to find the salesperson with a particular phone number you now have to search two columns. As a result, it will take longer to get the information.

Consider another solution: using two rows to store information about Doris Anderson. Repeat all of the data elements belonging to Anderson, except for her first phone number in the new row. Then enter the second phone number in the second row. The revised table looks like that in Figure 1.11.

The revised Salesman table in Figure 1.11 shows that Anderson is assigned two different identification numbers, S0 and S1. This is necessary because each row must have a unique identification number if it is to be used in a master table that can be linked to another table, as you will see later in this chapter. But, by assigning Anderson two different identification numbers, essentially you are treating her as two different salespeople. It is confusing. Furthermore, using two rows to hold data elements belonging the same salesperson can cause other types of problems, such as if you have to determine how many salespeople you have by tallying the rows in the table. Obviously, you will get an erroneous head count.

As you can see, these solutions both introduced new problems. But do not despair. There is a solution to *all* these problems. It involves separating the phone numbers from the Salesman table and saving them to another table. As an example,

```
Table: Salesman (Revised)

Salesman ID    Last Name    First Name    Phone No    Hire Date    Salary

S0             Anderson     Doris         123-4567    07/01/86     2,800
S1             Anderson     Doris         987-6543    07/01/86     2,800
S2             Bell         George        234-3456    10/12/88     2,400
S3             Carter       Jack          456-9023    05/14/87     2,550
S4             Davidson     Edward        234-5645    06/04/90     1,500
S5             Evans        Henry         635-2345    03/08/88     2,000
S6             Ford         Ida           345-2345    11/22/87     2,600
S7             Gilbert      Fred          234-4576    04/15/87     2,300
S8             Harvey       Candy         555-2323    12/01/89     2,450
S9             Iverson      Albert        123-3333    10/25/88     2,200
S10            Jones        Betty         342-4567    09/26/89     2,500
```

Figure 1.11 Adding another row to the Salesman table

we split the original Salesman table into two tables: Salesman and Phone, as shown in Figure 1.12. You then link them together when you need to know the phone numbers of anyone on the sales staff.

After splitting the Salesman table, you treat the first as a master table and the second as a table to be linked with the master table as needed. All data elements associated with saleswoman Anderson, except for her phone numbers, are found on the master Salesman table. To locate her phone numbers, you first find her identification number (S0) in the master table and then go to the Phone table to retrieve all the phone numbers associated with that identification number. But, if you want to retrieve *every* data element that is associated with a particular salesperson, you can link the two tables by using the identification number as a linking key, an operation we will discuss later in this chapter.

OTHER DESIRABLE CHARACTERISTICS

We have mentioned some basic requirements that must be followed when designing a good relational database. They can be summarized as follows:

- Plan your data needs well and in advance.
- Anticipate information needs and store only relevant data.
- Group data elements logically in columns.
- Use tables to store all data elements and relations.
- Never allow duplicate rows in any table.
- Place only a single data value in a cell.
- Avoid blank cells if at all possible.

```
Table: Salesman

Salesman ID    Last Name    First Name    Hire Date    Salary

S0             Anderson     Doris         07/01/86     2,800
S1             Bell         George        10/12/88     2,400
S2             Carter       Jack          05/14/87     2,550
S3             Davidson     Edward        06/04/90     1,500
S4             Evans        Henry         03/08/88     2,000
S5             Ford         Ida           11/22/87     2,600
S6             Gilbert      Fred          04/15/87     2,300
S7             Harvey       Candy         12/01/89     2,450
S8             Iverson      Albert        10/25/88     2,200
S9             Jones        Betty         09/26/89     2,500


Table: Phone:

Salesman ID    Phone No

S0             123-4567
S0             987-6543
S1             234-3456
S2             456-9023
S3             234-5645
S4             635-2345
S5             345-2345
S6             234-4576
S7             555-2323
S8             123-3333
S9             342-4567
```

Figure 1.12 Splitting the Salesman table into two tables

In addition to these requirements, there are other desirable characteristics you may want to build into your database. These are:

- Make database structure flexible to accommodate changes.
- Reduce redundant data to a minimum.
- Keep tables logically indexed.
- Keep data tables as simple as possible.

Making Data Structures Flexible

In structuring data tables, you should try to include all columns that are associated with a data entity in the same table. These columns should be logically divided to anticipate future needs. Such a structure should be sufficient for all future applications, as well. That is, all the information about every data entity should be available from the data table. If your data tables are flexible enough to accommodate all the data manipulation and query needs, you will not need to restructure them each time you require a new report or a different kind of information. Restructuring data tables not only takes time, it often necessitates changing many related objects.

Therefore, if initially you decide to save the names of your customers in your data table, for example, you should consider at the same time how to structure the table to make it workable for later use. Consider the following: Should you save the first and last names as one data element in a single column? Or should you save the first name and last name in two separate columns? How about middle initials? Should they be stored in a separate column or as part of the first name? Answers to these questions depend on the way the data elements are to be used in your applications. If you plan to search the data records using last names, you may want to save the last names in a separate column. If you need to produce a form letter in which you will address your customers by their first names, you must store all the first names in an independent column, too. If you do not take all potential applications into consideration, it will be much more difficult and time-consuming to extract information from your tables.

Avoiding Redundant Data

A good relational database design does not have any single data element appearing more than once anywhere in the database. Recall that in Figure 1.10 we added the Phone #2 column in order to accommodate Anderson's second phone number. This, as also mentioned, is highly undesirable if you are to conserve valuable storage space and make searching and updating your records as efficient as possible. Therefore, try to avoid, at any cost, redundant data in your database.

The exceptions to the redundancy rule are those data elements that are to be used as linking keys. In order to link two data tables together, the rows must share the same identification number; therefore, this type of data duplication is necessary. Look at Figure 1.12. Notice that Salesman ID appears in both tables. These numbers are to be used as the linking keys when you need to join the tables together. They are necessary for relating the data elements in both tables.

Indexing Data Logically

Indexing is an operation that you can use to order data records in a predetermined sequence. When you add data records to your data tables, they are usually stored in the order in which they are entered. However, this order may not be the one you desire when you later search for a record. To speed up your search, it is often preferable to arrange your tables in an order *other* than entry order. Say you would like to find a salesperson by his or her first name, but that the names were entered last name first. Naturally, the search process would be quicker if those records could now be arranged in first name order. Therefore, if you know ahead of time that you might at some later date like to search your data records in other than entry order, it is very beneficial to index that data according to specific data values.

FoxPro makes it very easy to index your records using one or more of your columns as key fields. You can arrange your database in ascending or descending order. You can even use a compound index key that consists of a combination of key values. We will discuss the details of the indexing operation in a later chapter. For now, all you have to keep in mind is the concept of indexing.

Keeping Data Tables Simple

In most database management applications, you need a set of data tables to hold all of your data elements. Ideally, try to keep these tables simple by holding to a minimum the number of columns. The fewer the columns in the table, the quicker you can retrieve necessary information from them. It is also easier to maintain data in a small table than a large one.

The number of columns in a data table should be determined by the nature of your data elements. As stated earlier, try to group related columns that are associated with a data entity in the same table. However, good relational database design does not *require* that you store all the data elements of a data entity in the same table. In some cases, when there is a very large set of columns necessary to describe the properties of a data entity, you can place them in more than one table. This is especially applicable when some of these data elements are likely to be used later as a group. Nevertheless, you *do* need to maintain a proper balance between the number of data tables and the size of these tables. Keep in mind, however, that the number of rows has a far greater impact on processing time than the number of columns in sequential operations.

RELATING DATA

To reiterate, relations among data elements are the backbone of a relational database. They are the links to the data elements, and once you learn how to link tables together, you will have the freedom to structure very flexible data tables. For example, if the number of columns in a table becomes unduly large, you can split them into more than one table. Then, when you need to associate the data elements scattered in these tables, you can join them again to provide the necessary information. In addition, if there are many-to-many relations among your data elements, you can create the relation table to join them.

The way that you structure your data table to accommodate relations depends on the type of relations that exist among your data elements. Again, the three basic types of relations are: one-to-one, one-to-many (or many-to-one), and many-to-many. Each type of relation requires a different structure to accommodate it.

Handling One-to-One Relations

The simplest form of relation is the one-to-one. This type of relation associates one object with one other unique object, which may consist of one or more data elements. For example, you can assume that each salesperson has only one hire date. Therefore, a salesperson's last name has a one-to-one relation to his or her hire date. If you also assume that a salesperson will be assigned to one and only one sales office, then there would be a one-to-one relation between a salesperson and the office to which he or she belongs.

When you have one-to-one relations among data objects, you can include them in the same table. Recall that in Figure 1.1 we assumed the following one-to-one relations among the three salespeople, Anderson, Bell, and Carter, and the three sales offices B1, B2, B3. Anderson is assigned to office B1 (New York), Bell to B3 (Los Angeles), and Carter to B2 (Chicago). To accommodate these three one-to-one relations, you can store data elements about these salespeople and offices in the same table, as shown in Figure 1.13. (In order to fit the table on this page, we've eliminated the Salesman ID, the Office ID, and the phone numbers of the offices.)

Notice in this figure that each row contains data elements about not only a salesperson, but also about his or her sales office. This is possible only if there are one-to-one relations among the three salespeople and their sales offices. If different types of relationships existed among these data objects, then you would need to structure the table accordingly.

Handling One-to-Many Relations

When there are one-to-many relationships among data objects, you cannot store all the associated data elements in the same table if you are to avoid duplicate data.

```
Table: Salesman (including data for sales offices)

Last      First   Hire      Salary Address          City         ST Zip
Name      Name    Date

Anderson  Doris   07/01/86  2,800  100 Park Avenue  New York     NY 10016
Bell      George  10/12/88  2,400  200 Lake Drive   Chicago      IL 60607
Carter    Jack    05/14/87  2,550  500 Century Blvd. Los Angeles CA 94005
```

Figure 1.13 Handling one-to-one relations in the same table

```
Table: Salesman (including data for sales offices)

Last      First   Hire     Salary Address           City        ST Zip
Name      Name    Date

Anderson  Doris   07/01/86 2,800  100 Park Avenue   New York    NY 10016
Davidson  Edward  06/04/90 1,500  100 Park Avenue   New York    NY 10016
Gilbert   Fred    04/15/87 2,300  100 Park Avenue   New York    NY 10016
Jones     Betty   09/26/89 2,500  100 Park Avenue   New York    NY 10016
Bell      George  10/12/88 2,400  200 Lake Drive    Chicago     IL 60607
Carter    Jack    05/14/87 2,550  500 Century Blvd. Los Angeles CA 94005
```

Figure 1.14 Handling one-to-many relations in one table

If you assign more than one salesperson to a given office, obviously you would have to repeat the data elements about the office more than once in the table. For example, if you assign four salespeople—Anderson, Davidson, Gilbert, and Jones—to the same New York office (B1), the Salesman table would look like that in Figure 1.14.

As you look at this table, notice that redundant data appears in the second through fourth rows. Since the first four salespeople belong to the same New York office, data elements about that office appear in four different rows. If each office is occupied by several salespeople, the problem of redundant data becomes more severe. And, if you try to accommodate all the one-to-many relations, as shown earlier in Figure 1.2, the amount of repeated data becomes very significant, as you can see in Figure 1.15. These repeated data elements waste storage and endanger the accuracy of information in the database and should be avoided.

One way to eliminate these redundancies is to structure the table so that data elements about a given office appear in only one row in the database. To do this in the new structure, save all the data elements associated with the sales offices in one table and leave those data elements about sales personnel in another table. To provide the link between these two tables, add a column in the Salesman table to hold the office identification number for the associated sales office. In Figure 1.16, you can see how these two tables are structured.

Notice that the Office ID column appears in both the Salesman and Office tables. It provides the link between these two tables. Consequently, when you want information about a given office that belongs to a salesperson, first go to the Salesman table to find the salesperson either by his or her last name or identification number. After finding the row for that person, retrieve the office number from the Office ID column. Using the office number, then go to the Office table to find the information about a particular office. All these tasks can be done by linking the data elements in the two tables. In this example, the Salesman table is considered the master table, and the Office table is referred to as the linkup table.

```
Table: Salesman (including data for sales offices)

Last       First   Hire     Salary Address          City         ST Zip
Name       Name    Date

Anderson   Doris   07/01/86 2,800  100 Park Avenue   New York    NY 10016
Davidson   Edward  06/04/90 1,500  100 Park Avenue   New York    NY 10016
Gilbert    Fred    04/15/87 2,300  100 Park Avenue   New York    NY 10016
Jones      Betty   09/26/89 2,500  100 Park Avenue   New York    NY 10016
Bell       George  10/12/88 2,400  200 Lake Drive    Chicago     IL 60607
Evans      Henry   03/08/88 2,000  200 Lake Drive    Chicago     IL 60607
Harvey     Candy   12/01/89 2,450  200 Lake Drive    Chicago     IL 60607
Carter     Jack    05/14/87 2,550  500 Century Blvd. Los Angeles CA 94005
Ford       Ida     11/22/87 2,600  500 Century Blvd. Los Angeles CA 94005
Iverson    Albert  10/25/88 2,200  500 Century Blvd. Los Angeles CA 94005
```

Figure 1.15 All one-to-many relations in the Salesman table

Linking Keys

The Office ID column, which serves as a linking key for joining the two tables, is called a foreign key in the Salesman table because it provides a link to those data elements stored in another data table.

```
Table: Salesman (after adding the Office_ID column)

Salesman ID   Last Name   First Name   Hire Date   Salary   Office ID

S0            Anderson    Doris        07/01/86    2,800    B1
S1            Bell        George       10/12/88    2,400    B3
S2            Carter      Jack         05/14/87    2,550    B2
S3            Davidson    Edward       06/04/90    1,500    B1
S4            Evans       Henry        03/08/88    2,000    B3
S5            Ford        Ida          11/22/87    2,600    B2
S6            Gilbert     Fred         04/15/87    2,300    B3
S7            Harvey      Candy        12/01/89    2,450    B3
S8            Iverson     Albert       10/25/88    2,200    B2
S9            Jones       Betty        09/26/89    2,500    B1

Table: Office

Office ID  Address            City         State Zip    Phone #

B1         100 Park Avenue    New York     NY    10016  800-123-5555
B2         200 Lake Drive     Chicago      IL    60607  800-234-5555
B3         500 Century Blvd.  Los Angeles  CA    94005  800-456-5555
```

Figure 1.16 Relating Office to Salesman

Remember, a good relational database is one in which all the rows in a data table are indexed according to specific values in one or more columns. The Salesman ID column can be used for such a purpose in this example. Since each salesperson number is unique, it provides a quick and precise reference to a particular row relating to a given salesperson. Such a column is often referred to as a primary key in a master table. Similarly, the Office ID column in the Office table is considered a primary key, as it provides unique identification and reference for those rows in that table.

In summary, each data table should have a primary key. In order to link to another data table to handle one-to-many relations, you also must have a foreign key column that relates to the linking table. Of course, you may have more than one foreign key if you are to link one master table to several linking tables.

Handling Many-to-Many Relations

Earlier examples proved that if only one-to-one relations exist among data objects, you can use a single data table to organize data elements. When you have one-to-many or many-to-many relations, however, you need to use at least two tables to accommodate the relations in order to avoid redundant data. But, if you have many-to-many relations among data objects, you must define and create one or more relation tables to handle these relations.

A relation table looks exactly like a regular data table; it is, in fact, a data table. As such, it contains a number of rows and columns. What is different is that, in a relation data table, you save the data elements that specify the link between two objects. Each row of the table associates one primary key of one table with another primary key of the other table. The relation table may not have a a primary key column.

Examples of many-to-many relations are apparent among the data elements in the original Salesman and Region tables in Figure 1.3. For quick reference, these relations are repeated in Figure 1.17. Contents of the original Salesman and Region tables are shown in Figure 1.18.

In Figure 1.17, notice that saleswoman Harvey has three sales regions (R4, R5, and R6) assigned to her, while each of these three regions in turn belongs to other salespeople. That is, sales regions R4 and R6 are assigned to Evans as well; Region R5 is assigned to Bell in addition to Harvey. If you were to structure all of these relations in a single table with data elements referencing the sales staff and their sales regions, it might look in part like that in Figure 1.19.

There are a lot of redundant data in this figure. The redundant data are necessary, however, to relate data associating salespersons Harvey, Evans, and Bell to the regions R4 (Southcentral), R5 (Northwest), and R6 (Southwest). The complete table showing all the relations among the salespeople and their assigned sales

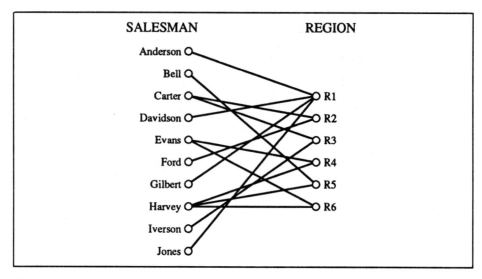

Figure 1.17 Relations between Salesman and Region

```
Table: Salesman

Salesman ID    Last Name    First Name    Hire Date    Salary

S0             Anderson     Doris         07/01/86     2,800
S1             Bell         George        10/12/88     2,400
S2             Carter       Jack          05/14/87     2,550
S3             Davidson     Edward        06/04/90     1,500
S4             Evans        Henry         03/08/88     2,000
S5             Ford         Ida           11/22/87     2,600
S6             Gilbert      Fred          04/15/87     2,300
S7             Harvey       Candy         12/01/89     2,450
S8             Iverson      Albert        10/25/88     2,200
S9             Jones        Betty         09/26/89     2,500


Table: Region

Region ID    Region            Manager

R1           Northeast         Alice F. Gibson
R2           Southeast         Bob L. Major
R3           Northcentral      John K. Freed
R4           Southcentral      Cathy M. Wilson
R5           Northwest         Chris C. Hall
R6           Southwest         Helen T. Taylor
```

Figure 1.18 The original Salesman and Region tables

```
Table: Salesman (including data elements for sales regions)

Last    First   Hire       Salary  Region        Manager
Name    Name    Date

Harvey  Candy   12/01/89   2,450   Southcentral  Cathy M. Wilson
Harvey  Candy   12/01/89   2,450   Northwest     Chris C. Hall
Harvey  Candy   12/01/89   2,450   Southwest     Helen T. Taylor
Evans   Henry   03/08/88   2,000   Southcentral  Cathy M. Wilson
Evans   Henry   03/08/88   2,000   Northwest     Chris C. Hall
Bell    George  10/12/88   2,400   Southwest     Helen T. Taylor
```

Figure 1.19 Relating Salesman and Sales Region in a data table

regions has even more redundant data. Obviously, the table is not properly structured to conform to the requirements of a relational database.

To eliminate redundant data in the table, you must store the data elements for the sales staff and the sales regions in separate tables, as shown in Figure 1.18. In each of these tables, data elements associated with each object appear only once. That is, data about a salesperson is saved in one and only one row in the Salesman table, and each of the sales regions occupies a single row in the Region table. But, in order to relate the objects in these two tables, you have to build a relation table that specifies the link between them. In the relation table, all you have to do is show

```
Table: Assignment

Region ID   Salesman ID

R1          S0
R1          S3
R1          S6
R1          S9
R2          S2
R2          S5
R3          S2
R3          S8
R4          S4
R4          S7
R5          S1
R5          S7
R6          S4
R6          S7
```

Figure 1.20 The relation table associating sales staff and regions

the relations between the sales staff and the sales regions. In the table, each association between a salesperson and his or her sales region(s) is saved as one row. The Assignment table in Figure 1.20 is such a relation table.

Here you can see that the first four rows show the association between region R1 and the four salespeople assigned to it. The Assignment table has two columns, each of which can be linked to a data table. Thus, you can use the Salesman ID column to link to the Salesman table, or use the Region ID to link to the Region table.

Chapter Summary

This chapter explained the fundamentals of a database management system and database design, including the basic ingredients and units of a database and the relations among them. Three data models for organizing data elements were introduced, with the focus directed at the relational data model. The desirable characteristics of a relational database also were described. This knowledge will serve as the foundation on which to build as you design and develop your own database system. In the next chapter, you will get an overview of FoxPro for Windows.

2
An Overview of FoxPro for Windows

An Overview

FoxPro for Windows is one of the most user-friendly, yet powerful software programs that you can use for designing and developing relational database management systems (RDBMS). The comprehensive menu system is the center of the FoxPro user interface, and by selecting appropriate options from it, you can perform virtually all of your data management functions. This chapter provides an overview of this system as well as other major components of the FoxPro user interface.

What Is FoxPro for Windows?

FoxPro for Windows is database software that utilizes a graphical user interface (GUI) to enhance its ease of use, but that can be used for designing and developing virtually any relational database application that runs on a personal computer. Because of its sound design and superior performance, it has been widely recognized as one of the best database management software programs in the industry. FoxPro for Windows operates on all IBM PCs and compatible single-user, stand-alone machines, or multiple-user local area networks (LANs).

FoxPro for Windows represents a significant improvement over the early versions of FoxPro and FoxBase+. If you have developed your database files with these programs, you should be able to use them in FoxPro for Windows without major changes. In addition, all database files created in dBASE III Plus and dBASE IV are compatible with those used in FoxPro for Windows.

FoxPro for Windows assumes a relational data model in which you organize all data elements in data tables. To link elements in these data tables, you create relation tables and then store all the data and relation tables on disk as database files.

The data contained in the database files can be processed using two different modes: interactive mode and batch mode. Interactive processing can involve extensive use of the menu interface. In interactive mode, the FoxPro menu interface becomes the focal point of the data manipulation. Menu options represent operations that are carried out on the databases, creating and manipulating them at the click of the mouse or touch of a key. Instead of working with the menus, appropriate FoxPro commands also can be used to govern and alter the database in interactive mode.

Programs written in the FoxPro command language are the vehicle of FoxPro batch command processing. These programs consist of a set of FoxPro commands and functions. They manipulate data elements and extract information as specified by the commands, producing the desired results without interruption. There are two ways to use the batch processing method: You can execute a custom tailored program you've written or execute a program generated by FoxPro. For example, to produce a customized report, you can write and execute a program that designs and prints the report. Alternatively, you may use the Report Writer provided by FoxPro to lay out the report. After the layout is saved, a program file is automatically generated by FoxPro that you can simply run in order to create and print the report.

The FoxPro User Interface

Thanks to its powerful and easy-to-use interface, FoxPro for Windows is one of the most user-friendly database management software programs available. Even an end user without any programming knowledge can perform most data management functions with the user interface.

The heart of the user interface is the versatile and logically organized menu system. By choosing the appropriate options from the menu, you can instruct FoxPro to carry out any operations that are required for managing your database. Once you have selected a given menu option, it returns a set of option windows, dialog boxes, check boxes, push buttons, radio buttons, etc. that you use to give further instructions to FoxPro.

THE MENU SYSTEM: MENU BAR AND MENU PADS

The FoxPro menu system consists of four basic components: a menu bar, menu pads, menu popups, and menu options (see Figure 2.1). The menu bar is usually

An Overview of FoxPro for Windows   31

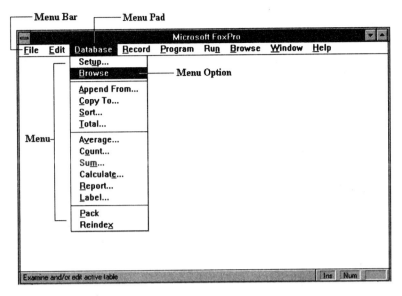

Figure 2.1 The FoxPro menu system

the first thing that you see when you enter FoxPro. Each item displayed is called a menu or a menu pad. The actual number of available menu pads varies depending on precisely what you are using FoxPro to do. For example, a Browse menu pad will be displayed only after you have selected an existing database file and have opened a Browse window for it. Similarly, when you are designing a report, the Report menu pad will be added to the menu bar.

Each menu pad contains a set of options for performing certain related data management functions. The Database menu pad contains the set of options used to manipulate data in the current database file, for instance. You can select a menu pad either by clicking on it with your mouse; by holding down the Alt key and pressing the highlighted letter in the menu pad's name (for example, the D in Database); or by holding down the Alt key, moving the cursor to the menu pad, and pressing Enter. When you select a menu pad, a menu popup opens. It is a rectangular box that shows all the available options.

Depending on the current status of the database file, not all of the options may be selectable. The options that can be selected are displayed differently from the disabled options. An enabled option is indicated by the highlighting of one of its key letters. When the letter "u" of the Setup option on the Database menu pad is highlighted, it is selectable. Other options, such as Append From, Copy To, etc., are disabled when no database file is in use. If you are using a color monitor, disabled options are displayed with dimmed labels or in a different color.

You can select an item from a menu popup in much the same way you would select an option on the menu bar: either click on it with your mouse, press the highlighted letter (called the hotkey) on your keyboard, or cursor to the item with the up- and down-arrow keys and press Enter. Once you have selected an option, FoxPro usually will present you with an array of interface objects that either carry out your selection or allow you to define more precisely just what you would like FoxPro to do.

DIALOGS

FoxPro most commonly uses dialog boxes to get additional information for the menu option chosen. When you choose a menu option that is followed by an ellipsis (...), FoxPro responds with a dialog. For instance, when you select the Open... option from the File menu pad, you will be presented with the dialog box shown in Figure 2.2.

Here you can see that the File Open dialog asks you to provide FoxPro information on the current disk drive, the file directory, and the type of file you would like to open. You supply this information by using a number of objects provided by FoxPro and included in the dialog: popups, scrollable lists, push buttons, check boxes, and text boxes.

Dialog Popups

Note in Figure 2.2 that the Open File dialog has two dialog popups: Drive and List Files of Type. (A popup is also called a drop-down list in the normal Windows environment.) The Drive popup is for choosing the disk drive, and the List Files of Type popup is for selecting the type of file you want to open. Like a menu popup,

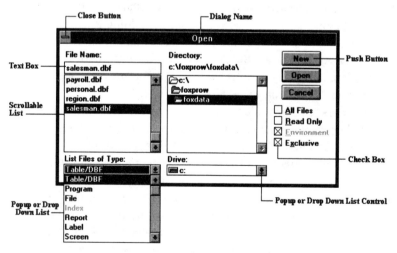

Figure 2.2 The Open File dialog box

a dialog popup, once selected, presents a list of data objects from which to choose. Select the List Files of Type dialog and a list of file types will be displayed. The size of a dialog box depends on the number of data objects in the list. If there are more objects than can be shown in the box, you can use the Scroll Down button to see the hidden items. When you are at the lower portion of the list, you can use the Scroll Up button to reveal the items in the upper portion of the list.

Unlike a menu popup, the initial contents of the dialog popup's frame, when it is not selected, represent the current setting. For example, in Figure 2.2, FoxPro will use drive c: as its currently logged drive and Foxdata as the current directory. These can be changed, of course, by using the popup dialog to make another selection.

List Boxes

In addition to popups, you often will find a list box within a dialog box. A list box allows you to select a data object from among a number of alternatives. In Figure 2.2, for example, the rectangular window beneath File Name: is a list box; it displays available files and you use it to select the file you would like to open. Another example is the Directory list box for selecting and identifying the current file directories.

When there are more items than can be shown in the list box at a single time, FoxPro displays a scrollable list box. This is very similar to a list box, except that a scroll bar with a set of control buttons is present on the right side of the box. The up and down arrows can be used to scroll upward or downward, while the square-shaped object (called a thumb button) roughly indicates the position of the items displayed in the total list. In addition, the thumb button can be used to rapidly move from one part of the list to another.

Push Buttons

A set of push buttons also is displayed in a dialog box. These buttons, also called text buttons, are used to carry out certain operations. To create a new file, for example, you would select the New text button. Disabled buttons are displayed in a different or dimmed color. A default button is one whose name is enclosed in a dotted rectangle (in a latter example).

Check Boxes

Another common object in dialogs is a check box. Check boxes are used to turn particular dialog box options on or off. In the Open dialog, note that four different check boxes are provided: All Files, Read Only, Environment, and Exclusive.

34 Understanding FoxPro 2.5 for Windows

Select a check box option either by clicking on it or by highlighting it and pressing the Spacebar. FoxPro then indicates that the option is in effect by displaying an X in the check box. In Figure 2.2, for example, the Exclusive box contains an X; this indicates that an exclusive condition is in effect. On the other hand, the Read Only check box is not checked, which indicates that this option has not been selected.

Radio Buttons

Closely related to check boxes are radio buttons. Radio buttons also indicate whether an option is turned on or off; FoxPro indicates this by placing a dot within the parentheses to the left of the button. However, unlike check boxes, radio buttons occur in groups, one for each mutually exclusive option. Therefore, one of them must be turned on at all times. In Figure 2.3, for example, you can select Table/DBF as the type of new file to be created by turning on the Table/DBF radio button. Turn on or off a radio button by clicking the mouse on it, or, with the keyboard, first use the Tab key to select one of the radio buttons and then use the up- or down-arrow key to move between the radio buttons. Then press the Space key to toggle it on and off.

Nested Dialogs

When FoxPro requires additional information, it presents a dialog. This is true when you choose some of the push buttons as well as when you select any object that displays ellipses (. . .).

You can see in Figure 2.4 that the Field Picker dialog is nested in the Setup dialog. The dialog is displayed after you select the Fields... push button in the Setup dialog. Be aware that it is possible to have dialogs nested several levels deep.

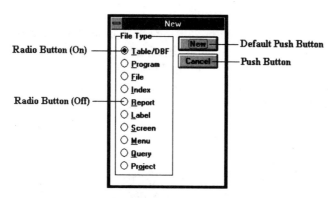

Figure 2.3 Radio buttons

An Overview of FoxPro for Windows   35

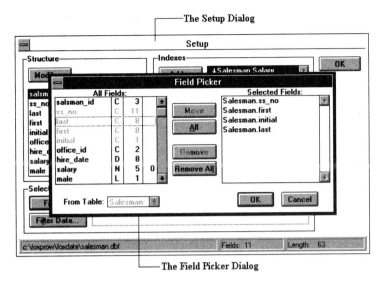

Figure 2.4 The Field Picker nested in the Setup dialog

Warning Dialogs

FoxPro sometimes uses a dialog box to display warning and confirmation messages so that you have a chance to cancel your action if you so desire. If you decide to delete a file, for instance, FoxPro will ask you to confirm your action in a dialog box (see Figure 2.5).

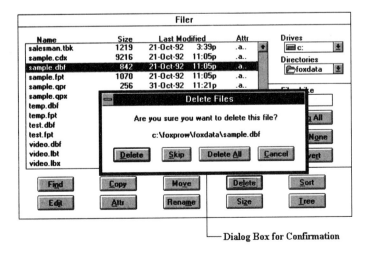

Figure 2.5 A warning dialog

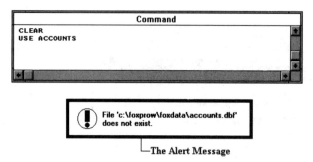

Figure 2.6 A FoxPro Alert

ALERTS

FoxPro also displays a warning or informs you of an error by returning Alert messages, which are different from warning dialogs. In a dialog, you normally are given the option to continue or cancel the current process, while an Alert usually informs you of an unexpected condition causing the action to be aborted. If you try to use a nonexisting database file, for example, an Alert stating "File does not exist" will be returned (see Figure 2.6).

WINDOWS

A window is another object that you can use to communicate with FoxPro. It is a screen area reserved for displaying a particular kind of information. There are a number of windows that you can use to perform different data management operations. You can select the database files that you plan to process in the View window, design a custom report by laying out the report form in a Report Design window, or view the contents of your database files in Browse windows.

You can float (move) most windows around the screen; change their size from a full-screen display to a minimum size of one line high, 16 characters wide; or simultaneously open multiple, overlapping windows on the same screen. Then you can close the windows you have finished using or make a window invisible by temporarily hiding it. Alternatively, you can reduce windows to their minimum size and dock them somewhere on the screen (without closing them) for later use.

There are many different types of windows that you can use in FoxPro for performing various data management functions. Each of these windows has its own set of characteristics and interface objects. In the forthcoming sections, we will examine these windows individually and in detail.

Components of a FoxPro Window

A window usually contains a title bar and a number of controls and buttons. A layout of a typical window is shown in Figure 2.7. The title bar that appears on the

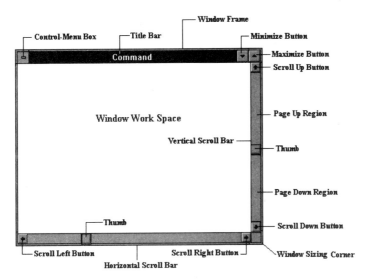

Figure 2.7 FoxPro window components

top of the window is used for identifying the window. The Control box at the upper left-hand corner of the window is used for closing the window.

At the upper right-hand corner are two buttons: one for maximizing the window, the other for minimizing the window. A maximized window fills the entire screen. There are two scroll bars, one on the vertical right-hand side of the window, the other at the bottom of the window. The buttons within the scroll bars enable you to scroll the contents of the window so that you can view the area that is hidden. The lower right-hand corner can be used to adjust the size of the window. Some windows have a status bar at the bottom for displaying infromation about the current state of the application you're processing.

There are many types of windows that are used in FoxPro for displaying different kinds of information. Not every window contains all the components mentioned above. However, at the minimum, all windows have a title bar and a Control box. And, while you can always move a window around on the screen, some windows do not have the scroll bar that enables you to scroll the contents of the windows or a maximizing button that allows you to enlarge the window.

The View Window

The View window permits you to open the databases you will be using in individual work areas. It also can be used to establish the relations among different database files. Or you can perform a number of operations on an opened file by choosing one of the text buttons provided (see Figure 2.8).

38   Understanding FoxPro 2.5 for Windows

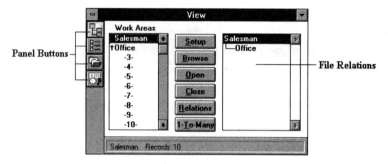

Figure 2.8 The View window

You can see that the View window, like all windows, is identified by a title bar showing its name (i.e., View). Figure 2.8 also shows that two database files, Salesman and Office, are open in work areas 1 and 2. The currently selected database file (e.g., Salesman) is highlighted in the work area. These two files are also shown linked together in the relation box on the right of the window.

Objects such as push buttons and scrollable list boxes also exist in a window. In the center of the View window is a set of push buttons that enable you to perform designated operations, such as the Browse button that, when chosen, allows you to view the contents of the currently selected database file.

The View window, like all windows, also has a Control box located on the upper left-hand corner of the window. The Close option is included in the Control box. Once you have closed a window, you can no longer view its contents.

Browse Windows

As noted above, a Browse window is used to display the contents of a database file. The Browse window in Figure 2.9, in addition to its title bar and Control box, contains many other types of controls that assist in displaying data. They include the maximize and minimize buttons, scroll bar and buttons, and a Window Splitter (see Figure 2.9).

Zoom Control

The Zoom control, shown in the upper right-hand corner of the window, enables you to switch between a full-screen and a window display. When you switch to the full-screen display, the other objects that were on your screen are still there, but are hidden behind the zoomed window.

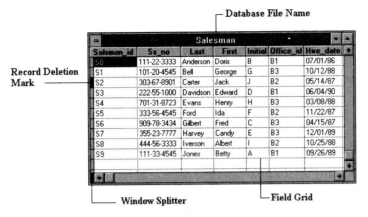

Figure 2.9 A Browse window

Size Control

In the lower right-hand corner of the Browse window is the Size control, which is used to resize the window.

Scroll Control

Two sets of controls enable you to scroll window contents: Use the Up and Down arrows to scroll vertically to reveal hidden data fields, and the Left and Right arrows to scroll horizontally to reveal hidden items in the window. You also can use the Thumb control on the right side of the window to scroll up and down the window more quickly, and the Thumb control on the bottom of the window to scroll left and right in the window.

Window Splitter

The Window Splitter, shown in the lower left-hand corner of the window, is a special control provided by the Browse window. It opens a second "window pane" that duplicates the window's contents, thus displaying two views of the same database. Unlike most windows, the Browse window permits you to view the contents of a database file in one of two modes. In Browse mode, data fields are shown as vertical columns, and data records are displayed as rows. In Change mode, each data field occupies its own row, and each data record is shown as a block. You also can use the Window Splitter to display a database file in both modes simultaneously in the same window (see Figure 2.10).

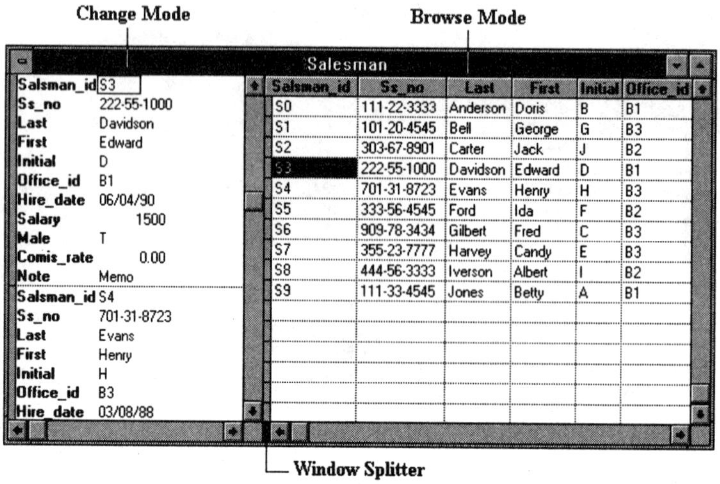

40   Understanding FoxPro 2.5 for Windows

Figure 2.10 Using the Window Splitter

The Memo Window

FoxPro for Windows allows you to save a block of text in a special type of data field called a memo field. Data stored in a memo field cannot be displayed with the other fields of a record in the Browse window; it only can be shown in a Memo window (see Figure 2.11).

This figure shows that a Memo window is used to display the contents of the memo field NOTE for a given data record. In addition to viewing the contents of the memo field, you also can modify the text shown in the Memo window.

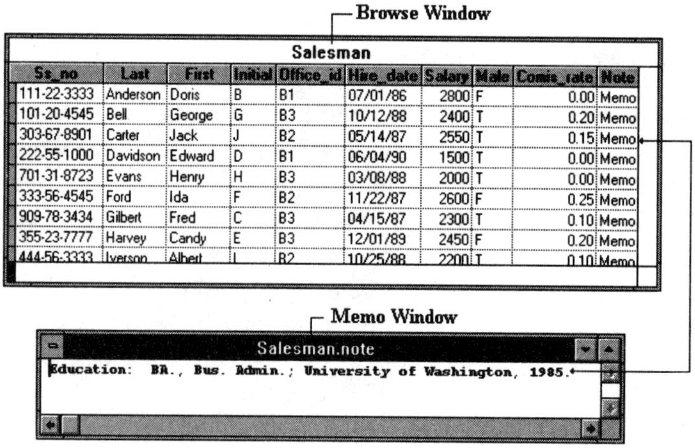

Figure 2.11 A Memo window

An Overview of FoxPro for Windows   41

You'll also find the Control box, Zoom, and Size controls in a Memo window, which enable you to resize the window, place it anywhere on the screen, and close it when you have finished using it.

The RQBE Window

One of the most significant enhancements of FoxPro for Windows over the early versions of the program is the implementation of the powerful Relational Query By Example (RQBE). With the RQBE builder, you can create a query by which you are able to search and extract meaningful information from one or more database files. Using RQBE, you provide FoxPro with an example of the kind of information you are looking for, and FoxPro takes over and finds the most efficient way to extract the information without the user's intervention.

FoxPro uses a separate Relational Query By Example window, shown in Figure 2.12, that displays all the information and the options that are required to carry out the query operation.

Note in Figure 2.12 that the RQBE window includes list boxes for defining the files used and their output data fields, plus a popup for selecting the output destination. It also includes a number of check boxes and push buttons for defining the query settings. At the bottom of the window is an area for defining the selection criteria for the query.

The Screen Design Window

FoxPro provides a number of standard form-based windows in which you can view and modify the contents of a database file. You can, for instance, display a file's

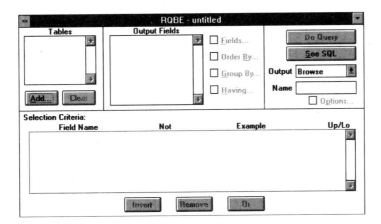

Figure 2.12 An RQBE window

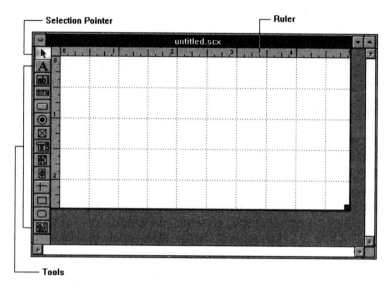

Figure 2.13 The Screen Design window

contents in a Browse window for viewing and editing purposes. In addition, you can use the Browse window to enter data elements into a new data record.

While the standard forms provided by FoxPro are sufficient for many data entry operations, FoxPro also offers the Screen Builder, a tool that allows you to design customized, enhanced entry forms that include a variety of interface objects such as push buttons, check boxes, and radio buttons. Graphics features such as lines and boxes also can be drawn to further accentuate data entry forms.

When you use the Screen Builder to design a customized entry screen, FoxPro opens the Screen Design window shown in Figure 2.13. As shown here, you can lay out all the data fields and interface objects on the screen in the format you choose. These objects can include field labels, check boxes, radio buttons, lines, and boxes.

The Report Layout Window

The Report Layout window is provided by the Report Writer for designing custom reports. It is here that you lay out all the objects related to the report in the format of your choice. The report form is divided into a number of bands used for defining the report title, page heading, record details, footers, and summary statistics (see Figure 2.14).

The Label Layout Window

FoxPro for Windows Label Designer is used to produce mailing labels of different sizes and formats by extracting data elements from database files. You lay out a

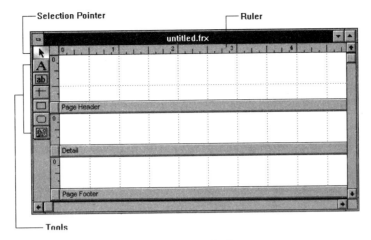

Figure 2.14 The Report Layout window

mailing label form in the Label Layout window where you specify the size of the mailing label, the placement of the data fields and text, and the height and width of the labels, along with the size of the margins and spaces between the labels.

The Label Layout window looks identical to that of the Report Layout window because a label is very similar to a form report. All the data fields used to create a mailing label are specified in the Detail band of the layout form.

The Menu Design Window

An attractive feature of the FoxPro user interface is its menu system. All the menu options are logically organized on the System menu bar as menu pads. By choosing the appropriate menu options, you can perform the designated data management operations without any programming knowledge.

The power of the menu interface extends beyond the System menu, however. FoxPro also allows you to design and create a customized menu system tailored to your database applications, instead of using only those options included in the System menu pads. This is done in the Menu Design window (see Figure 2.15).

Project Windows

The Project window is the interface provided by the FoxPro Project Manager. If you are a software developer, you can use the Project Manager to create a FoxPro application. After you have created all the components of a database management system, the next step is to organize them into a project; the components of the system are specified in the Project window (see Figure 2.16).

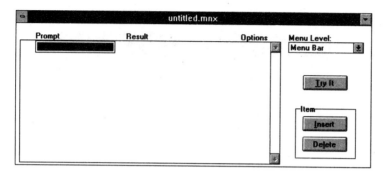

Figure 2.15 The Menu Design window

The Command Window

The Command window displays and executes the FoxPro commands that are issued either by a user or by FoxPro itself. When you perform data management functions interactively by issuing FoxPro commands, you enter those commands in the Command window. As a matter of fact, even when you choose a menu option to carry out a data management operation, FoxPro usually translates that choice into an equivalent FoxPro command. As a result, the command is displayed in the Command window as if you had entered the command directly (see Figure 2.17).

The Command window in Figure 2.17 shows a list of FoxPro commands that were used to carry out certain management functions. They could have been entered by a user or issued by FoxPro after you selected the corresponding menu options.

Text Editing Windows

A program is a collection of commands grouped together in a single file that will perform one or more database management functions. This program file can be created and edited in a number of ways and with a wide range of text editors,

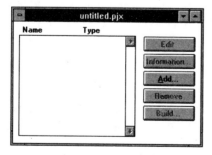

Figure 2.16 The Project window

An Overview of FoxPro for Windows   45

Figure 2.17 The Command window

including the text editor offered by FoxPro for Windows. When you select the editor, FoxPro opens a Text Editing window like the one shown in Figure 2.18.

You can see that the Text Editing window shows a listing of the program named GENMENU.PRG. You can make any modifications you want to the program listing in this window.

Help Windows

FoxPro provides a comprehensive help facility that you can access at any time by simply pressing the F1 function key. Usually, help is context-sensitive—that is, the contents of the Help window that FoxPro opens in response to your request for help are related to what you are doing in FoxPro at that particular time.

If FoxPro cannot determine what you are doing or cannot find any information related to where you are in the FoxPro program, it displays the topics-level Help window shown in Figure 2.19. You can then scan the list of topics and select the one in which you are interested. Otherwise, FoxPro opens a details-level Help

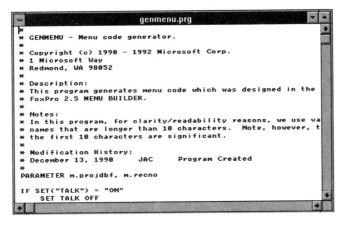

Figure 2.18 A Text Editing window

46 Understanding FoxPro 2.5 for Windows

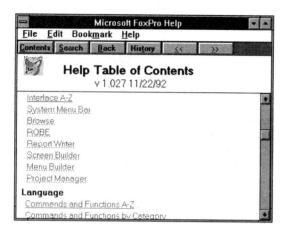

Figure 2.19 A Help window

window that provides you with information about the task that you are currently performing. For example, if you press the Help (F1) key while using the Calculator, FoxPro will open a Help window that displays information about the operation of the Calculator desktop accessory.

The Major Components of FoxPro

The most important component of any relational database management system is, of course, its data and the associated tables for organizing the relations among data elements. And FoxPro naturally offers the capability to create and maintain database files and a number of different kinds of index files.

This potentially valuable data is meaningless, however, without tools that will allow you to ensure its integrity and to extract the information you desire. Consequently, FoxPro offers more than the capability to create and maintain files; as a comprehensive environment for relational database management, it provides all the tools you need to create, maintain, and extract your data. Besides its file system, these tools, some of which we've already discussed, form the components of the system and include:

- Relational Query By Example (RQBE), a powerful tool for extracting information quickly and efficiently.

- The Screen Builder, a tool that creates customized data entry forms. It facilitates data entry and modification and can be used to ensure the integrity and accuracy of your data.

- The Report Writer, a flexible tool that allows you to format output in the way you desire.

- The Label Designer, a tool that handles labels of virtually all sizes easily and elegantly.
- The Menu Builder, which allows you to replace FoxPro's menu system with a customized one that is tailored to a particular application. This allows users who have little or no knowledge of how FoxPro works to use the program.
- The Project Manager, a tool that links all these diverse components to an integrated database management system.

In the following section, we will survey these components in greater detail.

THE FILE SYSTEM

Data and relational tables make up one major component of a relational database. Data elements are organized in tables by data fields and records. These tables are saved on disk as database files in FoxPro. In addition to data elements, these files also contain information about the structure of the data tables.

Index files also play an important role in a database management system. They provide information for arranging the data in database files. There are two types of index files that you can use in FoxPro: standard and compound.

Each type of disk file is given a unique file extension; FoxPro database files are assigned .DBF. If you need to store large blocks of text in a data table, you can save them in memo fields, which FoxPro saves to a separate disk file with .FPT as the file extension. If you decide to create a database file in FoxPro to store the data table named SALESMAN in Chapter 1, it would contain six data fields and ten records (see Figure 2.20).

The database file named SALESMAN.DBF contains all its data elements in a data table. In addition, it contains information about the database structure (see Figure 2.21). The data structure contains a memo field named NOTE that is used for storing a block of text describing a salesperson's specifics such as hobbies, educational background, etc. Contents of this memo field are saved in the memo file named SALESMAN.FPT.

THE RQBE BUILDER

As described earlier, the RQBE Builder allows you to create a data query for finding the information you want. This tool opens an RQBE window in which you specify all the conditions and select the options and settings that are required by the query operation. An RQBE window is shown in Figure 2.22.

In this window, you select the database files from which the query will extract information. You can see in Figure 2.22 that the query uses two database files: SALESMAN.DBF and OFFICE.DBF. At the lower portion of the window are the conditions for linking the database files and for defining the selection criteria for

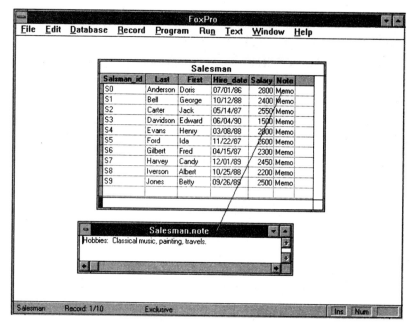

Figure 2.20 A sample database file

the query. The first condition is used to link the two database files using the common data field, OFFICE_ID. The second and third conditions specify the selection criteria, indicating that only those salespeople earning a salary of more than $2,500 or less than $2,000 will be chosen. When you carry out the query, it returns from the selected database file the data elements that satisfy the selection conditions.

Other settings in the RQBE window are for specifying and organizing the results returned from the query. They are used to identify the data fields to be returned by the query and how they should be arranged and grouped. You can also direct the

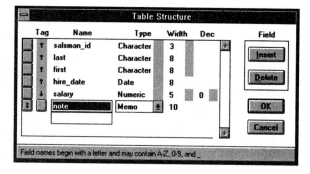

Figure 2.21 A database structure

An Overview of FoxPro for Windows 49

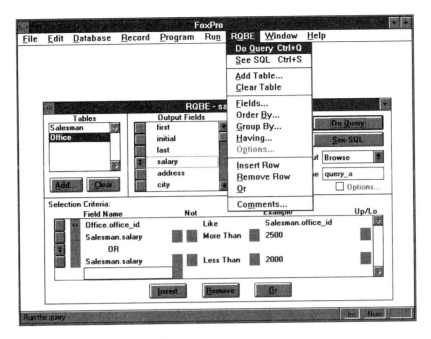

Figure 2.22 An RQBE window

query results to a number of destinations, including on screen, saved to a database file, or sent to a report.

THE SCREEN BUILDER

When you create a database file, FoxPro provides two modes that you can use to enter data elements into the data table, as well as view and edit the contents of your database files. These two modes are Browse and Change.

In Figure 2.23, you can see that the data fields in SALESMAN.DBF are shown as columns in Browse mode, while each data record is displayed as one row. Conversely, in Change mode, each data record is shown as a group of rows, each of which shows the contents of a data field. By default, the sequence of the data fields is determined by the order in which they are saved in the data structure.

Although Browse mode and Change mode are sufficient for many data entry operations, from time to time you probably will need a customized form for data entry or browsing. It may be that you simply find the arrangement of the data entry window to be unattractive and would like some alternative to it. Or perhaps the organization of the window in Browse mode is not conducive to rapid data entry. Or possibly, in browsing records, you would like to highlight certain information so that it readily stands out.

In the past, designing a custom screen required a knowledge of programming. But even more importantly, it was a cumbersome process. The programmer first

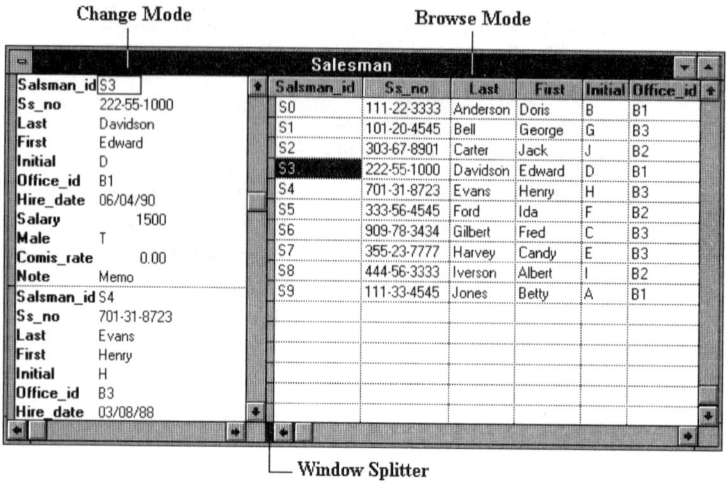

Figure 2.23 Browse and Change modes

used a text editor to write some code, then used the database management system to inspect the results. This process was repeated any number of times, until the screen finally conformed to the programmer's original intention.

FoxPro for Windows, however, provides a tool, the Screen Builder, that allows you to create your own customized data entry and browsing forms. In contrast to the techniques used in the past, the Screen Builder offers important advantages:

- You do not have to know programming to design attractive, functional screens. The Screen Builder is easy to use.

- You can design your screen visually by placing, moving, and sizing objects on the screen. Designing a screen is no longer a two-step process.

The Screen Builder permits you to determine the data entry order of individual fields, include calculated fields, and incorporate a number of graphics (like lines and boxes) and interface objects (push buttons, check boxes, radio buttons) into your forms. The Screen Builder is very flexible.

Figure 2.24 shows a custom screen created with the Screen Builder. Notice that the data fields are organized in the order of the user's choice. A check box identifies whether the salesperson is male or female, a radio button specifies the office to which the salesperson belongs, and a box displays the contents of a memo field. Figure 2.25 shows the same screen in the process of being created with the Screen Builder.

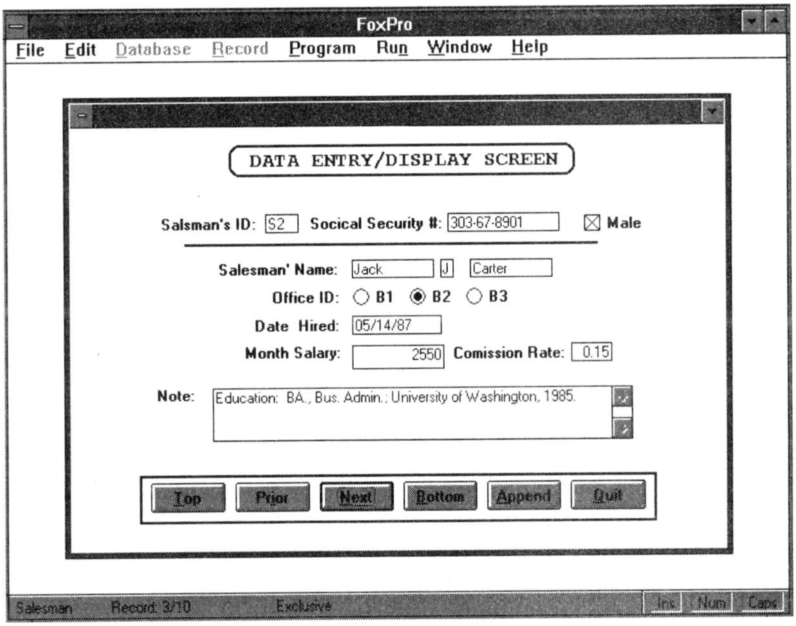

An Overview of FoxPro for Windows 51

Figure 2.24 A custom screen

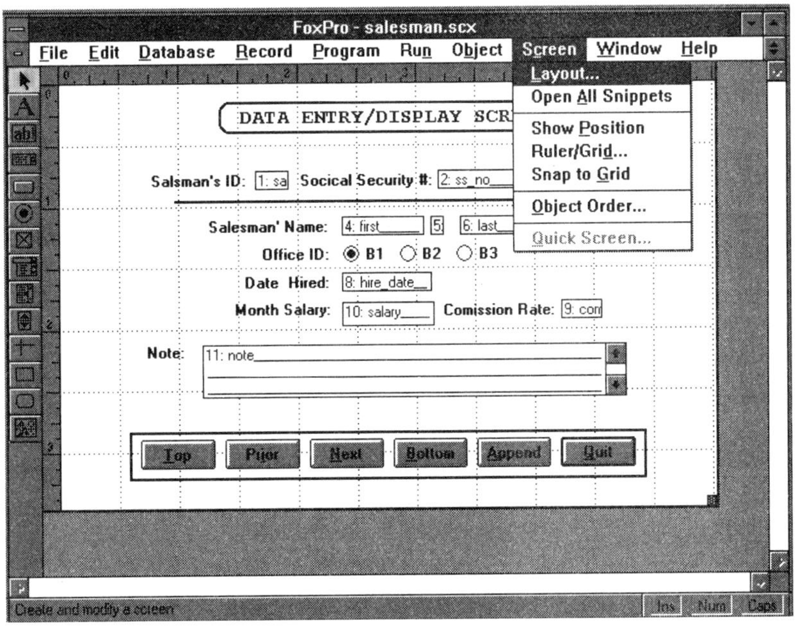

Figure 2.25 Creating a custom screen

THE REPORT WRITER

FoxPro's Report Writer is one of the most versatile report generators provided by a database management system. It allows you to produce professional reports with very little effort. You can choose either a columnar or a form report format. In a columnar report, values appear in columns; each row corresponds to a data record. Summary statistics (like totals) are shown at the bottom of the report (see Figure 2.26).

In a form format, text can be mixed with the contents of data fields in a free form. This is an efficient way to produce computer form letters when you need to move information from your database files into precomposed text.

A report in either format can be designed by using the Report Layout window provided by the Report Writer. In the report layout, you specify the data fields in the Detail band. The necessary field labels are added to the Page Header band. Data is grouped and summary statistics are generated in the Summary band. A footnote can be placed in the Page Footer band.

Figure 2.27 shows the report layout used to produce the report shown in Figure 2.26. In the figure, you can see some of the basic components of a report layout, including report title, column heading, data fields, and summary statistics.

Figure 2.28 shows an example of a form letter that was produced by using the Report Writer in a form format. In this letter, the names of salespeople Doris B. Anderson and George B. Bell are taken from SALESMAN.DBF and inserted into a block of text. The form letter also extracts data from other data fields such as HIRE_DATE and SALARY. To produce these form letters, you simply place the text and data fields in the location desired in the Report Layout (see Figure 2.29).

Page 1
12/06/92

COMPENSATION SUMMARY REPORT

Name of Salesperson	Date Hired	Salary	Commission
Doris B. Anderson	07/01/86	$2,800	0%
George G. Bell	10/12/88	$2,400	20%
Jack J. Carter	05/14/87	$2,550	15%
Edward D. Davidson	06/04/90	$1,500	0%
Henry H. Evans	03/08/88	$2,000	0%
Ida F. Ford	11/22/87	$2,600	25%
Fred C. Gilbert	04/15/87	$2,300	10%
Candy E. Harvey	12/01/89	$2,450	20%
Albert I. Iverson	10/25/88	$2,200	10%
Betty R. Jones	09/26/89	$2,500	0%
TOTAL		$23,300	

Figure 2.26 A columnar report

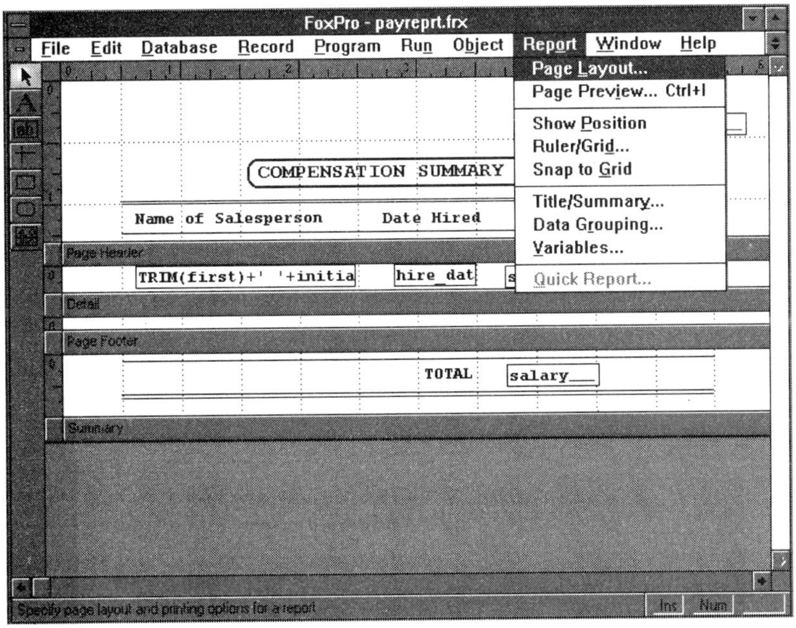

Figure 2.27 A report layout

To: **Ms. Doris B. Anderson**

From: Human Resource Department

Date: December 31, 1992

Please take a moment to verify the followion information and report any descrepencies to us at your earliest convenience:

Date of Employment:	**07/01/86**
Current Monthly Salary:	**$2,800**
Commission Rate:	**0%**

To: **Mr. George G. Bell**

From: Human Resource Department

Date: December 31, 1992

Please take a moment to verify the followion information and report any descrepencies to us at your earliest convenience:

Date of Employment:	**10/12/88**
Current Monthly Salary:	**$2,400**
Commission Rate:	**20%**

Figure 2.28 A form letter created in the Report Writer

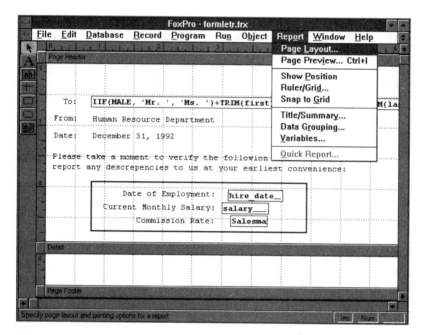

Figure 2.29 Using the Report Writer

THE LABEL DESIGNER

The Label Designer is provided by FoxPro for the design and production of mailing labels of various sizes and formats. You can define the number of labels across and the space between labels (see Figure 2.30).

These labels are produced by using the design specified in the Label Design screen shown in Figure 2.31. The Label Design window is very similar to the Report Writer screen. A mailing label can be considered as a special form of a

```
Ms. Doris B. Anderson          Mr. George G. Bell
100 Park Avenue                500 Century Blvd.
New York NY  10016             Los Angeles CA  94005

Mr. Jack J. Carter             Mr. Edward D. Davidson
200 Lake Drive                 100 Park Avenue
Chicago IL  60607              New York NY  10016

Mr. Henry H. Evans             Ms. Ida F. Ford
500 Century Blvd.              200 Lake Drive
Los Angeles CA  94005          Chicago IL  60607

Mr. Fred C. Gilbert            Ms. Candy E. Harvey
500 Century Blvd.              500 Century Blvd.
Los Angeles CA  94005          Los Angeles CA  94005
```

Figure 2.30 Sample labels

An Overview of FoxPro for Windows 55

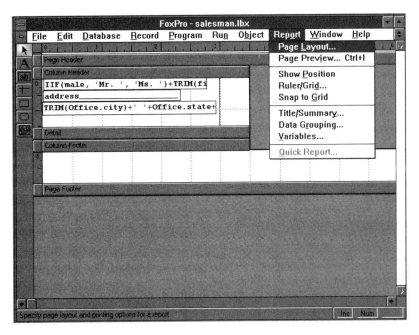

Figure 2.31 The Label Design window

report that is divided into a number of columns. You can use the same set of Report Writer's tools to design the mailing labels.

THE MENU BUILDER

The Menu Builder gives you the capability to design and create a menu system that is tailored to your applications. You can include some of the options from the System menu and create additional menu options for performing specific data manipulation operations. Your menu system will have the same appearance as the System menu, complete with menu pads, popups, and options.

The Menu Builder comes with a Menu Design window in which you lay out the menu structure. Besides the Menu Design window, the Menu option on the System menu provides additional options for creating a customized menu system. You begin by defining the menu pads to be included in the custom menu bar that will replace the FoxPro System menu. For each menu pad defined, you then define its associated options as a submenu.

Figure 2.32 shows a custom menu that has six menu pads, each of which performs a certain function. For example, in the Edit Data menu pad you can include options for editing the contents of different databases. Similarly, you can choose to include in your menu pad any of the system options that are normally found in the FoxPro menu pad (e.g., Help, Filer, Calculator, Calendar/Diary, etc.).

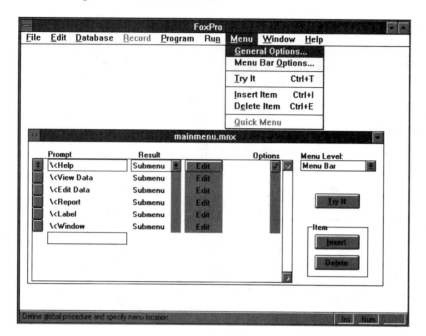

Figure 2.32 A custom menu

As a result, it will show only those options selected when you invoke your menu system (see Figure 2.33).

In this figure, you can see the six menu pads on the custom menu bar as defined in the Menu Builder. When you select the Edit Data menu pad, five menu options are displayed in its menu popup.

THE PROJECT BUILDER

To develop an integrated data management system, you use the tools provided by FoxPro to design and develop various components of the system: create the necessary database files for organizing data elements, design the screens for the data entry and data display operations, and create custom reports and label forms. To facilitate information searches, you create the necessary data queries. In addition, you create a custom menu for carrying out the data management functions with these components.

Finally, you integrate all the components into a project with the Project Builder. If you are a software developer, you can use the Project Builder to create a database application for the end user; using your application, the end user can access all the database components through the custom menu system without using the general user interface provided by FoxPro. In the Project Builder, you identify the name and type of management components to be included in the Project window. Then

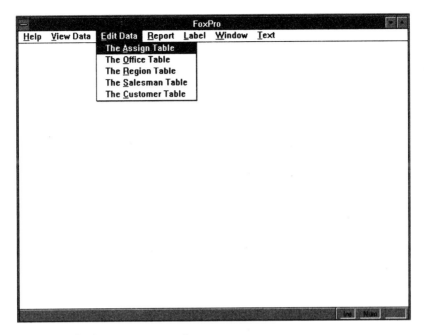

Figure 2.33 A custom menu bar

choose the appropriate options from which to build your project in the Project menu pad (see Figure 2.34).

THE DESK ACCESSORIES

In addition to providing the tools for managing your databases, FoxPro gives you a set of handy desk accessories. You access these accessories, which include a Filer, a Calculator, and a Calendar/Diary, by choosing from the options in the Help menu pad. (Note, however, that these accessories won't appear in the Help menu if you did not select them during Custom setup when you installed FoxPro. They are automatically included in the Help menu pad if you chose Express setup.) In addition, the Help menu provides options for getting help in using the software.

The Filer

The Filer is a utility tool that helps you to manage your disk files efficiently. With the Filer you are able to perform all file manipulation operations by choosing the appropriate text buttons (see Figure 2.35).

In the Filer, you can rename, copy, and delete an existing file; create a file directory; and move files between directories. You can sort files by their attributes,

58   Understanding FoxPro 2.5 for Windows

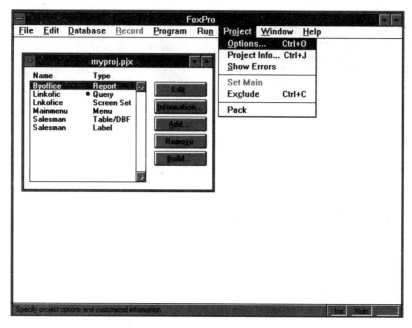

Figure 2.34 Defining a project with the Project Builder

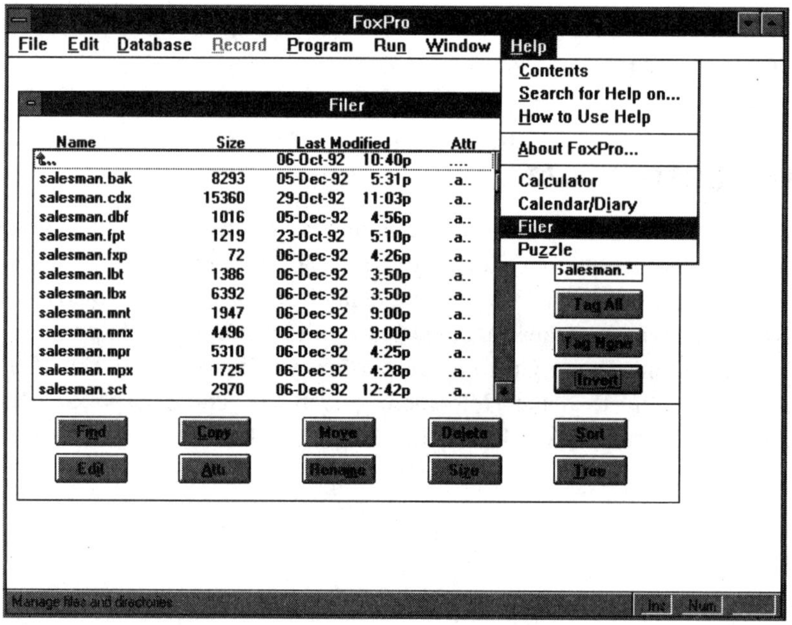

Figure 2.35 The Filer

An Overview of FoxPro for Windows   59

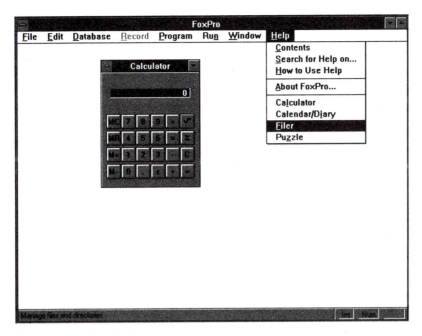

Figure 2.36   The Calculator

examine your file structure in a given directory by displaying the structure in a tree diagram, and perform some directory and file operations.

The Calculator

When you choose the Calculator option from the Help menu popup, a simple calculator appears on the screen (see Figure 2.36). You can invoke this handy tool while you are in most FoxPro operations. Once you are done using it, just close it and return to other operations.

The Calendar/Diary

The Calendar/Diary option, which you invoke by choosing it from the Help menu popup, allows you to view the calendar and enter appointments for a given date in the diary. In Figure 2.37, you can see that some events and appointments have been entered into the diary for December 21, 1992. Use the text buttons to display a different month or year on the calendar.

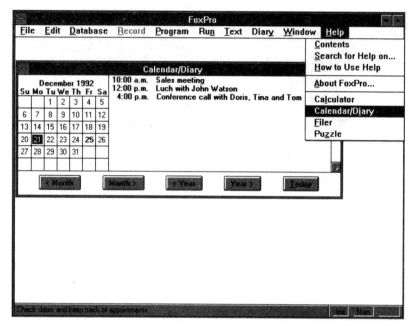

Figure 2.37 The Calendar/Diary

FOXPRO FILES

FoxPro follows the DOS file-handling convention of identifying a file by a name and a file extension. The first part is a symbolic name that describes the object; the file extension identifies the file type. For example, the filename SALESMAN.DBF indicates that it is a database file (.DBF) containing data about sales personnel.

Some files containing information about the same data object are saved in different forms with different file extensions. For example, the layout of a data form created in the Screen Builder is saved in a file with an .SCX extension. Before it generates the data form, the screen layout is translated into a set of FoxPro commands as a program and saved in a file with an .SPR extension. Furthermore, the compiled version of the program, which contains instructions coded in a machine language that can be understood by the computer, is saved in another file with an .SPX extension.

The types of FoxPro files can be summarized as follows:

File Type (Extension)　　　　　　*Description/Contents*

Database Files
    Database (.DBF)　　　　　　Data structure and table
    Database Backup (.BAK)　　　Backup of .DBF and others
    Memo (.FPT)　　　　　　　　Contents of memo fields
    Memo Backup (TBK)　　　　　Backup of .FPT

File Type (Extension)	*Description/Contents*
Index Files	
Standard Index (.IDX)	Standard indexes
Compound Index (.CDX)	Compound indexes
RQBE Files	
Generated Query (.QPR)	SQL commands of the query
Compiled Query (.QPX)	Compiled version of .QPR
View Files	
View (.VUE)	Open .DBF files and relations
Label Files	
Label (.LBX)	Layout of labels
Label Memo (.LBT)	Memo of the .LBX
Report Files	
Report (.FRX)	Layout of report
Report Memo (.FRT)	Memo of the .FRX
Screen Files	
Screen (.SCX)	Screen layout of data form
Screen Memo (.SCT)	Memo of the .SCX
Generated Program (.SPR)	Command file about the .SCX
Compiled Program (.SPX)	Compiled version of .SPR
Menu Files	
Menu (.MNX)	Layout of menu structure
Menu Memo (.MNT)	Memo of the .MNX
Generated Program (.MPR)	Command file about the .MNX
Compiled Program (.MPX)	Compiled version of .MPR
Project Files	
Project (.PJX)	Listing of project components
Project Memo (.PJT)	Memo of the .PJX
Generated Applications	
Generated Application (.APP)	Application program
Executable Program (.EXE)	Stand-alone executable program
Memory Variable Files	
Memory Variable Save (.MEM)	Memory variables
FoxPro Command Files	
Program (.PRG)	FoxPro commands
Compiled Program (.FXP)	Compiled version of .PRG

File Type (Extension)	Description/Contents
Text Files	
Text (.TXT)	Textual information
Macro Files	
Macro (.FKY)	—
Window Files	
Window (.WIN)	—
Working Files	
Temporary (.TMP)	—
FoxPro System Files	
Executable (.EXE)	—
Overlay (.OVL)	—

System Capacities

The maximum number of files that can be saved on your disk is limited by the amount of disk storage you have on your hard disk. The system capabilities for the objects to be discussed in this book can be summarized as follows:

	FoxPro Base	FoxPro Extended
Database files on disk	unlimited	unlimited
Database files open at one time	225	225
Data records per database file	1 billion	1 billion
Data fields per data record	255	255
Characters per data record	4,000	4,000
Characters per data field	254	254
Characters per standard index key (.IDX)	100	100
Characters per compound index key (.CDX)	254	254
Memory variables	3,600	65,000

Chapter Summary

This chapter presented the basic design philosophy and major components of FoxPro for Windows. In addition to the powerful user interface, you were introduced to the RQBE Builder, Screen Builder, Label Designer, Report Writer, Menu Builder, and Project Builder.

This chapter also discussed the comprehensive FoxPro menu system and its set of tools for working with the menu system. These tools include dialogs, alerts, popups, scrollable lists, push buttons, radio buttons, and various kinds of windows. In the forthcoming chapters, you will use these tools to effectively design, develop, manage, and safeguard the integrity of your relational databases.

3
Getting Started

An Overview

You are now ready to begin using FoxPro for Windows. But before you can design and develop your database management system, you first must install the program on your disk. This chapter outlines the steps involved in the installation process. You will learn how to navigate the FoxPro interface and its tools to carry out data manipulation operations.

Installing FoxPro for Windows

The installation process involves setting up the necessary file directories and copying the program files from the distribution diskettes into these directories. This process is simple and automatic—FoxPro even checks to make sure that you have enough disk space.

Since FoxPro for Windows is designed to be used in the Windows environment, it can only be set up inside Windows. As a result, if you have not installed Windows on your hard disk you, must do that before you can install FoxPro for Windows. After you have installed Windows and you bring up the Program Manager window, the desktop will look similar to that shown in Figure 3.1.

In Figure 3.1, you can see that icons are displayed in program groups. Each software application has its own window containing the icons representing the application program. For example, the Word for Windows window contains two icons, one for the word processor program, Microsoft Word, and another for the Word Setup program. After you have set up FoxPro for Windows, a similar window will be added to the desktop containing the icons for the associated programs.

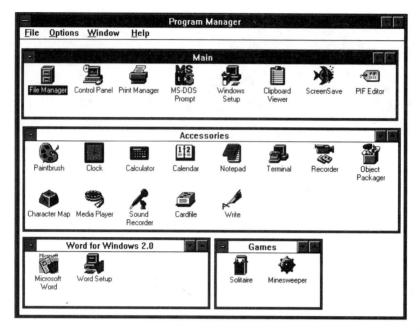

Figure 3.1 The Program Manager window

To begin the installation, first select the Run option from the File menu in the Program Manager. With the mouse, click on the File menu and you will see the list of options provided by the File menu. Select Run by clicking on the option. In return, you will be asked in the Run dialog to enter the command for installing the FoxPro for Windows program (see Figure 3.2). At this point, insert the first distribution disk in either drive A (or B), then type in one of the following commands:

```
A:\setup
```

or

```
B:\setup
```

Next, press the Enter key or select the OK button. This begins initializing the setup process. The process may take few minutes. (The actual amount of time depends on the type of computer you use.)

You will then be asked to enter your name and your company name. Next, you will be asked to specify where you would like to save the FoxPro files on the disk. By default, the program will be installed in drive c: under the foxprow directory (c:\foxprow). The name of the Program Manager Group is assumed to be FoxPro for Windows (see Figure 3.3). Of course, you can install it in a different directory and assign a different name to the program group simply by editing the input entries. Otherwise, just press the Continue button to proceed.

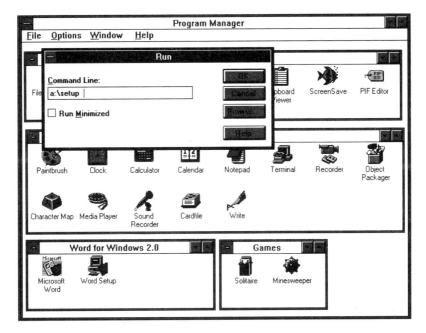

Figure 3.2 The Run dialog

At this stage, the program checks for available disk space. The amount of disk space required varies according to the optional components you choose to install. You may choose to install all or some of the components by selecting one of the three installation types: Complete, Custom, or Minimum (see Figure 3.4)

If you have plenty of disk space and would like to install all of the optional files, including all the sample and tutorial files provided by FoxPro, choose the Complete Installation option. This option requires at least 17 MB disk space. If you want to install only those files that are necessary to run FoxPro, select the Minimum Installation button. You can also install some of the optional files by choosing the Custom Installation option, in which case, you will be asked to select the optional files you want to install.

Once you have selected an installation option, FoxPro will check the available disk space. If you do not have enough for the installation option you have chosen, it will ask you to choose a different option that may require less disk space, or it will instruct you to cancel the installation process if you do not have sufficient disk space to continue.

If you have enough disk space to continue, FoxPro will prompt you to configure the program to use either Windows-style keystrokes or DOS-style keystrokes (see Figure 3.5). To take advantage of the Windows environment, choose the Windows-Style Keystrokes option to continue.

At this point, the program will begin copying files from the distribution disks to the FoxPro directory. You will be asked to insert the appropriate disks to complete

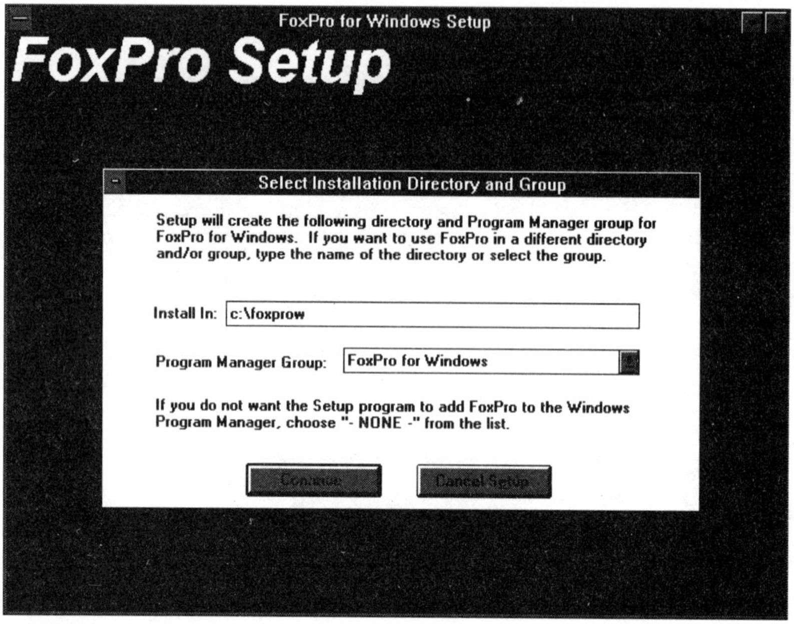

68 Understanding FoxPro 2.5 for Windows

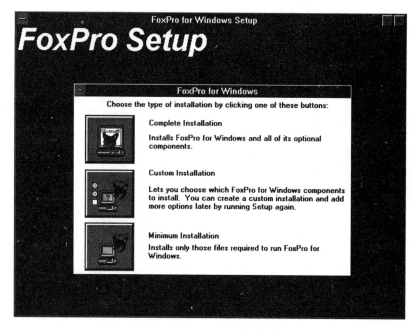

Figure 3.3 Defining the Installation Directory and Group

Figure 3.4 Selecting the installation type

Getting Started 69

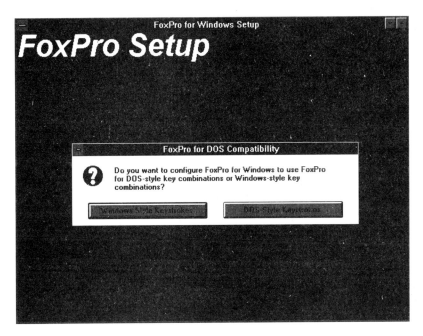

Figure 3.5 Selecting the style of keystrokes

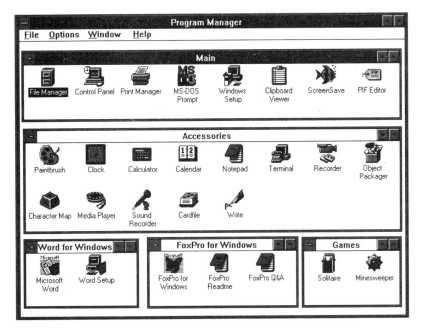

Figure 3.6 Showing the FoxPro for Windows icons

the installation process. Once the program is successfully installed, a group of icons will be displayed in the FoxPro for Windows group window in the Program Manager (see Figure 3.6)

Getting Ready

Before starting to work with FoxPro, it is highly recommended that you create a special subdirectory for saving all the disk files that you will create for your database. You can assign a name of your choice to that directory or name it foxdata. Create this subdirectory within the foxprow directory that was set up during the installation process. (If you already know how to do this, skip the next section and create the foxdata directory.)

CREATING THE DATA DIRECTORY

To create the foxdata subdirectory within the foxprow directory, you need to be at the DOS prompt. To access the DOS prompt, choose the Exit Windows option from the File menu in the Program Manager or choose the MS-DOS Prompt icon from the Main program group to open a DOS session and leave Windows running in the background. In either case, you will be at the DOS prompt in a directory that reads something like c:\windows where Windows is installed. Then you can switch to the foxpro directory by typing the following:

```
CD \FOXPROW
```

When you are in the c:\foxprow directory, issue this command to create a directory at the prompt:

```
MD FOXDATA
```

To return to the Windows directory, issue the following command:

```
CD \WINDOWS
```

Now you can return to the Windows environment to run FoxPro. If you exited Windows earlier by choosing the Exit Windows option from the File menu, you can restart Windows as follows:

```
CD \WINDOWS
WIN
```

If you temporarily left Windows by choosing the MS_DOS Prompt icon, return to Windows by issuing this command:

```
EXIT
```

Once you return to Windows and the Program Manager, you are ready to run the FoxPro program.

FILE ORGANIZATION

During the installation process, a number of subdirectories were created in the foxprow directory. In each of these subdirectories are disk files or more subdirectories. The contents of these subdirectories depend on the components you chose in the installation process.

INSTALLING THE MOUSE

To take advantage of FoxPro's powerful user interface, it is highly recommended that you use a mouse. When you set up Windows, the files necessary to operate the mouse are automatically installed. Therefore, when you are in Windows, you should see the mouse cursor active. If you have trouble activating your mouse, or if you are using some other type of mouse, consult the user's manual.

Starting FoxPro for Windows

When you are in the Program Manager, you can start FoxPro for Windows by opening the FoxPro for Windows program group icon and selecting the FoxPro for Windows icon and double clicking on it. As a result, you will be in FoxPro for Windows, indicated by the appearance of the program logo (see Figure 3.7).

Now, you can begin using FoxPro for Windows to design and develop your data management system. Before you actually can create the necessary database files, however, you need to learn the basics of working with the FoxPro user interface.

MOUSE BASICS

The mouse is a pointer device used for selecting objects to perform data manipulation operations in FoxPro. Although there are many different brands of mice, they all have at least two buttons: left and right. Most mouse techniques involve four basic actions, namely, pointing, clicking, double clicking, and dragging.

Pointing

When the mouse is active on the screen, a mouse cursor (or mouse pointer) in the shape of an arrow is visible. As you move the mouse, the cursor moves in the same direction and the same relative distance. Therefore, you can point your mouse cursor at any object on the screen simply by moving your mouse in the direction

Figure 3.7 The initial FoxPro for Windows screen

of the object. As you point the mouse cursor at different elements in a FoxPro window, its shape may change depending on the object at which it is pointing. The shape identifies the operation that can next be performed with the mouse. For example, when you are viewing data in a Browse window and you point your mouse at the Window Splitter, the cursor becomes a double cross with double arrows, which allows you to divide the Browse window into two panes. Similarly, when you point the mouse cursor at the lower right-hand corner of a window, the mouse cursor changes to a double arrow symbol, allowing you to resize the window.

Clicking

The clicking action involves pressing the mouse button once quickly and then releasing it. In FoxPro, normally you click only on the left button; rarely is the right button used. The clicking action usually follows pointing, so you would click the mouse button after you have pointed the mouse cursor at the selected object. This combined point-and-click action allows you to select an object without using the keyboard. As an exercise, point and click your mouse at the Help menu in the FoxPro menu bar. As a result, the Help menu options will be displayed in its popup (see Figure 3.8).

In Figure 3.8, you can see the list of options shown in the Help menu popup. At this point, you can use the point-and-click technique to select a menu option. To

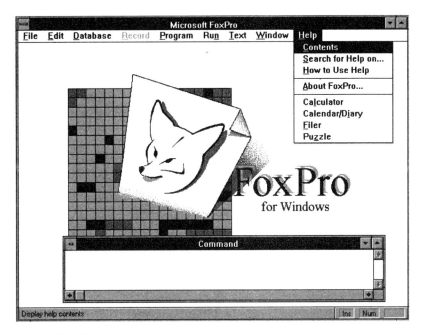

Figure 3.8 Selecting the Help menu pad

bring up the Calculator, for example, point and click on the Calculator option, and the Calculator is displayed on the screen.

Use the same point-and-click action to enter the number and operators (+, −, *, /, =, etc.) for the Calculator. After you are finished, close the Calculator by pointing and clicking on its Control box at the upper left-hand corner.

Dragging

Dragging involves holding down the mouse button (again, in most cases, the left button) and simultaneously moving the mouse in the direction and distance desired. You normally use the dragging action to select a menu option from a menu pad or to move an object around on the screen. You can also use the dragging operation to resize an object (such as a window or a report band, etc.)

To select a menu option, first point and click on a menu pad. When the menu popup appears, drag your mouse cursor to the menu option of your choice and then release it. As an exercise, point and click on the Window menu pad, and when its popup appears, drag the mouse cursor to the Clear option and then release the mouse button. After this, the FoxPro logo disappears and the work space is cleared.

To move an object around, first point the mouse cursor at the object that you want to move. Then use the dragging action to move it to another location. To move the Command window to a different location, for instance, first point the mouse cursor at the title bar (where the word Command appears) and then drag the mouse. As you drag the mouse, the window moves with it to a location of your choice.

To resize an object, point the mouse cursor at the right window frame, for example, and then drag it to the right to widen it or to the left to narrow it. Position the mouse cursor over the top window frame and drag it up to lengthen the window, and drag it down to shorten it. You can enlarge the window horizontally and vertically at the same time by pointing the mouse cursor at the lower right-hand corner of the window and dragging it toward the lower right-hand corner of the screen. As an exercise, use the dragging action to resize the Command window. Point the mouse cursor at the lower right-hand corner of the window and then drag it in the direction of your choice.

Double Clicking

Double clicking means pressing the mouse button twice in rapid succession and then releasing it. In some cases, double clicking can serve as a shortcut to pointing and clicking. For example, you can select an object from a scrollable list in two ways: either point and click on an object to select it, and then point and click on a push button to confirm the selection; or, point the mouse cursor at the object and then double click the mouse button. As an exercise, close the Command window by double clicking the Control box.

KEYBOARD BASICS

As stated, because FoxPro for Windows is designed for the Windows environment, a mouse is highly recommended, if not mandatory. Although many data entry functions require use of the keyboard, many other operations can be performed far more efficiently with the mouse than with the keyboard. For example, selecting a FoxPro object (a menu option, a button, etc.), can be done very easily by using the mouse; it is more cumbersome to use the keyboard for this same process in FoxPro for Windows.

In addition to the "typewriter" keys that you expect to find on the keyboard, there is a set of keys specially designed for computer use. These special-purpose keys are Esc, Alt, Ctrl, Shift, and Enter. Many of them are also used in conjunction with other keys.

There is another set of cursor keys, which include Home, End, PgUp (Page Up), PgDn (Page Down), and four arrow keys that are used for moving the cursor on the screen. These keys come in handy when you are editing data in a data table. They allow you to position your cursor at a specific location on the screen and edit the selected data items. Other useful editing keys are Ins (insert) and Del (delete).

Function Keys

There are ten function keys on a standard computer keyboard and they are labeled F1 through F10 (some keyboards may have more than ten, although these extra keys are generally not operational). Function keys are programmed by FoxPro to perform certain predefined operations while you are in the program:

Function Key	*Function*
F1	Help
F2	SET
F3	LIST
F4	DIR
F5	DISPLAY STRUCTURE
F6	DISPLAY STATUS
F7	DISPLAY MEMORY
F8	DISPLAY
F9	APPEND
F10	Activate/Deactivate FoxPro menu bar

Thus, if you press the F1 key when in FoxPro, the Help screen will appear. Depending on where you are in the program, it displays help messages pertinent to the current operation. Similarly, if you press F10, you activate or deactivate the menu bar. Other function keys are used for issuing FoxPro commands. Pressing F4, for example, is equivalent to issuing the DIR command in the Command window; as a result, FoxPro displays the list of database files in the current directory.

The Esc Key

The Esc key is usually used to exit from the current operation and return to your previous location. For example: If, after you have finished using the Calculator, you press the Esc key, you will exit from the Calculator and return to the FoxPro menu bar. You also can use Esc to abort the current operation. Say you are viewing your data in the Browse window and you want to abort the operation: Simply press the Esc key. Be aware, however, that if you do this, you interrupt the current operation, and the actions you have already taken will be canceled and the results will be voided. So, if you were editing data in a data field in the Browse window before you pressed the Esc key, all the changes you made would not be recorded or saved.

The Enter Key

The Enter key, which is also called the Return key, is similar to a carriage return on a normal typewriter. It signifies that you are at the end of a string of characters that you have entered. For example, when you are entering a data element to a data field, press the Enter key to complete the field and move on to the next field.

In FoxPro, the Enter key is often used to accept or to confirm an action. To use it in this way, select an object from the menu, position the cursor at the object and then press the Enter key to accept it.

Cursor Keys

Besides the mouse cursor (or mouse pointer), FoxPro maintains a second cursor in the form of a blinking dash. This is the keyboard cursor. It shows the location at which input from the keyboard will be placed.

The position of the keyboard cursor can be changed by using any of a number of cursor keys. These include the four arrow keys—the left, right, up, and down arrows. When you press one of these keys, the cursor moves in the designated direction. The distance you move depends on the operation: for example, when editing data, pressing the left or right arrow key moves you one character to the left or right respectively; pressing the up and down arrows moves you up or down one line. There are, however, exceptions to these processes. When a menu popup is displayed, for example, you still move up and down by pressing the up and down arrows, but if you press the left and right arrows at this time, the current menu popup is closed and the menu popup of the menu pad to the left or right of the current one is opened.

To move more than one line or one character at a time, use the PgUp, PgDn, Home, and End keys. By pressing the PgUp and PgDn keys, you move to the top and bottom, respectively, of a data block, which may occupy the whole screen or only a section of the window. By pressing the Home and End keys, you move to the beginning and end of a block, which may be a data record or a data field, etc. Again, these keys are used to move the cursor to a different location depending on the mode you are in. For example, if you are viewing data in Browse mode, you would move to the top of the screen by pressing the PgUp key. You would jump from the beginning to the end of a data field by pressing the End key. Likewise, when you press the Home key you would jump from the end to the beginning of the data field.

The Tab Key

The Tab key is used to move around objects in FoxPro. Each time you press the key, the cursor cycles from one object to another. Depending on where you are in a FoxPro session, the type of objects that you can cycle with the Tab key varies. In some cases, you can use the Tab key to cycle among the push buttons for performing certain operations. In others, you may move among the items in a table or list. In most cases, you can point to an object with the Tab key in the same way that you would with a mouse. The object of the current cursor is highlighted; to select the highlighted object, just press the Enter key.

The Ctrl Key

The Ctrl (Control) key is always used in combination with one or more keys for carrying out various operations. For example, after you have closed the Command window, you can redisplay it by pressing the F2 key while holding down the Ctrl key. If there are multiple windows displayed on the screen, use the Ctrl+F1 key combination to cycle among these windows. Every time you press this key combination, the next window will become active, a state that is indicated with a different color in the title bar.

The Alt Key

Like the Ctrl key, the Alt key is always used with one or more other keys. These key combinations are usually used to select a menu pad from the FoxPro menu bar by holding down the Alt key and pressing the highlighted letter in the menu pad name. As an exercise, press the Alt+F key combination to bring up the File menu popup and press the Alt+W key combination to select the Window menu pad from the FoxPro menu bar.

The Shift Key

In addition to using the Shift key to switch between upper- and lowercase, you also can use it with one or more other keys to perform certain functions. For example, pressing Shift and one of the arrow keys enables you to select a block of text when you are in Edit mode. And, in the same way that you use the Tab key to cycle through objects on the screen from top to bottom and left to right, pressing the Shift+Tab key combination cycles you through the objects in a reverse direction, from bottom to top and right to left.

WORKING WITH WINDOWS

Because FoxPro offers a graphics-based windowing interface, windows play a very important role in FoxPro. Among other things, FoxPro opens a window to allow you to browse or edit data. Windows are also used when you define data entry forms and reports. FoxPro windows are movable; that is, by clicking and dragging on a window's title bar, you can position it anywhere on the screen. FoxPro windows are also sizable; they can be maximized to take up the full screen (thus hiding other windows behind them). Most windows can be sized both horizontally and vertically. This is particularly important because FoxPro allows you to have multiple windows open and displayed on the screen simultaneously. To avoid a cluttered screen, you can reduce the size of your windows and position them in the way that you find most convenient. And, once you have finished using a window, you can remove it from the screen by closing it. It is important to note that, although you can have multiple windows open on the screen simultaneously, only one window may be active at a time.

Opening Windows

There are a number of ways to bring up a window, and a common one is to select one or more menu options. For example, if you want to view the contents of an existing database file, you could open the Browse window by selecting the Browse menu option from the Database menu popup after you have opened the database file in a work area. Or you could first bring up the View window by choosing the View menu option from the Window menu popup, and, when it appears, open the database file in a work area and then select the Browse push button.

As an exercise, open the Browse window to display the contents of a sample database file named CUSTOMER in the Tutorial subdirectory. (If you do not have enough disk space to install the tutorial files, open any .dbf file in another directory for the exercise. The procedure for opening a database file is the same.) Choose the View menu option from the Window menu popup after you have selected the Window menu pad from the menu bar. In response to the menu selection, you will see the View window appear on the screen (see Figure 3.9).

In the View window, select a work area in which to open your database file. If you want to open the CUSTOMER database file in work area 1, for instance, double click your mouse on that work area. If you are using the keyboard, press the Enter key when work area 1 is highlighted. In response, the Open dialog will appear to prompt you to select the database file to be opened in that work area (see Figure 3.10).

In Figure 3.10, you can see that all the subdirectories in the foxprow directory (c:\foxprow) are displayed in the Directory list (some are hidden from view). Since the database file is stored in the c:\foxprow\tutorial subdirectory, you need to select that directory in the Open dialog. Click the mouse on the down button in the scroll bar of the Directory list to reveal the tutorial subdirectory. When that subdirectory appears, select it by double clicking on it. As a result, the subdirectory will be highlighted, and all the database files stored in that subdirectory are displayed in

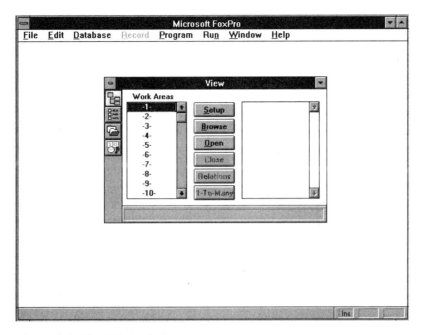

Figure 3.9 The View window

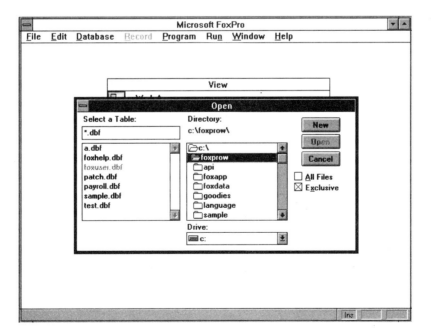

Figure 3.10 The Open dialog

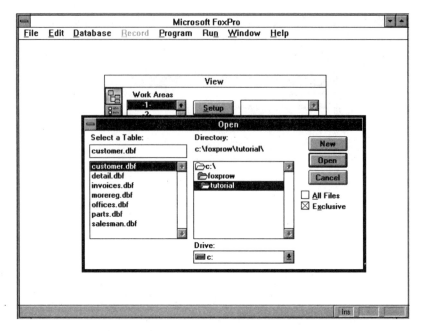

Figure 3.11 Highlighting a database file in a subdirectory

the Select a Table list. At this point, click on customer.dbf to highlight it (see Figure 3.11). Then select the Open button to open the database file and return to the View window.

When you return to the View window, the CUSTOMER database file will be open in work area 1. To view the contents of that file, select the Browse push button by clicking your mouse once on that button. Alternatively, you can double click on the Customer file. On the keyboard, use the Tab key to highlight the push button and press Enter to accept it. As a result, you will see the contents of the CUSTOMER database file displayed in a Browse window in Browse mode, which is a columnar format (see Figure 3.12).

If your screen shows the database file in Change mode (in which data fields are displayed in rows), you can switch to Browse mode by selecting the Browse option from the Browse menu popup. Do not be concerned if the location and size of your window on the screen differ from that shown in Figure 3.12. You will be able to relocate and resize it later.

Moving Windows

Because FoxPro allows you to have several windows displayed on the screen at one time, some may be hidden and overlapped by others. You can reveal the hidden windows by moving them around on the screen with your mouse or the keyboard.

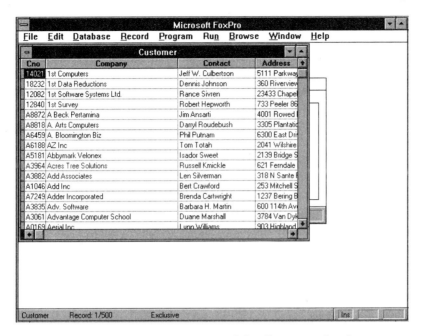

Figure 3.12 Displaying the contents of the Customer database

To move a window with the mouse, point it on the title bar of the window and then drag it to a new location. To move the CUSTOMER Browse window to the right, for example, point the mouse on the title bar (where the database filename CUSTOMER appears) and then drag it to the right.

If you are using the keyboard, press the Ctrl+F7 key combination. As a result, the window will be framed with a dotted line. Now move the window in the desired direction by using the cursor keys; in this case, the right arrow key. When you are done, press the Enter key to accept the new window location (see Figure 3.13).

Sizing Windows

The size of a window also can be changed either with the mouse or the keyboard. You can make the window shorter, longer, narrower, wider, smaller, or larger. Experiment making the CUSTOMER Browse window shorter and longer by pointing the mouse at the Size control (the box at the lower right-hand corner of the window) and then dragging it up and down, respectively. To make the window narrower and wider, drag the mouse to the left and right accordingly. The window becomes smaller (shorter and narrower at the same time) when you drag the mouse to the upper left, and larger (longer and wider) when you drag the mouse to the lower right.

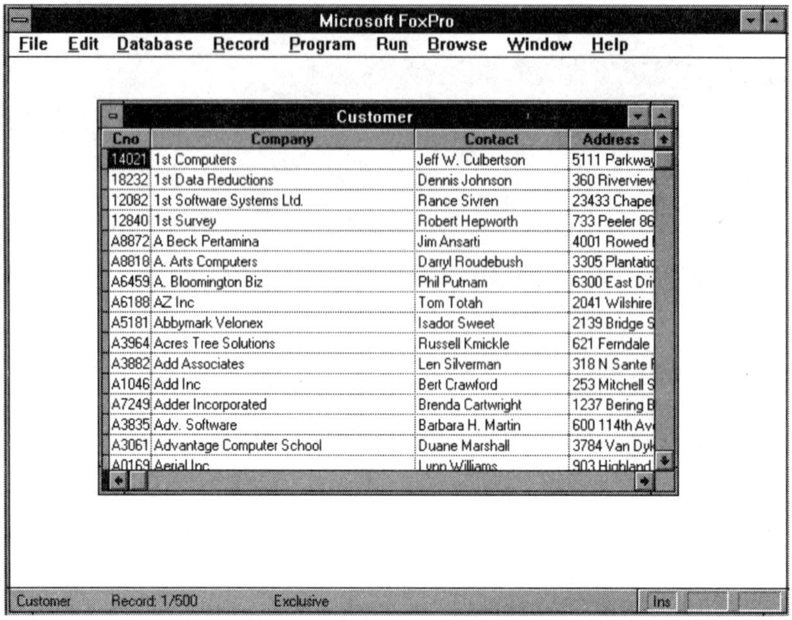

Figure 3.13 Moving the Customer window to a new location

Note that you can also resize a window by positioning the mouse cursor over any side of its window frame. When the mouse cursor changes into a double arrow, simply drag in the direction in which you would like to expand or contract the window.

To resize a window using the keyboard, press the Ctrl+F8 key combination. When the window is framed by a dotted line, press the up and left arrow keys to make the window shorter and narrower, and the down and right arrows to make the window longer and wider (see Figure 3.14).

Maximizing Windows

You can enlarge a window to its maximum size, thereby displaying its contents on the whole screen. To use the full screen to display the contents of the CUSTOMER database file, click your mouse on the maximize button (labeled with an up arrow) at the upper right-hand corner of the window; or, on the keyboard, press the Ctrl+F10 key combination. As a result, the Browse window fills the whole screen (see Figure 3.15).

To return the maximized window to its original size, click the mouse on the Restore button (the button with an up-and-down arrow that is located directly below the maximize button). With the keyboard, press the Ctrl+F5 key combination.

Getting Started 83

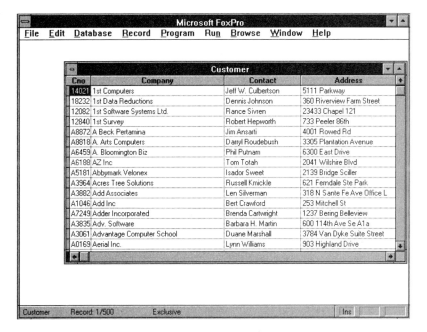

Figure 3.14 Resizing the Customer window

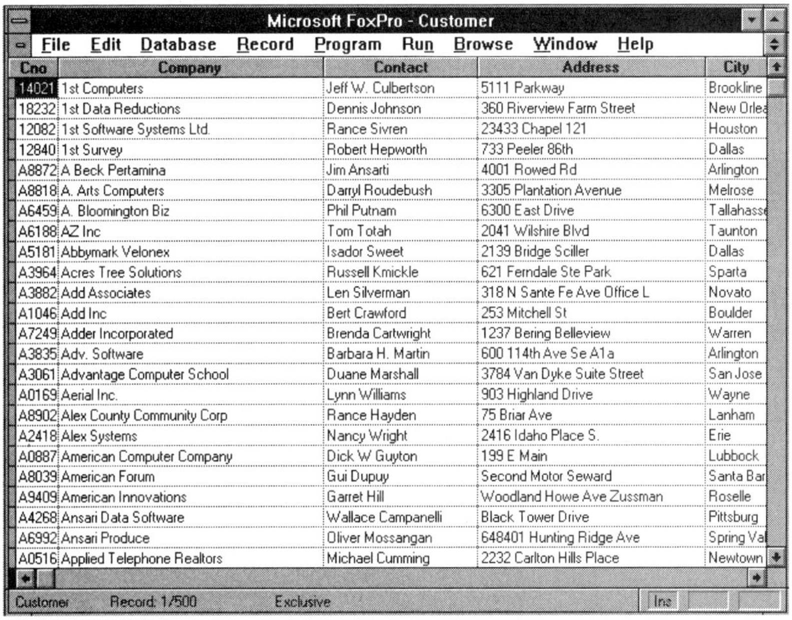

Figure 3.15 Maximizing the Customer window

Minimizing Windows

Minimizing windows also can be achieved, and is done usually in order to free up screen space and to display other objects without closing any windows. When a window is minimized, it is reduced to an icon and displayed in a small block that is 1 line high and 18 characters long.

To minimize a window, click on the minimize button of the window you would like to shrink. To continue with our example, minimize the CUSTOMER Browse window by double clicking your mouse on the minimize button (labeled with a down arrow) that appears to the left of the Maximize button. If you are using the keyboard, press the Ctrl+F9 key combination. You'll see the CUSTOMER Browse window displayed as an icon (labeled as Customer) in the lower left-hand corner of the work space. (see Figure 3.16). To return the minimized window to its original size, double click the mouse on the Customer icon; on the keyboard, press the Ctrl+F5 key combination.

Arranging Window Icons

There will probably be times when you are working with several windows on the screen at the same time, and you will want to minimize and display them as icons in order to free up screen space. To do that, first minimize the windows and then rearrange them with the mouse or keyboard. To move a window icon, point the

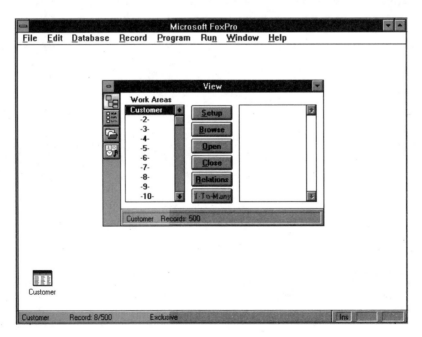

Figure 3.16 Minimizing the Customer window

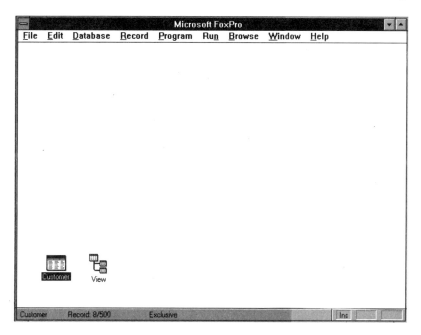

Figure 3.17 Rearranging the Window icons

mouse cursor at the icon and then drag it to a new location. With the keyboard, use the Ctrl+F1 key combination to highlight the icon to be moved, then press the Ctrl+F7 to select it. As a result, a four-arrow cross will appear on the icon selected. At this point, use the cursor keys to move it to a new location, then press the Enter key to anchor it at the new location. Use this procedure to minimize the Customer Browse window and the View window. After they are minimized, move them around so that they form a stack on the screen (see Figure 3.17).

In Figure 3.17, you can see that the Customer and View windows have been minimized and arranged in the lower left-hand corner of the screen so that the work space in the FoxPro window is clear.

Activating Windows

When you have several windows open on the screen at the same time, only one window may be active. The active window is indicated by a different color in the title bar and by the presence of its Control box and Close and Zoom control buttons. The title of the active window is always highlighted, and its controls and buttons are always visible. In contrast, the titles of inactive windows are not highlighted, and their window controls are not visible. If the windows overlap, the active one is always displayed in the foreground, and the inactive windows are hidden in the background.

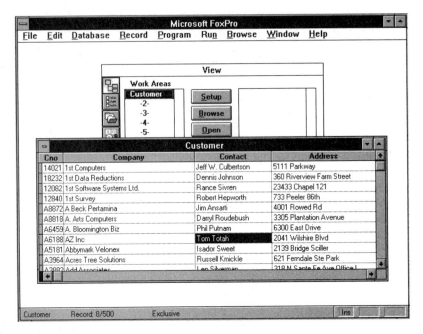

Figure 3.18 Showing overlapped windows

In Figure 3.18, you can see that the Customer window is active in the foreground, and its Control box and the Maximize and Minimize buttons appear in the window. On the other hand, the View window is in the background, and its Control box and the Maximize and Minimize buttons are missing.

It is simple to activate a window if its title bar or its border is visible—just click on the bar or the border. Otherwise, move the window that's in the foreground to reveal the hidden one. Alternatively, press Ctrl+F1 to cycle among the windows until the one you would like to make active appears. You can also bring up the Window menu popup to select the window you want. For example, while the CUSTOMER and View windows are inactive, you will find that the CUSTOMER window is displayed at the bottom of the window popup when you select the Window menu pad (see Figure 3.19).

To activate the CUSTOMER Browse window, select it from the menu popup. Activate the View window in the same manner. Once this is done, you can return them to their original size if they have been minimized.

Closing Windows

After you have finished using a window, you can remove it from the screen by closing it. Either click the mouse on the close option in the Control box that appears in the upper left-hand corner of the screen; or, if you are using the keyboard, press

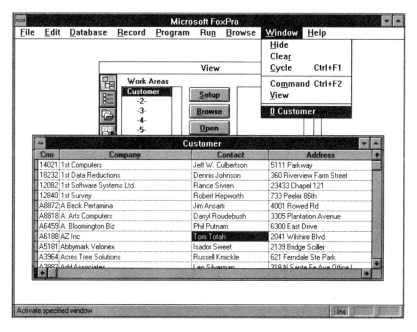

Figure 3.19 Designating an active window

the Ctrl+F4 key combination. As an exercise, close the Customer window with the mouse or the keyboard.

SETTING SCREEN COLORS

Since FoxPro for Windows runs in the Windows environment, the color scheme used in the program is controlled by the environment. As a result, you must use the tools provided by Windows to set the colors that display various FoxPro objects, such as the components of a window, dialogs, text, etc.

To define screen colors, you must temporarily leave the FoxPro window and bring up the Program Manager. Press the Alt+Tab key combination to cycle the windows until the Program Manger window appears. At this point, double click the Control Panel icon to bring up the Control Panel window (see Figure 3.20). Double click the Color icon to bring up the Color dialog (see Figure 3.21).

The Color dialog in Figure 3.21 shows a Color Schemes drop-down list. A color scheme defines a set of colors for displaying window objects. A default is assumed when you first bring up Windows, which provides a set of pleasant basic colors for displaying FoxPro objects. You can select a different color scheme that better suits your taste or choose individual colors for each selectable screen object. This is a more tedious process, to be sure, but it means you can customize the screen colors to your exact specifications. For example, in order to reproduce the screen figures

88   Understanding FoxPro 2.5 for Windows

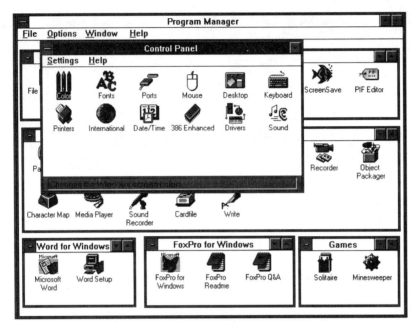

Figure 3.20   The Control Panel window

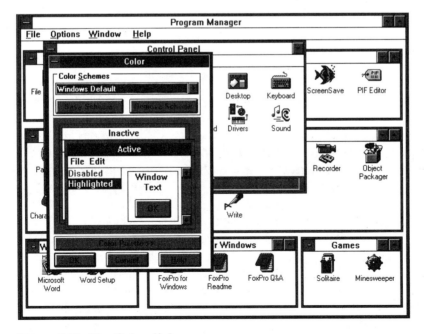

Figure 3.21   The Color dialog

in a black-and-white scheme for this book, a set of custom colors were chosen. As a result, you may note minor variations in some screens between what you see on the screen and what you see reproduced on paper.

In the Color dialog, you can select another predefined color scheme in the Color Schemes list. Experiment to find what works best for you or a given project.

After selecting a color scheme, return to FoxPro by pressing the Alt+Tab key combination. When the FoxPro window appears, if you are not satisfied with the color scheme you have chosen, return to the Color dialog by again pressing the Alt+Tab key combination.

If you cannot find a predefined color scheme that you like, you can define your own colors for each part of the window. To do that, press the Color Palette button to bring up the color palette in an enlarged Color dialog for defining the screen elements (see Figure 3.22).

On the right-hand side of the enlarged Color dialog, you will find a set of colors for displaying a given screen element. To define a color for a particular Windows interface, first select the object and then select a color from the color palette. For example, to display the title bar of an active window in red, first click on the title bar (the bar labeled "Active") on the left-hand side of the dialog and then click on the small red color square. Similarly, to choose yellow to display your buttons, click on the OK push button (the button that appears directly below the Window

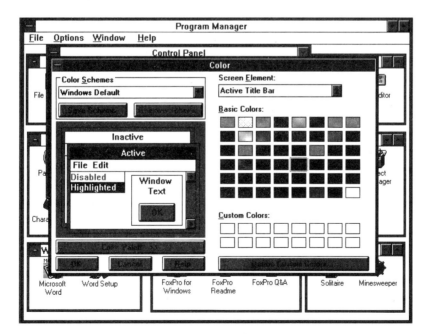

Figure 3.22 Defining a custom color scheme

Text label) and then click on the yellow color square. As a result, the selected object will be displayed in the chosen color.

In most cases, the set of basic colors provided by Windows probably will be sufficient for defining your screen elements. If not, blend your own colors. Select the Define Custom Colors button to proceed. For details on this subject, refer to the Windows user's manual.

SETTING UP PRINTERS

When you are in FoxPro for Windows, you can display your data and processed results on the screen or route them to a printer. But before using a printer, you must tell FoxPro the kind of printer you intend to use, because each type of printer has its own operating characteristics. Characteristics of specific printers are contained in a program file called a printer driver. A set of commonly used printer drivers was included at the time you installed Windows. It is from this set of printers that you activate the printer or printers that you are planning to use. You can do this any time prior to using the printer. You also can set up more than one printer at the same time and change them as often as you wish.

To set up printers, begin at the Program Manager window. Again, to return to the Program Manager from FoxPro, press the Ctrl+Tab key combination until it appears. Then double click on the Control Panel; next, double click on the Printers icon in the Control Panel window. As a result, the Printers dialog appears, showing the list of installed printers and the default printer (see Figure 3.23).

If the printer you would like to use in FoxPro is displayed as the default printer, select the Close button to leave the Printers dialog and return to the Control Panel and then to the Program Manager. Otherwise, choose another printer from the Installed Printers list by clicking on it. Then select the Set As Default Printer button to make it the default printer.

If you do not find the printer you need in the list, select the Add button to install the printer you need. Select the Connect button to connect your printer to a printer port (e.g., LPT1:, LPT2:, COM1:, etc.). If you have problems in setting the default printer, select the Help button.

When you are done setting the default printer, select the Close button to return to the Control Panel. Then close the Control Panel window and return to the Program Manager. To return to the FoxPro for Windows program, press the Ctrl+Tab key combination until the FoxPro window appears.

After you have returned to FoxPro, you can verify the default printer by selecting the Print Setup... option from the File menu pad in the FoxPro menu bar. When the Print Setup dialog appears, you can verify the information about the default printer (see Figure 3.24). At this point, you can select another printer if you do not want to use the default printer. To do that, click on the radio button labeled Specific Printer and then select another printer from the popup or drop-down list.

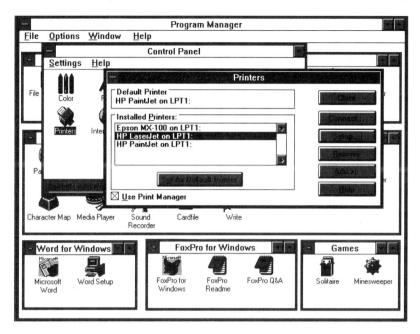

Figure 3.23 The Printers dialog

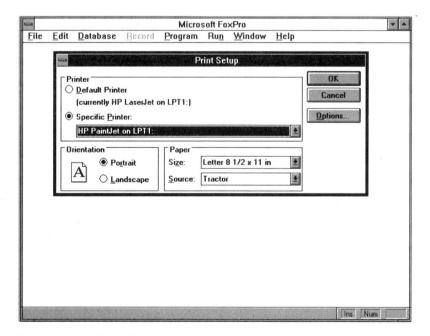

Figure 3.24 The Print Setup dialog

In the Print Setup dialog, you can change the print orientation by selecting either the Portrait or the Landscape radio button. To print the output in a normal layout (8 1/2" x 11"), choose the portrait orientation. If you choose landscape orientation, output will be printed horizontally across the longer axis of the page. You also can specify the paper size by selecting the appropriate measurement in the Size popup list in the Print Setup dialog and the source of paper (upper paper tray or tractor feed mechanism).

Setting Default Data Directory

When you installed the FoxPro for Windows program, all the files associated with the program were written to the foxprow directory and its subdirectories. To better organize your files, it is highly recommended that you create a subdirectory under the foxprow directory for saving all the databases and their associated data files. In this chapter, we created the foxdata subdirectory (c:\foxprow\foxdata) under the foxpro directory. Use this subdirectory as the default data directory, and all databases and related files that will be created in subsequent exercises will be stored there.

To select a data directory as the default data directory, select the View option from the Windows menu in the FoxPro menu bar. When the View window appears, notice the four panel buttons located in the upper left-hand portion of the window (see Figure 3.25).

The first button returns you to the default View window display after you have selected another panel. The second button brings up the Set Option On/Off panel. Below this button is the File Selection button used for displaying the File Selection panel, where you define the default disk drive and working directory, etc. The last button is for bringing up the Set Miscellaneous Values panel, which is used to define the default format for displaying dates, monetary values, etc. (You will learn how to use these panels in detail in later chapters.) To set the default data directory,

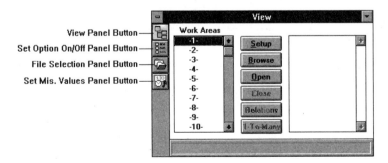

Figure 3.25 The Panel buttons in the View window

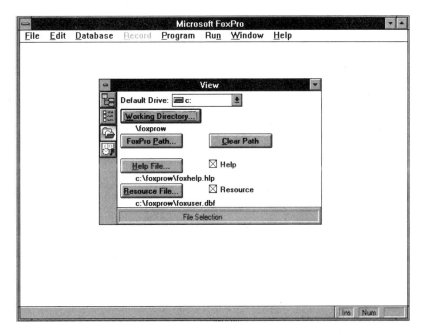

Figure 3.26 The File Selection panel

double click the third, the File Selection panel button. As a result, the File Selection panel will be displayed in the View window (see Figure 3.26).

In the File Selection panel, select c: as the default disk drive and Foxdata as the working directory. In addition, define the path for the FoxPro files. (Do not be concerned with where the Help and Resource Files are stored. They are saved in the directory in which the FoxPro is installed.)

To specify the working directory, select the Working Directory... button to display the Select Directory dialog (see Figure 3.27). In this dialog, select the directory. Choose the foxdata subdirectory under the foxprow directory by double clicking on it. When the subdirectory is highlighted, click on the Select button and return to the View window. At this point, the working directory reads \foxprow\foxdata; the default drive reads c:.

To return the View window to its normal display, click on the View panel button. To close the View window, click on the Control box or press the Ctrl+F4 key combination.

Getting Help

If you need help while you are in FoxPro for Windows, press the F1 function key. Most help is context-sensitive, meaning that the help messages returned by FoxPro are related to the operation you are conducting when you pressed the function key.

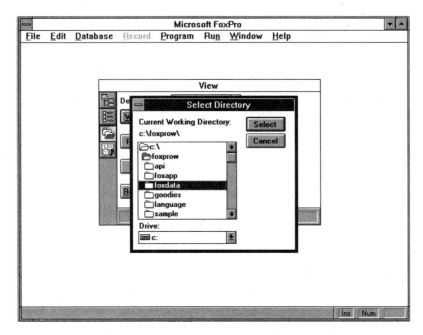

Figure 3.27 The Select Directory dialog

Thus, if you press F1 while you are viewing a database's contents in a Browse window, a help message regarding the process of browsing appears. Use the scroll controls to reveal any portion of the message that is hidden from view.

The Help window contains a number of push buttons. Use them to navigate through the subjects and to find help on a specific subject. If you need to learn more about Help, select one or more of the options from the Help menu pad in the FoxPro menu bar: Contents, Search for Help on..., and How to Use Help. They are self-explanatory.

Exiting FoxPro

After you have completed a FoxPro for Windows session, you can leave the program and return to the general Windows environment by choosing the Quit option from the File menu popup. *Do not exit the program by turning off or rebooting (pressing Ctrl+Alt+Del key combination) the computer.* Failure to exit the program properly will damage your database files, and you risk losing valuable data.

Chapter Summary

This chapter prepared you to make efficient use of the tools provided by FoxPro for Windows for designing and developing a database management system. You learned how to customize screen colors and to set up printers correctly. You also became familiar with the basic techniques for using either the mouse or keyboard to work with the FoxPro menu system and the Windows interface. In the next chapter, you will begin using these techniques to create your database files.

4

Creating Databases

An Overview

You are now ready to begin to develop a relational database. This chapter will show you the correct procedures for setting up data tables to hold your data elements.

Defining the structure of a data table is the first step. The structuring procedure involves identifying and specifying all of the attributes of the data fields that you would like to include in the data table. The character differences of your data elements require that you set up different data fields to accommodate them.

The first part of this chapter describes the types of data fields and how to define them when structuring a database. Once a table structure is properly defined, data can be entered. (The procedure for entering data into data tables is covered in the latter part of the chapter.) All of these procedures are explained and illustrated in detail by incorporating some of the data tables introduced in Chapter 1. You are advised to take a hands-on approach, and doing the exercises as you read.

Defining the Data Structure

As defined in Chapter 1, a data table is the basic unit of a relational database. It is where all of the data elements associated with a data entity in a data table are stored. You may recall from Chapter 1 that data columns are also called data fields. They form the segments of the data structure that accommodate those data elements describing the properties of the data entity.

IDENTIFYING DATA FIELDS

The first step in structuring a data table is to identify its data fields. Each data field is chosen to describe a unique property of the data entry associated with the table. For example, the Salesman table introduced in Chapter 1 has the following columns:

Identification Number
Last Name
First Name
Hire Date
Monthly Salary

Each of these columns describes a property about each salesperson and will therefore be structured as a data field in the Salesman table. And, as just noted, because the types of data elements to be saved in the table are different, the data fields must be set up with different attributes. For instance, the first three data fields are set up to accommodate strings of alphabetic and numeric characters only. A different format must be used to hold the hire dates. The salary data field can hold only numeric values, so it has to be set up in yet another way. In addition to these types of data fields, there are other kinds of data fields—logical and memo fields—that are necessary for many data structures. In order to demonstrate how they are set up, let's add the following two data fields to the Salesman table:

Commission status—called COMMISSION
Reference note—called NOTE

The commission status column reveals whether or not a salesperson is compensated with a commission; the reference note field holds information such as the hobbies and educational background (or any other pertinent data) of each salesperson.

DEFINING DATA FIELD ATTRIBUTES

Once you have identified the necessary data fields for your table, you can define the attributes for each of these fields. The attributes of a data field are:

- the name of the field
- the type of data to be stored in the field
- the size or width of the data field

A field name is used to refer to the columns as a whole. The field's data type determines how the data field can be used, as well as the format in which the data is stored in the field. For example, the data elements in the last name and first name character fields will probably be used only as textual information for identifying a salesperson, while values in the salary field will most likely be used for computations and to provide summary statistics; dates will be used for still other purposes. Finally, the size or width of a field determines the number of characters or numbers that can be stored in it.

Naming a Data Field

The rules governing the naming of a data field may vary among different database software, but this book is concerned only with the conventions prescribed by FoxPro. Its rules state:

- A field name may be no more than 10 characters long.
- It can be made up of a combination of alphabetic letters, numeric digits, and underscores (_), but it must begin with a letter.
- Blank spaces *cannot* be included, nor can most symbols such as commas, periods, dollar signs, colons, semi-colons, and question marks.

You should always try to create names that help to define the nature of the data elements, and make them as descriptive as possible. Obviously, due to the width limit, you may need to abbreviate them; and, if the name includes more than one word, separate them with underscores for clarity (e.g., area_code, acct_name, etc.).

If your database has more than one data table, assign unique field names to them. For example, use SALSMAN_ID in the Salesman table and OFFICE_ID in the Office table. Avoid using just ID or ID_NO to represent the identification number fields for both the Salesman and Office tables. This eliminates potential confusion and allows you to distinguish one field from another whenever you need to. And FoxPro will not allow you to duplicate field names in the same database.

When you are defining field names with alphabetic characters, case is ignored. You may use either upper- or lowercase letters, and FoxPro will automatically convert them to lowercase. Here are some examples of acceptable field names, some of which you've already seen used in this book:

SALSMAN_ID
ACCOUTNAME
ACCT_NAME
HIRE_DATE
ADDRESS_1
ADDRESS_2
BIRTHDATE
AREA_CODE
PHONE_NO
UNIT_COST

Specifying Field Type

As already stated, different types of data elements are saved in different formats in data fields. A salesperson's monthly salary takes the form of a number, like 2500, while a date value is normally expressed as 07/04/91. You must tell FoxPro for Windows what type of data element you intend to store in each field. There are eight different types of data fields from which you can choose to hold your data elements. They are:

C	Character Fields
N	Numeric Fields
D	Date Fields
L	Logical Fields
M	Memo Fields
F	Float Fields
G	General Fields
P	Picture Fields

Of these eight data fields, you probably will be concerned with only the first five, the most common ones. The float data field is designed for saving scientific data when very large or very small values are involved. You can do without this type of data field in most business-related applications, since most numbers you are likely to encounter can be accommodated by the regular numeric data fields. Picture fields are reserved for holding graphic images which can only be generated outside of FoxPro for Windows; coverage of these fields is beyond the scope of this book. Picture fields are also designed to hold external graphic images; however, support for this type of field has not been implemented in FoxPro 2.5 for Windows.

Character Fields

A character data field is used to hold a string of characters consisting of a combination of alphabetic letters, numeric digits, and symbols, which include most of the punctuation marks and symbols that you would find on a regular computer keyboard. Any foreign alphabet and graphic symbols for drawing boxes and borders also can be included.

A maximum of 254 characters can be stored in a character field. Examples of character strings are sales staff identification numbers, addresses of customers, first and last names of individuals, telephone numbers, etc. The string in a character field is used primarily for holding textual information; even if it contains numbers, these are not intended to be used for calculations.

Numeric Fields

Numeric fields hold numbers in data tables. Numbers can take the form of integers or values with decimal points. Any values used in business applications can be stored in these fields; negative values are expressed with leading minus signs.

Although it is necessary to display monetary values with dollar signs and grouped by commas (e.g., $123,4456.78) in your reports, dollar signs or commas cannot be included in a numeric field. They must be added to the screen display or reports as needed.

The maximum width of a numeric field is 20, including places for the plus or minus sign and the decimal point. You can specify the desired number of places after the decimal point in order to include, for example, the values of 123.45 or -123.45, which occupies six and seven places, respectively, in a numeric field with two places after the decimal point. Data elements stored in numeric fields can be used in formulas for calculations and for providing summary statistics.

Date Fields

Date fields are used to save calendar dates. Internally within the database file, each date is always stored in a field with a length of eight characters in the form YYYYMMDD, where YYYY, MM, and DD are formats representing the year, month, and day, respectively. However, the format in which dates are displayed and entered into the database is usually different from this. The default format for entering dates is MM/DD/YY. But you also can display and enter dates in formats such as DD-MM-YY, YY.MM.DD, or MM/DD/YYYY.

In addition to representing calendar dates, dates can be used in calculations. You can compute, for example, the number of days between any two dates by taking the difference between the two dates (e.g., DATE1 – DATE2). You will learn more about this capability later.

Logical Fields

A logical field is a special kind of data field for saving answers to a true/false (yes/no) type of question. It occupies only a one-character width in the form of T (true) or F (false). Say you want to store the answer to the question, "Is (a given salesperson) compensated with commission?" A logical field would be used to save T (for yes) or F (for no). You also can use this type of field to hold answers regarding whether an employee is male or female, an account is invoiced or not, etc. Logical fields play a very significant role in a data structure. When properly defined, they provide a useful means for efficiently dichotomizing data elements.

Memo Fields

Memo fields are set up to hold text information. They can hold character strings composed of the same elements as character fields. However, there are two major differences between a memo field and a character field. The first difference is structural; a character field can hold a fixed number of characters, while a memo field can hold a variable number of characters. The second difference is one of usage; while a character field is intended to be used for storing a fixed kind of information, memo fields are used to store information that is more free-form in its character.

Often, memo fields contain text that is used for reference purposes. A memo field occupies a 10-character width in a table structure, but the actual contents of the memo field are saved in a separate file instead of in the data table where the field is defined.

Note that although FoxPro allows you to find a substring in a memo field, its primary purpose is not for query operations. Character fields are better candidates for those operations because searching a large memo field can be a very slow process, and the number of ways in which you can manipulate a memo field is very limited.

Creating a Data Table

With the basic components of a data structure in mind, let's create a data table. We'll call it SALESMAN, and it will consist of the following data fields with the following attributes:

Field Name	*Field Type*	*Field Width*	
SALSMAN_ID	Character	3	
LAST	Character	8	
FIRST	Character	8	
HIRE_DATE	Date	8	
SALARY	Numeric	5	0 (decimal places)
COMMISSION	Logical	1	
NOTE	Memo	10	

Table names used in this book have, until now, been spelled with initial capitalization only, e.g., Salesman, Office, Region, etc. These are ordinary descriptive names assigned to a proper object. From this point on, however, in order to follow the naming convention adopted by FoxPro for Windows, all uppercase letters will be used for the names of actual data tables.

Notice above that the first data field is named SALSMAN_ID instead of SALESMAN_ID. In order to stay within the 10-character width limitation, abbreviation is necessary here. The fields LAST and FIRST refer to the sales staff's first and last names. For now, we are ignoring middle initials. They will be added to the database structure later. As an example of readability in naming conventions, note the underscore (_) used to separate the two words in the HIRE_DATE field. Of course, it could have been called hiredate as well. And recall from the beginning of the chapter that COMMISSION is the logical field that identifies the commission status of each saleperson, and NOTE stores reference information about the sales staff.

The procedure for setting up a data structure with these data fields involves the following steps:

Creating a new database file
Defining the structure
Assigning a name to the table
Saving the structure

CREATING A NEW DATABASE FILE

To set up a new database file, begin by selecting the File option from the menu pad. (Refer to Chapter 3 if you need to refresh your memory regarding the steps used to select an option from the menu pad with a mouse or the keyboard. You may also want to review the procedures needed to open a window, enter text in a dialog box, and select and use the control buttons. Knowledge of these procedures is necessary for setting up a new data table.) After selecting the menu option, a menu popup is displayed. From that, select the New option and then specify the type of file you would like to create (see Figure 4.1).

In this instance, because the default is a database file, you need not select a file type; simply press the Enter key to accept the default. If you are using a mouse, point its cursor on the New button and then click once to accept the default file type.

(If you decide not to create a new database, exit the dialog and return to FoxPro by choosing the Cancel option or by pressing the Esc key. If you are using a mouse, place its cursor on the Cancel button and click once.)

SPECIFYING FIELD ATTRIBUTES

Once you have accepted the default option, the Table Structure dialog box showing a data structure definition form appears, as shown in Figure 4.2. This form provides the space in which to enter the attributes for all the data fields you intend to include in the table.

The screen also shows the name of the structure at the lower left-hand corner of the dialog box. Note that currently it is labeled "untitled.dbf." You will be asked later to assign a name to the table when you try to save it.

104 Understanding FoxPro 2.5 for Windows

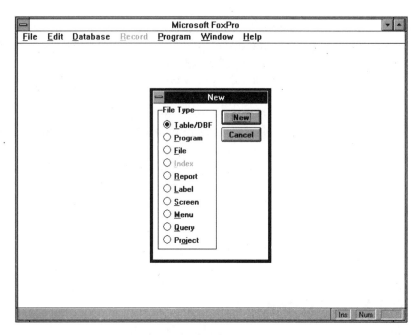

Figure 4.1 Creating a new database file

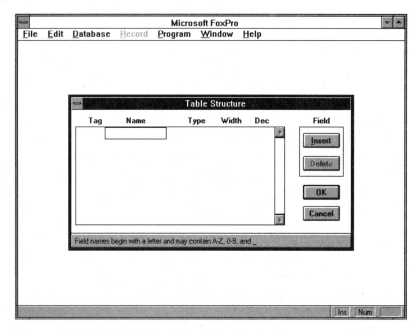

Figure 4.2 The Table Structure dialog box

Creating Databases 105

At the bottom of the form in the status bar, FoxPro displays some statistics on the database you are now defining. There are also two buttons, OK and Cancel. OK lets you accept the structure after you have completed defining it. You can always quit this step and exit the procedure by using the Cancel push button or by pressing the Esc key on your keyboard.

Once in this form, you can specify your data fields. Begin by typing in the name of the first data field, followed by the field type and the appropriate width. To continue with the creation of the SALESMAN table, enter SALSMAN_ID as the first field name; then press the Tab key. Do not press the Enter key. If you did by mistake, press Esc to return the structure definition screen. The cursor moves to the column for defining the field type. Here the default field type "Character" is shown. To accept this, press the Tab key, which moves the cursor to the Width column. The default width of 10 appears for the width field. To change it, just type in the desired width. In this case, enter 3 and then press the Tab key. Alternatively, you can press the up- or down-arrow key to increase or decrease the width of the field. If you are using the mouse, click the up or down arrow in the spinner box to increase or decrease the field width. When you are finished defining the first data field, it should look like Figure 4.3.

In general, when determining the width of a character field, you should plan ahead by anticipating the maximum number of characters you might need for your

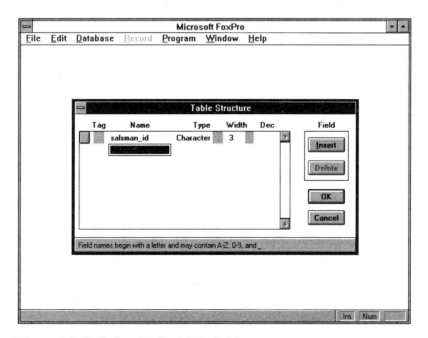

Figure 4.3 Defining the first data field

data elements in that field. FoxPro then uses that fixed number of characters that you define in the structure to hold your character strings. Consequently, regardless of the number of characters a string may actually have, the field will always occupy a fixed number of characters. Unused spaces become blank spaces in the data table; extra characters become truncated. You should keep the field width as small as possible in order to conserve disk space and reduce processing time. Do not worry about setting it too small now, however, as it can be changed later.

If you make mistakes in entering the field names and field width, use the Tab key or the Shift+Tab key combination to move between field name and column width. Pressing the Tab key moves the cursor to the next item, and pressing the Shift+Tab key combination moves it back to the previous item. As the field name or field width column is highlighted, you can enter the new field name or field width. With a mouse, point and click the cursor on the spot at which you would like to make a correction and then type in the changes.

Now define the second (named LAST) and third (named FIRST) fields. Because they are all character fields, you can follow the procedure you used to define the SALSMAN_ID field. Note that the width of each field is 8. To specify the HIRE_DATE field, however, you must choose a date field instead of the default character field. To do that, either press D or select Date from the Type drop-down list. The list of acceptable field types can be displayed in the Type drop-down list by pressing the Space key or by clicking your mouse on the down-arrow in the list (see Figure 4.4). You can use the up- or down-arrow key to select the field type you want, followed by pressing the Space key. With the mouse, you can click on the field type you want.

The width of a date field is always set to 8 characters automatically. Just press the Tab key to accept the date type and move on to the next field.

When you define the numeric salary field, type in its name (SALARY), define the field type as numeric, and specify the field width as 5 with 0 decimal places. By specifying the number of decimal places as 0, you are indicating that the salary values are to be treated as integers. Otherwise, you would set Dec to 2 to accommodate the dollar and cents format for most monetary values.

To define the commission field, type in its name (COMMISSION) and enter L to specify a logical field. Remember that the width of a logical field is always set to 1 by FoxPro.

The NOTE memo field is automatically set to a width of 10. This completes the definition process for the structure of the SALESMAN table (see Figure 4.5).

If, when you are defining fields, you find you have skipped one by mistake, you can insert a new column at the cursor position. First position the cursor in the field *below* where you want to insert the field. Then choose the Insert push button. In response to the button selection, a new space will open up for defining the new field. Similarly, you can delete a field at the current cursor position by choosing the Delete push button.

Creating Databases 107

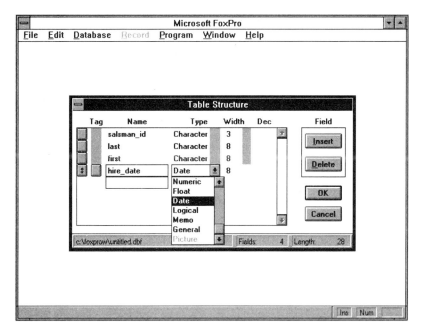

Figure 4.4 Selecting a data field type

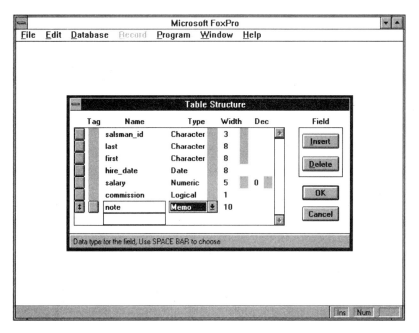

Figure 4.5 Data structure for SALESMAN table

SAVING A DATA STRUCTURE

To save the structure you have just defined, point your mouse cursor on the OK button and click it once, or press the Tab key to move your cursor to the OK button and press Enter to accept it.

Now the Save As dialog box appears, and you are required to assign a name to the database file. The upper left-hand corner of the dialog box asks for the database name. Type in the table name SALESMAN in either lowercase or uppercase (see Figure 4.6).

The dialog box also shows you the disk drive (c) and the directory (\foxprow\foxdata\) to which FoxPro will save your table. The default disk drive is shown in the Drive drop-down list box at the bottom of the screen. Above it is the directory definition box in which the default directory is displayed. (Setting up the default drive and directory were covered in Chapter 3.)

To change to a different disk drive, open the Drive drop-down list box and select the drive you want. With a mouse, point the mouse cursor on the down arrow, hold down the mouse button, and drag it to the desired disk drive; then release the button. With the keyboard, press the Tab key until the Drive drop-down list is highlighted, then press the Space key to open the list box. Finally, use the cursor key to select the desired disk drive. To close the Drive drop-down list box, press the Space key.

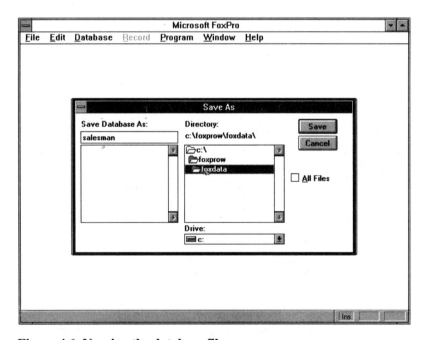

Figure 4.6 Naming the database file

To select the directory, use the Tab key to first highlight the root directory and press the Enter key to bring up its subdirectories. Then use the up or down arrow key to highlight the subdirectory you want. When you have found the directory of your choice, press the Enter key to accept it. If you need to go down to the next level of directories, follow the same procedure until you have found the subdirectory you need. For example, if you would like to store your data table in the c:\foxprow\foxdata\ directory, first highlight the foxprow directory and press the Enter key. When the foxdata subdirectory appears, highlight it and then press the Enter key to select it. With the mouse, first double click on the disk drive (c:\) in the directory box to display all subdirectories of the root directory. Then double click on the subdirectory of your choice to display its subdirectories until the subdirectory you want is visible and can be highlighted.

Assuming for now that you intend to save the SALESMAN table to the default disk drive and directory, choose the Save button. Of course, you can return to the Table Structure dialog (the previous step) by pressing the Esc key from the keyboard or by choosing the Cancel button with your mouse. After selecting Save, a data table named SALESMAN with the structure you have specified is saved to the disk. You are then asked in a dialog box whether or not you intend to begin entering data values in the table (see Figure 4.7).

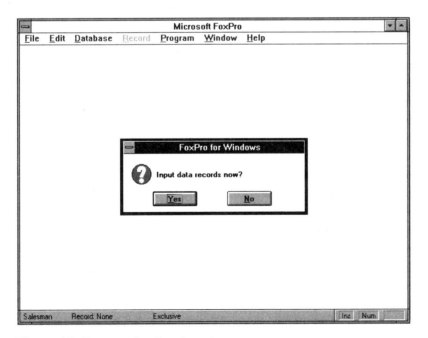

Figure 4.7 Request for data input

ENTERING DATA VALUES

If you decide to enter data to the SALESMAN data table at this point, select Yes as the response to the prompt, "Input data records now?" A default data entry form is displayed (see Figure 4.8).

Data can now be entered into the table, one record at a time. Begin by typing the data value S0 in the first data field, SALSMAN_ID. As you fill the field, the cursor will automatically move to the next field. Otherwise, you can press the Enter key or the Tab key to finish a field and move down to the next field. Next, type Anderson in the field named LAST and Doris in the field named FIRST. Type in a date, 07/01/86, in the HIRE_DATE field without entering the slashes. Enter a numeric value (2800) in the SALARY field. (Don't forget: Do not include a dollar sign or commas in the salary figure. If you make a mistake, use the left or right arrow key to move within a data field, or use the up or down arrow key to move between data fields to make the corrections. With a mouse, point to the particular position and click to make any changes.)

When you come to the COMMISSION logical field, enter F (see Figure 4.9). You *must enter either T (or Y) or F (or N)* in this field. If you enter Y or N, it will automatically be converted to T or F. No other letters are accepted in a logical field.

The procedure for entering text in a memo field differs slightly from that for other fields. When you move the cursor to the memo field, the field will show

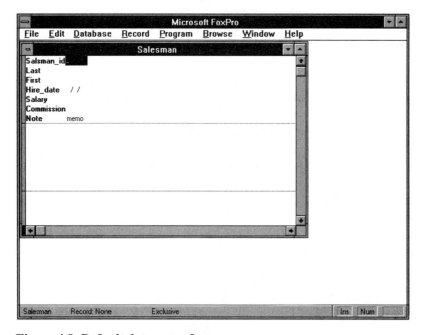

Figure 4.8 Default data entry form

Creating Databases 111

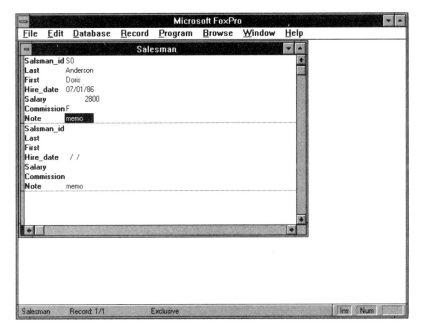

Figure 4.9 Entering data to character, date, and numeric fields

"memo," indicating the type of data field. To enter text in that field, you must use the FoxPro text editor. To open the text editor with a mouse, point the mouse cursor on the memo field and double click. With the keyboard, press the Ctrl+Home key combination while the cursor is resting on the memo field. As a result, a text window opens. The name of the window is the name of the data table and the memo field with a period separating them (Salesman.note). At this point, type in the text that you want to save to the memo field (see Figure 4.10).

Once you have entered all the text you want, close the window with the mouse by clicking on the Close option inside of the Control box. With the keyboard, press the Ctrl+W key combination. Once the text window is closed, you are returned to the data entry form. At this point, notice that the memo field displays "Memo" (instead of "memo" as before) in the field. This change indicates that there is something stored in that field; "memo" shows that the memo field is empty.

Now you can clearly see that the actual text in the memo field is not shown with the rest of the field values. To view its entire contents again, reopen the text editor window.

You may continue to enter the next data record by repeating the same procedure. The contents of the memo fields for the ten records in the SALESMAN table are shown in Figure 4.11. It is recommended that you enter the contents of these fields in your SALESMAN table as shown, as they will be used for exercises in later chapters.

112 Understanding FoxPro 2.5 for Windows

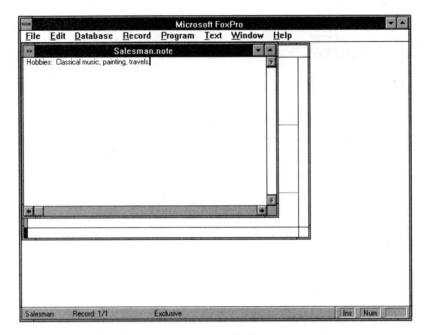

Figure 4.10 Entering text to a memo field

Entering Data in Change Mode

The default data form provides space in which to enter data for a new record. This is Change mode. In this mode, the number of records that you can view at a single time on the same screen depends on the number of data fields per record and the size of the open window. As discussed in Chapter 3, the window can be enlarged to show the maximum number of records. In our example, you can fit three full

Salesman	Contents of the *note* data field
Anderson	Hobbies: classical music, painting, travel
Bell	Hobbies: fishing, hunting, country music
Carter	Education: BA, Bus. Admin., University of Washington, 1985
Davidson	Citizenship: Canadian
Evans	Education: BA, Marketing, UCLA, 1986
Ford	Hobbies: classical music, sailing, travel
Gilbert	Hobbies: classical music, opera, foreign travel
Harvey	Hobbies: ballet, classical music, travel
Iverson	Hobbies: hunting, fishing, sailing
Jones	Education: BA, Social Studies, University of Oregon, 1987

Figure 4.11 Contents of memo fields

Creating Databases   113

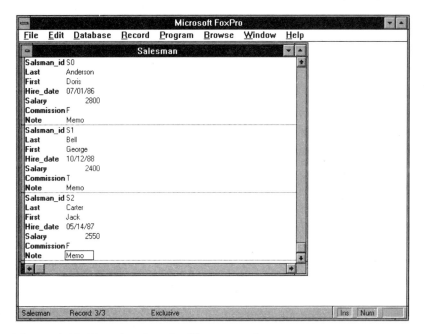

Figure 4.12 Entering data in Change mode

records per screen (see Figure 4.12). The exact number of records shown may vary, depending on the kind of monitor you have.

Press the Enter key after entering data in the last field of the third record (or the last record displayed on your screen). The form will scroll up, providing space to enter values for the next record.

In Change mode, each data field is shown as a line in the data entry form. All the data fields for a record are grouped and separated from the next record by a horizontal line. When you are in Change mode, it is usually possible to see the complete contents of the record being entered (unless the fields are too long or too numerous to fit on the same screen), but you can view only a limited number of records at any one time on the screen.

Entering Data in Browse Mode

To be able to see more records on the screen, switch to Browse mode by choosing the Browse option from the Browse menu pad. In response to this menu option selection, the records in the SALESMAN table will be displayed in a Browse window. If the window is too small to show all the data fields, you can resize or maximize it. To change the size of the window, move the mouse pointer to the side, bottom, or corner window border. When the pointer becomes a double arrow, hold the mouse button down, drag the border to the desired size, then release the button.

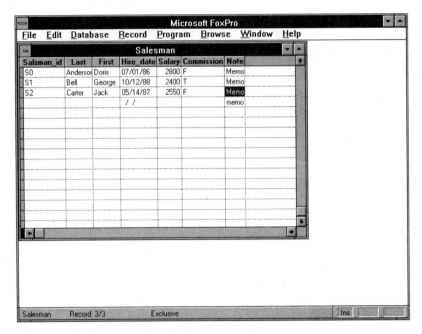

Figure 4.13 Entering data in Browse mode

To maximize the window, click on the Maximize button (the upward triangle) in the upper-right corner of the window. In Browse mode, each record is displayed as a row; data fields are displayed as columns in table form (see Figure 4.13).

Continue entering the rest of the data records into the table. As in Change mode, use the arrow keys to move within a field or between records. To move between fields, use the Tab or Shift+Tab keys. The same procedure applies for entering text in memo fields.

SAVING DATA RECORDS

After you have entered all ten records to the SALESMAN table (Figure 4.14), save the records by exiting from the data entry operation. With a mouse, close the Browse window by double clicking on the Close option in the Control box. If you are using a keyboard, press the Ctrl+End key combination to terminate the data entry operation.

Using FoxPro Commands

So far we have set up a data structure for the SALESMAN table and filled it with ten data records. We accomplished these tasks by using the FoxPro for Windows

Creating Databases   115

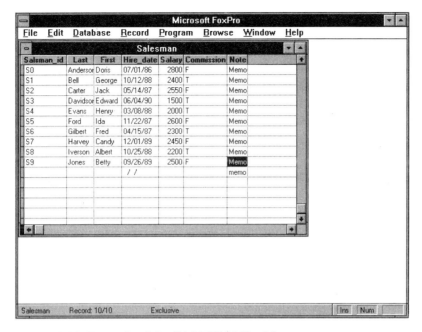

Figure 4.14 Records of the SALESMAN table

menu interface. The initial step of setting up the data structure was done by choosing the File option from the menu pad. After that, you chose the appropriate menu option, control buttons, etc., to complete the task.

The setup procedure to create a new data table or database file also can be initiated by entering a FoxPro command in the Command window. Practice this option now by going to the Command window. You can then decide which method works best for you.

If you cleared the screen and closed the Command window before you created the SALESMAN table, bring it back by pressing the Ctrl+F2 key combination or by choosing the Command option from the popup menu under the Window menu pad. As a result, the Command window will reappear. Its actual location and size on the screen will be the same as when you closed it.

Now let's create another data table called OFFICE by using a FoxPro command. This table will hold data elements for the sales offices discussed in Chapter 1. The command for creating a new database file is CREATE, followed by the name of the database file:

```
CREATE <database filename>
```

The brackets are used to describe the object to be created; do not enter them in the command. To create the OFFICE database file, type CREATE OFFICE in the Command window (see Figure 4.15).

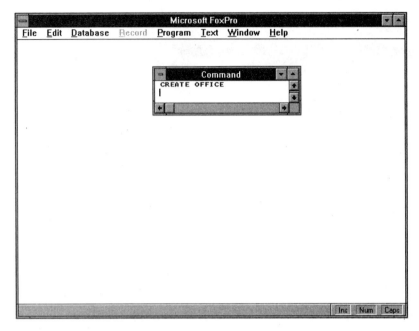

Figure 4.15 Creating the OFFICE table

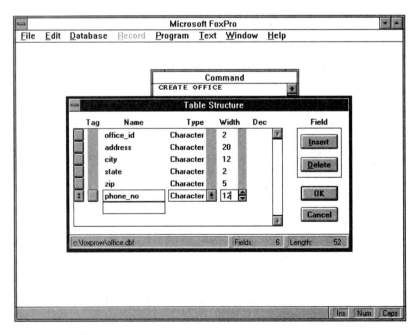

Figure 4.16 Data Structure of the OFFICE table

Creating Databases 117

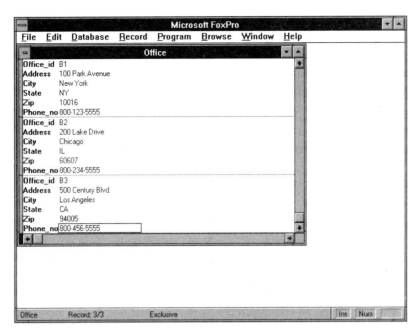

Figure 4.17 Records in the OFFICE Table

In response to the command, a new Table Structure dialog is displayed as before. From this point on, follow the same steps used for creating the SALESMAN table. The OFFICE database file contains six character fields for describing the properties of the sales office entity (see Figure 4.16).

After defining and saving the data structure OFFICE, enter the three records in the database file (see Figure 4.17). Then close the Browse window. Finally, select the Exit option from the File menu popup to leave FoxPro. As a result, the OFFICE table will be closed and you will exit FoxPro for Windows and return to Program Manager. After that, you may return to FoxPro by using the same procedure discussed earlier.

Chapter Summary

This chapter detailed the procedure for creating a new database file, including the setup of a proper data structure and the insertion of all the necessary fields. The SALESMAN table was used as an example to show all the steps for creating the database file with the FoxPro menu interface. Finally, the FoxPro command that enables you to do the same thing was used to create the OFFICE database.

In the next chapter, you will learn how to view and display the contents of the database files that were created in this chapter.

5

Displaying Data

An Overview

In Chapter 4, you learned how to create a database file, which involved first defining its data structure and then filling the data table with the necessary records. The first part of this chapter will show you how to display the data structure of an existing database file. You will then learn how to display the contents of all the data fields in every record of a database file.

Because in many applications you will want to look at only a selective set of the data records in a table, this chapter will then explain how to filter out unwanted records. You will also learn how to select only designated data fields without displaying all the data fields in a database file.

In addition, this chapter will demonstrate how all the data display functions can be executed easily by using the FoxPro menu interface, then it will discuss how to display data using the appropriate FoxPro commands.

Displaying File Directories

Chapter 2 explained that all of your data files are saved and organized in various directories on your disk. For example, the FoxPro program stores all of its files in the FOXPRO directory (c:\foxprow). Further, it was recommended that all database files and other related disk files be saved in a subdirectory named foxdata under the foxprow directory (c:\foxprow\foxdata). As an example, all the database files created in Chapter 4 were saved in that subdirectory.

USING THE FILER

To view all of your disk files in the FOXDATA subdirectory, choose the Filer option from the Help menu. In response, the Filer displays all the files in the current subdirectory of the default disk drive.

If your screen does not appear like Figure 5.1, this indicates that FoxPro is displaying the files in the current directory, which is a directory other than c:\foxprow\foxdata. In all probability, it is the contents of the c:\foxprow directory that Filer is displaying. In this case, simply double click on the foxdata folder, and Filer should change the current directory and display the files in c:\foxprow\foxdata.

Figure 5.1 shows Filer displaying the contents of the c:\foxprow\foxdata directory. As you can see, the default disk drive is c: and the current subdirectory is foxdata (under the foxprow directory). Other information on the screen relates to other types of file management functions that we will discuss elsewhere. The list shows the names and extensions of all the disk files in that subdirectory, together with their sizes (in bytes), and the date and time the files were last changed. The specification that determines which files are displayed is indicated by *.* in the Files Like text box. The asterisks are called wildcard parameters and indicate that everything is to be included. Thus, *.* means that you want to list all files in the subdirectory, regardless of their names and types. If you would like to list only files with a .dbf file extension, you would change the text in the Files Like text box to

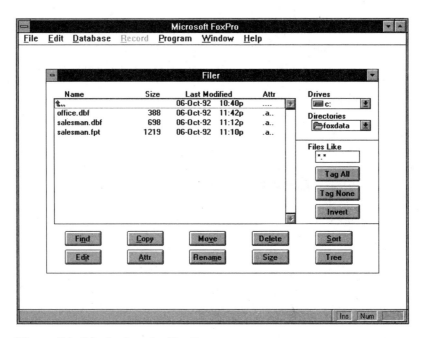

Figure 5.1 Displaying the file directory

Displaying Data   121

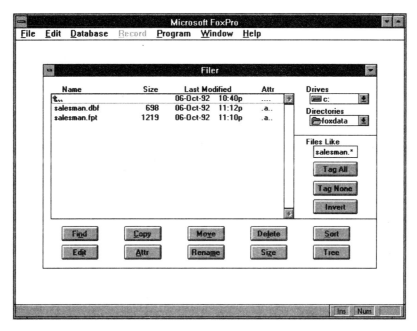

Figure 5.2 Listing of selected files

.dbf. Likewise, as shown in Figure 5.2, by specifying salesman. in the Files Like text box, you would get a list of those files named salesman that have different file extensions.

Information displayed in the Filer window is very useful when you need to know what data files you have created. From the directory list in Figure 5.1, you can see that two database files (SALESMAN.DBF and OFFICE.DBF) have been created. In addition, it is apparent that the SALESMAN database file contains one or more memo fields because the contents of the memo fields are saved in the SALESMAN.FPT file.

To switch to a different disk drive, select the disk drive in the Drives drop-down list box. Similarly, you can change the subdirectory by selecting the desired directory from the Directories drop-down list box.

To exit from the Filer, close the Filer window by pressing the Esc key on the keyboard; or, exit with the mouse by double clicking on the Control box on the Filer window or by choosing the Close option from the Control Menu.

Using FoxPro Commands

You also can invoke the Filer by issuing the FILER command in the Command window. In response, the Filer window of Figure 5.1 appears. (Recall that if the Command window is hidden, you can display it by pressing the Ctrl-F2 key combination.)

122   Understanding FoxPro 2.5 for Windows

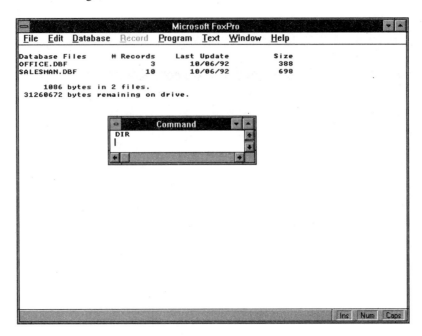

Figure 5.3 Using the DIR command

An alternative to using the Filer to list the disk files in the current subdirectory of the default disk drive is to list them by issuing the appropriate FoxPro command. To list all the database files, issue the DIR command. As a result, information about the database files will be displayed on the screen (see Figure 5.3).

Notice that the DIR command displays only database files (files with a .DBF file extension) and ignores other types of disk files. To list every disk file in the current subdirectory, issue the DIR *.* command (see Figure 5.4).

If you would like to look only at a specific type of file, issue the DIR command and specify a file extension. For example, to view only memo files, issue the following command:

```
DIR *.FPT
```

Similarly, if you would like to list all the files named SALESMAN, regardless of their file extension, issue the following command:

```
DIR SALESMAN.*
```

After viewing the database file list, you can clear the screen by issuing the CLEAR command.

Notice that the DIR *.* command produces only a list of filenames with their file extensions. When you issue the DIR command along with a file specification, the resulting file list does not contain any information about the size of the files. Neither does it show the time and date you changed the files. To view detailed information about these files, use the Filer.

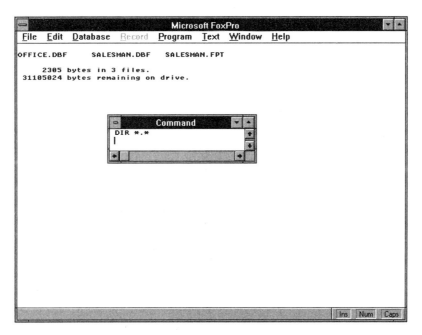

Figure 5.4 Listing all the disk files

Viewing Database Files

As discussed, to create a database file, you begin by defining its structure and then fill it with your data records. You save the data structure with its records in the database file you name. To view the structure of that or of any existing database file, or to manipulate your data in any way, you must first open it in a work area.

A work area is a temporary space reserved for storing data in an open database file. There are 225 different work areas from which you can choose to hold your database files. A work area can be identified with a number ranging from 1 through 225. The first ten work areas can also be identified with a letter from A through J. It is possible to open—at one time—up to 225 database files that do not contain memo fields. The number of database files with memo fields that can be opened is 75. Furthermore, you can switch from one work area to another while you are working.

INVOKING THE VIEW WINDOW

There are a number of ways to open a database file in a work area. One is to choose the View menu option from the Window menu, after which a View window appears on the screen (see Figure 5.5).

The View window can serve as a general control center for handling your database files. Among other functions, it enables you to open database files in work

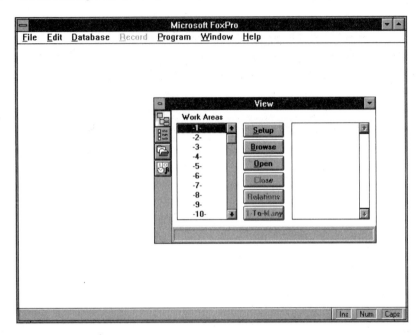

Figure 5.5 The View window

areas and to link your files together, a topic that will be discussed in Chapter 8, "Linking Databases." In the center column of the window, there are six buttons: Setup, Browse, Open, Close, Relations and 1-To-Many. These buttons are for invoking various functions. While you will learn in detail later how to use these buttons, we will briefly discuss them here.

The Setup Button

The Setup button is used to open the Setup dialog box, which allows you to view and modify an existing data structure. But before you can bring up the Setup dialog box, you must open a database in a work area. If no database file is open when you select the Setup button, FoxPro displays the Open File dialog box asking you to open a database file. (We will continue with the Setup dialog after you have learned to open a database file in a work area in the next section.)

The Browse Button

By pressing the Browse button, you can view the records in a database file. Like the Setup button, you need to open a database file before using the Browse button. Again, if you have not opened a database file in a work area, FoxPro will display the Open File dialog box, indicating that you must select a database file before initiating the Browse operation. You will learn how to use the Browse button to view your data records later in this chapter.

The Open Button

Pressing the Open button in the View window is another way to open a database file. Other procedures for opening a database file involve using the FoxPro menu interface and FoxPro commands, both of which are covered in the next section.

The Close Button

The Close button provides the means for removing an open database file from a work area. The button is active only when there is at least one database file open in a work area. Closing a database file is very important for some database file manipulations. For example, you can make a duplicate copy of a database file only if you have first closed the file.

In the View window, in addition to the six buttons, there are four picture buttons that are located below the Control box in the upper left-hand corner of the window. You can use these buttons to display different types of panels. They are, from top to bottom: the View panel button, which causes the View panel that is first displayed when you select the Window View menu option to be redisplayed; the Set Options On/Off panel button, which allows you to change a number of FoxPro's system

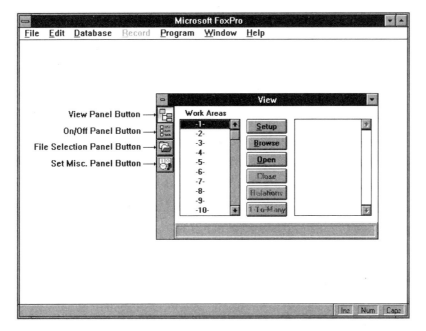

Figure 5.6 The Panel Buttons

settings; the File Selection panel button, which allows you to control where FoxPro looks for a variety of files; and the Set Miscellaneous Values panel button, which allows you to change a number of additional system settings (see Figure 5.6).

The View Panel

The View panel, which is shown in Figure 5.5, displays information on which database files are open in particular work areas. By default, FoxPro for Windows displays the View panel when you select the Window View menu option. If you display some other panel by selecting its picture button, you can return to the View panel by selecting the View panel button, the topmost picture button on the left side of the View window.

The Set Options On/Off Panel

The Set Options On/Off panel displays a series of check boxes, each of which represents the value of a FoxPro control variable or an environmental variable that can be either set on or off. This panel is shown in Figure 5.7, and is accessed by clicking the On/Off picture panel button in the View window. You can use this panel to set the values of a number of variables that control the precise way in which various features of FoxPro for Windows operate. A variable is turned on when its check box is checked, and is turned off when no check appears in the check box. For example, you can set the Clock option to On and continuously display the system time in the lower right corner of the FoxPro window by clicking on the check box; the check box will then contain an "x." To turn the clock display off, click on the check box once more; the "x" will disappear from the check box, and the clock will no longer be displayed.

The File Selection Push Button

The File Selection panel shows information about the default disk drive and working directory, etc. To display this panel, click the mouse on the File Selection panel picture button in the View window. You can use the File panel to view and modify the current disk drive, the working directory, the directory path, and other information (see Figure 5.8). In Figure 5.8, you can see the current default disk drive and working directory are displayed. If you need to change the current drive, select it from the Default Drive drop-down list box. You can specify the data directory by double clicking your mouse on the Working Directory button and then making your selection from the Select Directory dialog box. Likewise, you can specify a different directory path by first double clicking on the FoxPro Path button and then entering the path.

Displaying Data 127

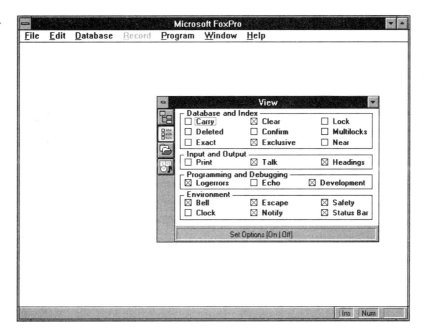

Figure 5.7 The On/Off Panel

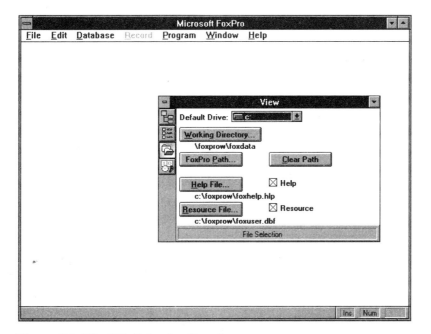

Figure 5.8 The File Selection Panel

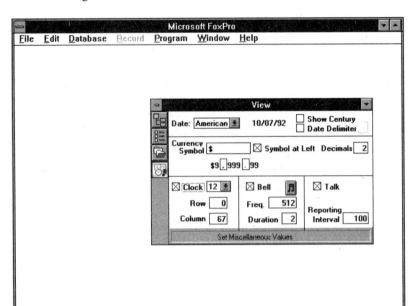

Figure 5.9 The Set Miscellaneous Panel

The Set Miscellaneous Values Panel

The Set Miscellaneous Values panel shows values for various display functions in FoxPro (see Figure 5.9). For example, you can use it to determine how the date is to be displayed (e.g., in the American convention, such as 07/04/93), or whether or not to display the century (07/04/93 vs. 07/04/1993). You can display the clock in a 12-hour or 24-hour format. You can also specify the format for displaying a monetary value. The Set Miscellaneous panel can be displayed by clicking the mouse on the Set Miscellaneous panel button in the View window.

OPENING DATABASE FILES

To reiterate, there are a variety of ways to open a database file in a work area. One is to select the Open button from the View window by clicking on it with your mouse or by pressing the letter "O" on your keyboard. Alternatively, you can simply move the highlight to a work area that does not have an open file and press Enter.

In either case, FoxPro will respond by opening the Open File dialog, as Figure 5.10 shows. This dialog shows the names of the database files available for opening. At this point, select the one you would like to open. With a mouse, double click on the database file; with the keyboard, use the up- and down-arrow keys to highlight the file and then press Enter to open it. Alternatively, after you have

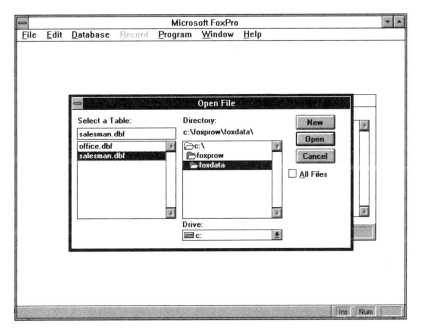

Figure 5.10 Selecting the database file to be opened

highlighted the file, select the Open button. The name of the database file opened is then displayed in the indicated work area; in Figure 5.11, for example, we've opened SALESMAN.DBF. You also can see that the name of the database file that was opened in the highlighted work area appears at the bottom of the View window, together with its number of records.

You can open more than one database file at a time, as long as each is opened in a separate work area. For example, you also can open OFFICE.DBF in work area 2 after opening SALESMAN.DBF in work area 1.

Another method for opening a database file is to double click the mouse button on an unused work area in the View window. Use this method to open OFFICE.DBF in work area 2—point and double click the mouse on the number 2 in the work area; or, if you are using the keyboard, use the down arrow to highlight work area 2 and then press Enter to access the File Open dialog. In either case, when the File Open dialog appears, select OFFICE.DBF and open it. As a result, there are now two database files open in work areas 1 and 2 (see Figure 5.12). Note that, although you can have more than one database file open at the same time, only a single database can be active at any given time. This active database is also referred to as the current or selected database; it is the database to which FoxPro for Windows will apply all database and file operations. The active database is indicated in the View window by the highlight. In Figure 5.12, for example, OFFICE.DBF, the database that we have just opened, is the active database.

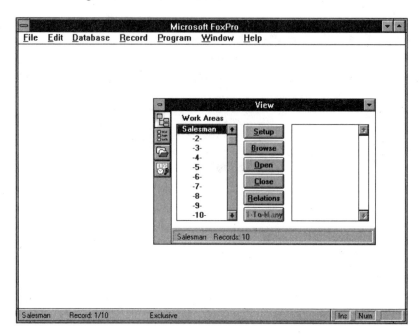

Figure 5.11 Displaying an open database file in a work area

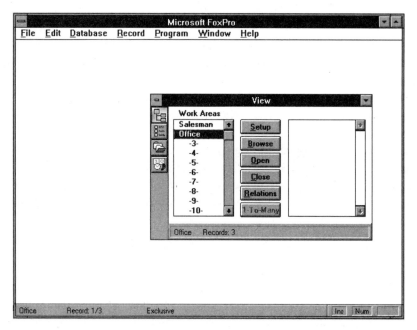

Figure 5.12 Opening two database files in different work areas

Displaying Data 131

CLOSING DATABASE FILES

A database file remains open until you close it, and you should get into the habit of closing files once you have finished using them. Open files are more susceptible to the accidental loss of data as a result of power failure, for example, since the contents of a database can be damaged when the power goes down. In addition, there are some operations (such as file copying and deletion) that cannot be carried out on an open file.

To close a database, select the Close button by pressing the letter "C" or by clicking the mouse on the button. As an exercise, close OFFICE.DBF. First, highlight the OFFICE database file in work area 2 and then select the Close button. After you select the button, OFFICE.DBF is removed from work area 2. Now the View window shows that only SALESMAN.DBF remains open in work area 1.

DISPLAYING DATABASE STRUCTURES

Once a database file is open in a work area, you can view its structure or its contents by selecting the appropriate buttons.

To display the structure of an existing database file, all you have to do is open it in a work area and then select the Setup button. To display the structure of SALESMAN, select the Setup button while the database file is open in work area 1 by pressing the letter "S" or by clicking on the button when the database file is highlighted. (After you closed OFFICE.DBF in work area 2, highlight SALESMAN.DBF in work area 1 to make it the active database.) In response, the data structure associated with the open database file is displayed in the Setup dialog (see Figure 5.13).

You can see in this figure that all the data fields defined in the open SALESMAN.DBF are displayed in a list, along with their type, width, and number of decimal places. There are other items displayed in the Setup dialog box, but they will be discussed later; you do not have to be concerned with them at this point.

After viewing the structure, exit from the Setup dialog and return to the View window by clicking the OK button, by pressing the Esc key, or by double clicking on the Control menu bar.

VIEWING DATA RECORDS

Recall from Chapter 4 that when you were entering data into a database file, you could choose one of two views: Record view or Browse view. From the View window, you also can choose one of two display modes for showing the data records in an existing database: Change or Browse. When data is displayed in

132   Understanding FoxPro 2.5 for Windows

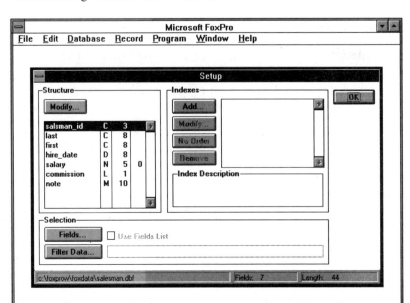

Figure 5.13 Displaying a data structure in the Setup dialog

Record view, it is in Change mode, so called because it is the usual mode for making changes to data records. Otherwise, it is in Browse mode.

Using Change Mode

To switch from Browse mode to Change mode, select the Change option from the Browse menu popup. In response to the menu selection, FoxPro displays the data records in Change mode. Again, you can adjust the window size to reveal as many records as possible (see Figure 5.14).

Because you can see only a few records at a time in Change mode, you will have to scroll up and down to bring hidden records into view. Either click on the Scroll control or use the PgUp and PgDn keys to advance forward and backward.

Now that you have seen how data records are displayed in Change mode, return to Browse mode, since it offers many desirable features that you can use for displaying your data.

Switching to Browse Mode

To switch from Change to Browse mode, select the Browse option from the Browse menu popup, and you will be returned to Browse mode. Remember, though, if you changed the window while you were in Change mode, the size and location of the Browse window will now reflect those alterations.

Displaying Data   133

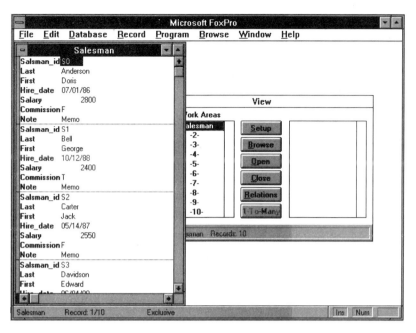

Figure 5.14   Displaying data records in Change mode

Using Browse Mode

Browse mode displays data records in table form, using one row per record and one column for each data field. To bring up Browse view, select the Browse button in the View window when an open database is selected. For example, try clicking on the Browse push button or pressing the letter "B" while SALESMAN is open in work area A. Watch as the records of the SALESMAN database are displayed in Browse mode (see Figure 5.15). However, your records may initially be displayed in Change mode. This happens because you had last used Change mode to display your data records prior to selecting the Browse button. To change back to Browse mode, select the Browse option from the Browse menu.

The size and location of the Browse window are carried over from the previous application. Because of this, your Browse window may look different from that shown in Figure 5.15. If it is too small to display all the data fields in the SALESMAN table, you can resize the window to display as much data as the window allows. (The procedures for moving and sizing a window were covered in Chapter 2. You may want to review them before proceeding to the next section.)

One advantage to using Browse mode is that you can view many records on one screen, because each record occupies only one line. But if your data table has a large number of data fields, you may not be able to view all of them on the same screen without scrolling the data fields. In this case, you may want to view your

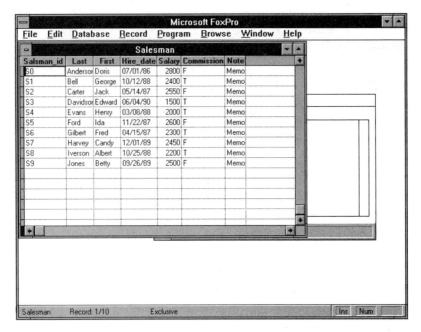

Figure 5.15 Displaying data records in Browse mode

records in Change mode, which enables you to display more fields on the screen. Of course, you can view only a more limited number of records per screen.

Sizing Browse Columns

In Figure 5.15, you saw that data fields are displayed in columns in the Browse window. The default width of the column is determined by the length of the field name or the field width specified in the database structure, whichever is greater. For example, even though the SALSMAN_ID field is defined as three characters long in the database structure, the field occupies ten spaces in the Browse window because that is the length of its field name. On the other hand, the LAST field occupies an 8-character wide column—the size of the field in the database structure—even though the field name itself has only four letters.

Because of this, you may want to adjust the width of a column so that you can display its data more suitably. Then, if some columns in the Browse window appear to be too crowded, you can widen them so that the data fields appear in a more pleasing format. Or, if you want to display more data fields on the same screen in the Browse window, you can narrow some of the columns.

You can size a column either by using the mouse or by choosing a menu option with the keyboard. It is important to remember that changing the size of a Browse column does not affect the actual field width in the data structure.

To resize a Browse column with a mouse, first position the mouse cursor on the right vertical grid line in the field name column until a double-arrow cross symbol appears. Then, hold down the left mouse button and drag it to the right to widen the column or to the left to narrow the column. You can go back and forth until you have achieved the desired column width. As an exercise, place the mouse cursor on the right-hand grid line of the LAST column (for the salesperson's last name) and drag it several spaces to the right.

To resize a column with the keyboard, first position the cursor on the column you would like to size. Then choose the Size Field option from the Browse menu. Press the right- or left-arrow keys to widen or narrow the column. Finally, press Enter to confirm the changes and establish the new column width or press ESC to cancel them. As a demonstration of this method, widen the FIRST column, which displays salespeople's first names. First, position the cursor anywhere in that column (regardless of the row or character position), then choose the Size Field option from the Browse menu. In response, the First column is highlighted. Next, press the right arrow key several times to widen the column until you have achieved the desired width (see Figure 5.16).

When you look at the Browse window in Figure 5.16, notice that widening these two columns did not change the window size. Sometimes, data fields may become hidden as a result of your widening some columns. To view the hidden data fields, you can widen the Browse window if there is sufficient space on the screen to do so. Otherwise, you will have to scroll the data fields to view those hidden fields.

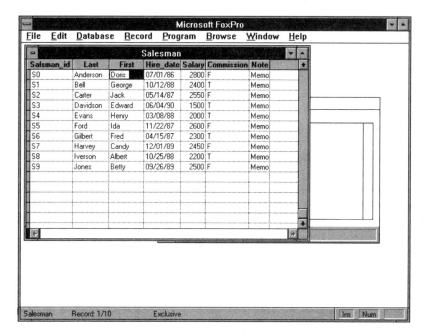

Figure 5.16 Widening the LAST and FIRST columns

Scrolling Data Fields and Records

In Browse view, you can scroll to the left or right to reveal any data fields that are hidden from the Browse window. Similarly, if you have more records than can be displayed on the same screen in the Browse window, you can also scroll up and down the window to reveal hidden records.

If you are using a mouse, click on the left or right arrows in the horizontal scroll bar at the bottom of the window. This allows you to scroll left and right along the data fields. Or point your mouse cursor at the thumb button in the scroll bar and drag it to the left or right to reveal the hidden data fields. With the keyboard, press the Tab or Shift+Tab key to move to the right or left one data field. After you have reached the last column shown in the window, FoxPro will reveal the hidden fields as you continue to press one of these keys.

To scroll data records up and down, use the vertical scroll bar on the right of the window. Similarly, by pressing the up- and down-arrow keys, you move up and down one record at a time in the window. FoxPro reveals the hidden records after you have moved to the top or bottom of the Browse window.

Hiding Data Fields

Browse view displays all of the data fields defined in the database structure, but if you would like to view only selected data fields, you can choose one of two options: either select only those data fields to be included in Browse view (you will learn how to do this later in the chapter) or hide those fields you don't want to see in Browse view.

The procedure to hide a data field is the same for narrowing a Browse column. By shrinking a column to its minimum width, you hide its contents. As a test, try shrinking one of the data columns in Browse view until it is hidden. To redisplay the hidden column, widen the column again to the desired width.

Removing Column Grids

By default, Browse mode uses a vertical grid to divide the columns for showing your data fields. But you can remove the grid lines by toggling (turning off) the Grid option from the Browse menu. To replace the grids, simply toggle the Grid option again from the Browse menu.

Moving Data Fields

In its default layout, Browse view displays all the data fields in the order in which they are defined in the database structure. But you can rearrange them in whatever order you choose by moving the data fields around in the Browse window.

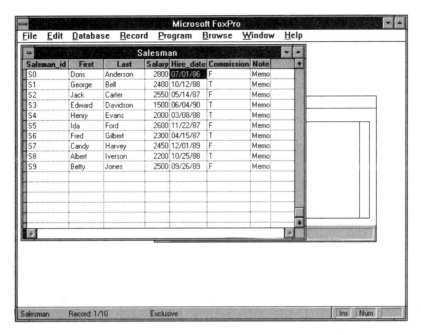

Figure 5.17 Moving the FIRST and HIRE_DATE data fields

Moving a data field with a mouse is very simple. All you have to do is first place your mouse cursor on the name of the field you would like to move. Then hold down the left button and drag to the field's new position. For example, if you would like to move the FIRST field to the left of the LAST field, position your mouse cursor on the column label, e.g., FIRST. Then hold down the left mouse button and drag it to the left until First appears to the left of Last. When you release the mouse button, the order of these two fields will be reversed.

You also can move a field by using the keyboard. To do so, first place your cursor anywhere in the field to be moved by using the Tab or Shift-Tab keys and then choosing the Move Field option from the Browse menu. Next, use the left- or right-arrow keys to move to the left or right in the window. Pressing Enter completes the operation. As a test, try moving the HIRE_DATE field to the right of the SALARY field by first placing your cursor in the HIRE_DATE column and then choosing the Move Field option from the Browse menu. In response to the menu choice, the column name is highlighted. Now, press the right-arrow key until the HIRE_DATE field appears to the right of the SALARY field (see Figure 5.17). Finally, press Enter to complete the operation.

Maximizing the Browse Window

In some situations when you would like enlarge the Browse window to display the maximum amount of data in it, you may choose to maximize the window size. To

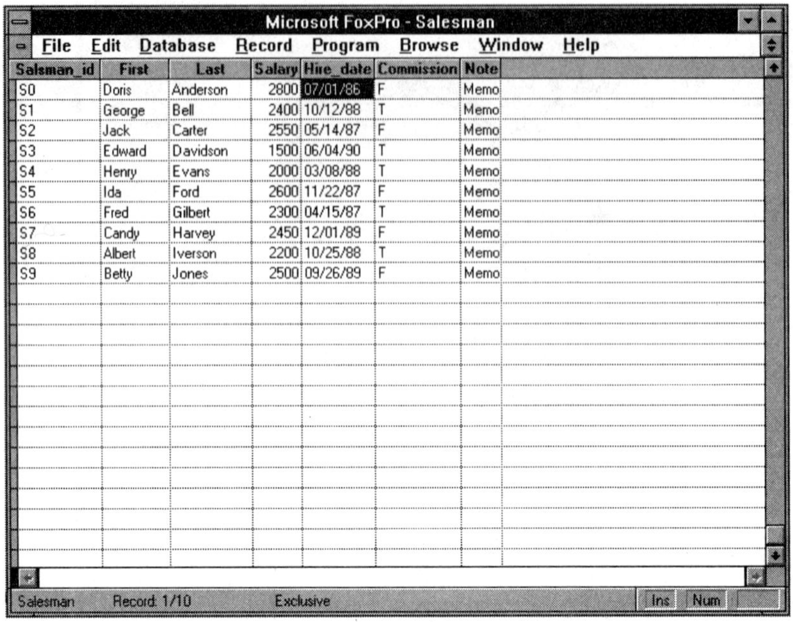

Figure 5.18 Maximizing the Browse window

do that, click the mouse on the Maximize button in the upper right-hand corner of the window. Or you can select the Maximize option from the Control menu. With the keyboard, you can also press the Ctrl+F10 key combination to maximize the window. As a result, the contents of the Browse view will be displayed in the entire FoxPro window (see Figure 5.18).

In Figure 5.18, you can see that the records of SALESMAN.DBF are shown in a Browse window that fills the entire FoxPro window. To restore the Browse window to its previous size, click the mouse on the double-arrow button in the upper right-hand corner of the Browse window (below the maximize button for the entire FoxPro window), or press the Ctrl+F9 key combination. Now, use the mouse or keyboard to return to the original Browse window.

Minimizing the Browse Window

If you would like to temporarily put aside the Browse window while freeing the screen to view other data, you can choose to minimize the active Browse window. To do that, click on the Minimize button at the upper right-hand corner of the Browse window or press the Ctrl+F9 key combination. As a result, the Browse window will be reduced to an icon and placed at the lower left-hand corner in the FoxPro window. The name of the icon will be the name of database being displayed in the Browse window (see Figure 5.19). To return the Browse window to its

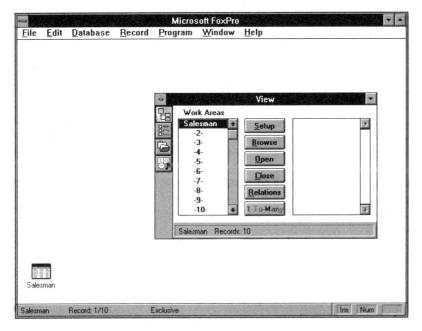

Figure 5.19 Minimizing the Browse window

previous size, double click the mouse on the icon or press the Ctrl+F5 key combination. Now, practice pressing the Minimize button to shrink the Browse window and then return it to its original size. Then, to prepare for the next exercise, maximize the Browse window now.

Partitioning the Browse Window

In those situations when you have a data table with a large number of data fields, you may want to view groups of fields in sections of the Browse window. You can do this by partitioning the Browse window into two sections, each of which shows a group of data fields. Or you may want to view data records in Record and Browse views simultaneously on the same screen. This requires splitting the window into two parts.

You can partition a Browse window by using either the mouse or the keyboard. With the mouse, first position the mouse cursor on the Window Splitter button, which appears at the bottom left-hand corner of the window, next to the left-arrow scroll button. When a double cross with double arrows and double vertical lines appears, hold down the button and drag it to the right. As a result, the Browse window splits into two sections (see Figure 5.20).

You also can partition the Browse window or change the size of the partitions with the keyboard by first selecting the Partitions option from the Browse menu

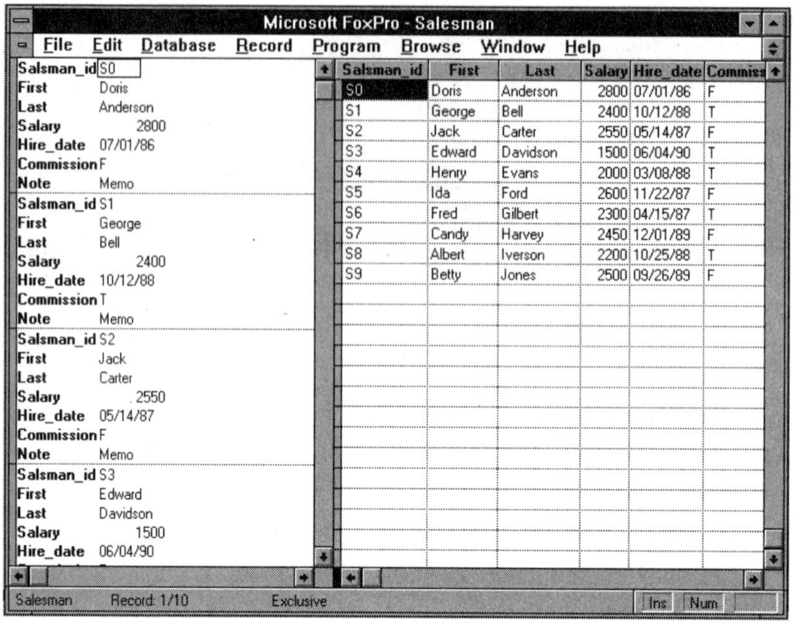

Figure 5.20 Partitioning the Browse window

popup. Then press the left or right arrows to resize the partitions. When you have finished, press the Enter key to accept the new partitions.

When you split the Browse window into two sections, each section may be in a different view. In Figure 5.20, you can see that the left section is in Change mode while the right section is in Browse mode. You can move from one section to another by moving your mouse cursor or by pressing the Ctrl+H key combination. With one section of the split window active, you can switch that partition of the Browse window from Browse mode to Change mode or vice versa by selecting the appropriate option on the Browse menu popup.

When you split a Browse window into two sections, the data records displayed in the partitions can be linked or unlinked, depending on the last window settings you have saved. (Note: When you first invoke FoxPro, records are linked together by default.) In linked partitions, any movement from one record to another in one partition also occurs in the other partitions. The same record is always highlighted in both partitions, and the highlighted record, along with assorted records surrounding it, is always displayed in both partitions. If you move the highlight to a record that is displayed in one partition but not in the other, FoxPro will immediately update the records being displayed in the second partition to include the highlighted record and the records immediately around it.

On the other hand, when two partitions are unlinked, it is still true that the same record is always highlighted in both partitions. But, if there are more database

Displaying Data 141

records than can fit in a window, requiring that the records in the partition be scrolled, the same highlighted record is not necessarily displayed in both partitions. Unlinking partitions allows you to scroll one partition while maintaining a stationary display of the records in the second partition.

It is important to note that unlinking does not allow you to highlight a different record in each partition. In Figure 5.20, for example, the highlighted record in the Change mode partition is the same as that highlighted in the Browse mode partition. In addition, because the partitions are linked, a comparable set of records is displayed in the two partitions. As you move around the records in one partition, the corresponding records in the other partition will be highlighted. If you would like to hold records stationary in one partition while you move around the records in the other partition, you can unlink them. All you have to do is toggle (select) Link Partitions from the Browse menu popup. As a result, when you move around the records in one partition, the records in the other partition will remain stationary once you have moved beyond the current screen of records being displayed (see Figure 5.21).

In Figure 5.21, you can see that on the left partition record S9 is highlighted in Change mode, while the same record is invisible in the right partition, where records are displayed in Browse mode.

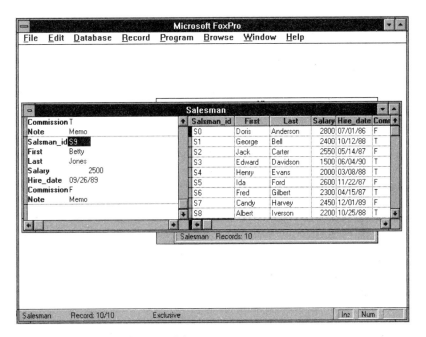

Figure 5.21 Unlinking partitions

Viewing Memo Fields

(To prepare for the next exercise, close the left partition and display the records in Browse view. To use the mouse to do this, simply position the mouse cursor on the Window Splitter button, which now appears in the lower left-hand corner of the right partition. When a double cross with a double arrow and a double vertical line appears, hold down the mouse button and drag to the left until there is only one partition. With the keyboard, select the Resize Partitions option from the Browse menu popup. Then continue to press the left-arrow key until only one partition remains on the screen and press the Enter key.)

In our previous examples, the contents of the memo fields are hidden in both Change and Browse modes. Instead, only the word "Memo" appears in the memo field, indicating that there is text stored in that field. This is because a memo field is a variable-length field and requires special handling. All other FoxPro field types—character, numeric, float, date, and logical—are fixed-length fields. The length of these fields is declared in advance, at the time that the database structure is defined. All data stored to a particular field will have the same length. In contrast, memo fields, which are intended to store free-form textual information, are not assigned a fixed length at the time the file is created. The actual length of a memo field depends on the amount of text that has been stored to that memo field for a particular record. The advantage of a memo field is that vastly different amounts of information can be stored to each record of a database without wasting disk

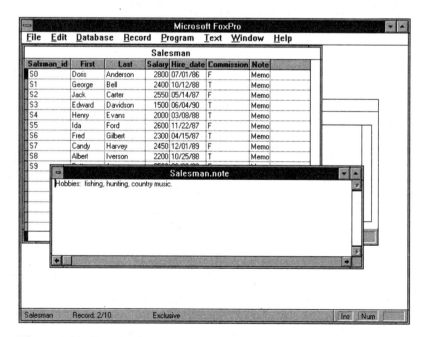

Figure 5.22 Showing contents of a memo field

storage space. The disadvantage is that FoxPro stores memo fields in a separate file apart from the database file itself.

To view the memo field contents, bring up the Memo window by pressing the Ctrl+Home (or Ctrl+PgUp key combination) after placing your cursor on the memo field you would like to view. If you are using a mouse, double click on the memo field.

To view the contents of the NOTE memo field for salesman Bell, place the cursor on the word "Memo" in the second record and then press Ctrl-Home. Alternatively, double click your mouse on that word. The contents of that memo field are displayed in the Memo window (see Figure 5.22). The size and location of the Memo window are set by the last application. You can resize and rearrange the window on the screen to best fit the contents of your memo fields.

After viewing the Memo window, close it by double clicking the mouse on the Control box at the upper left-hand corner of the window, or by pressing the Ctrl+W key combination.

VIEWING DATA RECORDS IN MULTIPLE DATABASE FILES

As mentioned, you can open database files in up to 225 work areas at a time in FoxPro. While the files are open, you can view any of them in either Change or Browse mode. As a result, you are able to view multiple files on the same screen simultaneously with overlapping Browse windows. If the contents of your database files are small, you can size and arrange the windows so that you can view them all on the same screen.

If you would like to view more than one database file at a time, all you have to do is use the View window to open, one at a time, those you want in separate work areas. Once the files are open in their respective work areas, you can then select the Browse button to display them in sequence.

To view the SALESMAN and OFFICE databases, open SALESMAN.DBF in work area 1 and OFFICE.DBF in work area 2. Because you already opened the SALESMAN database in a previous exercise and displayed its records in Browse mode, if it is now open and its records are currently displayed in a Browse window, all you have to do now is bring up the View window. To do that, if it is partially visible in the background, click anywhere on the View window to bring it to the foreground. Otherwise, move the Browse window in the foreground to reveal the View window before clicking on it. Or choose the View option from the Window menu popup to bring the View window to the foreground.

Alternatively, you can press the Ctrl+F1 key combination to cycle between the Browse and View windows. Once the View window appears, you can open the OFFICE database in work area 2. You can display the records of the OFFICE database file in the Browse window by selecting the Browse button when the

144 Understanding FoxPro 2.5 for Windows

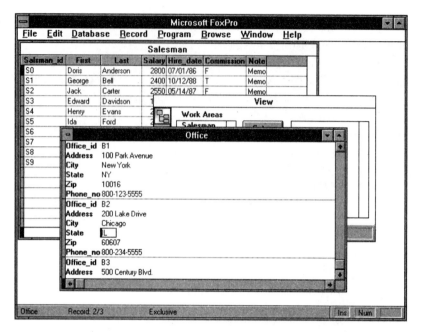

Figure 5.23 The second Browse window

OFFICE database is highlighted. The records of the database file will then be displayed in a Browse window on top of the one showing the records from the SALESMAN database file. (see Figure 5.23). You can see in this figure that the records of the OFFICE database file are displayed in Change mode while the records of the SALESMAN database file are shown in Browse mode.

Of course, you can switch from Change mode to Browse mode and vice versa by using the procedure you learned earlier. While you are in the OFFICE Browse window, you can choose the Browse option from the Browse menu popup to make the switch. You also can clean up the screen by removing the View window from the screen. To do that, close the View window by first bringing the window to the foreground and then double clicking on the Control box with the mouse; or press the Esc key. You also could choose the Hide option from the Window menu popup when the View window is highlighted to close the View window. Later, you can resize the Browse windows so that you can view records in the SALESMAN and OFFICE database files on the same screen (see Figure 5.24).

Switching between Browse Windows

When database files are displayed in more than one Browse window on the screen, you can switch from one to the other by using either the mouse or the keyboard.

Displaying Data   145

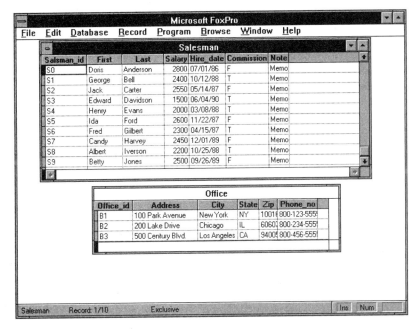

Figure 5.24 Showing SALESMAN and OFFICE databases in Browse windows

The current active window is indicated by a highlighted window title bar and by the presence of the Control box at the upper left-hand corner of the window. In addition, the active window is shown in the foreground if the Browse windows overlap.

If you are using a mouse, click it anywhere within the Browse window that you would like to be active. With the keyboard, switch from one Browse window to another by selecting the Cycle option available on the Window menu popup or by pressing the Ctrl+F1 key combination. In response to the menu selection, the other Browse window will become the active one. If you have overlapping Browse windows open when you select the Cycle option, it will bring the active window to the foreground.

When database files are displayed in Browse windows, their names are shown at the bottom of the Window menu popup (see Figure 5.25). Because of this, you can designate the database file that you would like to display in the active Browse window by selecting it from the Window menu popup accordingly. Thus, while the OFFICE database file is displayed in the active window, you can choose the SALESMAN database file from the Window menu popup to make it the active window. This option is very useful when you are displaying a number of database files in multiple Browse windows. It allows you to go to a specific database file directly without cycling through other Browse windows or without having to click on a window that is completely hidden underneath other open windows.

146 Understanding FoxPro 2.5 for Windows

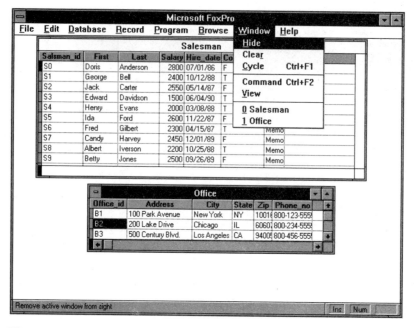

Figure 5.25 Switching between Browse windows

Setting Type Font

While you are viewing data in the Browse window, you can choose a specific font to display the contents of your database records. In addition to MS Sans Serif, the default font that we have used so far to display the records in the SALESMAN and OFFICE databases, you can choose from a list of fonts provided by FoxPro. To select a new font, first choose the Font option from the Browse menu to bring up the Font dialog. (Figure 5.26). In the Font dialog, you can choose the type, style, and size of the font for displaying the records in the active Browse window. As an exercise, make the salesman Browse window active and then choose the Font option from the Browse menu. Then select Courier as the font type, Bold as the font style, and 10 as the font size. After your selection, select the OK button or press the Enter key to accept the font. As a result, the records in the salesman Browse window will be displayed in the selected font, while the records in the office Browse window will continue to be shown in the default font. (see Figure 5.27). To return the Browse window to the default font, select the Font option from the Browse menu and select MS Sans Serif as the font, Regular as the style, and 8 as the font size. However, in the event that you cannot remember the font that you would like to restore and do not want to close the window, there is an undocumented trick. Simply convert the window from Browse mode to Change mode by selecting the Change option from the Record menu. When the window's records are arranged

Displaying Data 147

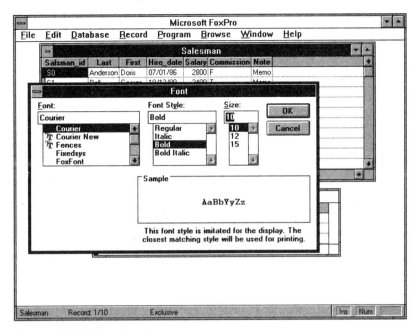

Figure 5.26 Selecting fonts

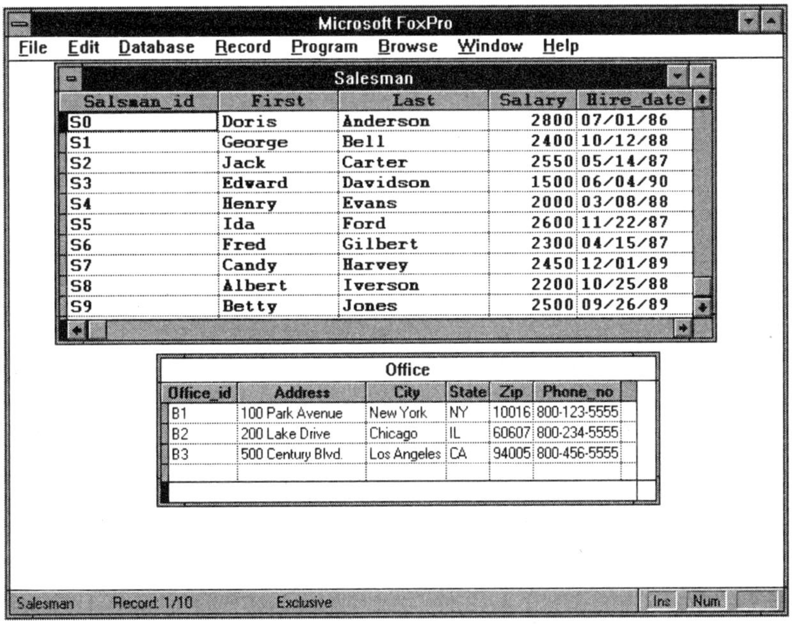

Figure 5.27 Showing records in Courier font

in Change mode, the default font will be restored. The Browse window can then be placed in Browse mode once more.

VIEWING SELECTIVE FIELDS

When you view the contents of a database file in Browse or Change mode, all of the records and data fields in the database file are displayed. If you would like to view only selective data fields or records, you have to let FoxPro know before opening the Browse window.

Earlier in this chapter, you learned how to hide Browse columns and show only those data fields that you want to see. But you can do this only in Browse mode; in Change mode, FoxPro shows *all* the existing data fields. Therefore, if you want to display only selective data fields in either mode, you must specify those data fields.

To select the data fields to be displayed in the Browse window, use the Setup dialog, which is available by choosing the Setup button in the View window. Let's say that you want to display only the LAST, FIRST, and SALARY fields of the SALESMAN database file. First, bring up the View window and close the OFFICE database so that only the SALESMAN database remains open in work area 1. In addition, select the SALESMAN database as the current database. In the View window, select the Setup button to bring up the Setup dialog (see Figure 5.28).

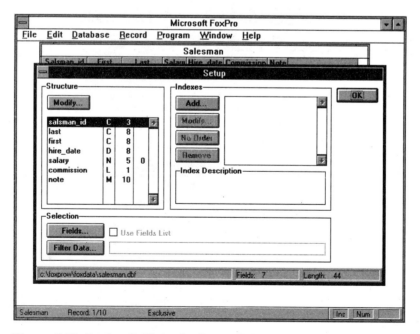

Figure 5.28 Setting fields in the Setup dialog

Displaying Data   149

The Setup dialog, in addition to showing the structure of the database file, has many controls, including two buttons that are located at the bottom left side of the dialog. These buttons—Fields and Filter Data—allow you to select the data fields to be displayed and determine which kinds of records are to be displayed.

Picking Data Fields

To pick the data fields that you would like to display, select the Fields button by clicking your mouse on the button. With the keyboard, use the Tab key to move the highlight to the button and press the Enter key. Now the Field Picker dialog appears (see Figure 5.29).

There is a set of four buttons in this dialog—Move, All, Remove, and Remove All—which are for selecting or deselecting one or all of the data fields in the database file. The OK button lets you exit from the dialog with the selected data fields, and Cancel enables you to exit from the dialog without completing the field selection. The left-hand side of the dialog contains the All Fields list box; this displays the database structure, including all of its fields. On the right is the Selected Fields list box, which will contain a list of the fields that will eventually be displayed in the Browse window. The Field Picker dialog operates by allowing you to select from among the fields whose names are displayed in the All Fields list box and place them in the Selected Fields list box.

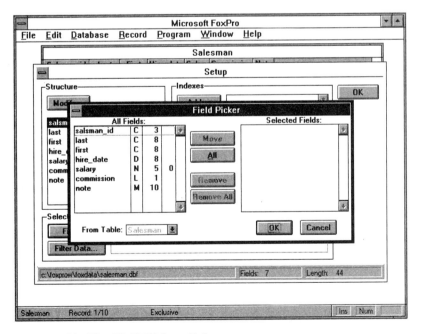

Figure 5.29 The Field Picker dialog

150 Understanding FoxPro 2.5 for Windows

To include all the data fields in the display, select the All button either by clicking the mouse on the button or by pressing the letter "A." To deselect all the data fields, press the letter "l" or click the mouse on the Remove All button. Notice that the Remove All button becomes active only when at least one field has been placed in the Select Fields list box.

An easy way to select an individual data field for display is to double click your mouse on the field you want to pick. With a keyboard, first highlight the field name by pressing the Tab key continuously until the first field name is highlighted and then use the down-arrow key to select the field you want to pick. Press the Enter key to select it, and the field name is moved to the list of selected fields on the screen. To select another data field, use the up- or down-arrow keys to highlight another data field and press the Enter key.

Now you can use the mouse or keyboard to select the FIRST, LAST, and SALARY fields, in that order. The selected data fields are then displayed in the Selected Fields list box (see Figure 5.30).

If you make a mistake, just double click your mouse on the field you would like to deselect. On the keyboard, you must first highlight the field in the Selected Fields list box (with Tab and arrow keys) and then press the Enter key.

After you select all the data fields—but before you display the data—you must exit from the Field Picker dialog by selecting the OK button. FoxPro then returns you to the Setup dialog (see Figure 5.31). Notice in this figure that the Use Fields

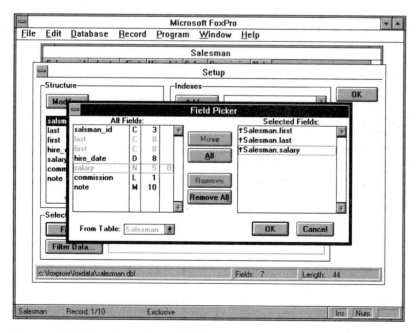

Figure 5.30 Showing selected fields

Displaying Data 151

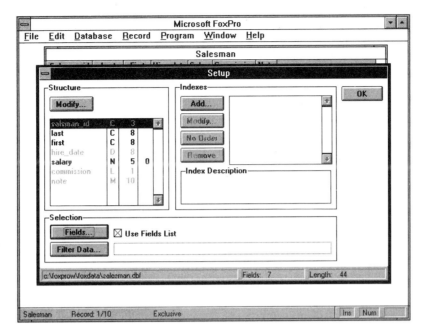

Figure 5.31 Showing the Fields list

List box has been checked. Now you can bring up the Browse window to display the selected data fields. To do that, select the OK button from Setup dialog. This returns you to the View window, at which point you choose the Change option from the Record (not the Browse) menu to display the data fields you have selected in Change mode in the Browse window; this is shown in Figure 5.32. To display the selected fields in the Browse window in Browse mode, simply press the Browse push button.

Whether the records are displayed in Browse mode or Change mode, note that the order of the data fields in the Browse window is determined by that field's ordinal position in the data structure, and not by the sequence in which the field was picked. To rearrange the order of fields in the Browse window, use the procedure that was discussed earlier in this chapter in "Moving Data Fields."

Resetting Data Fields

After examining the data in the selected fields, you can change the list of selected fields by returning to the Setup dialog from the View window and invoking the Field Picker dialog to revise the Selected Fields list. After you have made the necessary change(s), bring up the Browse window again to display the data. Note, however, that when you return to the Browse window, the original set of selected data fields will remain on the screen. To update the screen for showing the revised

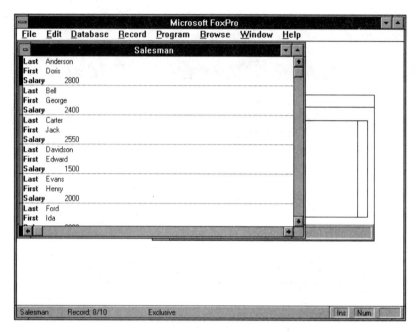

Figure 5.32 Displaying the selected data records

list of selected data fields, select the Change option from the Record menu popup. The Browse window will be placed in Change mode, and the display will be updated to reflect the fields that you selected from the Field Picker dialog. Note that simply pressing the Browse push button once more, or selecting the Change option on the Browse menu pad, will not update the display accordingly. The fields displayed will continue to be based on the old fields list.

Similarly, if you would like to redisplay all the data fields in the database file, you must return to the Setup dialog and use the Field Picker dialog to deselect the data fields that you picked earlier. But remember that when you return to the Browse window, you must select the Change option from the Record menu popup to update the screen. Now, select all the data fields and display them in the Browse window.

VIEWING SELECTIVE RECORDS

Now that you have learned how to pick the data fields you would like to browse, we'll show you how to select and view only a subset of the records in a database file. This procedure is very similar to that for picking fields. It requires that you bring up the Setup dialog so that you can define filter conditions—i.e., the criteria that will be used to screen out the unwanted records and select only those you want.

Using Filter Conditions

Filter conditions are written in the form of expressions made up of the following: the names of your data fields, any logical operators, and values for the data fields. Examples of such expressions are:

```
salary >= 2500
salary >= 2000 AND salary <= 2500
salary > 2500 OR salary < 2000
first = 'Jack' OR first = 'John'
hire_date > {01/01/88}
hire_date > {01/01/88) OR salary >2600
commission = .T.
BETWEEN(salary,2000,2400)
```

The first expression, salary >= 2500, for example, specifies the name of the data field (SALARY), the logical operator (>=, indicating greater than or equal to), and the filter value (2500). The expression means that you would like to select only those records whose value in the SALARY field satisfies the filter condition (equal to $2,500). AND is used as a connector to join two conditions; it means that both conditions must be true for the record to satisfy the filter condition. So in the case of the second expression, those records in which salary is greater than or equal to 2,000 as well as in which salary is less than or equal to 2,500 will satisfy the filter criteria. In other words, since both conditions must be met, this filter effectively selects records whose salaries fall in the range from 2,000 to 2,500.

OR is another connector that joins two conditions; it means that at least one condition must be true for the record to satisfy the filter condition. In the case of the third expression, those records that have a value less than 2000 or greater than 2500 in the salary field will meet the filter condition.

You also can define your expressions with character, date, and logical fields, but remember to enclose the filter string in quotation marks for the character field, such as FIRST = "Jack"; and use curly brackets to define the date value for the filter condition, such as HIRE_DATE > {01/01/88}. For logical fields, use either .T. or .F. as a filter value in the expression, such as COMMISSION = .T.

In addition to field names, logical operators, and filter values, you also can use mathematical functions in an expression. The last expression, BETWEEN(salary, 2000, 2400), is an example. BETWEEN is a function that evaluates the value in the SALARY field to determine whether it lies between the two limits (2000 and 2400). If you specify the filter condition with this expression, it will select those salaries between $2,000 and $2,400 inclusively.

There is a large set of functions that you can use to define your expressions, and we will discuss them in more detail in later chapters. For now, all you need to be concerned with are the more simple expressions.

Defining Filter Conditions

To specify filter conditions for viewing selective records, first bring up the Setup dialog from the View window. Let's assume that you have SALESMAN.DBF open in a work area in the View window, and that you have selected the Setup button so that the Setup dialog appears. Now, select the Filter Data button at the bottom of the screen with the mouse or the keyboard. (The Setup dialog was shown earlier in Figure 5.28.) After selecting the Filter Data button, the Expression Builder dialog appears (see Figure 5.33).

The Expression Builder is a special dialog that allows you to define an expression—a formula that, when evaluated, generates a new value with a data type of character, numeric, logical, or date. The Expression Builder contains a number of drop-down lists for selecting the expression's functions and logical and relational operators. These drop-down lists make it extremely easy for you to build expressions. It also contains a text box for defining the filter expression itself. The Expression Builder's overall ease of use is enhanced by the Verify button, which instructs FoxPro to check the expression that you have created to make sure that it is valid and to report any errors to you.

On the top of the Expression Builder, four drop-down lists are visible: String, Math, Logical, and Date. Open these drop-down lists by clicking the mouse on the down arrow at the right side of the list. With the keyboard, use the Tab key to

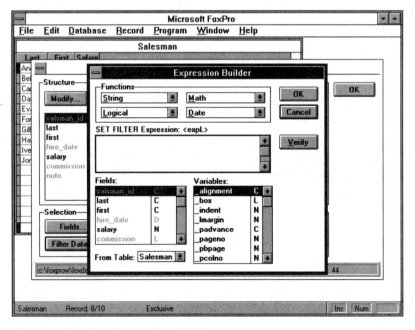

Figure 5.33 The Expression Builder

highlight the drop-down list and press the Space key to display the list. When the drop-down list is shown, select an item of your choice by clicking on it. Or use the down-arrow key to highlight the item and select it by pressing the Enter key.

The Math drop-down list shows the numerical functions and operators that are available for inclusion in your expression. Likewise, all the functions and operators for string manipulation appear in the String drop-down list, and all the logical functions and operators are in the Logical drop-down list. And, if you intend to use a function for manipulating your date fields in an expression, open the Date drop-down list. To familiarize yourself with these popups, open each of them and take a look at their contents. You will learn to use some of them in later exercises.

Entering Filter Expressions

In the center of the Expression Builder is the text box in which you specify your filter expression. The easiest way to enter an expression is to type it in on the keyboard. For example, if you want to view only those records whose values in the SALARY field are greater than or equal to $2,500, type in the appropriate filter expression (see Figure 5.34).

After you have completed defining the filter expression, select the Verify button to check its validity. If the expression is invalid, FoxPro will display an alert dialog

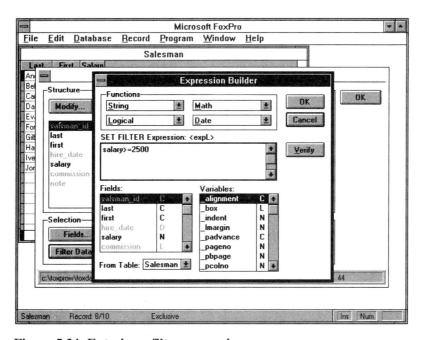

Figure 5.34 Entering a filter expression

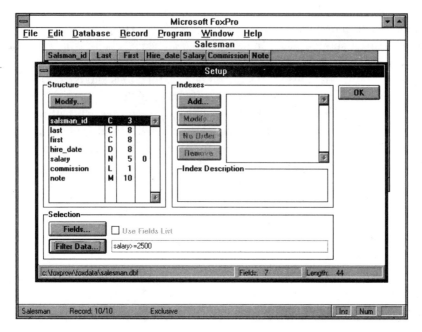

Figure 5.35 Filter expression in the View window

that attempts to diagnose the problem. Clicking anywhere on the screen or pressing any key will clear the dialog and allow you to correct the expression. If you decide at any time that you do not want to correct it, you can exit the dialog by selecting the Cancel button. Otherwise, if the expression is valid, choose the OK button to exit from the Expression Builder and return to the Setup dialog. At this point, the filter expression you entered appears next to the Filter Data... button (see Figure 5.35).

Now, you can proceed to display the records in the Browse window by returning to the View window and selecting the Browse button. The new Browse window will display only those records that satisfy the conditions specified in the filter expression (see Figure 5.36).

Modifying Existing Filter Expressions

After displaying the selected records, you may decide you want to look at a different set of records, a procedure easily accomplished by revising the filter expression. To do so, return to the Expression Builder and change the current filter expression by modifying it. Or, if you would like to write an entirely new expression, just press the Del key to erase the existing expression. So, to replace the current expression with the new expression, HIRE_DATE > {01/01/88} OR SALARY > 2600, type it in after erasing the existing one.

Displaying Data 157

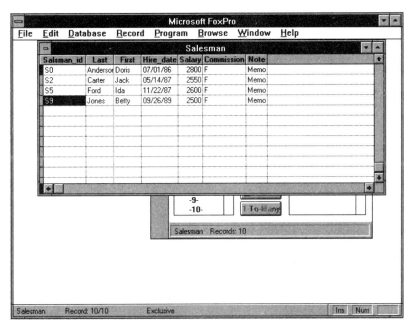

Figure 5.36 Showing selected records

Another way to define a filter expression is to build it with the components selected from the field list and options from the drop-down lists. To build a new expression in this way, follow these steps:

1. First, select the HIRE_DATE field from the Fields list (double click the mouse at the field or use the Tab and arrow keys to highlight it; then press the Enter key). The name of the selected field will be added to the expression.

2. Choose the > operator from the Logical drop-down list.

3. Type in the filter value {01/01/88} for the HIRE_DATE field from the keyboard.

4. Choose the OR operator from the Logical drop-down list.

5. Select the SALARY field from the Fields list.

6. Select the > operator from the Logical drop-down list.

7. Finally, type in the filter value of 2600 for the salary field.

Although blank spaces are not important in an expression, for clarity purposes, you may want to insert blank spaces between components. Case also is not important in an expression. Field names, for example, can be in either lowercase or uppercase letters. However, logical operators such as AND and OR are usually expressed in uppercase letters for easy identification (see Figure 5.37). If the expression is too long to be displayed in the expression box, it will scroll and leave

158 Understanding FoxPro 2.5 for Windows

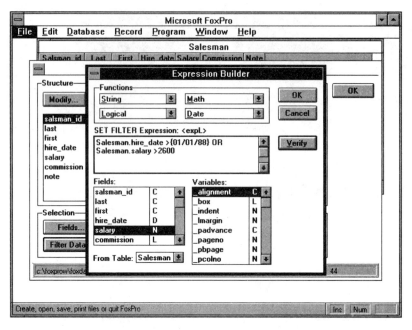

Figure 5.37 Building a filter expression

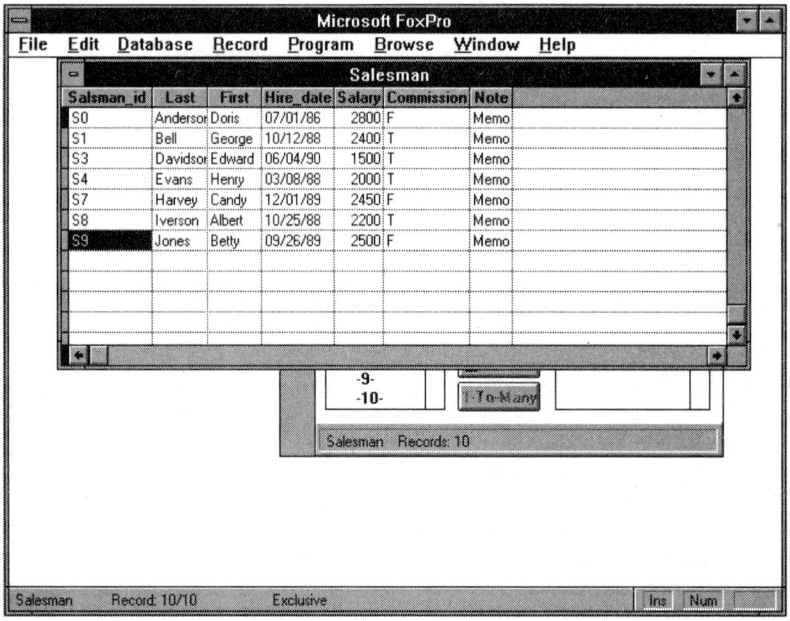

Figure 5.38 New set of selected records

a part of the expression hidden from your view. (To access the hidden portion of an expression, simply use the up- and down-arrow keys or the scroll bar to the right of the text box.)

After verifying its validity, use the filter expression to display those records you want; in this case, the records refer to those salespeople who were hired after January 1, 1988 or whose salaries are greater than $2,600 (see Figure 5.38).

PRINTING DATA

The procedures you have learned so far allow you to display your data on the screen only. And, although there is a Print menu option in the File menu popup, it is used primarily for printing reports and labels. (You will learn these printing operations in later chapters.) But if you would like to route displayed data to a printer, you can do so with the appropriate FoxPro Commands described in the next section.

Using FoxPro Commands

So far in this chapter, we have used the menu interface for viewing data. But you can accomplish most of the same tasks by issuing the appropriate FoxPro commands. And, once you have mastered the FoxPro commands, you may find you prefer to use them as a shortcut to the menu interface.

OPENING A DATABASE FILE

The FoxPro command to open a database file in a work area has the following format:

```
USE <name of database file>
```

Use brackets to describe the object you need to enter. In this case, the object is the database file you would like to open in a work area. So, to open SALESMAN.DBF, issue the following command:

```
USE SALESMAN
```

You do not need to include the file extension. The USE command automatically assumes .DBF. And, if you do not specify the work area, 1 is assigned by default.

You can open more than one database file in different work areas, but to do that you must select the work area for the database file before you issue the USE command, as in this example:

```
SELECT A
USE SALESMAN
```

```
SELECT B
USE OFFICE
```

These four commands open SALESMAN.DBF in work area 1 (also referred to as work area A) and OFFICE.DBF in work area 2 (or work area B).

If you want to use FoxPro commands to open more than one database, you can actually use fewer commands by telling the USE command both the name and database file that you want to open and the work area in which it is to be opened. For example, instead of the four commands listed above, the following two commands achieve an identical result:

```
USE SALESMAN IN 1
USE OFFICE IN 2
```

CLOSING DATABASE FILES

After you have finished using your database files, close them by using the following command:

```
CLOSE DATABASES
```

This command closes all the open database files in all the work areas. However, if you need to close an individual database file, you must use two commands instead of a single CLOSE DATABASE command. In this case, it is necessary to select the work area in which the open database is to be closed and then to issue the USE command without naming a database file. This tells FoxPro that the database file currently open in that work area is to be closed. For example, assuming that we have opened the two database files shown in the previous example, we could close them as follows:

```
SELECT A
USE
SELECT B
USE
```

For now though, let's close all the open database files before proceeding to the next exercises.

LISTING DATA RECORDS

When you want to list all the records in the current database file, use the LIST command. It lists all of the records on the screen, one line for each record, with the field names shown on top as labels or headers (see Figure 5.39).

Displaying Data 161

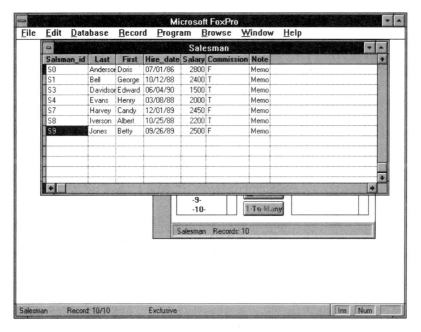

Figure 5.39 Listing every record in SALESMAN.DBF

You can see that all of the records in that database file are displayed, and that the list includes their record numbers. But, if you would like to omit the column of record numbers, simply add the keyword "OFF" in the LIST command so that it reads LIST OFF (see Figure 5.40).

Listing Selected Fields

To list only those data fields you want to view, add the FIELDS keyword in the LIST command. Following the keyword, specify the names of those data fields, separated by commas. For example, if you would like to view the FIRST, LAST, SALARY, and HIRE_DATE data fields, the command would read:

```
LIST FIELDS FIRST, LAST, SALARY, HIRE_DATE
```

As a result, these fields will be listed in the order they are specified, with all the records in the database file (see Figure 5.41).

As a shortcut, you can omit FIELDS in the LIST command for displaying records of selective data fields. The command would then read:

```
LIST FIRST, LAST, SALARY, HIRE_DATE
```

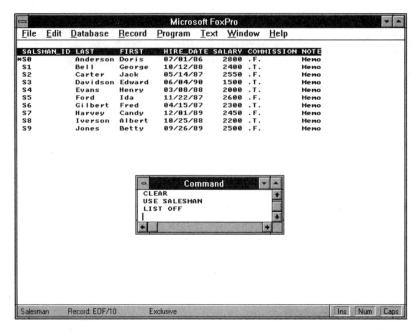

Figure 5.40 Omitting record numbers in record list

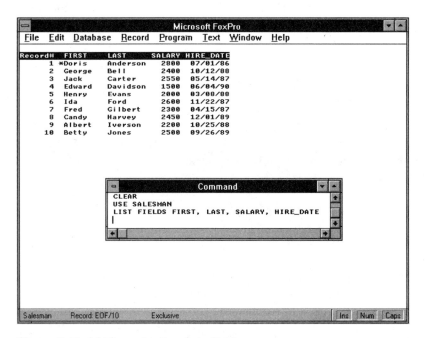

Figure 5.41 Listing selective data fields

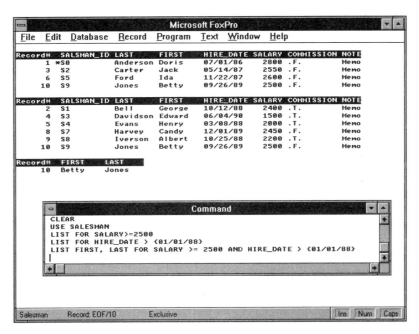

Figure 5.42 Adding the FOR clause to the LIST command

Listing Selected Records

If you would like to display only a subset of the records in the current database file, add a FOR clause in the LIST command to qualify the records. The format of such a LIST command is:

```
LIST [FIELDS] [<field names>] FOR <conditions>
```

The qualifying conditions are the same as the filter conditions you saw earlier. The objects in the square brackets ([ ]) are optional. Examples of these commands and their results are shown in Figure 5.42.

In this figure, you can see that different sets of records are listed in response to the filter conditions specified in the LIST commands. The first set shows those salaries that are greater than or equal to $2,500. Those records having hire dates after January 1, 1988 are listed in the second set. The third command specifying the joint conditions resulted in only one record, the salesperson whose salary is $2,500 and was hired on September 26, 1989.

LISTING MEMO FIELDS

When you display data records with the LIST command, the contents of the memo fields will not be listed because memo fields are organized and stored differently

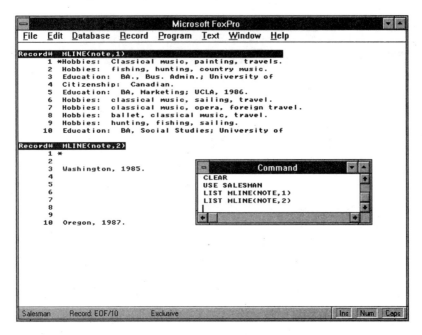

Figure 5.43 Listing contents of the NOTE memo field

than the other types of data fields. When viewing the contents of the memo fields, you must include the MLINE function in your LIST command to show a specific line of the memo text. It has the following format:

```
MLINE(<memo field name>, <line #>)
```

For example, if you would like to list the first line of the NOTE memo field in SALESMAN.DBF, issue the following command:

```
LIST MLINE(NOTE,1)
```

Text in a memo field is divided into lines, each of which is set to a default width of 50 characters. If the text width is greater than the default width, it is pushed to the next line. Therefore, you may want to display the second line of the memo field as well (see Figure 5.43).

Changing Memo Field Width

You can change the width of the memo field in the display by issuing the SET MEMOWIDTH command in the following format:

```
SET MEMOWIDTH TO <number of characters>
```

So, if you would like to set the memo width to 65 characters, issue the command SET MEMOWIDTH TO 65 accordingly (see Figure 5.44). Note in this figure that,

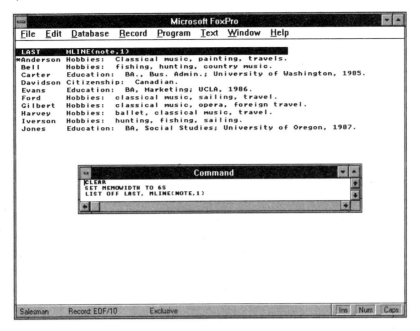

Figure 5.44 Setting a memo field's display width

after changing the memo field display width to 65, the contents of the NOTE memo field are displayed in full. The memo field contents also are listed. (Add the keyword OFF if you don't want the record numbers to appear.)

DISPLAYING THE DATA STRUCTURE

The command for showing the data structure of the current database file is:

```
DISPLAY STRUCTURE
```

Issue this command after selecting the database file and opening it in a work area with the USE command (see Figure 5.45).

Using the Display Command

In addition to the LIST command, FoxPro provides another command for displaying data. In most cases, you can use DISPLAY in place of LIST in the command, as in the following:

LIST Command	*DISPLAY Command*
`LIST`	`DISPLAY ALL`
`LIST FIELDS ...`	`DISPLAY ALL FIELDS ...`
`LIST ... FOR`	`DISPLAY ... FOR`

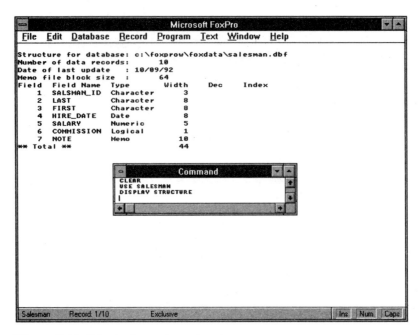

Figure 5.45 Displaying a data structure

Examples of valid DISPLAY commands are:

```
USE SALESMAN
DISPLAY ALL
DISPLAY ALL FIELDS LAST, FIRST, SALARY, HIRE_DATE
DISPLAY ALL LAST, FIRST, SALARY, HIRE_DATE
DISPLAY FOR SALARY >= 2500
DISPLAY FOR SALARY >= 2500 AND HIRE_DATE >= {01/01/88}
DISPLAY ALL MLINE(NOTE,1)
DISPLAY ALL FIRST, LAST, MLINE(NOTE,1)
```

But there are a few differences. First, DISPLAY ALL, like LIST, shows all the records in the database file. However, in databases whose records will fill more than one screen, DISPLAY ALL pauses after displaying each screen of data, while LIST does not. So, when you use LIST to view a large number of records, they may scroll out of sight before you actually have a chance to examine them. Unlike LIST, which by default works with all the records of a database, the command DISPLAY alone shows only the contents of the current record. And to display a specific record, you must first go to that record before issuing the DISPLAY command. To go to the very first record in a database file, use the GO TOP command; to go to the very last record, use the GO BOTTOM command. To go to a specific record, specify the record number in the GOTO <record number>

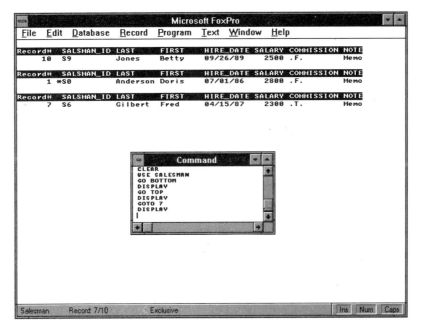

Figure 5.46 Displaying a specific data record

command (see Figure 5.46). Another difference is that you cannot include the keyword "OFF" in a DISPLAY to omit record numbers.

SETTING FILTER CONDITIONS

When you use the FOR clause in the LIST and DISPLAY commands, you are qualifying the records before they are displayed. There is, however, another way to filter out unwanted records—use the SET FILTER command before issuing the LIST and DISPLAY command, in this format:

```
SET FILTER TO <filter conditions>
```

There is a significant difference between the effect of including the filter condition in the FOR clause and that of including it in the SET FILTER TO command. The effect of the former is limited only to the command that includes the FOR clause, while the filter condition included in the SET FILTER TO command will affect all the operations thereafter.

For example, to display only those records whose values in the SALARY field are greater than or equal to $2,500, use the following filtering command:

```
SET FILTER TO SALARY >= 2500
```

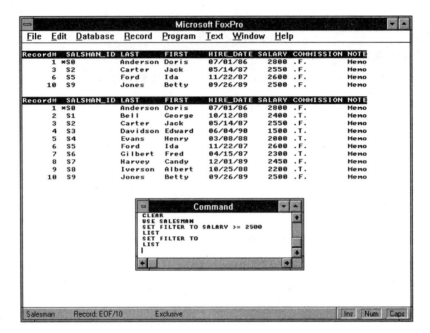

Figure 5.47 Setting filter conditions

After executing the SET FILTER command, only those records satisfying the the filter condition will be subject to subsequent operations. To remove the filter conditions, simply issue the SET FILTER TO command and leave out the filter conditions (see Figure 5.47).

Note that, after issuing the filter conditions, only records satisfying those conditions will be the subject of the subsequent LIST command. After removing the filter conditions with the SET FILTER TO command, all the records become available for the LIST command.

DIRECTING DISPLAYED DATA TO PRINTERS

The LIST and DISPLAY commands are used to display the structure and records of your database files on the screen. To then route the displayed data to your printer, add the TO PRINT clause to your LIST or DISPLAY commands, as in these examples:

```
USE SALESMAN
LIST TO PRINT
LIST LAST, FIRST TO PRINT
LIST LAST, FIRST, SALARY FOR SALARY >=2500 TO PRINT
DISPLAY ALL TO PRINT
DISPLAY FOR SALARY >= 2500 TO PRINT
```

```
DISPLAY ALL MLINE(NOTE,1) TO PRINT
DISPLAY ALL FIRST, LAST, MLINE(NOTE,1) TO PRINT
```

An alternative is to print your data by issuing the SET PRINT ON command to activate your printer. Once the printer is activated, all the displayed data will be routed to the default printer. (They will be displayed on the screen as well.) After you have finished printing your data, remember to issue the SET PRINT OFF command to deactivate the printer; otherwise, results of subsequent commands will be directed to your printer as well.

BROWSING DATA

You can bring up the Browse window for displaying your data with the BROWSE command. Without adding any other keywords or filter conditions, the BROWSE command displays all the records and data fields in the current database file in the current Browse window. In Figure 5.48, for example, the Browse window displays all of the existing records. The location and size of the Browse window are carried over from the last exercise.

Like the DISPLAY and LIST commands, the BROWSE command allows you to view multiple records. However, it offers three major advantages over DISPLAY and LIST. First, since it presents its data in a window, it offers a more attractive, formatted display. Second, it allows you to scroll among the records in a database.

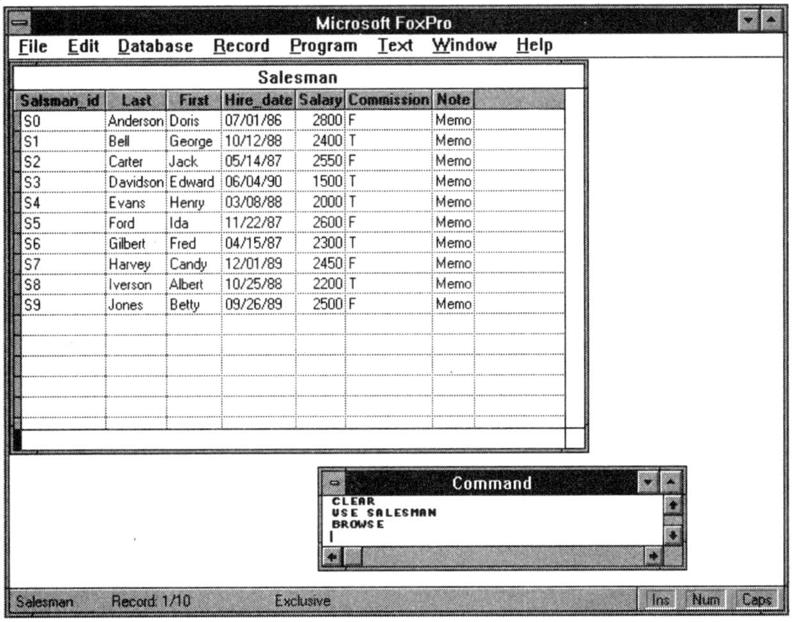

Figure 5.48 Invoking the Browse window

Finally, BROWSE allows you to modify the contents of your database, whereas DISPLAY and LIST only show the contents of fields and records.

Browsing Selected Data Fields

It is possible to display selected data fields and records with the BROWSE command by adding the keyword "FIELDS" and the data fields you would like to view. The command would read:

```
BROWSE FIELDS <field list>
```

For example, you can specify the data fields in SALESMAN.DBF that you would like to display in the Browse window by listing the fields in the BROWSE FIELDS command, as shown in Figure 5.49. Notice that the order of the displayed data fields is determined by what was specified in the BROWSE command.

Browsing Selected Records

As with the LIST and DISPLAY commands, you can also add filter conditions in the BROWSE command to select only those data records that you need. Just specify the filter conditions as an expression in a FOR clause, such as:

```
BROWSE [FIELDS <field list>] FOR <filter conditions>
```

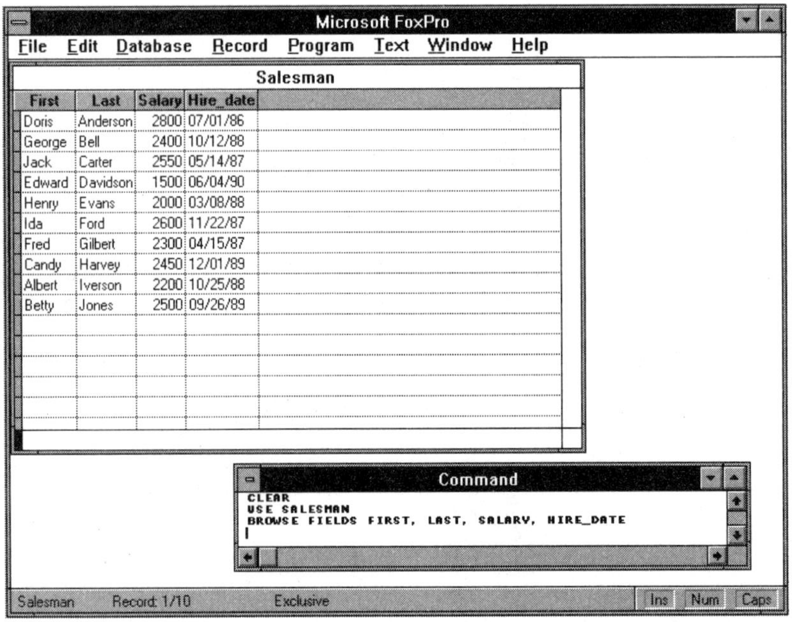

Figure 5.49 Browsing selective data fields

Displaying Data 171

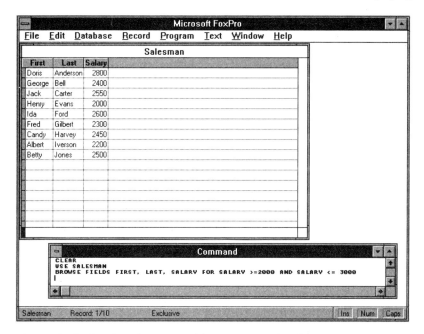

Figure 5.50 Adding filter conditions to a BROWSE command

Here are some examples:

```
BROWSE FOR COMMISSION = .T.
BROWSE FOR HIRE_DATE >= {01/01/88}
BROWSE FIELDS LAST, SALARY FOR SALARY >= 2500
BROWSE FIELDS LAST, SALARY FOR SALARY >= 2000 AND SALARY <=
3000
```

When the last BROWSE command is executed, it displays only those records that satisfied the filter conditions (see Figure 5.50).

Of course, you also can issue the SET FILTER TO command to screen your records before issuing the BROWSE command to display selected records, in which case you would replace the final BROWSE FIELDS command with the following commands:

```
SET FILTER TO SALARY >=2000 AND SALARY <= 3000
BROWSE FIELDS LAST, SALARY
```

DEFINING CUSTOM WINDOWS

As you have seen in all the examples, the size and location of the Browse window are retained from their previous use. You can use the mouse or the appropriate menu options to resize and move the window, or you can use a FoxPro command to define the exact size and location of the window. The command for setting up a custom window is:

```
DEFINE WINDOW <custom window name> FROM <row,column> TO
<row,column>
```

In this command, you must supply the name of the window that you are setting up. In addition, it is necessary to specify the screen locations for the upper left- and lower right-hand corners of the window. Each location is defined by a pair of numbers indicating the row number and the column number. When you display text on the screen, it is divided into 25 rows and 80 columns. Rows are numbered from 0 to 24, columns from 0 to 79. This is a sample command for setting up a custom window named BWINDOW:

```
DEFINE WINDOW Bwindow FROM 3,10 TO 20,40
```

The window defined here has its upper left-hand corner at the intersection of the third row from the top and the tenth column from the left. The lower right-hand corner of the custom window is located at the twentieth row from the top and fortieth column from the left. As a result, the size of the window is 18 rows high and 31 columns wide.

Browsing Data in a Custom Window

After a custom window is defined, you use it in the BROWSE command in the following format:

```
BROWSE WINDOW <window name> ......
```

You can add the necessary keywords and filter conditions to the command as well (see Figure 5.51).

Pay particular attention to this figure, because there is an important difference between a custom window and a regular Browse window. A custom window cannot be resized or moved. Note that it does not have the Size control at the lower right-hand corner of the window. In order to change the custom window, you must redefine it with the DEFINE WINDOW command.

To display data in a regular Browse window, just issue the BROWSE command without the WINDOW clause in it. You can resize and move the Browse window after it appears.

Browsing Memo Fields in a Custom Window

The custom window you set up with the DEFINE WINDOW command also can be used to display the contents of memo fields. Instead of using the default window carried over from the last application, just use the custom window that you defined.

Displaying Data 173

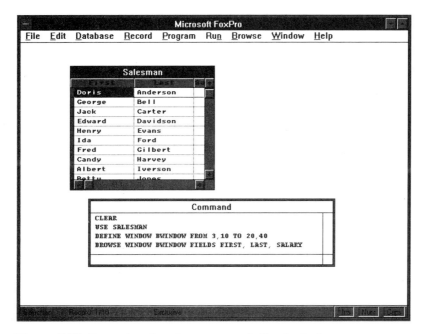

Figure 5.51 Browsing data in a custom defined window

To do that, designate the custom window as your Memo window with the SET WINDOW OF MEMO TO command:

```
SET WINDOW OF MEMO TO <window name>
```

Here is an example:

```
DEFINE WINDOW MWINDOW FROM 19,5 TO 22,70
SET WINDOW OF MEMO TO Mwindow
BROWSE
```

When the BROWSE command is executed, the records of the current database file are displayed in the normal Browse window, and the contents of the memo field are shown in the custom window (see Figure 5.52).

In this figure, you can see that the contents of the NOTE memo field of the first record are displayed in the custom window. Remember, to view the memo field, click the mouse twice on the field, or press the Ctrl+PgUp key while the memo field is highlighted.

Closing Custom Windows

After you have finished using the custom defined windows, you can close them by closing the database file. When you close the database file, all its associated windows will be closed. If you do not want to close the database file, you can

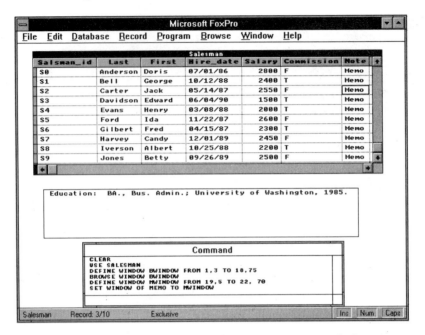

Figure 5.52 Memo fields displayed in a custom memo window

reissue the BROWSE command. As a result, the records of the database will be displayed in the default Browse window, and all the custom windows will be closed.

Browsing Multiple Database Files

Recall that it is possible to have more than one database file open in different work areas at the same time. Likewise, you can view these database files in multiple Browse windows. First, open the database files in their respective work areas and then issue the BROWSE command to display their contents. Try using the following commands to open and browse the contents of the SALESMAN.DBF and OFFICE.DBF databases:

```
SELECT A
USE SALESMAN
BROWSE
SELECT B
USE OFFICE
BROWSE
```

After executing these commands, two Browse windows appear, each of which is used to display the contents of a database file. These windows overlap, the last one appearing on top of the first.

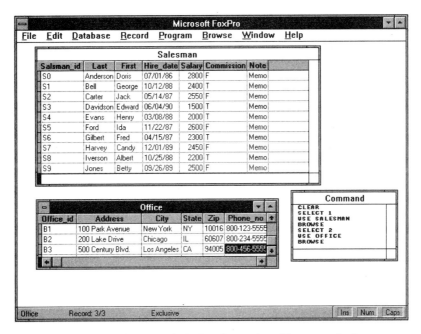

Figure 5.53 Browsing multiple databases in a Browse window

The Browse window that includes the records of OFFICE.DBF appears on top of the SALESMAN.DBF Browse window, because OFFICE.DBF was opened and browsed *after* you opened and browsed SALESMAN.DBF. Obviously then, the database that you browse last becomes the active window. At this point, you can resize and rearrange the windows so that they can display the data in a layout of your choice (see Figure 5.53).

Abbreviating Command Keywords

Earlier in the chapter, we introduced a list of keywords common in FoxPro commands: LIST, DISPLAY, FIELDS, STRUCTURE, SELECT, BROWSE, etc. As a shortcut, you can abbreviate all the longer keywords to only the first four letters. That is, replace DISPLAY with DISP, FIELDS with FIEL, STRUCTURE with STRU, SELECT with SELE, and BROWSE with BROW. Commands would then read:

```
SELE A
USE SALESMAN
DISP ALL
DISP STRU
BROW FIEL LAST, FIRST, SALARY
DEFI WIND Bwindow FROM 5,5 TO 20,20
BROW WIND Bwindow
```

Chapter Summary

In this chapter, you learned how to display the data structure and records of your database files. You also were made aware of the option to use either Browse or Change modes to view your data in a Browse window.

We showed that the Browse window provided by FoxPro is a very powerful tool for displaying data. In it, you can display all or some of the records of your database files and, if necessary, you can partition it so that you can display various parts of a database file on the same screen. In addition, you can display multiple database files in several Browse windows simultaneously.

Furthermore, you can issue the LIST or DISPLAY commands to display data on the screen. Then, by adding the TO PRINT clause to the LIST or DISPLAY commands, you can direct the displayed data to your printer as well.

This chapter also clarified how data records are displayed—in the order that they were entered into the database file. Then you learned that you could rearrange these records into a specific order (e.g., in ascending or descending order) by sorting or indexing your database file. These operations—sorting and indexing—are the subject of discussion in the next chapter.

6

Sorting and Indexing Data

An Overview

As discussed in Chapter 5, when data in a database file is displayed in either Change or Browse mode, its records are arranged in the order in which they were entered into the database file. This arrangement will not work for all applications, such as when you want to display the records according to the values contained in specific data fields. Sorting and indexing are the two methods that enable you to reorder your data records.

There are advantages and disadvantages to both of these methods. Depending on your objectives, you will decide on one over the other for different applications. In the beginning of this chapter, we will explore the strengths and weaknesses of both methods; later, you will learn how to apply them.

Ordering Data Records

As seen in earlier examples, a relational database stores and organizes its data elements in table form. Data records are entered into the table after its data structure has been set up. The order in which the records are added to the table determines the order in which they will be displayed in the Browse window, unless other steps are taken to alter their order.

In Figure 6.1, for example, all of the records are displayed in the order in which they were entered. Although no sorting operation has been performed on the table, the records in SALESMAN.DBF are in the order of salesperson identification number and last name. It is not unusual to arrange data records in such a manner

178 Understanding FoxPro 2.5 for Windows

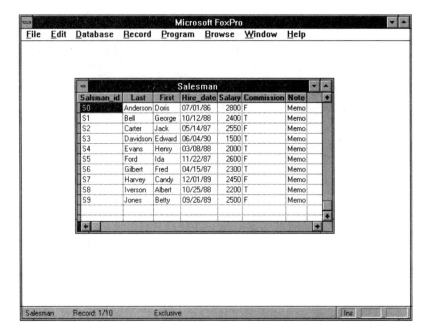

Figure 6.1 Data records in original order

before entering them into a table. For example, we arranged the data records alphabetically by last name and assigned a sequential identification number (from S0 to S9) for each of the 10 salespeople. But from this point on, all data records that you append to the table will appear as they are entered and will not follow the original alphabetic order. So, if a new salesperson named Charles Gilmore is hired and you enter his data into the table as the eleventh record, with S10 as his identification number, the records in SALESMAN.DBF will no longer be alphabetical by last name.

In addition, in some applications you will want your records displayed in an order that is determined by the values in only some of the data fields. You may want, for example, to arrange the records in chronological order by the values in the HIRE_DATE field. Or you might want to produce a roster showing the sales staff's names, ordered according to their salaries. Obviously, you need to be able to order your records according to a set of predetermined criteria, and both sorting and indexing allow you to do this.

SORTING VS. INDEXING

Sorting involves physically rearranging records in a database file according to a predetermined order, using one or more data fields to define the sort order. The values in these fields determine the order of the records. Sorted records are saved in a separate database file with a different name. Then, if you need to view the sorted records, you select the sorted file.

The indexing method arranges records according to the values in one or more fields, which is called an index key. But the indexing operation does not actually *rearrange* the records in a database file. Instead, it creates a separate index file whose records are arranged based on the values of the index key. Each time you need to view the records in a database file in a particular order, the index file is used. You can create a number of index files, each of which is set up according to an index key, and you can later use the existing index files to display your records in a number of different ways.

One advantage to using the sorting method is that sorted records are created and stored in separate files which you can access at any time to show the ordered records. You don't have to re-create the files as long as the contents of the original database remain unchanged. But, sorting a database also has some enormous drawbacks. If you do modify the contents of the original database file, the sorted file is not updated automatically. You must re-sort the original database file and replace the sorted file with the new set of sorted records. This process can require great amounts of time when working with large databases. It can also lead to enormous confusion if you forget to re-sort a modified database file, or, if you make different changes to both the sorted and the unsorted data.

In addition, because sorting results in the creation of another file, valuable disk space is taken up for the storage of each new sorted file. And this is an especially important point to remember if the database file has a large number of records containing numerous data fields.

The indexing operation, on the other hand, rearranges the data records according to the information in the index files each time that you need to order the records. The index file contains only the information necessary for arranging the data records in the database file; it is used for ordering the actual records. It is easier to keep an index file updated each time you modify the contents of the database file because whenever you modify your records in a database file in FoxPro, the corresponding index files are updated automatically as long as the index files remain open. It is possible, however, to corrupt the contents of an index file if you fail to open it before making changes to its associated database file. To preclude such a risk, FoxPro provides a special index file called a structural index file that automatically opens when you open its database file. You will learn about this later.

Moreover, in an indexing operation, the original index file occupies a small amount of disk space because the index file contains only the values of the index key and is relatively small.

Finally, because sorting is much slower than indexing, indexing is a more desirable method for ordering data records in most applications. An exception is when you have a relatively small database file and you do not expect to make any changes to its contents.

SORTING DATA RECORDS

You can use either the menu interface or FoxPro commands to sort a databas. First, we'll discuss the procedure for sorting records with the menu interface.

The first step in sorting data records is to open the database file in a work area. You can use the View window to open a database file in any one of the 225 work areas. Or choose the Open option from the File menu and select the database file to be opened from the Open dialog. When you open a database file this way, the file is always opened in the default work area—1. If you subsequently open another database file using the same Open menu option, the current open file will be closed automatically and the new database file will be opened in work area 1. This method is very useful when working on only one database file.

As an exercise, open SALESMAN.DBF in work area 1 by choosing the Open option from the File menu. Next, select the SALESMAN.DBF file from the Open dialog (see Figure 6.2). In addition to the three buttons (Open, New, and Cancel), the Drive drop-down list, and the Directory selection list, there is a List Files of Type drop-down list at the bottom left of the dialog box, which indicates the types of files that you can open. In this case, we want it to read "Table/DBF." If it does not, simply open the drop-down list and select the correct file type.

Once you have opened SALESMAN.DBF, the Open dialog disappears. To sort the data records in the database, choose the Sort option from the Database menu. When the Sort dialog appears, specify the sort order and identify the file to which

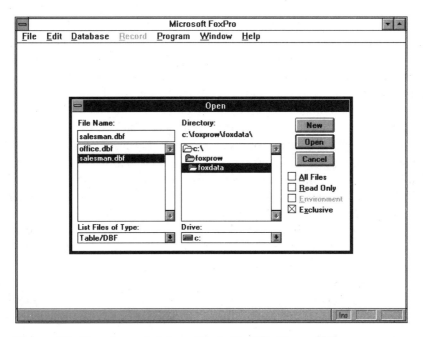

Figure 6.2 Opening a database file in the File Open dialog

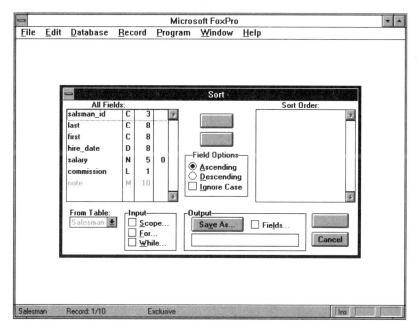

Figure 6.3 Sort dialog

you would like to save the sorted records. This dialog also is where you define the filter conditions for selecting the data records that you would like to save to the output file, as well as the list of data fields to be included in the sorted file (see Figure 6.3).

The name of the database file being used (e.g., SALESMAN) is displayed in the lower left-hand corner of the dialog. Next to it in the Input box are three check boxes (Scope..., For..., and While...), which are used to specify the filter conditions for selecting the data records that you would like to sort. Above these check boxes is the list of data fields in the database file. One or more of these fields can be used to define the sort order.

The Move and Remove buttons are provided so that you can move the data fields from the All Fields list into the Sort Order list to the right of the buttons. Use one of the two radio buttons (Ascending or Descending) to specify how you would like the sorting operation to be carried out. The Ignore Case check box gives you the option to ignore case when sorting character strings. These radio buttons and the check box are in the Field Options box.

Finally, the Output box at the bottom center of the dialog box is where you specify the name of the output file for the sorted records in the Save As... dialog. Next to it, in the Fields check box, is where you select the data fields to be included in the output file.

The usual OK and Cancel buttons are in the lower right-hand corner of the dialog box.

Defining Sort Order

Before you sort data records, you must specify the sort order. This involves selecting the data fields whose values will be used to determine the order.

Almost any type of data field may be used as a sort field, with the exception of the values in a memo field. Each of the sortable fields can have its values arranged either in ascending or descending order. Therefore, you can arrange the character strings in a character field alphabetically from A to Z (ascending) or from Z to A (descending). Similarly, you can sort a numeric field from smallest to largest, or from largest to smallest. You also can arrange dates chronologically from earliest to most recent (ascending) or from most recent to earliest (descending). But when you sort a logical field, the records are grouped into those having .T. (True) and .F. (False) values.

Sorting Character Fields

When sorting character strings, remember that case is important. Uppercase and lowercase letters are treated differently, and the order follows that of the ASCII (American Standard Code for Information Interchange) code in which uppercase and lowercase letters are assigned different codes. Although you can find a copy of the complete ASCII table showing all of the characters in their predefined order in Appendix A of this book, a brief definition is necessary here: In ascending order, the set of capital letters A–Z appears *before* the lowercase letters a–z; digits 0–9 appear before letters; and blank spaces appear before letters and digits. For example:

Ascending Order	*Descending Order*
100 MAIN STREET	Peterson
100 Main Avenue	PETER
1000 MAIN STREET	monkeys
DAVID	Monkey
DAVIDSON	Jackie
David	Jack
Davidson	JOHN
JOHN	Davidson
Jack	David
Jackie	DAVIDSON
Monkey	DAVID
monkeys	1000 MAIN STREET
PETER	100 Main Avenue
Peterson	100 MAIN STREET

As an exercise, let's sort the SALESMAN.DBF records in ascending order by using the contents of the FIRST (for first name) data field. First, select the data field whose values you intend to sort by, then choose the sort order by turning on the radio button for either ascending or descending. To turn on a radio button, either click your mouse button once on the name of the radio button or press the underlined letter "A" or "D" to turn on the Ascending or Descending radio button. In our exercise, because we want to sort the FIRST data field in ascending order, turn on Ascending (indicated with a dot inside the parentheses).

For this procedure, you must decide whether case is important in sorting the character strings selected. If you do not want to differentiate between upper- and lowercase letters in the sorting operation, select the Ignore Case check box. Do this by clicking the mouse button on the box or by pressing the letter "I" and then Enter on the keyboard. Our exercise requires that this box be checked because the first names are composed of upper- and lowercase letters.

After the field options are defined, select the data field from the All Fields list and move it to the Sort Order list by double clicking your mouse on the field name. With the keyboard, position the cursor on the data field and then press Enter. If you make a mistake, you can remove the selected data fields using exactly the same procedure. With that in mind, move the FIRST data field into the Sort Order box (see Figure 6.4). The Sort Order box now has the FIRST data field listed. The up arrow that appears in front of the field name indicates an ascending sort order.

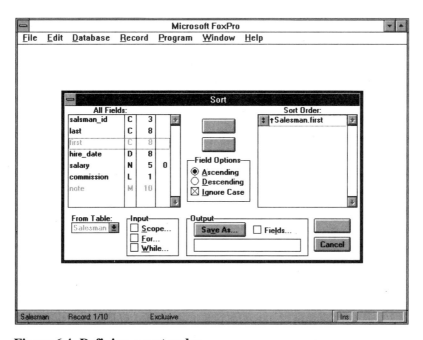

Figure 6.4 Defining a sort order

184   Understanding FoxPro 2.5 for Windows

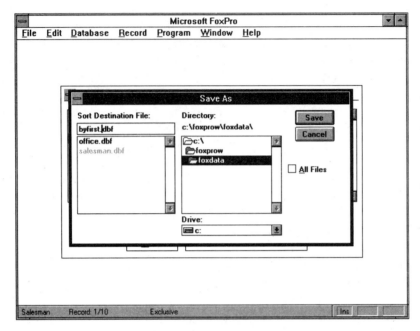

Figure 6.5 Naming a sorted output file

To specify the name of the database file that will contain the sorted records, either use the mouse or press the letter "v" to select the Save As... button. Next, enter the name of the output file (BYFIRST.DBF) accordingly in the Sort Destination File box of the Save As dialog (see Figure 6.5).

After you have specified the output filename and selected the Save button, FoxPro returns you to the Sort dialog. At this point, the output filename appears at the bottom of the Output box (see Figure 6.6).

If you are using a mouse, you can enter the output filename directly into the Output box without going through the Save As dialog. Double click on the location where the name of the output file should appear (in the text box, below the Save As... button). When the cursor appears, enter the filename with the keyboard.

The sorting operation is now defined. It is time to actually sort the records: Just select the OK button. Watch as the records in SALESMAN.DBF are sorted in ascending order according to the contents of the first data field. When the sorting operation is finished, the message "10 records sorted" appears briefly in the status bar.

Viewing the Sorted Records

After the records in SALESMAN.DBF are sorted, the output file named BYFIRST.DBF contains the sorted records. To view them you must open the

Sorting and Indexing Data   185

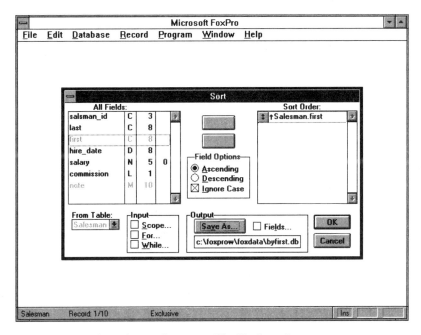

Figure 6.6 Name of sorted output file displayed

BYFIRST.DBF file. Remember: The records in SALESMAN.DBF remain unchanged.

To view *only* the sorted records, open just BYFIRST.DBF in work area 1. You can, however, open both the original and sorted files in the View window and then verify their contents in the Browse windows (see Figure 6.7).

Sorting Numerical Fields

To use the sorting operation to rank records according to the values in a numerical data field, choose either ascending order (numbers arranged from the smallest to the largest values), or descending order for the reverse. Utilizing the sorting operation in this way enables you to produce, for example, a roster of sales personnel from the SALESMAN.DBF database ranked by salary in descending order based on the values in the salary data field (see Figure 6.8).

When you view the sorted records in the BYPAY.DBF output file, you can see that the records are arranged in this way. As a result, you can quickly tell which salesperson earns the highest salary (see Figure 6.9).

Sorting Date Fields

Records also can be arranged by the date values in a date field; in ascending order, they are listed from earliest to most recent date, and in descending order, from most

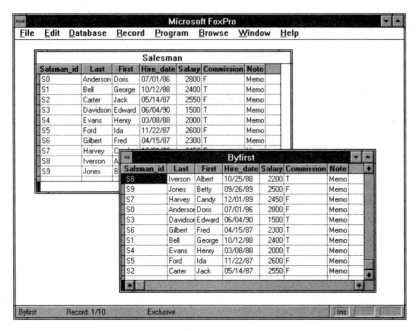

Figure 6.7 Comparing the original and sorted databases

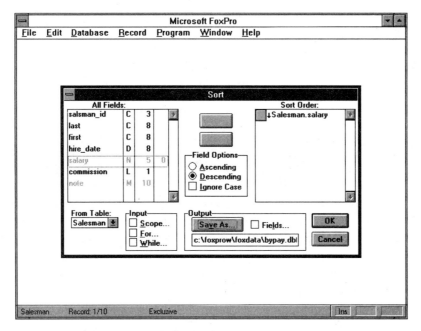

Figure 6.8 Sorting the Salary numerical field

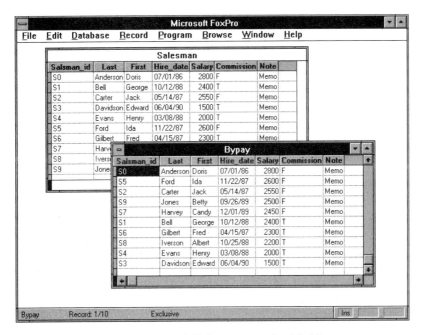

Figure 6.9 Viewing the sorted Salary numerical field

recent date to earliest. Say that you want to arrange the records in the SALESMAN database in ascending order by the date values in the HIRE_DATE field. To do that, turn on the Ascending radio button in the Field Options box. After that, select HIRE_DATE as the sort field and move it to the Sort Order box. Finally, enter BYDATE.DBF as the name of the output file (see Figure 6.10). As a result, the sorted records in the output file named BYDATE.DBF are arranged from the earliest to the most recent (see Figure 6.11).

Sorting Logical Fields

Values in a logical field are expressed in the form .T. or .F. and, hence, you can sort your records into these two groups. When you are using a logical field as the sorting key, the group of records having .F. values always appears first in the sorted database.

As an exercise, let's sort the records in the SALESMAN database according to the logical values in the COMMISSION field and save them to the BY-COMMIS.DBF output file (see Figure 6.12).

When you view the BYCOMMIS.DBF output file, note that all of the records with the value .F. in the COMMISSION field appear first. The others appear in the second group of sorted records (see Figure 6.13).

188 Understanding FoxPro 2.5 for Windows

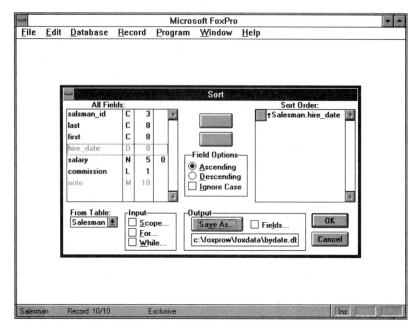

Figure 6.10 Sorting the HIRE_DATE date field

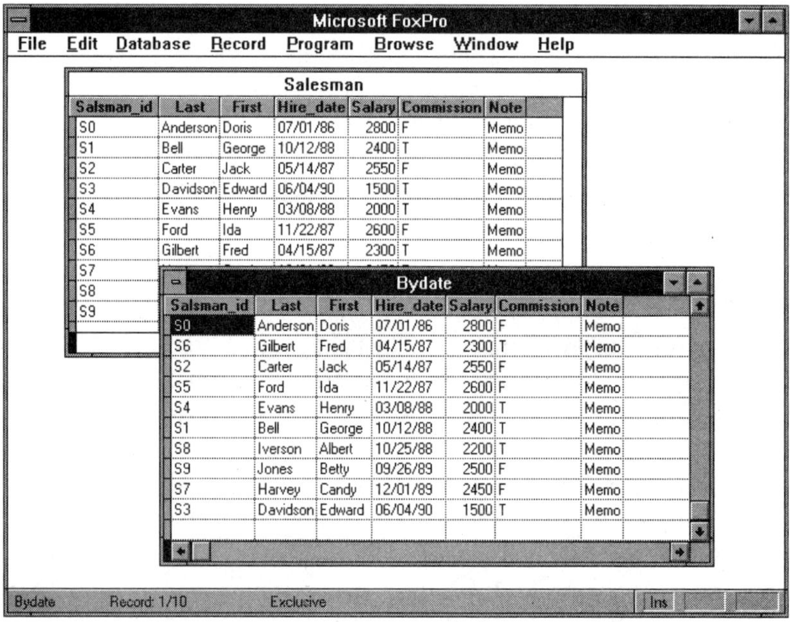

Figure 6.11 Viewing the sorted HIRE_DATE date field

Sorting and Indexing Data 189

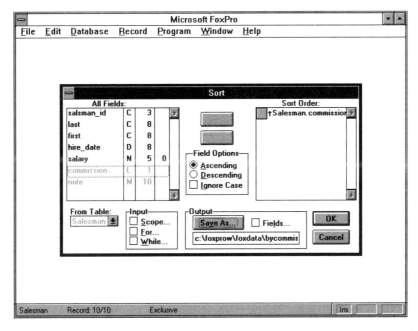

Figure 6.12 Sorting the COMMISSION logical field

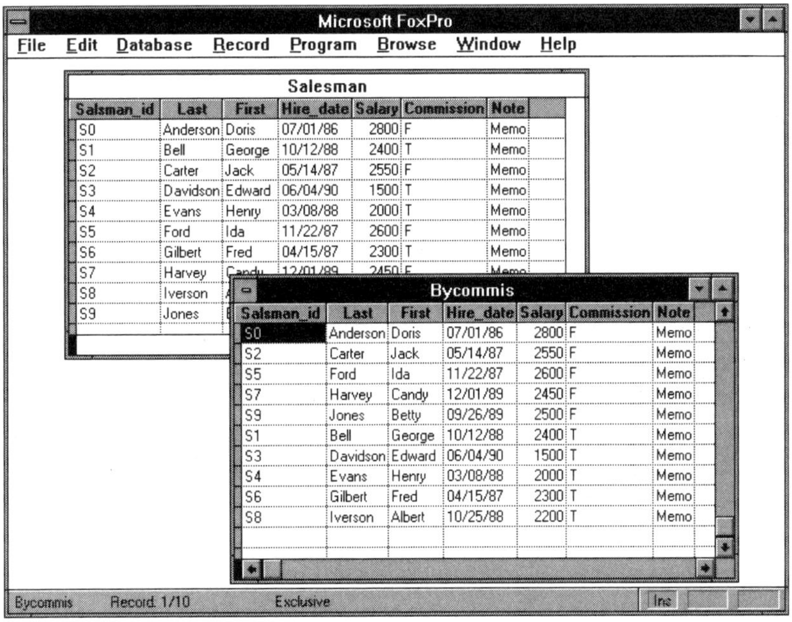

Figure 6.13 Viewing the sorted COMMISSION logical field

Sorting Multiple Fields

When you define a sort order, it is possible to include more than one data field as the sorting key. In such a situation, the records will be sorted in sequence. For example, if you select two data fields as the sort order, the records initially will be arranged according to the values in the sorting field you specify first. Those records having the same value in the first sorting field will then be arranged by the values in the second sorting field.

As an exercise, let's sort the records in SALESMAN.DBF using the COMMISSION and SALARY fields. Choose descending order for the SALARY sorting field and save the sorted records to the output file COMISPAY.DBF (see Figure 6.14).

When the sorting operation begins, it first separates the records in SALESMAN.DBF into two groups according to the values in the COMMISSION logical field. Those records in the group with an .F. value in the logical field are then sorted into descending order based on their values in the SALARY field. As a result, the largest salary for the salesperson not earning any commission appears on the top of the first group. Likewise, the salesperson who earns a commission and has the highest salary is shown at the beginning of the second group (see Figure 6.15).

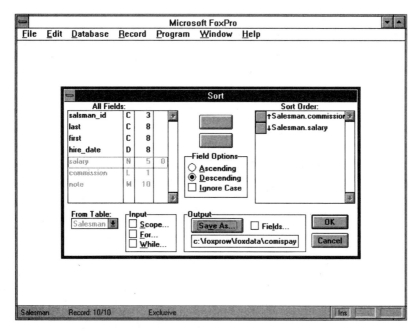

Figure 6.14 Sorting the COMMISSION and SALARY fields

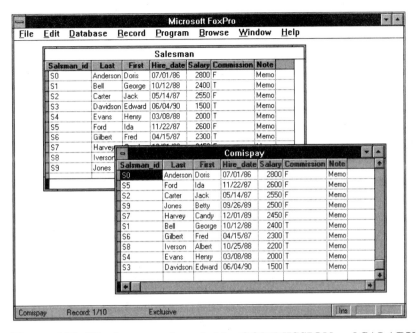

Figure 6.15 Viewing records sorted by COMMISSION and SALARY

Saving Selected Data Fields

In the preceding examples, the sorted output files that we saved contained every data field in the original database file, by default. It also is possible to save only selected data fields by choosing the Fields check box in the Sort dialog when you define the contents of the output file.

As an exercise, use the same sort order as shown in the previous example and sort the COMMISSION field in ascending order and the SALARY field in descending order. Then, instead of saving all of the data fields in the output file, save only the FIRST, LAST, COMMISSION, and SALARY data fields. To select these fields for the output file, choose the Fields... check box; the Field Picker dialog appears. Now choose the data fields you would like to include in the Sort Destination File (see Figure 6.16). The procedure for selecting data fields is identical to the one defined earlier. After selecting your output data fields, select the OK button to continue.

Defining Filter Conditions to Save Selected Records

Following a sorting operation, the sorted output file normally contains all of the data records in the original database file. But if this is not what you want, you can

192 Understanding FoxPro 2.5 for Windows

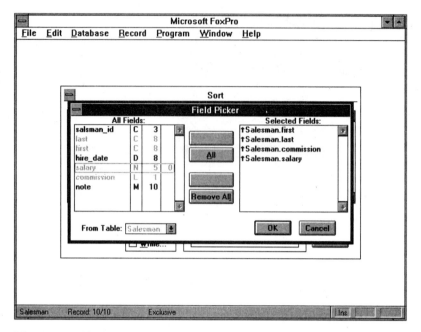

Figure 6.16 Selecting data fields for the Output File

save a subset of these records to the output file by defining the appropriate filter conditions in the Sort dialog.

First, select the For check box in the Input box of the Sort dialog either by clicking your mouse button on the check box or by pressing the "F" key. As a result, FoxPro presents you with the Expression Builder, where you enter the filter condition that determines the records that are subject to the sorting operation. (This Expression Builder is identical to that covered in Chapter 5.) So, if you want to save only the records for those salespeople whose salaries are between $2,000 and $2,500, you would enter the filter conditions as shown in Figure 6.17.

After building the filter expression, check its validity by selecting the Verify button. If the expression is valid, you then can exit from the Expression Builder by choosing the OK button.

When you return to the Sort dialog, you can see that the For check box has been selected, together with the Fields... box you marked earlier (see Figure 6.18).

Now you are ready to sort your records. Choose the OK push button in the Sort dialog. The records saved in the output file BYPAY01.DBF contain only those data fields you selected earlier, along with those records that satisfy the filter conditions (see Figure 6.19).

You can see that BYPAY01.DBF contains only the four data fields that you selected: FIRST, LAST, COMMISSION, and SALARY. Consequently, the output

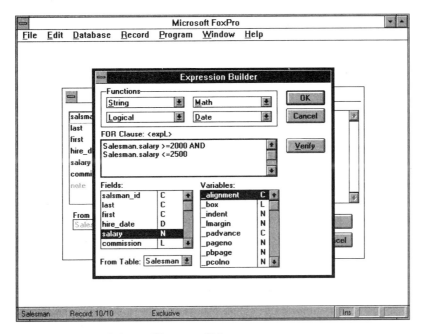

Figure 6.17 Defining a filter condition

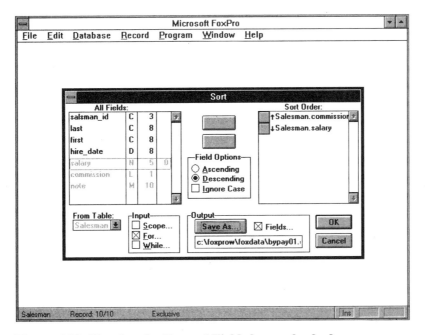

Figure 6.18 Showing the For and Fields boxes checked

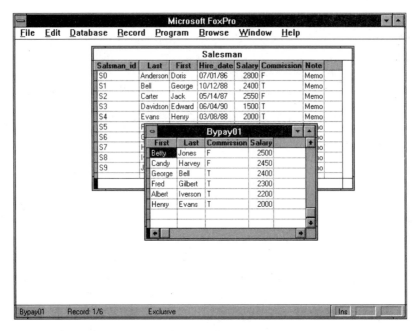

Figure 6.19 Viewing records in BYPAY01.DBF

file contains only those records whose values in the SALARY field range from $2,000 to $2,500.

SORTING WITH FOXPRO COMMANDS

As stated, you also can perform the Sort operation by issuing the appropriate FoxPro commands. The command for sorting a database file uses the following format:

```
SORT TO output filename ON field list
```

The field list can contain one or more sort fields. If you intend to sort on several data fields, you must separate them with commas. Thus, to sort the records in the SALESMAN database by first name, issue the following SORT command:

```
SORT TO SORTED01 ON FIRST
```

In this command, you sort on the FIRST data field and save the sorted records to SORTED01.DBF. After the sort is complete, you can view the contents of the output file by issuing the LIST and USE commands (see Figure 6.20).

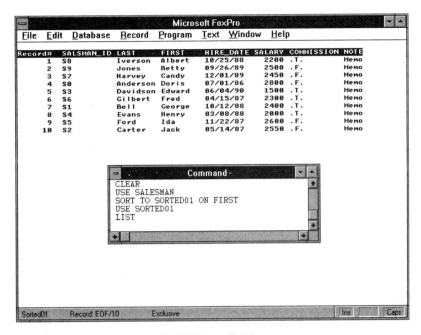

Figure 6.20 Sorting the FIRST data field

Specifying Sort Order

The FoxPro SORT command sorts records in ascending order by default. You can reverse that order simply by placing /D (for descending) at the end of the sort field name. Then if you decide to arrange the records in descending order by the values in the FIRST field, issue the following command:

```
SORT TO SORTED02 ON FIRST /D
```

Alternatively, you can spell out the sort order (DESCENDING or ASCENDING) following the sort field:

```
SORT TO SORTED02 ON FIRST DESCENDING
```

Of course, you can abbreviate the word DESCENDING to DESC or /D:

```
SORT TO SORTED02 ON FIRST DESC
```

Regardless of which method you choose, the records in the database will be arranged by first name in the FIRST field in descending order, from Z to A (see Figure 6.21).

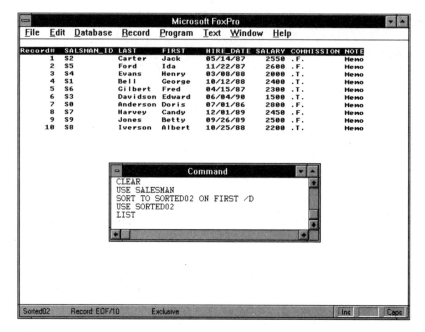

Figure 6.21 Sorting the FIRST field in descending order

Sorting Multiple Fields

It is possible to sort more than one data field at a time in a database using the SORT command. Just list the sort fields following the keyword ON in the command. But remember to separate the sort fields with commas. And, if you intend to sort the data field in descending order, specify the sort order in the field list as well. For example:

```
SORT TO SORTED03 ON COMMISSION, SALARY /D
```

This command will result in records that are arranged first in ascending order based on the values in the COMMISSION field; then, for each commission group, the records will appear in descending order according to SALARY (see Figure 6.22).

Saving Selected Data Fields and Records

In a SORT command, you can specify the data fields that you would like to save to the sorted output file by adding the FIELDS clause:

```
SORT TO output filename ON field list
     FIELDS output field list
```

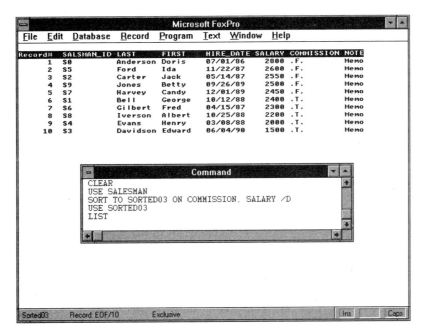

Figure 6.22 Sorting multiple data fields

Similarly, you can define a filter condition for screening the data records that you would like to sort. Filter conditions are specified with a FOR clause:

```
SORT TO output filename ON field list
[FIELDS output field list]
FOR filter conditions
```

Here is an example:

```
SORT TO SORTED04 ON COMMISSION, SALARY/D
FIELDS FIRST, LAST, COMMISSION, SALARY /D
FOR SALARY = 2000 AND SALARY = 2500
```

The resulting output file contains only those records that satisfied the filter conditions; it has only the four data fields specified in the FIELDS clause, as shown in Figure 6.23.

The SORT command in the example above is a long one. Look again at Figure 6.23 and you can see that it is too long to be fully displayed in the Command window. As you enter this command, continue typing even when you reach the end of the display line. The maximum length of a command line is 255 characters. You can scroll left and right to view the command line in its entirety.

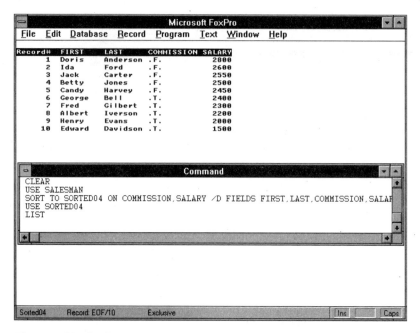

Figure 6.23 Saving selected data fields and records

INDEXING DATA

Unlike sorting, indexing does not create another database for saving sorted records. Instead, it creates an index that contains information that indicates where the actual records are located in the original database file.

A database index is comparable to the subject index located at the end of this book. It arranges alphabetically all the keywords describing the subjects covered in the book. Following each subject keyword are page numbers indicating where in the book the subject is mentioned. These page numbers represent a set of pointers that you use to refer to the subjects.

A subject index can be used in a variety of ways. The most common way to read the material in a book is to go through it page by page from beginning to end, but it is not the only way. For instance, although it is not recommended, you could read this book by choosing from the subjects that are listed alphabetically in the index, going down the subject list and finding the page numbers associated with particular subjects. You would then read just the sections of text related to those subjects, jumping from one section to another in the book. In a sense, then, you would be using the subject index to arrange the subjects you would like to read in the order in which you would like to read them.

Another way to use a subject index is to seek out only the subject that you would like to read and ignore the rest. In this case, you would be using the subject index as a quick way to retrieve information on a specific topic in a book.

In a database index, each record can be treated like a subject in a book, and, like reading a book from beginning to end, you can view your data records in the order in which they were entered; or you can read them in a different order based on the values in a certain data field. Say you want to view the records in the SALESMAN database in descending order based on the values in the SALARY field. In this case, you would create an index that contains the actual locations of the records, arranged by salary values.

Although the contents of a database index are very similar to that of a subject index of a book, the major difference is that a database index does not contain the actual subjects. Instead, it holds only the reference information to help you find the actual subjects in the database. And while the subject index of a book lists reference page numbers, an index created for a database file contains pointer information about the actual data records in the database file.

Index Keys

A database index can be created using one or more data fields to form an index key. The values in the index key determine how the data records are to be arranged. For example, you can use the SALARY field in the SALESMAN database as an index key for creating an index file; therefore, the index will contain pointers indicating the locations of the records that are arranged by the values in the SALARY field.

If you use more than one data field as an index key, the data records are arranged according to the *combined* values of the data fields. So, if you create an index using the FIRST and LAST data fields in the index key expressed as

```
FIRST+LAST
```

the combined value of this expression will be used to arrange your data records.

You can create as many as 25 indexes for the same database file, and each index will be defined with an index key which may contain one or more data fields. Once these indexes are created and saved in one or more index files, they can be used later to arrange your data records. Remember, however, that when you change the contents of a database file, you must open and update its associated index files as well. Otherwise, you will get erroneous results because you used an outdated index file for ordering the records.

FoxPro Index Files

In FoxPro, there are two kinds of index files: the standard index file using the .IDX file extension and a compound index file with the .CDX file extension.

The .IDX standard index file has been around since the early versions of FoxPro and FoxBASE+. It contains only one index, and that index is made up of only one index key that, in turn, may consist of one or more data fields.

The compound index file, on the other hand, is an enhanced feature of FoxPro 2.0 and FoxPro for Windows, and it can contain multiple indexes, each of which may be made up of one or more data fields. Each index in a compound index file is called an index tag. If your index tag contains only one data field, FoxPro, by default, automatically names the index tag after the data field. But if the index tag is made up of multiple data fields, you must provide a name for the tag.

When working with a compound index file, only one index tag at a time is used, and that one tag is called the master index. Obviously then, when an index file contains multiple tags, you must designate one index tag as the master index. The other tags remain open in the background. If you choose to rearrange your records in a different order later, you must designate another index tag as the master index if one exists, or create a new index tag if one does not.

Saving Index Files in a Compact Format

In FoxPro, all compound index (.CDX) files are saved in a compact format; standard index (.IDX) files can be saved either in a compact or regular format. In the compact format, the size of index files is reduced to approximately one-sixth, and this reduction results in a much shorter processing time. Therefore, if you want to speed up indexing time, save your index files in a compact format (assuming that you are using standard indexes). There is one exception, however. Early versions of FoxPro accept only standard format, so if you want to export your standard indexes from 2.0 to these earlier versions, you may need to save your .IDX files in standard format.

Saving Compound Index Files in a Structural Format

Compound index files also can be saved in a structural format, and there are many advantages for doing so. First, using an existing compound index in a structural format is automatic; that is, when you open a database file in a work area, it automatically opens its associated compound index file. You do not have to remember to open the index file yourself. As a result, you are able to use any index tags in the index file as long as the database file remains open.

This is not the case when you save an index file in a normal format where you must open your index file *after* you have opened your database file. If you do not, the index file will not be updated after you have made changes to the database.

This causes the database to be corrupted because you used an outdated index file for the index operation.

Another advantage to maintaining index tags in a structural compound index file is that the process is simple and systematic. Whenever you modify the contents of the database file, all the associated index tags in the index file are automatically updated. You do not have to rebuild the index tags to reflect the changes in the database file. If your compound index file is not saved in a structural format, you must remember to update the standard index file after you have made changes to the contents of the database file.

Because of these advantages, a structural compound index file is the preferable method for indexing data, and you should try to use structural compound index files for most of your index operations. One more thing: There is a unique reference between the database file and its associated structural compound index file—they share the same filename, but with different file extensions. So, if you create a structural compound index file for the SALESMAN.DBF file, the index file is automatically named SALESMAN.CDX. In addition, FoxPro saves all structural compound index files in a compact format, thereby improving processing speed.

Creating a Structural Compound Index File

In the next exercise, we create a structural compound index file to hold a set of index tags, which is used to arrange data records in the SALESMAN database.

First, open your database file in a work area. Once it is open, bring up the Setup dialog. When the dialog appears, define the index tags that will become the components of the compound index file that you are creating.

For example, if you intend to use indexes to arrange the records in SALESMAN.DBF, you must create a compound index file to hold all the index tags that you will create. Later you will choose one as the master index for ordering your records.

For this exercise, we'll display records in the SALESMAN database according to the values in the SALARY and HIRE_DATE fields, respectively. First, we'll set up two index tags and save them to an index file. The first index tag is made up of the SALARY field, and the second uses HIRE_DATE as the index key.

Once these tags have been set up, you'll choose the appropriate one for arranging your records; that is, designate the first one as the master index if you want your records arranged according to salary values. Choose the second if you want your records arranged according to the values in the HIRE_DATE field.

To create your new compound index file, use the View option from the Window menu to open the SALESMAN database and bring up the Setup dialog (see Figure 6.24).

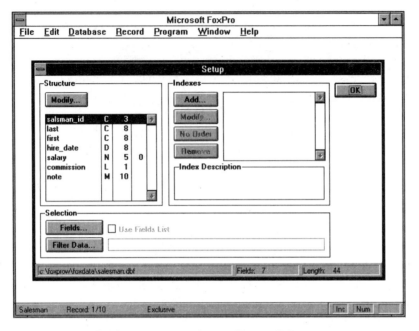

Figure 6.24 Defining index tags in the Setup dialog

In the middle of the Setup dialog is a space for displaying your index tags. Four buttons are shown on the right-hand side of the dialog: Add..., Modify..., No Order, and Remove. Their functions are:

Add...	Adds and opens a new index file
Modify...	Modifies existing index tags
No Order	Designates the master index
Remove	Closes an open index file

Note in Figure 6.24 that only the Add button is active. The other three buttons will become active only after an existing index is present. In addition, the No Order button will be changed to Set Order when index tags are available for use as a master index (you will learn about this later).

Creating an Index Tag

The first time you create an index file, set up a new index tag by choosing the Add... button from the Setup dialog. This brings up the Open File dialog (see Figure 6.25). At this point, choose the New button to add a new index tag to the index file. The Index dialog appears (see Figure 6.26). Now you can define the new index tag.

Sorting and Indexing Data 203

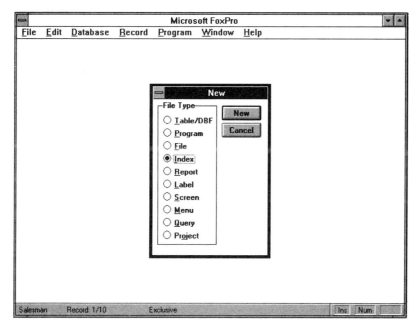

Figure 6.25 The Open File dialog

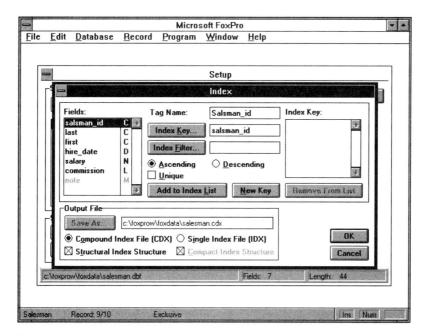

Figure 6.26 The Index dialog

To construct the index tag, choose from the names and types of data fields on the left-hand side of the dialog. Then specify index order by selecting either the Ascending or Descending radio button in the middle of the dialog.

Below the radio buttons is a Unique check box. Select it if you want to exclude duplicate values from the index tag. The name of the index tag that you are creating will be displayed in the Tag Name text box. As you highlight a field in the Fields list, the field will be chosen as a default index tag. As a result, the field name will be entered in the Tag Name text box. Below the Tag Name text box you will find the Index Key... text box for displaying the index key of your choice. The default index key is set to the highlighted field in the Fields list. Select the Index Filter... button to define the filter condition for selecting the data records to be affected by the index operation.

The Add to Index List button enables you to select a data field from the Fields list and move it to the Index Key list for defining an index tag. Choose the Remove From List button to reverse the field selection. The New Key button is used for selecting a new index key. When this button is pressed, the Tag Name and Index Key... text boxes will be cleared so that you can enter a new index tag and key.

At the bottom of the Index dialog is an Output File box where you choose the type of index file by turning on either the IDX or CDX radio button. If you are creating a standard index (.IDX) file, check the Compact box to specify the index file format; if you are creating a compound index, check the Structure box instead. Finally, the name of the index file is displayed in the Save As... text box. The default is a compound index file (.CDX) with a structural index structure.

Now, create the first index tag for the SALESMAN.DBF file. This will consist only of the SALARY data field, sorted in descending order. First, turn on the Descending button either by clicking your mouse on the button or by pressing the letter "D." Then, select the SALARY data field to be included in the index tag by double clicking your mouse on that field. Or, on the keyboard, use the Tab and arrow keys to highlight the data field and then press the Enter key. As a result, the data field selected appears in the Index Key list.

At this point, note that the Tag Name and Index Key... text boxes are cleared. If your index key is made up of a single field, as in this example, you would want to assign the field name to the index tag and the index key. To do that, you can type the field name in the Tab Name and Index Key... text boxes. As a shortcut, click the mouse once on the field name in the Index Key list. As a result, the field name will be copied into the Tag Name and Index Key... text boxes (see Figure 6.27). (Remember that you must name the index tag yourself when it is composed of more than one data field.)

Next, look at the Output File box. Because you are allowed only one structural compound index file for each database file, the name of the index file will automatically be set to that of the database file—in our example, c:\foxprow\foxdata\salesman.cdx.

Sorting and Indexing Data 205

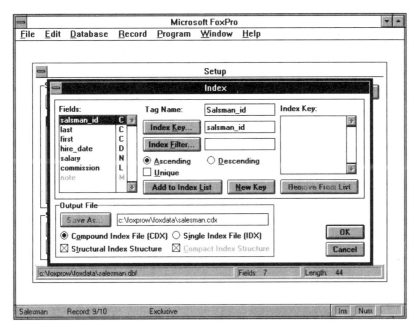

Figure 6.27 Creating an index tag with the SALARY field

At this point, you either can exit from the Index dialog or create another index tag. If you would like to create another index tag, repeat the same process. Try creating another index tag by selecting HIRE_DATE as the index key. First, click on the New Key button and accept Ascending as the index order (the default). Then, double click on the HIRE_DATE in the Fields list to move it to the Index Key list. Click on HIRE_DATE in the Index Key list to enter the field name in the Tag Name and Index Key... text boxes (see Figure 6.28).

Using Multiple Data Fields in Index Tags

As just mentioned above, an index tag can be defined with a single data field or with more than one data field. If you intend to sort your records according to the combined character strings in the FIRST and LAST fields, for example, you would define the index tag as:

```
FIRST+LAST
```

Specify the tag with an index expression by selecting the Index Key... button in the Index dialog with the mouse or keyboard. This causes the Expression Builder dialog to appear; it has the same format as the Expression Builder that you were introduced to earlier. Build the index expression with the data fields (FIRST, LAST) and the necessary mathematical operator (e.g., +) as shown in Figure 6.29.

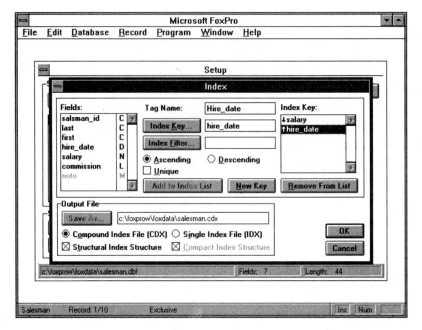

Figure 6.28 Creating an index tag with the HIRE_DATE field

Verify the expression and then return to the Index dialog by choosing the OK button. When you return to the dialog, you can see that the index key appears in the Index Key... text box (see Figure 6.30). Now you can enter a name (let's call it Fullname) to the index tag in the Tag Name text box. After that, select the Add to Index List to move the index expression into the Index Key list. (see Figure 6.30).

Like a field name, the name of an index tag may have as many as 10 characters. It must begin with a letter or an underscore, but may consist of any combination of letters, digits, or underscores.

Saving Index Tags to a Compound Index File

To save the index tags you have created to a structural compound index file, first verify the type and format of the index file. Make sure that the CDX radio button has been turned on (indicated with a dot) and then verify that the Structural check box has been selected.

Now you can proceed to create the index file and exit from the Index dialog by selecting the OK button. FoxPro then creates all the index tags in the file. As each index tag is created, the following message appears in the status bar:

```
10 records indexed
```

Sorting and Indexing Data 207

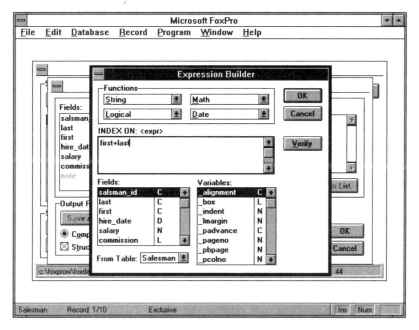

Figure 6.29 Defining the expression for an index tag

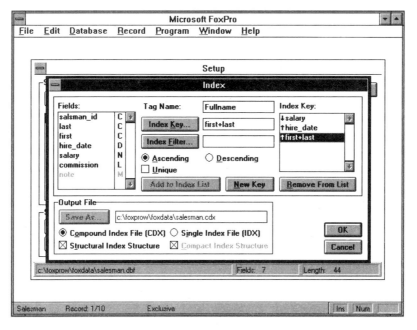

Figure 6.30 Creating an index tag with an index expression

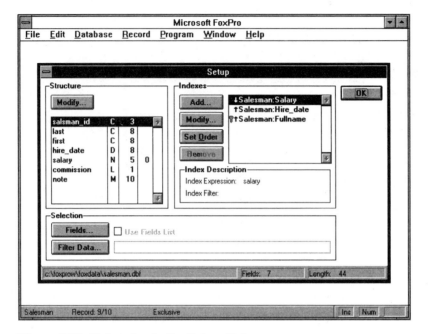

Figure 6.31 Returning to the Setup dialog

Of course, the number of indexed records is determined by the number of records in any given file. Afterwards, you will return to the Setup dialog (see Figure 6.31).

All the index tags that were created are now visible in the Indexes list box in this figure. Each index tag name is preceded by the name of the compound index file. Notice that the symbol of a key appeared to the left of the index tag most recently created (Salesman:Fullname). The key symbol indicates that that index tag is the current master index and that the records in the database file are now being arranged according to the values of that tag.

At this point, if you want to view the ordered records, leave the Setup dialog by choosing the OK button. Display the records in the SALESMAN database now by selecting the Browse option. You can see that they are arranged in alphabetical order by the character strings in the FIRST and LAST data fields, i.e., alphabetically arranged by first name (see Figure 6.32). Because there are no duplicate first names, the index tag of FIRST+LAST yielded the same results as an index tag using only the FIRST data field.

If there had been more than one record sharing the same first name, their associated last names would have been alphabetized accordingly. Thus, if you had John Smith, John Albertson, and John Nelson in the database file, they would have been arranged as follows:

```
Albertson    John
Nelson       John
Smith        John
```

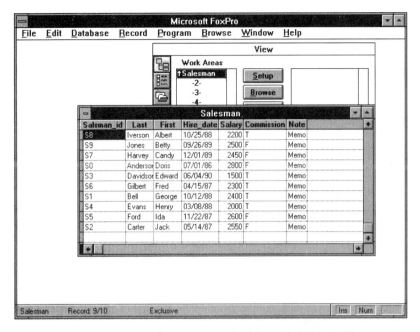

Figure 6.32 Viewing indexed records in SALESMAN.DBF

Designating the Master Index

Although you can *save* multiple index tags in a compound index file, you can *use* only one of them at a time to arrange your data records. The one in use is called the master index.

You can designate any one of the index tags as the master index by using the Set Order operation. Recall that when you returned to the Setup dialog after you had created the index tags, it automatically designated the last index tag as the master index, which was indicated with a dot.

To designate a different index tag as the master index, return to the Setup dialog and select any other index tag as the master index by using the mouse or the keyboard. With a mouse, first click on the index tag that you want to select. With the keyboard, use the arrow keys to move the cursor to the index tag you want to select. It is then highlighted and its associated index expression is displayed below the Indexes list box. Next, select Set Order to designate this index tag as the master index.

As an exercise, designate the salary index tag as the master index. Click your mouse on that tag in the Indexes box. Watch as it is highlighted and the index expression (in this case, the SALARY data field) is displayed in the Index Description text box (see Figure 6.33). Finally, select the Set Order button to designate the selected index tag as the master index. A symbol of a key now appears to the left of the salary index tag (see Figure 6.34).

210   Understanding FoxPro 2.5 for Windows

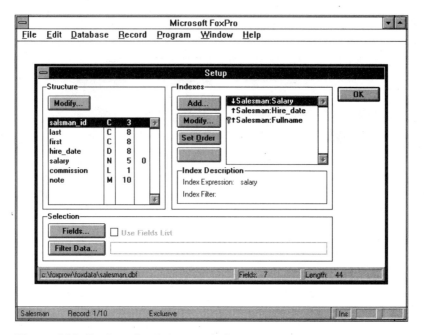

Figure 6.33 Designating a master index

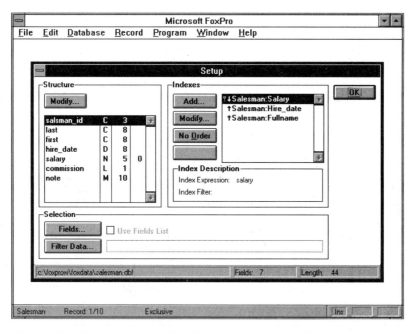

Figure 6.34 Designating SALARY as the master index

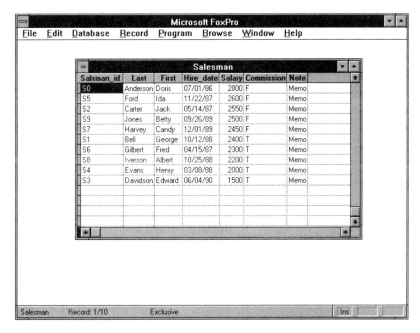

Figure 6.35 Viewing records indexed by a new master index

After you have designated your new master index, select the OK button to exit from the Setup dialog and then select the Browse option to display the records as they are arranged by the master index (see Figure 6.35). Notice that all of the records in SALESMAN now are ordered according to the values in the current master index, SALARY.

Modifying Compound Index Files

After creating a structural compound index file, you can modify its contents to accommodate your new indexing needs. Add a new index tag to the index file when you need to arrange your records in a different order or remove existing index tags that you no longer need. You also can change the index expression that makes up an existing index tag.

There are a number of ways to enter Edit mode in order to alter the contents of an existing structural compound index file. The simplest is to choose the Modify... button in the Indexes box of the Setup dialog. Follow this procedure to change the contents of SALESMAN.CDX. FoxPro opens the Index dialog, which enables you to see all of the index fields and expressions that you used to define the existing index tags (see Figure 6.36).

212 Understanding FoxPro 2.5 for Windows

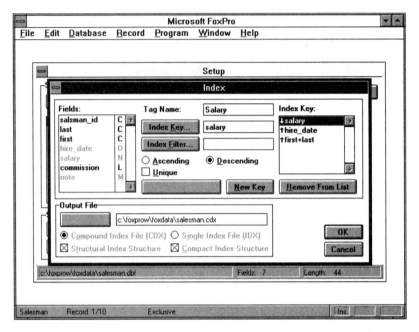

Figure 6.36 Showing the existing index tags

Adding New Index Tags

To add a new index tag to a structural compound index file, follow the same procedure that you learned earlier. Using the SALSMAN_ID data field as the index key, first select the New Key button and then move the field into the Index Key list (accept the default, ascending order, for this example). Note that the data field selected now is displayed in the Index Key list for the new index tag (see Figure 6.37).

If the index tag that you would like to add requires an index expression, define that expression in the Expression Builder dialog using the same procedure described earlier. That is, select the Index Key... button to bring up the Index Expression Builder.

After defining the new index tag, either exit from the Index dialog or continue to add new index tags. If you select the OK button, you will be returned to the Setup dialog after the new index tag is added to the index file. Otherwise, you may stay in the Index dialog so that you can make other changes to the index tags.

After you have made all the changes that you want, exit the Index dialog by choosing the OK button. At that point, the contents of the index file will be updated. Do that now: Select the OK button to create the new index tag. Watch as the following message is displayed briefly in the status bar:

```
10 records indexed
```

indicating that the new index tag has been created and added to the index file.

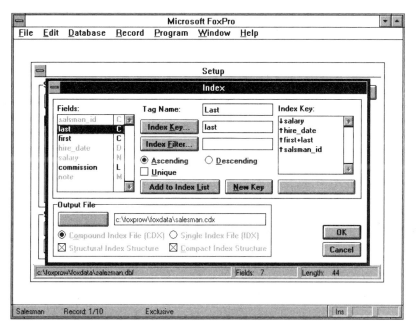

Figure 6.37 Adding a new index tag

Removing Existing Index Tags

The procedure to remove an existing tag from the index file is very simple. Return to the Index dialog by selecting the Modify... button from the Setup dialog. Once there, remove any existing index tags either with the mouse or keyboard.

If you are using a mouse, double click on an existing index tag to remove it from the index file. To remove the index tag SALSMAN_ID, for example, double click on the index key SALSMAN_ID in the Index Key list. You are then prompted for confirmation (see Figure 6.38). If you choose Yes, the index tag named SALSMAN_ID will be eliminated. But because we do not want to remove it from the index file, answer No to abort the action.

If you are using the keyboard, remove an existing tag by first highlighting the index tag and then pressing the Enter key or the letter "R" (for the Remove From List button). You are prompted for confirmation as above. Answer either Yes or No to continue.

At this point, you can choose to return to the Setup dialog or remain in the Index dialog. For our purposes, stay in the Index dialog for the next exercise.

Modifying Existing Index Tags

In addition to adding a new tag or removing an existing tag, you also can modify an existing index tag. This involves first removing the index tag that you intend to

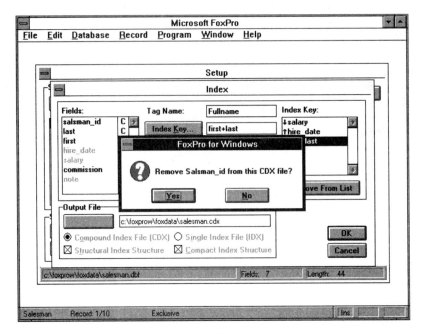

Figure 6.38 Removing an existing index tag

modify and then redefining it with another index key. There are two ways to accomplish this. For this exercise, let's assume that you are going to modify the index tag Fullname by replacing its current index expression, first+last, with a new expression that consists only of the FIRST data field. The first method is to use the procedure that you have just learned—remove the Fullname index tag and then add a new index tag by choosing the FIRST data field as an index key. This method is adequate for this example because it is easy to redefine the index expression for the new index tag after you have removed the old one.

But, if you would like to create a new index by editing the existing index expression, there is an easier way. Highlight the index tag to be modified in the Index Key list and then select the Index Key... button. When the Expression Builder dialog appears, edit the INDEX ON expression accordingly (see Figure 6.39). Then, select the OK button to return to the Index dialog to change the index tag name from Fullname to First in the Tag Name text box (see Figure 6.40).

Finally, select the OK button to confirm the change by choosing the Yes button from the Prompt:

```
Remove Fullname from this CDX File?
```

When you return to the Setup dialog, you will note that the new index tag First now replaces the Fullname tag (see Figure 6.41).

Sorting and Indexing Data 215

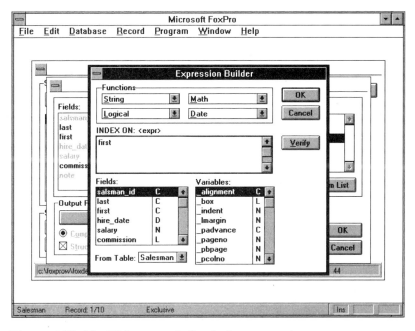

Figure 6.39 Modifying an existing index expression

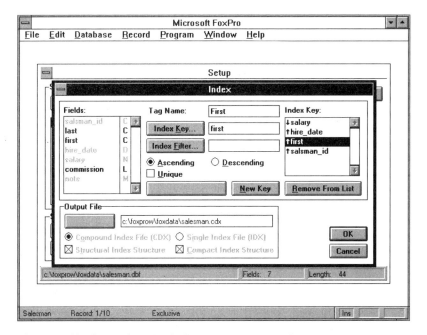

Figure 6.40 Changing the index tag name

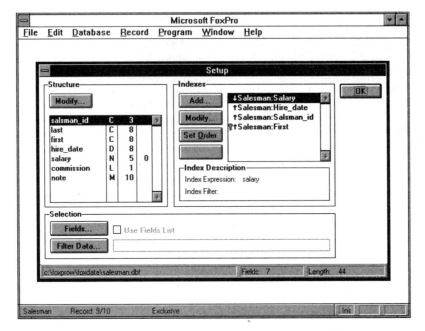

Figure 6.41 Showing the changed index tag

If you remove all the index tags from the structural compound index (.CDX) file, the index file will automatically be deleted from the disk. This is one way to delete a structural compound index file. Another way to delete it is by using the Filer. We will discuss it later.

Creating Index Tags in the Data Structure

Up to this point, you have seen how to create a compound structural index (.CDX) file using the Index dialog. Using this method, you can create index tags that consist of one or more data fields as index keys. If all your index tags contain single data fields as keys, there is a shortcut to create the compound structural index file—define your index tags in the data structure. For example, to arrange the records in the OFFICE.DBF according to the values in the OFFICE_ID and ZIP data fields, you would create three index tags with these fields and save them in the OFFICE.CDX file.

You can define index tags in a data structure when you are creating the structure, or you can add the index tags to the structure after it has been created. This involves modifying an existing data structure. For example, to add index tags to the existing structure of OFFICE.DBF, first bring up the Setup dialog while the database file is open in the current work area (see Figure 6.42). Then, select the Modify button in the Structure box to bring up the Table Structure dialog in which the structure of the OFFICE.DBF is displayed (see Figure 6.43).

Sorting and Indexing Data 217

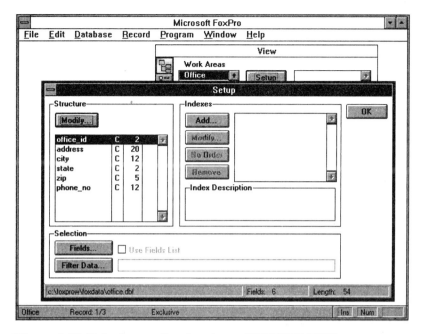

Figure 6.42 Bringing up the structure of OFFICE.DBF

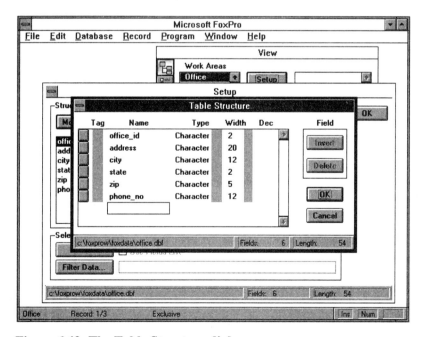

Figure 6.43 The Table Structure dialog

In Figure 6.43, you can see that the attributes of all the existing data fields are shown in the Table Structure dialog. In addition, to the left of the Name column is a column labeled Tag. This is where you define the order of an index tag that uses the adjacent data field as the index key.

To add an index tag that uses an existing data field, first highlight the field with the mouse or press the Tab key. When a data field is highlighted, an additional Tag box is displayed in the Tag column. This new Tag box is used to define either an ascending or a descending order for the index tag. To define the order, click your mouse on the Tag box. An up arrow will appear, indicating an ascending order to the index tag. If you click on the Tag box again, it will show a down arrow, assigning a descending order to that index tag. To remove the tag, click the mouse a third time. To create an index tag in the data structure using the keyboard, when the data field is highlighted, use the space key to assign either an ascending or descending order to its corresponding index tag.

As an exercise, let's create an index tag in ascending order using the OFFICE_ID field and an index tag in descending order using the ZIP field. First, highlight the OFFICE_ID field with the mouse or by using the Tab key. Click your mouse on the Tag box to show an up arrow. With the keyboard, press the space key to display an up arrow in the Tag box. Follow the same procedure to display a down arrow in the Tag box next to the ZIP data field (see Figure 6.44). Then select the OK button to modify the structure to include the index tags defined. Select the Yes button in response to the Prompt:

```
Make structure changes permanent?
```

When you return to the Setup dialog, note that the two index tags that you defined in the data structure caused the creation of a compound structural index file (named OFFICE.CDX). The index tags named Office:Office_id and Office:Zip are shown in the Indexes list box in the Setup dialog. You can then select the master index by using the Set Order button. As an exercise, choose Office:Zip as the master index (see Figure 6.45). Select the OK button to exit from the Setup dialog.

If you look at the records in the OFFICE.DBF using the Browse window now, you will see that they are arranged in a descending order according to the values in the ZIP field (see Figure 6.46).

Creating Standard Index Files

In general, it is recommended that you use structural compound index files. Standard .IDX and nonstructural compound .CDX index files should be reserved for special occasions, such as if you intend to use different sets of indexes for different applications. Then you may want to save these indexes in several .IDX

Sorting and Indexing Data 219

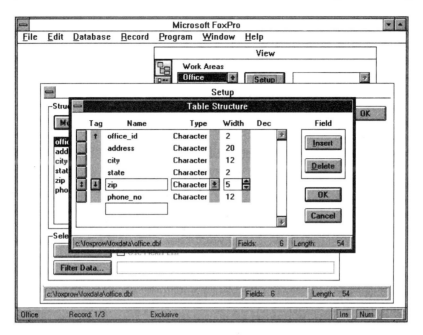

Figure 6.44 Defining an index tag with the ZIP field

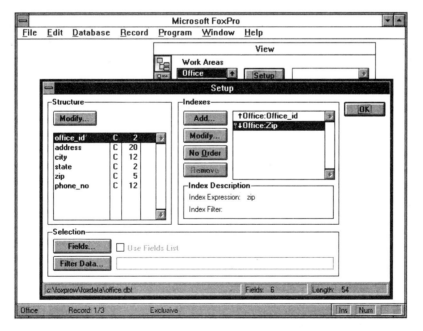

Figure 6.45 Designating ZIP as the master index

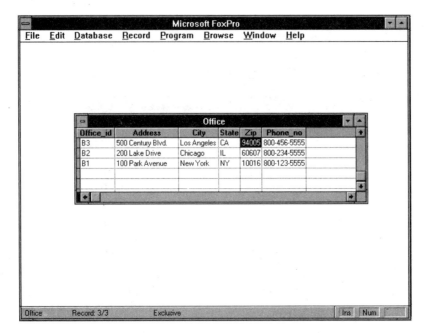

Figure 6.46 Viewing records in zip code order

and nonstructural compound index files, instead of in a structural compound index file. If this is the case, open those indexes only when you need them and do not keep all your indexes open at the same time. And remember to update your indexes before using them.

To reiterate: Unlike compound index files that may contain multiple indexes, a standard index file can have only one index, and that index is expressed as a key consisting of one or more data fields. And because you can create only one structural compound index file for a database file, this index file is always named after its associated database file. On the other hand, you may create several standard .IDX index files and nonstructural compound index files for the same database file; therefore, unique names must be assigned to each index file.

Although there are a number of ways to create a new standard index file, a simple one is to select the New option from the File menu after you have opened its associated database file in a work area. When the New dialog appears, select Index as the type of file to be created. With a mouse, click on the Index radio button to turn it on. If you are using the keyboard, highlight the Index radio button with the Tab key and then press the Spacebar to turn it on (see Figure 6.47).

Next, select the New button to bring up the Index dialog, and when it appears, begin defining the new index file. First, select the Single Index File (IDX) radio button. Then assign a name to the index file, and before saving it, define its associated index key.

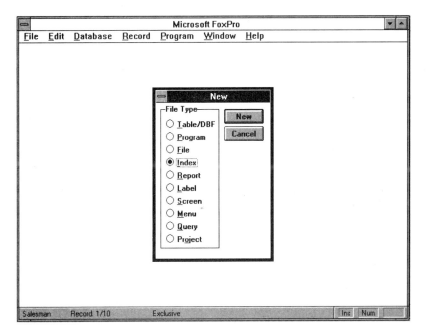

Figure 6.47 Creating a new single index (.IDX) file

To create a sample .IDX index file named BYLAST using the LAST data field from the SALESMAN.DBF database as its index key, first turn on the Single Index File (IDX) radio button. To conserve disk space, save the index file in compact format (the default format). If you do not want this feature, remove the check mark from the Compact Index Structure check box.

After selecting the index type, assign a name to the index file by typing in the filename (e.g., BYLAST) in the text box in the Output File box. Alternatively, bring up the Index File Name dialog by choosing the Save As... button and then enter your filename.

Now you are ready to define the index key for the file that you are creating. Follow the same procedure that you learned earlier in this chapter for this step. As an exercise, select the LAST data field and move it to the Index Key list to define the index key (see Figure 6.48). As this point, note that the Tag Name text box is inactive. You cannot define an index tag for a single index (IDX) file.

After defining the index file, select the OK button to exit from the Index dialog. Consequently, the .IDX index file is created and saved to disk. At the same time, the index file is opened and added to the active indexes. You can verify this by bringing up the Setup dialog (see Figure 6.49).

A standard .IDX index file is displayed differently from an index tag of a compound index file. Whereas an .IDX file is listed by its filename, an index tag

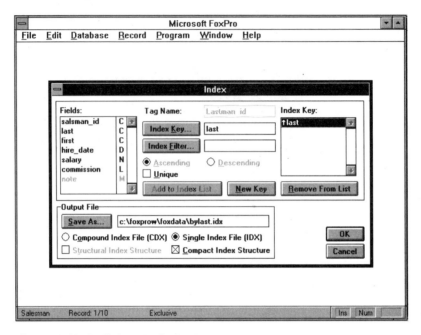

Figure 6.48 Defining the index key

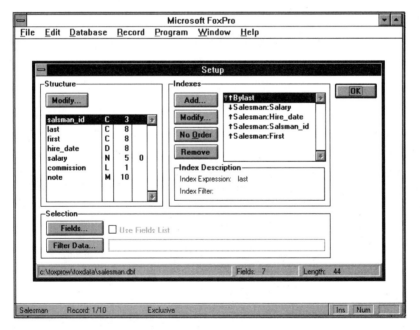

Figure 6.49 Verifying the BYLAST.IDX index file

is displayed in two parts: the name of the .CDX file and the name of the index tag. Also note the key symbol displayed to the left of the BYLAST.IDX index file.

Removing Index Files

To remove a standard .IDX index file from the current indexes, simply select the Remove button in the Setup dialog while the index file is highlighted. Highlight the index file that is to be removed either with the mouse or by using the Tab key.

Another way to remove a standard .IDX index file from the current indexes is to close its associated database file and then reopen it. When you close a database file, all of the .IDX files that are currently open will be closed automatically. When you reopen the database file, only the index tags in the structural compound index file will be opened. However, removing it from the current Indexes list does not erase it permanently from the disk. You can retrieve it by selecting the Add button in the Setup window. To permanently delete a single index (.IDX) file, use the Filer. As an exercise, remove BYLAST.IDX in the Setup dialog by choosing the Remove button while the Bylast index file is highlighted in the Indexes list.

Creating Nonstructural Compound Index Files

In addition to standard .IDX index files, you can also create nonstructural compound index files. A nonstructural compound index file is very similar to a structural compound index file; it too stores multiple indexes as index tags. But there are minor differences between them. First, while the name of a structural compound index file is always the same as that of its associated database file, a unique name can be assigned to a nonstructural compound index file. As a result, for a database file, you can create different nonstructural compound index files, each of which can consist of a different set of index tags. Second, when you open a database file in a work area, its associated structural compound index file is automatically opened; this is not true for nonstructural compound index files. They must be added to the currently open indexes if they are to maintain their index tags.

To create a nonstructural compound index file, follow the same procedure for creating a standard .IDX index file. The only difference is that when you define the index file, choose .CDX as the output file and do not select the Structural Index Structure check box in the Output File box.

Deleting Index Files

Any index file that you have created may be erased from your disk. The procedure for doing this is the same as for deleting any disk file. Choose the Filer option from

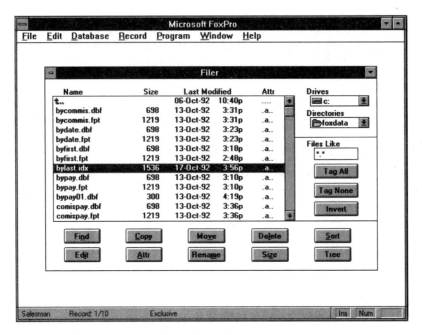

Figure 6.50 Tagging the file to be deleted

the Help menu. From there, choose the Delete button after you have tagged the files you intend to delete. Remember though, before you can delete a disk file, it must be closed. Therefore, to delete an index file, close it first; otherwise, the Filer will not allow you to tag that file.

As an exercise, delete the BYLAST.IDX index file. First, highlight the index file with your mouse or the keyboard. (see Figure 6.50), then choose the Delete button either by clicking your mouse on that button or by pressing the "L" key. You are then prompted to confirm your action (see Figure 6.51). At this point, select the Delete button to confirm the deletion, and the tagged file is permanently removed from your disk.

You may use this procedure to delete a compound index file; however, after you have deleted a structural compound index (.CDX) file with the Filer, the next time you open its associated database file, you will see the message:

```
Structural CDX file not found
```

In this case, select the Ignore button to continue. As an exercise, delete the OFFICE.CDX file by using the Filer so that we can re-create the structural compound index file using the FoxPro commands described in the next section.

Sorting and Indexing Data 225

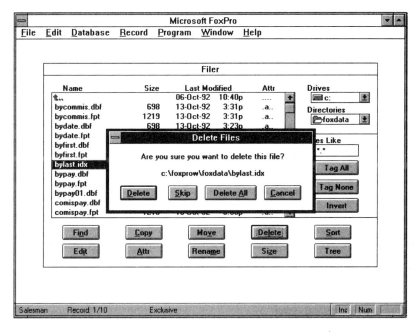

Figure 6.51 Confirming deletion of the index file

INDEXING WITH FOXPRO COMMANDS

Index operations also can be performed by issuing the appropriate FoxPro commands. These commands enable you to create any type of index file (including standard .IDX files and structural and nonstructural compound .CDX index files). You can use a command to add an index tag to the index file of a compound index file; likewise, you can remove any existing index tag from a compound index file or designate an existing index tag as the master index.

Creating Structural Compound Index Files

To create a structural compound index file with a FoxPro command, you must first issue the USE command to open the database file whose records you want to order. Then, issue the INDEX ON command in the following format:

```
INDEX ON expression TAG index tag name [DESCENDING] [UNIQUE]
```

In this command, you define the expression that serves as the index key and specify the index tag name. If you are using a single data field as your index key, name the index tag after that data field. Otherwise, assign a unique name to any index tag that represents an expression consisting of more than one data field.

Like a field name, the name of an index tag may be any combination of letters, digits, or underscores up to 10 characters long, and it must begin with a letter or an underscore.

Use the DESCENDING (or just DESC) keyword to change the default (ascending) order for arranging your records. To ignore duplicate values in the index key, add the UNIQUE keyword to the INDEX ON command.

Although the INDEX ON command defines an index tag, it creates its associated structural compound index file if the index tag is the first tag you are creating for the file. Here is an example:

```
USE OFFICE
INDEX ON OFFICE_ID TAG OFFICE_ID
```

The INDEX ON command sets up the index tag, OFFICE_ID, using the OFFICE_ID field as an index key. Because this is the first index tag you have defined, FoxPro creates a structural compound index file to hold the index tag (remember that we deleted OFFICE.CDX with the Filer in the last exercise.) The index file will be named after its associated database file (i.e., OFFICE.CDX).

Displaying Index Status

After creating the structural compound index file, you can verify its existence in a variety of ways. Either use the procedure that you learned earlier in this chapter—bring up the Setup dialog (see Figure 6.52)—or issue the following command:

```
DISPLAY STATUS
```

This command directs FoxPro to display information about the status of your current database, and it may take several screens to display all the information. On the first screen, among other items, FoxPro will list all of the database files that are currently open, along with their associated structural compound index files (see Figure 6.53).

Figure 6.53 shows OFFICE.DBF as currently open in work area 1. The index tag, OFFICE_ID, (which uses OFFICE_ID as the index key) is also shown, along with the name of its structural compound index file, OFFICE.CDX.

Information about other items is displayed on subsequent screens, but because they are related to subjects we will discuss in later chapters, skip them at this point by pressing the Esc key.

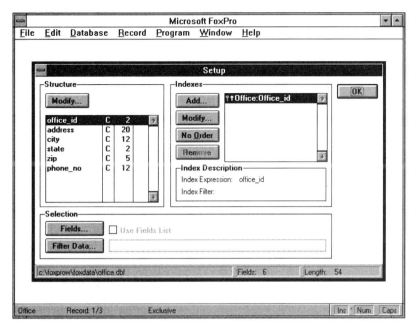

Figure 6.52 Verifying the index file in the Setup dialog

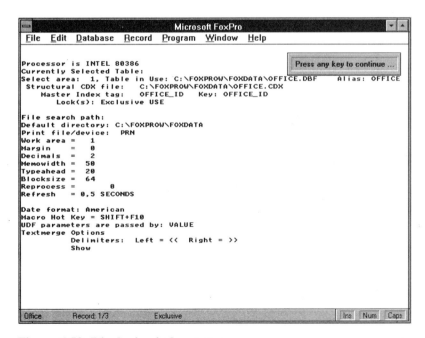

Figure 6.53 Displaying index status

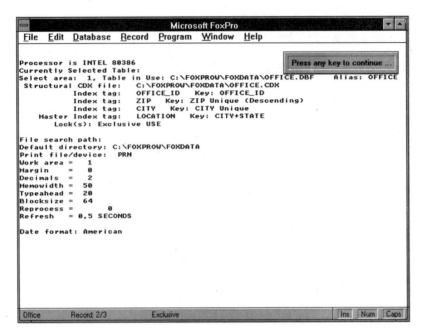

Figure 6.54 Showing added index tags

Adding Index Tags

Once you have created a structural compound index file, use the INDEX ON command to add more index tags to the file. For example, the following three commands will add three different index tags to the OFFICE.CDX index file:

```
INDEX ON ZIP TAG ZIP DESCENDING UNIQUE
INDEX ON CITY TAG CITY UNIQUE
INDEX ON CITY+STATE TAG LOCATION
```

As an exercise, enter these commands to add the three index tags to the index file. Next issue the DISPLAY STATUS command to verify them (see Figure 6.54). This figure lists all of the new index tags. Notice that the most recently created index tag, LOCATION, has been designated as the master index.

Designating the Master Index

If you have more than one index tag in a structural compound index file, any one of them can be designated as the master index by using the SET ORDER command:

```
SET ORDER TO index tag name
```

To designate the index tag ZIP as the master index, issue the following command:

```
SET ORDER TO ZIP
```

If you issue the DISPLAY STATUS command again, the ZIP index tag will be labeled as the Master Index.

Removing an Index Tag

When you no longer need it, remove an existing index tag from a structural compound index file with the command:

```
DELETE TAG index tag name
```

For example, issue the following command to remove the index tag LOCATION from the OFFICE.CDX index file:

```
DELETE TAG LOCATION
```

Modifying Index Tags

DELETE and INDEX ON are the commands to invoke if you want to modify an existing index tag in a compound index file. Issue the DELETE command to remove the index tag earmarked for modification and then use the INDEX ON command to create another one. Note: There is no command that enables you to edit the definition of an existing index tag.

Creating Standard Index Files

The FoxPro command to create a standard .IDX index file is INDEX ON used in the following format:

```
INDEX ON index key TO name of .IDX file [COMPACT] [UNIQUE]
```

Here is an example:

```
USE OFFICE
INDEX ON STATE TO BYSTATE COMPACT
```

This command will create a standard .IDX index file named BYSTATE that uses the STATE data field as its index key for arranging the data records in ascending order (descending order is not allowed in .IDX file). The file is to be saved in a compact format.

Creating Nonstructural Compound Index Files

The command to create a nonstructural compound index file is similar to that for creating a structural one, but it requires that you assign a name to it in the INDEX ON command:

```
INDEX ON expression TAG index tag name OF name of .CDX
file [UNIQUE]
```

The following command will set up an index tag named BYPHONE and create the OFPHONE.CDX compound index file and save it in a compact format:

```
USE OFFICE
INDEX ON PHONE_NO TAG BYPHONE OF OFPHONE
```

After executing the INDEX ON command, you may issue the DISPLAY STATUS command to verify the index file's existence. The DISPLAY STATUS command will display the nonstructural compound index file, along with the structural compound index file (see Figure 6.55).

Figure 6.55 shows that the nonstructural compound index file just created (OFPHONE.CDX) is listed below the structural compound index file (OFFICE.CDX). If you bring up the Setup dialog now, you also will see that all the index tags of the compound index files are displayed in the Indexes list (see Figure 6.56).

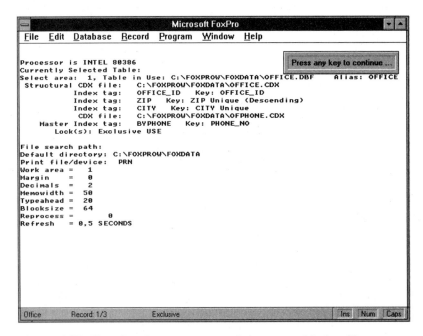

Figure 6.55 Showing the nonstructural compound index file

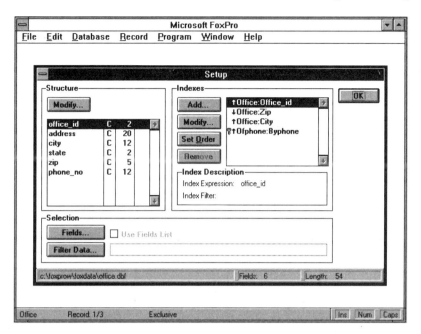

Figure 6.56 Showing the nonstructural OFPHONE.CDX file in the Setup dialog

At this point, you can choose any index tag in either index file as the master index. But, if you no longer need the nonstructural index file, you can remove it by first closing OFFICE.DBF and then reopen it with these commands:

```
USE
USE OFFICE
```

The first command closes the database file that is currently open in default work area 1. When you reopen the OFFICE database with the USE OFFICE command, only the structural compound index file will be reopened. Consequently, any previously opened standard .IDX and nonstructural compound .CDX index files will not be opened.

Deleting Index Files

To permanently remove any index files from your disk, invoke this command:

```
ERASE filename
```

It deletes any type of index file, but you must specify the filename with its file extension. For example:

```
ERASE XYZ.IDX
ERASE ABC.CDX
```

The ERASE command allows you to remove standard .IDX and nonstructural compound .CDX index files that you no longer need in order to conserve storage space. Remember that you must close these index files before you can erase them.

Although it is not recommended, it also is possible to erase a structural compound index file. If you do, you will be warned about the absence of the index file when you try to open its associated database file:

```
      Structural CDX file not found
Ignore                        Cancel
```

When this happens, choose the Ignore button to continue.

Chapter Summary

This chapter detailed the two methods for ordering records in a database file: sorting and indexing. In discussing the strengths and weaknesses of both methods, you learned that sorting causes the creation of duplicate files, which take up valuable disk space. Therefore, it is faster to order records with the indexing operation, and unless you need to work repeatedly with sorted records, you should choose the indexing operation.

You also learned how to create different types of index files, but it was made clear that you should always try to use a structural compound index file for your indexing operations because of its power and ease of use. With a structural index file, whenever you open a database file, all the index tags in that file will be opened and updated automatically. As a result, the task of using and maintaining your indexes with a structural index file is simple and automatic.

Indexing plays a very important role in manipulating data in a database. Besides speeding up the process of data query, it allows you to build the links for joining different database files together. Indexing also allows you to group data elements so that you can produce summary reports. Furthermore, by arranging your data records with the indexing operation, you are able to systematically edit your data in the database. In the next chapter, you will learn how to modify the contents of your database files.

7
Editing Data

An Overview

In preceding chapters, you learned how to create database files and order their records. This chapter explains how to make changes to database files, which includes modifying the database structure and editing the contents of its data records.

Modifying a database structure enables you to add new data fields to and remove existing data fields from an existing database file, as well as change the attributes of existing data fields. In addition to showing you how to modify data structures, this chapter will discuss potential problems. Then, you will learn how to add new records to and permanently remove existing records from your database files; finally, you'll learn how to edit the contents of those records.

Modifying the structure of a database file and its data records can be done either with the menu interface or the appropriate FoxPro commands, and both methods will be detailed in this chapter.

Copying Database Files

Although the primary focus of this chapter is on modifying the structure and contents of existing database files, it is important to address the process of copying database files because modifications become permanent once they are carried out, and you may want to make a copy of your original files to use for reference and as backup files. Copying files gives you the opportunity to return to the original contents of a database file at any time, which is a necessary option if you discover that you have made mistakes in your changes or simply decide to discard all the changes that you have made and start over.

There are two ways to make a copy of an existing database file. One is to use the System's Filer utility to copy an existing database file to a new database file. The other is to select the Copy To option from the Database menu.

USING THE SYSTEM'S FILER

To make a copy of an existing database file using the System's Filer utility, select Filer from the Help menu popup. When the Filer window appears, it contains all of the disk files stored in the current directory. At this point, tag the database file that you would like to copy with either the mouse or the keyboard. Note, however, that you can tag only those files that are *not* currently open in a work area. Therefore, you must close any open files that you would like to copy before selecting the Filer option. After you have tagged a file, select the Copy button and assign a name to the duplicate file.

As an exercise, make a copy of SALESMAN.DBF. First, tag that file by highlighting it with the mouse or the keyboard. Click the mouse button on SALESMAN.DBF in the file list in the Filer dialog or, with the keyboard, move the cursor to that file with the arrow keys and press the Spacebar (see Figure 7.1).

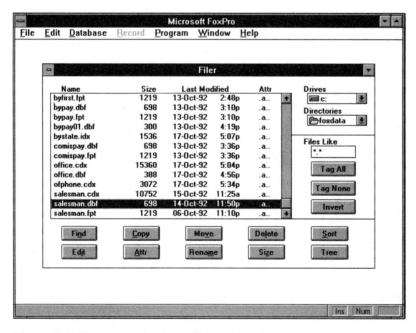

Figure 7.1 Tagging a database file

If you try to tag a file whose name appears in light gray in the file list, there will be no response because that file is currently open in a work area. If this is the case, exit the Filer and close the file. Then you can return to the Filer and continue the copy operation.

If you tag the wrong file, just move to a different file and tag it. Or you can select the Tag None button to remove the current tag and then tag the one you want.

Once the file is tagged, create the duplicate file by clicking the mouse on the Copy button or by pressing the Alt+C key combination. The Copy dialog appears, showing the directory and filename of the duplicate copy (see Figure 7.2). To save the duplicate file to a directory that is different from that shown in the dialog, change it accordingly.

In Figure 7.2, you can see that the default setting of the Copy Tagged Files As text box is *.*. This allows you to copy an entire set of tagged files at one time. You will learn how to use this feature in later exercises, but here, because you are copying only SALESMAN.DBF, replace *.* with the name of your duplicate file (e.g., OLDFILE.DBF).

Two check boxes are provided in the Copy dialog: Replace existing files and Preserve directories. If you check Replace existing files, any files with the same name as the duplicate in the target directory will be overwritten. Otherwise, you will be warned about the existence of a file with the same name before the file is

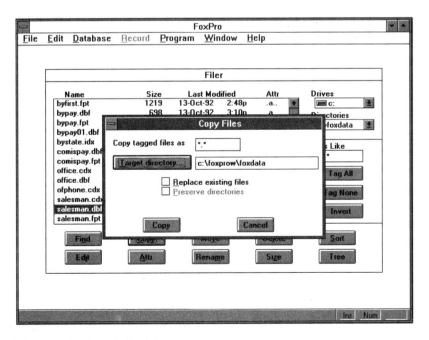

Figure 7.2 Target directory

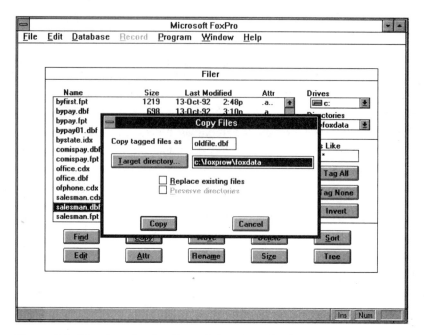

Figure 7.3 Naming the duplicated database file

overwritten. If you check the Preserve directories box, the current directory structure will be copied to the target directory. For this exercise, however, you do not need to check either box because you will be saving the duplicate file in the current directory with a different filename (see Figure 7.3).

After naming your output file and specifying the target directory, select the Copy button to create the duplicate file. You will return to the Filer window and see the duplicate file (OLDFILE.DBF) listed in the window (see Figure 7.4).

Copying Associated Files

When you make a copy of an existing database that contains memo fields, you may not be able to use the duplicate database file unless you also have copied its associated memo file. For example, if you attempt to open OLDFILE.DBF at this point, the following error message would result:

```
MEMO file is missing/invalid.
```

The reason for this is that the contents of the memo fields are saved in the SALESMAN.FPT memo file. Therefore, to use SALESMAN.DBF, you also must make a copy of SALESMAN.FPT and save it as OLDFILE.FPT.

Similarly, if the database file you are copying has a structural compound index file, you will want to duplicate its .CDX file as well. Otherwise, you must re-create the structural compound index file.

Editing Data   237

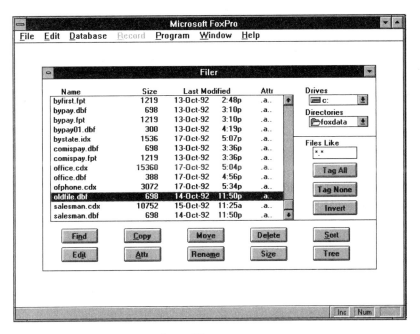

Figure 7.4 **Duplicate database file**

Copying Multiple Files

There is a shortcut that enables you to copy all the files that are associated with a database file: Collectively tag all the files that you need to copy and then copy them as a group. The wildcard character (*) is used to select all the files sharing the same filename as SALESMAN. For example, to make a copy of all the files that are associated with SALESMAN.DBF (including SALESMAN.FPT and SALESMAN.CDX), specify SALESMAN.* in the Files Like text box in the Filer dialog (see Figure 7.5) and select the Copy button. As a result, the Filer displays only those files that are associated with SALESMAN.DBF. At this point, choose the Tag All button to tag all these files (see Figure 7.6). You also can tag multiple files by pressing the Shift key while clicking the mouse successively on each of the filenames. This method is very useful when you have different filenames that you need to tag as a group.

After tagging your files, choose the Copy button. When the Copy dialog appears, enter the names for the target files (e.g., OLDFILE.*) in the Copy tagged files as text box (see Figure 7.7). Since we created the OLDFILE.DBF in our last exercise, you will be prompted to overwrite it. In this case, select the Yes button to re-create OLDFILE.DBF with its associated files.

After the target files are named, select the Copy button to create the duplicate files and exit the Copy dialog. When you return to the Filer, you can change the Files Like text box to OLDFILE.* to view the files you have just created (see

238   Understanding FoxPro 2.5 for Windows

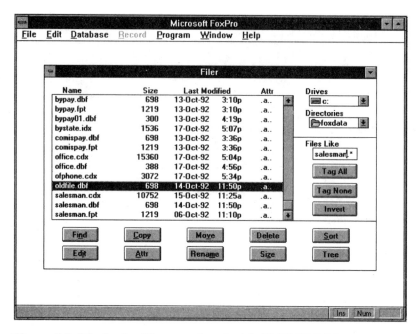

Figure 7.5   Displaying files associated with OFFICE.DBF

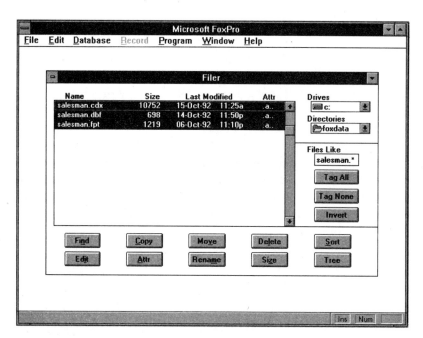

Figure 7.6   Tagging files associated with OFFICE.DBF

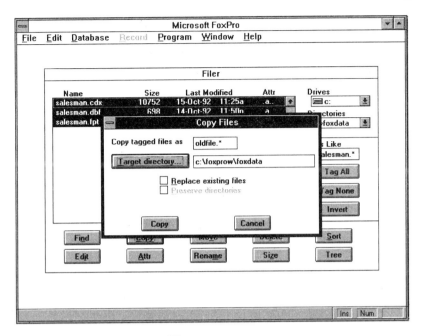

Figure 7.7 Naming target files

Figure 7.8). In Figure 7.8, you can see that OLDFILE.DBF, OLDFILE.FPT, and OLDFILE.CDX have been created with the copying operation.

USING THE COPY TO MENU OPTION

Instead of using the Filer, a copy of an existing database file also can be made by choosing the Copy To option from the Database menu popup. This option allows you to create a copy of the current database file. It creates a new structure and then copies all the data records from the existing database file to the new structure. If the database file contains memo fields, it copies the memo fields to a memo file as well. Note that it does not copy the associated structural compound index file.

As an exercise, use the Copy To option to make a copy of SALESMAN.DBF and its associated .FPT memo file. Then, name the duplicate files TEST.DBF and TEST.FPT, respectively. To do that, open SALESMAN.DBF in the current work area and then choose the Copy To option from the Database menu popup. When the Copy To dialog appears, assign a name to the duplicate file. You can do this by entering the filename in the Copy filename text box in the Save As dialog after selecting the Save As... button (see Figure 7.9).

In the Save As dialog, you also can verify the drive and directory for the duplicate file; then select the OK button to return to the Copy To dialog. When you return to

240 Understanding FoxPro 2.5 for Windows

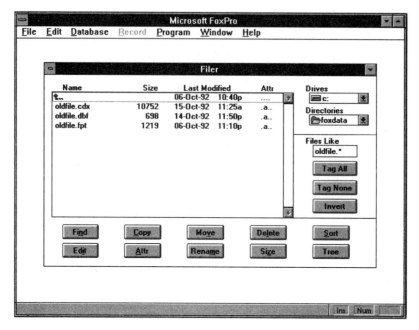

Figure 7.8 Listing duplicated files

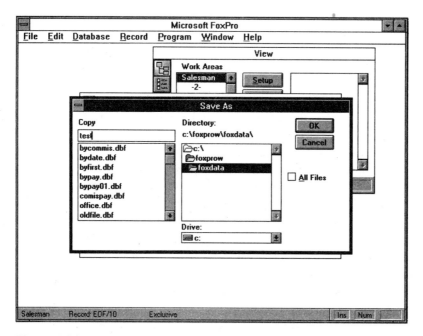

Figure 7.9 Naming the duplicate database file

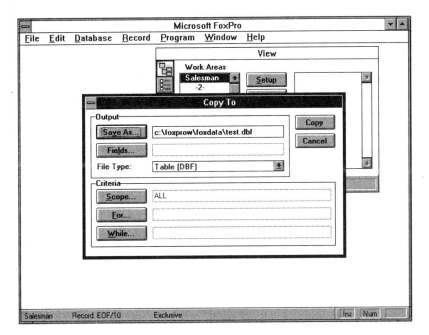

Figure 7.10 The Copy To dialog

the Copy To dialog, you will see that the name of the duplicate file is shown in the Save As... text box (see Figure 7.10). You also can enter the filename directly to the Save As text box using the Save As... button. To make sure the duplicate file is saved in the correct drive and directory, include the drive and directory with the filename.

When you enter the filename directly to the Save As... text box, it is not necessary to specify the file extension. When "Table(DBF)" appears in the File Type drop-down list, the file that you are creating will have .DBF automatically assigned as its file extension. Its associated memo file with the same root filename also will be created. It is important to remember that the Copy To option will not duplicate the structural compound index file belonging to the database file you have just copied. You must use the Filer to duplicate and save it.

Select the Copy button in the Copy To dialog to begin copying SALESMAN.DBF and SALESMAN.FPT to TEST.DBF and TEST.FPT. Afterward, bring up TEST.DBF to verify its contents.

Copying Selected Data Fields and Records

In the preceding example, the Copy To option was invoked to make a copy of an existing database file that had the same data structure and included all the data

242   Understanding FoxPro 2.5 for Windows

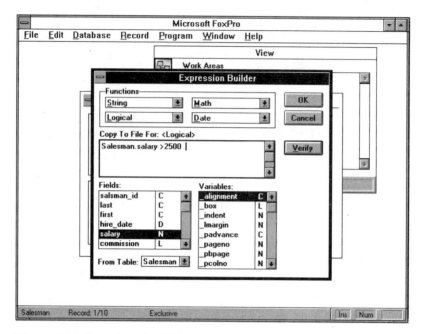

Figure 7.11 Defining the filter condition

records of the original database file. This same option allows you to copy selected data records to your target file by specifying a filter condition to identify the designated records that you want to copy; this also is possible for data fields.

As an exercise, assume that you want to copy to a file named HIGHPAY.DBF records for members of the sales staff in SALESMAN.DBF whose salaries are greater than $2,500. In addition, you want to include only the LAST and SALARY fields in the target file. To do that, again open the SALESMAN database in the current work area and select the Copy To option from the Database menu pad to bring up the Copy To dialog.

When the Copy To dialog appears, check the For box to bring up the Expression Builder. Use the Expression Builder to specify the filter condition for selecting the records that fit the parameters given above—in this case, SALARY > 2500 (see Figure 7.11). After defining the filter condition, select the OK button to exit from the Expression Builder dialog.

To choose the data fields to include in your target file, select the Fields button when you return to the Copy To dialog. When the Field Picker dialog appears, select the data fields that you want to copy. For this exercise, select LAST and SALARY and move them to the Selected Fields list, as shown in Figure 7.12.

After you have defined the field list, exit from the Field Picker dialog by selecting the OK button. When you return to the Copy To dialog, enter the name of the target file (e.g., c:\foxprow\foxdata\highpay.dbf) in the Save As... text box. Note at this point that the For and Fields text boxes have been filled (see Figure 7.13).

Editing Data 243

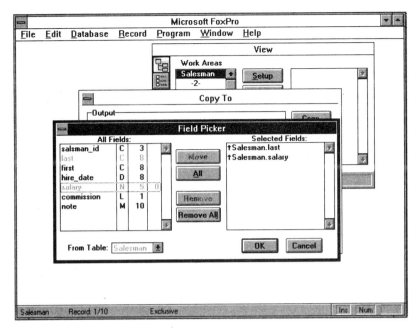

Figure 7.12 Selecting data fields to copy

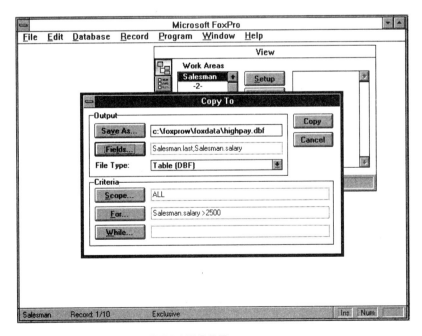

Figure 7.13 Saving HIGHPAY.DBF

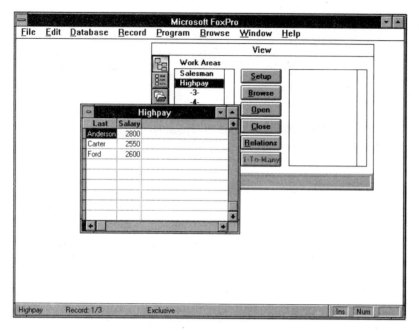

Figure 7.14 Viewing the records of HIGHPAY.DBF

The final step in the creation of the duplicate file HIGHPAY.DBF is to select the OK button. Now you can open and view the contents of the duplicate file in the usual way. Do that now and compare your screen with Figure 7.14 to see that the file contains three data records and two fields from the SALESMAN database.

Renaming Database Files

There may be occasions when you want to change the filename of a database. This involves using the Filer and choosing the Rename operation to assign a new name to an existing database file (remember to rename its associated memo and index files, as well).

You may want to try this procedure using the duplicate file named TEST.DBF that you created in an earlier exercise. Because SALESMAN.DBF has its associated memo file named SALESMAN.FPT, the Copy To operation also created a corresponding TEST.FPT memo file. To rename the TEST.DBF file to BACKUP.DBF, you must also rename the TEST.FPT to BACKUP.FPT. If this is not done, you will not be able to open BACKUP.DBF without its associated memo file.

To rename TEST.DBF and its associated TEST.FPT memo file, bring up the Filer dialog by selecting the Filer option from the Help menu popup. (Make sure

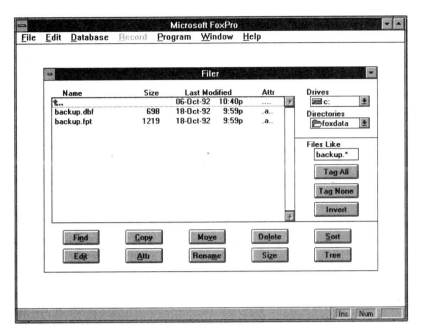

Figure 7.15 Listing the renamed files

that the files you want to rename are not open.) When the Filer dialog appears, select the files you would like to rename by specifying TEST.* in the Files Like text box and press the Enter key. When the files you have specified appear, select the Tag All button to tag them. Next, choose the Rename button by pressing the Alt+M key combination or by clicking the mouse on the button. When the Rename dialog appears, you are asked to assign a name to each of the files that you tagged—in this exercise, TEST.DBF and TEST.FPT. After you have renamed the two tagged files, you can verify the operation by listing Files Like BACKUP.* in the Filer.

In Figure 7.15, you can see that TEST.DBF and TEST.FPT have been renamed as BACKUP.DBF and BACKUP.FPT, respectively. Also notice that the Rename operation did not alter the sizes of the renamed files, nor did it change the time and date when the files were last modified.

Deleting Database Files

The System's Filer also can be used to permanently remove any files that you no longer need. First, tag the files that you want deleted and then choose the Delete button. It's a good idea to also delete all the memo and index files that are associated with the database files that you are deleting. Again, remember that you must close

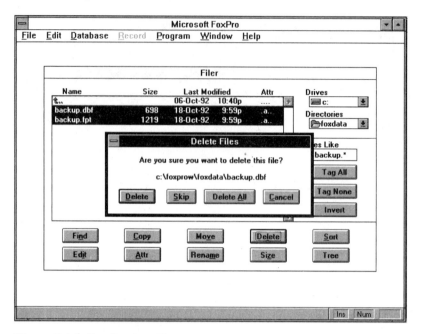

Figure 7.16 Confirming file deletion

the database files before you can delete them; you cannot delete any database file that is open in any of the work areas.

The procedure for deleting a set of files is very similar to that for renaming files. After you have tagged your files, choose the Delete button by pressing Alt+L or clicking your mouse on the button. A prompt appears asking you to confirm your decision to delete the tagged files. Try this process with BACKUP.DBF and BACKUP.FPT. Once you have tagged the two files in the Filer dialog and chosen Delete, you can respond to the confirmation prompt by choosing either the Delete button or by selecting the Delete All button (or press the A key) to delete all the files you have tagged at one time (see Figure 7.16).

It is important to be aware that the deletion of a file is permanent. Once you have deleted a file, it cannot be recovered by FoxPro. (It may, however, be possible to recover files through the use of special utilities such as UNDELETE in DOS 5.0 or The Norton Utilities.) Nevertheless, always be careful when deleting files.

Modifying the Database Structure

When you create a database file, every effort should be made to ensure that its data structure is correctly set up. It should include the correct data fields with the properly defined attributes enabling you to use the structure to organize your data elements efficiently for most, if not all, data management applications.

Sometimes, however, because of unforeseen changes in data requirements, you will need to modify your database structure at a later date to accommodate these changes, which may require the addition of new data fields or the deletion of others. Or you may need to change the attributes of some data fields to satisfy the new data requirements.

FoxPro accommodates the inevitability of changes to a database structure, and its procedure for modifying a data structure is simple. Open the View dialog by selecting the View option found in the Window menu pad. Open the database whose structure you want to modify in a work area. Next, select the Setup button by clicking on it or pressing the ALT-S key combination. From the Setup dialog, you select the Modify button to change the database structure.

During modification of a database structure, you can edit all the attributes of your existing data fields. Although you should be careful in making changes, do not worry about making mistakes in the process. You will be given the opportunity to cancel any changes that you make to the structure and will be asked if you want the modifications to be made permanent after you have finished the editing process. And in some cases, as a safety feature, you are able to return a structure to its original form.

To modify the structure of the SALESMAN database, invoke the Setup dialog after opening the database file in a work area by choosing the Setup button from the View window. Alternatively, select the Setup option from the Database menu popup. In response to your selection, FoxPro displays the Setup dialog—the same Setup dialog used in the exercises in Chapter 6. There it was used to create the index tags for your structural compound index file. Now it is invoked to modify the structure of the database file. Choose the Modify button by clicking on it, by pressing the letter "y," or by clicking your mouse on the button. In return, FoxPro displays the current structure of the database file (see Figure 7.17).

All the information about the existing data structure is visible in the Table Structure dialog shown in Figure 7.17: the name of the database file, the type and width of each of its data fields, and the data fields that have been used as index keys (identified with either an up arrow for ascending order or a down arrow for descending order).

ADDING NEW DATA FIELDS

There are three types of changes that you can make to a data structure. Of the three, two can be carried out by choosing the Insert and Delete buttons in the Table Structure dialog. Their use is fairly obvious: Select the Insert button to insert a new

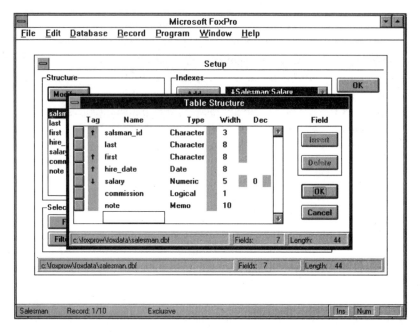

Figure 7.17 Viewing the existing data structure of SALESMAN.DBF

data field at the cursor position; select the Delete push button to delete an existing data field in the same way.

For practice, choose the Insert button to add the following three new data fields to the structure:

Name	Type	Width
SS_NO	Character	11
INITIAL	Character	1
MALE	Logical	1

The data field SS_NO is used for storing social security numbers for the sales staff, INITIAL is for middle initials, and the MALE logical field is used to code gender.

The order in which data fields appear in a structure is not an important factor in determining how you organize your data. You will learn in later chapters that you can display your data fields in whatever order you choose in the Browse window or in custom reports. Therefore, when you add new data fields to the structure, their order is really a matter of personal preference.

You do need to be aware, however, that you can insert data fields in the structure only one field at a time. Position your cursor where you would like to insert the data field, then choose the Insert button to open a row for the new data field. To

Editing Data 249

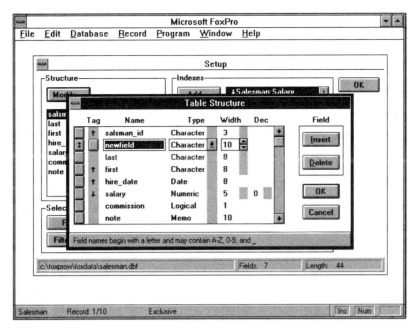

Figure 7.18 Inserting a new data field

insert the SS_NO field between the SALESMAN_ID and the LAST data fields, for instance, first place your cursor on the LAST field by pressing the Tab key until the symbol in front of the LAST field is highlighted. Or click your mouse immediately to the left of the LAST field name. Then select the Insert button. As a result, a new field with the default name of NEWFIELD is displayed at the current cursor position (see Figure 7.18.)

You can see that the new data field is set to a character field with a default width of 10 characters. At this point, you can change the name and the other attributes of the field that you inserted. Just type your changes over the default values provided for the new data field. Use the left- or right-arrow key to move to the left or right 1 character; press the Tab or the Shift-Tab key combination to move one column to the left or right. In this case, replace newfield with SS_NO and change its field width from 10 to 11 (see Figure 7.19).

Insert the new INITIAL and MALE fields in the structure in the same way. So that your screen looks like Figure 7.20, place the INITIAL character field between the LAST and FIRST fields, and MALE above the COMMISSION field. The widths of these two new fields are set to 1; MALE is a logical data type. If you make a mistake and insert the new fields in the wrong place, you can rearrange them later.

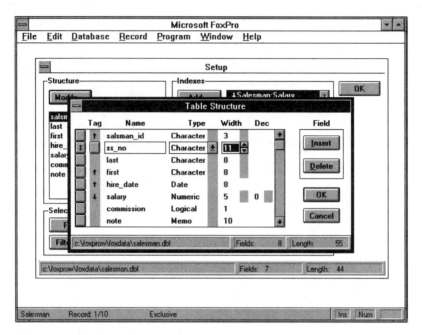

Figure 7.19 Defining the inserted data field

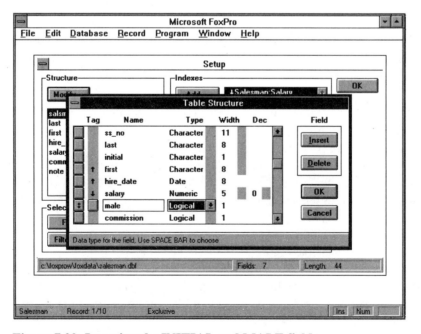

Figure 7.20 Inserting the INITIAL and MALE fields

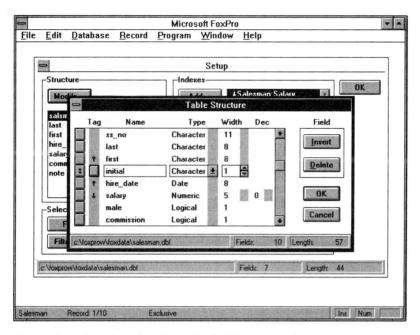

Figure 7.21 Moving the INITIAL field to a new location

REARRANGING EXISTING DATA FIELDS

The actual order of the data fields in the structure is not an important issue. You can always rearrange them to meet your specifications. For example, after inserting the INITIAL field in the SALESMAN.DBF data structure, you can move it to a new position, say, below the FIRST field. To move a data field, click the mouse on the button that appears to the left of the Tag button of the field. When a double-arrow symbol appears, hold down the mouse button and drag it to the new position.

As an exercise, click the mouse on the button to the left of the Tag button of the INITIAL field, drag it below the FIRST field, then release the button. With the keyboard, first use the Tab key to highlight the initial field. Then, while holding down the Ctrl key, press the up- or down-arrow key to move the field below the FIRST field. After the move, the order of the data fields should look like that shown in Figure 7.21.

DELETING EXISTING DATA FIELDS

The procedure for removing an existing data field from the database structure is very simple. All you have to do is select the data field to be deleted and then choose the Delete button. For example, to delete the COMMISSION field from the current

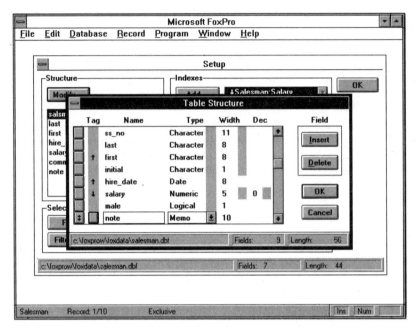

Figure 7.22 Deleting an existing data field

structure, select that field either with your mouse or the keyboard. Then, select the Delete button and the COMMISSION field is removed from the structure (see Figure 7.22). If you made the mistake of deleting the wrong data field, choose the Cancel button to exit from the Table Structure dialog without making any changes and start over.

REDEFINING EXISTING DATA FIELDS

The third type of change that you can make to a structure is the redefinition of existing fields. This may include renaming existing data fields, changing their field widths, and redefining their field types. Some of these operations can be carried out by editing field attributes; others require replacing the existing data fields with new data fields.

Renaming Data Fields

You can rename an existing data field just by editing its current name in the structure. As long as the new field name follows FoxPro's naming convention, the program will modify the existing field names. You may want to try renaming some of the data fields as an exercise. Afterward, however, change them back to their original names so that you can follow the next set of exercises.

Resetting Field Widths

You can also modify the width of existing character and numeric fields if your data requirements change. A longer last name, for example, would require that you widen the LAST data field in the structure. To do that, simply increase its field width. On the other hand, if you have set the field width too wide, you may want to narrow it to conserve storage space. (Note: You cannot change the widths of the date, memo, or logical fields, because they are determined by FoxPro.)

Widening an existing character data field adds blank spaces at the end of that field for each record. This has no effect on existing field values, except that the field will take up more space in the screen display. But, if you narrow its field width, you may lose part of the field's contents for some records—FoxPro will truncate the field by deleting the outermost right columns. Therefore, you must be careful not to narrow the field width when those fields contain character strings that are longer than what the new field width can accommodate.

Changing the width of a numeric field also allows you to store larger or smaller values in the redefined field. But again, you must not narrow the width of an existing field so that it becomes too small to accommodate existing values. If you do, some of the values will be lost. When you try to view these lost values, they will be displayed as a string of asterisks.

Changing Field Types

Although you can rename an existing data field and reset its width by just editing its field name and field width in the database structure, it does not necessarily make sense to redefine its field type in the same way. Each type of data field is set up to hold a specific type of data element in a predetermined format. And, even though FoxPro will permit you to modify the database structure in this way, the result frequently will be a complete loss of the original data in that field. In cases where you intend to replace one field with another that has a completely different type of data (in other words, in cases where changing the field type is a shortcut for deleting an existing field and inserting a new one), this data loss is acceptable. In other cases, however, you may discover that you incorrectly defined the original field type, or that particular items of information can be handled more efficiently if their field type is changed. Let's assume, for example, that you've defined ZIP as a five-digit numeric field. You will probably find that it is easier and more efficient to handle this data element as a character data type. In cases such as these, a precise understanding of how changing the field type affects the data contained in the field will allow you to choose the best method for modifying the database structure.

The following specific changes in the field type will not cause a loss of data or will result in a minimal loss of data:

- Character fields to memo fields—character fields can be safely and accurately changed to memo fields without risking a loss of data.
- Character fields that contain numeric strings (0 through 9, –, and . only) can be successfully changed to numeric or float fields with a minimal loss of data. Any leading zeros, however, will be lost, and the numeric data will be right justified.
- Character fields that contain dates can be changed to date fields with no data loss.
- Character fields can be converted to logical fields if they contain Yes, Y, or T (which are converted to a logical true value), or if they contain No, N, or F (which are converted to a logical false).
- Numeric fields can be changed to float fields with no loss of data.
- Float fields usually can be changed to numeric fields with no data loss.
- Numeric or float fields can be changed to character fields with no loss of data. Leading zeros will not be added to the character string.
- Date fields can be successfully changed to character fields only.
- Logical fields can be changed only to character fields without losing data. A logical true will become the letter T; a logical false will become F.

In all other cases, when you do not want to discard the information in the field and simply changing the field type will not preserve the contents of the data field, the best method is to modify the database structure: add a new field, enter data into the new field, and finally delete any field that is no longer needed.

For example, to change the COMMISSION logical field to a numeric field named COMIS_RATE (for saving rates of commissions), you cannot just edit the attributes of the COMMISSION field. Instead, you must first delete the existing field and then insert a new data field. But because we deleted the COMMISSION logical field in the last exercise, just insert the COMIS_RATE as a new numeric field in its place. Set the width of the numeric field to 5 characters with 2 decimal places (see Figure 7.23).

SAVING MODIFIED DATA STRUCTURES

After you have made all your changes to the existing data structure of a current database file, it is important to save the changes by choosing the OK button. Until

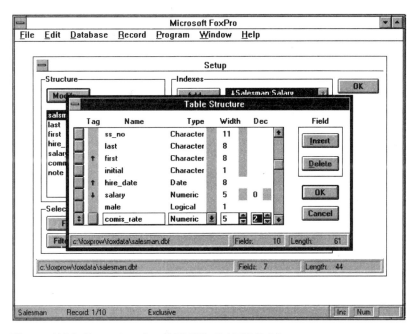

Figure 7.23 Inserting the COMIS_RATE field

you take that step, all the changes you have made up to this point are temporary. (This means that you can still discard these changes by choosing the Cancel button to exit the Modify Structure dialog.) Once you select the OK button, you are prompted to confirm that you want to save these changes permanently:

```
Make structure changes permanent?
```

Answer Yes to the prompt and all the changes are saved, and you will be returned to the Setup dialog. At this point, the Setup dialog will display the modified data structure (see Figure 7.24).

VIEWING RECORDS IN MODIFIED DATA STRUCTURES

After you have modified the structure of a database file, you can view the original data records in the new structure. To do that, first close the database file; otherwise, FoxPro may display the data records with the previous database. After you reopen it, you can view the data records in the new structure in the Browse window in either Browse or Change mode.

The records of the revised SALESMAN database are displayed in Browse mode in Figure 7.25. Notice that all the new data fields are blank. These fields will be filled with appropriate data elements later.

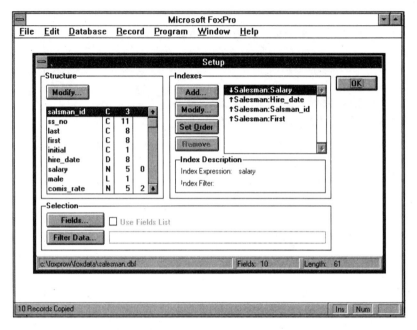

Figure 7.24 Viewing the modified data structure

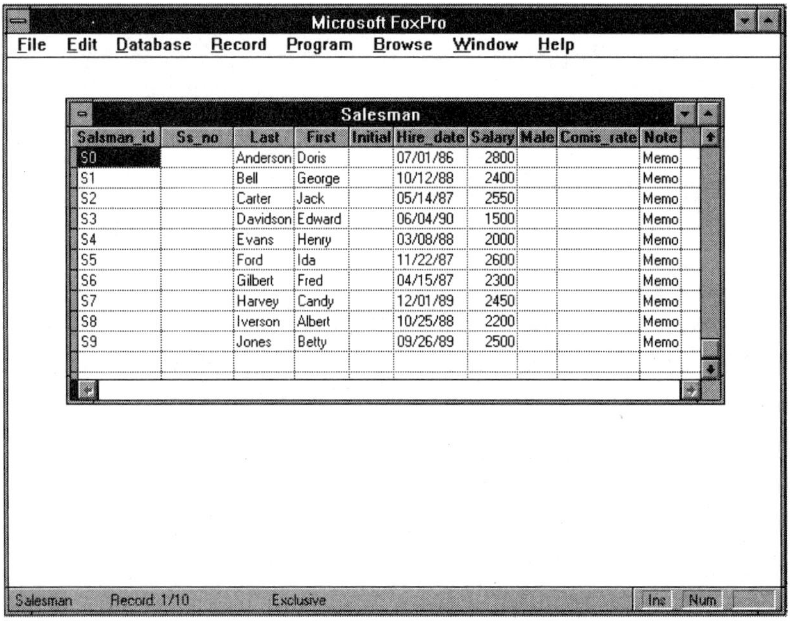

Figure 7.25 Viewing records in the modified database

CANCELING STRUCTURAL CHANGES

FoxPro is a very forgiving program. It allows you to reverse many actions you have taken. For example, during the process of making changes to the data structure, you had several opportunities to abort the process by choosing the Cancel button. Even after the changes were made permanent, the option was offered to return your database file to its status prior to the last structural change. This is possible because FoxPro always saves a copy of the original database file in a backup file. The backup file is named after its original file, but with .BAK as its extension. If the database file has an associated .FPT memo file, FoxPro creates a corresponding backup file with a .TBK file extension.

For example, after making your structural changes to SALESMAN.DBF, two new files were created: SALESMAN.BAK and SALESMAN.TBK. These two new files store the original records in the database structure (see Figure 7.26). Therefore, if you wanted to return the SALESMAN database to its original form, you would delete the current files in SALESMAN.DBF and SALESMAN.FPT. Then you would rename SALESMAN.BAK to SALESMAN.DBF and SALESMAN.TBK to SALESMAN.FPT. But to continue with our exercises, do not reverse the modifications made to SALESMAN.DBF and SALESMAN.FPT.

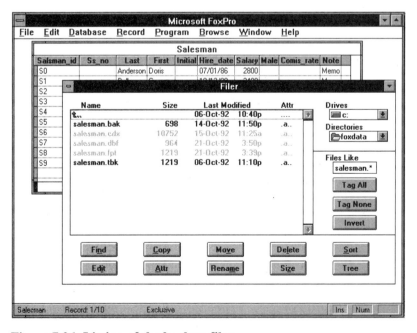

Figure 7.26 Listing of the backup files

REBUILDING INDEXES

When you modify a data structure, it is very important that you update all associated index files as well; and when you delete any existing data fields from a structure, you must also remove those indexes that used the deleted fields as index keys.

When you use a structural compound index file to hold all your index tags, index upkeep is automatic. When you open a database file in a work area, its associated structural file also will be opened. After you have finished modifying the data structure, the index tags will be automatically updated to reflect the changes. All the index tags that referred to any of the deleted data fields will be removed from the structural compound index file as well. This is a major advantage of using a structural compound index to hold all your indexes.

If you have added new data fields to a database structure, you can build new index tags that include any of these new fields. To do that, just modify the contents of the structural compound index file, adding the new index tags. For example, because we added the SS_NO field to the SALESMAN database structure in the last exercise, you also may want to add a new index tag, SS_N0, to its structural compound index file (see Figure 7.27).

If, however, you use other types of index files, you must modify them yourself to accommodate any changes that you make to the data structure. Any standard .IDX files that are no longer valid after the structural changes must be removed. Similarly, the contents of those nonstructural compound index files that contain index tags that use the deleted data fields also must be revised.

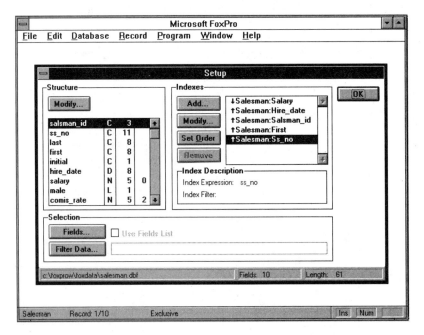

Figure 7.27 Updating indexes after modifying the data structure

Modifying Data Records

To accommodate changes in your data elements, you may find it necessary to modify the contents of your database records. This may involve editing the field values of existing records, adding new records to the database, and/or deleting existing records from the database.

EDITING RECORD CONTENTS

The contents of existing records in a database file can be edited while on display in the Browse window. Data values can be added to blank fields and alternate values can replace existing field values; these changes can be done either in Browse or Change mode.

Editing Records in Change Mode

As an exercise of the editing process, let's assign values to the fields we added in the last exercise—SS_NO, INITIAL, MALE, and COMIS_RATE. First, display the records in the Browse window. Note that the new structure has more fields than can be shown on the same screen in Browse mode; therefore, let's switch to Change mode to complete the exercise. Just select the Change option from the Browse menu popup (see Figure 7.28).

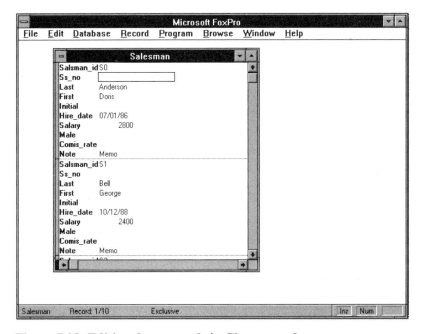

Figure 7.28 Editing data records in Change mode

This screen shows that currently, the fields that you created during the restructuring process are blank and ready to have appropriate values entered into them. It is important to remember that the order in which the records are displayed is determined by the master index that you designate. If you choose SALSMAN_ID as the master index, the data records are displayed according to the values in that field; if you designate SALARY as the master index, the records would be arranged by those values. But, for this exercise, keep SALSMAN_ID as the master index.

When you are ready to edit the field values, use your mouse to position the cursor on the field that you intend to change. On the keyboard, use the arrow keys to select the field earmarked for editing; with the cursor positioned on the correct data field, use the following keys for editing:

Key	Function
Left arrow	Move 1 character to the left
Right arrow	Move 1 character to the right
Up arrow	Move to the beginning of the previous field
Down arrow	Move to the beginning of the next field
Shift+Tab	Move to the beginning of the previous field
Tab	Move to the beginning of the next field
Home	Move to the beginning of the current field
End	Move to the end of the current field
PgUp	Move up one record
PgDn	Move down one record
Esc	Abort editing
Ctrl+End	Save changes and exit

After you have finished editing one record, move to the next. (As soon as you move the cursor beyond the last data field in the record you are editing, you will move to the next record.) To skip the next record, press the PgDn key; to return to the preceding record, press the PgUp key.

If you make mistakes during the editing process, you either can reedit the changes or abort all the changes made to that field by pressing the Esc key to exit from the Edit operation. If necessary, you can return to the data records to continue modifying the field values. But do not *close* the Browse window, because that step will render all the changes (mistakes included) permanent.

Editing Records in Browse Mode

Although more data fields can be viewed at one time in Change mode, editing records in Browse mode gives you the advantage of viewing more records on the same screen at one time, thus making it easier to move between existing records. One way to make use of both modes (using SALESMAN as an example) is to edit

Editing Data   261

the first record in the SALESMAN database in Change mode, and then switch to Browse mode by choosing the Browse option from the Browse menu popup.

While you are in Browse mode, use these keys to edit your records:

Key	Function
Left arrow	Move 1 character to the left
Right arrow	Move 1 character to the right
Up arrow	Move one record up
Down arrow	Move one record down
Shift+Tab	Move to the beginning of the previous field
Tab	Move to the beginning of the next field
Home	Move to the beginning of the current field
End	Move the the end of the current field
PgUp	Move to the first record on the screen
PgDn	Move to the last record on the screen
Esc	Abort editing
Ctrl+End	Save changes and exit

Other ways to manipulate the contents of a database for display are:

- Use the scroll control to display most of the data fields on the same screen.
- If you cannot display all the fields you want on the screen, rearrange them in the manner that best suits your editing needs. The procedure for rearranging displayed fields was discussed in Chapter 5.

So that you can continue with the exercises in this chapter, fill in the first five blank fields with the values shown in Figure 7.29 and then close the Browse window.

Editing Selected Data Fields

When you have a database that has more data fields than can be displayed in the same Browse window, you have the option of displaying only those fields that you need to edit. This is achieved by selecting the data fields earmarked for editing in the Setup dialog *before* displaying them in the Browse window.

We'll use this procedure to finish adding values to the blank fields for the last five records. Therefore, instead of showing all the data fields, we'll display in Browse mode only those fields that are related to your editing needs. They are: SS_NO, INITIAL, MALE, and COMIS_RATE. Other fields—the SALSMAN_ID and LAST fields—should be displayed to provide a reference point.

To select the data fields to be shown in Browse mode, check the Set Fields button after you have invoked the Setup dialog from the View window. Then, select the

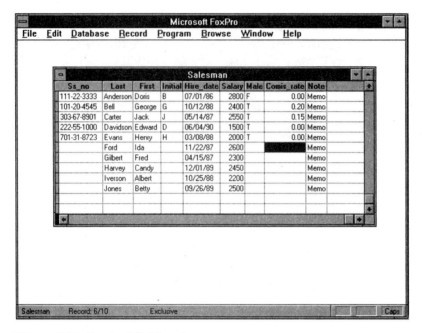

Figure 7.29 Revised fields values

fields you want in the Field Picker dialog. Figure 7.30 shows six data fields selected.

When you return to the Setup dialog, note that the Use Fields List box is checked. At this point, select the OK button to exit the Setup dialog and return to the View window; then select the Browse option. You'll see that only those data fields that you selected are displayed, whether you are in Browse or Change mode. Now, you can continue entering values in those blank fields for the last five records, as illustrated in Figure 7.31.

If you want to display all the data fields after you have completed the browsing or editing operation, you must exit the Browse window and return to the Setup dialog. Next, select the Fields... button and then select the Remove All button to clear the Selected Fields list box. Finally, click on the OK button to return to the Setup dialog. When you exit the Setup dialog and return to the View window, you may select the Browse option to display all of the data fields. Do this before the next exercise so that the Browse window will display all the fields in the SALESMAN database.

Editing Selected Data Records

The previous exercise showed you how to use the Set Fields operation to display only those fields that you need for editing your data records. Similarly, you can

Editing Data 263

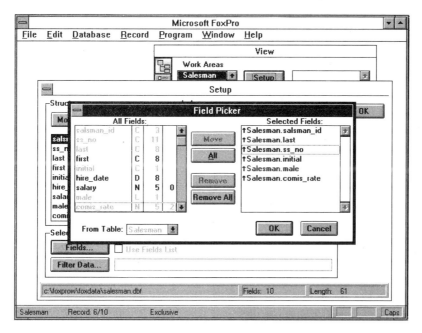

Figure 7.30 Selecting fields to be edited

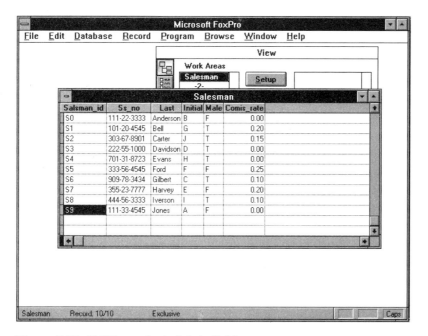

Figure 7.31 Editing selected data fields

display in the Browse window only a certain set of data records that you would like to edit. This is done by specifying a filter condition that screens the data records. Simply select the Filter Data button in the Setup dialog to gain access to the Expression Builder dialog. Then, follow the procedure that you learned in Chapter 6 for creating a filter condition to display selected records.

Saving Edited Data Records

Any changes made to a data field during the editing process are considered temporary until you save them. So be aware that if you press the Esc key in the middle of editing a field, you will lose all the changes that you have made to the field so far. To save these changes, either exit the Browse window view by double clicking on the Control box or by pressing the Ctrl+End key combination; or move the cursor to another field or record in the Browse window.

ADDING NEW DATA RECORDS

In addition to editing existing records, you also can add new records to a database file by selecting the Append option from the Record menu popup. This option is available after you have opened a database file in a work area, regardless of whether or not you are in the Browse window. In every case, when you select the Append option, a blank data entry form will be displayed in Change mode.

In order not to disturb the contents of SALESMAN.DBF, let's copy its records to a temporary database file (to be named SAMPLE.DBF) for the next set of exercises. To do that, use the Copy To operation that you learned earlier in this chapter. The resulting database, SAMPLE.DBF, will be an exact duplicate of SALESMAN.DBF. Remember, the Copy To operation will automatically copy the memo file, SALESMAN.FPT, to SAMPLE.TBK.

To create the structural compound index for SAMPLE.DBF, you must copy SALESMAN.CDX to SAMPLE.CDX using the Filer (close SALESMAN.DBF first). Then, you must add SAMPLE.CDX to the database's index files using the Setup dialog. To do that, select the Add button from the Setup dialog. As a result, the Open File dialog appears. At this point, open SAMPLE.CDX and return to the Setup dialog. When you return to the Setup dialog, you will see that all the index tags are copied from SALESMAN.CDX to SAMPLE.CDX (see Figure 7.32). This step is necessary if you intend to use the indexes to arrange the records in SAMPLE.DBF.

There is, incidentally, a somewhat more efficient method to copy these files. If the SALESMAN database is open, use the View window to close it. Then open the Filer. Select the three files—SALESMAN.DBF, SALESMAN.FPT, and

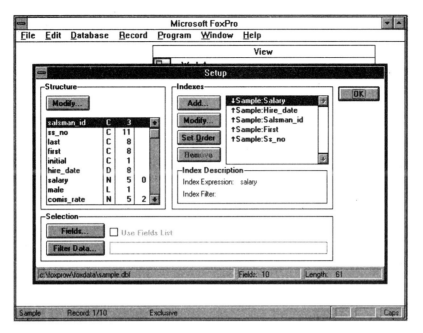

Figure 7.32 Creating the SAMPLE.CDX index file

SALESMAN.CDX—and make a copy of them, specifying the names of the copies as SAMPLE.*. Then, return to the View window and open SAMPLE.DBF. When you click on the Setup button to open the Setup dialog, you will notice that the structural compound index file also has been opened automatically.

To add new records to the SAMPLE database, choose the Append option from the Record menu popup after you have opened the database file in a work area. In response to selecting this menu option, a standard data entry form for a new record will be displayed. Note that in order to show as many data fields as possible, FoxPro always displays the data entry form in Change mode. You can switch to Browse mode by selecting the Browse option from the Browse menu popup. But in this case, because the SAMPLE database has too many data fields to be shown on the same screen, it is better to use Change mode for entering your data values.

Enter data values in the new record by using the editing keys discussed earlier. You may enter as many new records as needed. You'll see that as soon as one record begins to fill, the data entry form for the next new record will begin to show. As an exercise, add the two new records that are shown in Figure 7.33 to the SAMPLE database. Leave their memo fields blank.

New records will always be appended to the end of the file. If, however, you view them in Browse mode, the order in which they are displayed is determined by the master index that you designate. If you did not designate an index tag as the master index, the records would be displayed in the order in which they were

266 Understanding FoxPro 2.5 for Windows

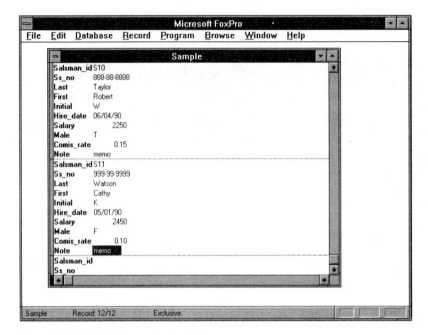

Figure 7.33 Adding new records

entered. In this case, however, the records were entered in the order based on values in the SALESMAN_ID field, as illustrated in Figure 7.34.

If you had chosen another index tag as the master index, they obviously would be displayed in that order. Say you selected SALARY as the master index in the Setup dialog. When you returned to Browse mode, the records would be ordered by their salary values, as shown in Figure 7.35.

Notice in this figure that a line is open at the end of the table for appending another new record. You could continue adding new records to the file at this stage, or you could save the new records either by closing the Browse window or by pressing the Ctrl+End key combination.

If you set SALSMAN_ID as the master index, you may find that the records in SAMPLE.DBF will be arranged in an order that places the records of S10 and S11 between records S1 and S2 (see Figure 7.36). This is because the character string S2 is considered to be greater (in ASCII value) than that of S11 and S10. Therefore, if you would like to arrange SALSMAN_ID in a natural numeric order, you must change S0 to S00, S1 to S01, S2 to S02, etc. Since the records in the SAMPLE database are entered in a natural numeric order according to SALSMAN_ID, you can display them in that order by not selecting any index tag as the master index. For the next exercise, display the records in SAMPLE.DBF in the original order by deselecting salary as the index tag in the Setup dialog.

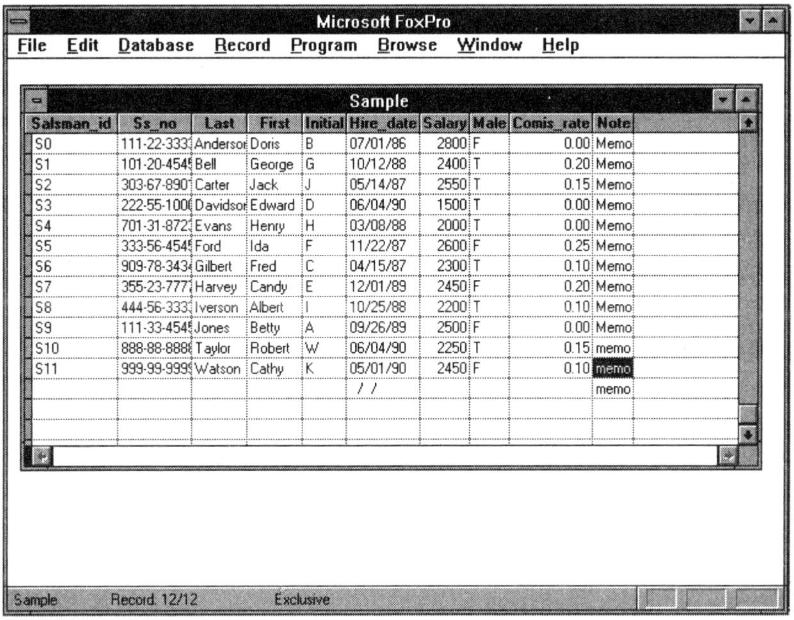

Figure 7.34 Appended records

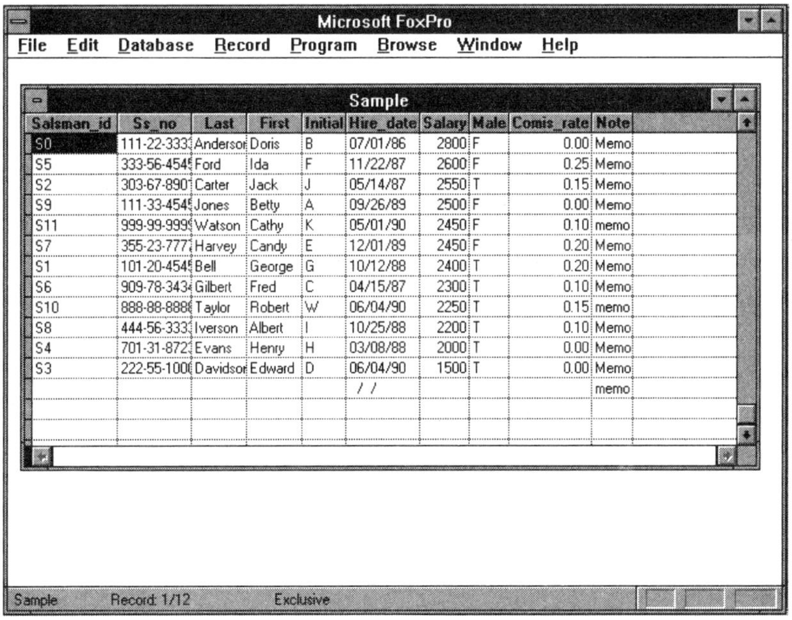

Figure 7.35 Ordering new records by SALARY master index

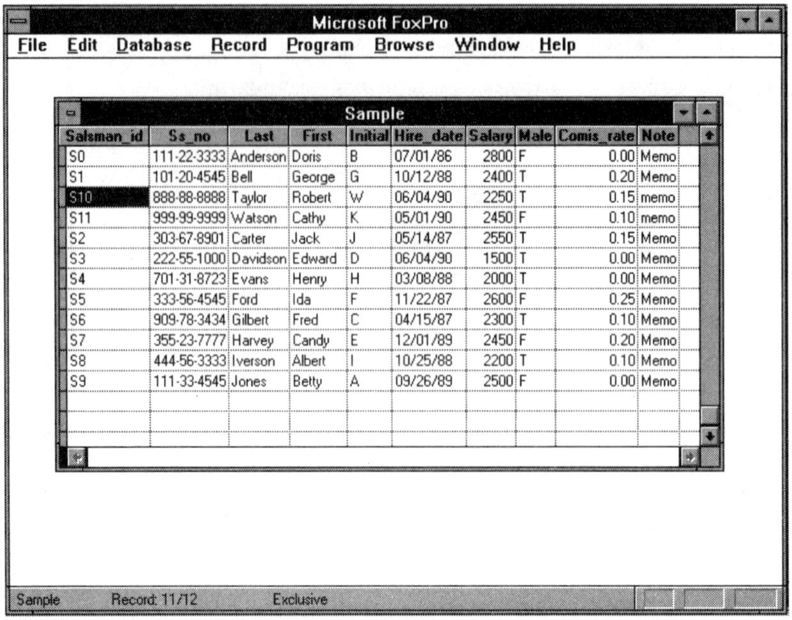

Figure 7.36 Ordering new records by SALSMAN_ID master index

DELETING EXISTING DATA RECORDS

Any records that you no longer need can be deleted permanently from a database file by following a two-step process: mark the records to be deleted, and then perform the Pack operation that physically removes records marked for deletion. These procedures are detailed in the next sections. (Note: Until you pack the database file, any records marked for deletion can still be recalled. This is a safety feature that guards against deleting the wrong data records by accident. Once the database file is packed, all the records that were marked for deletion will be permanently removed; you will not be able to recover them using FoxPro.)

Marking Data Records for Deletion

There are a number of ways to mark records for deletion: one at a time, as a group, by defining the record Scope, or by specifying the appropriate filter condition.

To delete an individual record, just mark that record in either Browse or Change mode by using the mouse or the keyboard. Using the mouse, simply click on the column between the window frame and the record's first field. Try this on the fourth record (SALSMAN_ID = "S3"). Click the mouse in front of the "S3" field value; the small vertical rectangular box to the left of the record will be shaded, indicating that it is marked for deletion (see Figure 7.37). If you click the mouse on the same

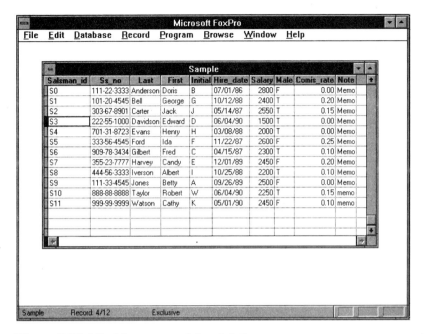

Figure 7.37 Marking a record for deletion

location again, the deletion mark will be removed. If you are using the keyboard, choose the Delete option from the Record menu popup after highlighting the record. As an exercise, use the down arrow to highlight record S5 and then choose the Delete option from the Record menu. As a result, the Delete dialog appears.

You are next asked to define the scope and filter condition to identify the records to be deleted. In this case, all you want to delete is the highlighted record, so simply choose the Delete button to mark the record, as shown in Figure 7.38. The highlighted record is then marked for deletion—indicated by the shaded vertical rectangular box in front of it.

Marking a Group of Records for Deletion

You can delete more than one record at a time by defining either the record scope or the filter condition to select a group of records for deletion. The record scope specifies a section of records and includes one or more contiguous records; the filter condition screens the records for deletion.

Defining the Record Scope

To delete a set of records, select the Delete option from the Record menu, regardless of which record is highlighted. When the Delete dialog appears, select the Scope...

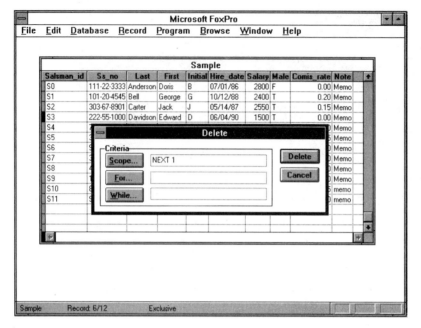

Figure 7.38 The delete dialog

button to select the range of contiguous records to delete. A Scope dialog appears that contains the following four radio buttons, as shown in Figure 7.39:

- All—marks every record in the database for deletion. The result will be an empty database file that contains only the database structure.

- Next—marks a block of consecutive records starting from the current cursor position. The default value of NEXT is 1, meaning that only the current record will be deleted; however, you can enter any number you choose.

- Record—marks a specific record for deletion by prompting you to enter the record number in a text box. The text box will appear next to the radio button once the button is selected.

- Rest—marks for deletion all the records from the current record to the end of the file.

Specifying Filter Conditions

To mark a set of records for deletion by specifying a filter condition—let's say all the records belonging to the male sales staff—select the For... button after you select the Delete option from the Record menu popup; then use the Expression Builder to define the filter condition.

Editing Data 271

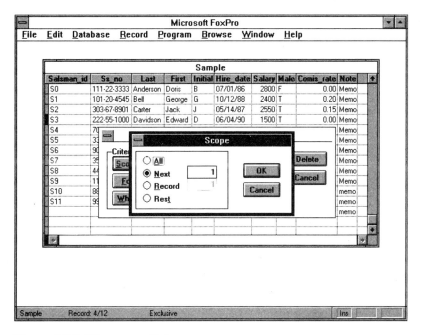

Figure 7.39 The scope dialog

To continue with our example, if you would like to delete all the records belonging to the male salespeople, you would define MALE = .T. as the filter condition (see Figure 7.40). After selecting the OK button to return to the Delete dialog, select the Scope button to bring up the Scope dialog and select the All radio mark to subject all the records to the filter condition. When you return to the Delete dialog, select the Delete button to mark the set of records. As a result, all the male records (in addition to records S3 and S5, which were marked earlier) are marked for deletion, as illustrated in Figure 7.41.

It is important to note that when using filter conditions to select records for deletion, in most cases, you will want to set the Scope to All because this subjects all the records in the database file to the filter conditions; otherwise, only the highlighted record will be subjected to the filter conditions. The For filter determines which records are deleted within the range of records defined by Scope.

Recalling Marked Data Records

Once you have marked a record for deletion, the deletion tag remains attached to the records until you take one of two actions: remove the marked record permanently from the database file or remove the deletion tag by recalling the marked records. Otherwise, the deletion marks (and the deleted records) will remain even after you close the database file.

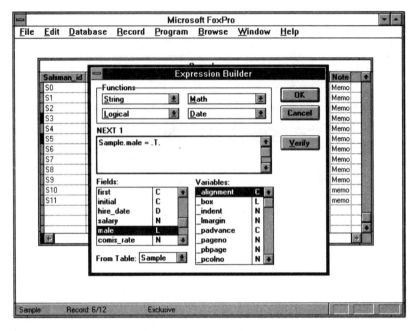

Figure 7.40 Defining deletion filter condition

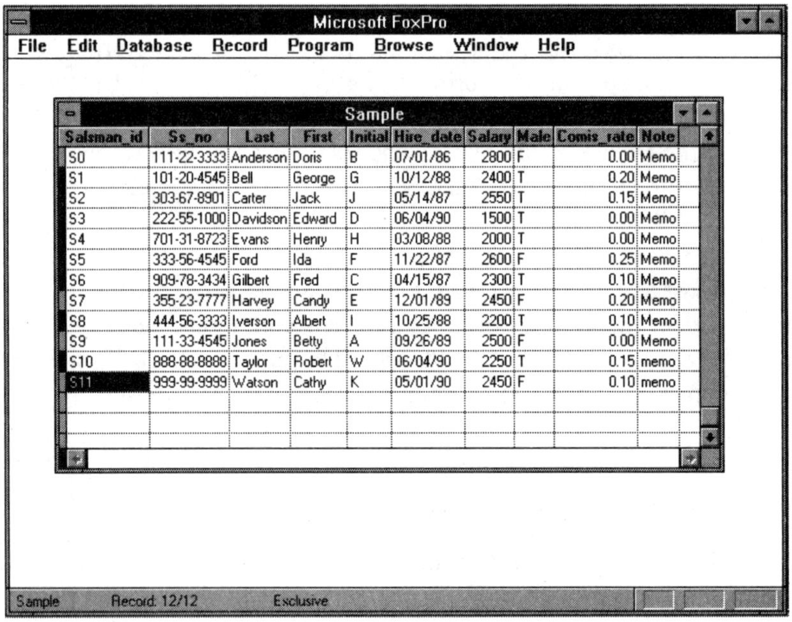

Figure 7.41 MALE records marked for deletion

The first way to recall a record marked for deletion is to select the Recall option from the Record menu popup and then define the record scope and filter condition. The second is to remove the deletion marks from records one by one while you view the records in the Browse window. For example, if you decide to recall some of the records that are marked for deletion in the SAMPLE database, select the Recall option from the Record popup. FoxPro then displays the Scope, For, and While check boxes from which you can specify the record scope and filter conditions for selecting the records that you intend to recall.

The process of defining the record scope and filter conditions for restoring records is identical to that used to select the records for deletion. Any marked records that satisfy the filter condition and are within the scope will be recalled.

So, to recall some of the records that we marked for deletion above—let's say those belonging to male salespeople whose salaries are at least $2,400—specify the record scope and filter condition accordingly. That is, select the All radio button after checking the Scope box, then click on the For... button to enter SALARY => 2400 as the filter condition. As a result, when you view the records in the SAMPLE database, you can see that some of the records that were marked for deletion have been recalled. Compare Figure 7.42 with Figure 7.41. The records for Bell (S1) and Carter (S2) have been recalled.

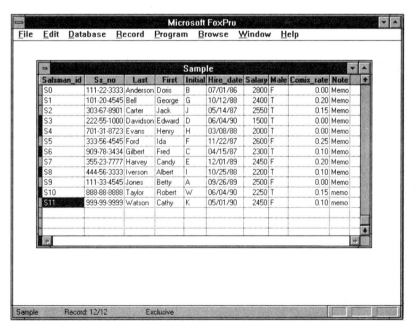

Figure 7.42 Recalling selected records

Recalling records one by one while they are displayed in the Browse window has the advantage of allowing you to review the records that you think you want to recall. To use this method, simply click your mouse on the deletion mark next to the record you intend to remove; repeat this process for each record that you are going to recall. Try this method by recalling the record S4. Click your mouse on the deletion mark next to the record. Note that there are now only four records marked for deletion.

Removing Marked Records

The Pack operation should be used only after you are sure that the records that you have selected are the ones that you want to delete from the database file. Select the Pack option from the Database menu popup and you will see the following prompt that requires you to confirm your action:

```
Pack c:\foxprow\foxdata\sample.dbf?
```

Answer Yes to the prompt, and all the marked records will be permanently removed from the database file. Display the contents of SAMPLE.DBF now and you will see that only eight records remain (see Figure 7.43).

Remember, the Pack operation is permanent, so it is a good idea to make a backup copy of your database file before packing it. To repeat: Once the Pack operation is complete, there is no way to recover the deleted records.

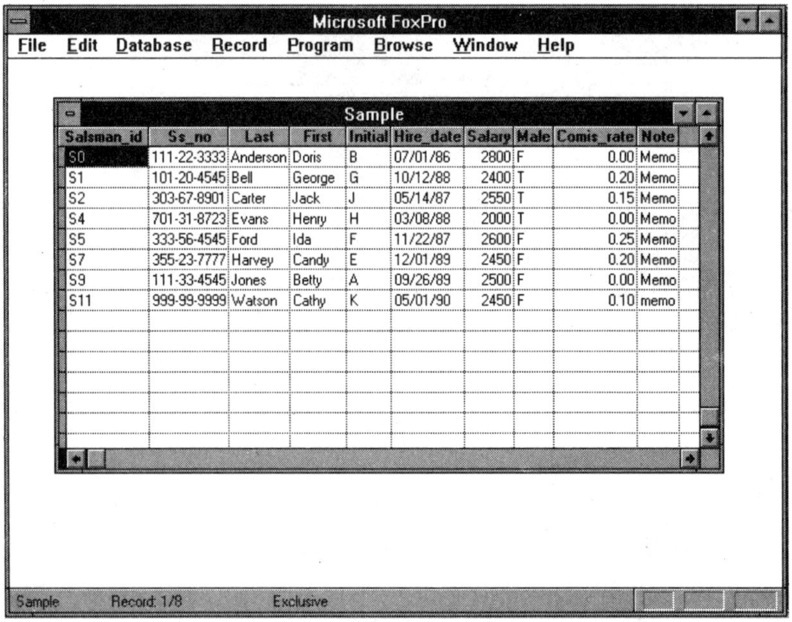

Salsman_id	Ss_no	Last	First	Initial	Hire_date	Salary	Male	Comis_rate	Note
S0	111-22-3333	Anderson	Doris	B	07/01/86	2800	F	0.00	Memo
S1	101-20-4545	Bell	George	G	10/12/88	2400	T	0.20	Memo
S2	303-67-8901	Carter	Jack	J	05/14/87	2550	T	0.15	Memo
S4	701-31-8723	Evans	Henry	H	03/08/88	2000	T	0.00	Memo
S5	333-56-4545	Ford	Ida	F	11/22/87	2600	F	0.25	Memo
S7	355-23-7777	Harvey	Candy	E	12/01/89	2450	F	0.20	Memo
S9	111-33-4545	Jones	Betty	A	09/26/89	2500	F	0.00	Memo
S11	999-99-9999	Watson	Cathy	K	05/01/90	2450	F	0.10	memo

Figure 7.43 Data records remaining after pack operation

REPLACING DATA FOR MULTIPLE RECORDS

There are a number of ways to replace individual field values in one or more data records. One is to edit the existing records individually with the procedure discussed earlier in this chapter so that they contain new values in the data fields. But another—easier—way to replace a set of values in a given field is to select the Replace option from the Record menu popup.

Let's say that as the result of a decision to award a 10-percent salary increase to those salespeople who were hired before December 31, 1988, you have to change the salaries for several members of the sales staff. There are two ways to do this. The first way—a tedious process—is to edit the value in the SALARY field for each salesperson who qualified for the increase. The better way is to systematically replace all the field values involved as a group. To do that, first choose the Replace option from the Record menu popup. When the Replace dialog appears, select from the field list the data field whose existing value you would like to replace with a new value. In the With... text box, enter the new value in the form of an expression. Use the Scope, For, and While check boxes to specify the record scope and filter condition for selecting the records involved.

For this exercise, select SALARY as the data field whose values you would like to replace. Then, enter the expression that will create the new value in the With... text box, in this case:

```
salary*1.10
```

which represents a 10-percent increase in the value of the existing SALARY field (see Figure 7.44). Note that clicking on the With... button leads to the Expression Builder, where you can build and verify a valid expression.

If you were to select the Replace button at this point to make the change, only a single record would be affected because the Replace option by default operates only on the current record. But because you want to make changes to multiple records, you must define the record scope and filter condition for the data records whose values you are replacing. First, check the Scope box and, because you want to make changes to all the records in the database that meet a specific condition, select All for the record scope. Next, because you want to change the contents of the SALARY fields for only some of the records—namely, those showing the hire date as on or before December 31, 1988—select the For... button and enter HIRE_DATE <= {12/31/88} as the expression in the FOR Clause text box in the Expression Builder (see Figure 7.45).

Select the OK button to return to the Replace dialog. To start the Replace operation, choose the Replace button; the values in the SALARY field for all the records that you selected will be replaced with the new values (see Figure 7.46).

In this figure, you can see that the salary values for the first five salespeople in the SAMPLE database have changed because they were hired before December

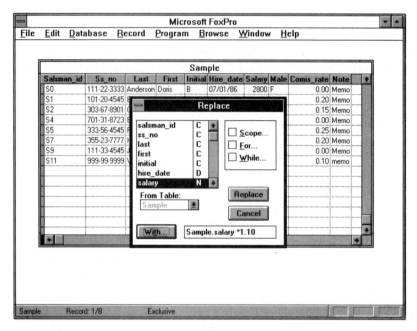

Figure 7.44 Defining the expression for replacing a value

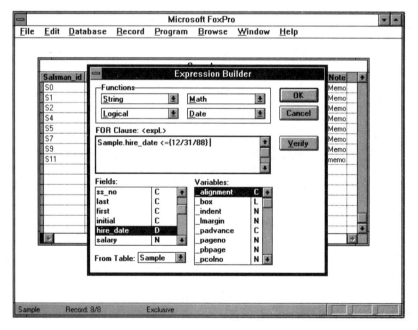

Figure 7.45 Defining filter conditions for replacing records

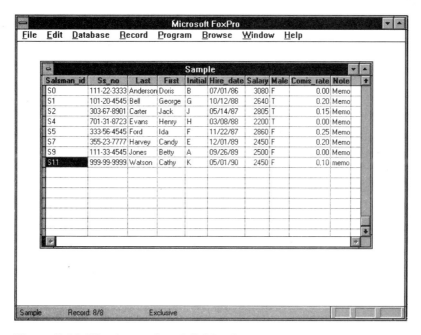

Figure 7.46 Viewing replaced field values

31, 1988; the salary for Anderson has changed from $2,800 to $3,080, an increase of $280 (10 percent of $2,800).

IDENTIFYING AND REMOVING DUPLICATED RECORDS

In a database file, there may be duplicate values in different records for the same data field. Some of these duplicate values are necessary and acceptable; others may represent data entry errors. For example, while it is acceptable to have more than one record with the same state code in the state data field, the same social security number obviously should not appear in the SS_NO data field in more than one record. Such a duplicate field value means either that you have mistyped the social security number in a new record or that you have entered a duplicate record to the database file. In either case, you should correct the error.

Obviously, if a database file has a large number of records, it can be difficult to spot any duplicate records. One possible solution is to index the database on the data field in which you think the duplicate field values may occur. When this index is designated as the master index, all the records will be arranged by their values in this field. As a result, it is easier to notice any duplicate values in the index field. For example, if the SS_NO index tag is set as the master index, a new record entered with a duplicate value in the SS_NO field of the SALESMAN database will be displayed right below an existing record with the same social security number, making it easy to spot.

Once you have found the records with duplicate field values, you can either edit them or remove them from the file. If you choose to remove the records, use the procedures discussed earlier to mark and then delete them with the Pack operation.

Another method for removing duplicate records is to copy the unique records in the database file to another database. To do that, again index the database on the data field that contains duplicate values. This time, however, select the Unique option. As a result, all the records with duplicate values in the index field will be ignored and only unique values in the indexed field will remain. Therefore, if you copy these records to a new file, the file will no longer contain any duplicate records. You can then replace the original database file with the file just created.

As an exercise, add a duplicate record to the SAMPLE file for Anderson, as shown in Figure 7.47. Notice that records S0 and S12 are identical except for their identification numbers—every record entered, regardless of its contents, receives a different identification number. To remove the duplicate record, index on one of the data fields where duplicate values occur. In this example, choose SS_NO as the key field. Because an index tag named SS_NO was set up earlier, you can modify the tag by choosing Unique as the indexing option (see Figure 7.48).

Before you exit from the Index dialog, designate SS_NO as the master index. As a result, when you view the records in the SAMPLE database, the duplicate record (S12) is no longer there (see Figure 7.49).

In Figure 7.49, all the records are now arranged in ascending order by social security number. As you can see, the duplicate record (S12) has been excluded from the Browse view. It is important to note, however, that this record is still physically present in the database file. The unique index that we generated governs our access to records in the physical database. Since we have created a unique index on the SS_NO field, all records with duplicate social security numbers are hidden from view. To remove those duplicate records that are not shown in Browse view, copy the records in Browse view to a temporary file named TEMP.DBF by selecting the Copy To menu option from the Database menu popup (see Figure 7.50).

There are a number of ways to perform the next step, which involves replacing the records in the SAMPLE database with those in TEMP.DBF. You can use FoxPro's Filer, or you can first delete all the records in the SALESMAN database and then append records from TEMP.DBF.

To empty the records in the SAMPLE database, open the View window (if it is not already open), select the work area in which SAMPLE is the open database, and click on the Setup push button. When FoxPro displays the Setup dialog, make sure that SS_NO is not the master index (denoted by a key in the first column of

Editing Data 279

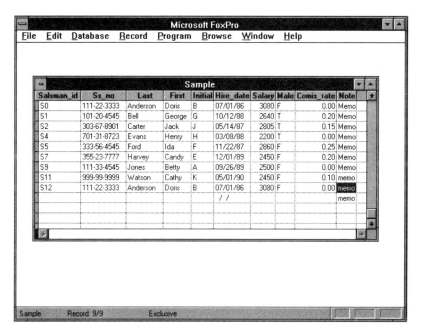

Figure 7.47 Duplicate records

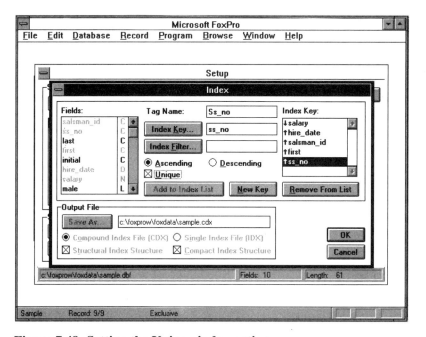

Figure 7.48 Setting the Unique index option

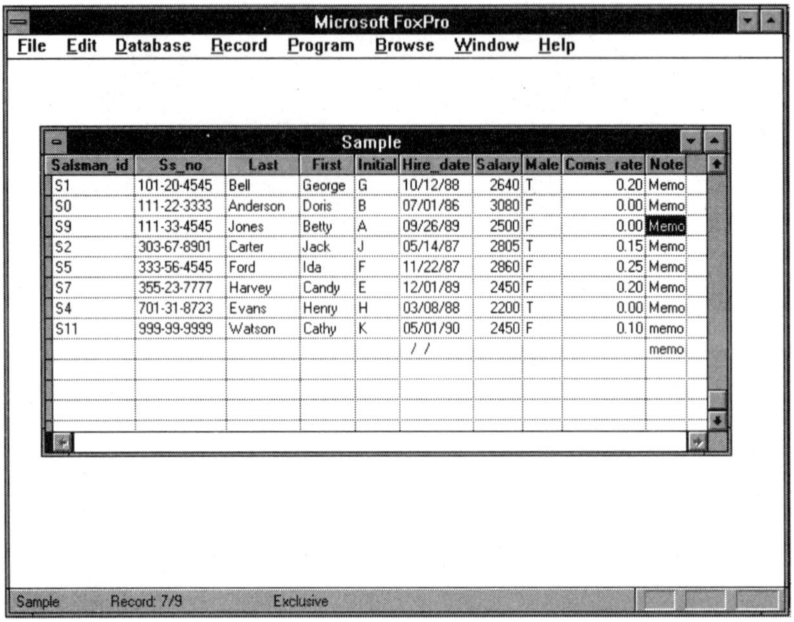

280   Understanding FoxPro 2.5 for Windows

Figure 7.49 Showing unique records

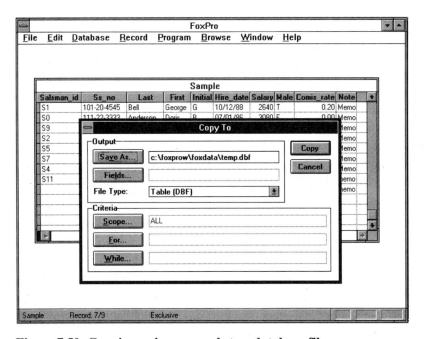

Figure 7.50 Copying unique records to a database file

Editing Data 281

the Indexes list box. If it is, select any of the other indexes and click on the Set Order push button. (We'll see why this step was necessary shortly.) After you click on the OK push button to close the Setup dialog, choose the Delete option from the Record menu popup and set the record scope to All; this marks all the records in the database for deletion. You can then remove them by selecting the Pack option from the Database menu popup.

To delete all the existing records in the SAMPLE database, it was necessary for us to change the master or controlling index in order to ensure that all records in the database were actually tagged for deletion. All unique indexes (i.e., indexes generated with the Unique check box selected) hide duplicate records from view. When the unique index is the master index, FoxPro can perform file operations only on records that are visible to the master index. Hence, in our example, deleting all records when SS_NO is the active index would leave one record—the duplicate record that was originally invisible—in the SAMPLE database.

Finally, select the Append From option from the Database menu popup. When the Append From dialog appears, specify TEMP.DBF as the source database file (see Figure 7.51). As a result, FoxPro adds all the records in TEMP.DBF to the SAMPLE database. After the Append operation, SAMPLE.DBF contains all the original unique records.

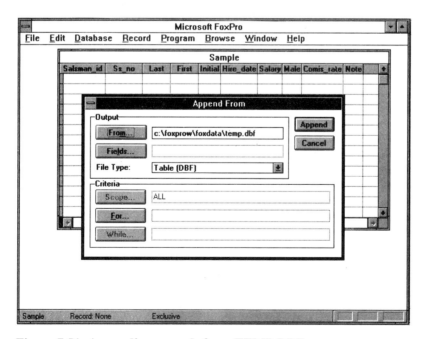

Figure 7.51 Appending records from TEMP.DBF

Splitting Database Files

When you design a good relational database, it is wise to keep your database files simple. If a database file becomes too large and contains too many fields, you may want to split it into two or more database files. Then, each file will contain a subset of the data fields in the original database. But to provide links among themselves, these database files should share a common data field.

The SALESMAN database contains 10 fields describing the attributes of a company's sales staff. Some fields contain personal data, while others contain payroll information. Although the database file is not too large and would not be divided in a real situation, as an exercise, let's split it into two files: PERSONAL.DBF and PAYROLL.DBF. The former will hold the personal data, while the latter will contain the payroll information. The two database files contain the following data fields:

Database File	*Data Fields*
PERSONAL.DBF	SALSMAN_ID
	LAST
	FIRST
	INITIAL
	HIRE_DATE
	MALE
	NOTE
PAYROLL	SALSMAN_ID
	SS_NO
	SALARY
	COMIS_RATE

The easiest way to split the file is to create the two database files using the Copy To operation discussed earlier. So, to create PERSONAL.DBF, select the Copy To option from the Database menu popup after you have opened the SALESMAN database in the current work area. To select the fields to be included in PERSONAL.DBF, choose the Fields... button to bring up the Field Picker, as shown in Figure 7.52.

After selecting the fields, create the PERSONAL database containing the selected fields by entering the name of the output file as PERSONAL in the Save As text box of the Copy To dialog. Follow the same procedure to create the PAYROLL database file. You can verify the contents of these two files in the Browse window (see Figure 7.53).

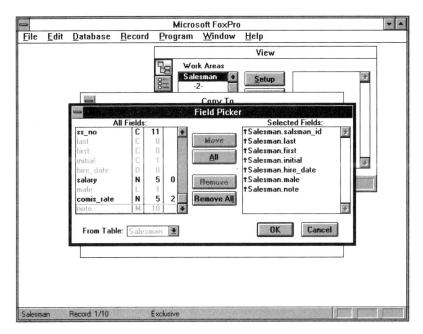

Figure 7.52 Selecting fields for PERSONAL.DBF

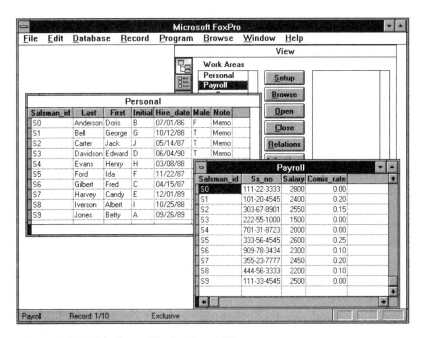

Figure 7.53 Viewing split database files

Using FoxPro Commands

In the preceding sections we used FoxPro's menu interface to modify the structure and contents of database files in a number of ways: We made duplicate copies of database files and renamed or restructured them; in addition, we edited the contents of databases, including adding new records to and removing existing records from existing database files. Many of these same tasks can be done by issuing the appropriate FoxPro commands.

COPYING DATABASE FILES

FoxPro offers a number of ways to copy database files with commands. One command for making duplicate copies of an existing database file follows this format:

```
COPY FILE source filename TO target filename
```

Note that the source filename and the target filename parameters must include their file extensions. To copy SALESMAN.DBF to BACKUP.DBF, the command would read:

```
COPY FILE SALESMAN.DBF TO BACKUP.DBF
```

To copy the associated memo and compound index files, the commands would be:

```
COPY FILE SALESMAN.FPT TO BACKUP.FPT
COPY FILE SALESMAN.CDX TO BACKUP.CDX
```

No wildcard characters—* or ?—can be used with the COPY FILE command. Wildcards can, however, be used with the DOS COPY command. For example, to copy SALESMAN.DBF and its associated files to a new group of target files with the root name of BACKUP, you could issue the DOS COPY command within FoxPro in the following format:

```
RUN COPY SALESMAN.* BACKUP.*
```

The RUN command opens a DOS window, and the DOS COPY command executes normally, displaying the names of the source files as it copies them. When the command has finished executing, close the window by selecting Close from the Control box and return to FoxPro.

To verify the existence of the duplicate files, issue one of these commands:

```
DIR BACKUP.*
RUN DIR BACKUP.*
```

The COPY FILE and RUN COPY commands make a duplicate copy of each source file. If the file is a database file with a .DBF extension, the database as a whole will be duplicated, including its database structure and all of its records; you cannot copy only selected data fields or selected records with these commands. To do that, you must use FoxPro's COPY TO command. Its format is:

```
COPY TO .dbf filename
        [FIELDS field list]
        [scope]
        [FOR expression]
```

The COPY TO command allows you to copy a certain portion of the currently selected database file. To include selected fields from the source file in the target database, add the FIELDS clause to the COPY TO command; to include selected records in the target database, specify the filter condition in a FOR clause; use the scope clause to define the scope for the records to be copied.

To create a duplicate copy of the SALESMAN database, for example, you would issue the following commands:

```
USE SALESMAN
COPY TO TEST
```

The COPY TO command creates a duplicate copy of the database file and its associated memo file. The files created here, TEST.DBF and TEST.FPT, have the same structure as the SALESMAN database and contain all of its records. Note, however, that the COPY TO command will not create a copy of its associated structural compound index file.

A command to copy only selected data fields to the target file using the FIELDS clause, as described above, would read:

```
COPY TO TEST FIELDS LAST, FIRST
```

And, to define a filter condition with a FOR clause for selecting data records, a sample command would read:

```
COPY TO TEST FOR MALE = .F. AND COMIS_RATE = 0
COPY TO TEST FIELDS LAST, FIRST, COMIS_RATE FOR COMIS_RATE   0
```

To specify a scope to select a range of records that you would like to copy, the command would read:

```
USE SALESMAN
GOTO 2
COPY TO TEST NEXT 5
```

In this example, the GOTO 2 command positions the cursor at the beginning of the second record. The NEXT 5 clause in the COPY TO command copies the next five records, beginning from the current record to the target file.

RENAMING DATABASE FILES

The command for assigning a new filename to an existing database file follows this format:

```
RENAME old filename TO new filename
```

The RENAME command does not accept the DOS wildcard characters * and ?. In addition, it requires that you include .DBF as its file extension, as in:

```
RENAME BACKUP.DBF TO TEST.DBF
```

This command also can be invoked to rename other types of files. The following commands rename the memo and compound index files that are associated with BACKUP.DBF to TEST.FPT and TEST.CDX:

```
RENAME BACKUP.FPT TO TEST.FPT
RENAME BACKUP.CDX TO TEST.CDX
```

You can use the DOS RENAME command inside of FoxPro to rename a group of files that share the same name. The following DOS RENAME command accomplishes the same tasks as multiple RENAME commands:

```
RUN RENAME TEST.* TEST1.*
```

MODIFYING DATA STRUCTURES

The command to bring up an existing data structure so that it can be modified is MODIFY STRUCTURE. As shown in the example below, it redefines the SALESMAN.DBF data structure:

```
USE SALESMAN
MODIFY STRUCTURE
```

The resulting data structure will be displayed as in Figure 7.54. It can then be edited with the procedures you learned earlier.

EDITING DATA RECORDS

The command to modify the contents of records is EDIT. This command provides a great deal of flexibility. By using its FIELDS clause, you can select only certain data fields to edit, edit only selected data records by specifying the appropriate filter conditions, or define the scope of those records that you would like to edit. In addition, you can limit the movement of the cursor to selected data fields with the FREEZE clause. The format of the EDIT command is:

Editing Data   287

```
EDIT [FIELDS field list]
     [scope]
     [FOR expression]
     [FREEZE field]
```

To edit the records in the SALESMAN database, for instance, issue the following commands:

```
USE SALESMAN
EDIT
```

If you do not include a clause that specifies individual records to be edited, all records are subjected to the Edit operation. As a result, in executing the EDIT command, FoxPro will display the first record of the SALESMAN database in an editing window in Change mode (see Figure 7.55).

At this point, you can edit the contents of the first record and then continue to the next. You can abort the Edit operation at any time by pressing the Esc key. To save the changes, either close the window or press the Ctrl+End key.

To position the cursor at a specific record before issuing the EDIT command, use the GOTO command. The sample commands below direct the operation to begin editing from record #5:

```
GOTO 5
EDIT
```

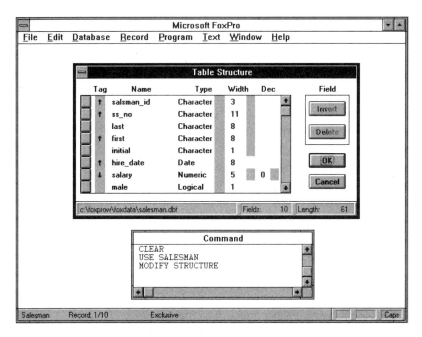

Figure 7.54 Modifying data structure

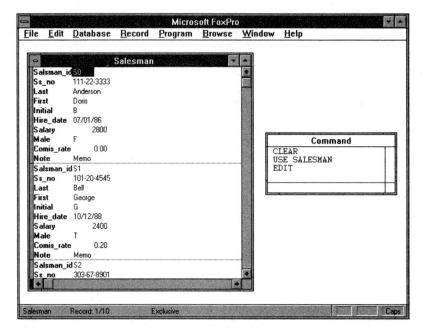

Figure 7.55 The data edit window

The same task can be accomplished by issuing the following command:

```
EDIT 5
```

This command begins the Edit operation at record number 5 (S4 in SALESMAN.DBF). FoxPro will display all subsequent records until the end of the file.

Alternatively, you can define filter conditions for any records that you would like to edit. The following command would be used to edit the records of those salespeople who were hired on or before December 31, 1988:

```
EDIT FOR HIRE_DATE = {12/31/88}
```

Similarly, the next command lets you edit all the records belonging to male salespeople:

```
EDIT FOR MALE = .T.
```

You can display selected data fields to be edited by adding a FIELD clause, such as:

```
EDIT FIELDS FIRST, LAST, SALARY, COMIS_RATE
EDIT FIELDS LAST, SALARY FOR SALARY >= 2000
```

As a result, you can move among the data fields specified in the EDIT command.

Editing Data   289

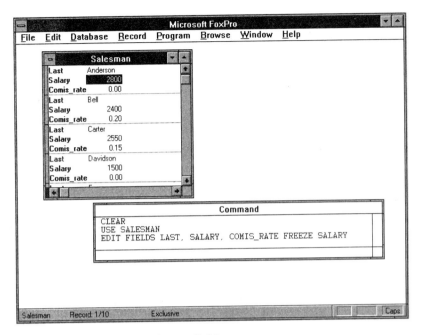

Figure 7.56 Editing the freeze field

Some of the fields, however, such as LAST and FIRST, are displayed primarily for reference purposes, and you probably would not want to edit them. Instead of moving around in reference fields such as these, you can freeze the cursor at a specific field during editing; to do this, use the FREEZE clause in this way:

```
EDIT FIELDS LAST, SALARY, COMIS_RATE FREEZE SALARY
```

In executing this command, FoxPro displays the contents of only the LAST, SALARY, and COMIS_RATE fields (see Figure 7.56). When the edit form appears, the cursor is positioned in the frozen field, and FoxPro will permit you to edit only the frozen field. You cannot move around within a record, and pressing the Enter key will not advance you to a new field or a new record. Instead, you can move from record to record by pressing the Page Up and Page Down keys in Change mode, and by pressing the up-arrow and down-arrow keys in Browse mode or by clicking your mouse on the record to which you would like to move.

ADDING NEW DATA RECORDS

If you need to add new records to the end of a database file, issue the APPEND command, which has the following format:

```
APPEND
```

To add new records to the TEST database, for instance, issue the following command:

```
USE TEST
APPEND
```

In return, FoxPro displays a data form for the new record that will be added to the end of the file. You can then enter the field values for the new record. After you are finished entering data, you can continue adding more records.

DELETING DATA RECORDS

You can mark any records for deletion by using the DELETE command in the following format:

```
DELETE [scope]
       [FOR expression]
```

Use the scope and filter condition to select the records that you would like to mark. For example:

```
USE TEST
DELETE NEXT 3
DELETE FOR MALE = .T.
DELETE FOR SALARY = 2000 AND HIRE_DATE <= {01/01/89}
```

The NEXT 3 scope clause in the first DELETE command marks three records starting from the current record. The last two commands use the FOR clause to define the filter condition for selecting the records to be deleted.

To permanently remove the marked records from the database file, issue the following command:

```
PACK
```

If you decide to unmark records flagged for deletion, issue the RECALL command in the following format, but only *before* issuing the PACK command:

```
RECALL [scope]
       [FOR expression]
```

Here are some examples:

```
USE TEST
RECALL ALL
RECALL NEXT 5
RECALL FOR MALE =.T.
RECALL FOR SALARY >= 2000 AND HIRE_DATE <= {01/01/89}
```

Ordinarily, to delete all the records in a database, you must first mark them for deletion and then pack the database, as discussed earlier. There is a shortcut, however—the ZAP command. This command, used in the format shown, would enable you to delete all the records from TEST.DBF:

```
USE TEST
ZAP
```

This command results in a warning prompt asking you to confirm your action. It reads:

```
Zap c:\foxprow\foxdata\test.dbf?
```

If you answer Yes to the prompt, all the records in the database file will be permanently removed.

DELETING DATABASE FILES

Although the DELETE and ZAP commands will permanently delete records from your database files, they will not remove the data structure. To delete the database file from the disk, you must issue the ERASE command. To permanently remove TEST.DBF from your disk, issue the following command:

```
ERASE TEST.DBF
```

You can use this command to delete other files that are associated with the erased database file, as well. For example:

```
ERASE TEST.FPT
ERASE TEST.CDX
```

Before erasing these files, however, you must first close them. FoxPro will not allow you to erase any files that are in use. You also can choose to erase your files with the DOS DELETE or ERASE command in formats such as:

```
RUN DELETE TEST.DBF
RUN DELETE TEST.*
RUN ERASE TEST.DBF
RUN ERASE TEST.*
```

BORROWING EXISTING DATA STRUCTURES

The COPY TO and ZAP commands enable you to borrow an existing data structure for a new database file. For example, the following commands will create a database file named TEST.DBF by borrowing the structure from SALESMAN.DBF:

```
USE SALESMAN
COPY TO TEST
USE TEST
ZAP
```

Of course, you can borrow selected data fields from the existing database, as well. Here is an example:

```
USE SALESMAN
COPY TO ROSTER FIELDS LAST, FIRST
USE ROSTER
ZAP
```

The resulting ROSTER.DBF will have a data structure containing only the LAST and FIRST fields.

Chapter Summary

This chapter defined the procedures necessary to modify the contents of database files. You learned how to modify the data structure of an existing database file, insert new fields in the existing data structure, and remove existing data fields; you also learned how to redefine the attributes of existing fields.

This chapter also covered the editing processes that enable you to change the contents of your data records using either Browse or Change modes in the Browse window. You were introduced to methods for adding new records to the file and deleting records that are no longer needed. It was pointed out that most of the procedures covered in this chapter can be carried out either by using the menu interface or by issuing the appropriate FoxPro commands.

You learned how to make duplicate copies of your database files before you begin modifying them. This important safety precaution means that you can revert to the original copies if you decide to cancel all the changes you make to the database.

To this point, you learned the procedures related to creating and maintaining your database files. In the next chapter, you will begin to see how you can efficiently retrieve useful information from the database.

8
Linking Databases

An Overview

In illustrating how to create and maintain data in your database files, the preceding chapters assumed that you were working with a single file at a time. Although it is perfectly acceptable to use FoxPro in this way, FoxPro is also a powerful relational database management system. As you may recall from the discussion of relational database concepts in Chapter 1, a relational database management system allows you to store related information in multiple files. Designing your database system in this way provides the most efficient storage for your data, while ensuring its integrity.

It is through file linking that you are able to take advantage of FoxPro's power as a relational database management system. To manage or display related information from separate database files, FoxPro temporarily links data records in these files. Once their records are linked, their contents can be manipulated simultaneously. The capability to link different database files is vital to your success in managing relational databases. It enables you to efficiently organize data elements and to produce useful and complex reports.

This chapter will introduce you to FoxPro's relational database capabilities by demonstrating how to link data elements in different database files. Because some of the procedures for linking database files can be carried out only by using FoxPro commands, this chapter will show you how to link database files both through FoxPro's menu interface and by issuing FoxPro commands.

Relating Database Files

If the information you need for an application is stored in more than one data table, a link field—a field whose value is common to at least two databases—must be incorporated to relate them. How these databases are linked depends on the exact relationship between the databases. If there are one-to-one and one-to-many relations (defined below) between two database files, they can be linked directly through a common link field. Otherwise, when many-to-many relations exist between two database files, they may need to be linked through information in a third relation table.

HANDLING ONE-TO-ONE RELATIONS

One-to-one relations exist when each record in a database file corresponds to one—and only one—record in another database file. As noted above, to link two database files with one-to-one relations, the two files must share a common field, called a link field, that provides the information for relating one file to another. You can, for instance, link the PERSONAL and PAYROLL files using SALSMAN_ID as the link field. PERSONAL.DBF, to which you want to link PAYROLL.DBF, is called the parent. PAYROLL.DBF, the file that you want to link with the parent, is called a child. With a one-to-one relationship, however, the designation of the child and parent files is arbitrary, depending on which one is in control. The relationship between these two database files is depicted in Figure 8.1.

As you can see in this figure, one-to-one relations exist between PERSONAL.DBF and PAYROLL.DBF because each record in the parent can be uniquely linked to a record in the child. That is, you can relate each PERSONAL.DBF record that has a unique value in the link field (SALSMAN_ID) to a unique record in the PAYROLL file.

After linking these two files, each record in the parent that has a unique value in the link field will be related to a child record having the same value in that field. Once the two files are linked, data elements in the two related records can be treated as if they are in the same record.

Before you try to link the database files, though, you must index the child on the link field. In this case, it means that, before you begin linking PERSONAL.DBF and PAYROLL.DBF, you must index the latter on the SALSMAN_ID field. If you have already set up the index tag with the link field, designate that tag as the master index (see Figure 8.2). The parent, however, need not be indexed on the link field—it can be indexed on any field in the database or on none at all.

The first step in linking is to bring up the View window. When it appears, open the parent in a work area. Then, choose the Relations operation and link it to the child that is open in *another* work area. As an exercise, we will link PER-

```
Parent: PERSONAL.DBF
SALSMAN_ID   LAST       FIRST     INITIAL   HIRE_DATE   MALE   NOTE
S0           Anderson   Doris     B         07/01/86    .F.    Memo
S1           Bell       George    G         10/12/88    .T.    Memo
S2           Carter     Jack      J         05/14/87    .T.    Memo
S3           Davidson   Edward    D         06/04/90    .T.    Memo
S4           Evans      Henry     H         03/08/88    .T.    Memo
S5           Ford       Ida       F         11/22/87    .F.    Memo
S6           Gilbert    Fred      C         04/15/87    .T.    Memo
S7           Harvey     Candy     E         12/01/89    .F.    Memo
S8           Iverson    Albert    I         10/25/88    .T.    Memo
S9           Jones      Betty     A         09/26/89    .F.    Memo

    Child: PAYROLL.DBF
    SALSMAN_ID   SS_NO          SALARY     COMIS_RATE
    S0           111-22-3333    2800       0.00
    S1           101-20-4545    2400       0.20
    S2           303-67-8901    2550       0.15
    S3           222-55-1000    1500       0.00
    S4           701-31-8723    2000       0.00
    S5           333-56-4545    2600       0.25
    S6           909-78-3434    2300       0.10
    S7           355-23-7777    2450       0.20
    S8           444-56-3333    2200       0.10
    S9           111-33-4545    2500       0.00
```

Figure 8.1 One-to-one relation between PERSONAL.DBF and PAYROLL.DBF

SONAL.DBF and PAYROLL.DBF. First, use the View window to open PERSONAL.DBF as the parent in work area 1. Then, select the Relations button, which causes the relation symbol (an arrow) to appear (see Figure 8.3).

Next, open the child, PAYROLL.DBF, by clicking on work area 2 and selecting the database from the files list box. At this point, FoxPro will open the Set Index Order dialog and ask you to select the link field from the child's available index tags. (see Figure 8.4). (If FoxPro cannot find any index files for the child, the message "Table is not ordered" will appear, and FoxPro will not permit you to link the files.) Since SALSMAN_ID is the only index tag in PAYROLL.CDX, it becomes the default master index. Select the OK button to accept the default, and FoxPro takes you to the SET RELATION Expression Builder. If you had previously selected SALSMAN_ID as the master index, FoxPro skips the Set Index Order dialog and takes you straight to the SET RELATION Expression Builder.

You are then asked to define the link field in the SET RELATION expression dialog. When the dialog appears, it shows the indexed field as the default link field

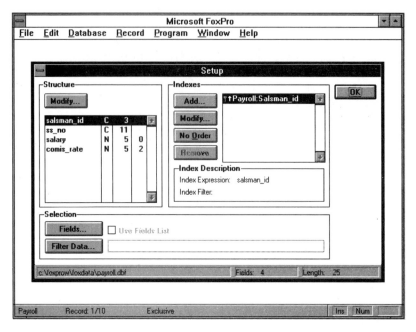

Figure 8.2 Indexing PAYROLL.DBF with the SALSMAN_ID index tag

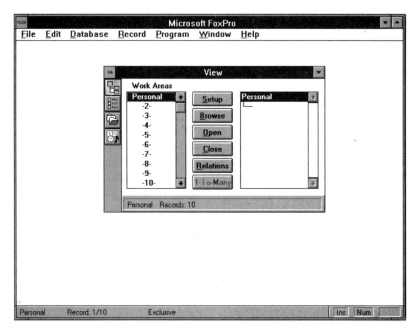

Figure 8.3 Opening the parent file in Work Area 1

Linking Databases 297

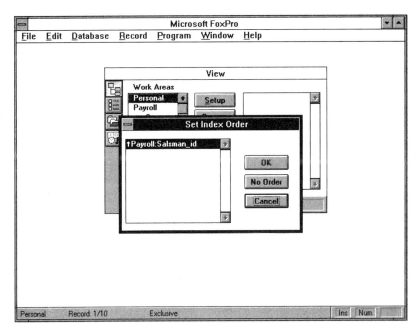

Figure 8.4 Indexing the child file

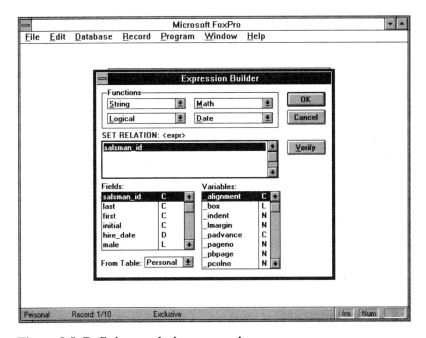

Figure 8.5 Defining a relation expression

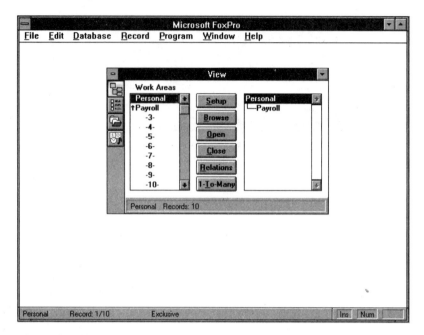

Figure 8.6 Showing linked files in a View window

(see Figure 8.5). After verifying its validity, accept the relation expression by choosing the OK button. As you return to the View panel, note that SALESMAN.DBF and PAYROLL.DBF are linked, indicated by the arrow joining the two files (see Figure 8.6). This graphically identifies the PERSONAL database as the parent and the PAYROLL database as the child. Database files also can be linked by issuing FoxPro commands directly in the Command window. The command invoked for this purpose is SET RELATION, which has the following syntax:

```
SET RELATION TO <<link field INTO <<child>>
```

Before you issue this command, however, the parent must be open in one work area and the child in another. In addition, the child must be indexed on the link field.

When you specify the child in the SET RELATION TO command, use either its filename or its alias. A file alias is represented by a letter or digit representing the work area in which the file is open (e.g., A or 1). However, it is better to use a letter as an alias, because in other commands (such as LIST, DISPLAY, etc.) you can refer to an alias only by a letter. For example, the following commands will establish the relationship between PERSONAL.DBF and PAYROLL.DBF:

```
SELECT A
USE PERSONAL
SELECT B
```

```
USE PAYROLL
SET ORDER TO SALSMAN_ID
SELECT A
SET RELATION TO SALSMAN_ID INTO B
```

The first two commands open the parent, PERSONAL.DBF, in work area A (which is equivalent to work area 1). Then the child, PAYROLL.DBF, is opened in work area B (corresponding to work area 2). Before issuing the SET RELATION command, the child's controlling index is set to the link field, SALSMAN_ID. And, as noted above, the file to be linked may be identified in the SET RELATION command either by its filename or by its alias. That is, the last command also can be written as

```
SET RELATION TO SALESMAN_ID INTO PAYROLL
```

As a result, the same relationship between the PERSONAL.DBF and PAYROLL.DBF will be established, which we succeeded in defining using FoxPro's windowing interface (see Figure 8.7).

Viewing Related Data Records

Once the database files are linked and you view a record in the parent, you also are able to view its related records in the child. Thus, as long as the PERSONAL and

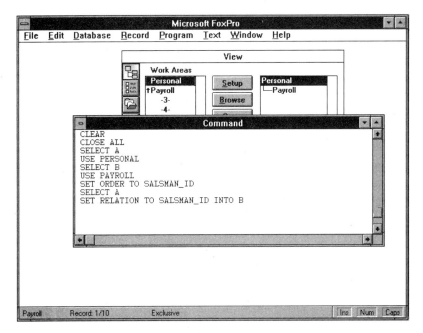

Figure 8.7 Establishing a link with FoxPro commands

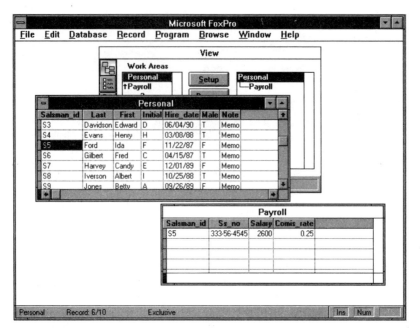

Figure 8.8 Viewing related records in linked files

PAYROLL database files are linked, you can view the related records in both files simultaneously in separate Browse windows. To do this, use the View window to open separate Browse windows for the PERSONAL and PAYROLL databases and make the Browse window for PERSONAL.DBF the active window. Then, when you place the cursor on a record in PERSONAL.DBF, its related record in PAYROLL.DBF automatically is displayed (see Figure 8.8).

Because there is a one-to-one relation between PERSONAL.DBF and PAYROLL.DBF, each record in the parent shows only one record in the child. Notice in Figure 8.8, that when you highlight the S5 record in PERSONAL.DBF, PAYROLL.DBF shows its related record. If you highlight another record in the PERSONAL file, it will display its related record in PAYROLL.DBF.

It is important to note that you can move only among the records in the parent for the change to be reflected in the child; FoxPro will not allow you to move among the records in the child's Browse window. For example, when you display records from the PERSONAL and PAYROLL files in the Browse windows, you can highlight only different records in the PERSONAL file. When you attempt to position the cursor in PAYROLL.DBF, it remains on the record related to the record that is highlighted in PERSONAL.DBF. You cannot move to a different record in PAYROLL.DBF. To move among the records in PAYROLL.DBF, you must designate it as the parent when you link it to PERSONAL.DBF.

If you are using FoxPro commands, selected related fields from the two database files may be displayed simultaneously. After relating PERSONAL.DBF and

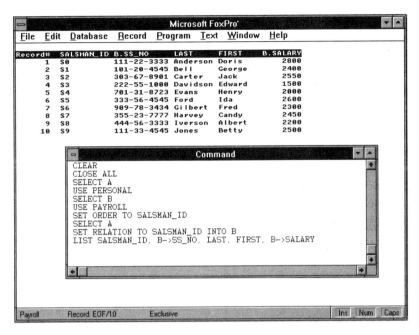

Figure 8.9 Listing records in linked files

PAYROLL.DBF, for example, you can display records that belong to either database file. Here is an example:

```
SELECT A
USE PERSONAL
SELECT B
USE PAYROLL
SET ORDER TO SALSMAN_ID
SELECT A
SET RELATION TO SALSMAN_ID INTO B
LIST SALSMAN_ID, B->>SS_NO, LAST, FIRST, B->>SALARY
```

In the LIST command, some of the fields are taken from the parent (PERSONAL.DBF in work area A), while others are extracted from the child (PAYROLL.DBF in work area B). To identify a field, add the file alias in front of the field name if you are not in that work area. Use B->>SS_NO to identify the SS_NO field in work area B (where PAYROLL.DBF is open) if you are working in A. The results of the LIST command are shown in Figure 8.9.

Saving Relations to View Files

When you link two database files in this manner, their relationship is temporary. It remains intact only as long as the two files remain linked in the View panel.

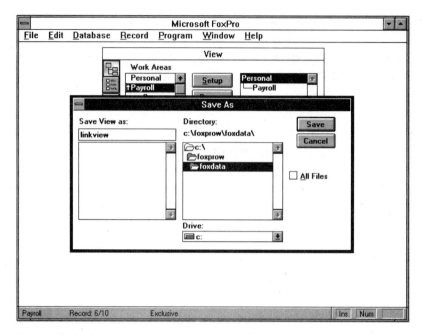

Figure 8.10 Saving a relation to a View file

When you close one or both of the related files or exit from FoxPro, the link is destroyed. The one-to-one link of PERSONAL.DBF and PAYROLL.DBF will be canceled if either of these two files is closed, for example. Therefore, in order to relate the two files for use in another application, their relationship must be set up again.

FoxPro does, however, make accommodations for cases in which you intend to use the same relation repeatedly: It allows you to save the relation to a view file. This prevents the necessity of re-creating the relationship from scratch each time. To save an established relation to a view file, select the Save As... option from the File menu popup while the relation remains valid in the View panel. When the Save View dialog appears, enter the name of the view file (in this case, LINKVIEW) in the Save View as: filename text box (see Figure 8.10).

The view file you have created will be given a default file extension of .VUE. The information contained in this file will be used later solely to reestablish the relationship between the two database files; the view file does not contain any records belonging to any of the related database files.

Another way to save relations to a view file is to issue the CREATE VIEW command in the following format:

```
CREATE VIEW <<name of view file>>
```

Then, while all the database files are still linked, issue the following command to save their relations:

```
CREATE VIEW LINKDBFS
```

The resulting view file, LINKDBFS.VUE, will contain all the information needed to re-create the relations between the PERSONAL AND PAYROLL database files.

Using Existing View Files

Once you have saved an established relation to a view file, the database files can be closed. The same relationship can be reestablished later by opening the view file. In the last exercise, for instance, we saved the relationship between the PERSONAL and PAYROLL databases to the LINKVIEW.VUE view file. To reestablish that relationship now, choose the Open option from the File menu popup and, when the Open dialog appears, select View as the file type in the List Files of Type: drop-down list and then open the view file of your choice (see Figure 8.11).

When an existing view file is opened, the information in the file will be used to set up the relation that you have saved. The database files do not need to be opened

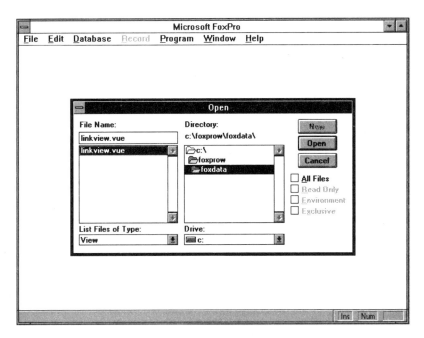

Figure 8.11 Opening an existing View file

individually. Opening the view file also opens all the related database files in the appropriate work areas and reestablishes the previous relationship. The effect is the same as if you had reset the relationship between the database files all over again.

To reestablish relations that were previously saved in a view file using a FoxPro command, issue the SET VIEW TO command:

```
SET VIEW TO <<name of view file>>
```

To reestablish the relation that was set up in LINKDBFS.VUE, issue the following command:

```
SET VIEW TO LINKDBFS
```

As a result, all the linked databases (PERSONAL.DBF and PAYROLL.DBF) will be opened in separate work areas and then linked using the information stored in the view file.

HANDLING ONE-TO-MANY RELATIONS

A similar procedure is used to relate database files that have one-to-many relationships. In linking files that have a one-to-many relationship, however, it is critical that you properly designate the parent. Otherwise, related records in the child cannot be identified or displayed correctly. To demonstrate how to link two database files having one-to-many relations, we will use the OFFICE (created in Chapter 4) and SALESMAN files. The relationship between the two database files is depicted in Figure 8.12.

OFFICE.DBF contains information on the location of each sales office and its accompanying identification code. Note that each record in the parent (OFFICE.DBF) corresponds to one or more records in the child (SALESMAN.DBF). For example, record B1 (in OFFICE_ID) in the OFFICE file relates to records S0, S3, and S9 (in SALSMAN_ID) in SALESMAN.DBF.

Before you can link OFFICE.DBF and SALESMAN.DBF, you must insert a new data field, OFFICE_ID, into the SALESMAN.DBF data structure. Select the View option from the Window menu pad and press the Setup button. When the Open dialog appears, open the SALESMAN.DBF table. Once you're in the Setup dialog, select the Modify (structure) button, and insert the OFFICE_ID field before the HIRE_DATE field with the following structure:

Tag	Name	Type	Width
↑	OFFICE_ID	character	2

Either the Spacebar or the mouse can be used to create the new index tag, OFFICE_ID, in ascending order by selecting the up arrow for the tag field in the

Parent: OFFICE.DBF

OFFICE_ID	ADDRESS	CITY	STATE	ZIP	PHONE_NO
→ B1	100 Park Avenue	New York	NY	10016	800-123-5555
B2	200 Lake Drive	Chicago	IL	60607	800-234-5555
B3	500 Century Blvd.	Los Angeles	CA	94005	800-456-5555

Child: SALESMAN.DBF

SALSMAN_ID	SS_NO	LAST	FIRST	INITIAL	OFFICE_ID	...
→ S0	111-22-3333	Anderson	Doris	B	B1	...
S1	101-20-4545	Bell	George	G	B3	...
S2	303-67-8901	Carter	Jack	J	B2	...
→ S3	222-55-1000	Davidson	Edward	D	B1	...
S4	701-31-8723	Evans	Henry	H	B3	...
S5	333-56-4545	Ford	Ida	F	B2	...
S6	909-78-3434	Gilbert	Fred	C	B3	...
S7	355-23-7777	Harvey	Candy	E	B3	...
S8	444-56-3333	Iverson	Albert	I	B2	...
→ S9	111-33-4545	Jones	Betty	A	B1	...

Figure 8.12 One-to-many relations between OFFICE.DBF and SALESMAN.DBF

same manner you learned in a preceding chapter. The OFFICE_ID field contains the office identification code representing the office to which each salesperson is assigned (see Figure 8.13). It will serve as the link field for relating OFFICE.DBF and SALESMAN.DBF. OFFICE_ID is considered the "primary field" in the parent database (OFFICE.DBF) and a "foreign field" in the child database (SALESMAN.DBF). After you've finished modifying the data structure, return to the View dialog, open the Browse window, and enter the values for the OFFICE_ID field for each record. The revised records are shown in Figure 8.14.

Use the View panel to establish the relationship between the OFFICE and SALESMAN database files in a manner similar to that detailed previously: Open OFFICE.DBF as the parent in work area A and SALESMAN.DBF as the child in work area B. Next, using the Setup dialog, make the OFFICE_ID index tag the controlling index of the SALESMAN database. Then, link the two databases by using this common field. To do this, select the OFFICE database, then the Relations button, and click on the SALESMAN database. FoxPro will then open the Expression Builder and select OFFICE_ID as the field to which to set the relation. After verifying the expression, selecting OK should cause the View window to appear as it does in Figure 8.15. Once the two database files are linked, each record in the OFFICE file is automatically related to its corresponding records in the SALESMAN file. If you view their records in the Browse windows, you will see that for

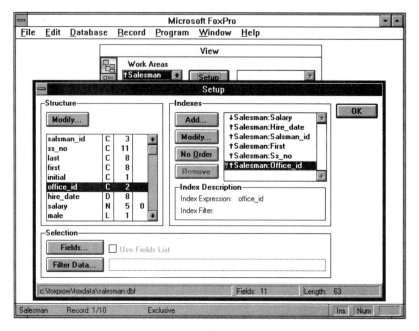

Figure 8.13 Adding the OFFICE_ID field to SALESMAN.DBF

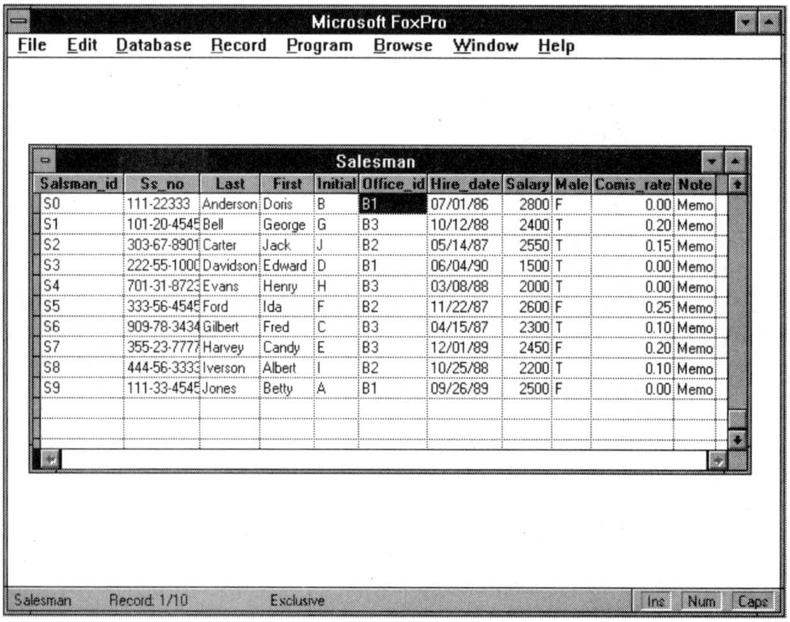

Figure 8.14 Revised records of SALESMAN.DBF

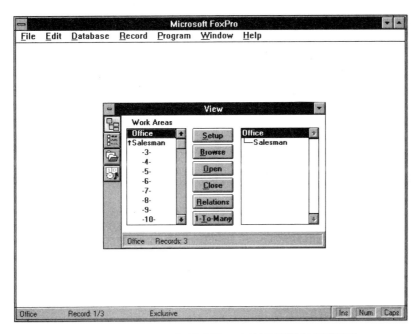

Figure 8.15 Relating OFFICE.DBF and SALESMAN.DBF

each record you choose in the parent, its corresponding records in the child are displayed (see Figure 8.16).

To watch this happen, highlight the first record (B1) in OFFICE.DBF in one Browse window. All of its corresponding records (S0, S3, and S9) in SALESMAN.DBF are displayed in another Browse window. Highlight another record in the parent, and all the records in the child relating to that record will be displayed accordingly.

The FoxPro commands required to relate the OFFICE and SALESMAN database files are:

```
SELECT A
USE OFFICE
SELECT B
USE SALESMAN
SET ORDER TO OFFICE_ID
SELECT A
SET RELATION TO OFFICE_ID INTO B
```

While the two database files are linked, related records may be listed by invoking the LIST or DISPLAY commands. But, for each record in the OFFICE file that you list, only the first record from the SALESMAN file relating to the record in OFFICE.DBF will be displayed; the remaining related records will not be

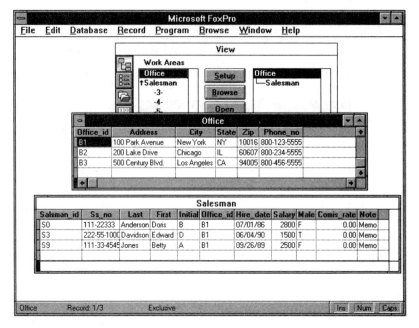

Figure 8.16 One-to-many related records

displayed. To confirm this, issue the following command after you have linked the two database files:

```
LIST OFFICE_ID, B->>SALSMAN_ID, B->>LAST FOR OFFICE_ID = "B1"
```

The results of the LIST command are shown in Figure 8.17. Although record B1 in OFFICE.DBF corresponds to three records (S0, S3, and S9) in SALESMAN.DBF, only the first (S0) record is displayed.

There is, however, a workaround that will allow you to show the multiple records that correspond to a single parent record when working with FoxPro's command-driven interface: The SET RELATION TO command establishes the one-to-many relationship by reversing the parent and child databases and selecting a common index expression to order both databases. The FoxPro commands necessary to do this with our sample databases are as follows:

```
SELECT A
USE SALESMAN
SELECT B
USE OFFICE
SET ORDER TO OFFICE_ID
SELECT A
SET RELATION TO OFFICE_ID INTO B
LIST OFF SALSMAN_ID, LAST, B->>OFFICE_ID FOR OFFICE_ID = "B1"
```

Figure 8.17 Showing only one salesman in office B1

The results of this LIST command can be seen in Figure 8.18, where you can see that all the salespeople in office B1 are shown by the LIST command. Records S0, S3, and S9 in SALESMAN.DBF are linked to the same B1 record from the OFFICE database file.

Also note that because we reversed the parent and child databases to mimic a one-to-many relationship, you no longer can directly view the one-to-many relationship in the Browse window. You may highlight only one record at a time in the parent file Browse window. Therefore, you can see only one record in the child Browse window that is related to the highlighted record in the parent (see Figure 8.19). There is a trade-off: In order to view all the related records via the LIST command, you relinquish the capability to view all related records in the Browse window.

HANDLING MANY-TO-ONE RELATIONS

You can view many-to-one relations in a way that is similar to viewing one-to-many relations. As you can see in Figure 8.19, many-to-one relations exist between SALESMAN.DBF and OFFICE.DBF. To link the two tables, you have to designate SALESMAN.DBF as the parent and OFFICE.DBF as the child. As a result, while they are linked, you can view a single record in the child when you highlight a record in the parent table.

Figure 8.18 Showing all the salespeople in B1

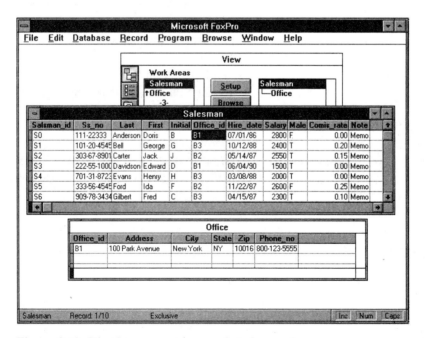

Figure 8.19 Viewing many-to-one related records

HANDLING MANY-TO-MANY RELATIONS

Many-to-many relationships are the most complex connections that exist between any two data entities. You learned in Chapter 1 that one way to link two data entities is to use one or more relation tables. Many-to-many relations may exist, for example, between SALESMAN.DBF and REGION.DBF—one salesperson may be assigned to more than one sales region, and one sales region may be assigned to several salespeople. To properly link these two database files, a relation table must be created; for this example, we will name it ASSIGN.DBF. It contains information about which salespeople are assigned to various sales regions.

Before learning how to define many-to-many relationships, you must create the necessary sample database files. In addition to the existing SALESMAN database file, you need to create the ASSIGN.DBF relation table and the REGION database file for holding data associated with the sales regions.

The data structure of REGION.DBF is:

Field	Field Name	Type	Width	Dec
1	region_id	Character	2	
2	region	Character	12	
3	manager	Character	15	

After you have defined the database structure, you should also create a structural compound index with a tag for the REGION_ID field. This will allow the REGION database to be used as the child database when you link databases.

As an example, the database file might contain the following records:

Record#	REGION_ID	REGION	MANAGER
1	R1	Northeast	Alice F. Gibson
2	R2	Southeast	Bob L. Major
3	R3	Northcentral	John K. Freed
4	R4	Southcentral	Cathy M. Wilson
5	R5	Northwest	Chris C. Hall
6	R6	Southwest	Helen T. Taylor

Each of these records holds data elements associated with a given sales region and contains the identification of each sales region and the name of the manager in charge of that region.

To relate the records in REGION.DBF to those in SALESMAN.DBF, a relation table, ASSIGN_DBF, also must be created with the following data structure:

Field	Field Name	Type	Width	Dec
1	REGION_ID	Character	2	
2	SALSMAN_ID	Character	3	

When you finish defining the database structure, you also should create a compound index with tags for the REGION_ID and SALSMAN_ID fields. Each record in the ASSIGN file relates a sales region to a salesperson. If you assign more than one salesperson to a sales region, use separate records to represent assigned sales regions in ASSIGN.DBF:

Record#	REGION_I	SALSMAN_ID
1	R1	S0
2	R1	S3
3	R1	S6
4	R1	S9
5	R2	S2
6	R2	S5
7	R3	S2
8	R3	S8
9	R4	S4
10	R4	S7
11	R5	S1
12	R5	S7
13	R6	S4
14	R6	S7

The ASSIGN.DBF relation table provides the necessary link between the REGION and SALESMAN database files and allows you to find many-to-many relations. Records in the REGION and SALESMAN databases now can be linked to provide more comprehensive information. You can find, for example, all the sales regions that have been assigned to a given salesperson or all those salespeople who are supervised by the same regional manager. Figure 8.20 shows how to relate the REGION and SALESMAN database files using ASSIGN.DBF as their link.

Figure 8.20 also shows that a SALESMAN.DBF record may be related to more than one record in REGION.DBF, and vice versa. For example, record S2 of SALESMAN.DBF is related to records R2 and R3 in REGION.DBF. Likewise, record R2 in REGION.DBF is related to records S2 and S5 in SALESMAN.DBF.

To set up these many-to-many relationships between salespeople and sales regions, first bring up the View panel and open SALESMAN.DBF as the parent. Next, select the Relations button to establish the relation between SALESMAN.DBF and its child, ASSIGN.DBF. Link SALESMAN.DBF and ASSIGN.DBF using SALSMAN_ID as the link field. Then, select ASSIGN.DBF as the parent for the next linking operation. Select the Relations button again to establish the relation between ASSIGN.DBF and its child, REGION.DBF, using REGION_ID as the link field. When all three databases are linked, your screen should look like that shown in Figure 8.21.

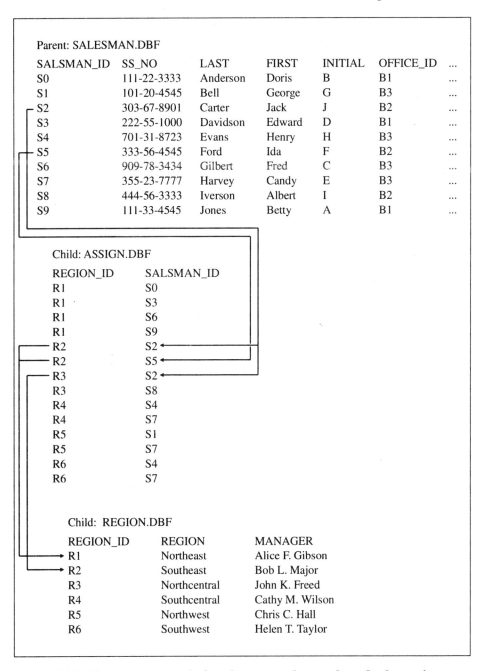

Figure 8.20 Many-to-many relations between salespeople and sales regions

This figure depicts the relations as a relation chain. SALSMAN_ID is used as the link field to relate SALESMAN.DBF and ASSIGN.DBF. ASSIGN.DBF and REGION.DBF are linked through the REGION_ID field.

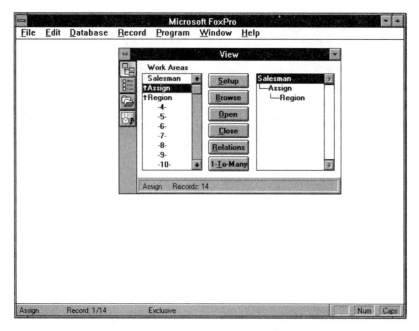

Figure 8.21 Linking SALESMAN.DBF and REGION.DBF through ASSIGN.DBF

Once these files are linked, the related records can be displayed in different Browse windows. When you move among the records in the parent, the related records in its children are displayed. Highlight record S4 in SALESMAN.DBF, for instance; its related records, R4 and R6 in ASSIGN.DBF, are displayed (see Figure 8.22).

Notice, however, that only one record is displayed in the REGION Browse window; you would have expected two to be displayed. The reason is that there are direct one-to-many relations between SALESMAN.DBF and ASSIGN.DBF, and FoxPro is able to successfully handle these. But the REGION database is the child of the ASSIGN database; many-to-one relations exist between ASSIGN.DBF and REGION.DBF. FoxPro does not provide direct many-to-many relations between SALESMAN.DBF and REGION.DBF. As a result, their relations have to be expressed indirectly through the set of one-to-many relations between SALESMAN.DBF and ASSIGN.DBF and the set of many-to-one relations between ASSIGN.DBF and REGION.DBF. FoxPro is unable to graphically depict these latter many-to-one relationships.

In order to show the record in the REGION Browse window corresponding to the record in ASSIGN.DBF, that record must be highlighted in the ASSIGN Browse window. Therefore, to see the information about region R6 in REGION.DBF, highlight R6 in the ASSIGN Browse window (see Figure 8.23).

Linking Databases 315

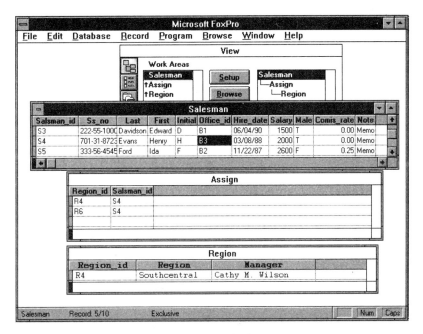

Figure 8.22 Linked many-to-many relations

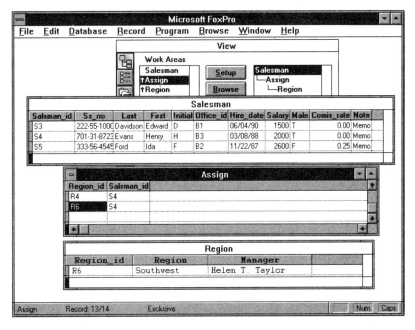

Figure 8.23 Related records between ASSIGN.DBF and REGION.DBF

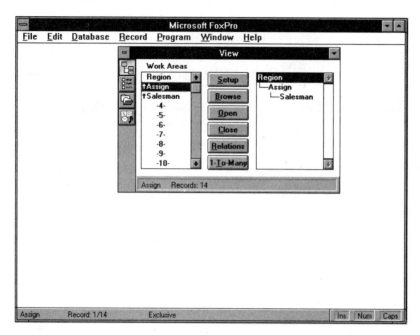

Figure 8.24 Designating REGION.DBF as the parent in the relation chain

In short, relating databases in this way—with ASSIGN as the child of SALESMAN and REGION as the child of ASSIGN—allows you to focus on the regions to which a given salesperson is assigned. But, to view information regarding all the salespeople assigned to a given region, choose REGION.DBF as the parent in the relation chain (see Figure 8.24) and designate the REGION_ID tag as the index controlling the ASSIGN database.

As a result, all the records related to a given sales region can be displayed in ASSIGN.DBF. When you highlight the R1 record in the REGION Browse window, for example, four records are displayed in the ASSIGN Browse window linking S0, S3, S6, and S9 in SALESMAN.DBF (see Figure 8.25).

To view detailed data for a specific record displayed in the ASSIGN Browse window, simply highlight that record. In return, all the fields about that record in SALESMAN.DBF will be displayed in the SALESMAN.DBF Browse window accordingly.

The three database files also can be linked using FoxPro commands. Use the following commands to link the SALESMAN and REGION database files through the ASSIGN.DBF relation table:

```
SELECT A
USE SALESMAN
SELECT B
USE ASSIGN
```

```
SET ORDER TO SALSMAN_ID
SELECT C
USE REGION
SET ORDER TO REGION_ID
SELECT A
SET RELATION TO SALSMAN_ID INTO B
SELECT B
SET RELATION TO REGION_ID INTO C
```

After setting up the relations, their related records can be viewed in the Browse windows. Alternatively, issue the LIST command to display records in the related database files. If, for example, you want to know all the salespeople who are supervised by the manager named Alice F. Gibson, issue the following LIST command:

```
SELECT A
LIST LAST, C->>MANAGER, C->>REGION FOR C->>MANAGER='Alice F. Gibson'
```

The LIST command displays all the records in the parent (SALESMAN.DBF in work area A) related to the records having values 'Alice F. Gibson' in the MANAGER field of the child (REGION.DBF in work area C). The results of the LIST command are shown in Figure 8.26.

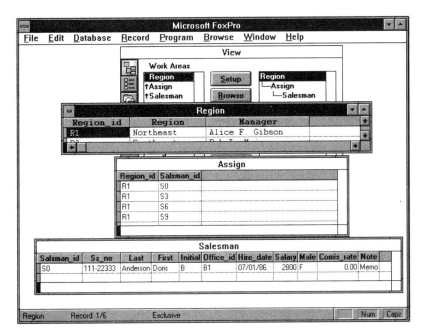

Figure 8.25 Relating records in REGION.DBF and SALESMAN.DBF

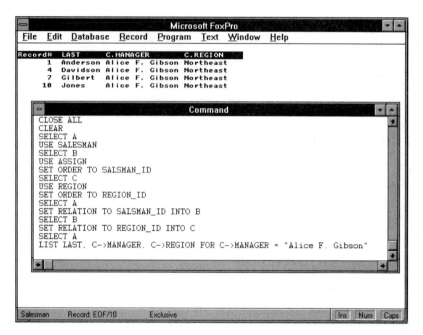

Figure 8.26 Showing the salesperson managed by Gibson

Be aware, however, that the power of the LIST command is limited and results produced may be incomplete. To find all the managers for the sales regions assigned to salesperson Harvey, issue the following commands:

```
SELECT A
LIST LAST, C->>MANAGER FOR LAST = 'Harvey'
```

When you execute this command, you will see only the name of one regional manager displayed, even though Harvey has been assigned to more than one sales region:

Record#	LAST	C.MANAGER
8	Harvey	Cathy M. Wilson

Although Harvey has been assigned to regions R4, R5, and R6, only the manager of Region R4 is displayed as her regional manager. Managers for Regions R5 (Chris C. Hall) and R6 (Helen T. Taylor) are not displayed. Obviously, the LIST command is not always an appropriate command for extracting information from within multiple related database files. Instead, you would use the data query technique discussed in the next chapter to find the information you want from the related files.

Chapter Summary

This chapter detailed the procedures for combining data fields and records from different database files. You learned how to temporarily relate records in these database files so that their data elements can be manipulated. This capability is the most powerful tool that you can use to manage relational databases. With it, you are able to efficiently access all data elements that are logically organized in different database files. In subsequent chapters, you will learn how to use this tool to find information and produce reports from multiple database files.

9

Querying Data

An Overview

So far, we have covered a variety of topics that relate to creating, organizing, and putting information into databases. But of real interest to most database users is how to find and get information out of databases. In this chapter, you will learn different and creative ways to retrieve your most precious resource—your data.

We will focus primarily on FoxPro's powerful Relational Query By Example (RQBE) techniques, which enable you to locate a set of records from one or more database files that provide the information you want. In addition, you will learn how to use the Locate and Seek operations to quickly extract records from a current database file for viewing and editing purposes.

Locating Data Records

For each database file that you open, FoxPro maintains a *record pointer* that is responsible for keeping track of where you are in the file. The record pointer indicates the *current record* to FoxPro—this is the record with which FoxPro is actually working at any given time. When you open a database file, the record pointer is placed on the first record in the database. Then, when you move to the next record in the database, the record pointer is positioned accordingly on the second record. When you are using the FoxPro interface to interactively browse a database, for example, the current record is the one that is highlighted.

There are two ways of moving the record pointer from one record to another: sequentially or directly. When FoxPro traverses a database file sequentially, it moves the record pointer from one record to the next, very much as you might move the cursor record by record through a database while searching for a particular record in the Browse window. As it traverses the database, it singles out each record for attention, and the record pointer is positioned at each record for a certain period of time. To search a database sequentially, FoxPro provides the Locate operation.

In some cases, you will want FoxPro to move the record pointer directly from the current record to another record that you identify. This ability to move from one record directly to the record that you specify requires that the database be indexed and that you are seeking a value that corresponds to all or a portion of the index expression. FoxPro offers the Seek operation to allow you to move the record pointer directly from the current record to a noncontiguous record.

The Locate and Seek operations both are designed to allow you to pinpoint records in a database file. While the Seek operation tends to work much faster than the Locate operation, it also requires that the database be indexed. The Locate operation, although it can be significantly slower than seeking, also can be much more versatile.

USING THE LOCATE OPERATION

To use the Locate operation in a current database file to find a record that meets certain criteria, choose the Locate option from the Record menu while the database is open in the current work area. Then provide the selection criteria that will enable FoxPro to identify the record for which you are looking.

The Locate operation searches sequentially from the beginning (top) to the end (bottom) of a database file until it finds the first record that satisfies the criteria specified. When it finds a record, it places the record pointer on that record, at which time it becomes the current record. If Locate fails to find any record that satisfies the search criteria, it places its record pointer after the last record in the database file, and the "End of Locate Scope" message is displayed in the status bar.

The Locate option may be selected as long as the database file that you are searching is open in the current work area. Although it is not required, normally you would choose the option while the data records are displayed in the Browse window.

Once the Locate operation has found a record, it is available for examination and/or modification. As an exercise, use the Locate operation to point out Davidson's salary record in SALESMAN.DBF. Open the database in the current work area and then choose the Locate option from the Record menu. FoxPro displays the Locate dialog (see Figure 9.1), where the search criteria is defined by selecting the Scope... and For... buttons. Note: If you are searching *all* the records in the database file, it is not necessary to select the Scope button because its default

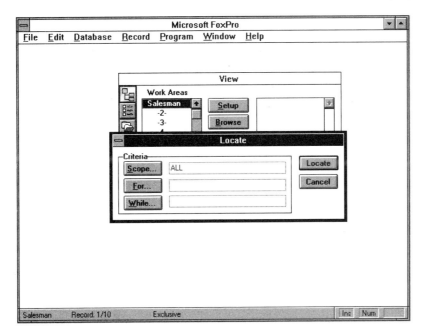

Figure 9.1 The Locate dialog

setting is All. If you are not searching all records, select Scope and then select the records to be searched by turning on the appropriate radio button in the Scope dialog (see Figure 9.2).

Selecting the All radio button means that all the records in the current database will be subjected to the Locate operation; Next directs the Locate operation to act on a range of records beginning with the current record and continuing for the number of records specified in the text box next to the radio button. To select a specific record for the Locate operation, enter the record number in the box next to the Record radio button after selecting that button; select Rest to direct the Locate operation to act on the range of records beginning with the current record and ending with the last record in the current data file.

Defining Search Conditions

The For... and While... buttons are used to define search conditions. Selecting the For... button enables you to define the expression that directs the Locate operation. All the records that satisfy the conditions defined in the expression will be searched by the Locate operation. Select the While... button to define another search condition. The Locate operation continues searching the records only as long as the condition remains true. As soon as it encounters a record that fails to meet the While condition, the search is halted. If you define both the For and While

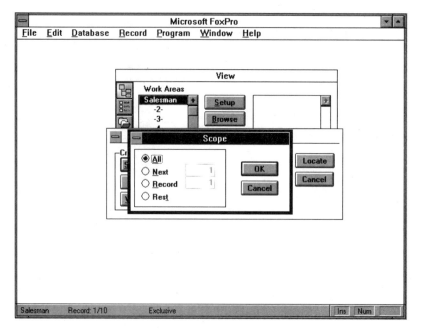

Figure 9.2 The Scope dialog

conditions, only those records that satisfy both conditions will be included in the results of the Locate operation. Note that the While condition is valid only when the data scope is set to All.

The Expression Builder is used to specify both For and While conditions. To define a For condition, select the For... button to bring up the Expression Builder. Then define the expression in the For text box, describing the search conditions in the same way that you defined record filter conditions. Any type of data fields may be included in the expression, along with the necessary mathematical and logical operators.

Searching for Character Strings

Records can be searched by comparing a search string with the contents of a database field. To find Davidson's record, for example, define LAST = "Davidson" or SALESMAN.LAST = "Davidson" as the search condition (see Figure 9.3).

When the Locate operation is executed, it compares each string with the search string ("Davidson") in the LAST character field until it finds an acceptable match. Once it does, it displays a message (e.g., Record = 4) in the Status Bar showing its record number. If the Browse window is open, the record pointer will move to the record that FoxPro has located. If the Browse window is not open, the record found by the Locate operation will be highlighted when it is opened (see Figure 9.4). Note

Querying Data 325

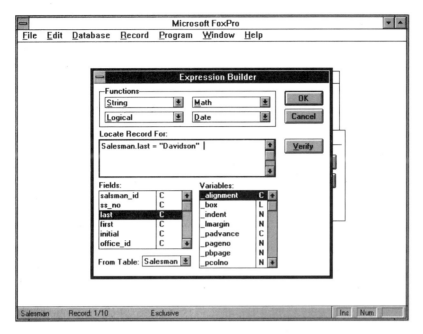

Figure 9.3 Searching for a specific character string

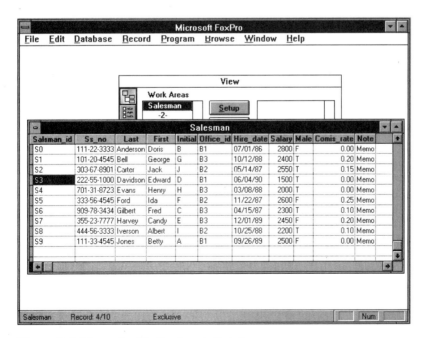

Figure 9.4 Record with the located string

that the record with "Davidson" in the LAST field is highlighted in both Browse and Change modes. At this point, you may choose to view or edit its contents.

In this example, the Locate operation found the character string "Davidson" in record S3 when it compared the string with the search string "Davidson". This happens to be an exact match; that is, every character in the LAST field of record S3 matched those in the search string. But the Locate operation will accept a partial match as long as all the characters in the search string match, character by character, the string in the data field against which it is compared. The string in the data field may contain more and different characters beyond those contained in the search string. With these parameters then, it is possible to find "Davidson" in the LAST field by using any one of following search conditions:

```
LAST = "Davids"
LAST = "David"
LAST = "Dav"
LAST = "D"
```

The above are acceptable because as soon as a string in the data field that is being searched matches, character by character, the search string, it is considered an acceptable match. This partial match requirement often makes the search process less restrictive; you do not have to remember the whole string in order to find it. Be aware, however, that if you use LAST = "Dav" as the search string, you may find a character string such as "Davis"; or a search string of "D" may find the first character string beginning with "D".

One restriction on defining a search string in a data field is that the string must appear *after* the data field. Therefore, all of the following search conditions are unacceptable:

```
"Davidson" = LAST
"David" = LAST
"D" = LAST
```

The Exact Setting

If you require an exact match of the search condition, select the Set Option panel button (the second button on the far left) from the View dialog. When the default View window setting is replaced by the Set Option panel, check the Exact box (SET EXACT ON). SET EXACT OFF is the default value. (See Figure 9.5.)

In order to locate the data record of the person(s) whose first name is "John," not "Johnny," define the following search condition after setting Exact on:

```
FIRST = "John"
```

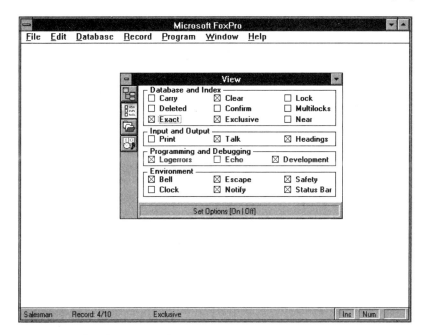

Figure 9.5 Setting Exact On

Ignoring Case

When search strings are specified, case is important. You will not find "Davidson" if you type "davidson" or "DAVIDSON". To ignore case, convert the strings in the data field either to all upper- or all lowercase letters by creating an expression that uses the UPPER() or LOWER() function. (A function tells FoxPro to return a predefined value. The object enclosed in the parentheses is called an argument. A function argument may be a data field or an expression. You will learn more about this in a later chapter.) UPPER(LAST), for instance, will return a string in which the contents of the LAST field have been converted to uppercase. Similarly, the function LOWER(LAST) will return a string that consists of the LAST field in lowercase letters only. Therefore, any one of the following expressions may be used as a search condition for finding a record in which the LAST field has been entered as "Davidson", "DAVIDSON", or "davidson":

```
UPPER(LAST) = "DAVIDSON"
LOWER(LAST) = "davidson"
```

The UPPER(LAST) function in the first search condition returns a string in which all the letters in the LAST data field are converted to uppercase before it is compared with the search character string "DAVIDSON". As a result, case is ignored in the character string in the LAST data field. The second search condition works the same way by converting the character string to lowercase before it is compared with the character string "davidson".

Two additional points that relate to ignoring case when searching a database are worth noting: First, an expression like UPPER(LAST) that converts the contents of a database field into a new string does not actually modify the contents of the database field itself. Second, a frequent cause of error in searching a database occurs when the search string and the database field expression are in different cases. For example, if you are attempting to make the search case-insensitive by using the UPPER function to convert the contents of a particular field, the search string also must be entirely in uppercase. As a result, the following search conditions will not succeed in locating the desired record:

```
UPPER(last) = "Davidson"
LOWER(last) = "DAVIDSON"
```

Searching for Numeric Values

The Locate operation also can be used to find a numeric value in a current database file. To find a salesperson who has a monthly salary of $2,000 or less from SALESMAN.DBF, the search condition would be defined as SALARY <= 2000. Upon execution, the Locate operation finds in the SALARY field the first record having a salary that is less than or equal to $2,000 (see Figure 9.6).

You can see that record S3 (the fourth record or Record=4) was found by the Locate operation. It is important to note that if there is more than one record in the SALARY field satisfying the search criterion, the record pointer will be placed on the first record that satisfies the search condition. The Locate operation does not return a set of records; it stops searching once the first record that satisfies the search criterion is found.

To find the next record that satisfies the search criterion, select the Continue option from the Record menu. As a result, the record pointer is positioned on the next record that satisfies the search criterion if there are no additional records that meet the criterion; otherwise, the pointer is positioned after the last record in the database. If, as an exercise, you select the Continue option from the Record menu now, the next record—S4, SALARY <= 2000—is highlighted (see Figure 9.7).

Searching for Dates

Extracting a specific date from a data field in a database file is similar to finding a character string or a numeric value. But, when you specify a search criterion for a date value, it must be enclosed in a pair of braces ({ }). So, to find the salesperson

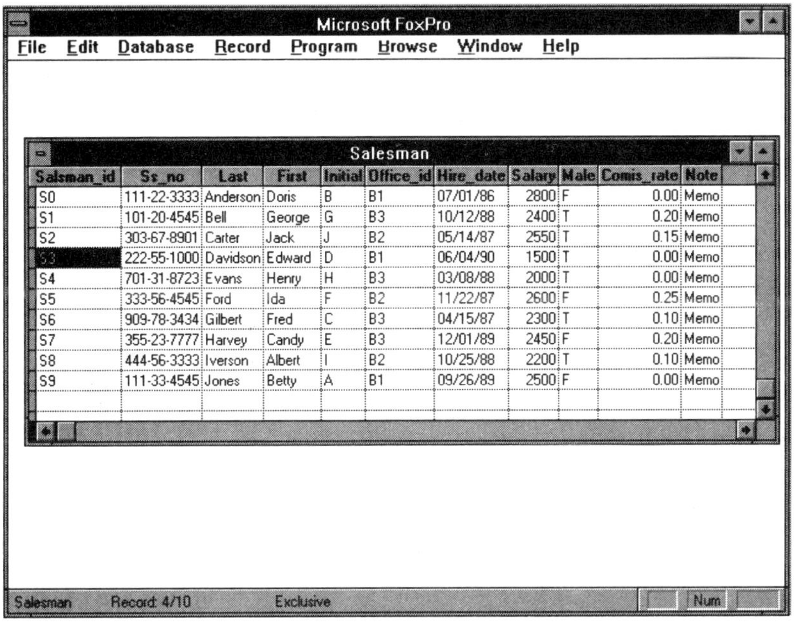

Querying Data 329

Salsman_id	Ss_no	Last	First	Initial	Office_id	Hire_date	Salary	Male	Comis_rate	Note
S0	111-22-3333	Anderson	Doris	B	B1	07/01/86	2800	F	0.00	Memo
S1	101-20-4545	Bell	George	G	B3	10/12/88	2400	T	0.20	Memo
S2	303-67-8901	Carter	Jack	J	B2	05/14/87	2550	T	0.15	Memo
S3	222-55-1000	Davidson	Edward	D	B1	06/04/90	1500	T	0.00	Memo
S4	701-31-8723	Evans	Henry	H	B3	03/08/88	2000	T	0.00	Memo
S5	333-56-4545	Ford	Ida	F	B2	11/22/87	2600	F	0.25	Memo
S6	909-78-3434	Gilbert	Fred	C	B3	04/15/87	2300	T	0.10	Memo
S7	355-23-7777	Harvey	Candy	E	B3	12/01/89	2450	F	0.20	Memo
S8	444-56-3333	Iverson	Albert	I	B2	10/25/88	2200	T	0.10	Memo
S9	111-33-4545	Jones	Betty	A	B1	09/26/89	2500	F	0.00	Memo

Figure 9.6 Using Locate to find a numeric value

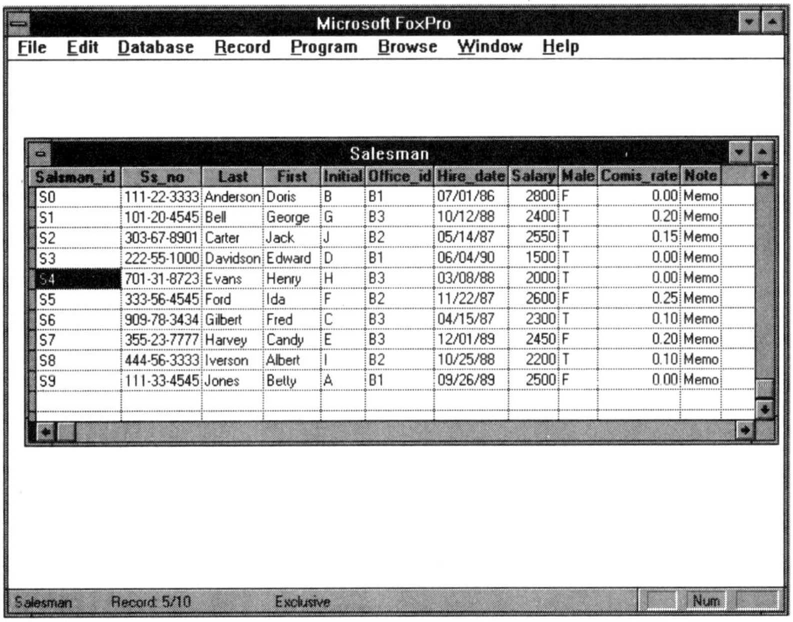

Salsman_id	Ss_no	Last	First	Initial	Office_id	Hire_date	Salary	Male	Comis_rate	Note
S0	111-22-3333	Anderson	Doris	B	B1	07/01/86	2800	F	0.00	Memo
S1	101-20-4545	Bell	George	G	B3	10/12/88	2400	T	0.20	Memo
S2	303-67-8901	Carter	Jack	J	B2	05/14/87	2550	T	0.15	Memo
S3	222-55-1000	Davidson	Edward	D	B1	06/04/90	1500	T	0.00	Memo
S4	701-31-8723	Evans	Henry	H	B3	03/08/88	2000	T	0.00	Memo
S5	333-56-4545	Ford	Ida	F	B2	11/22/87	2600	F	0.25	Memo
S6	909-78-3434	Gilbert	Fred	C	B3	04/15/87	2300	T	0.10	Memo
S7	355-23-7777	Harvey	Candy	E	B3	12/01/89	2450	F	0.20	Memo
S8	444-56-3333	Iverson	Albert	I	B2	10/25/88	2200	T	0.10	Memo
S9	111-33-4545	Jones	Betty	A	B1	09/26/89	2500	F	0.00	Memo

Figure 9.7 Using the Continue menu option

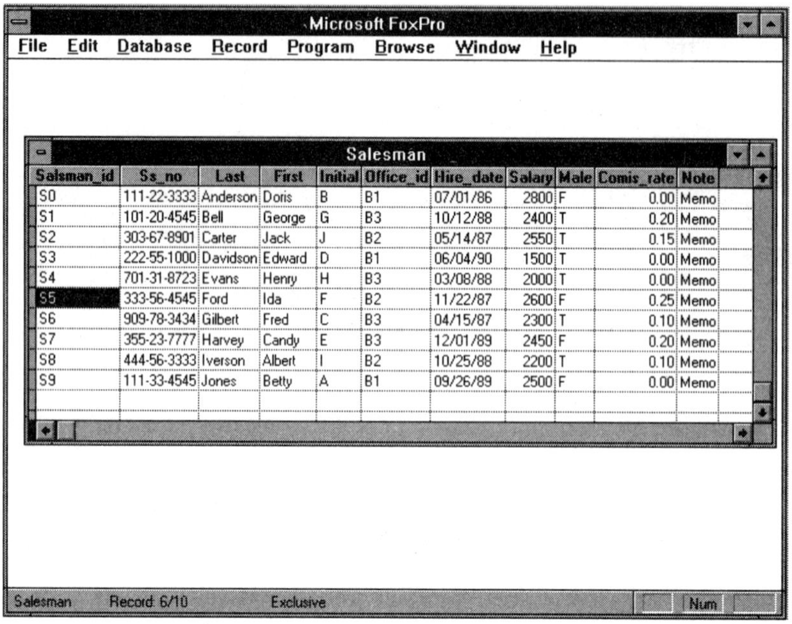

![Figure 9.8 showing the Salesman table in FoxPro with record 6/10 (Ida Ford) highlighted]

Figure 9.8 Record with the Located date

who was hired on November 22, 1987, define the search criterion as HIRE_DATE = {11/22/87}.

When the Locate operation is carried out with this search criterion, FoxPro moves the record pointer to the first record it finds with 11/22/87 as the value in the HIRE_DATE field; in our sample database, that record belongs to Ida Ford (see Figure 9.8).

Searching for Logical Values

If you want to locate the first record in a current database file with the value of either true (.T.) or false (.F.) in one of its logical fields, simply define the search criterion for the Locate operation by including periods around the logical value. To find the first record belonging to a male salesperson in SALESMAN.DBF, specify MALE = .T. as the search criterion for the Locate operation. Then execute Locate; it scans the values in the MALE logical field until it finds the first record having a true value. In our sample database, as Figure 9.9 shows, it is the record for George Bell.

If there is no record satisfying the search criterion, the record pointer is placed at the last record in the database file.

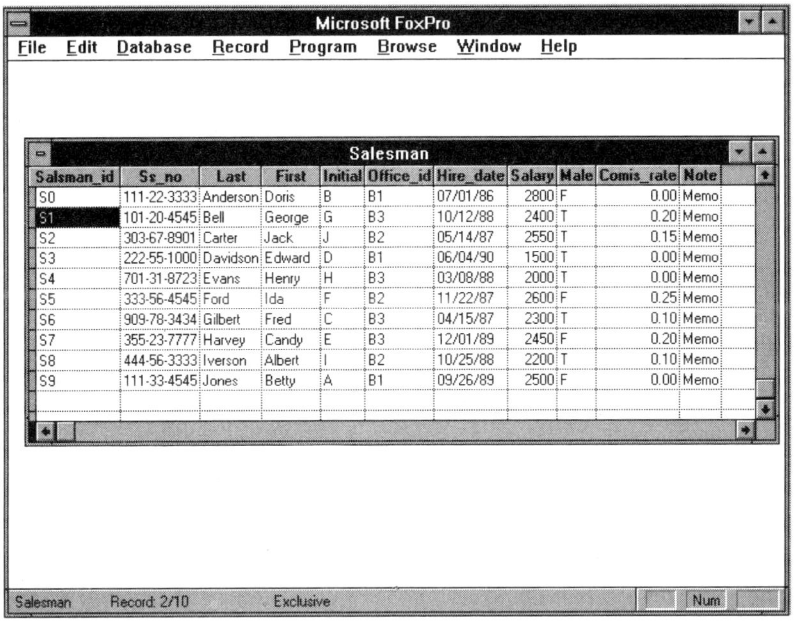
Microsoft FoxPro
File Edit Database Record Program Browse Window Help
Salesman
Salesman Record: 2/10 Exclusive Num

Salsman_id	Ss_no	Last	First	Initial	Office_id	Hire_date	Salary	Male	Comis_rate	Note
S0	111-22-3333	Anderson	Doris	B	B1	07/01/86	2800	F	0.00	Memo
S1	101-20-4545	Bell	George	G	B3	10/12/88	2400	T	0.20	Memo
S2	303-67-8901	Carter	Jack	J	B2	05/14/87	2550	T	0.15	Memo
S3	222-55-1000	Davidson	Edward	D	B1	06/04/90	1500	T	0.00	Memo
S4	701-31-8723	Evans	Henry	H	B3	03/08/88	2000	T	0.00	Memo
S5	333-56-4545	Ford	Ida	F	B2	11/22/87	2600	F	0.25	Memo
S6	909-78-3434	Gilbert	Fred	C	B3	04/15/87	2300	T	0.10	Memo
S7	355-23-7777	Harvey	Candy	E	B3	12/01/89	2450	F	0.20	Memo
S8	444-56-3333	Iverson	Albert	I	B2	10/25/88	2200	T	0.10	Memo
S9	111-33-4545	Jones	Betty	A	B1	09/26/89	2500	F	0.00	Memo

Figure 9.9 Using Locate to find a logical value

Using Logical Connectors

When the search criteria are defined, logical connectors such as AND and OR can be included to define more complex conditions. These connectors enable you to specify compound search conditions that may include multiple fields.

AND as the Logical Connector

The AND connector is used to combine two or more search conditions to form the search criteria. A record is then selected by the Locate operation only when it satisfies all the conditions in the criteria. Here are some examples of expressions incorporating the AND connector:

```
MALE = .T. AND COMIS_RATE > 0.10
SALARY > 2500 AND HIRE_DATE >= {01/01/89}
MALE = .T. AND SALARY <= 2500 AND COMIS_RATE > 0.10
```

The first two expressions use AND to join search conditions involving two different fields. The Locate operation will find the first record that satisfies both these conditions simultaneously. The first expression uses AND to join the MALE = .T. condition with the COMIS_RATE > 0.10 condition; FoxPro will search for those salespeople who are male and receive a commission of more than 10 percent. Similarly, the second expression joins SALARY > 2500 and HIRE_DATE >= {01/01/89} with the AND logical connector; and FoxPro searches for the records of salespeople hired on or after January 1, 1989 and whose salaries exceed $2,500. AND also may be used to join more than two search conditions. The third expression above joins three search conditions using two logical AND connectors. FoxPro will locate the first record for which all three conditions are true.

OR As the Logical Connector

Using OR as the logical connector to define compound search conditions for the Locate operation results in a record that is selected as long as one of the two conditions is met. Here is an example:

```
MALE = .T. OR COMIS_RATE > 0.10
```

This expression uses OR to connect the MALE = .T. and COMIS_RATE > 0.10 conditions. As a result, a record will be selected when either the MALE = .T. or the COMIS_RATE > 0.10 condition is true. Of course, if both conditions are met in the same record, the record will be selected as well. As with AND, more than one OR connector may be included in an expression to build complex search conditions:

```
MALE = .T. OR COMIS_RATE > 0.10 OR HIRE_DATE >= {01/01/89}
```

In this case, a record will be selected as long as one of the three conditions in the expression is true.

Furthermore, AND and OR may be combined in an expression to define search conditions. But, to avoid confusion, you may want to use parentheses to clearly define the conditions. For example:

```
(MALE =.T. OR SALARY < 2200) AND (MALE = .F. OR SALARY > 2800)
```

The parentheses are used to group the conditions and determine which is to be evaluated first. If there is more than one pair of parentheses in an expression, evaluation is from left to right. Therefore, when the above condition is evaluated, the expression contained in the first pair of parentheses, (MALE = .T. OR SALARY < 2200), will be evaluated before the expression (MALE = .F. OR SALARY > 2800) in the second pair of parentheses.

The placement of parentheses is important, because search conditions can have different meanings if you eliminate or rearrange them. If, for example, you eliminate all the parentheses in the preceding expression, the search condition will have a different meaning.

Nested parentheses also may be used to define the search criteria, in which case the expression in the inner parentheses is evaluated before the expression specified in the outside parentheses. Therefore, in the expression:

```
(MALE = .T. OR (SALARY >= 2000 AND SALARY <= 4000))
```

(SALARY >= 2000 AND SALARY <= 4000) will be evaluated first. The records that satisfy the condition defined by this expression will be evaluated with the MALE = .T. condition.

Using LOCATE Commands

As an alternative to choosing the Locate option from the Record menu, a database file can be directed to search for records by invoking the LOCATE command. The search conditions then would be defined as an expression in the FOR clause:

```
LOCATE FOR <expression>
        [<record scope>]
```

The LOCATE command sequentially searches the current database file for the first record that satisfies the conditions specified in the FOR expression. The optional record scope can be added to identify the records that are subjected to the search. Here are examples of LOCATE commands:

```
USE SALESMAN
LOCATE FOR LAST = "Davidson"
LOCATE FOR UPPER(FIRST) = "DORIS"
LOCATE FOR MALE = .F. AND SALARY > 2500
LOCATE FOR HIRE_DATE > {01/01/89} OR COMIS_RATE > 0.20
```

USING SEEK OPERATIONS

Because the Locate operation scans through the database file sequentially from top to bottom and examines each record in passing, the amount of time it takes to find a record depends largely on the number of records in the database file. If your database file has fewer than a thousand records, it may be acceptable to use the Locate operation to find your records. But the search process becomes unacceptably slow if the database file has a very large number of records. For such large files, the Seek operation is much faster; it works with an indexed database file whose records have been ordered, and, therefore, provides direct access to the first record meeting the search criteria.

To find records with the Seek operation, the database file must first be indexed on the key expression whose values you are searching for. Usually, this is done by designating as the master index an existing index tag whose key field matches the search expression. (It also is possible to create the appropriate index tag and make

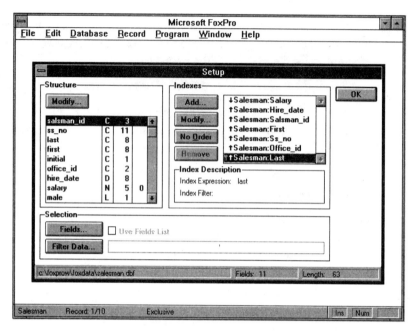

Figure 9.10 Setting Last Name index tag as master index

it the current master index, but this is done less frequently because it is too time-consuming.) All you need to do to find a record is specify the value of the index tag. You do not have to specify the complete expression as the search criteria. To find a salesperson by his or her last name in SALESMAN.DBF, for example, set the LAST index tag as the master index in the Setup window (see Figure 9.10).

Once the database file is ordered appropriately, choose the Seek option from the Record menu to begin the record search. In response to the menu option selection, you are asked to specify the value you are seeking in the expression text box provided. If the value is a character string, enclose the string in a pair of double quote marks (see Figure 9.11).

Figure 9.11 displays the current index key in parentheses (e.g., Index = LAST). Remember: The value entered for the Seek operation must be of the same type as the index key. In this case, because the LAST index tag consists of the LAST field, a character type and only a character string may be entered as a seek value (e.g., "Davidson"); if you enter an incorrect value type, FoxPro will display a message informing you that "Expression must be of type C" (or whatever type is correct). Once executed, the Seek operation searches the indexed file for the first occurrence of a record whose index key expression matches the expression you have specified. Unlike the Locate option, however, Seek uses the index file to search the database. This difference means that Seek has nearly direct and immediate access to the first

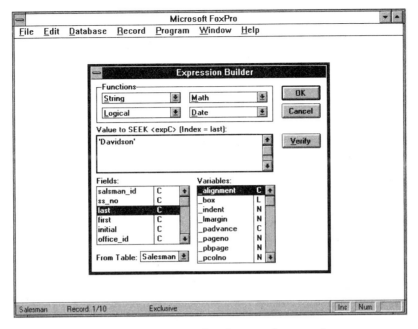

Figure 9.11 Defining the expression for a seek operation

record whose key meets the Seek expression. If you view the records in SALESMAN.DBF at this point, you would find that the record selected by the Seek operation is highlighted and belongs to salesperson Davidson (see Figure 9.12). Seek highlights the first record that meets the selection criteria.

Like the Locate operation, the Seek operation accepts a partial match unless Exact is set to on. Thus, if you specify "David" as the Seek value, it will find Davidson in the LAST data field in the file.

The index key does not have to be a character string. Seek accepts date, numeric, and logical values as well. It is important to stress once again, however, that the data type of the index key and the search expression must correspond. When searching for a date value, enclose it in braces (e.g., {01/01/89}); for numeric values, just specify the value as the Seek expression itself; when expressing a logical value, include the periods (e.g., .T. or .F.) in the Seek expression.

Using SEEK Commands

The Seek operation, too, may be executed by issuing a FoxPro command in the following format:

```
SEEK <expression>
```

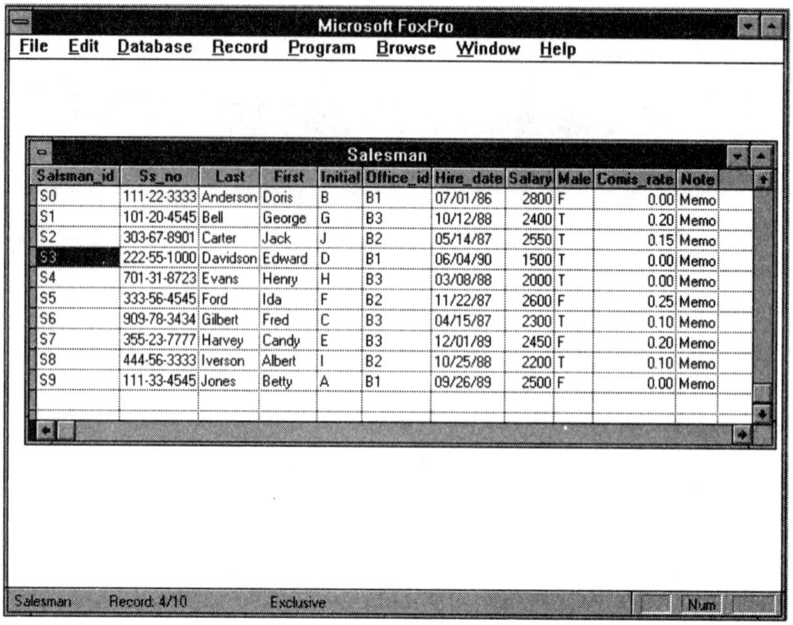

Salsman_id	Ss_no	Last	First	Initial	Office_id	Hire_date	Salary	Male	Comis_rate	Note
S0	111-22-3333	Anderson	Doris	B	B1	07/01/86	2800	F	0.00	Memo
S1	101-20-4545	Bell	George	G	B3	10/12/88	2400	T	0.20	Memo
S2	303-67-8901	Carter	Jack	J	B2	05/14/87	2550	T	0.15	Memo
S3	222-55-1000	Davidson	Edward	D	B1	06/04/90	1500	T	0.00	Memo
S4	701-31-8723	Evans	Henry	H	B3	03/08/88	2000	T	0.00	Memo
S5	333-56-4545	Ford	Ida	F	B2	11/22/87	2600	F	0.25	Memo
S6	909-78-3434	Gilbert	Fred	C	B3	04/15/87	2300	T	0.10	Memo
S7	355-23-7777	Harvey	Candy	E	B3	12/01/89	2450	F	0.20	Memo
S8	444-56-3333	Iverson	Albert	I	B2	10/25/88	2200	T	0.10	Memo
S9	111-33-4545	Jones	Betty	A	B1	09/26/89	2500	F	0.00	Memo

Figure 9.12 Record resulting from the Seek operaton

So, to find and edit the record belonging to the salesperson who was hired on March 8, 1988, the following commands may be invoked:

```
USE SALESMAN
SET ORDER TO HIRE_DATE
SEEK {01/01/88}
EDIT
```

The SET ORDER command is issued to designate the existing index tag named HIRE_DATE as the master index. The index tag uses the HIRE_DATE data field as the index key. If you have not set up a HIRE_DATE index tag, you can create one and add it to the compound index file, SALESMAN.CDX. Although it is not a good practice, you may create a standard HIREDATE.IDX index file, as shown below, to order your records before carrying out the Seek operation.

```
USE SALESMAN
INDEX ON HIRE_DATE TO HIREDATE
SEEK {12/01/89}
EDIT
```

Querying Data with RQBE

RQBE is a flexible tool that enables you to easily and efficiently isolate the information you would like to extract and then determine how and where you would like it to appear. RQBE, by incorporating what Fox Software calls Rushmore Technology, executes most queries very quickly; this is particularly important if you are working with large databases.

In addition to its speed and flexibility, RQBE offers a number of other attractive features:

- *Ease of use.* Selection criteria are defined by providing an example of the kind of records you would like to include in the query.
- *Optimization.* When choosing between the Locate and Seek options to query databases, a decision has to be made—deliberate or not—about how the results of a query should be found. RQBE relieves you of this responsibility. It examines your query and the data and decides on the best available access path to the data.
- *Set Orientation.* In contrast to Seek and Locate, which find one record at a time, RQBE returns all of the records that meet your selection criteria. These can then be manipulated as a set, rather than individually.

CREATING RQBE QUERIES

The process of querying data with RQBE requires several steps. First, bring up the RQBE window and specify a number of query settings. These settings determine which database files to use, which fields to include in the output from the query, how to organize that output, and where to send it. The next step involves defining the selection criteria for the query operation. This requires identifying the query field and specifying the query conditions. Finally, the query is saved and executed.

The RQBE Window

The first step in creating a new query is to bring up the RQBE window. To do that, first open the database file you need in the current work area. (Although you can open other database files later, FoxPro requires that at least one file be open before it allows you to access the RQBE window.) To query data in the SALESMAN database file, for example, open it in work area 1; then select the New option from the File menu, followed by selecting Query as the type of new file to create. As a result, the RQBE window appears (see Figure 9.13).

338 Understanding FoxPro 2.5 for Windows

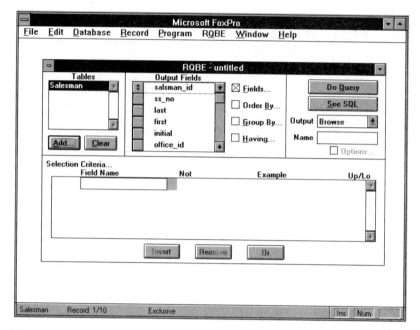

Figure 9.13 The RQBE window

In the upper left-hand corner of Figure 9.13 you can see the database files that are available for the query operation. In this example, because SALESMAN.DBF is open in the current work area, it is shown in the Tables list box. Below that are two buttons: Add and Clear. If you need to use more than one database file, use the Add button to insert the others to the list box; to remove an existing database file from the list box, choose the Clear button.

In the top center of the window are the selected output fields that will be included in the query results. By default, FoxPro includes all the data fields associated with the selected database files in the Output Field list. But you may change the output fields list by selecting the Fields... check box that appears next to the Output Fields list box.

Below the Fields... check box are three more check boxes: Order By..., Group By..., and Having.... Use one or more of these to order and organize your query results.

In the upper right-hand corner of the RQBE window is an Output drop-down list that is used to specify where the results of your query will appear. By default, output is sent to a Browse window after FoxPro carries out the query operation. You may choose, however, to create a formatted report or labels that FoxPro will print, display, or write to a file; you also may store the results of the query in either a permanent or a temporary database file.

Querying Data   339

The lower portion of the RQBE window is used for defining the selection criteria for the query operation. Define one selection criterion per line in the text box provided; to build a compound selection criteria, use one or more of the three buttons provided: Insert, Remove, and Or.

Finally, the Do Query button is provided for executing the operation after all the query settings and search conditions have been specified.

At this point, take note of the See SQL button just below the Do Query button. If you select this button, you will see that FoxPro has translated all the query instructions into a set of Structured Query Language (SQL) commands. This is an excellent way to learn about SQL commands if they are of interest to you. If, however, you do not intend to familiarize yourself with the SQL language, this button may be ignored.

Selecting Output Data Fields

After opening the RQBE window, the first step in defining a query is to identify the data fields that you would like to include in the output. To include all the existing data fields of the selected database file, do nothing. By default, all of the existing data fields of the open database file are selected automatically by FoxPro as output fields, and, subsequently, are shown in the Output Fields list.

To select only some of these data fields for output, check the Fields... box. The RQBE Select Fields dialog, which is used to select data fields, appears. Then, to maintain only the FIRST, INITIAL, LAST, and SALARY fields from the database file, remove the unwanted fields from the selected fields list: Double click on the unwanted field in the Selected Output drop-down list or, with the keyboard, use the Tab key to move the highlight into the list and select the field with an arrow key; press Enter. To remove all the fields in the list, select the Remove All button or press the "L" key. If you have mistakenly removed a field, you can retrieve it from the Fields In Table list to the Selected Output list by selecting the Move button and following the same procedure.

In Figure 9.14, only four fields remain after removing the unwanted fields from the Selected Output box. This list determines the order in which fields will appear in the final output, as well as if a field is included in the query. If you would like to change the order of the selected data fields, there are two ways to do so. First, although this is somewhat cumbersome, you could remove all the data fields from the selected fields list and then select them again in the order you want them to appear in the final output. The second, preferable method is to rearrange the order of the selected fields in the Output Fields list box or in the Selected Output list box. This can be accomplished with either the mouse or the keyboard. With the keyboard, first position the cursor on the field you would like to move. Press

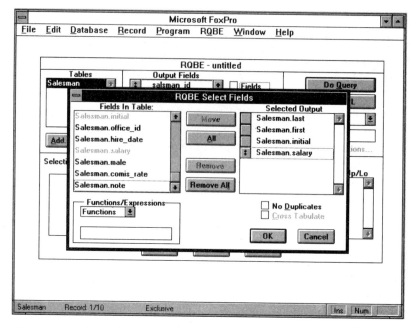

Figure 9.14 Selecting output data fields

Ctrl+PgUp to move the record up one position or Ctrl+PgDn to move it down one position. (On some keyboards, you can press Ctrl+UpArrow and Ctrl+DownArrow, as well.) With the mouse, select the field you intend to move, position the mouse pointer on the double arrow immediately to the left of the field name and drag it to the desired position.

To position the LAST field between the INITIAL and SALARY fields in this example, move the LAST field down two lines. If you are using the mouse, point it on the double-headed arrow to the left of the LAST field and then drag it to its new position. With the keyboard, use the Tab and arrow keys to highlight the LAST field and then press the Ctrl+PgDn (or Ctrl+DownArrow) key combination to move it to its new position. To move the selected field list up, use the Ctrl+PgUp (or Ctrl+UpArrow) after you have highlighted the field you want to reposition.

The RQBE Select Fields dialog also provides the No Duplicates check box that makes it possible to eliminate duplicate records from query results. This option is very useful for removing redundant information from the database. If, for example, you have entered duplicate records for the same salesperson in the SALESMAN database, simply choose this option to discard the extraneous record. Another situation that can be solved by checking the No Duplicates check box is to eliminate records containing the same values in the data fields selected by the query. For example, although no two records in the original database have the same values for all the data fields, some of the data fields share the same data values in some

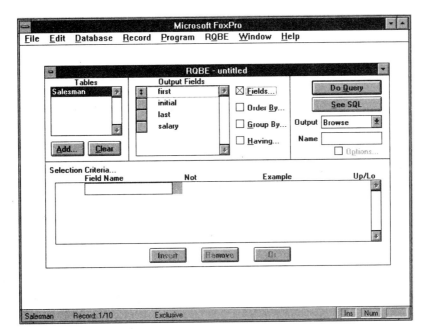

Figure 9.15 Selected output fields

records. When you select these data fields for query output, the query produces duplicate records. The No Duplicates option can eliminate these records.

In our example, however, there are no records in the SALESMAN file that share identical data values in the data fields selected, so there is no need to check the No Duplicates box.

After you have finished selecting the data fields in the order of your choice, select the OK button to exit from the RQBE Select Fields dialog. When you return to the RQBE window you will see that the selected data fields are displayed in the Output Fields box in the order specified (see Figure 9.15). Note that, as long as the Output Fields list box contains the fields whose values you want to appear in your query, you can use it to rearrange the order of the selected data fields by employing the same techniques that you applied to the Selected Output list box of the RQBE Select Fields dialog.

Identifying Output Destinations

After selecting the fields for which FoxPro will *return* information for each record that matches your selection criteria, you also can determine where FoxPro is to *send* the information about these records. You may choose to view the resulting records in a Browse window, or you can save them in a temporary or permanent database file. In addition, you can use the resulting records to produce reports and mailing labels.

There are four possible destinations—Browse, Report/Label, Table/DBF, Cursor—that you can choose from the Output popup in the RQBE window to channel the query results. To view the resulting records in a Browse window, choose that option as the output destination; a Browse window is, in any case, the default destination for all RQBE output. If you intend to use the query results in custom reports and mailing labels, choose the Report/Label option.

If you need to save the resulting records in a database file, choose either the Cursor or the Table/DBF option. If you choose Cursor as the destination, all the resulting records will be saved in a temporary database file that FoxPro will open automatically. Once you close this database, FoxPro will erase it, effectively removing all its records in the process. But, if you intend to use the resulting records from the query operation later, they should be saved in a permanent database file with a name of your choice. To do that, choose the Table/DBF option as the output destination. In return, you will be asked to name the database file.

Ordering Query Results

If the query operation returns more than one record, you can specify how you would like to order those records in the RQBE window by selecting the Order By... check box. In return, you are asked to select the order in which the resulting records are to be arranged. To arrange the resulting records in descending order by the values in the SALARY field, move the SALARY field to the Ordering Criteria list and select the Descending radio button in the RQBE Order By dialog (see Figure 9.16).

Multiple ordering criteria can be specified as well. If the SALESMAN database were much larger, for instance, there easily could be a number of salespeople with the same last names. In this case, you would want the records ordered by last name and, for those records with the same last name, by first name as well. To specify multiple ordering criteria in this way, decide which fields will determine the order of the report, then choose them in the Selected Output list and select the Move button to move them to the Ordering Criteria list box.

As was the case in the Selected Output list in the RQBE Select Fields dialog, the order in which field names appear in the Ordering Criteria list determines their sequence in the query ouput. This order can be changed by selecting a field name and either pressing CTRL+PgUp or CTRL+PgDn on the keyboard or clicking and dragging the adjacent double arrow with the mouse until the field is in the proper position.

If you do not specify an order for the output records, FoxPro will return the records in the order in which they are stored in the database file or in the order determined by the master index active at the time the query executes. Of course,

Querying Data   343

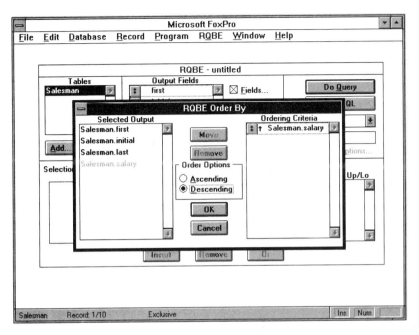

Figure 9.16 Ordering resulting records

if you expect the query operation to return only one record, you do not have to select the Order By... check box.

Defining Selection Criteria

The most important step in creating an RQBE query is to define its selection criteria. The lower half of the RQBE window is provided for this. Its basic purpose is to allow you to create queries that are more English than "computerese." To define selection criteria, select an item of information from your database (usually a field) and then provide an example of a value that would qualify a record for inclusion in the query. To find the record belonging to salesperson Davidson, for example, you would specify the following selection criterion:

Field Name	*Comparison Operator*	*Example (Criterion Value)*
SALESMAN.LAST	Exactly Like	Davidson

To enter this particular selection criterion, first choose the data field from the list of fields associated with the current database file. If you are using the mouse, click the button on the Field Name drop-down list and select the field you want. With the keyboard, use the Tab key to open the Field Name list and then select the field accordingly. Besides selecting a field, you can use the Field Name list to create an expression by selecting <expression...> at the bottom of the list and using the

344 Understanding FoxPro 2.5 for Windows

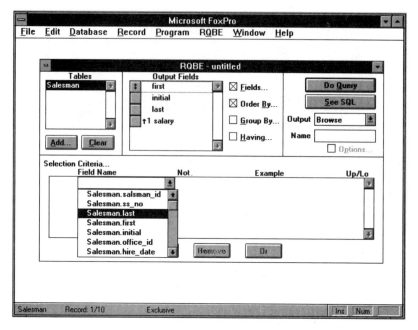

Figure 9.17 Selecting the Query data field

Expression Builder. As an exercise, select the LAST data field from the Field Name list (see Figure 9.17).

As soon as a field is entered into the Field Name text box, the default—Like—comparison operator appears. To use another comparison operator, select a different one from the comparison popup. FoxPro's RQBE window offers the following comparison operators:

- *Like.* A record will be selected if its field or expression matches the example. To select all salespeople whose last names begin with "D," for example, define the selection criterion as:

    ```
    SALESMAN.LAST    Like    D
    ```

- *Exactly Like.* A record will be selected if its field or expression exactly matches the example, character for character.

- *More Than.* A record will be selected if its field or expression is greater than the example. If the field is a character string, this means that it follows the example in alphabetical order.

- *Less Than.* A record will be selected if its field or expression is less than the example. If the field is a character string, this means that it precedes the example in alphabetical order.

- *Between.* A record will be selected if it falls between a range of values. To select all salespeople whose last names begin with the letters C, D, E, F, and G, for example, define the selection criteria as:

  SALESMAN.LAST   between   "C,G"

- *In.* A record will be selected if its field value is included in a list of example values. For example, to select salespeople with the first names Doris, George, or Henry, define the selection criteria as:

  SALESMAN.FIRST   in   Doris, George, Henry

(These options will be discussed in greater detail later in this chapter in the section, "More on Selection Criteria.") In this case, because you want to find the record belonging to salesperson Davidson, select Exactly Like as the comparison operator (see Figure 9.18).

Finally, enter the criterion value in the Example text box. If the criterion value is a string of characters (including spaces), just enter the character string (e.g., Davidson) without enclosing it in quotes (see Figure 9.19). If, however, the character string includes commas, it must also be enclosed in quotation marks to avoid confusion, because a comma is used to separate characters strings when the Between or In comparison operator is used in selection criteria.

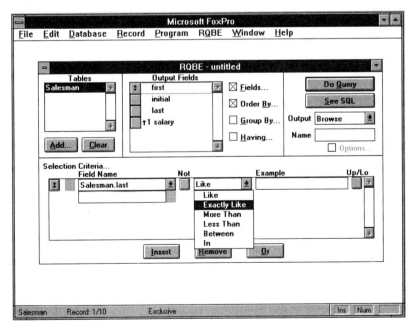

Figure 9.18 Selecting comparison type

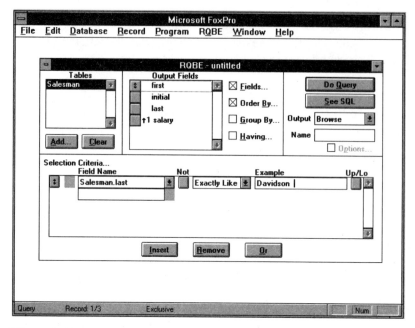

Figure 9.19 Selecting criterion value

EXECUTING RQBE QUERIES

After you have specified all the query settings and defined the selection criteria, you are ready to execute the query operation. To do that, select the Do Query button. FoxPro then searches through the records in SALESMAN.DBF and finds the records that meet the selection criteria you have specified. They are then sent to the destination selected. In this example, Browse was chosen as the destination for the query results, so FoxPro displays the selected records in a Browse window (see Figure 9.20).

If you want to return to the RQBE window to perform other operations after you have viewed the query results, close the Query Browse window by pressing the Esc key. If you are using a mouse, select the Close option in the Browse window's Control box or double click on the Control box. Once the window is closed, the results of the query are lost. In order to retrieve those same records, you must run the query again.

SAVING THE CURRENT QUERY TO A FILE

As just stated, to terminate the query operation, close the RQBE window. But, if you expect to repeat the current query at a later date, you should save all the query settings and selection criteria in a permanent query file by selecting the Save As... option from the File menu. In return, you will be asked to assign a name (e.g.,

Querying Data 347

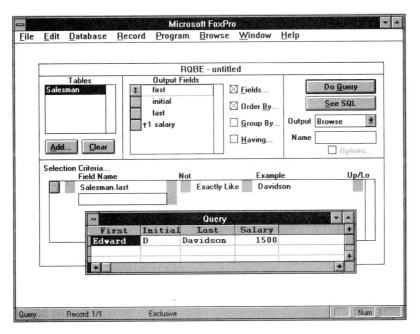

Figure 9.20 Showing the record selected by the query

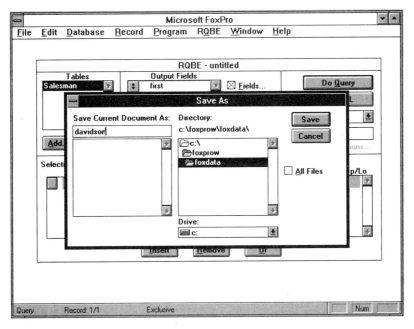

Figure 9.21 Naming a query file

DAVIDSON) to the query file (see Figure 9.21). Note that FoxPro automatically assigns a .QPR file extension to your query unless you explicitly specify some other file extension.

FoxPro uses an UNTITLED.QPR file to *temporarily* hold the settings and selection criteria for the current query. If you exit from the RQBE without saving the query to a permanent file, the UNTITLED.QPR temporary file will be closed and all information about the query will be lost. Therefore, you must save the query to a permanent query file if you plan to repeat the same query at a later date. Once you have done this, you can exit from the RQBE window by pressing the Esc key or by double clicking the mouse on the Control box.

REPEATING AN EXISTING QUERY

To repeat the query about salesperson Davidson, simply recall the DAVIDSON.QPR query file by selecting the Open... option from the File menu. When the Open file dialog appears, select Query in the List Files of Type: drop-down list and then open DAVIDSON.QPR accordingly. As a result, you are returned to the RQBE window and the query settings and selection criteria previously saved will be intact. You can then carry out the query as if you had created it anew.

MODIFYING EXISTING QUERIES

If you need to change the query settings and selection criteria for an existing query, bring it up in the RQBE window by opening its associated query file. When the RQBE window appears, make all the necessary changes to the query. As an exercise, recall DAVIDSON.QPR to explore ways of using different comparison operators in defining selection criteria.

MORE ON SELECTION CRITERIA

Working interactively with FoxPro to query a database can be frustrating if you do not have a basic working knowledge of how FoxPro searches a database. Such factors as the Exact setting or case-sensitivity must always be considered when searching a database. In contrast, a major strength of RQBE is that it allows you to select the records that interest you by specifying conditions that are more intuitive and easily understandable. At the same time that RQBE attempts to make it easier for you to define selection criteria, the comparison operators and pattern symbols that we will examine in this section make it a flexible and powerful tool for querying a database.

Using the Like Comparison Operator

In one of the previous exercises, Exactly Like was selected as the comparison operator with which to define the selection criteria. In that case, a record was selected if and only if the character string in the LAST field exactly matched the example character string "Davidson". Exactly Like requires that every character in the field string matches that of the example character string, including any blank spaces in the field. Therefore, it is obvious that this operator may be used only if you know precisely what the character string looks like; otherwise, FoxPro cannot find the records.

If you cannot recall exactly the makeup of a character string, the Like operator can be used to find a partial match. Thus, you can find Davidson in the LAST field if you use any one of the following examples:

Field Name	*Operator*	*Example*
SALESMAN.LAST	Like	David

or

SALESMAN.LAST	Like	Davids

or

SALESMAN.LAST	Like	Dav

FoxPro will select the records as long as the character string specified in the example matches the first set of characters in the query field. Similarly, if you specify "111-" as the example string for searching the values in the SS_NO data field and by adding the SS_NO field to the Output Fields list box, you would find all the social security numbers beginning with 111- displayed in the Query Browse window (see Figure 9.22).

Ignoring Case

Ordinarily, RQBE is sensitive to case when comparing example strings with character fields. So, in our original example, defining a selection criterion such as:

SALESMAN.LAST	LIKE	DA

would not have returned any records. If you do not remember whether a character string is in upper- or lowercase letters, select the Up/Lo check box to direct FoxPro to search the field strings while ignoring case. Then, the salesperson whose first name is Doris can be found by using "doris" as the example string in the selection criteria (see Figure 9.23).

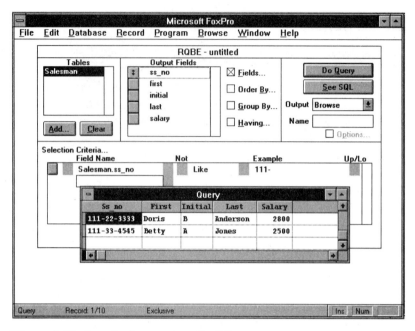

Figure 9.22 Results from using the Like operator

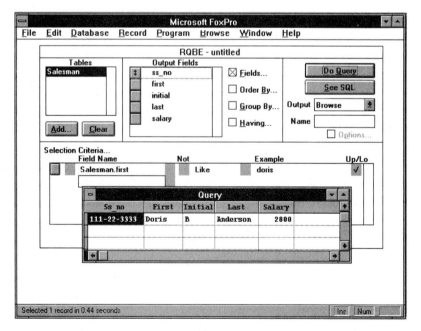

Figure 9.23 Ignoring case in searching character strings

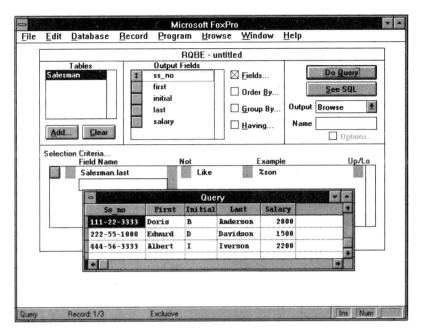

Figure 9.24 Using pattern symbols in selection criteria

Using Pattern Symbols

When searching character strings, it often is helpful to specify a certain pattern without being concerned about the exact position of the character string that you are looking for. For example, to find all the salespeople whose last names end with "son," use the percent (%) symbol to describe the pattern of the character string as %son (see Figure 9.24).

Use the percent symbol to denote any sequence of zero or more characters that are to be ignored in the comparison. In this way, the %son pattern selects any last names that end with "son." Figure 9.24 shows that the query returned the records belonging to Anderson, Davidson, and Iverson.

As another example, if %333% is used as the pattern for searching the character strings in the SS_NO field, all the records having "333" in their social security number would be returned (see Figure 9.25). The query returned three social security numbers: 444-56-3333, 333-56-4545, and 111-22-3333. Notice, however, that if the selection criterion is specified as:

```
SALESMAN.SS_NO   Like   %333
```

FoxPro will return only two records—those belonging to Albert Iverson (SS_NO=444-56-3333) and Doris Anderson (SS_NO=111-22-3333). The percent sign serves as a substitution or wild card symbol for any number of characters at

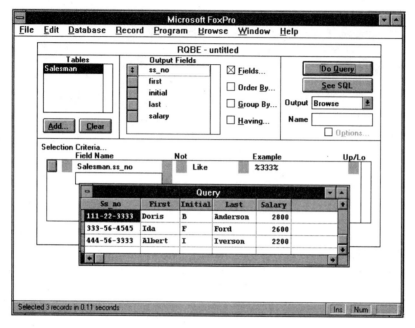

Figure 9.25 Second example using pattern symbols

one end of the string only. So, to search for a string located at the end of a field, the pattern should be specified as:

`%<string>`

If you want to find a substring that can be located anywhere within a larger string, you must specify the search pattern as:

`%<string>%`

Comparing Numeric Values

The Like and Exactly Like operators also can be used for comparing numeric values, dates, and logical values. But pattern symbols may not be included in the example value.

When comparing numeric values, the Like and Exactly Like operators produce the same effect as "equal to." This means that to find the salesperson who has a monthly salary of $2,200, the selection criterion would be defined as:

Field Name	*Operator*	*Example*
SALESMAN.SALARY	Like	2200

or

Querying Data 353

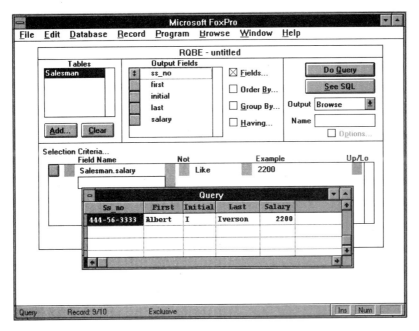

Figure 9.26 Comparing numeric values in query

Field Name   *Operator*   *Example*

SALESMAN.SALARY   Exactly Like   2200

and both of these selection criteria would return the same records (see Figure 9.26).

Comparing Dates

In a similar fashion, the Like and Exactly Like operators may be incorporated to compare dates in selection criteria, in order to find the records belonging to those salespeople who were hired on a certain date (see Figure 9.27). Remember that the date value must be enclosed in braces in the selection criterion (e.g., {03/08/88}).

Comparing Logical Values

When comparing logical values in selection criteria, periods must be included for defining the values. To find information about the female sales staff, for instance, define .F. as the example value in the selection criteria. You may use either the Like or Exactly Like operator for comparing the example value with that in the MALE logical data field (see Figure 9.28). This figure shows that the query returned all the records belonging to saleswomen in the Browse window.

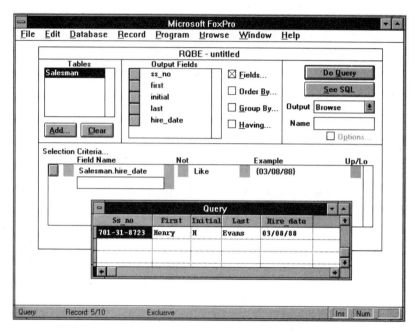

Figure 9.27 Comparing dates in query

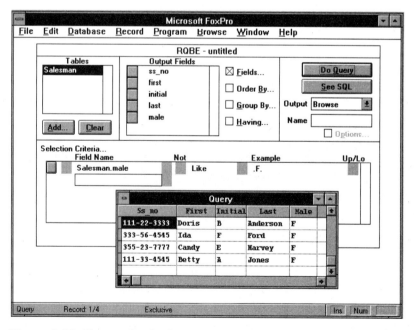

Figure 9.28 Comparing logical values in query

Using the Not Operator

To reverse the result of a given comparison, select the Not check box. In this case, to find information about all the male sales staff, define the selection criteria as:

Field Name	*Operator*	*Example*
SALESMAN.MALE	Not Like	.F.

Selecting the Not check box reverses the comparison. In Figure 9.29, for example, you are searching for all records that do not have a false value in the MALE field—in other words, for all records belonging to males.

The NOT operator can be used with other data types as well. When combined with the pattern symbols and the various comparison operators provided by RQBE, it allows you to define some very precise and powerful queries. For example, if you are interested in salary extremes—those employees at both the low and high end of the salary scale—you could combine the Not operator and the Between comparison operator (which we will discuss later in this section) to formulate your selection criteria as:

Field Name	*Operator*	*Example*
SALESMAN.SALARY	Not Between	2000,2500

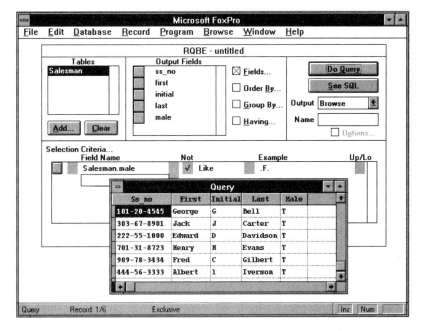

Figure 9.29 Using the Not operator

Using the More Than/Less Than Operator

When selecting records using numeric values, it is often useful to set the maximum or the minimum value as the query criterion. Therefore, to find information about those salespeople who are making a certain minimum amount as their monthly salaries, use the More Than operator in the selection criteria for the query operation (See Figure 9.30). The selection criteria in this figure instructs FoxPro to accept any records that have a value greater than $2,500 in the SALARY field; as a result, it returned three records. It is important to note that the More Than operator did not select the record belonging to Betty Jones whose salary is equal to $2,500. If you would like to include the minimum value, you could use the Not and Less Than operators jointly in the selection criteria (see Figure 9.31). You can see in this figure that the record with 2500 in the SALARY field was chosen by the Not Less Than selection criterion. (This selection criterion also could be expressed as SALESMAN.SALARY Greater Than 2499.)

More Than and Less Than can be used for evaluating character strings as well. For example, if you want to find all the last names that begin with C through Z, you would define the selection criteria as shown in Figure 9.32. (Alternately, it could be defined as SALESMAN.LAST Greater Than B.)

Similarly, the More Than and Less Than operators may be used for comparing dates in selection criteria. When the More Than operator is used, FoxPro selects the dates that are one day or more after the example date. So, to find information

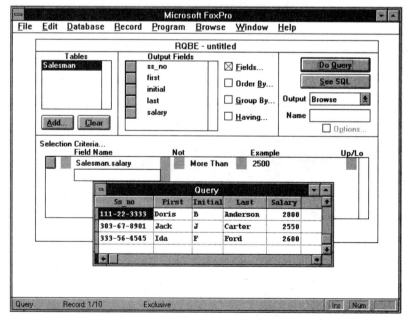

Figure 9.30 Using the More Than operator

Querying Data 357

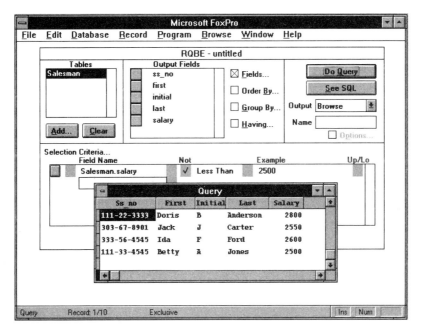

Figure 9.31 Using the Not Less Than operator

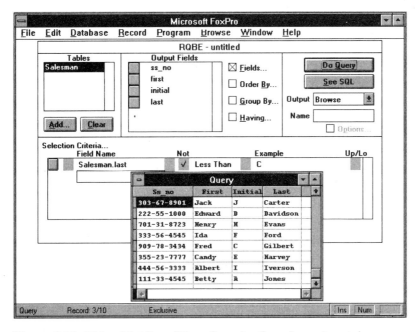

Figure 9.32 Using Not Less Than for selecting character strings

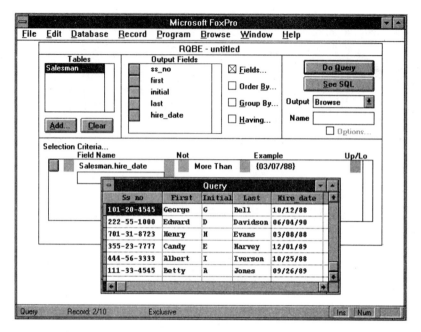

Figure 9.33 Using the More Than operator for comparing dates

about salespeople who were hired after March 7, 1988, define {03/07/88} as the example date in the selection criteria (see Figure 9.33).

Using the Between Operator

To retrieve records with field values that are within a given range, use the Between operator. When this operator is used, the lower and upper limits of the range must be specified. Therefore, to find the salary values that fall in the range $2,200–$2,600, identify in the selection criteria the lower and upper limits as two example values separated by a comma (see Figure 9.34).

Notice that the query returned all the salaries between $2,200 and $2,600 and included the two end values (e.g., 2200 and 2600). The Between operator also may be incorporated when comparing character strings and dates. Here are examples of such selection criteria using the Between operator:

Field Name	*Operator*	*Example*
SALESMAN.LAST	Between	C, G
SALESMAN.HIRE_DATE	Between	{01/01/88}, {12/31/88}

Querying Data   359

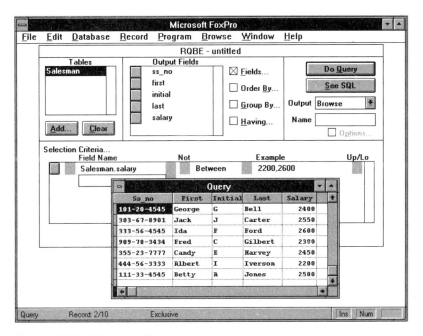

Figure 9.34 Using the Between operator

Using the In Operator

As discussed, when using the Like and Exactly Like operators, a *single* example value is specified in the selection criteria; the Between operator requires that limits for a *range* of values be set. But, to find records with a set of individual values, the In operator is chosen. To find those salespeople whose first names are George, Doris, and Betty, for instance, specify those first names in the selection criteria, as shown in Figure 9.35.

This operator also is used to locate dates and numerical values as detailed in these examples:

Field Name	*Operator*	*Example*
SALESMAN.SALARY	In	2200, 2500, 2550, 2400
SALESMAN.HIRE_DATE	In	{05/14/87}, {09/26/89}

Using Formulas in Selection Criteria

In addition to using data fields in selection criteria, a formula may be included to define conditions. To find those salespeople who have been with the company for more than three years (say, 1095 days), the criterion would read:

Field Name   *Operator*   *Example*

{10/25/91} - SALESMAN.HIRE_DATE   More Than   1095

In this criterion, the formula {10/25/91} - HIRE_DATE returns the number of days between the two dates specified. If the current date is October 25, 1991, the formula calculates and returns the number of days since the HIRE_DATE. As a result, the query returns all the hire dates that occurred more than 1095 days (three years) from the current date. To specify the formula, select the <expression...> button from the bottom of the Field Name drop-down list (see Figure 9.36).

When the Expression Builder appears, enter the formula in the text box as the selection expression. Note: If you are querying from more than one database when entering a data field, it is best to include the name of the database as the prefix, such as SALESMAN.HIRE_DATE. If you are querying from only one database, however, you do not have to include the prefix; there would be no question to which database you are referring. When more than one database is involved in the query, the prefix identifies which is currently being used. This is especially important if an identical field name appears in more than one database.

When you return to the RQBE window, finish defining the selection criteria by adding the comparison operator and the example value (see Figure 9.37). When executed, the query returns all the records belonging to salespeople who were hired more than three years ago (see Figure 9.38). This figure also shows that the records

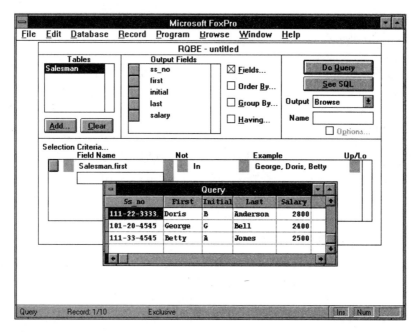

Figure 9.35 Using the In operator

Querying Data 361

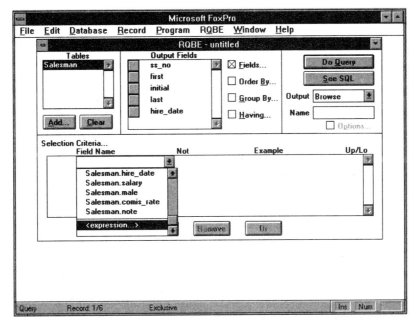

Figure 9.36 Selecting Field Name for query expression

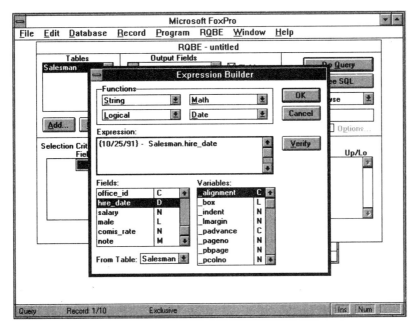

Figure 9.37 Entering a formula as selection criterion

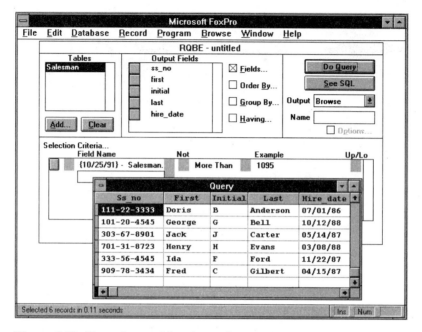

Figure 9.38 Records resulting from the query

returned by the query include hire dates that occurred more than three years prior to the present date ({10/25/91}).

Using Functions in Selection Criteria

Any of FoxPro's many functions may be included in a formula that is part of a selection criteria. In previous chapters, you became familiar with such functions as AVG(), MAX(), MIN(), SUM (), and DATE() that returned summary statistics. As an exercise of how functions are used here, include DATE() in the selection criterion. When the function is executed, it returns the current system date. You do not have to specify an argument in the parentheses. The selection criterion should look like this:

Field Name	*Operator*	*Example*
DATE() - Salesman.hire_date	More Than	1095

The DATE() function is used to replace the current date, in this case, {10/25/91}. When you carry out the query with this selection criterion, it will always return the records of employees who have been employed for more than three years (assuming that the computer's system date is correct).

Specifying Compound Selection Criteria

In all of the preceding examples, we used a single selection criterion for selecting records. Each criterion had only one search condition involving one data field. Although many data query operations require only simple selection criteria, other data search tasks may need compound criteria, which in turn require more than one search condition involving multiple data fields in one or more database files.

Defining Joint Search Conditions

Compound selection criteria instruct the query operation to find records that satisfy *all* the specified conditions simultaneously. If you want to find those female members of the sales staff who are earning a monthly salary of more than $2,500, for instance, specify the following conditions in the selection criteria for the query operations:

Field Name	*Operator*	*Example*
SALESMAN.MALE	Like	.F.

and

SALESMAN.SALARY	More Than	2500

To find the same information with a RQBE query, enter these two conditions jointly in the selection criteria (see Figure 9.39). This figure shows that these two search conditions were entered on two separate lines in the Selection Criteria text box. If you need more than two conditions, you may continue entering additional conditions on subsequent lines. The query operation will select only those records that satisfy all the joint conditions. The query in Figure 9.39 returned two records that met the conditions specified in the selection criteria, i.e., records belonging to those salespeople who are female and earn a monthly salary of more than $2,500.

Using the OR Logical Connector

In the preceding example, records that met a set of multiple conditions simultaneously were retrieved. Sometimes, however, you may be interested in finding records that meet at least one of the conditions specified in the selection criteria. To do that, use the OR logical connector to link the conditions in the criteria. Then, for example, you can find those salespeople who are either female or who earn a monthly salary of more than $2,500. In such a case, enter the two conditions that are connected by OR in the selection criteria (see Figure 9.40). The two conditions that occupied a separate line in the selection criteria box are linked by the OR connector.

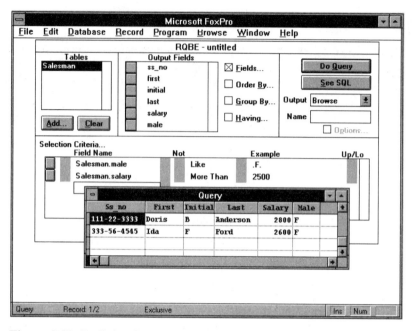

Figure 9.39 Defining joint search conditions

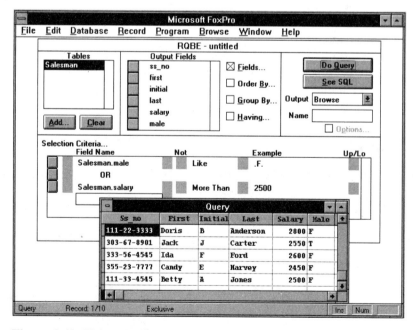

Figure 9.40 Using the OR logical connector

Querying Data

You can either enter the OR line at the cursor position by selecting the Or button or move it up and down by using the mouse or keyboard. If you are using the mouse, click on the double-headed arrow to the left of the line containing OR and then drag it to its new position. With the keyboard, use the Tab and arrow keys to highlight the line and then press the Ctrl+UpArrow or Ctrl+DnArrow key combinations to move it to its new position.

When two conditions are joined by OR, the query operation returns those records that meet any one or both of these conditions. You can see in Figure 9.41 that the query selected four records, each of which satisfied at least one of the two search conditions specified. If there are more than two conditions linked by the OR connector, continue inputting the additional conditions on subsequent lines. When you execute the query, FoxPro will return all the records that meet any of the specified conditions.

To create a more complex selection criteria, define multiple joint search conditions (i.e., search conditions joined by the AND connector) and connect these search conditions using one or more OR connectors, as shown in Figure 9.41. In this example, the selection criteria include three search conditions. The query operation will select those records that satisfy either the first two joint conditions or the third condition. This query returned four records belonging to the salespeople who are female and earn more than $2,500 per month or who were hired prior to December 12, 1987.

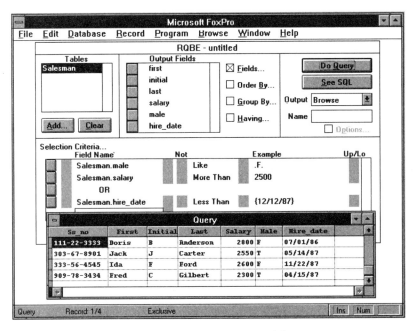

Figure 9.41 Example of multiple search conditions

In general, regardless of the number of conditions you specify, FoxPro will evaluate conditions linked by the AND connector before it evaluates conditions linked by OR.

Using Multiple Database Files in RQBE Queries

One of the most powerful features of RQBE is its capability to join several database files so that you can retrieve information from more than one database file using a single query. As a result, you are able to query data from any data field in the joined database files as if they were in the same database file.

In our sample database files, information about a fictional sales staff is stored in SALESMAN.DBF. Information about members' sales offices is saved in another database file, OFFICE.DBF. The SALESMAN file includes OFFICE_ID as a foreign field, which was used as a link to OFFICE.DBF. Because these two databases can be linked, you are able to extract information from them with a RQBE query. Therefore, by linking SALESMAN.DBF and OFFICE.DBF in a query, you can find out information about a salesperson (e.g., Davidson) and his sales office at the same time.

To create such a query, open the first database file, SALESMAN.DBF, in work area 1. Then select the New option from the File menu popup and select Query as the file type to bring up the RQBE window. As the RQBE window appears, note that SALESMAN.DBF is selected as the database for the query operation. Now join it with the second database file, OFFICE.DBF, by selecting the Add... button. When the Open File dialog appears, open OFFICE.DBF from the Select a Table list box (see Figure 9.42).

You will be asked in the RQBE Join Condition dialog to specify the join condition for linking OFFICE.DBF to SALESMAN.DBF. The join condition involves identifying the linking field that is common to the two files. Since there is only one data field that is common to the two database files, FoxPro automatically selects that common field (OFFICE_ID) from OFFICE.DBF and places it in the left drop-down list. It also selects the OFFICE_ID from SALESMAN.DBF and places it in the right drop-down list. The middle drop-down list is for selecting a comparison operator from FoxPro's choices of Like, Exactly Like, More Than, Less Than, Between, and In. Most join operations require either the Like or Exactly Like operator (see Figure 9.43).

After defining the join condition, return to the RQBE window by selecting the OK button. Once you are back in the RQBE window, note that the join condition is displayed as a part of the selection criteria and is indicated by a horizontal double-arrow symbol (↔) to the left of the field name (see Figure 9.44). You now can add any search condition to the selection criteria. If, for example, you want to find out information about salesperson Davidson and his sales office, search the

Querying Data 367

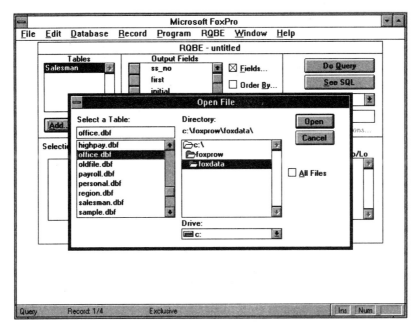

Figure 9.42 Adding a database to the query

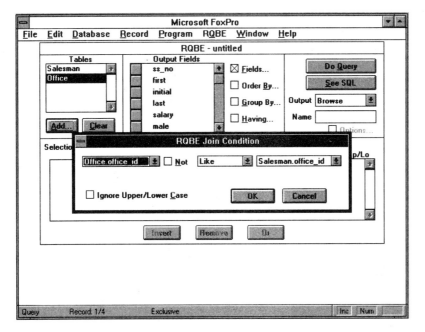

Figure 9.43 Defining the join condition

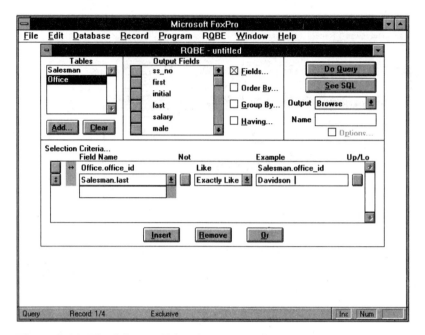

Figure 9.44 The join condition in the selection criteria

database by last name, looking for a match with "Davidson," as shown in Figure 9.44.

At this point, select the data fields for your output from the joined database files. To do that, choose the Fields... check box. When you are in the Field Selection dialog, you may select any fields from the two database files. For example, you can select the FIRST and LAST fields from SALESMAN.DBF, and the ADDRESS, CITY, STATE, ZIP, and PHONE_NO fields from OFFICE.DBF (see Figure 9.45).

After selecting the output destination (e.g., Browse), carry out the query operation by clicking in the Do Query button. As a result, the query returns the records from the joined database files that satisfy the selection criteria (see Figure 9.46).

This figure shows that the query returned data fields extracted from SALESMAN.DBF and OFFICE.DBF. The FIRST and LAST fields are from SALESMAN.DBF; the rest are from the OFFICE database file. The query first found the record with "Davidson" in the LAST field in the SALESMAN database, then it used the value in the linking field (e.g., "B1") to find the associated record for the New York office in the OFFICE file. As another exercise, join SALESMAN.DBF and OFFICE.DBF in a query to find all salespeople who are either in the New York or Chicago sales offices (see Figure 9.47).

In Figure 9.47, two search conditions are joined by the OR connector. As a result, the query returned all salespeople belonging to either the New York or Chicago

Querying Data 369

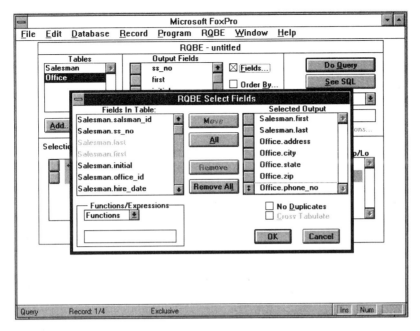

Figure 9.45 Selecting fields from joined database files

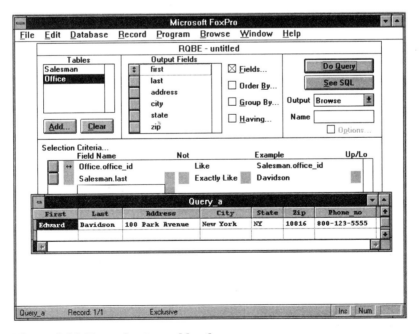

Figure 9.46 Record returned by the query

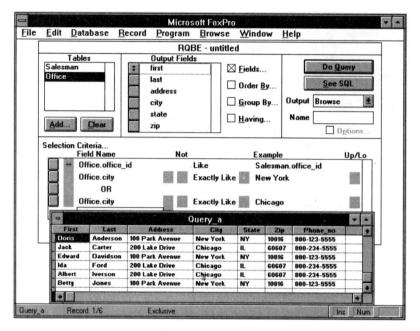

Figure 9.47 Extracting information from joined databases

sales offices. The first two fields were extracted from SALESMAN.DBF; the rest were taken from the OFFICE database file.

DISPLAYING CALCULATED DATA FIELDS

The output from a query operation usually consists of data fields in the database files used. But a query also can be instructed to calculate values that are based on the existing data fields and functions. To do that, incorporate a formula when defining an output field. Let's assume, for instance, that you want to examine the monthly withholding taxes for the sales staff and that these taxes total 20 percent of their monthly salaries. The following formula would be used to define the output field:

```
SALESMAN.SALARY * 0.2
```

To continue with our example, use the Clear button under the Tables dialog to remove the OFFICE database and enter the formula SALESMAN.SALARY * 0.2 as an output field, then select the Fields check box from the RQBE window. When FoxPro displays the RQBE Select Fields dialog, simply enter the formula in the Functions/Expressions text box (see Figure 9.48). When you press the Enter key to accept the formula, you will be prompted to include it as an output field:

```
Include SALESMAN.SALARY * 0.2?
```

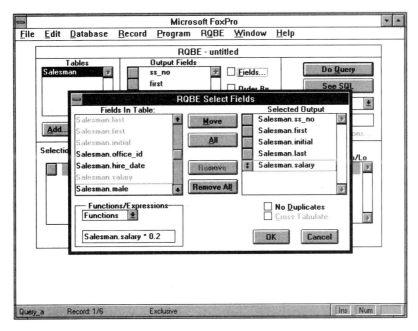

Figure 9.48 Using a calculated output field

By answering Yes, the calculated field will be moved to the Selected Output list.

After defining the output fields, add the necessary search condition to the query. When the query is executed, the value of the output field is calculated according to the formula (see Figure 9.49).

The calculated field is labeled automatically by FoxPro as EXP_6, indicating that it is the sixth field in the output and was the result of evaluating an expression (formula). You cannot specify a custom label for the output field in the query, so if you want to display the calculated field with a more descriptive label, you must manipulate the output outside the query operation. One way to do this is to present the query results in a report where custom labels can be assigned to all the output data fields. (This topic is covered thoroughly in Chapter 11.) Alternatively, you may save the query results in a database file and then rename the calculated fields in the data structure.

DISPLAYING SUMMARY STATISTICS

Because FoxPro allows you to use functions in an expression and define the result of that expression as an output field, you can produce summary statistics from the values of particular database fields. Thus, you can use the AVG(SALESMAN.SALARY) function to calculate and display the average salary for all or some of the sales staff.

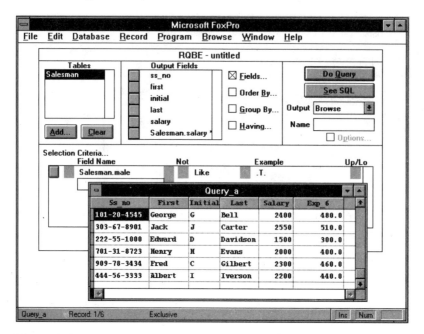

Figure 9.49 Results of using a formula in an output field

By allowing you to define a calculated field that will display a summary statistic, FoxPro substantially enhances your flexibility in generating queries of various kinds. All the sample queries generated so far have been record-oriented; that is, they have returned a set of records that meet some selection criteria. In working with summary statistics, in contrast, we are no longer interested in the contents of individual records. Indeed, all individual fields should be removed from the Selected Output list box in the RQBE Select Fields dialog, because we are exclusively interested in generating a single figure that characterizes a set of records.

To generate such a summary query, define an output field with a function as an expression. Enter the function directly into the Functions/Expressions text box in the RQBE Select Fields dialog, which is accessed by selecting the Fields... check box in the RQBE window. Alternatively, select the AVG() function from the Functions drop-down list, followed by highlighting the numeric field (e.g., SALESMAN.SALARY) as the function argument (see Figure 9.50). After highlighting the function argument, select it by pressing either the Enter key or by double clicking on the mouse. The function selected appears in the Functions/Expressions text box. Add it to the Selected Output list with the Move button.

If there is the possibility of duplicate records in the database (i.e., records with identical values in every field), you should decide whether or not to exclude the duplicate values from the calculation of summary statistics. Do this by selecting the version of the appropriate function that contains DISTINCT as an argument.

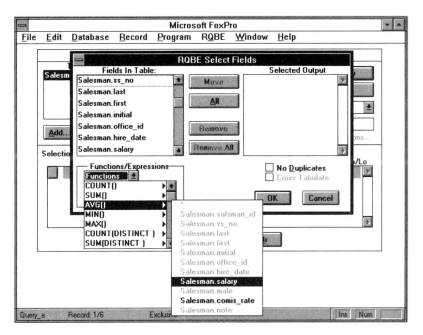

Figure 9.50 Selecting a function from the Functions list

In this example, select AVG(DISTINCT). When the query operation is executed, it calculates the average salary from the selected records and displays it in a calculated field (see Figure 9.51). Notice that the query returned only one record in the calculated field, AVG_SALARY. The calculated value (e.g., 2158.33) was computed from the values of all the records in the SALARY field belonging to the male sales staff.

Multiple output fields containing functions can be used to display several summary statistics. To find out the salary range for the male sales staff, for example, use MAX() and MIN() as the output fields to display the highest and lowest salary values. Use the COUNT() function to determine the number of records selected by the query; use SUM() to total the values in an existing or calculated field. Several kinds of summary statistics are shown in Figure 9.52. This figure shows that the query returned summary statistics that were calculated with the following functions in the output fields:

Output Field	Functions used in the Expression
CNT	COUNT(SALESMAN.SALARY)
MIN_SALARY	MIN(SALESMAN.SALARY)
MAX_SALARY	MAX(SALESMAN.SALARY)
EXP_4	MAX(SALESMAN.SALARY) - MIN(SALESMAN.SALARY)
SUM_SALARY	SUM(SALESMAN.SALARY)
AVG_SALARY	AVG(SALESMAN.SALARY)

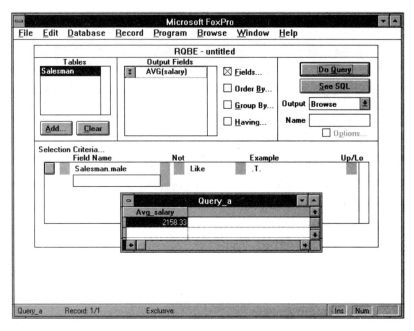

Figure 9.51 Showing average salary

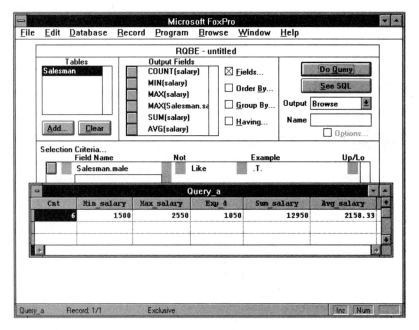

Figure 9.52 Using multiple summary functions

The output field labeled as EXP_4 represents the salary range and was calculated by taking the difference between the maximum salary and the minimum salary. Note that the returned records belong only to male salespeople as a result of the selection criteria specified. If you later need to display the summary statistics for the female group, carry out a similar query by changing the selection criteria to SALESMAN.MALE Like .F. or by selecting the NOT check box.

PRODUCING GROUP SUMMARY STATISTICS

It is possible to produce separate sets of summary statistics, each of which is calculated using a specific group of records selected by the query. To do that, group the records in the database file according to a specified criterion. You can group the records in SALESMAN.DBF by the values in the MALE field and then produce summary statistics for each of the two groups, for example. As a result, you are able to compare the summary statistics between the male and female groups.

To divide records into groups for the query operation, select the Group By... check box in the RQBE window. When the RQBE Group By dialog appears, select the field whose values you want to use to group the records. For example, to divide the sales staff into male and female groups, choose the MALE data field (see Figure 9.53).

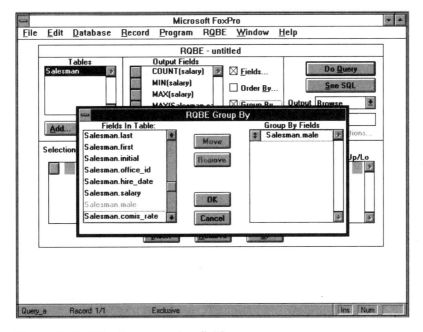

Figure 9.53 Selecting grouping fields

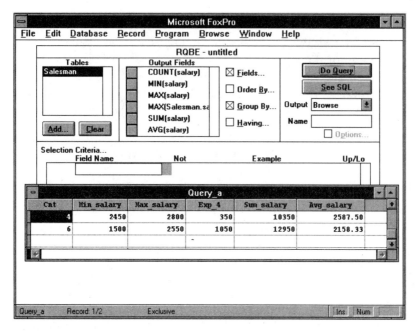

Figure 9.54 Showing group summary statistics

You must add the MALE data field to the selected output field list to identify which set of summary statistics belongs to which group. In addition, because we are now interested in including all records for the two groups in our summary statistics, no selection criteria should be specified. When you execute the query, it will return separate summary statistics that were calculated from the records belonging to the groups of male and female salespeople (see Figure 9.54).

Records were grouped according to their distinct values in the field that was specified for the grouping operation. Because the MALE data field has only two distinct values (.T. and .F.), RQBE provides summary statistics for these two groups. As a result, Figure 9.54 shows that the query returned two records, each showing a set of summary statistics for a given group. The first record shows the number of female salespeople in the field labeled CNT; the next three fields show their minimum, maximum, and average salaries. Concomitantly, the second record shows all the summary statistics for the male salespeople.

It also is possible to screen the results so as to display only those summary statistics that meet certain requirements. For example, in Figure 9.54, the query returned two average salaries: 2587.50 for the female group and 2158.33 for the male group. You may want to display only the summary statistics for groups with an average salary that is greater than $2,500. To do this, choose the Having... check box to specify the screening conditions for the summary statistics.

Querying Data 377

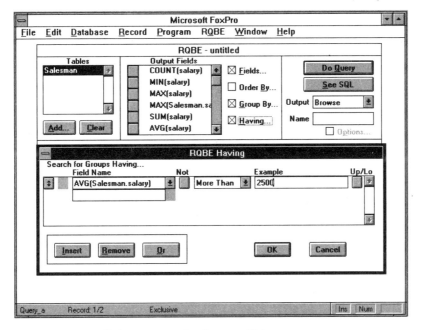

Figure 9.55 Defining groups having conditions

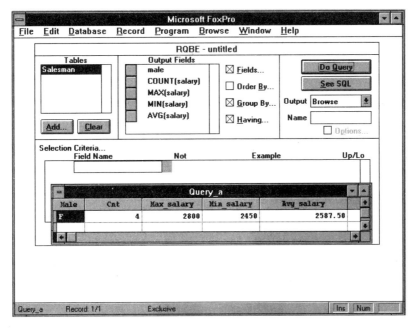

Figure 9.56 Screened group summary statistics

In response to checking the Having... box, the RQBE Having dialog box appears. Enter the following condition in the text box provided as shown in Figure 9.55.

Fields	Operator	Example
AVG(SALESMAN.SALARY)	More Than	2500

When this query is executed, it returns summary statistics for only those groups whose average salaries are greater than $2,500. As a result, only the summary statistics belonging to the female sales staff are displayed in the query results (see Figure 9.56).

Using FoxPro Commands

If you prefer to use commands, you can create a new query by using the FoxPro CREATE QUERY command in the following format:

```
CREATE QUERY <name of the query file>
```

After opening the SALESMAN database file in the current work area, issue the following commands to create a new query named SAMPLE.QPR:

```
USE SALESMAN
CREATE QUERY SAMPLE
```

FoxPro opens the RQBE window in which the current database is selected for the query operation (see Figure 9.57). From this point on, continue to specify the query settings, define the query selection criteria, and then execute the query by selecting the <Do Query> button. Save the query to a file by following the procedure defined in the last section.

After saving the query to a query file, it can be recalled for the purpose of repeating the query or for inserting modifications. To do that, issue the MODIFY QUERY command:

```
MODIFY QUERY <name of the query file>
```

In order to recall the query that has been saved in the SAMPLE.QPR file, issue the following command:

```
MODIFY QUERY SAMPLE
```

After the command is executed, FoxPro displays the query in the RQBE window with all the previously defined settings and selection criteria intact. If necessary, modify the query settings and selection criteria; otherwise, just repeat the existing query.

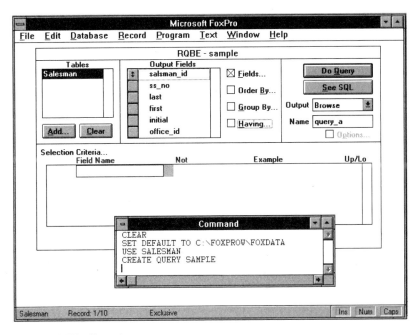

Figure 9.57 Creating a new query

QUERYING MEMO FIELDS

Although memo fields provide an efficient means for saving large blocks of text in a database file, you cannot use them in RQBE query operations or specify them as part of selection criteria. Therefore, if you need to find information in memo fields, the Locate operation must be used. So, to find those salespeople who enjoy fishing, for example, use the following search conditions with the Locate option:

```
FOR "fishing" $ SALESMAN.NOTE
```

The dollar sign can be interpreted as the "is contained in" operator. FoxPro will search the contents of the memo field SALESMAN.NOTE, which contains all the information about the hobbies of the sales staff. As a result, the condition will be met if the search string "fishing" is found in any record of the memo field. Records may be searched in this way by using the menu interface or by issuing the appropriate FoxPro commands. If you select the Locate option from the Record menu, define the search condition in the Locate Record For text box (see Figure 9.58). When Locate is executed, FoxPro locates the first record containing a memo field with the search string "fishing" in it (see Figure 9.59).

The Locate operation also can be invoked by issuing the LOCATE command:

```
CLEAR
USE SALESMAN
LOCATE FOR "fishing" $ NOTE
```

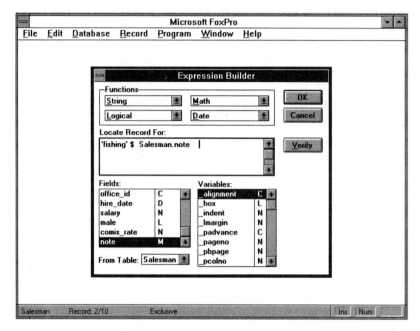

Figure 9.58 Searching memo fields

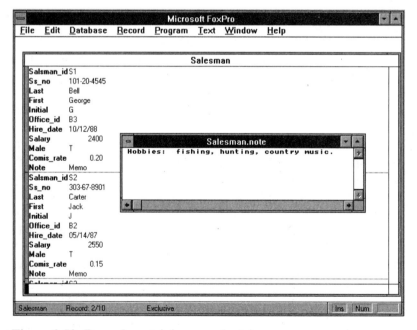

Figure 9.59 Record containing search string

Querying Data   381

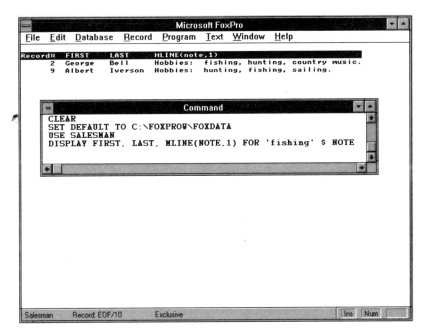

Figure 9.60 Displaying contents of memo fields

Once the record is found, it can be displayed in a Browse window for viewing or editing.

It is important to remember that the Locate operation finds only the first record that satisfies the search condition. It does not show any other records that also satisfy the condition. To list all the records satisfying the search condition, use the DISPLAY command accompanied by the condition for locating a given string in the memo field. For example, the following DISPLAY command will show the names of all salespeople who list fishing as their hobby:

```
DISPLAY FIRST, LAST, MLINE(NOTE,1) FOR "fishing" $ NOTE
```

Remember that MLINE(NOTE,1) is used to display the first line of the memo field, NOTE. When this command is executed, it lists all the records that satisfy the search condition specified in the FOR clause (see Figure 9.60).

Chapter Summary

This chapter explored the ways to extract useful information from databases. The Locate and Seek operations can be used to find a record that meets certain search conditions: Locate allows you to find a record from any database file; to search for a record with the Seek operation, however, the database file must be indexed on the search expression.

This chapter also detailed how to query data with the powerful RQBE tool. With a RQBE query, you can find a set of records that satisfy a selection criterion that you specify. Your selection criterion can be defined by using data fields that are from one or more database files. In the next chapter, you will discover how to create and use memory variables and how to use FoxPro's built-in function to manipulate your database.

10

Using Memory Variables and Built-In Functions

An Overview

So far, this book has shown you how to design database files and access the data that they contain. Frequently, however, your database may not contain the precise information that you need. In some cases, the necessary information must be derived from data stored in the database. Let's assume, for example, that you are interested in the total annual payroll of your sales force, and that the only information available to you in SALESMAN.DBF consists of the monthly salary of each salesperson. In order to obtain the information you need, you must total the monthly salaries of all the salespeople and multiply that figure by 12.

In other cases, data may not be in the precise format that is needed or wanted. Let's assume that you have decided to store all of the names in a contact database in uppercase. You now want to create some personalized letters, but do not want the letters to look anything like the following:

```
Dear MICHAEL:

    We appreciate you taking the time to call us with your
inquiry. We hope that our customer service department was ...
```

To create an attractive, personalized form letter, you must convert the contact's first name to a combination of upper-and lowercase letters.

In this chapter, we will examine two features of FoxPro—memory variables and built-in functions—that you can use to extract precisely the kind of information that you want from your database. Their utility will become fully apparent to you in later chapters, but, for now, just be aware that they increase enormously your flexibility in working with FoxPro databases.

Memory variables are individual data elements that are temporarily stored in the computer's memory, rather than in a database file. This makes them ideal for a number of uses, including:

- Temporarily storing intermediate results generated in the course of an application. It might be useful, for example, to total the monthly salaries of all the salespeople in our sample database to a memory variable before multiplying it by 12 to derive the total annual salary.
- Retaining summary statistics about your data.
- Passing information from one part of your application to another.

Built-in functions are provided by FoxPro as tools to manipulate data in a wide variety of ways. A function generally takes a particular value—such as the contents of the LAST field in SALESMAN.DBF—and converts (or returns) it to a different value, like an uppercase string. You have already been exposed to several built-in functions, including AVG(), SUM(), MAX(), and MIN(), that are included in the Expression Builder for defining search and filter conditions. However, FoxPro provides a large number of built-in functions that can be used for such purposes as:

- Generating summary statistics
- Transforming data for subsequent manipulation
- Displaying data in a format that you select

Memory Variables

Memory variables are individual memory locations that are set aside for holding separate data elements. A memory variable is similar to a data field in many ways: It is used to hold a character string, a numeric value, a date or a logical value; and, like a data field, each memory variable is assigned a symbolic name that describes its contents.

There are, however, three major differences between a data field and a memory variable.

1. A data field, because it is stored as part of a larger database file, has a definite structure that is defined when the database is created. In contrast, a memory variable, because it is simply stored at a location in memory, does not have a predefined structure. As a result, although you must access the correct database and record in order to access the correct element in a data field, memory variables can be accessed independently of one another and of the contents of database files.

2. Whereas a data field takes on a different value for each record in the database, a memory variable can take on only a single value at any given time.
3. A data field is a permanent part of a database file; its contents are stored in a permanent disk file when you close its database or exit from FoxPro. A memory variable, on the other hand, is a temporary location in memory; unless you decide to save a memory variable to a permanent disk file, its contents are erased when you exit from FoxPro.

The contents of a memory variable can be changed. In fact, any time you store a new data value to the memory variable, its existing contents will be replaced with the new value. Therefore, the same memory variable may be used repeatedly.

Memory variables have many uses. Often, they are used to retain intermediate results of data manipulation for later processing. In addition, they are used to pass data values among different data manipulation operations. You also may include memory variables in expressions to define search conditions and selection criteria for data manipulation operations. For example, a character string that you locate in a data field can be stored in a memory variable and used in the FOR clause to define a search condition.

Another important use of memory variables is to pass values to custom reports. Summary statistics that are computed and held in memory variables enable you to produce more versatile reports. You could, for example, produce a summary salary report that shows the salaries of individual salespeople as percentages of the total salary. To do so, however, requires a two-pass process. First, you must compute the total salary by adding up all the individual salaries; then, you must compute the percentages by dividing the salary values by the total. This is where the value of using a memory variable becomes obvious. Because the report generator allows only a single-pass process, you can pass the salary total as a memory variable to the report before the process begins. The salary total can be computed from the database and saved in a memory variable prior to bringing up the report generator. Once you are in the report generator, you can access the memory variable accordingly.

TYPES OF MEMORY VARIABLES

There are different types of memory variables available for use in FoxPro. The commonly used ones are character, numeric, date, and logical. A character memory variable holds character strings, a numeric memory variable saves values that can be integers or decimal numbers, date memory variables store dates, and logical memory variables hold logical values in the form of .T. or .F. Be aware that when building expressions in FoxPro, you cannot mix different types of memory variables and data fields in the same expression.

As already stated, every memory variable is identified by a symbolic name. The variable type is determined only by the type of data element you store in it. For example, once you have stored a character string to a memory variable, it becomes a character memory variable. The memory variable remains of that type until you replace its contents with a different type of data element.

NAMING MEMORY VARIABLES

Like a data field name, a memory variable name can have up to ten characters, which may be a combination of letters, digits, and underscores (_), but the first character of a memory variable *must* be a letter. Although it is not mandatory, for quick reference purposes, you are advised to assign descriptive names to your memory variables that will help you identify their contents.

Case is irrelevant in memory variable names, because FoxPro stores them all in uppercase. You may decide, however, to incorporate lowercase letters when naming memory variables to help differentiate them from data field names that also appear in uppercase. Here are examples of acceptable memory variable names:

unit_cost
total_wage
avg_salary
net_profit
tax_withld
fullname
invoice_no

When you assign names to memory variables, avoid using words that have been reserved by FoxPro for its commands, functions, and system variables. Do not use such command words as DISPLAY, LIST, TOTAL, MODIFY, etc., to name your variables. You can, however, alter command names to clarify the difference, calling them NAME_LIST and TOTAL_PAY, for instance. And, instead of using function names such as SUM, AVG, MAX, MIN, change them to read as SUM_VALUE, AVERAGE, MAX_SALARY, or MIN_COST. Also avoid beginning your memory variable names with an underscore (_), because FoxPro names its system variables that way—_PAGENO is a FoxPro system variable that keeps track of report pages, for example.

Although FoxPro does not prevent you from doing so, you should not name a memory variable with an existing field name. Besides being confusing, only the data field will be recognized if the database file containing the data field is currently selected. When the data field is active, the contents of the memory variable will be ignored. For certain data manipulation operations, however, it often is useful to store the value that is currently in a data field in a memory variable. If this is the case, assign the memory variable a name that is related to the corresponding data field by adding a letter, such as "m," in front of the name. Then *msalary*, for example, would represent the memory variable holding the value in the SALARY data field.

STORING DATA IN MEMORY VARIABLES

There are two ways to assign a data element to a memory variable, and both require that you issue a FoxPro command; *a memory variable cannot be created by using FoxPro's menu interface.*

Using the STORE Command

STORE is one of the two commands that can be invoked to assign a data element to a memory variable. Its format is:

```
STORE <data element> TO <memory variable name>
```

The data element can be a character string, a numeric value, a date, or a logical value. The command instructs FoxPro to save the data element in the memory variable specified, which can be a new or an existing one. If it is a new variable name, FoxPro creates a new memory variable and then saves the data element to it accordingly. Otherwise, the data specified in the command element will replace the current contents of the memory variable.

Let's say that you would like to save the string 'Hello' in the memory variable named *greeting*. You would issue the following command:

```
STORE 'Hello' TO greeting
```

Because 'Hello' is a character string, it must be enclosed in quotation marks. And because a character string is stored to *greeting*, the memory variable becomes a character variable, as defined earlier. Once this command is executed, a memory location is set aside to hold the character string. When this is done, its contents are displayed on the screen for verification.

After you have stored a data element to a memory variable, the contents of the variable can be displayed on the screen. To do that, you need to issue the following commands:

```
SET STATUS BAR OFF
SET TALK ON
```

The first command erases the Status Bar that normally appears at the bottom of the screen. As a result, messages that normally are displayed there will be shown in the desktop area of the screen.

If you do not want to see the value of the memory variable displayed after assigning a value to it (and if you do not want the results of a number of other commands displayed on the screen), turn off the TALK setting with the following command:

SET TALK OFF

To bring back the Status Bar, issue the following command:

SET STATUS BAR ON

In general, you must use a separate command to store each value that you would like to assign to a memory variable. This is illustrated in Figure 10.1 where we have issued a series of commands to fill memory variables with data elements.

In this figure, the first STORE command stores the character string 'George' to the memory variable named *friend*. The next three commands store values to numeric memory variables. You may assign a value (e.g., 25 or 29.95) to a memory variable (e.g., qty or price). You also may store the result of a formula or numeric expression (e.g., 8/100) to a numeric memory variable.

The fifth command saves the date, December 25, 1991, to the date memory variable named *xmas*. Note that the date must be enclosed in braces (e.g., {12/25/91}); without them, the date would be evaluated erroneously as a numeric expression (e.g., 12/25/91). As a result, the variable *xmas* would equal .01, the result of dividing the answer of (12/25) by 91.

The last command stores a logical value, .T., to the logical memory variable named *answer*.

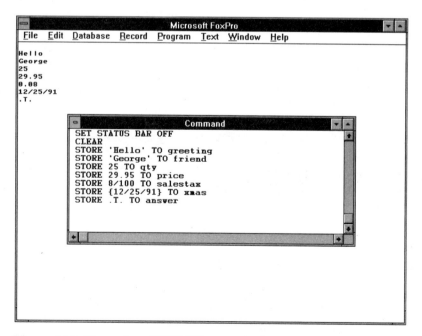

Figure 10.1 Examples of STORE commands

You can, in addition, store the same value to several variables using only a single command by separating the variable names with commas. For example:

```
STORE 25 to qty, oldqty
STORE 'George' to friend, newfriend
```

Using the = Command

Another way to assign a data element to a memory variable is to issue the = command in the following format:

```
<memory variable name> = <data element>
```

Examples:

```
greeting = 'Hello'
friend = 'George'
qty = 25
price = 29.95
salestax = 8/100
xmas = {12/25/91}
answer = .T.
```

The = command will produce the same result as that of the STORE command (see Figure 10.2); therefore, the two may be used interchangeably. Some programmers adopt a convention whereby they use STORE commands to initialize the values in memory variables and then use = commands to change their values. As a result, when they return to the commands issued, it is possible to tell when the memory variables were first set up.

ASSIGNING DATA FIELDS TO MEMORY VARIABLES

Previous examples illustrated how to assign a character string, a number, a date, and a logical value to a memory variable. This also can be done with the value in a current data field, using either a STORE or an = command in the following format:

```
STORE <data field name> TO <memory variable name>
```

or

```
<memory variable name> = <data field name>
```

You can store, for example, salesman Davidson's first name and salary in memory variables *mfirst* and *msalary* for later data manipulation purposes. To do that, first locate the record belonging to Davidson in SALESMAN.DBF. When the

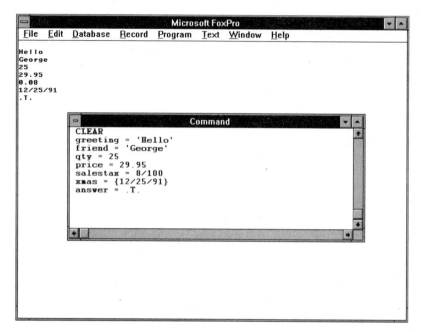

Figure 10.2 Using the = command

Locate operation returns the record, issue the command to assign the field values to the appropriate memory variables (see Figure 10.3).

In Figure 10.3, the Locate operation found Davidson's record (Record=4). Then, the contents of the database FIRST were stored to a memory variable named *mfirst*, while a memory variable named *msalary* was created to hold the contents of the SALARY field. Notice that in each case, we avoided naming the memory variable after the field simply by adding an "m" to the field name. Although by no means obligatory, this convention has several advantages. First, it "documents" the memory variable; we can easily tell that the value of a memory variable beginning with an "m" has been assigned from a database field. But this convention also avoids confusing FoxPro. If a memory variable and a database field have the same name and you refer to it, FoxPro will be able to access only the value of the current data field. If, for example, you had instead named the memory variable *salary*, the same as the data field, when you try to view the value in the memory variable, it will show only the value of the SALARY data field.

DISPLAYING MEMORY VARIABLES

When you enter data elements to memory variables, they are stored temporarily in the computer's memory. The contents of these memory variables can be viewed in

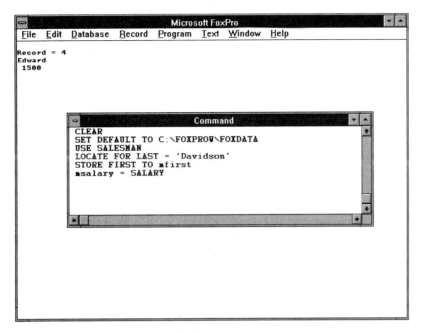

Figure 10.3 Assigning data fields to memory variables

two ways. You may list some or all of the current memory variables by using the DISPLAY MEMORY command. Or you may display the value of an individual memory variable with a ? command.

Using the DISPLAY MEMORY Command

Use the DISPLAY MEMORY (or DISP MEMO) command to show the names of all the current memory variables and their values. If, for example, you issue the DISPLAY MEMORY command now, you would be able to view the values of all the memory variables you have created (see Figure 10.4).

You can see in this figure the list of current memory variables returned by the DISPLAY MEMORY command. In addition to listing their names and the values, FoxPro also shows what type of variables they are. For example, all character variables are indicated by a letter "C"; numeric, date, and logical variables are indicated by letters "N," "D," and "L," respectively.

Memory variables are also classified as either public or private. A public variable is one that is accessible anywhere while you are in FoxPro, whereas private variables are accessible in certain applications or programs only. When memory variables are created in the Command window, they are classified as public and indicated by "Pub" in the variable list. You don't have to worry about private variables at this point.

```
                    Microsoft FoxPro
 File  Edit  Database  Record  Program  Window  Help
GREETING      Pub    C    "Hello"
FRIEND        Pub    C    "George"
QTY           Pub    N             25  (             25.00000000    Press any key to continue ...
PRICE         Pub    N             29.95 (           29.95000000)
SALESTAX      Pub    N             0.08  (           0.08000000)
XMAS          Pub    D    12/25/91
ANSWER        Pub    L    .T.
MFIRST        Pub    C    "Edward    "
MSALARY       Pub    N             1500  (           1500.00000000)
      9 variables defined,      40 bytes used
    247 variables available

Print System Memory Variables

_ALIGNMENT    Pub    C    "LEFT"
_BEAUTIFY     Pub    C    "D:\FOXPROW\BEAUTIFY.APP"
_BOX          Pub    L    .T.
_CALCMEM      Pub    N             0.00  (           0.00000000)
_CALCVALUE    Pub    N             0.00  (           0.00000000)
_CONVERTER    Pub    C    "D:\FOXPROW\CONVERT.FXP"
_CUROBJ       Pub    N             -1    (          -1.00000000)
_DBLCLICK     Pub    N             0.50  (           0.50000000)
_DIARYDATE    Pub    D    10/28/92
_DOS          Pub    L    .F.
_FOXDOC       Pub    C    "D:\FOXPROW\FOXDOC.APP"
_FOXGRAPH     Pub    C    ""
_GENGRAPH     Pub    C    ""
_GENMENU      Pub    C    "D:\FOXPROW\GENMENU.PRG"
_GENPD        Pub    C    ""
_GENSCRN      Pub    C    "D:\FOXPROW\GENSCRN.FXP"
_GENXTAB      Pub    C    "D:\FOXPROW\GENXTAB.PRG"
_INDENT       Pub    N             0     (           0.00000000)
_LMARGIN      Pub    N             0     (           0.00000000)
_MAC          Pub    L    .F.
_MLINE        Pub    N             0     (           0.00000000)
```

Figure 10.4 Displaying current memory variables

Notice the list of system memory variables in Figure 10.4. These variables are used by FoxPro to hold data values for its internal use. For example, FoxPro keeps track of the page number in the system variable _PAGENO. Although most of these system variables are of no direct interest to you, you can use some of them in your applications and reports, as you will learn in the next chapter. There is a large set of system variables requiring several screens to show them all. After viewing one screen, press any key to continue until you have viewed them all.

To display only selected memory variables, use the LIKE operator in the DISPLAY MEMORY command. For example, to display all the memory variables whose names begin with the letter "m," issue the following command:

```
DISPLAY MEMORY LIKE m*
```

As a result, the command will display the memory variables such as *mfirst*, *msalary*, etc. The asterisk is a wildcard that accepts any string of characters in its place.

Using the ? Command

To display the value of a memory variable, invoke the ? command in the following format:

```
? <memory variable list>
```

Using Memory Variables and Built-In Functions 393

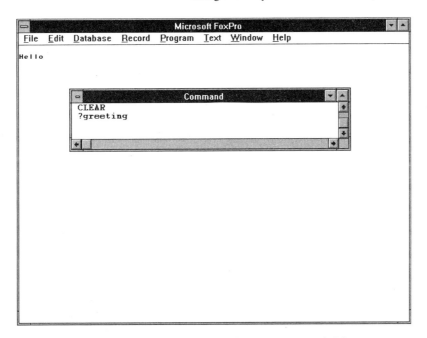

Figure 10.5 Displaying the contents of a memory variable

To view the contents of the memory variable named *greeting*, for example, issue the following command:

```
?greeting
```

Upon execution of the command, the value of the memory variable is displayed, as shown in Figure 10.5. The contents of more than one memory variable may be displayed in the same command. To do that, specify the memory variables and separate them by commas (see Figure 10.6).

SAVING MEMORY VARIABLES TO MEMORY FILES

Memory variables are temporary storage locations that have been set aside in the computer's RAM. As soon as you exit from FoxPro, the memory variables you have created will be erased and their memory spaces released. You may, however, save memory variables to a permanent file if you intend to use them again later. If they are not saved, obviously they will have to be re-created later. The command for saving memory variables to a memory file is:

```
SAVE TO <memory filename>
```

This command saves all the current memory variables (excluding system variables) to a memory file with a .MEM file extension. For example, if you would like to

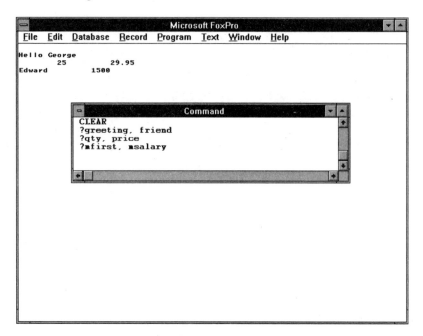

Figure 10.6 Displaying the contents of multiple variables

save the memory variables that you have created to the SAMPLE.MEM memory file, issue the following command:

```
SAVE TO SAMPLE
```

Upon execution, the command creates the memory file named SAMPLE.MEM to hold the current memory variables. To verify the existence of this file, issue the DIR SAMPLE.MEM command (see Figure 10.7).

The SAVE TO command saves every memory variable to the specified memory file. If you need to save memory variables selectively, use the LIKE qualifier in the SAVE command. For example, to save all the variables whose names begin with the letter "m," issue the following command:

```
SAVE ALL LIKE m* TO MEMFILE
```

The wildcard character, *, stands for any series of characters in the variable names. As a result, the command will save such memory variables as *mfirst* and *msalary* to the MEMFILE.MEM file.

You also may use another wildcard character, ?, to select the variables to be saved. Each ? represents a single character in the memory name. For example, if you would like to save a series of memory variables that all have seven-character names and contain the string "rate" as the second through fifth characters of their

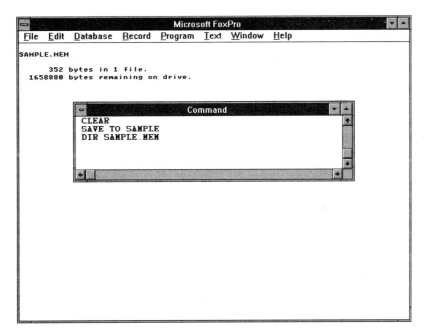

Figure 10.7 Saving memory variables to a file

name (for example, *yrate01*, *yrate02*, *mrate01*, *drate01*), issue the following command:

```
SAVE ALL LIKE ?rate?? TO TESTFILE
```

This command will save only those memory variables with names of seven characters and with rate occupying the second through fifth positions, regardless of what characters occupy the other positions.

You also may use the EXCEPT qualifier to exclude a set of memory variables to be saved to a file. To save, for example, all memory variables whose names do *not* begin with the letter "m," issue the following command:

```
SAVE ALL EXCEPT m* TO TESTFILE
```

DELETING MEMORY VARIABLES

Although an individual memory variable does not take up much memory space, it is a good practice to delete those variables that are no longer needed for the current session. When you do this, it frees the computer's valuable memory space to be used for other operations. After you no longer need your memory variables or you have saved them to a disk file, some or all of them can be erased from the computer's memory with the RELEASE command. To erase one or more memory variables from memory, specify the name(s) of the memory variable(s) as follows:

```
RELEASE <memory variable list>
```

For example:

```
RELEASE mfirst
```

If you are erasing more than one variable, they must be separated with commas in the RELEASE command, as in the following:

```
RELEASE greeting, friend, qty
```

To erase all the memory variables from memory, use the following command:

```
RELEASE ALL
```

In executing this command, all the current memory variables will be erased and their memory locations released for other use. The LIKE or EXCEPT clauses also may be used to selectively erase certain memory variables. Examples:

```
RELEASE ALL LIKE m*
RELEASE ALL LIKE cost*
RELEASE ALL LIKE ?rate??
RELEASE ALL EXCEPT m*
```

In using the RELEASE ALL LIKE command, however, be careful not to precede the memory variable name or skeleton with the global wildcard character (*), because this releases *all* memory variables. For example, the following two commands are identical in the effect they have:

```
RELEASE ALL LIKE *COST
RELEASE ALL LIKE *
```

It is important to know that the RELEASE command deletes only the memory variables from the computer memory, not the contents of any memory files.

RESTORING MEMORY VARIABLES

You may retrieve any memory variables that have been saved in a memory file and then place them into memory with the RESTORE FROM command:

```
RESTORE FROM <memory filename>
```

When the command is issued, any memory variables in memory are erased and replaced with those retrieved from the memory file. Here is an example:

```
RESTORE FROM MEMFILE
```

When the preceding command is issued, all the current memory variables will be released, and the contents of the MEMFILE.MEM file will be placed into the current memory. As a result, the memory will contain only two memory variables: *mfirst* and *msalary* (those saved with the SAVE ALL LIKE m* TO MEMFILE command).

To add the memory variables from a memory file to the current memory without erasing the existing memory variables, attach the ADDITIVE clause at the end of the command, as in this example:

```
RESTORE FROM SAMPLE ADDITIVE
```

This command will retrieve all the memory variables from SAMPLE.MEM and then add them to memory. The contents of the existing memory variables will not be disturbed unless the restored variables share the same name as any of the existing variables. If that occurs, the values of the existing variables will be replaced with the values retrieved from the memory file.

DELETING MEMORY VARIABLES FROM MEMORY FILES

The RELEASE command may be invoked to delete memory variables from memory only; it cannot be used to remove any memory variables that are saved in a memory file. To delete some or all of the memory variables that have been saved to a memory file, they must first be retrieved from the file by using the RESTORE command; then they can be deleted with the RELEASE command. When that action is complete, again save the remaining memory variables to the memory file. As an exercise, use the following commands to remove the memory variable *mfirst* from the memory file named MEMFILE:

```
RELEASE ALL
RESTORE FROM MEMFILE
RELEASE mfirst
SAVE TO MEMFILE
```

or (better):

```
RESTORE from MEMFILE
RELEASE mfirst
SAVE TO MEMFILE ALL LIKE M*
```

Built-In Functions

Functions in FoxPro provide a "built-in" way of performing mathematical and string manipulation on different types of data elements. A function takes values that are passed to it and performs a predefined operation on them. The function then returns the result of the operation. For example, ABS(-123.45) returns the absolute value (i.e., 123.45) of the number that is passed to it in the argument (the value in the parentheses, i.e., -123.45). Similarly, the function RTRIM(FIRST) takes the character string in the FIRST (first name) data field, trims off all the trailing blank spaces, and returns the trimmed string.

Functions are divided into groups according to the types of data they return and the kinds of operations they perform. Character and string functions select parts of a character string for use in searching, sorting, and indexing operations. Other string functions can insert blank spaces in a character string or trim off unwanted blank spaces. Date manipulation functions display dates in a number of formats that are used in business data processing applications. Numeric functions can round a decimal number to the integer, compute the square root of a value, and perform many other mathematical operations on the values. Statistical functions can be used to produce summary statistics by using the values in data records.

A built-in function is identified by a symbolic name followed by a pair of parentheses:

```
<function name>([<argument>])
```

The name indicates the type of data manipulation the function performs. The object of the function, which is enclosed in the parentheses, is called an argument. The argument is used to pass the value to the function. With few exceptions, most functions require an argument. Here is an example of a built-in function:

```
SUM(SALARY)
```

It instructs FoxPro to add the values in the data field SALARY and return the sum. The argument in this case is represented by a data field name. Recall from previous chapters that functions may be used in expressions, and the value of a function may be assigned to a memory variable. Here is an example:

```
STORE 1234.567 TO x
STORE INT(x) TO y
```

The function INT(x) will convert the value in the argument to an integer by eliminating the digits to the right of the decimal point. As a result, the value assigned to variable *y* will be 1234 (see Figure 10.8).

Although most functions require an argument, some do not. TIME() is one that does not. When executed, it returns the current system time. Similarly, DATE() returns the current system date (see Figure 10.9).

There are many types of functions. Many, like SUM(), perform mathematical operations; others manipulate character strings. The SUBSTR() function, for instance, is used to locate a subset of a character string within a character string.

Using Memory Variables and Built-In Functions   399

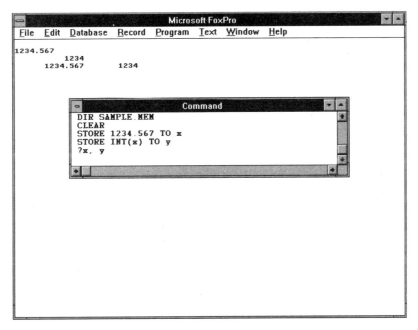

Figure 10.8 Assigning a function to a memory variable

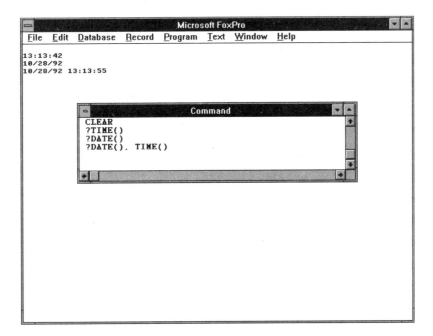

Figure 10.9 TIME() function

Still other types of functions process dates. DTOC(), for example, converts a date to a character string.

Because of the different operations they perform, the argument or arguments that must be supplied to the functions are different. In addition, different types of functions return different types of data values. For example, a date is supplied in the argument for the DTOC() function, and it returns a character string, while the CTOD() function takes a character string as an argument and returns a date.

FoxPro provides a wealth of built-in functions that enable you to manipulate data. This chapter covers only some of the most commonly used ones, but once you have mastered these, you should have no trouble learning the others.

CHARACTER STRING FUNCTIONS

A large set of built-in functions is provided in FoxPro for Windows that enable you to manipulate a character string that is specified in a function argument. There is a function to remove unwanted blank spaces in the string, another to include a string of blank spaces, one to convert letters from lowercase to uppercase and vice versa, and still another to convert a string of digits into a value. It also is possible to find and return a subset of a character string with one of these functions.

Most functions require one or more character strings as an argument. In general, each argument also can be supplied to the function as a character expression. A character expression is a combination of character strings, character data fields, and character memory variables joined by one or more operators (such as the plus sign). You also can include a character string returned by another built-in function in the function argument. A simple character expression, on the other hand, can be only a character string, a character data field, or a character memory variable.

RTRIM(), TRIM()

The RTRIM() (or TRIM()) function allows you to trim off the trailing blank spaces in a character string. The format of RTRIM() and TRIM() is:

```
RTRIM(<character string>)
TRIM(<character string>)
```

The character string to be trimmed can be specified in the function argument as a character expression. The function returns a character string without the trailing blanks.

The TRIM() or RTRIM() function is most commonly used to eliminate trailing spaces from the character values stored in database fields. When a character string is stored in a data field, FoxPro adds blank spaces to the end of the string to fill out the field width. As a result, when you display the contents of the data field, they

Using Memory Variables and Built-In Functions   401

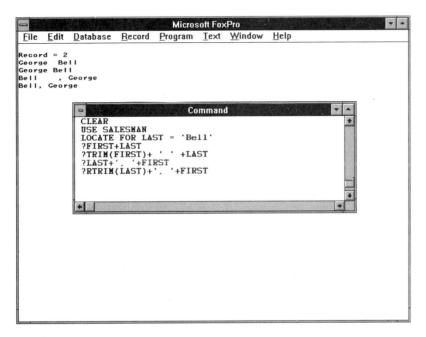

Figure 10.10 TRIM() function

will include the blank spaces. For example, in SALESMAN.DBF, every first and last name stored in the FIRST and LAST data fields contains eight characters because both of their field widths are set to eight characters. If a salesperson's first name has fewer than eight characters, FoxPro will fill the remainder of the field width with blank spaces. It will do the same for a last name that is shorter than the field width. As a result, when the string in that field is displayed, it will occupy 8 spaces. To trim off those trailing blank spaces, use the TRIM() function as detailed in Figure 10.10.

You can see in this figure that the ?FIRST+LAST command displays the first and last names of George Bell as eight characters each, with two trailing blanks added to the first name. You also can see that the TRIM(FIRST) function is used to remove the blank spaces between the first and last names. You also could use the RTRIM(LAST) function to display last name, comma, and first name.

LTRIM()

The LTRIM() function is similar to TRIM() and RTRIM(). It is used to remove leading blanking spaces in a character string. The format of the function is:

```
LTRIM(<character string>)
```

Figure 10.11 Using LTRIM()

The function returns a character string without the leading blank spaces, as shown in this example:

```
STORE '    Johnson' TO LASTNAME

STORE '   Mary'    TO FIRSTNAME

STORE ' K. ' TO INITIAL

LTRIM(FIRSTNAME)+INITIAL+LTRIM(LASTNAME)
```

This function could be used to remove the leading blank spaces in the *firstname* and *lastname* memory variables (see Figure 10.11).

It is important to remember that a blank space is considered a valid character. And, when searching for or comparing character strings, leading blanks are important. If, for example, you store '   Johnson' in the LAST data field, you would not be able to find the record by using 'Johnson' as the search string with the following command:

```
LOCATE FOR LAST = 'Johnson'
```

Instead, to find '   Johnson', you must remove the leading blanks from the LAST data field before comparing it with the search string 'Johnson':

```
LOCATE FOR LTRIM(LAST) = 'Johnson'
```

Figure 10.12 Using ALLTRIM()

ALLTRIM()

ALLTRIM() removes all the leading and trailing blank spaces from a character string. The format of the function is:

```
ALLTRIM(<character string>)
```

An example of ALLTRIM() is shown in Figure 10.12. ALLTRIM(fullname) removes all the blanks before and after a character string stored in the memory variable *fullname*.

The ALLTRIM() function is very useful when you do not remember whether a character string was stored with any leading or trailing blanks. For example, the following LOCATE command will be able to find all the records belonging to Doris, regardless of whether there are leading or trailing blanks stored in the FIRST data field:

```
LOCATE FOR ALLTRIM(FIRST) = 'Doris'
```

UPPER()

The UPPER() function converts to uppercase all characters in the expression specified as an argument. Its syntax is:

```
UPPER(<character expression>)
```

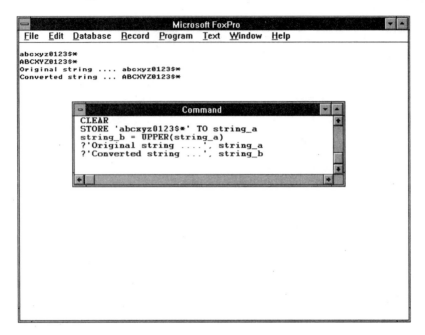

Figure 10.13 Using UPPER()

The following command, then, converts the character string in memory variable *string_a* to uppercase and stores it to another variable named *string_b*:

```
STORE 'abcXYZ0123$*' TO string_a
string_b = UPPER(string_a)
```

After executing the commands, all the lowercase letters in the memory variable *string_a* will be converted to uppercase (see Figure 10.13). Notice that UPPER() has no effect on uppercase letters or such symbols as $ and *.

Similarly, you may convert all the last names in the LAST data field to uppercase letters in a database file by using the following command:

```
REPLACE ALL LAST WITH UPPER(LAST)
```

You may also use the UPPER() function to find character strings by ignoring case. For example, if you are unsure of how a salesperson's first name was saved in the FIRST data field, you would use the following command to list all salespeople whose first name is 'Doris':

```
LIST FIRST, LAST FOR UPPER(FIRST) = 'DORIS'
```

This command will list all first names in the forms of 'doris', 'Doris', or 'DORIS', etc.

LOWER()

LOWER() is the opposite of UPPER(). It converts uppercase letters in a character string to lowercase letters. The format of the function is:

```
LOWER(<character string>)
```

The function returns a character string after converting all the uppercase letters in the string represented by the character expression. Here is an example:

```
STORE 'abcXYZ0123$*' TO string_a
string_b = LOWER(string_a)
```

After executing the commands, the memory variable *string_b* contains only lowercase letters, in addition to the numeric digits and special symbols (see Figure 10.14).

Like UPPER(), you may use LOWER() in the REPLACE command to convert all existing character strings in a data field to lowercase. The following command, for example, will convert all the FIRST names in the first data field to lowercase:

```
REPLACE ALL FIRST WITH LOWER(FIRST)
```

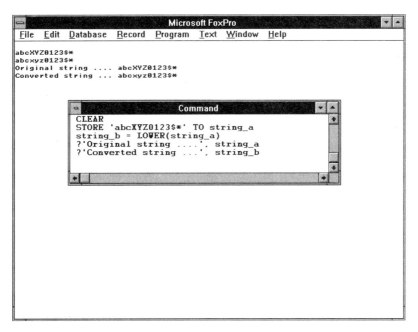

Figure 10.14 Using LOWER()

More practically, LOWER() may be used to search character strings by disregarding case entirely. It converts a character string to lowercase before comparing it with a search string in lowercase. Here is an example:

```
LOCATE FOR LOWER(LAST) = 'davidson'
```

This command will find last names 'Davidson', 'DAVIDSON', or 'davidson'.

SPACE()

A string of blank characters may be created in two ways. One is to enclose the blanks in quotation marks for the string such as:

```
STORE '     ' TO fivespaces
```

or

```
fivespaces = '     '
```

Another way is to use the SPACE() function, which allows you to create a string composed of a specified number of blank spaces. The number of blank spaces is specified in the function argument:

```
SPACE(<number of spaces>)
```

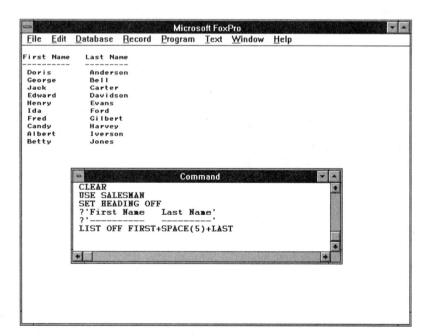

Figure 10.15 Spacing output items

Use SPACE(5) to create a string of five blank spaces, and then use it to assign a character string to a memory variable, as in this example:

```
STORE SPACE(5) TO fivespaces
```

or

```
fivespaces = SPACE(5)
```

SPACE() also can be used to space output on the screen. SPACE(5) in the following command will insert five blank spaces between the first and last names:

```
LIST OFF FIRST + SPACE(5) + LAST
```

Working with the SALESMAN database file, then, this command can be used to display the sales staff's first and last names. The keyword OFF is used to suppress the display of the record number (see Figure 10.15). Notice that issuing the SET HEADING OFF command precluded the display of the field names. The ? commands enable you to display your own column headings.

STUFF()

The STUFF() function allows you to replace a portion of a character string with another character string. The portion to be replaced is identified by two parameters: the beginning character position and the number of characters to be replaced. The portion of the character string that is to be replaced is specified as the first string in the function argument, followed by the parameters that will replace it. The replacement character string is specified as the last item in the function argument:

```
STUFF(<first character string>, <beginning position>,
      <number of characters to be replaced>,
      <replacing character string>)
```

Here is an example:

```
STORE 'John J. Smith' TO old_user
new_user = STUFF(old_user, 6,2, 'K.')
```

The STUFF() function will return a new character string after replacing two characters in the *old_user* string, beginning from the sixth character with the string '*K*'. As a result, the *new_user* memory variable will hold the string '*John K. Smith*' after executing the second command (see Figure 10.16).

SOUNDEX()

Often, when comparing strings or searching for a database value, you may know how a string sounds without knowing how it is spelled. In such cases, a useful

Figure 10.16 Using STUFF() to replace character strings

function is SOUNDEX(), which returns a phonetic representation of a character string. Its syntax is:

```
SOUNDEX(<character string>)
```

Here is an example:

```
?SOUNDEX('John')
```

The function will return a phonetic index code (e.g., J500) representing the sound of the character string. Strings that sound alike will have the same phonetic code (see Figure 10.17).

SOUNDEX() lets you determine whether two strings sound alike by comparing their phonetic codes. Figure 10.17 shows that the strings '*john*', '*John*', '*JOHN*', '*jon*', '*Johnny*', and '*Johnie*' resulted in the same phonetic index code (J500), while the string '*Jack*' produced a different code.

The SOUNDEX() function is very useful for locating character strings whose spelling you do not remember. The following commands will list all the first names saved in the FIRST data field as JOHN, John, Johnny, etc.:

```
LIST FIRST FOR SOUNDEX(FIRST) = SOUNDEX('john')
```

or

```
LIST FIRST FOR LIKE(SOUNDEX(FIRST), SOUNDEX('john'))
```

Using Memory Variables and Built-In Functions   409

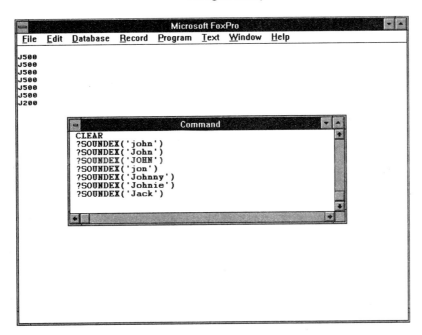

Figure 10.17   Examples of phonetic index codes

DIFFERENCE()

The DIFFERENCE() function compares the SOUNDEX() value of two specified character strings and returns a numeric index indicating how much they sound alike. The index value returned ranges from 0 to 4. The more closely they sound alike, the higher the returned index value. An index value of 4 indicates that the two strings sound very much or exactly alike. If the two strings sound completely different, the function returns an index value of 0. The format of the function is:

```
DIFFERENCE(<character string>,<character string>)
```

As examples, the SOUNDEX difference between the strings '*Jim*' and '*Jimmy*' is 4, whereas the difference between '*Jim*' and '*Tim*' is 3. The SOUNDEX difference between '*Jim*' and '*Albert*' obviously is 0. Figure 10.18 gives more examples of these values. DIFFERENCE() also can be invoked to find character strings that sound similar. The following would be used, for example, to find those first names in the FIRST data field that sound like '*Jim*':

```
LIST FIRST FOR DIFFERENCE(FIRST,'Jim') >= 3
```

This command will return all first names such as Jim, Tim, and Jimmy.

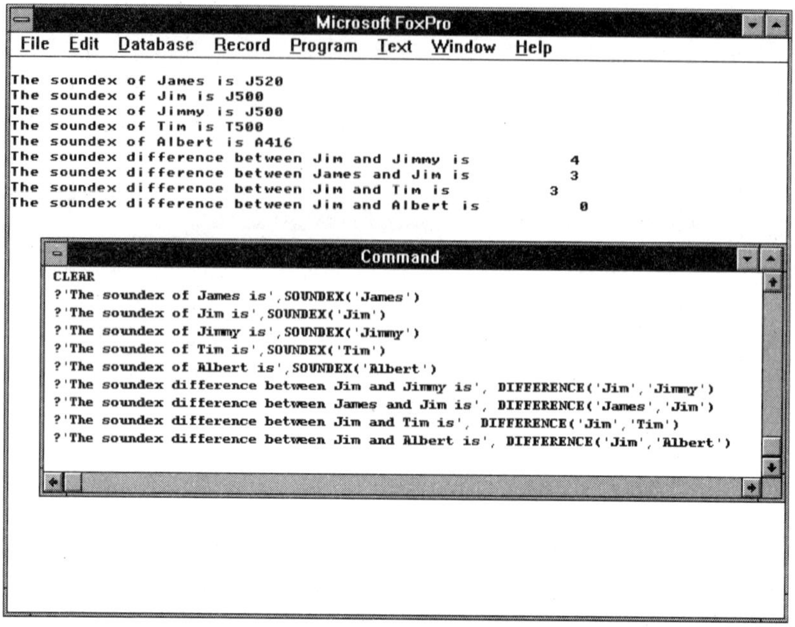

```
                    Microsoft FoxPro
File  Edit  Database  Record  Program  Text  Window  Help
The soundex of James is J520
The soundex of Jim is J500
The soundex of Jimmy is J500
The soundex of Tim is T500
The soundex of Albert is A416
The soundex difference between Jim and Jimmy is        4
The soundex difference between James and Jim is        3
The soundex difference between Jim and Tim is       3
The soundex difference between Jim and Albert is       0

                    Command
CLEAR
?'The soundex of James is', SOUNDEX('James')
?'The soundex of Jim is', SOUNDEX('Jim')
?'The soundex of Jimmy is', SOUNDEX('Jimmy')
?'The soundex of Tim is', SOUNDEX('Tim')
?'The soundex of Albert is', SOUNDEX('Albert')
?'The soundex difference between Jim and Jimmy is', DIFFERENCE('Jim','Jimmy')
?'The soundex difference between James and Jim is', DIFFERENCE('James','Jim')
?'The soundex difference between Jim and Tim is', DIFFERENCE('Jim','Tim')
?'The soundex difference between Jim and Albert is', DIFFERENCE('Jim','Albert')
```

Figure 10.18 SOUNDEX differences between strings

LEFT(), RIGHT()

The LEFT() and RIGHT() functions enable you to find and view the first or last few characters of a character string. They return a number of characters from the left or right respectively, and have the same argument format:

```
LEFT(<character string>, <number of characters from the left>)
RIGHT(<character string>, <number of characters from the right>)
```

The following LEFT() function will return the character string '*John*', the first four characters from the left of the specified string '*John J. Smith*':

```
?LEFT('John J. Smith', 4)
```

Similarly, the last four digits (e.g., 7890) of a phone number (e.g., 123-456-7890) are displayed by using the RIGHT() function:

```
?RIGHT('123-456-7890',4)
```

LEFT() and RIGHT() are most commonly used to find a substring of characters in a character data field; to list, for example, those social security numbers in the SS_NO data field that begin with '111' or that end with '3333' (see Figure 10.19). Use the SET HEADING ON command to display the names of the data fields as headings.

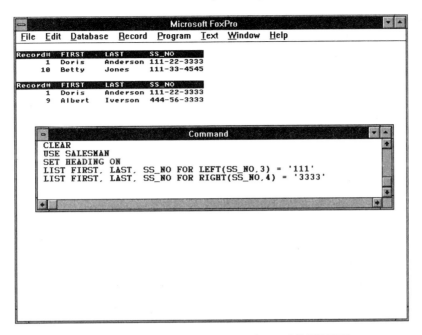

Figure 10.19 Locating records with LEFT() and RIGHT()

SUBSTR()

SUBSTR() is used to extract a portion of a specified character string. The character string, the beginning character position of the portion to be extracted, and the number of characters to be extracted are specified in the function argument:

```
SUBSTR(<character string>, <begin character position>,
       <number of characters to be extracted>)
```

The following command, for example, will extract from the string '*123-45-6789*' two characters beginning from the fifth character position:

```
?SUBSTR('123-45-6789',5,2)
```

The characters extracted from the character string by the SUBSTR() function will be '45'.

Like LEFT() and RIGHT(), SUBSTR() can be used to locate a substring within a character field. For example, to find all those salespeople in the SALESMAN database whose middle two digits of their social security numbers are '56' or '33,' issue the following LIST command:

```
LIST LAST, SS_NO FOR SUBSTR(SS_NO,5,2)='56' OR
SUBSTR(SS_NO,5,2)='33'
```

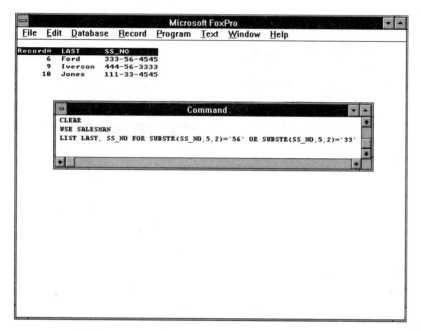

Figure 10.20 Locating substrings with SUBSTR()

A list of social security numbers satisfying the search condition is shown in Figure 10.20.

PROPER()

The PROPER() function returns a character string with the first letter in each word capitalized and the remainder in lowercase. The format of the function is:

```
PROPER(<character string>)
```

The function may be used to represent a proper name regardless of the case in which the name is stored. The following commands correctly display the country name by using the PROPER() function, whether the name is stored in lowercase or uppercase letters:

```
?PROPER('united states of america')
?PROPER('UNITED STATES OF AMERICA')
```

Thus, when these two commands are executed, they all will display the country name as United States Of America.

The PROPER() function is useful for ensuring that the names of people, cities, countries, etc. are displayed in a proper form. This function would come in handy to correctly display the names of salespeople in a report and and on mailing labels. Regardless of how the names are stored in the FIRST and LAST data fields, use

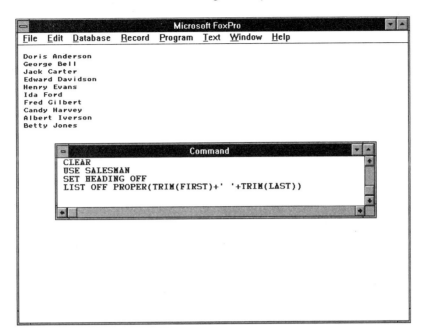

Figure 10.21 Using the PROPER() function

of the PROPER() function guarantees that they will be displayed in the proper format (see Figure 10.21).

AT()

The AT() function searches a character string for a specified substring. If the substring is contained in the string being searched, the function returns a number indicating the beginning character position of the substring in the larger string. If no such substring is found within the string, AT() returns a value of 0. The format of the function is:

```
AT(<substring>, <string to be searched>)
```

Here are two examples:

```
?AT('45', '123-45-6789')
?AT('56', '123-45-6789')
```

When the first command is executed, it will return a value of 5, indicating that the substring '*45*' is found in the fifth character position in the '*123-45-6789*' string. Because the string '*123-45-6789*' does not contain the substring '*56*', the second command will return a value of 0. The entire substring must appear consecutively in the searched string in order to be found.

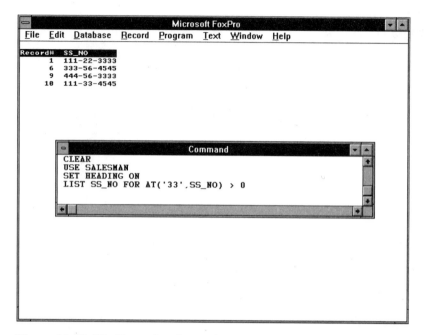

Figure 10.22 Finding substrings with the AT() function

AT() can be used to find a string of consecutive characters in a character data field. The following command, for example, will find all social security numbers containing the consecutive string of characters '33' in SALESMAN.DBF:

```
USE SALESMAN
LIST SS_NO FOR AT('33', SS_NO) > 0
```

When the LIST command is executed, it shows all social security numbers containing the substring '33' regardless of where the substring is found in the SS_NO data field (see Figure 10.22).

ASC()

As explained in Chapter 6, when character strings are sorted, their order is determined by their ASCII values. Each character is assigned a value that indicates its sequence number in the ASCII table. For example, in the ASCII table (see Appendix A), the uppercase letter 'A' has an ASCII value of 65; the lowercase letter 'a' has a value of 97.

The ASC() function returns the ASCII value of the first character of the string specified in the argument:

```
ASC(<character string>)
```

Using Memory Variables and Built-In Functions   415

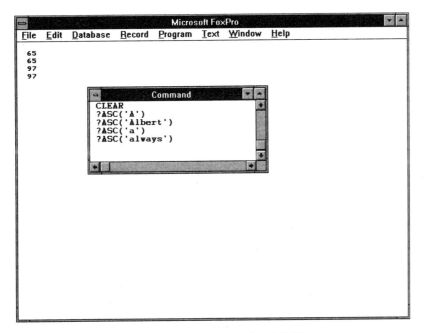

Figure 10.23 Displaying ASCII values with ASC()

Here are some examples:

```
?ASC('A')
?ASC('Albert')
?ASC('a')
?ASC('always')
```

The first two commands will return an ASCII value of 65, and the last two commands will return an ASCII value of 97 (see Figure 10.23).

ASC() also can be used to retrieve information about the ASCII value of a character. As with sorting, when indexing character strings, the order of a character is determined by its ASCII value. Although it is not necessary to know ASCII values for the index and sort operations, the information can be useful for understanding the results of the operations.

CHR()

CHR() is the opposite of ASC(). Where ASC() returns an ASCII value of a character, CHR() returns the character that has the specified ASCII value in the argument. The format of the function is:

```
CHR(<an ASCII value>)
```

Here are two examples:

```
?CHR(65)
?CHR(97)
```

The first command will display the uppercase letter 'A' and the second command will display the lowercase letter 'a'.

CHR() is useful for issuing printer control commands. You can control various aspects of printing with most printers by issuing an escape sequence before sending the output to the printer. If you are using an HP LaserJet II printer, for example, and want to print your report in Landscape mode (horizontally on the paper), you would issue the following command:

```
? CHR(27)+'&l1O'
```

where the ASCII value for the Esc key is 27. On some printers, you can issue CHR(13)+CHR(10), for example, to advance a page when the EJECT command does not work.

LEN()

The LEN() function returns the number of characters in the specified character string. The format of the function is:

```
LEN(<character string>)
```

The character string also can be represented by a character memory variable, a character field, or a memo field. If it is represented by a memory variable, the function counts all the characters including all the blanks stored in the variable. If it is a character field, the function will return the field width. When you specify a memo field in the function argument, the function will return the number of characters in the text, not including trailing blanks (see Figure 10.24).

You can see in this figure that the length of the string '*John J. Smith*   ' is 16, including trailing blanks. The length of the string in the LAST data field is always equal to the field width—8—regardless of the actual length of the string. The length of the contents of the memo field note, however, varies. The memo field of the first record contains 46 characters, whereas the memo field of the last record shows a length of 59.

Because the default width of a displayed memo field is 50 characters, the SET MEMOWIDTH command must be used to change the width in order to display a longer memo. The LEN() function allows you to determine the width necessary to accommodate the memo text.

Using Memory Variables and Built-In Functions   417

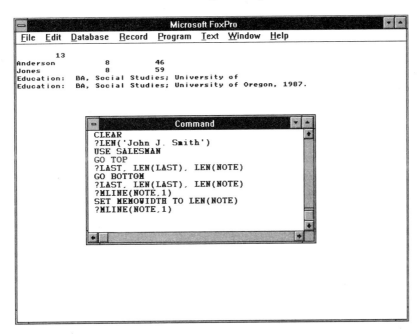

Figure 10.24 Determining string length with LEN()

NUMERIC FUNCTIONS

FoxPro provides a set of numeric functions that enable you to perform various mathematical operations on numeric values. These operations include calculating the square root of a number (SQRT()), taking the absolute value of a number (ABS()), converting a decimal value by truncating the decimal portion (INT()), or by rounding (ROUND()), and others such as LOG() and LOG10(). Most of these functions, except for ROUND(), follow this format:

    <function name>(<numeric expression>)

Each of these functions returns a numeric value after performing the mathematical operation on the value represented by the numeric expression supplied as an argument.

SQRT()

SQRT() finds the square root of a value; so, if you execute the following command, it will return the value of 10 (square root of 100):

    ?SQRT(100)

Of course, a negative value cannot be specified as the function argument—you cannot take the square root of a negative number as a real number.

ABS()

The ABS() function returns the absolute value of the value in the argument. It ignores the sign of the value; therefore, both of these commands will return the value of 123.45:

```
?ABS(123.45)
?ABS(-123.45)
```

INT()

The INT() function returns the integer portion of a decimal value. The integer value of 123 is returned when the following command is executed:

```
?INT(123.89)
```

It is important to note that the INT() function does not round the value to its nearest integer. It simply truncates the digits beyond the decimal point.

ROUND()

To round a decimal value to an integer, use the ROUND() function, which allows you to round a decimal value to a specified number of decimal places. The format of the function is:

```
ROUND(<numeric expression>, <number of decimal places>)
```

For example, to round the value of 123.6789 to its nearest integer, issue the following command:

```
?ROUND(123.6789,0)
```

The function will return the integer 124. Issue the following command, and it will return a value of 123.68:

```
?ROUND(123.6789,2)
```

The function rounds the value to two places beyond the decimal point.

LOG10()

The LOG10() function returns the common (base-10) logarithm value of the specified value. The following command, for example, returns the value of $2(10^2)$ as the common logarithm value of 100:

```
?LOG10(100)
```

LOG()

LOG() returns the natural (base-e) logarithm of the specified value. When the following command is executed, the LOG() function returns the value of 2.30259 as the natural logarithm value of 10:

```
?LOG(10)
```

STATISTICAL FUNCTIONS

FoxPro provides a set of statistical functions that you may use to calculate summary statistics such as average, variance, and standard deviation from values in a data field. With these functions, you can find, for example, the maximum and minimum value from a data field; or, count the number of records that satisfy certain filter conditions.

The summary statistics returned by these functions may be incorporated directly into a report or stored to memory variables for later use. To do that, use the CALCULATE command in the following format:

```
CALCULATE <statistical function
        TO <memory variable>
        [FOR <filter condition>]
```

Statistical functions that may be calculated include: CNT(), SUM(), AVG(), STD(), MAX() and MIN(). Except for CNT(), which needs no argument, every one of these functions requires a numeric expression as the function argument. The numeric expression must include one or more data fields.

The CALCULATE command offers the convenience of returning multiple summary statistics from a single CALCULATE statement. This ensures that all statistics returned by CALCULATE will be based on the same filter conditions. To have CALCULATE compute multiple summary statistics, you need to provide only the command with the list of functions, each separated by a comma. In addition, if you intend to store the values returned by the functions to memory variables, you must create a parallel memory variable list, with each variable name separated from the others by a comma. The syntax of this extended CALCULATE command is:

```
CALCULATE <statistical function list,...>
TO <memory variable list,...>
FOR <filter condition>
```

CNT()

Use CNT() to count selected records and save the result to a memory variable. CNT() could, for example, be used to determine the number of female salespeople

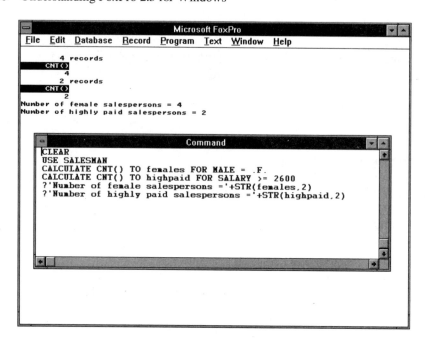

Figure 10.25 Counting records with CNT()

and the number of salespeople earning a salary of $2,600 or more. The functions would be included in CALCULATE commands and the results saved to memory variables as shown in Figure 10.25.

You can see that CNT() determined the number of records that satisfied the search conditions. The results were saved in the memory variables *females* and *highpaid*.

SUM()

The SUM() function is incorporated into a CALCULATE command to total the values in a numeric expression that includes one or more data fields. The sum is then saved to a memory variable. For example, the following CALCULATE command sums up the values in the SALARY data field:

```
USE SALESMAN
CALCULATE SUM(SALARY) TO totalpay
```

The SUM() function adds up all the values in the SALARY data field and saves the total to the memory variable named *totalpay*.

Instead of a single data field, you also may use a numeric expression in the function argument. Examples:

```
CALCULATE SUM(SALARY*.20) TO total_tax
CALCULATE SUM(QTY_SOLD*UNIT_PRICE) TO total_sale
```

Using Memory Variables and Built-In Functions   421

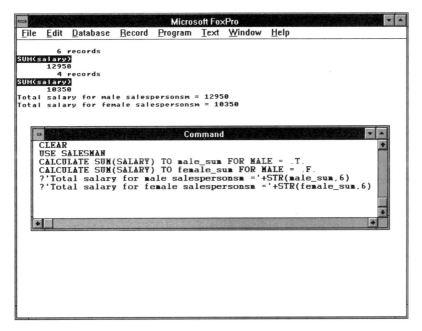

Figure 10.26 Totalling values in records with SUM()

The first command calculates the amount of withholding tax as 20 percent of the value in the SALARY data field. The second command calculates *total_sale* by multiplying the values in the QTY_SOLD data field by that in the UNIT_PRICE data field.

You also may add filter conditions to the CALCULATE command to sum up values in selected records (see Figure 10.26).

AVG()

Similar to SUM() is AVG(), which enables you to calculate averages in a CALCULATE command. The calculated averages are saved to specified memory variables. In the CALCULATE command, you may include one or more data fields in the function argument, with or without filter conditions. Examples:

```
USE SALESMAN
CALCULATE AVG(SALARY) TO avg_pay
CALCULATE AVG(SALARY*0.20) TO avg_tax
CALCULATE AVG(SALARY) TO male_avg FOR MALE
CALCULATE AVG(SALARY) TO female_avg FOR NOT MALE
```

When you execute these commands, they will calculate the averages with the values in the specified data fields for the selected records. The calculated averages are then saved to the memory variables (see Figure 10.27).

Figure 10.27 Calculating average values with AVG()

STD()

The STD() function calculates the standard deviation for the set of values represented by the numeric expression in the function argument. Standard deviation measures the average amount of deviation from the average value. As with the other mathematical functions, STD() is included in the CALCULATE command, and the result is stored to a memory variable, as shown in Figure 10.28. Examples:

```
USE SALESMAN
CALCULATE STD(SALARY) TO std_pay
CALCULATE STD(SALARY*0.20) TO std_tax
CALCULATE STD(SALARY) TO male_std FOR MALE
CALCULATE STD(SALARY) TO female_std FOR NOT MALE
```

MAX(), MIN()

MAX() and MIN() allow you to find the maximum and minimum value in a set of values represented by the numeric expression in the function argument. The functions are incorporated into the CALCULATE command. To find the highest

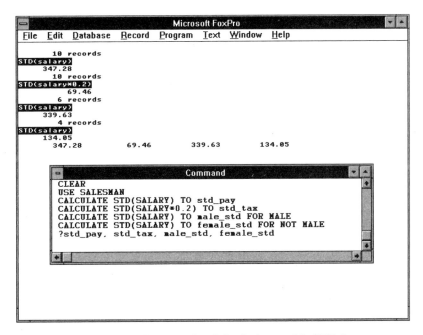

Figure 10.28 Calculating standard deviations with STD()

and lowest paid salesperson in SALESMAN.DBF, the following two commands would be issued:

```
USE SALESMAN
CALCULATE MAX(SALARY) TO max_pay
CALCULATE MIN(SALARY) TO min_pay
```

After executing the two commands, the memory variables *max_pay* and *min_pay* will contain the largest and smallest values in the SALARY data field. You also can find the salary range by taking the difference between the two memory variables (see Figure 10.29).

FINANCIAL FUNCTIONS

Two financial functions that may be of use to you are PAYMENT() and FV().

PAYMENT()

PAYMENT() computes the amount of payment to make on a fixed-rate loan over a period of time. The format of the function is:

```
PAYMENT(<loan amount>, <interest rate>,
     <number of payments>)
```

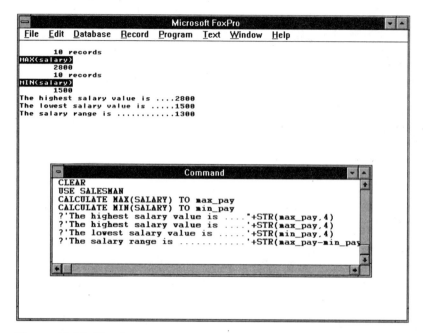

Figure 10.29 Finding maximum and minimum values with MAX() and MIN()

Let's say that you intend to borrow $100,000 and would like to repay the loan in 360 monthly payments at an interest rate of 12 percent per year (or 1 percent per month). To determine the monthly payment, use the following command:

```
?PAYMENT(100000, 0.01, 360)
```

When the command is executed, it will return a value of $1,028.61, representing the monthly payment necessary to pay off the loan in 360 months (30 years) at the prevailing interest rate of 1 percent (0.01) per month. If the annual interest were 9 percent (.09/12 per month) and you wanted to pay the loan off in 15 years (180 months), you would revise the command to read:

```
?PAYMENT(100000, 0.09/12, 180)
```

resulting in the amount of $1,014.27.

FV()

FV() calculates the future value of a series of equal periodic payments earning a fixed compounded interest. The format of the function is:

```
FV(<payment amount>, <interest rate>, <number of payments>)
```

Using this format, the following command will return the total investment value if you have made two payments at $100 each, earning 10 percent per year:

```
?FV(100, 0.10, 2)
```

The function returns the value of $210, representing the total value of the investment after you have made two payments of $100 each. The first payment earned $10 (10 percent of $100) and became $110 at the time the second payment was made. As a result, the total value is:

	Value At Beginning of	
	Period 1	Period 2
Payment #1	$100	$110
Payment #2		$100
Total Value		$210

Similarly, after making three payments of $100, the total value is $330:

	Value At Beginning of		
	Period 1	Period 2	Period 3
Payment #1	$100	$110	$121
Payment #2		$100	$110
Payment #3			$100
Total Value			$331

To calculate the future value, use the following FV() function:

```
?FV(100, 0.10, 3)
```

DATA CONVERSION FUNCTIONS

In preceding chapters we used expressions in a number of applications. Expressions were built as conditions for locating records, as selection criteria in query operations, and locate operations. Expressions may include data fields and memory variables, which must be of the same data type. You cannot, for example, mix a character data field with a date field in an expression. Therefore, to include data fields or memory variables of different types in the same expression, they must be converted to the same data type.

For this purpose, there is a set of built-in functions that convert data from one type to another.

CTOD()

The CTOD() function converts a character string to a date:

```
CTOD(<character string>)
```

For example, the CTOD() function will convert the character string '*12/25/91*' to a date and save it in the memory variable named *xmas*. As a result, the memory variable becomes a date variable:

```
STORE '12/25/91' TO string_a
xmas = CTOD('12/25/91')
```

The CTOD() function is necessary to store a date in a date variable. You cannot use the following command to assign a date into the date variable *xmas*:

```
xmas = '12/25/91'
```

As a result, the character string is stored to the variable *xmas*, and *xmas* becomes a character variable after the command is executed.

DTOC()

The DTOC() function converts a date to a character string:

```
DTOC(<date>)
```

Here is an example:

```
USE SALESMAN
LOCATE FOR LAST = 'Davidson'
?'Mr. '+TRIM(LAST)+' was hired on '+DTOC(HIRE_DATE)
```

After executing the commands, the output will be:

```
Record = 4
Mr. Davidson was hired on 06/04/90
```

DTOS()

There is another function that converts a date to a character string—DTOS(), used in the following format:

```
DTOS(<date>)
```

The function returns a string containing eight characters, indicating year (YYYY), month(MM), and day (DD) in the 'YYYYMMDD' format.

For example, the following DTOS() function will return a character string of '*19911225*' after you have executed the following command:

```
STORE {12/25/91} TO xmas
?DTOS(xmas)
```

You also may write the function as DTOS({12/25/91}). Remember, you must enclose the date in braces; otherwise, DTOS(12/25/91) will generate the syntax error "unrecognized phrase/keyword in command."

DTOS() comes in handy if you need to include a date in a character expression as an index key, because you cannot combine a date with a character string as an index key since all the data elements must be of the same type in an expression.

VAL()

A character string composed of digits can be converted to a numeric value with the VAL() function. The format of the function is:

```
VAL(<character string>)
```

The character string must contain only digits, with or without a leading positive or negative sign, and with or without a decimal point. Here are examples:

```
?VAL('123')
?VAL('123.45')
?VAL('-67.89')
```

After executing these commands, the output will be:

```
123.00
123.45
-67.89
```

The character string in the function argument must be enclosed in quotes; otherwise, no value will be returned. For example, if you execute the following command,

```
?VAL(123.45)
```

the error message, "Invalid function argument, type, or count" will result.

Commas or dollar signs may not be included in the character string that is to be converted to a value. For example, the following function argument will not return a correct value:

```
VAL('$12,345.67')
```

The function will return the value of 0 when the character string in the argument contains illegal symbols, such as a dollar sign and commas.

VAL() is useful for converting the contents of a character field to a set of numbers. For example, to store your account numbers (such as 101, 102, 103, etc.) as character strings in the character field ACCT_NO, you can convert the character strings to numeric values and use them for sorting operations. It is faster to sort a list of numeric values than a list of character strings.

STR()

The STR() function enables you to convert a numeric value to a character string. If the argument is an integer, STR() will return a string of digits corresponding to the integer. If the value is a decimal number, by default, it will convert the integer portion to a character string. But, as an option, you may specify the number of places after the decimal point that you would like to include in the return string. You also may choose the length of the returned character string. The format of the function is:

```
STR(<numeric value [,<length>, <decimal places>])
```

For example, the following two commands will return '-123' as a character string:

```
?STR(-123)
?STR(-123.45)
```

It will return the character string of '-123.45' if you specify the length of the character string as 7 and the number of decimal places as 2:

```
?STR(-123.45,7,2)
```

The STR() function is necessary for converting values in a numeric field so that it can be combined in a character expression as a key for the Index or Sort operations. For example, if you store your account identifications in a numeric field, the STR() function must be used if you want to include them in a character expression as part of an index key. You cannot combine a numeric field and other character strings as an index key.

DATE MANIPULATION FUNCTIONS

FoxPro's default format for representing dates is MM/DD/YY. But dates can be displayed in other formats. For example, the date {12/25/19}, once stored in a date variable named *xmas*, also can be displayed as December 25, '91 or December 25, 1991 by using one of the date manipulation functions. Other date manipulation functions allow you to extract the year, month, or day portion of a date for use as numeric values or character strings.

In addition, as we will see in a practical example at the end of this section, date manipulation functions are indispensable in using and incorporating dates into reports and labels. Most of these date manipulation functions (except for GOMONTH()) follow the same format:

```
<name of the function>(<date>)
```

The date value returned by the function may be a number or a character string depending on the type of function you use.

MDY()

The MDY() function converts a date to a character string in the Month DD, YY or the Month DD, YYYY format. The result will be Month DD, YY if the CENTURY system parameter is set to OFF (its default value). If SET CENTURY ON has been issued, the character string will be in the Month DD, YYYY format. For example, assuming the CENTURY setting is OFF, the following MDY() function returns the character string of '*December 25, 91*':

```
?MDY({12/25/91})
```

On the other hand, the function will return the character string of '*December 25, 1991*' after you have SET CENTURY ON:

```
SET CENTURY ON
?MDY({12/25/91})
```

YEAR(), MONTH(), DAY()

To extract the year, month, or day of a date and return it as a number or a character string, use one of the YEAR(), MONTH(), CMONTH(), or DAY() functions. Here are some examples:

```
STORE {'07/04/92'} TO holiday
?YEAR(holiday) ?MONTH(holiday)
?DAY(holiday)
```

?YEAR(holiday) will return a numeric value of 1991 regardless of whether the CENTURY setting is ON or OFF. ?MONTH(holiday) and DAY(holiday) return the values 7 and 4, respectively.

CMONTH()

CMONTH() enables you to extract the month from a date and returns a character string such as January, February, March, etc. The character string '*July*' is the result of the following command:

```
?CMONTH({07/04/92})
```

CDOW()

The day of a week can be determined by using the CDOW() function. It returns a character string, such as '*Monday*', '*Tuesday*', '*Wednesday*', etc., for the date specified in the function argument. The CDOW() function will return '*Saturday*' when the following command is executed:

```
?CDOW({07/04/91})
```

DOW()

DOW() also finds the weekday for a date, but while CDOW() returns a character string, DOW() returns a numeric value representing the day. The value range is between 1 and 7, representing Sunday through Saturday. Because July 4, 1992 is on Saturday, the following function will return a numeric value of 7:

```
?DOW({07/04/92})
```

GOMONTH()

The GOMONTH() function returns a date that is a specified number of months before or after a given date. The format of the function is:

```
GOMONTH(<date>, <number of months>)
```

If a positive number is specified, the function will return a future date; if you specify a negative number, it will return a past date. Examples:

```
?GOMONTH({12/25/91},3)
?GOMONTH({12/25/91},-6)
```

When these commands execute, they will return {03/25/92} and {06/25/91} which are, respectively, three months later and six months before the given date of {12/25/91}.

Chapter Summary

This chapter introduced the usefulness of memory variables and built-in functions in data manipulation. Memory variables make it possible to store intermediate results for later use. In addition, memory variables provide efficient means for passing data elements between databases and reports. Built-in functions are shortcuts for manipulating data elements. This chapter explained how to use character strings to manipulate the contents of character variables and character data fields. Similarly, the mathematical functions illustrated the methods for manipulating the numeric values in memory variables and data fields.

In preceding chapters, where expressions were used to specify search conditions and query selection criteria, all the data elements in them had to be of the same data type. This chapter described how to employ data conversion functions so that it is possible to include different types of data variables and data fields in the same expression.

The next chapter describes the procedures for creating custom reports and mailing labels, and some of the built-in functions discussed in this chapter will be used. In addition, you will learn how to pass summary statistics that are created and saved in memory variables to reports.

11
Producing Reports and Mailing Labels

An Overview

Perhaps the most important function of a database management system is to produce reports based on information extracted from the databases. This chapter details the procedures for designing and producing professional reports in a columnar or free-form format with FoxPro's Report Writer.

By the conclusion of this chapter, you will be able to create a quick report in the Report Layout window using FoxPro's default form or create a custom report based on a format of your own design. You also will be introduced to the procedure for generating mailing labels with FoxPro's Label Designer. Finally, you will learn how to output all these elements to the printer and the screen.

FoxPro Reports

After you have stored your data in database files, it is natural that you would want to extract useful information from them. A logical way to present this information is in professional reports that allow you to organize the extracted data elements in a consistent layout that shows precisely the kind of information you want to see.

The FoxPro Report Writer can be used to produce reports incorporating information that is taken from one or more database files. Depending on your application, you can choose either column or form reports. A column report obviously presents information in a column format, while a form report allows you to place information anywhere in the report. Most financial or accounting statistics are good candidates for column reports; computer-generated form letters are typical examples of form report output.

As a shortcut, you may choose to produce one of the two basic quick reports provided by FoxPro that present information in a default format. These quick reports label all data fields with their field names and place them in the report at a location determined by FoxPro. Alternatively, you may design a custom report over which you have full control of all the report objects and their placement on the page or screen.

The first step in creating a report is to determine its design in FoxPro's Report Layout window. This involves laying out all the necessary objects, which may include data fields taken from the database files, summary statistics computed from these field values, and text or graphics objects for describing or drawing attention to the information in the report. Once you have finished designing the report form, you can preview it on the screen before directing it to the printer.

Types of Reports

As mentioned, there are two types of report formats to choose from: column and form. Although they may contain the same data elements, information taken from the database is presented differently in each type of report. The report format you choose usually depends on the type of information that will be presented.

COLUMN REPORTS

A column report presents information in several columns, each of which contains data elements from one or more data fields. These data fields can be any of the valid data types supported by FoxPro: character strings, dates, logical values, and numeric values. A column report also gives you the capability to calculate summary statistics from the values in the columns and place them at the bottom of the columns. Data elements can be grouped in sections and group statistics can be displayed at the end of each section. An example of a column report is shown in Figure 11.1.

This sample report presents information about the salaries of the sales staff from the SALESMAN database. Social security numbers are presented in the column labeled "Soc. Sec. #." The Last Name and First Name columns display the last and first names of each member of the sales personnel. Monthly salaries are shown in the Monthly Salary column, and the Annual Salary column is calculated from the values in the Monthly Salary column.

Data elements in this report are divided into two groups: male and female sales personnel. Summary statistics, such as the monthly and annual salaries for each

	SALARY SUMMARY REPORT		Page 1 01/23/93

Soc. Sec. #	Last Name	First Name	Monthly Salary	Annual Salary
	Male Salespersons			
444-56-33	Iverson	Albert	$2,200	$26,400
909-78-34	Gilbert	Fred	$2,300	$27,600
701-31-87	Evans	Henry	$2,000	$24,000
222-55-10	Davidson	Edward	$1,500	$18,000
303-67-89	Carter	Jack	$2,550	$30,600
101-20-45	Bell	George	$2,400	$28,800
		Total	$12,950	$155,400
	Female Salespersons			
111-33-45	Jones	Betty	$2,500	$30,000
355-23-77	Harvey	Candy	$2,450	$29,400
333-56-45	Ford	Ida	$2,600	$31,200
111-22-33	Anderson	Doris	$2,800	$33,600
		Total	$10,350	$124,200
		Grand Total	$23,300	$279,600

Note: Figures updated 12/31/1992

Figure 11.1 A sample column report

gender group, as well as the grand total of the monthly and annual salaries, are calculated and placed at the end of the data section.

Three types of objects may be included in a column report: data fields, text, and graphic objects. Data fields are placed in the report to display information extracted from the selected database files. Text objects are used to describe information contained in the reports; they take the form of report titles, column or group headings, footers, etc. Graphics objects include boxes and vertical and horizontal lines that highlight the information in the report.

FORM REPORTS

If you decide to present the information extracted from the databases in a form report, you can include the same types of data objects as in a column report—data fields, text, and graphics objects. But be aware, there are significant differences between the two types of reports. Unlike a column report that displays information in a fixed format, a form report shows its information in a free-form layout, which means that data fields may be placed anywhere on the report page. And a column report displays the data taken from an individual data record in a row in the detail section of the report, whereas a form report displays the data from a single data record in a separate section or page. An example of a form report is shown in Figure 11.2.

This figure shows a portion of a form report that is produced using the information taken from the SALESMAN database. You can see that data fields are laid out in a free form. For example, the name of each salesperson is displayed as a character string taken from the FIRST, INITIAL, and LAST data fields of the record

```
┌─INFORMATION ABOUT OUR SALESPERSONS─┐     Page   1
                                            01/23/93

           Name of Employee: Albert I. Iverson
   Id. No.: S8    Social Security #: 444-56-3333      Male? [Y]

   Employment Date:  10/25/88      Office: B2
   Monthly Salary:    $2,200       Commission Rate:  10%
         Note: Hobbies:  hunting, fishing, sailing.


           Name of Employee: Fred C. Gilbert
   Id. No.: S6    Social Security #: 909-78-3434      Male? [Y]

   Employment Date:  04/15/87      Office: B3
   Monthly Salary:    $2,300       Commission Rate:  10%
         Note: Hobbies:  classical music, opera, foreign
               travel.


           Name of Employee: Henry H. Evans
   Id. No.: S4    Social Security #: 701-31-8723      Male? [Y]

   Employment Date:  03/08/88      Office: B3
   Monthly Salary:    $2,000       Commission Rate:   0%
         Note: Education:  BA. Marketing; UCLA. 1986.
```

Figure 11.2 A sample form report

belonging to that salesperson. Similarly, values from other data fields are scattered throughout the report. Descriptive text replaces field names in the report to describe information contained in the data fields. A page heading, including a page number and a report date, is added to the top of a report page for reference purposes.

A popular layout of a form report is an office memorandum, which mixes data fields taken from selected databases with other report objects. An example of this layout is shown in Figure 11.3.

An office memorandum such as this can be produced by mixing the information taken from the SALESMAN database and other report objects. In the memorandum, the name of the salesperson (Doris B. Anderson) is taken from the FIRST, INITIAL, and LAST data fields of her database record. Similarly, information about her employment date, monthly salary, and commission rate is extracted from the HIRE_DATE, SALARY, and COMIS_RATE data fields in the same record. These data field values are merged with the text necessary to convey the memorandum's message. In addition, a report date is inserted into the memorandum.

Report Components

A report consists of a set of components, some of which are found in all reports, while others may be included for special applications. These components tend to

```
                OFFICE MEMORANDUM

To:      Ms. Doris B. Anderson
From:    Human Resource Department
Date:    December 31, 1992
Subject: Personal Data
         Please take a moment to verify the following
         information and report any descrepencies to us
         at your earliest convenience:

            ┌─────────────────────────────────────┐
            │   Date of Employment: 07/01/86      │
            │   Current Monthly Salar: $2,800     │
            │      Commission Rate:       0%      │
            └─────────────────────────────────────┘

GTC: tjm
```

Figure 11.3 A sample form letter

be laid out in sections, and each serves to convey a specific kind of information. These report elements are as follows:

- A **report title** describes the information contained in the report. The report title should appear at the beginning of the report. If the report consists of several pages, subsequent pages may also include a **page heading** that describes the information on each page. In addition, a **footer** also may be displayed at the bottom of each report page. Report titles are included on almost all column reports and on many form reports.

- In a column report, a **detail section** displays the contents of database records. Information taken from data fields of selected database files is presented in various columns, each of which is identified with a **column heading**. Each data record is presented as a row in the detail section of a column report.

- In a column report, **summary statistics** are frequently placed at the end of data columns and summarize the data elements. If the data elements are divided into groups, **group statistics** are usually displayed at the end of each data group, and an overall statistical summary is placed at the end of the report. To describe the information in each group, reports also make use of a **group heading**. In a form report, on the other hand, the summary section may appear anywhere in the report.

- A sequential **page number** is usually included in multipage reports. The **report date** also is often displayed in the report. These two elements are incorporated both in column and form reports.

- Finally, a report may make use of various **graphics objects**, such as boxes and lines, that serve to highlight or to separate certain objects in the report.

For example, a rectangular box can be drawn around the report title to highlight it, and horizontal lines can be used to separate the column headings from the body of the report.

These components are depicted in the column report shown in Figure 11.4. The report title, SALARY SUMMARY REPORT, appears on top of the first page of the report with a box drawn around it as a highlighting device. Character strings taken from the SS_NO, LAST, and FIRST data fields of the SALESMAN database are displayed in the first three report columns. These are identified with the column headings "Soc. Sec. #," "Last Name," and "First Name," respectively. Values from the numeric field SALARY are shown in the column labeled Monthly Salary. The column with the Annual Salary heading displays values calculated from the SALARY data field. Two horizontal lines are used to separate the column headings from the field values.

Each row of the detail section in the report shows data elements taken from a data record of the selected database file. Records are grouped in two sections: one that lists data from salesmen and a second that lists data from saleswomen. Each group is identified with a label in the group heading.

Summary statistics, in the form of group totals, are computed and displayed at the end of each group of data records. Grand totals that are calculated from all the individual values listed in the Monthly Salary and Annual Salary columns are shown at the bottom of the two columns. Lines are drawn to separate the report detail and the totals. To complete the report, a footnote is included at the bottom of the report page.

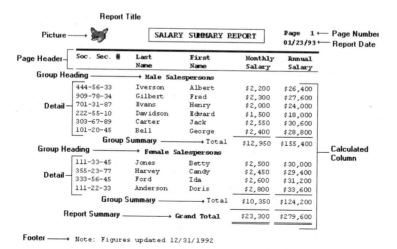

Figure 11.4 Components of a typical column report

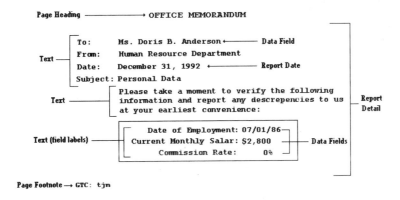

Figure 11.5 Components of a typical form letter

Although FoxPro allows you to include in a form report the same types of components as in a column report, different elements are usually chosen for a form report. In a form letter, **field labels** generally are used in place of column headings, and a **page heading** is used instead of a report title to describe the information in each form letter. And, because each form report is generated with data from an individual record, it does not usually include summary statistics.

Figure 11.5 shows an example of a form report. At the top of the report is the page heading. The report details include the data fields taken from the SALESMAN database and the accompanying labels that describe the field values. In addition to textual information, the report includes a report date and page footnote.

Creating Reports

To create a column or form report, use the FoxPro Report Writer. The process begins with designing the report form by laying out the report objects in the Report Writer's layout window and extracting selected fields from your database files and placing them in the report. After designing the report form, you may verify its contents by displaying it on the screen. If the report is satisfactory to you, the report can then be sent to the printer. If you choose to make additional changes, simply return to the layout window to make the necessary adjustments before printing the report.

Before designing a report, it is best to first select the database file or files that the report will incorporate. Data elements from one or more database files may be used in the same report. To simplify the explanation of the design process, however, let's assume that here you will use only one database file, SALESMAN.DBF, to create a report. To do that, select the database as the current database file in work

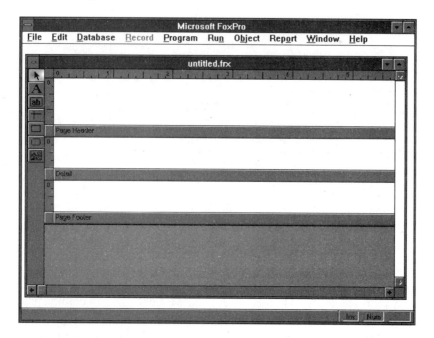

Figure 11.6 The Report Layout form

area 1. If you have not done this, FoxPro will prompt you to do so before you can begin designing your report.

To create a new report, select the New menu option from the File menu. When the New dialog appears, select the Report radio button, then select the New button. In return, a report layout form is displayed in the Report Layout window (see Figure 11.6). In addition, a Report menu is added to the menu bar in the FoxPro window, along with a set of tools that you can use to create graphic objects (such as lines, boxes, graphs, etc.) and place them in the report. The tools palette is shown to the left of the Report Design Window.

In Figure 11.6 you can see that the Report Design window is displayed within the Microsoft FoxPro window. If you need more working space so that you can display more report objects in the Report Design window, you can maximize the Report Design window to occupy the full screen. To do that, click your mouse on the Maximize control or press the Ctrl+F10 combination. As a result, the Report Design window becomes the only window displayed on screen, and the Report menu pad will be displayed with other menu pads on top of the window (see Figure 11.7).

THE REPORT MENU

You can use the options provided by the Report menu (see Figure 11.7) for laying out the report with a default quick report form or create one of your own design.

Producing Reports and Mailing Labels 441

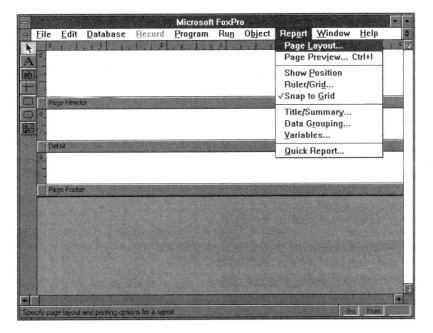

Figure 11.7 The Report menu options

With a menu option, you can preview the report on the screen before printing it. In addition, you can display the alignment grids and rulers so that you can easily align the report objects. The Report menu includes the following options:

- **Page Layout:** This option allows you to define the actual design of the report you are creating. You can specify the dimension of the report, the number and width of columns, and the margins and space between columns. You can define the printable area of the report, and the order of the printed columns. In this dialog, you also may choose the printer and the font for the printed text. You also can direct the program to save all the environment information related to this report (such as the databases used in the report, the indexes used, etc.).

- **Page Preview:** Use this option to display the report on the screen before directing it to the printer. You can scan through a multiple-page report, zero in on details, or view it in its actual layout.

- **Show Position:** This option allows you to display or hide the coordinates of the mouse pointer and the dimensions of the selected report objects in the status bar. By default, the mouse pointer and the dimensions are hidden.

- **Ruler/Grid:** The Ruler/Grid option provides for aligning report objects in the report form. The Ruler lines are visible upon request and can be measured in inches, centimeters, or pixels. The height and width of the grid can be customized.

- **Snap to Grid:** Use the Snap to Grid option to toggle on and off the grid alignment operation. When it is turned on, the Report Writer will automatically align report objects to their nearest grid lines.
- **Title/Summary:** Use this option to create a Title and Summary Band. In the Title band, you define the report title; in the Summary band, you can display summary statistics and related information. You will learn how to create these bands in later sections.
- **Data Grouping:** If you need to group information in a report, use this option to determine how it is to be done.
- **Variables:** In the last chapter, you learned how to store data or information in memory variables. You can use the Variables option to create memory variables so that you can use their values in the report.
- **Quick Report:** The Quick Report option provides a shortcut to laying out a report form. By using this option, you can quickly display data in a database file in a default format. You can choose either a column report or a form report.

Report Design Tool Palette

The report design Tool Palette is located in the upper left edge of the Report Design Window (see Figure 11.8). It consists of seven tools represented by icons, each of which can be accessed by pressing a button. These tools are:

Selection Pointer
Text Tool
Field Tool
Line Tool
Rectangle Tool
Round Rectangle Tool
Picture Tool

With the Selection Pointer button, you can select one or more report objects in the report form. Once the report objects are selected, you can move, resize, or delete them. The Text Tool is used to edit the labels and titles in the reports. You can place a data field in the report using the Field Tool button. You also can specify an expression and format of a data field placed in the report with this button. You can add graphic objects, such as lines, boxes, and pictures, with the Line, Rectangle, and Round Rectangle Tool buttons. If you need to place a graphic image (such as a logo or trademark, etc.) in the report, use the Picture Tool.

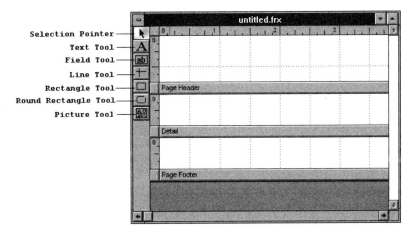

Figure 11.8 The Report Design Tool palette

Creating a Column Report

When you are in the Report Design window with a report layout, you may start placing report objects in the form. Choose the data fields from the selected database and place them in the report form; or choose a FoxPro default layout that places the data fields in the report using the quick report format. Although we will begin by creating a quick column report, we first will take a closer look at the layout of the FoxPro Report Writer.

REPORT BANDS

The FoxPro Report Writer divides a report into sections called report bands. Each band is used to hold certain kinds of report objects. In its default layout, as Figure 11.6 shows, the Report Writer displays three report bands: the Page Header band, the Detail band, and the Page Footer band. The name of a report band appears in a title line right below the band. In addition, other bands are available for placing different objects in a report. They include the Title band, the Group Header band, the Group Footer band, and the Summary band. Some of these bands are bound by a pair of title lines. Each report band, if it is present, occupies a certain amount of space in the column report.

Within a band, a number of vertial and horizontal grids can be used as a ruler to aid in the placement of report objects on the form. You can change the ruler measurement and grid lines specification by selecting the Ruler/Grid option from the Report menu. You also can eliminate the grid lines by selecting the No radio button in the Ruler Lines box in the Ruler/Grid dialog after you have selected the Ruler/Grid option.

You also can monitor the cursor position when you are working in the report form. Just select the Show Position option from the Report menu. As a result, at the bottom of the FoxPro window, the status bar line shows the location of the mouse cursor. The cursor location is represented by a pair of numbers showing the vertical and horizontal positions (in inches by default) related to the upper left-hand corner of the form.

Title Band

Typically, the Title band, when selected from the Title/Summary dialog, contains the report heading—the name of the report and any other descriptive text that applies to the entire report. The contents of the title band are displayed only once, at the beginning of the report.

Page Header Band

The Report Writer's Page Header band is used to hold the information that you intend to display at the top of each report page. In a column report, the Page Header band normally contains the column headings. It may also contain the page number or the report date, because the contents of the band will be repeated on each page of the report. In the quick report layout shown in Figure 11.9, for example, FoxPro places the names of the data fields in the Page Header band; these field names become the default column headings in a quick report.

In the default report layout, as shown in Figure 11.6, a certain amount of space is provided for showing the information in the Page Header band. The same amount of space will be displayed in the actual report. Within this space, you can display a number of report objects such as lines of text and graphic objects in the forms of lines, boxes, and pictures. The number of report objects that can be displayed in the band depends on the size of the objects. For example, when displaying text, the font size determines how many lines of text can fit in the space. In the default quick report format (see Figure 11.9), the Page Header band displays the field names in Courier font as the column heading in the Page Header band. The amount of space for displaying the page header information can be altered according to need, and you can change the height of the band with the mouse. To make the Page Header band wider, first point the mouse at the scroll box to the left of the band and then drag it down; drag the mouse upward to make the band narrower.

Detail Band

The Detail band in a column report displays the contents of selected data fields from the records in the database or databases. Because the Detail band displays information taken from one data record at a time, the band will be repeated as many

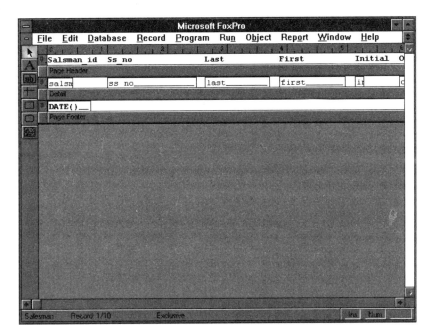

Figure 11.9 A Quick Report form layout

times as the number of records in the database. For example, in the quick report shown in Figure 11.9, data fields from the SALESMAN database are placed in the Detail band. Each data field is identified by the field name that you specified in the database structure. When you display the report, field values from each selected record will be extracted from the database and placed in the designated location.

Page Footer Band

The Page Footer is the last section of a report page. The information in this element will be displayed at the bottom of every page of the report. Usually, this consists of a footnote or a report date. In the quick report layout of Figure 11.9, for example, FoxPro places the report date—represented by the current system date, DATE( )—on the left-hand side of the Page Footer band. Similarly, if you scroll to the right-hand side of the quick report layout, you can see that the page number of the report is also placed in the Page Footer band. The report page number is identified by the label "Page," followed by a system variable, _PAGENO (which is partially hidden), that represents a sequential page number.

Group Header Band

If you divide records into groups and present them in different sections in a report, the group heading is placed in the Group Header band. Information placed in this band will be displayed at the beginning of the group. You will see an example of this in a later exercise.

Group Footer Band

Like the Group Header, the Group Footer band is used when data records are grouped for a report, and it is displayed at the end of each data group. Typically, the Group Footer band consists of text that describes the information in the group or summary statistics that relate to the group.

Summary Band

The Summary band is provided for placing summary statistics in a report. Because summary statistics are calculated using all selected records, they will appear only once at the end of the entire report.

CREATING QUICK REPORTS

To create a quick report using the Report Writer's default layout, choose the Quick Report option from the Report menu. In return, FoxPro displays the Quick Report dialog shown in Figure 11.10—if a database has been opened. If no database file is open, you will be asked to open a database in the current work area. For this exercise, open the SALESMAN database.

The Quick Report dialog shows two large text boxes and three check boxes. The large text boxes are used to select the type of report layout: column or form. The left text box shows FoxPro's default layout in which data fields are displayed horizontally in columns. The other format, represented in the right text box, shows the layout in which data fields are displayed vertically as rows. This layout can be used in a form report.

The Titles check box, which is selected by default, causes the names of selected data fields to be used as column headings. The Add Alias check box is also selected by default; it is used to include the database filename along with the name of the field for identifying a data field. For example, when the check box is selected, the data field FIRST will be identified as salesman.first in the report. In a quick report, you can select only those data fields you need for the report. This is done by checking the Fields check box. The Fields check box allows you to select only those data fields from the selected database that you would like to include in the report. Because the SALESMAN database has too many fields to be displayed on a single line of a column report, let's select only certain fields from the database to include in the report.

Producing Reports and Mailing Labels 447

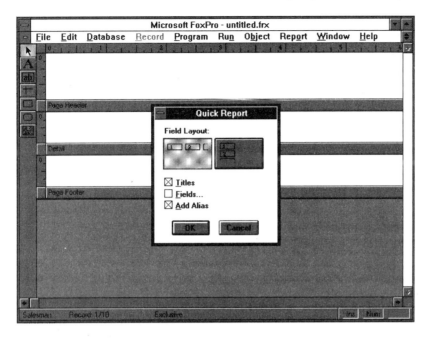

Figure 11.10 The Quick Report dialog

Selecting Data Fields

To select the data fields to include in a quick report, select the Fields check box. When the Field Picker dialog appears, select the following eight data fields in the order in which they are shown:

```
SALSMAN_ID
SS_NO
LAST
FIRST
INITIAL
OFFICE_ID
SALARY
MALE
```

When this is done, return to the Quick Report dialog and select the OK button to return to the Report Layout window. At this point, you can see that all the selected data fields are placed in the report, together with the column headings (see Figure 11.9). This figure shows the layout of the quick report and its report objects, along with all the selected data fields and text in the form of column headings for identifying these fields. It also displays other objects such as the report date.

Viewing Quick Reports

To view a quick report on the screen, select the Page Preview option from the Report menu or press the Ctrl+I key combination; the contents of the report will be displayed in the Page Preview dialog(see Figure 11.11).

In the Page Preview dialog, you can see the report displayed on the left-hand side of the dialog. On the right-hand side of the dialog, you will find a number of push buttons and a Page spinner. The Next and Previous push buttons allow you move forward and backward among report pages in a multiple-page report. You also can display a specific report page using the Page spinner. When the report is shown zoomed out or scaled down, you can choose the Zoom In button to enlarge the report image. To return the report to the scaled down image, select the Zoom Out button.

For example, the report as shown in Figure 11.11 is too small to be read, so select the Zoom In button. As a result, the report will be enlarged (see Figure 11.12). If the enlarged report is too big to fit in the box, you can use the scroll control to move vertically and horizontally to reveal the hidden portion of the report.

An alternative to using the Zoom In button is to focus on a select area of the report with the magnifying cursor. When the report is shown in a zoomed out (scaled down) image, as you move the mouse curor to the report image, the cursor

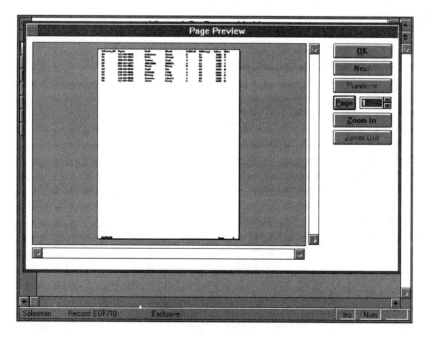

Figure 11.11 Previewing a quick report

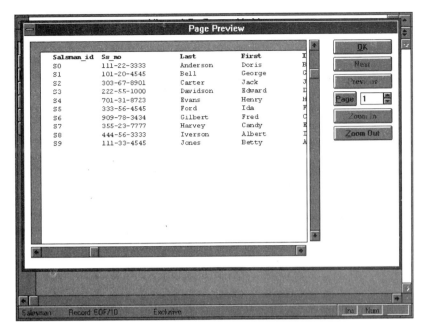

Figure 11.12 Zooming in a report section

becomes a magnifying lens. To enlarge a certain spot in the report, point the magnifying lens at the spot and then click the mouse. As a result, an enlarged image of that area will be shown in the Page Preview dialog.

The enlarged quick report in Figure 11.12 displays the column headings in the Page Header band on top of the report. The report body is represented by the information presented in the Detail band. Each line shows information taken from the fields of one record of the SALESMAN database.

After you have examined the report in the Page Preview dialog, you can return to the Report Layout screen by selecting the OK push button.

Producing Quick Reports

After viewing the quick report, it can be printed. But, before printing the report, the parameters that determine how the printed report page should look must be specified. These parameters set the length and margins of the report page. In addition, the printer driver to be used by FoxPro must be selected, and any printing options must be specified. Printing options determine whether FoxPro will issue a form feed before it prints the report, and whether it will omit the report detail and provide only summary statistics. In addtion, you can specify the scope and filter conditions to determine which records will be included in the report.

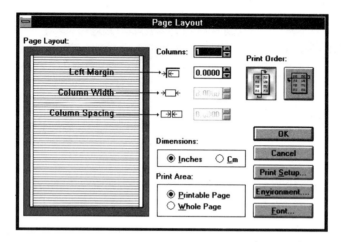

Figure 11.13 The Page Layout dialog

Specifying Page Layout

To specify the page layout for the report, select the Page Layout option from the Report menu after you have returned to the report layout screen. The report Writer displays the Page Layout dialog shown in Figure 11.13.

In the Page Layout dialog, you can see FoxPro's set of default values that determine the number and width of columns, the width of the left margin, and the space between report columns. In this dialog, you also can specify the dimension and printable areas of the report.

The left-hand side of the Page Layout dialog shows an image of the report, with the number of columns you specified (a single-column report—the default—is shown in Figure 11.13). In the middle of the dialog are four spinners:

- The first—Columns—is for determining the number of columns you want to use.

- The second is for specifying the width of the left margin.

- The third is for setting the width of columns when your report includes more than one. Note that all columns must be the same width.

- The fourth spinner is for assigning the amount of space you want to leave between columns in a multicolumn report.

All column widths and spaces can be measured in either inches or centimeters. Use the Dimension radio buttons in the dialog to determine those measurement units. Below the Dimensions radio buttons are two radio buttons that you can use to specify how the report is to be printed. When you choose the Printable Page, the report will be printed with the margins you have specified. If you choose the Whole Page radio button, the report will fill the whole page.

If the report is too big to be printed on a single page, it will be divided in sections and printed in sequence. You can choose to print the section vertically or horizontally by choosing one of the two Print Order buttons.

There are five push buttons in the lower right-hand corner of the Page Layout dialog. In addition to the OK and Cancel buttons, the Printer Setup button allows you to select the printer, orientation (portrait or landscape), and the page size, etc. If you need to save the environment information related to the report, select the Environment button. Enter the font and type size using the Font push button.

Selecting Printers

The next step is to select the printer. To do that, select the Print Setup button in the Page Layout dialog. When the Print Setup dialog appears (see Figure 11.14) you should see the default printer displayed in the Printer text box. To select a different printer that you have set up in Windows, choose the Specific Printer radio button and then select it from the printer list. Remember that the default and other printers were set up outside FoxPro in the Windows Program Manager. If you want to designate another printer as the default or change the list of printers, you must do that in the Program Manager.

After selecting the printer, as an exercise, select the Portrait radio button for the print orientation. Select 8 1/2 × 11 inches as the paper size. If you need to set

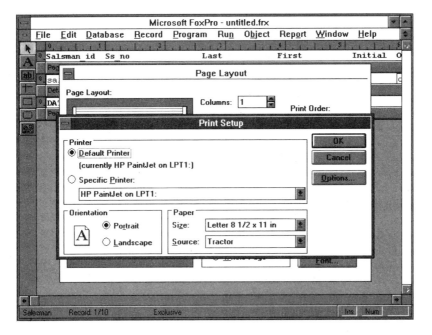

Figure 11.14 The Print Setup dialog

parameters for Dithering and Intensity control, select the Options button. For most print jobs, the default setting will be adequate. To return to the Page Layout dialog, select the OK button.

Saving the Report Environment

As mentioned, the Environment push button is used to control the information about the FoxPro environment that is to be passed to the report when it is executing. This information includes the names of all the databases that are open and any relations that have been established among them, the currently selected work area, and the names of all the indexes currently open, as well as the name of the current master index.

When you select the Environment button, the Environment dialog appears. The Save button in the Environment dialog saves the current report environment; the Restore button returns the report environment to its state *prior* to any changes made to it since the last time it was saved; Clear cancels all report environments previously saved. Normally, you would select Save to retain the current report environment for future use. This will allow you to modify or print the report in the future without first opening the necessary databases and index files and defining the necessary relations.

At this point, select the Save button to return to the Page Layout window. Then select the OK button to exit the Page Layout dialog and return to the Report Layout window. Now you may choose to output the report to the printer or save it to a file. A good habit to develop is to save the report layout to a file before printing it, in order to avoid the risk of damage in case the printing process is interrupted for any reason. If the printer is improperly connected or configured, for example, FoxPro may "freeze" the action and you will have to abort the printing process before continuing once again. If you have not saved your report form, it may be necessary to set it up again. If, however, you intend to use the report layout once and are certain the printer is properly installed and connected, it probably is safe to print the report without saving the layout to a file.

Saving Reports

To save the layout that appears in the Report Layout window as a report form, select the Save As option from the File menu popup. When the Save As dialog appears, enter the name of the report in the Save Report As text box; for example, type in QKREPORT, if that's the file you want to save. The report layout will be saved in a report form file with an .FRX extension (e.g., QKREPORT.FRX). At this point, if you didn't previously save the environment information, FoxPro for

Producing Reports and Mailing Labels 453

Windows asks if you would like to save the environment by displaying the following message before returning you to the Report Layout window:

```
Save Environment information?
```

For our purposes, select Yes. When you return to the Report Layout window, the name of the report will appear in the Title Bar of the window.

Printing Reports

When you are in the Report Layout window, the report can be printed by choosing the Report option from the Database menu popup, which causes the Report dialog to appear (see Figure 11.15).

Information in the Report dialog is displayed in two groups, each of which contains a number of check boxes and push buttons. The Input group contains the Form text box for identifying the report form (e.g., c:\foxprow\foxdata\qkreport.frx) to be used. While the Report Writer is the active window, the report form in it will be selected as the default report form. In addition, this group contains the Restore Environment check box and the Quick Report push button. If the Restore Environment check box is selected, FoxPro will restore any environment information that

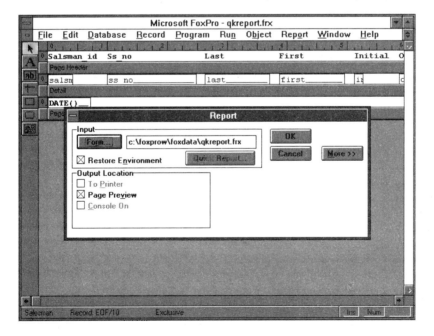

Figure 11.15 The Report dialog

had been previously saved with the report form. The Quick Report push button is disabled because the Report Writer is open and contains a custom report form, which will be used instead of FoxPro's default quick report.

The Output Location group contains three check boxes for routing the report to the desired destination. By default, Page Preview is selected. If you would like to print the report, click on the Page Preview check box and then check the To Printer box. If the report is going to either a printer or a file, you can monitor the output by clicking the Console On check box; leaving the Console On check box empty sends the report to the printer or a file, without the report being displayed in the desktop area on the screen.

Normally, these options are all that you need to print the quick report. However, there are other options that you can choose to control the contents of the report. You can display an extended Report dialog by selecting the More push button. As a result, you will see additional push buttons and check boxes in the Report dialog (see Figure 11.16)

In the extended Report dialog, there are a set of push buttons in the Output Options box. If you check First Page Heading Only, the report will print the information in the Page Header on the first report page only, not on subsequent pages. Normally, the printer will issue a page eject or a form feed before printing begins; this ensures that it will begin printing at the top of a new page. Choosing the No Initial Form Feed check box causes the printer to begin printing at the

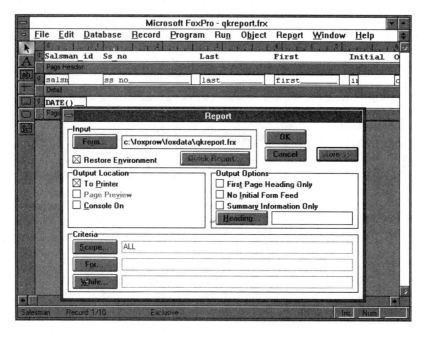

Figure 11.16 The extended Report dialog

current print position without first advancing to a new page. The Summary Information Only check box allows you to print only the information in the Summary band and suppress the printing of all detail information. An additional line may be added to the page heading on each report page and can be entered as text or an expression by selecting the Heading push button. This text will appear on a line below the information in the Page Header band.

In the Criteria box at the bottom of the extended Report dialog, you will find the Scope, For, and While buttons. They are used to select the records and fields to be printed in the same way as discussed previously.

As an exercise, print the quick report using the report form in the Report Layout window. Select the To Printer and Console On check boxes, then select the OK button in the Report dialog. In return, the Print dialog will appear (see Figure 11.17).

In the Print dialog, you can specify the print quality and number of copies. For a multipage report, you can select the range of report pages to be printed. In addition, you can determine whether or not to collate the report copies. After specifying the print settings, select the OK button to begin printing. A copy of the printer report is shown in Figure 11.18.

Another way to produce a report is to select the Report option from the Run menu after you have saved the report form in a file. Then, identify the name of report form (e.g. qkreport.frm) when the Open dialog appears. As a result, you will be asked to direct your report either on screen or to a printer in the Run Report

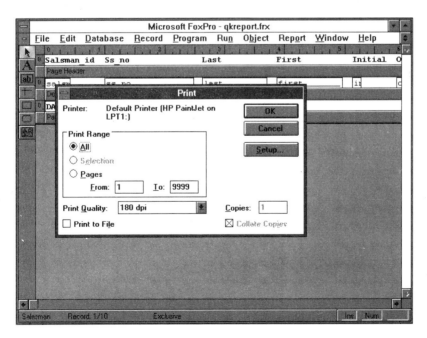

Figure 11.17 The Print dialog

```
Salsman_id  Ss_no         Last       First    Initial  Office_i  Salar  Male
S0          111-22-3333   Anderson   Doris    B        B1        2800   N
S1          101-20-4545   Bell       George   G        B3        2400   Y
S2          303-67-8901   Carter     Jack     J        B2        2550   Y
S3          222-55-1000   Davidson   Edward   D        B1        1500   Y
S4          701-31-8723   Evans      Henry    H        B3        2000   Y
S5          333-56-4545   Ford       Ida      F        B2        2600   N
S6          909-78-3434   Gilbert    Fred     C        B3        2300   Y
S7          355-23-7777   Harvey     Candy    E        B3        2450   N
S8          444-56-3333   Iverson    Albert   I        B2        2200   Y
S9          111-33-4545   Jones      Betty    A        B1        2500   N
```

Figure 11.18 A printed quick report

dialog (see Figure 11.19). If you select the To Print radio button in the dialog, the report in Figure 11.18 will be output.

When you inspect your quick report, you may want to modify the report form to produce a custom report. The custom report could, for example, incorporate descriptive text as column headings to describe the values in the report columns. You can add new data fields to the report or remove existing ones; you also can rearrange the order of the columns, change the column widths, and format the data values. You can add a report title to the beginning of the report that describes the information in the report, place the report date and page number in different places on the report, or add graphics objects such as boxes and lines to highlight the most important information in the report.

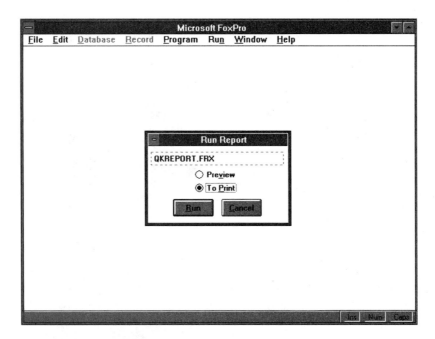

Figure 11.19 The Print Report dialog

CREATING CUSTOM REPORTS

There are two ways to create a custom report. One is to design the report form from scratch, individually defining and positioning all the report objects. Or you can modify an existing quick report that was generated by FoxPro, as in the example above. The latter approach often is a time-saver because the quick report provides a basic foundation on which to build. The quick report allows you to select the data fields that you would like to appear in the report, and you can quickly rearrange them in a custom report instead of placing each of them individually.

Modifying Existing Reports

To create a custom report using a previously defined report form, open QKREPORT.FRX so that it is displayed in the Report Layout window. If you have exited from the Report Writer, select the Open option from the File menu. When the Open dialog appears, select Report from the Type popup and then select the name of the report form file from the list. If you want to modify the report form QKREPORT.FRX that you have saved, select it from the file list in the Open dialog. The Open dialog also contains an Environment check box. Check this box to load the environment information that was stored with the report. By choosing this check box, the database file selected for the report will be opened automatically in the currently selected work area if you saved the environment with the report. Now, select QKREPORT.FRX. In return, the report form that was previously saved as QKREPORT.FRX is displayed in the Report Layout window. You can now begin to modify the report form.

Selecting Report Objects

During the report modification process, you may want to delete unwanted report objects or to move report objects from their current locations to new locations. To do that, select the objects you plan to delete or move (you may select one or more objects at a time with the mouse or using the keyboard).

To select a report object, first choose the Selection Pointer tool. Click your mouse on the object or press the Spacebar after positioning the cursor on the object. If you need to select several objects, click the mouse on each of the objects while holding down the Shift key. Selected objects are framed in boxes. If you make a mistake, click the mouse on an empty area of the layout, and all the selected objects will be deselected.

All report objects also may be selected by using a selection marquee, which allows you to define a rectangular area and select all objects within it. To draw the marquee, position the mouse pointer at any corner of a rectangular area that includes all the objects you wish to select and drag it to form the rectangle. As you do this, the selection marquee will appear as a rectangle with dotted lines. When you release the button, all the objects inside the marquee will be selected. Note: Be sure to position the pointer above and to the side of the objects before forming the rectangle.

Deleting Report Objects

Once you have selected one or more report objects, they can be removed from the report by selecting the Cut option from the Edit menu or by pressing the Del key. Although the Cut option and the Del key will remove the objects, it is preferable to use the Cut option because you can easily restore the objects if you have mistakenly removed them. Not all the objects can be restored if you use the Del key to remove them. Text, data fields, and graphics objects may be removed in this way; note, however, that data fields that have been removed from the report are also not deleted from the database.

As an example, to delete the column heading "Salsman_id," click the mouse on the heading and then select the Cut option from the Edit menu. Use the same procedure to remove the SALESMAN_ID data field in the Detail band from the report layout.

To delete the field MALE (labeled "ma") and the column heading "Male" as a group, hold down the Shift key, then click the mouse on the field and the column heading in sequence, and select the Cut option. It is possible to also delete a set of data fields and column headings using the selection marquee. For example, to remove the INITIAL and OFFICE_ID fields (labeled as "in" and "off") and their column headings ("Initial" and "Office_i"), first use the selection marquee to select the fields and column headings. Click the mouse just to the left of the column heading "Initial" and then drag the mouse just to the right of the data field labeled "of." As you do so, a dotted rectangular marquee appears, and all the objects within the marquee will be selected when you release the mouse button. In this case, the selected objects will be the two data fields and the column headings. To delete them, press the Del key. After removing these data fields and column headings, the report form will look like that shown in Figure 11.20.

Restoring Deleted Report Objects

Should you accidentally remove an object from your report, it is easy to restore it, provided that you notice and attempt to correct your mistake before making any further deletions. When a report object is removed from the Report Writer with the Cut option, it is not physically deleted immediately. Instead, FoxPro removes it

Producing Reports and Mailing Labels   459

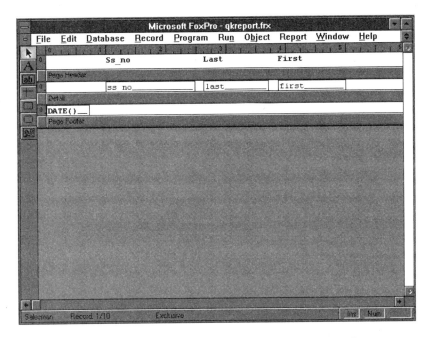

Figure 11.20 After removing data fields and column headings

from the screen and stores it in a temporary holding area called the Clipboard. As long as the contents of the Clipboard have not changed since you deleted the last report object or objects, you can restore them. To do this, select the Paste command from the Edit menu pad. FoxPro will retore the deleted objects to their original form.

It is worthwhile stressing, however, that deleted report objects can be restored only as long as they remain intact on the Clipboard. Once they are removed from the Clipboard—which happens when some other object is deleted or copied to the Clipboard, or when you exit FoxPro—they can no longer be recovered.

Another way to restore removed objects is by using the Undo operation. After you have carried out any operation, you can reverse the operation by selecting the Undo option from the Edit menu. For example, if you have accidentally removed a set of report objects, you can use the Undo operation to restore the removed objects. Another method of undoing changes to the report form is to select the Revert option from the File menu pad. FoxPro will display the following message:

```
Discard changes?
    Yes     No
```

Select Yes to discard all the changes made to the report since it was opened.

Moving Report Objects

Notice in Figure 11.19 that the space remains blank after the report objects are removed. Remaining objects will not be rearranged to fill the space. You may, however, move the remaining objects around yourself.

Any selected report objects may be repositioned in a report. To move a selected object with the mouse, point the mouse cursor at the object and then drag it to a new location. If a group of selected objects is to be moved, point the mouse cursor at any one of the squares surrounding the selected objects and then drag the group to the new location.

Let's say, for example, that you want to move the first column to the left: First select the SS_NO data field (labeled "ss_no") and the column heading "Ss_no." Then use the mouse to drag it left to the desired location. Use the same method to move the FIRST data field and its column heading closer to the LAST data field. Finally, move the SALARY field and its column heading closer to the LAST data field and its column heading. After moving the data fields and column headings, your report form should look like Figure 11.21.

Note that the column headings contain the names of their corresponding data fields. Because they do not fully describe the information contained in the columns, you may want to use more descriptive text to describe the data fields, which requires that you edit the text of each column heading that now appears in the Page Header band.

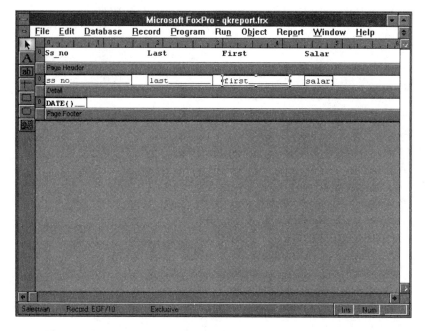

Figure 11.21 Rearranging report columns

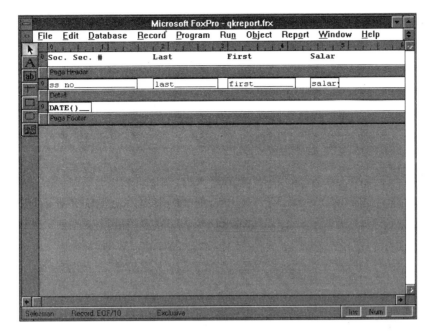

Figure 11.22 Editing column headings

Editing Text

Any text in a report can be edited by using the Text tool. To edit existing text, click on the Text Tool and then position the mouse cursor on the text to be edited. Insert a new string of characters to an existing text or type over the existing string of characters. For example, if you decide to change the heading of the first column from "Ss_no" to "Soc. Sec. #," position the mouse cursor and highlight the column heading after pressing the Text Tool button. Then, change the column heading to "Soc. Sec. #." After entering the new heading, click the mouse outside the text to anchor it. Your report form will now look like Figure 11.22.

Resizing Report Bands

In a default layout, the height of the report bands usually is set to a minimum. For example, the height of the Page Header band is set to accommodate only one line for displaying the column heading for the data fields. If you need to use multiline labels or to insert a blank space between the page heading and the detail band, you can resize the Page Header band. The procedure to resize any report band is the same: Click your mouse on the title line of the band and then drag it up or down to the new location. For example, if you need to insert text to the Page Header band, first click the mouse on the scroll box to the left of the band. As a result, the cursor

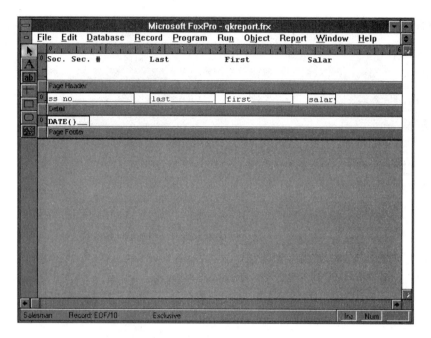

Figure 11.23 Resizing the Page Header band

becomes a double-arrow symbol. Drag the mouse downward until the band is at the desired height. Now the report layout may look like Figure 11.23.

Inserting Text

You can place text in the Report band with the same procecure as that used for editing existing text. First, select the Text Tool and position the cursor at the initial position of the text. Then simply type in the text from that position. Try this to enter the word "Name" below the current column headings of "First." Before making changes to the other column headings, be aware that it is possible at this stage to change the text font (you also can change it later). To do that, select the Font option from the Object menu. When the Font dialog appears (see Figure 11.24), select the font, font style, and size accordingly. A sample of the text with the selected font is shown in the Font dialog. After specifying the font, select the OK button to return to the report layout. Use the same procedure to edit the column heading so that it looks like Figure 11.25.

When you are using the Text Tool with the procedure outlined, each time you finish editing text, it automatically switches off and reverts to the Selection Pointer. The only way to keep the Text Tool in effect is to double click the Text Tool button; it will remain pressed (displayed in dark color) until you select another tool button.

Producing Reports and Mailing Labels   463

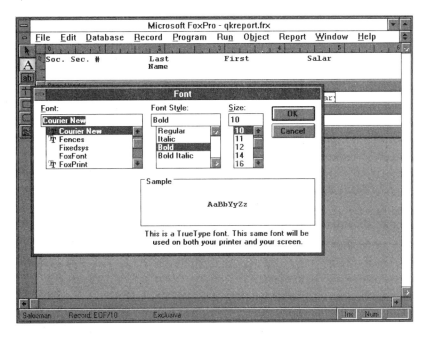

Figure 11.24 The Font dialog

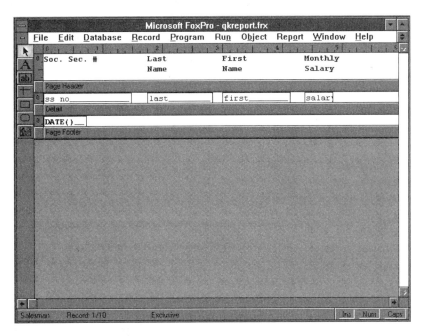

Figure 11.25 Inserting text to column headings

As a result, you won't have to press the Text Tool button each time you insert text to a column heading.

When you place text in a report, click the mouse outside the text to anchor it. Text entered in this way will be treated as one unit, and can then be selected independently later to move or delete. If, for example, you type an entire line before anchoring it, that whole line must be selected as a unit; you cannot select only a portion of it. Conversely, if you anchor each word in the line after entering it, the individual words then can be selected to move or delete.

Placing Data Fields

A new column can be created by using an existing data field from the selected database, or by defining an expression with values derived from one or more existing fields. To do that, select the Field Tool and then position the cursor at the location in the report where you want to place the field.

For example, you might like to add a column showing the annual salaries for the sales staff, which will be computed from the monthly salary values in the SALARY field of the SALESMAN database. To place the annual salary as a computed field in the report, first select the Field Tool and then click the mouse to the right of the Monthly Salary column in the Detail band. In return, the Report Expression dialog appears (see Figure 11.26).

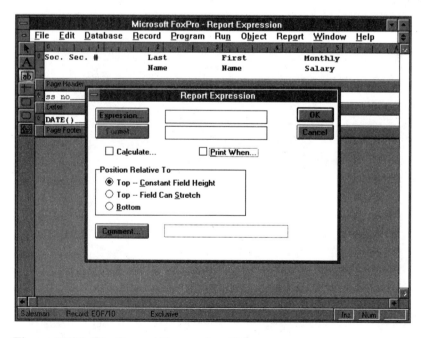

Figure 11.26 The Report Expression dialog

Producing Reports and Mailing Labels   465

In the Report Expression dialog are two push buttons labeled Expression and Format that are used to specify the expression and the format of the data field to be added to the report. Three radio buttons are provided to position the data field. Normally, you would keep the field height constant at the top of the band. Therefore, accept the default setting, selecting the Top -- Constant Field Height button. If Top -- Field Can Stretch radio button is selected, the band will stretch vertically to accommodate all data in the field. Use this option when data in the field varies in size. A memo field is a good candidate for this option. The Print When check box is used to specify special printing instructions. Click on the check box to bring up the Print When dialog (see the radio buttons and check boxes in the Print When dialog in Figure 11.27). For example, if you select the Yes radio button in the Print Repeated Values box, you would suppress displaying duplicate values in that data field. Return to the Report expression dialog.

The Calculate check box in the Report Expression dialog is used to place summary statistics as a field in the report. By selecting the Calculate check box, you can determine summary statistics such as sum, average, and standard deviation, and at what point a field will be set to 0 (reinitialized). When the Calculate dialog appears, select the type of summary statistics to be calculated by using the values in the field expression you have specified in the dialog.

The Comment check box is used to record a note for describing the data field. When this box is selected, the Comment dialog appears, in which you enter the reference note.

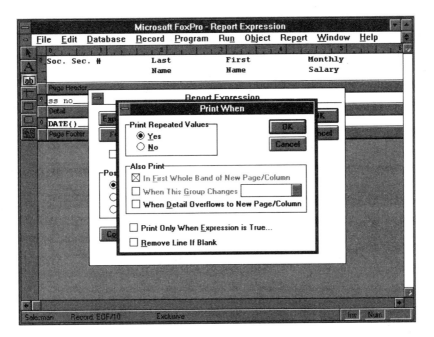

Figure 11.27 The Print When dialog

Defining Report Field Expressions

To continue with our example, the column that we add will contain values computed from the SALARY field by using the following expression:

```
salesman.salary * 12
```

Because the values in the SALARY field represent monthly salaries for the sales staff, multiplying it by 12 produces the annual salary. After selecting the Expr button, enter the expression in the Report Expression Builder and return to the Report Expression dialog; or type the expression directly in the text box next to the Expression button in the Report Expression dialog (see Figure 11.28).

Formatting Report Fields

FoxPro enables you to specify the format for a set of data values that are displayed in a report column. A monetary value, for example, can be displayed in the conventional format that includes the dollar sign and commas for grouping the digits (e.g., $1,234.45). A character string can be displayed in upper- or lowercase, right justified, and so on. Similarly, you can specify the format in which to display dates in the report.

To define the format for the annual salary column that we are adding to the report, select the Format button to bring up the Format dialog. In the Format dialog, select

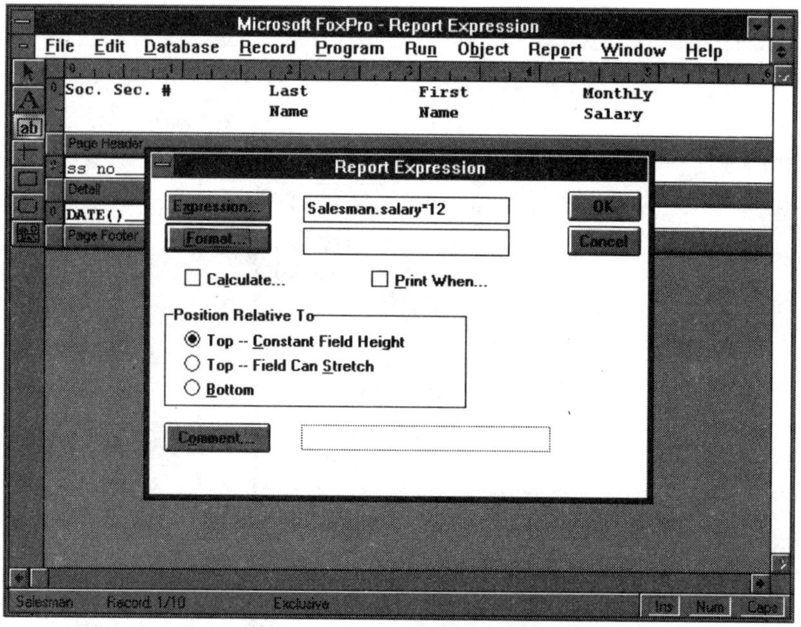

Figure 11.28 The Report Expression dialog

Producing Reports and Mailing Labels 467

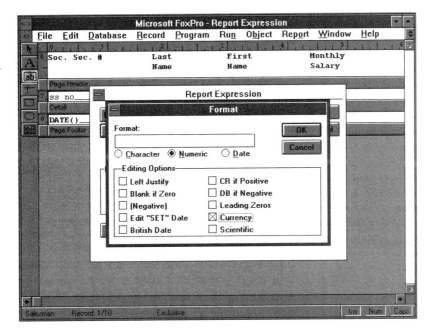

Figure 11.29 The Format dialog

one of the three radio buttons—Character, Numeric, Date—to identify the type of data. In addition, select one of the Editing Options check boxes to specify the display format for the field. Select the Currency check box to display values in a currency format, for instance (see Figure 11.29).

When you select the OK button and return to the Report Expression dialog, you will see the format string "@$" inserted in the Format text box. The string contains control characters that direct how the values are to be displayed (see Figure 11.30).

Select the OK button again to accept the report expression and you will return to the Report Layout window. At this point, you can add the text, "Annual Salary," to the page header for describing the new column. Now view the report on the screen by choosing the Page Preview option from the Report menu or by pressing the Ctrl+I key combination. Note that the annual salaries are displayed with leading dollar signs but without commas (see Figure 11.31). If you would like to add commas to values displayed in a currency format, you can define a field template in the field format.

Defining Field Templates

A field template is used to specify how particular values are to be displayed. A field template consists of a series of symbols that indicate the type of character that may

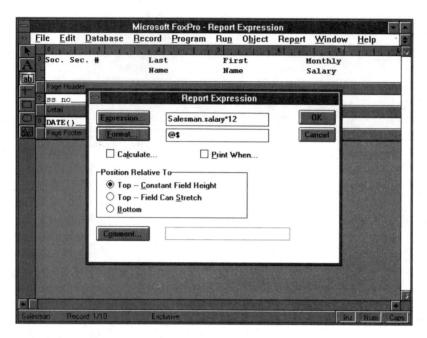

Figure 11.30 Defining a report field expression and format

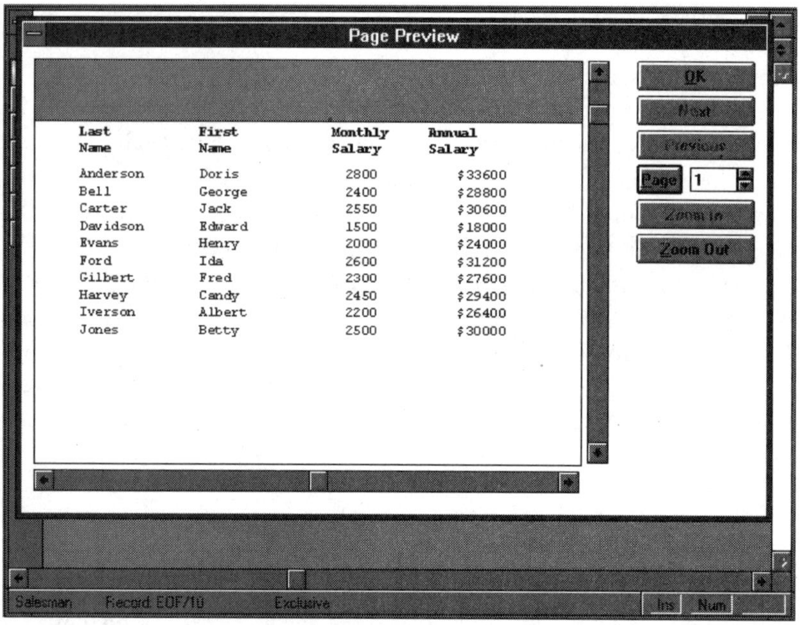

Figure 11.31 Previewing the Annual Salary column

be displayed in each position of a field value. In displaying a character field, the following are valid symbols in a field template:

- X   displays a character of any type
- A   displays a letter in lower- or uppercase (a–z, A–Z)
- #   displays a numeric digit (0–9)
- N   displays a letter, a digit, or an underscore (_)
- !   converts a letter to uppercase

Any other character used in the template that is not listed above is treated as a literal character; it will be displayed unchanged at the corresponding character position of the field. For example, !AAAAAAA might be the template for defining the format for a first name field of 8 characters. As a result, all the first letters of all the first names will be in uppercase. Similarly, if you use !!!!!!!! as a field template to format the last name field of 8 characters, all the last names will be displayed in capital letters. Valid symbols in a numeric field template are:

- 9   displays a digit (0–9) or a sign (+ or –)
- #   displays a digit
- *   displays leading zeros as asterisks
- $ displays a dollar sign in front of the value
- $$ displays a floating dollar sign in front of the value
- ,   displays a comma
- .   displays a period

In our example, you would use $999,999 or $$999,999 to display the values in the annual salary column in a conventional monetary format. As a result, monetary values will be displayed as:

Field Template Used:	$999,999	$$999,999
	$ 12,345	$12,345
	$ 6,789	$6,789

Note the difference between the two field templates: The left displays the dollar sign in a fixed location, while the right displays the dollar sign always next to the leading digit. To display the monetary values in dollars-and-cents format, use $$999,999.99 as the field template. To display a percentage value with the percent sign, use the field template: 999% or 999.9%.

Reformatting Report Fields

Although we have just defined the format for a field that we were adding to our report, it is also possible to view and modify the format for any fields that already have been placed in the report form. To view or modify an existing field in the

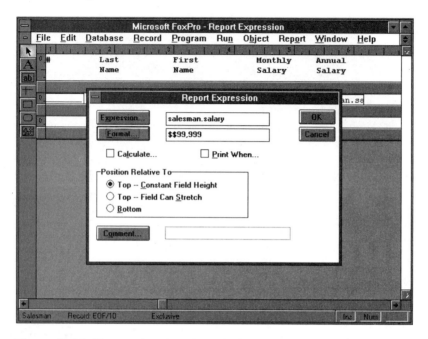

Figure 11.32 Formatting the Monthly Salary field

Detail band, double click the mouse on the field. To modify the format of the salary column, for example, return to the Report Layout window by choosing the OK button after viewing the report. Then double click the mouse on the SALARY field. When the Report Expression dialog appears, enter $$99,999 in the format text box (see Figure 11.32). Similarly, modify the annual salary column by using $$999,999 as the field template.

After you have made these changes in the field formats, the report should look like that shown in Figure 11.33. Note that the values in the Annual Salary column are displayed in a conventional monetary format with dollar signs and commas in their proper places. However, in the Monthly Salary column, strings of asterisks are displayed in place of the salary figures. A string of asterisks is used by FoxPro to indicate that the field width is set too narrow to accommodate the values plus the symbols (such as a dollar sign and commas). Therefore, we need to widen the field to show the monthly salary values.

Changing Report Column Widths

To change the width of an existing field in the report layout, use the mouse to stretch or shrink the rectangle that encloses the field name in the report layout. For example, to widen the SALARY field to accommodate the salary values, including

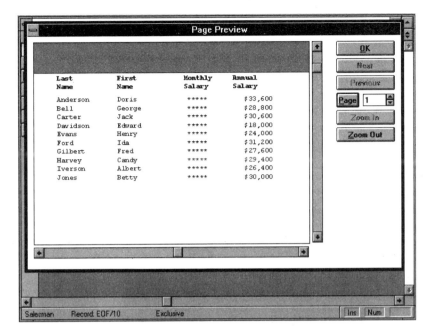

Figure 11.33 Previewing the formatted Salary column

the dollar sign and commas, select the SALARY field in the detail band. To do that, choose the Selection Pointer tool and then click on the field. As a result, the SALARY field box is framed in a rectangle with eight points—in addition to four corner points, there are two each of the horizontal and vertical lines. Use the two points at the center of the two horizontal lines to change the height of the field. The points at the middle of the two vertical lines are used to resize the field width horizontally. You can stretch or shrink a field from the left or the right. To widen the field from the right, click the mouse at the point on the middle of the right vertical line. When the cursor becomes a cross, drag it to the desired width. To make the field narrower, drag it to the left.

As an exercise, use the procedure outlined to widen the SALARY field to accommodate the monthly salaries. Similary, readjust the widths of other fields and realign their column headings so that they look the way you want. You may experiment with turning the Snap to Grid option (in the Report menu) on and off for positioning the objects. When Snap to Grip is selected, objects are positioned according to the alignment grid, which are set using the Ruler/Grid option in the Report menu. The alignment grid can be useful in aligning objects because it is sensitive to object size and positions. However, if you would like to move an object freely in the layout, turn the Snap to Grip option off. When you display the revised report on the screen, it should look like Figure 11.34.

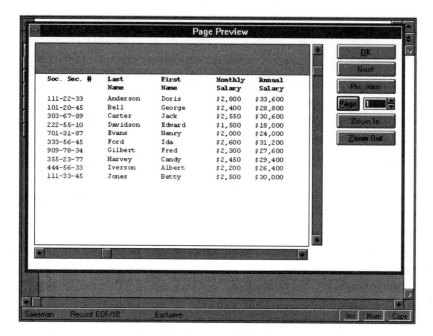

Figure 11.34 Previewing the reformatted Salary column

Adding a Report Title

To add a title to a report, choose the Title/Summary option from the Report menu. When the Title/Summary dialog appears, select the Title Band check box to add a Title band in the report layout and then select OK to return to the Report Layout window. As a result, a Title band will be inserted at the top of the report form. Then enter the text for the report title. For our example, let's add the title Salary Summary Report (use a larger, bold font). In addition, to improve the report's appearance, we should increase the space above the column headings (see Figure 11.35). To do that, make the Page Header band wider and move all the column headings down.

Adding Graphics Objects

Boxing selected elements in a report or incorporating vertical and horizontal lines to separate other elements often helps to make the information more easily understandable to the viewer. Furthermore, to enhance the appearance of the report you may also place a graphic object, such as a company logo, on the report.

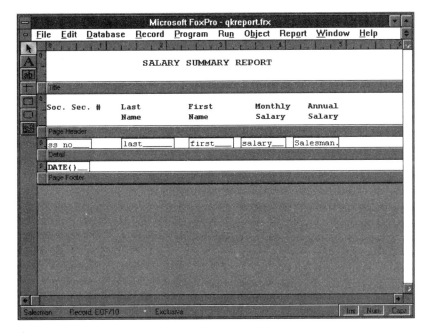

Figure 11.35 Adding the report title

Drawing Boxes

To draw a rectangular box, select the Rectangle Tool. Then, position the cursor on the location at the upper corner where you intend to begin drawing the box and drag the mouse in the lower right-hand direction. As a result, a rectanglar box will appear. When you release the mouse button, the box will be anchored. Don't worry if the box is not of the right size or not positioned correctly; you can easily redraw, resize, and reposition it.

To draw a box around the report title as an exercise, select the Rectangle Tool. Then point and click the mouse on the position that represents the upper left-hand corner of the box (a couple of characters to the left and above the report title). Drag the mouse right and down until the box reaches the desired size and encloses the report title. To anchor it, click the mouse outside the box.

If you make a mistake in drawing the box, choose the Undo option from the Edit menu. It will erase the box you have drawn. To resize or to reposition the box, click on the box after choosing the Selection Pointer. Use the same procedure for resizing fields and moving a report object to resize and move the box.

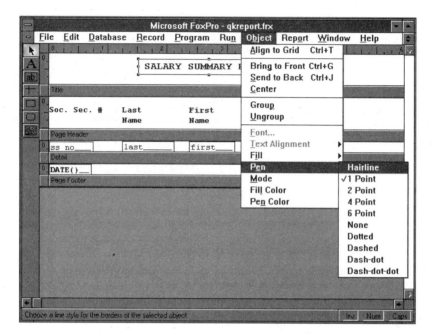

Figure 11.36 Selecting line thickness

By default, the box is drawn with a thin (1 point) solid line, but you also can use a different line width and line style to draw the box. To do that, choose the Selection Pointer and then double click on the box. Then select the Pen option from the Object menu (see Figure 11.36). From the Pen menu, you can select the size (from 1 to 6 point) and line style (dotted, dashed, etc.). For our example, choose 2 point as the line size. After you have done that, the report layout will look like that shown in Figure 11.37.

You can use the Fill option in the Object menu to shade the box with a certain graphic pattern. Using the Mode option can make the box opaque or transparent. If you would like to display the box in colors, choose the Fill Color or Pen Color option. Pen Color is used to select the color of the box. The color inside the box is determined using the Fill Color option.

To draw a double-line box, you have to draw one box within another. You may want to turn Snap to Grid off so that you can align the two boxes easily. The procedure for drawing a rounded rectangular box is identical to that of drawing a rectangular box, except you would select the Round Rectangle Tool.

Drawing Lines

To draw a line, select the Line Tool, position and click the mouse on the location where you would like to begin drawing the line, and then drag the mouse until the desired length is achieved. Release the mouse to anchor the line.

Producing Reports and Mailing Labels   475

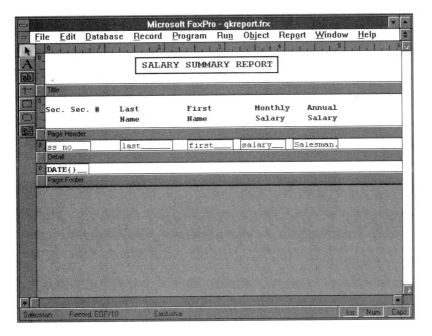

Figure 11.37 Drawing boxes around the report form

To place a line above the report heading, for example, select the Line Tool and then click the mouse above the first character in the first column heading and drag the mouse up a bit and continue to the right to form the line covering the column headings. Use the same method to draw a line below the column headings. While you are dragging the mouse, you may want to use the ruler to determine the exact location of the mouse cursor. If you make a mistake in drawing the line, undo it or resize and reposition it.

Again, you may use the Pen option from the Object menu to change the size and style of the line. For example, the line above the column headings shown in Figure 11.38 is drawn in 4 point. To draw a line in color, use the Pen Color option in the Object menu to select the color.

Adding Pictures

In a report, you can place a picture using the image saved in a graphic file in the bit-map (.bmp) format. For example, you could add the picture of a fox (the FoxPro logo) to the Title band on the SALARY SUMMARY REPORT. To do that, select the Picture Tool and then position the cursor at the location where the picture should appear. As the Report Picture dialog appears, identify the name of the graphic file (use the fox.bmp file in the \foxprow directory) and then select the Scale Picture -- Fill the Frame ratio button (see Figure 11.39). When you select the OK button to return to the report layout, a graphic image of a fox appears in the Title band.

476   Understanding FoxPro 2.5 for Windows

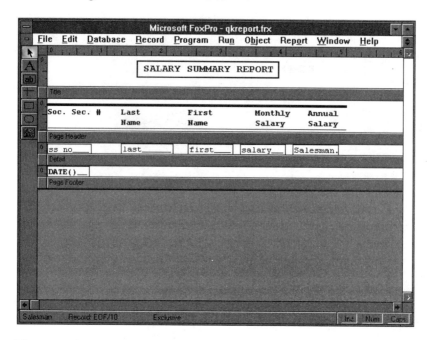

Figure 11.38   Drawing lines to the report form

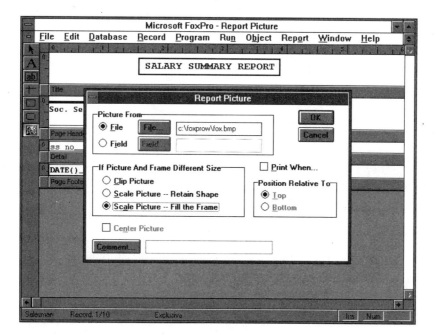

Figure 11.39   The Report Picture dialog

Producing Reports and Mailing Labels   477

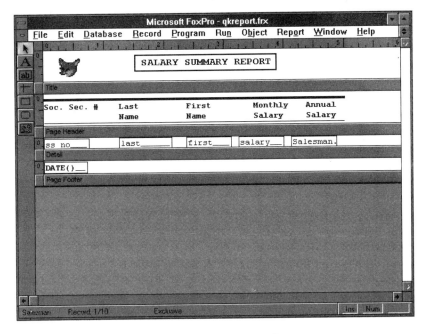

Figure 11.40 Adding a picture to the report form

You can then adjust its size and reposition it if necessary. After that, your report form should look like Figure 11.40.

Numbering Report Pages

In a multipage report, the Report Writer automatically keeps track of the current page number when the report is displayed or printed. This sequential page number is stored in a system variable named _PAGENO. In a quick report, the Report Writer displays the page number on the right-hand side of the Page Footer band by default. If you do not like FoxPro's default positioning of the page number, it can be moved in the same way that you move any report object. For example, to display the page number on top of each page, simply select both the _PAGENO variable and the "Page" text and drag them to the Page Header band. But, because our sample report contains only one page, let's move the page number to the Title band, to the right of the report title. In addition, adjust its size to accommodate up to 2 or 3 digits (see Figure 11.41).

The page number can be displayed in a format of your choice simply by modifying the format specification in the Report Expression dialog. To bring up the Report Expression dialog, double click the mouse on the _PAGENO variable.

478 Understanding FoxPro 2.5 for Windows

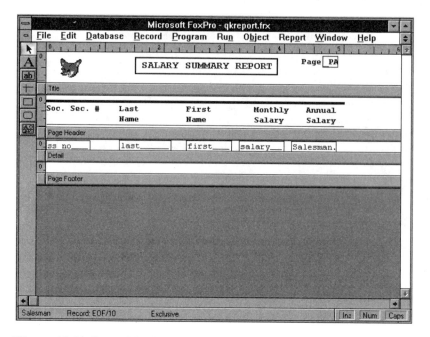

Figure 11.41 Repositioning the page number

Placing Report Dates

In a quick report, the Report Writer also will display the date the report was run on the left-hand side of the Page Footer band. To derive the current date, FoxPro uses the DATE( ) function, which returns the current system date. Like all objects in the FoxPro Report Writer, the date display can be moved anywhere on the report form, and its display attributes can be modified.

If you prefer that the date be displayed somewhere other than at the bottom of the report, you can move it to the Page Header, where it will be displayed at the beginning of each page, or to the Title band, where it will be displayed once at the beginning of the report. To continue our example, let's place it in the Title band, directly below the page number (see Figure 11.42).

Placing Footers

To position text used as a footer at the bottom of a page, place the text in the Page Footer band. An example is shown in Figure 11.40. The footer will be displayed at the end of every report page.

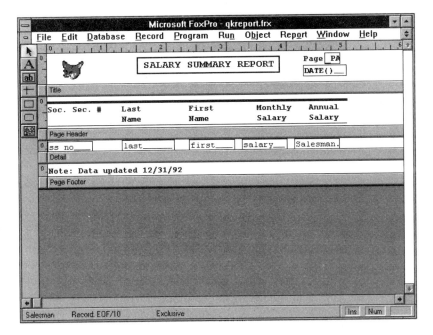

Figure 11.42 Repositioning the report date

Adding a Report Summary

The FoxPro Report Writer allows you to add descriptive statistics that summarize the information in an entire column of a report. Regardless of the data type, you can count the number of data items in the column and display the total amount at the bottom of the column. If the column contains numeric values, you also can calculate statistics such as the sum, the average, the standard deviation, and the minimum or maximum value, and place them in the report.

Because these statistics are computed using the values in the entire report, they are placed in a Summary band that is inserted at the end of the report. To add the Summary band to the report form, choose the Title/Summary option from the Report menu. When the Title Summary dialog appears, select the Summary Band check box and then the OK button to return to the Report Layout window. The Report Writer will insert a Summary Band at the end of the report form after the Page Footer band.

To insert a summary statistic in the Summary band, select the Field Tool and then position the cursor on the location at which you want the statistic to appear. When the Report Expression dialog appears, select the Calculate check box to bring up the Calculate Field dialog box. At this point, you can choose the type of summary statistic you would like to display.

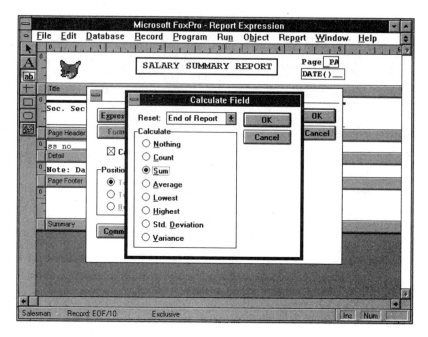

Figure 11.43 The Calculate Field dialog

To show, for example, the total of the Monthly Salary column, position the cursor in the Summary band at the bottom of the column after selecting the Field Tool. When the Report Expression appears, select the Calculate check box to bring up the Calculate Field dialog and check the Sum radio button before selecting the OK button to return to the Report Expression dialog (see Figure 11.43). At this point, take note of the Reset: list. It determines when FoxPro internally reinitializes the value of the statistic and begins to calculate it again. In this case, because we want a single total that applies to all the records displayed in the report, select the default choice, End of Report.

When you return to the Report Expression dialog, enter the name of the data field in the Expression text box for which you want a summary statistic computed (in our case, SALARY). In the Format text box, enter the field template ($$99,999) that will be used to display the statistic. When you return to the Report Layout dialog, the summary field will be placed on the report form as a line with three dots. Click on the middle dot and then drag it up or down to open the field. Then adjust the field width to accommodate the necessary digits, the dollar sign, and the commas. To align the sum with the salary values, turn on the Snap to Grid option while you move the calculated field around. For numeric values, you would want to align the fields to the right of the columns.

We should also add a summary field for the Annual Salary column. This is very much like adding the summary field for the Monthly Salary column, although, of

Producing Reports and Mailing Labels 481

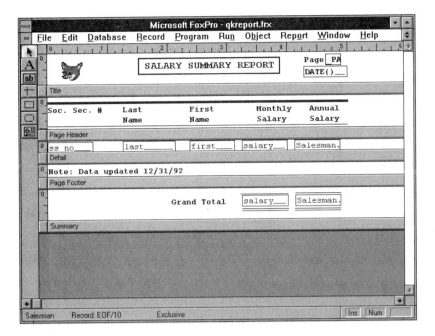

Figure 11.44 Showing the calculated fields on the report form

course, the annual salary is a computed value. After again selecting the Field Tool, click the mouse on the position at which you would like to place the field and bring up the Report Expression dialog. The summary statistic that we want the report to display is the sum of each employee's annual salary. To define it, enter SALARY*12 in the Expression text box and enter the field template ($999,999) in the Format text box. Next, select the Calculate check box to bring up the Calculate Field dialog and select the Sum check box. Accept End of Report as the default setting for the Reset option.

After you have finished positioning and defining the summary statistics, you can insert a line in the Summary band and draw lines above each of the summary statistics. In addition, you can add text ("Grand Total") to describe the statistics. After placing the summary statistics, move the column headings to align with the column values. To determine the exact locations for the column heading, try to view it on screen and then make the necessary adjustments. The final layout of the report should look like Figure 11.44. Then, when you view the final report on the screen, it will look like the professional report shown in Figure 11.45 (to see the footnote, scroll the report image in the Page Preview window).

Save the modified report form to disk by choosing the Save option from the File menu, and the revised report form will be saved in the file QKREPORT.FRX, replacing the form previously held in the file.

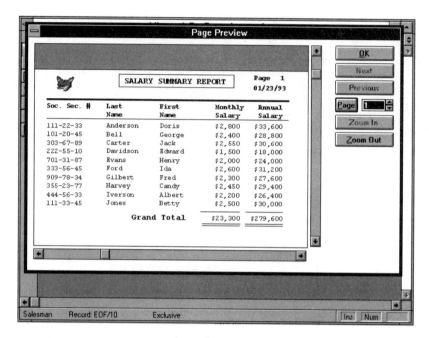

Figure 11.45 A printed report

Grouping Data

The salary report in Figure 11.45 shows the salaries for all sales personnel, listed in alphabetical order. This report might be of interest if we are concerned with examining how much each salesperson makes, or with knowing how much the total monthly or annual payroll is. Reports, however, also are used often to separate records into individual groups in order to compare them with each other or to gather summary statistics about individual groupings. For example, we might want to produce a salary report that groups employees by gender and shows the total monthly and annual salary paid to each group. Similarly, we might want a report that lists the level of salaries in each of the three regional offices; this is the report that we will develop in our next example.

With FoxPro, such a report can be created by adding a Group band to the report form. As a result, data records will be grouped together based on their value in a group field, and different groups will be broken out in the report.

To insert a Group band into the report, choose the Data Grouping option from the Report menu. When the Data Grouping dialog appears, select the Add button to bring up the Group Info dialog to specify the group field. To group the records according to their values in the OFFICE_ID data field, enter the field name in the text box next to the Group button (see Figure 11.46). (Alternatively, you may bring up the Expression Builder by selecting the Group button.)

Producing Reports and Mailing Labels 483

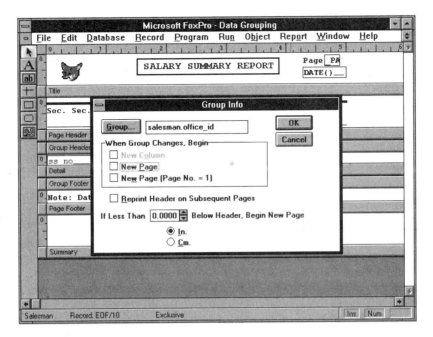

Figure 11.46 The Group Info dialog

When you return to the Report Layout window after selecting the OK button in both the Group Info dialog and the Data Grouping dialog, a Group band labeled 1:office_id is inserted both before and after the Detail band in the report. This Group band identifies the level of grouping (FoxPro allows you to further divide each group into subgroups) and contains the partial name of the group field.

Although we now have prepared a report that divides the detail records into groups based on their value in the OFFICE_ID field, the report will not actually show us the value of OFFICE_ID for any particular group. We could, of course, simply add the OFFICE_ID field to the Detail band, which means that its value will be displayed for each record listed in our report. This, however, is redundant, because each record in a group will have the same value. Instead, the best method is to identify the group by placing the value of the group field (in our case, OFFICE_ID) and any other descriptive text (like "Office:") in the beginning of the Group band, as we have done in Figure 11.47. In this way, the value of the group field will be displayed only when it changes.

· If we preview our report now, however, we will find that the results are somewhat unexpected. Records continue to be listed in alphabetical order and are not grouped according to common values in the OFFICE_ID field. This is because reports that use data groups expect records in the database to be arranged according to their values in the group field. Therefore, you must index the records on the group field (or fields, if subgroups are used in the report) before displaying or printing the report.

In our example, the database must be indexed on the OFFICE_ID field. Recall that we created an index tag named OFFICE_ID in the structural compound index file SALESMAN.CDX. In order to generate our report, we need to set only this index tag as the master index. To do this, select the Setup option from the database menu to bring up the Setup dialog. Then select Salesman:office_id from the Indexes list box and select the Set Order button to designate it as the master index. Return to the Report Layout window by selecting the OK push button. To avoid selecting the proper index whenever you run the report, you may want to store information about the database environment along with the report form. This information includes the name of the controlling master index file. To do this, select the Page Layout option from the Report menu. In the Page Layout dialog, select the Environment button and then select the Save button from the Environment dialog. Subsequently, whenever you use the report form in the future, FoxPro will automatically set the appropriate master index.

Besides displaying the individual records based on a common group value, you also can display summary statistics for all of the records that belong to each group. This is very similar to adding summary statistics to the report, except that summary statistics are placed on any line of the Group band that is below the Detail band. To continue embellishing our report, we now will add the monthly and annual salaries in each office and display the totals at the end of each group.

The method used to place these group statistics on the form is identical to the one used previously to create the summary statistics for the report as a whole. The only difference is that in the Reset list box of the Calculate Field dialog, the default option (which is the name of the group field, OFFICE_ID) should now be selected. Of course, you may also add text and boxes to the group lines to highlight the group totals as well. An example of such an enhanced group report form is shown in Figure 11.47. Figure 11.48 shows the printed report that was produced by using the report form.

Now save the revised report form to a file named BYOFFICE.FRX by choosing the Save As option from the File menu and then entering the name of the file in the Save As text box.

Grouping Data by Logical Values

Data records can be grouped in a report according to the values in any database or calculated field, regardless of its data type. In the previous example, data records were grouped according to their value in the character field OFFICE_ID. In that case, the value of the OFFICE_ID field was displayed as a group heading, but you may also group data records based on the values in a numeric or date field. In both

Producing Reports and Mailing Labels 485

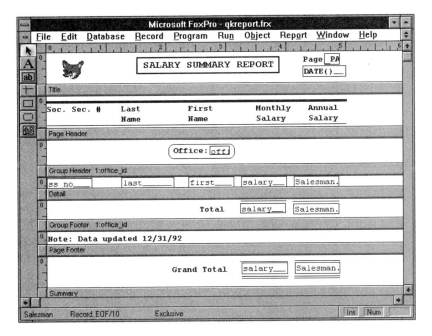

Figure 11.47 Showing the group heading on the Group Header band

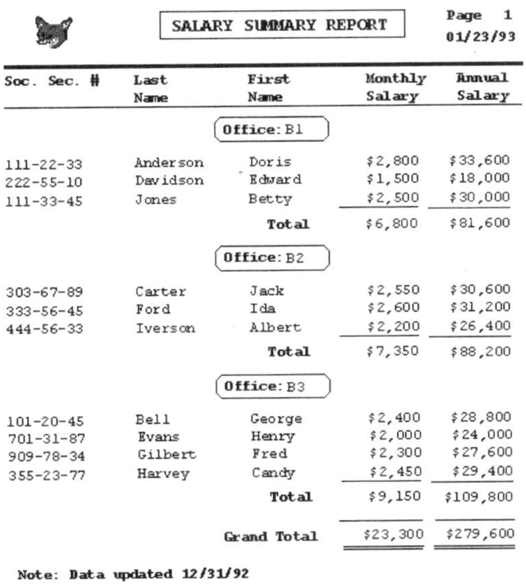

Figure 11.48 The printed group report

cases, the value of the numeric or date field provides sufficient information to describe the group.

This is not the case if data is grouped according to the values in a logical field where you can display only either "T" or "F" as the group heading. There is a way, however, to include more descriptive text in a logical field—let's say, to produce a salary report showing the sales staff's salaries grouped by sex. To describe the groups with more than the logical values of "T" or "F," use the IIF( ) function to display descriptive text instead of the logical values in the data field. The syntax of the IIF( ) function is as follows:

```
IIF(<logical field name>, <string1>, <string2>)
```

The IIF( ) function displays the first character string when the value of the specified logical field is true; otherwise, it displays the second character string. For example, you may use the following IIF( ) function to display the group headings for salary values that are grouped by the sex of the salesperson:

```
IIF(MALE, 'Male Salespersons', 'Female Salespersons')
```

By selecting the Field tool and clicking on an area in the Group band, you can access the Expression Builder and enter the above expression into the Expression text box. When you return to the Report Layout, your screen should look like Figure 11.49.

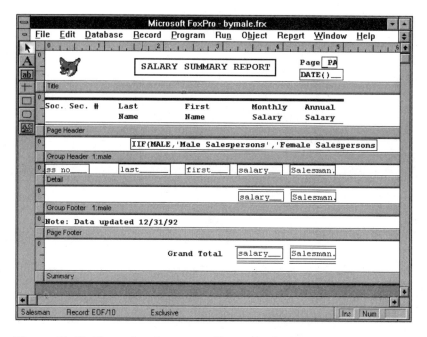

Figure 11.49 Grouping data according to logical values

```
              SALARY SUMMARY REPORT        Page  1
                                           01/23/93

Soc. Sec. #   Last        First       Monthly    Annual
              Name        Name        Salary     Salary
                    Male Salespersons
444-56-33     Iverson     Albert      $2,200     $26,400
909-78-34     Gilbert     Fred        $2,300     $27,600
701-31-87     Evans       Henry       $2,000     $24,000
222-55-10     Davidson    Edward      $1,500     $18,000
303-67-89     Carter      Jack        $2,550     $30,600
101-20-45     Bell        George      $2,400     $28,800
                                      $12,950    $155,400

                    Female Salespersons
111-33-45     Jones       Betty       $2,500     $30,000
355-23-77     Harvey      Candy       $2,450     $29,400
333-56-45     Ford        Ida         $2,600     $31,200
111-22-33     Anderson    Doris       $2,800     $33,600
                                      $10,350    $124,200

                          Grand Total  $23,300   $279,600
```

Figure 11.50 The printed report grouped by logical values

For this report to produce the desired results, you must, of course, insert a group band based on the value in the MALE field and index the database on the MALE field. Once you do this, you can preview the report, which should look like Figure 11.50. Note that the first group of records is labeled as "Male Salespersons" when the value in the MALE data field is "T." The second group of records with "F" in the logical field is identified as "Female Salespersons."

USING MEMORY VARIABLES IN A REPORT

In addition to data fields, you can also use the values of memory variables in a report. You can display the value of a memory variable as a report object or you can use a memory variable in an expression for placing a report field in the report. For example, you may use a memory variable to keep track of the running total of a certain data field and then display its value in the report. An example of such a report is shown in Figure 11.51.

```
           COMPENSATION SUMMARY REPORT      Page: 1
                                            01/23/93

  Name of Salesperson      Salary     Running Total
  Doris B. Anderson        $2,800        $2,800
  George G. Bell           $2,400        $5,200
  Jack J. Carter           $2,550        $7,750
  Edward D. Davidson       $1,500        $9,250
  Henry H. Evans           $2,000        $11,250
  Ida F. Ford              $2,600        $13,850
  Fred C. Gilbert          $2,300        $16,150
  Candy E. Harvey          $2,450        $18,600
  Albert I. Iverson        $2,200        $20,800
  Betty A. Jones           $2,500        $23,300
                 Total     $23,300
```

Figure 11.51 A report showing a column of running totals

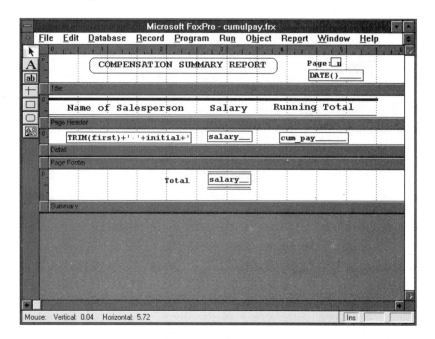

Figure 11.52 Placing a memory variable in the report form

You can see that the values in the Running Total column are computed by summing the value in the **salary** data field as displayed in the Salary column. The report form that was used to produce the report is shown in Figure 11.52. The report field for displaying the running total is defined by using the memory variable named *cum_pay*.

Before placing a memory variable in a report, you have to define and add it to the variable list. To do that, select the Variables option from the Report menu. As a result, the Report Variables dialog appears (see Figure 11.53). Select the Add button to define the memory variable to be added to the variable list. When the Variable Definition dialog appears, assign a name to the variable and specify the value of the variable and how it is to be computed (see Figure 11.54). You can see that we assigned *cum_pay* as the name of the variable. The value of the memory variable is calculated by summing the value in the **salary** data field as it is displayed in the detail band. The initial value of the variable is set to 0, and the variable is released at the end of the report.

CREATING FORM REPORTS

The procedure for producing a form report is almost identical to that for generating a column report. The steps for placing the objects in the report are the same, except

Producing Reports and Mailing Labels   489

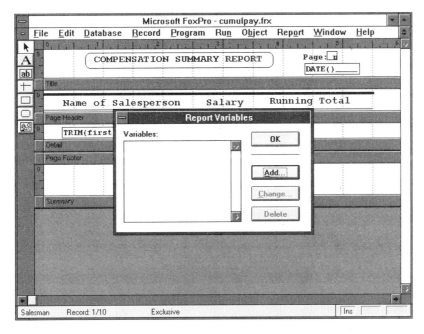

Figure 11.53 The Report Variables dialog

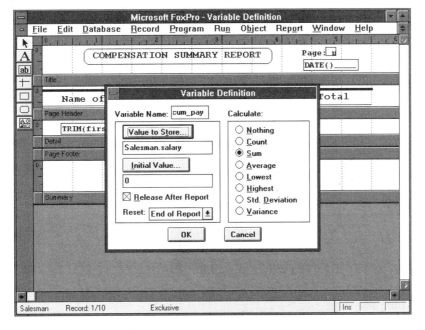

Figure 11.54 The Variable Definition dialog

that a form report allows you to place the fields anywhere in the form without lining them up in a column format. You may insert any additional text in the report to describe the information or incorporate graphics objects such as boxes and lines to outline or highlight various sections of the report.

Using Quick Report Layouts

The Report Writer provides a quick report format that you can use as the basis for your form report design. Simply select the Report radio button from the New dialog after you have selected the New option from the File menu. When the Report Layout window appears, select the Quick Report option from the Report menu. From the Quick Report dialog, choose the Form (also called Label) Layout radio button, which shows fields displayed vertically (see Figure 11.55).

Selecting this option means that all fields will be displayed in the default form layout in which data fields are placed sequentially according to their order in the data structure and labeled with the field names. The default layout of a quick report using all the data fields in the SALESMAN database is shown in Figure 11.56.

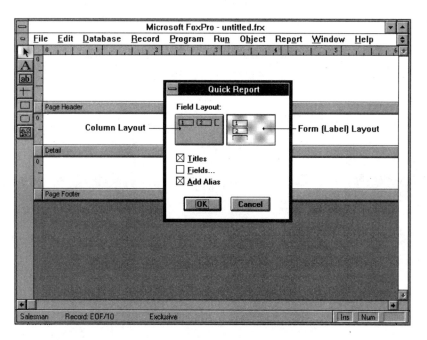

Figure 11.55 Choosing the form or label layout

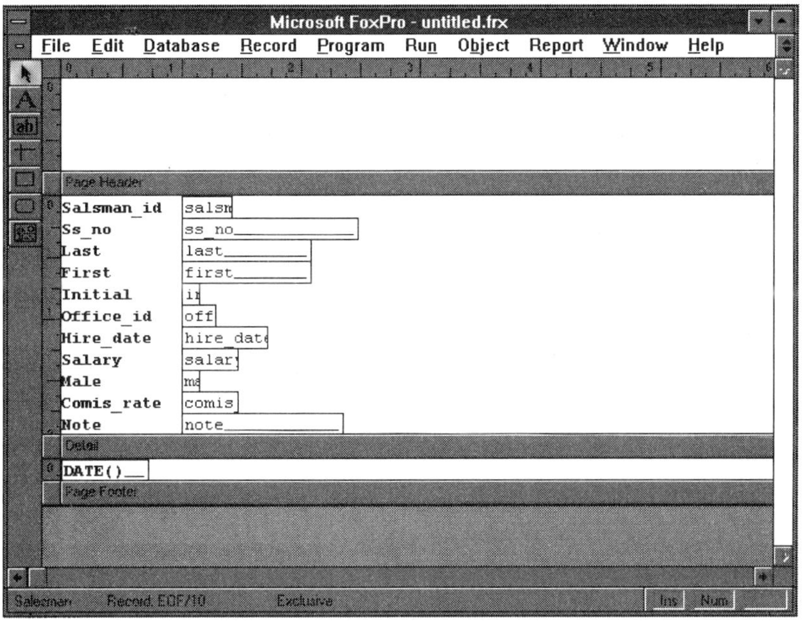

Figure 11.56 Default form layout of a quick report

Creating a Custom Form Report

To modify the default quick report provided by the Report Writer in order to create a form report of your own design, delete the data fields you don't need and create any calculated fields, then add the necessary descriptive text and graphics objects to the report. An example of such a custom report is shown in Figure 11.57.

In the report layout of Figure 11.57, you can see that the report title, report page number, and report date are placed in the Page Header band. In the Detail band, all the data fields appear in a free form and are placed in various sections of the report, where they are mixed with descriptive texts.

Incidentally, notice that in rearranging and modifying FoxPro's quick report to produce the report form shown in Figure 11.58, we have made liberal use of calculated expressions and have changed the formatting of the SALARY and COMMISSION fields to enhance the appearance of our report. It is possible, for example, to leave the first and last names and middle initial of each salesperson as separate fields. This, however, leaves blank spaces between the first name and middle initial of salespeople who have short first names. The solution is to delete the three fields and replace them with a single calculated field that uses the TRIM( )

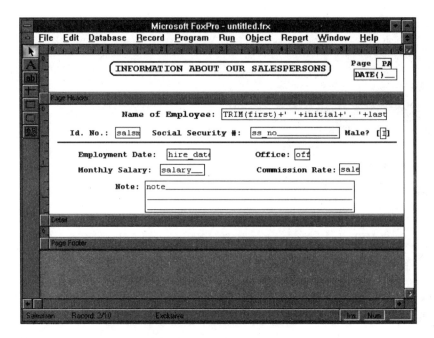

Figure 11.57 Layout of the custom form report

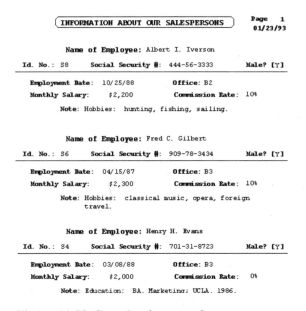

Figure 11.58 Sample of custom form report

function to remove trailing spaces from the first name. The following field expression will accomplish this:

```
TRIM(first)+' '+initial+'. '+last
```

The following table shows the expressions and format of the report items in the layout for producing the form report of Figure 11.58:

Report Object	Expression	Format
Name of Employee	TRIM(first)+' '+initial+'. '+last	default
Id. No	salsman_id	default
Social Security #	ss_no	default
Male	IFF(MALE, 'Y', 'N')	'Y'
Employment Date:	hire_date	default
Office:	office	default
Monthly Salary	salary	$$99,999
Commission Rate	comis_rate	99%
Note	note	

As in a column report, all the data fields placed in the Detail band of a form report are repeated for each data record in the selected database. There is a major difference between the two report forms, however. In a column report, field values of each record are displayed in rows, while in a form report, they are displayed in individual sections.

The layout of a form report is ideal for producing computer form letters, which mix text with information taken from selected database fields. You can, for example, create a letter in the form of an office memorandum addressed to each member of the sales staff, as illustrated in Figure 11.59.

```
                OFFICE MEMORANDUM

To:      Ms. Doris B. Anderson
From:    Human Resource Department
Date:    December 31, 1992
Subject: Personal Data
         Please take a moment to verify the following
         information and report any descrepencies to us
         at your earliest convenience:

           ┌─────────────────────────────────────┐
           │  Date of Employment: 07/01/86       │
           │  Current Monthly Salar: $2,800      │
           │     Commission Rate:     0%         │
           └─────────────────────────────────────┘
```

Figure 11.59 A form letter incorporating data

494 Understanding FoxPro 2.5 for Windows

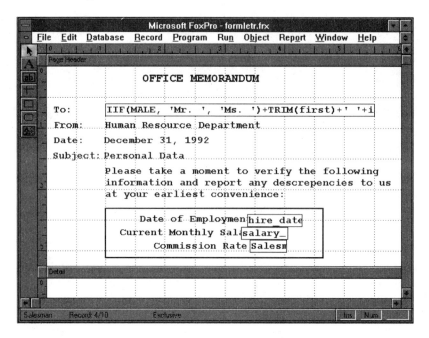

Figure 11.60 Layout of the form letter

Then, you may insert information taken from the data fields in the SALESMAN database into the text of the memorandum, as shown in Figure 11.60. Note that data elements from a number of data fields are taken from the SALESMAN database and inserted into the office memorandum: The name of the salesperson is displayed by using the values from the FIRST, INITIAL, and LAST data fields; information from the HIRE_DATE, SALARY, and COMIS_RATE fields is displayed at the end of the memorandum. In addition, the system date function, DATE( ), is used to display the memorandum date.

Figure 11.59 displays the office memorandum sent to Doris B. Anderson. You can see that information taken from her data record is displayed with the text placed in the Detail band in the report layout.

Creating Mailing Labels

The process of creating mailing labels is very similar to that of generating reports. It begins with laying out the data fields and any associated text in the Label Designer window. While you are in the Label Designer window, you can view the mailing labels on the screen to determine if any modifications are necessary. Once

Producing Reports and Mailing Labels   495

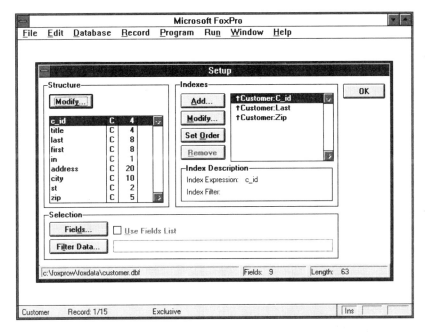

Figure 11.61 Data structure of CUSTOMER.DBF

you are satisfied with the label design, you can then output them on the printer. If you plan to use the same label layout again, save it to a label file.

As an example, we will be using the CUSTOMER database to illustrate the process of producing a mailing label. The data structure and the contents of CUSTOMER.DBF are shown in Figures 11.61 and 11.62, respectively.

DESIGNING MAILING LABELS

Because it is necessary to extract data from the database file to produce mailing labels, the CUSTOMER database file must be opened before designing the label form. In addition, if you would like the labels to print in a particular order, you must index the database.

To design the label form, select the New option from the File menu popup. When the New dialog appears, choose the Label radio button and select OK to bring up the New Label dialog (see Figure 11.63). The New Label dialog contains a label layout list that includes the Averg. No., height, width, and number of columns contained in the layout. Accept the default label layout and select the OK push button to bring up the Label Designer window.

When the Label Designer window first opens, it contains the default layout of a label form. Note that the Label Designer window looks almost exactly like that

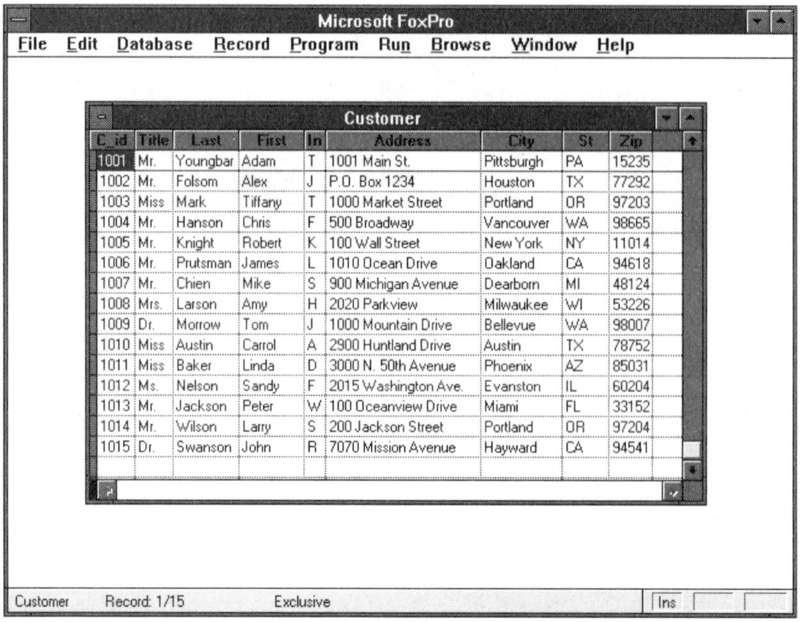

496 Understanding FoxPro 2.5 for Windows

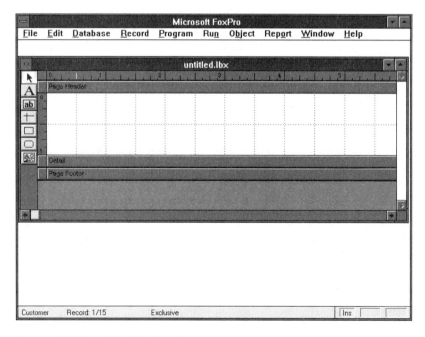

Figure 11.62 Data records of CUSTOMER.DBF

Figure 11.63 A label design form

of the Report Writer. It uses the same design tools and Report menu for laying out the label form. The options in the Report menu are the same too. In fact, to design a mail label, you use the same procedure that we used to lay out a report form: Use the same Text Tool to add text to the label form, use the Field Tool to place a field on the label form, and use the Line Tool, the Rectangle, Round Rectangle, and the Picture Tool to add graphic objects to the label form.

Defining Label Dimensions

A label form can be treated as a form report in a multiple-column format if you would like to print more than one label across the page. Use the Page Layout option in the Report menu to specify the number of labels across, and specify the width of the label and the horizontal spacing between labels. To determine the height of the mailing label and the vertical spacing between labels, adjust the Detail Band in the label form.

For example, if you would like to create mailing labels that look like those in Figure 11.64, you would lay out the label form as shown in Figure 11.65.

In the label form in Figure 11.65, you can see that the height of a mailing label is set to 1 3/4 inches, including the vertical spacing between labels. Three report fields are placed in the form. The first displays the name of a customer, using an expression that includes the TITLE, FIRST, IN (for middle initial), and LAST data

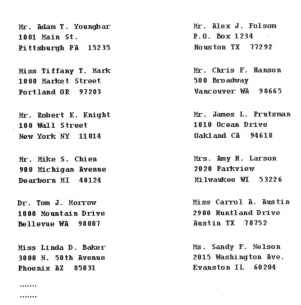

Figure 11.64 Sample mailing labels

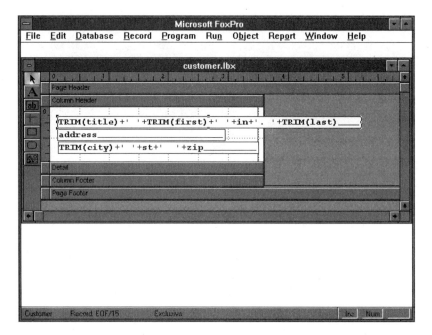

Figure 11.65 Layout of the mailing label form

fields in the CUSTOMER database. The second report field shows the ADDRESS field in the database; the last displays the address that uses the expression, including the CITY, ST (for state), and ZIP data fields in the database. Note that the report field expression can be extended beyond the label form in the layout. However, the actual size of the label must not be wider than the label width, which is set in the Page Layout option.

The width of a mailing label and the number of labels across is specified in the Page Layout dialog after you have selected the Page Layout option from the Report menu. In the Page Layout dialog, the number of labels across is set to 2 in the Columns spinner box, and the width of each label is set to 3.5 inches in the Column Width spinner box. The horizontal space between the two labels is set to 0.1 inches in the Column Spacing spinner box. When you want to edit the values shown in any spinner box, place the cursor at the end of the value and then use the Backspace key to strike out the existing digits; then type over a new value. FoxPro does not allow you to use the Del key to erase an existing value.

Viewing Mailing Labels on the Screen

To view mailing labels, select the Page Preview option from the Report menu or press the Ctrl+I key combination, and the labels will be displayed on-screen in sections. Use the scroll control to view the hidden section of the labels.

SAVING LABEL FORMS

Before saving the label form to a file, save the selected database as a part of the environment information. Choose the Save button in the Environment dialog after you have selected the Environment button in the Payout Layout dialog, which is accessed through the Page Layout option of the Report menu. This allows you to print or display the labels again without first opening the necessary database and defining a master index. To save the current label form to a disk file, select the Save As option from the File menu. When the Save As: dialog appears, assign a name to the label file (e.g., CUSTOMER.LBX).

After saving the label form to CUSTOMER.LBX, you may choose to print the mailing labels or close the window and run the labels at a later time. Let's exit the Label Designer window by closing the window after saving the label form.

PRINTING MAILING LABELS

To print mailing labels, select the Label option from the Database menu. When the Label dialog appears, select the Form button to retrieve the label form, customer.lbx (see Figure 11.66). Then select the To Printer check box, followed by the OK button.

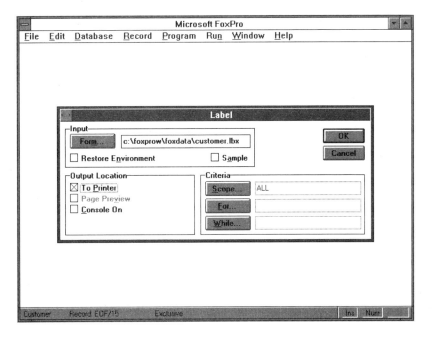

Figure 11.66 The Label dialog

PRODUCING REPORTS FROM MULTIPLE DATABASES

So far in this chapter, we have created a variety of reports and mailing labels using data from a single database file. It also is possible to produce column and form reports that extract information from multiple database files that are related to one another. It involves creating an RQBE query and directing the output of the query to a report or label form.

Extracting Data with RQBE Queries

To produce reports with multiple database files, you use the Relational Query by Example queries and the Report Writer. As you will see later, this is a two-stage process that ultimately results in the RQBE directly feeding the data that you have requested into the Report Writer, which in turn sends it to the output device you have selected.

The first step, then, is to obtain all data needed for the report by creating an RQBE query. In the process of defining the query, you must identify the database files that will be used and specify how they are linked. In addition, you can specify the data fields that will be used in the report and determine the order of the query results and how the records are to be grouped.

Let's assume, for instance, that you must produce a report showing the name of each salesperson and information about his or her sales office. Before designing the report form, the first step is to collect the information from the SALESMAN and OFFICE database files by using RQBE to create a query like the one shown in Figure 11.67.

To set up the query, first link the two database files by using the OFFICE_ID field as the link key. Then select the following data fields that are needed for the report:

```
From SALESMAN.DBF: FIRST, INITIAL, LAST
From OFFICE.DBF:   OFFICE_ID, ADDRESS, CITY, STATE, ZIP
```

This is done in the RQBE Select Fields dialog when you select the Fields button in the RQBE window (see Figure 11.68).

Normally, when you bring up the RQBE window, the Output list shows Browse as the destination. To produce a report, you need to select Report/Label as the Output option (see Figure 11.69). If you execute the query now, it would output the records to a report. However, before this happens, you need to provide the form for displaying the results from the query. To do that, check the Options check box to bring up the RQBE Display Options dialog. When the RQBE Display Options appears, select the Report radio button to indicate that you would like to produce a report with the query result. Then check the Quick Report box to create a quick report form for the report. As a result, the RQBE Quick Report dialog appears showing the two quick report forms (column versus form report) that you can

Producing Reports and Mailing Labels 501

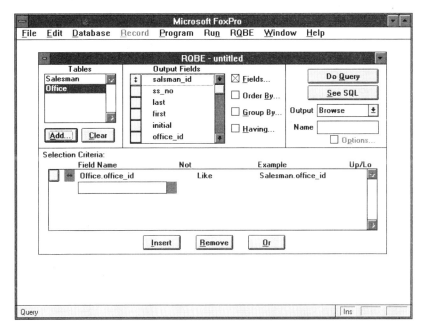

Figure 11.67 Using a RQBE to produce a report

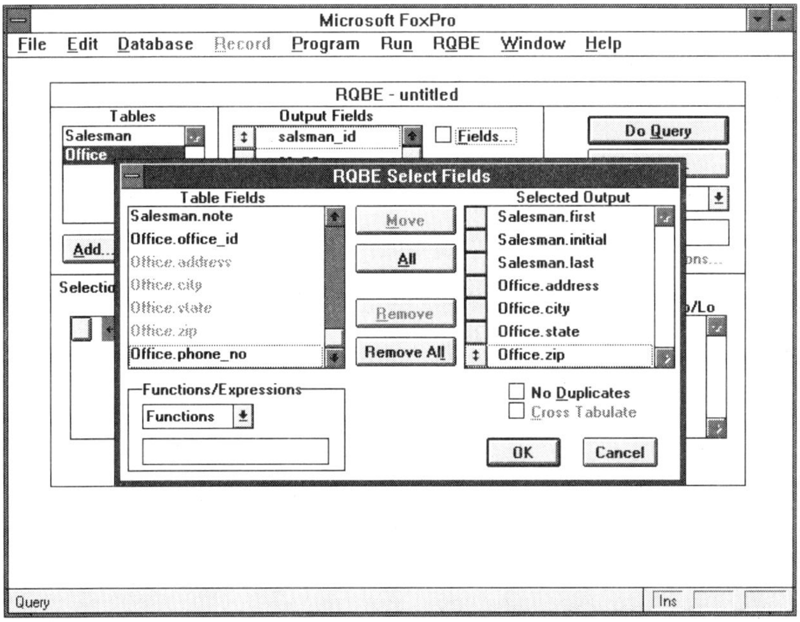

Figure 11.68 Selecting fields to include in a report

502 Understanding FoxPro 2.5 for Windows

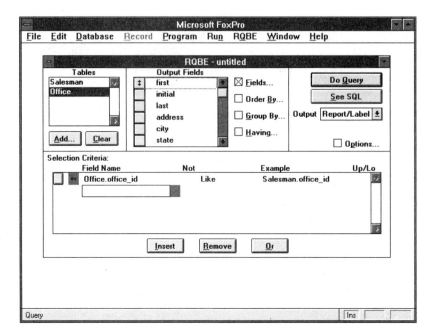

Figure 11.69 Selecting Report/Label to produce a report

choose (see Figure 11.70). To produce a column report, select the left report form button and then select the OK button to return to the RQBE Display Options dialog.

When you return to the RQBE Display Options dialog, you would find that FoxPro automatically saves the quick report form in a file named QUERY.FRX (see Figure 11.71). If you would like to preview the report later, check the Page Preview button as well. To return to the RQBE window, select the OK button.

After you return to the RQBE window and choose the Do Query button to execute the query, you will see the query results are displayed in a quick report form in the Page Preview window (see Figure 11.72).

REVISING THE REPORT FORM

A quick report is a convenient way to view the query results in a report. However, since the quick report form is always saved as QUERY.FRX, if you create another query later, its quick report form will replace an existing one. As a result, you need to bring up the quick report to save it under another filename to avoid its being replaced by a later report form name QUERY.FRX. In addition, you may want to modify the quick report to enhance its appearance.

To bring up the quick report form, select the Open option from the File menu. When the Open dialog appears, open the QUERY.FRX file. As a result, the quick report form will be displayed in the Report Writer window (see Figure 11.73). Now,

Producing Reports and Mailing Labels 503

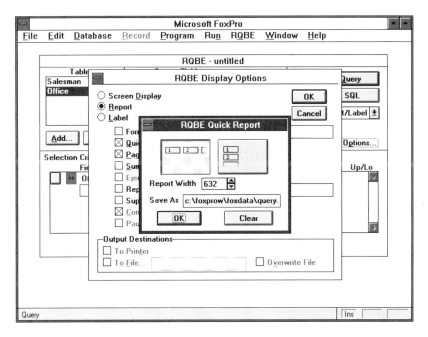

Figure 11.70 Changing the name of a report form file

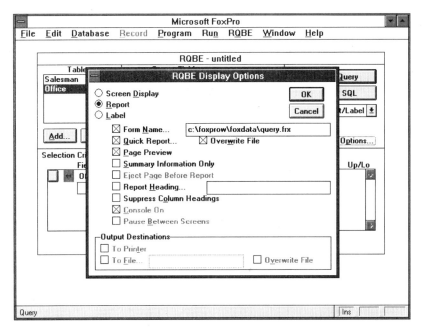

Figure 11.71 FoxPro automatically saves the quick report form.

504 Understanding FoxPro 2.5 for Windows

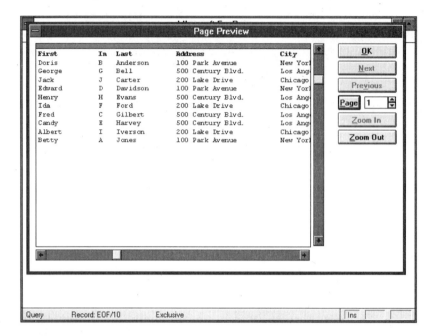

Figure 11.72 Query results displayed in a Page Preview window.

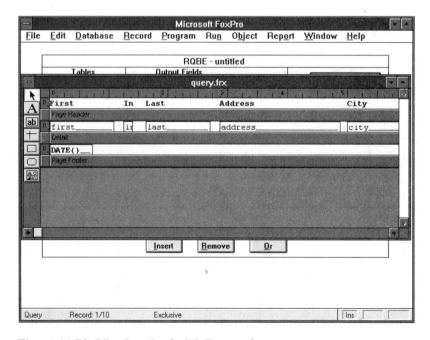

Figure 11.73 Viewing the Quick Report form

Producing Reports and Mailing Labels 505

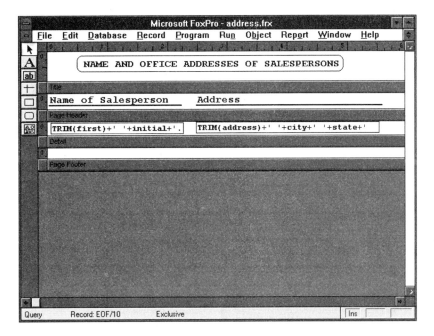

Figure 11.74 The modified Quick Report form

you can use the same procedure that you learned in this chapter to make the necessary changes. As an exercise, create a report form that looks like the one shown in Figure 11.74. For the name of the salesperson, use the following expression with the data fields taken from SALESMAN.DBF:

    TRIM(first)+' '+initial+'. '+TRIM(last)

For the address report column, use the following expression to define the report field using the data fields from the OFFICE.DBF:

    TRIM(address)+' '+city+' '+state+' '+zip

After making the changes, save the report form in a file named ADDRESS.FRX and close the Report Writer window to return to the RQBE window.

PRODUCING REPORTS

When you are at the RQBE window and you would like to output the query results to the modified report form named ADDRESS.FRX, check the Options box. When the RQBE Display Options dialog appears, modify the name of the report form in the Form Name box accordingly (see Figure 11.75). Afterward, when you execute the query, the query results will be displayed in the modify report form in the Page

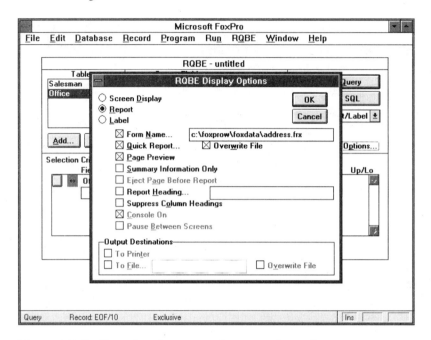

Figure 11.75 Changing the name of a report form file

Preview window (see Figure 11.76). After the report is produced within the RQBE, you can save the query with the environment information for a later use.

To produce a report with an existing query, select the Query option from the Run menu. The results of the query will then be displayed in the report forms specified in the query.

This completes our endeavor to use RQBE and the Report Writer to generate a multifile report. We have defined a query, ADDRESS.QPR, to generate the information we need for the report, and we have designed a report, AD-DRESS.FRX, to display that information. The query and the report work together by means of an intermediate database file, QUERY.DBF. As a result, when you use a report form in a query, the report form must be designed with the results from the query. That is, the data fields must be those generated from the query. Those report forms that are designed with data fields taken directly from a database and not from a query cannot be used for displaying a query. Therefore, care must be taken not to use a report form that is created outside the query for outputting the query results.

PRODUCING MAILING LABELS FROM MULTIPLE DATABASES

Earlier in this chapter you learned how to produce a report using data elements that were extracted from two linked database files. Labels can be produced in the same

Producing Reports and Mailing Labels 507

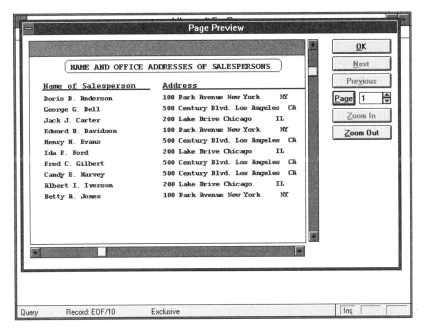

Figure 11.76 Previewing the modified report

way. To do that, use RQBE to link the data records and design a label form using the query results. Then, direct the query output to Report/Label and execute the query.

Using FoxPro Commands

The Report Writer and the Label Designer are powerful tools for creating custom reports and mailing labels. As already explained in this chapter, they can be invoked by selecting appropriate menu options. Reports and mailing labels also can be produced by issuing the appropriate FoxPro commands. In addition, you can create memory variables with the necessary commands and then pass their values to the Report Writer and Label Designer, so that you can include them in the reports and mailing labels.

CREATING AND MODIFYING REPORTS

To create a new report, issue the CREATE REPORT command from the Command window:

```
CREATE REPORT <name of report form>
```

To create a report named SALESRPT.FRX, issue the following command:

```
CREATE REPORT SALESRPT
```

Note that the database to be used for the report must be selected before issuing the CREATE REPORT command. Otherwise, you will be prompted to do so later.

When the command is executed, the Report Writer will be invoked and a blank report form will be displayed in the Report Layout window. After that, you can place all the report objects in the report form using the procedures described earlier in this chapter.

To make changes to an existing report form, issue the MODIFY REPORT command:

```
MODIFY REPORT <name of report form>
```

When this command is executed, FoxPro will locate and display the specified report form in the Report Layout window. If the specified report form does not exist, it will create a new report form with that name and display it in the Report Layout window. Therefore, you may use the MODIFY REPORT command to create a new report form as well.

To modify the report form named SALESRPT, issue the following command:

```
MODIFY REPORT SALESRPT
```

As a result, the report form SALESRPT.FRX will be displayed in the Report Layout window so that you can make the necessary changes to it.

PRODUCING REPORTS

After you have created the report form, produce the report by issuing the REPORT FORM command:

```
REPORT FORM <name of report form> [TO PRINT/PREVIEW]
```

To produce the report, using the report form BYMALE.FRX that was created earlier, issue the following command:

```
REPORT FORM BYMALE
```

Remember though, you will be prompted to select the database file to be used for the report if the environment was not saved with the report and the database file is not selected in the current work area. Of course, you can do this before issuing the REPORT FORM command in this form:

```
USE SALESMAN
REPORT FORM BYMALE
```

If you need to rearrange the records in the database before producing the report, you must issue the SET ORDER command to index the database file. For example, to arrange the records by sex in the database file, issue the following command to index the file by using the MALE index tag:

```
SET ORDER TO MALE
```

If, however, the indexing information is already an element of the report environment, you may skip this command.

To preview the report on the screen, add the keyword PREVIEW to the command as shown:

```
REPORT FORM BYMALE PREVIEW
```

This command is the equivalent of selecting the Page Preview option from the Report menu in the Report Layout window. After viewing the report on the screen, you can issue the command to print it by adding the TO PRINT clause at the end of the command:

```
REPORT FORM BYMALE TO PRINT
```

It is necessary to add either the PREVIEW or TO PRINT clause to the end of the command to view your report if it contains many records, because FoxPro's default screen preview scrolls by too rapidly to be of any viewing use.

USING MEMORY VARIABLES

Recall from the previous chapter that summary statistics can be created and saved to memory variables, so that their values can be passed to a report. The sample report shown in Figure 11.77 uses summary statistics that were saved in a memory variable.

The report displays the compensation of the sales staff as monthly salary values and as percentages of the total salary of the group. The percentages can be calculated only after the total salary value is computed. Due to the limitations of the Report Writer, however, it is not possible to compute the total salary and then calculate the percentages; a memory variable is required. This means, in our example, that you must calculate the total salary and save it to a memory variable before incorporating it in the report.

Thus, to calculate the total salary and save it in a memory variable named *total_pay*, issue the following command:

```
USE SALESMAN
CALCULATE SUM(SALARY) TO TOTAL_PAY
```

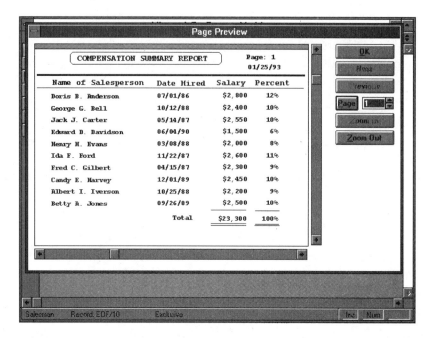

Figure 11.77 Report showing percent column

After that, bring up the Report Writer to create the report form you need. Figure 11.78 shows the report form (PERCENT.FRX) that was used to produce the percentage report shown in Figure 11.77.

When you are designing the report form, you can include the memory variable *total_pay* in the expression for defining a report field. Figure 11.79 shows the expression that was used to define the values for the report column named Percent.

When you are using memory variables in your reports, it is important to remember to create the variables *before* entering the Report Writer. You may use memory variables that have been saved in a disk file, but you need to first recall them by using the RESTORE command.

CREATING AND MODIFYING MAILING LABELS

To invoke the Label Designer so that you can create a new mailing label form, issue the following command:

```
CREATE LABEL <name of label form>
```

Then, to create the label form named CUSTOMER.LBX after selecting the database needed, issue the following command:

```
CREATE LABEL CUSTOMER
```

Producing Reports and Mailing Labels   511

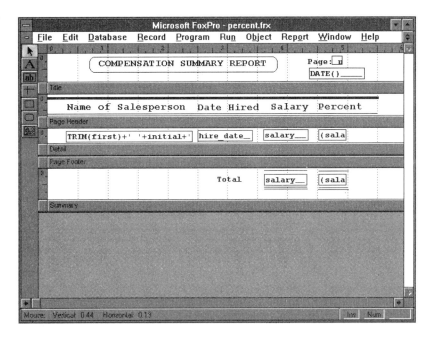

Figure 11.78 Report form showing percent column

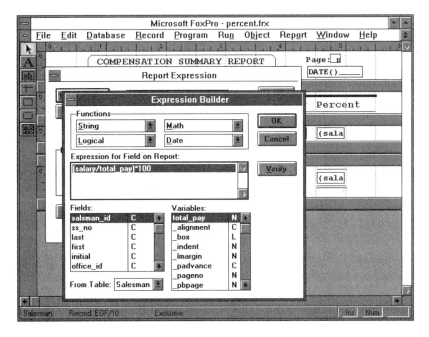

Figure 11.79 Defining the field expression using a memory variable

In response to the command, the Label Designer will display a new label form with the specified form name. After that, you can follow the same procedure outlined in this chapter to create your mailing labels.

To modify an existing label form, use the MODIFY LABEL command:

```
MODIFY LABEL <name of label form>
```

To make changes to the existing CUSTOMER.LBX label form, issue the following command:

```
MODIFY LABEL CUSTOMER
```

PRODUCING MAILING LABELS

The command to produce mailing labels using an existing label form is LABEL FORM:

```
LABEL FORM <name of label form> [TO PRINT/PREVIEW]
```

Add the PREVIEW keyword to the command to view the mailing labels on the screen before sending them to the printer. To print the mailing labels, add the TO PRINT clause to the LABEL FORM command. Examples:

```
LABEL FORM CUSTOMER PREVIEW
LABEL FORM CUSTOMER TO PRINT
```

Again, in this case, the database used for the mailing labels must be selected before issuing the LABEL FORM command. In addition, if you would like to rearrange the records in the database file before producing the mailing labels, remember to issue the commands to index the database file.

Chapter Summary

This chapter detailed the procedures for producing reports and mailing labels. To review: A report form is designed in the Report Layout window; a FoxPro report layout is divided into bands for organizing the information contained in the report, and various report objects can be placed in the report bands.

Information is displayed in a column format in a column report and data from an individual record is shown on a report line. All the information in a form report is displayed in a free form, and data from a record is displayed in a report section. Reports can be viewed on-screen before being sent to the printer.

This chapter also defined the processes that produce mailing labels. A label form is laid out in the Label Designer window; once the label's contents and form are defined, labels incorporating data from selected databases can be produced.

Information from multiple database files may be extracted to produce both reports and mailing labels by creating a RQBE query to link the database files and produce the data records to be used in the reports and mailing labels.

You should now be aware of the capabilities of the FoxPro Report Writer and Label Designer. In the next chapter, you will learn how to use the Screen Builder, another powerful FoxPro tool, to design custom data entry forms.

12
Using Custom Data Screens

An Overview

In previous chapters, the Browse window was used to view and edit data in Browse or Change mode. In either mode, the default screen provided by FoxPro was used to display data. There may be times, however, when the default screen layout in Browse or Change mode is simply not convenient to use. If you are using the Browse window primarily to view data, for example, it may present too much information in too compact an area. Or the layout of data on the screen may not harmonize well with the needs of data entry. Despite the flexibility that FoxPro offers in organizing data in the Browse window, you may find yourself wishing that you could replace FoxPro's default layout with one of your own creation; in fact, FoxPro allows you to do just that. It even allows you to add your own controls, like check boxes, popups, radio buttons, and push buttons. In this chapter, you will learn how to use the Screen Builder to create such custom screens, which can then be used for either viewing or entering data.

We will approach designing custom screens much like we approached designing custom reports and labels in the previous chapter. This chapter begins by illustrating how to design a custom data screen with the quick screen layout feature offered by the Screen Builder. Then, you'll learn how to modify the quick screen layout to create custom data screens that display data fields in an aesthetically pleasing layout.

CREATING CUSTOM DATA SCREENS

As you already learned, in FoxPro, data records can be viewed in a database by bringing up the Browse window, where they are then displayed in Browse or

Change mode. In either of these modes, it also is possible to modify data. Further, by choosing the Append option from the Record menu popup, you also can add new records to the database in the Browse window.

But data can be displayed in the Browse window only on a default screen where fields are identified by their names as defined in the database structure. No text may be added to the screen for describing the displayed data. In addition, all data fields are laid out on the default screen in a predetermined format that cannot be changed. These limitations often render the screen inadequate for satisfying the requirements of your data display and data entry operations.

Greater flexibility in laying out screens for viewing and entering data is provided by FoxPro's powerful Screen Builder, a tool that enables you to design custom screens. These custom screens can then be used for viewing and editing data in one or more databases, as well as for adding new data to an existing database.

The process of creating a data screen begins with laying out the screen objects in the Screen Design window provided by the Screen Builder. Like the Report Builder, the Screen Builder has all the tools needed to lay out screen objects. Data fields, text, graphics objects, as well as control panels, may be added to the screen to facilitate data viewing and data entry operations. The control panel may consist of a number of push buttons that you can use to select the data records to be displayed and edited. Furthermore, check boxes, radio buttons, spinners, and scrollable lists may be incorporated in a custom screen to display data field values.

After designing the data screen, the screen layout information is saved in a screen file that uses .SCX as its file extension; this actually is a special kind of database file that FoxPro uses to store screen information. The information is generated into a set of FoxPro commands and saved as a screen program with an .SPR file extension. When you want to use the screen layout to display data, you simply execute the screen program file. At that point, FoxPro compiles the FoxPro commands into computer machine codes and executes them to produce the data screen. The compiled program then is saved as another disk file with .SPX as its file extension.

TYPES OF DATA SCREENS

There are two kinds of screens on which to display data: a desktop screen and a window screen.

Desktop Screens

A desktop screen displays data in the desktop area of the screen, which is that area that underlies all system and user-defined windows. It is the screen that you see

Using Custom Data Screens

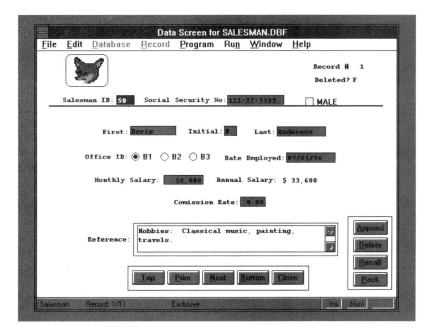

Figure 12.1 Sample desktop data screen

when you begin a FoxPro session. It also is the area in which FoxPro displays the results when it executes commands. For example, when you select the Clear option from the Window menu popup or enter the command "Clear" in the Command window, FoxPro clears the desktop screen.

Figure 12.1 shows an example of a desktop screen that displays all the data fields in the current record of the SALESMAN database. A desktop screen has a control that appears in the upper left-hand corner of the screen, which you can use to resize the screen or switch to another screen; you cannot close the desktop screen with that control, however. In addition to the data fields and their titles, the screen includes a number of screen objects, such as check boxes, push buttons, radio buttons, a record counter, record deletion indicators, and graphics objects.

Window Screens

A window screen displays data in a window similar to the Browse window. FoxPro allows you to choose from among four types of windows when creating window screens: user windows, system windows, dialogs, and alerts. Each of these is examined in greater detail below, but regardless of its type, a window can be categorized by the set of attributes it possesses. These attributes, in turn, determine how the window may be manipulated. FoxPro windows can be characterized by the presence or absence of the following attributes:

- *Float:* A window that possesses the float attribute is movable; otherwise, it is stationary.
- *Close:* A window that possesses the close attribute can be closed by selecting a menu option, clicking the mouse, or using the keyboard. A window without the close attribute generally is closed by selecting a designated push button.
- *Shadow:* A window defined with a shadow attribute has a darkened area behind it that resembles a shadow. A window without this attribute has no shadow.
- *Minimize:* A window with the minimize attribute can be reduced to 1 row by 16 columns that can be placed anywhere on the screen. A window without this attribute cannot be reduced or iconized in this way.

The Screen Builder allows you to create the four types of windows shown in the list below. The attributes of three of them—System, Dialog, and Alert—are fixed and cannot be changed. For example, the Dialog and Alert windows, which are primarily special-purpose windows used to display dialog boxes and alerts, are displayed with a double-line border (described below) and a shadow. In addition, they can be moved, but they cannot be minimized or closed. The attributes of the User window, on the other hand, are user-definable; although the user window's shadow attribute is selected by default, all four attributes may be set either on or off.

Window Type	Attributes	Default Settings
User	Close	Shadow
	Float	
	Shadow	
	Minimize	
System	Close	Close
	Float	Float
	Shadow	Shadow
	Minimize	Minimize
Dialog	Float	Shadow
	Shadow	Float
		Shadow
Alert	Float	Shadow
	Shadow	Float

In addition to possessing these four attributes, each window also can be framed by a particular type of border. FoxPro uses four different border patterns to frame a window: Single, Double, Panel, and System; or None may be specified. A Single border frames the window with a single line, a Double border with a double-line box; both the Panel and System borders display a wide window border, but any controls are hidden in a window with a Panel border, while they are visible in a window with a System border.

Similar to their window attributes, the border types of three kinds of windows—System, Dialog, and Alert—are predefined and cannot be changed. A System window has a System border, and the Dialog and Alert windows have a Double border. The border of a User window, on the other hand, is user-definable; by default, the User window has a Single border, but any of the five border types can be selected instead.

Because you are already familiar with a System window and the controls needed to manipulate it, we will use it to illustrate the operation of the Screen Builder in this chapter. Figure 12.2 shows such a System window that might be created to display the records in the SALESMAN database. The window has the normal control button to close it; it can be minimized and maximized in the regular manner, as well as moved anywhere on the screen. You may limit your screen to one or more of these controls by accessing a User window. In a User window, you can select one or more of these controls and define the screen border. Figure 12.3 shows the same data screen displayed in a User window in which the Close, Maximize, and Minimize controls are absent.

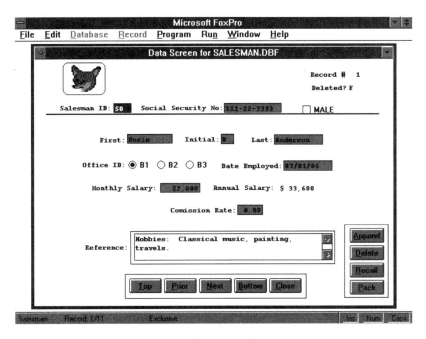

Figure 12.2 A data screen in a System window

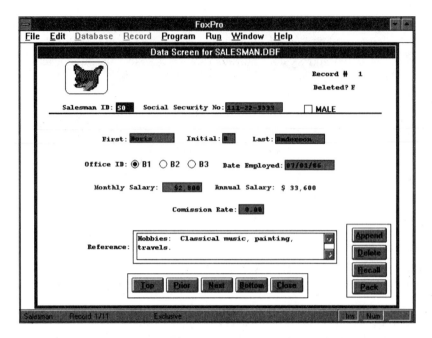

Figure 12.3 A data screen in a User window

The data window displays the values of all the data fields in the current record of the SALESMAN database. The values of some data fields are shown by using check boxes and radio buttons. In addition to graphics objects (boxes and lines), the data window has two sets of push buttons. In a User window, you can specify the type of controls you would like to have on the screen.

SCREEN LAYOUTS

The Screen Builder is used to create a data screen on which to lay out the objects in the screen form. As a shortcut, you can use the quick screen layout provided by the Screen Builder, where data fields are displayed in a column or row layout and are described with their field names as defined in the database structure. Or you can create a custom screen so that you can place the screen objects in any format. Then, in addition to descriptive texts and data fields, you can add graphics objects (boxes and lines) and controls (popups, radio buttons, push buttons, etc.) to the screen. A custom screen also can be created either by placing each object individually on the screen or by starting with the quick screen and then customizing it.

Creating Window Screens

The most useful screen type is a System window screen because it can be easily manipulated. And, because the procedure for producing other types of screens is very similar to that for producing a System window screen, we will focus our discussion on that type.

Before designing the screen layout, the necessary databases must be opened. If the screen will display only one database file, open it in the current work area and set the appropriate indexes accordingly. If you intend to display data from more than one database file, you must establish their relations in the View window before invoking the Screen Builder. In our example, to create a screen for displaying data in the SALESMAN database, open SALESMAN.DBF in work area 1.

The Screen Builder Window

To create a new screen, select the New option from the File menu popup. When the New dialog appears, select the Screen radio button and then the New push button. As a result, the Screen Builder window shown in Figure 12.4 appears. The screen being designed in the Screen Builder window is labeled untitled.SCX. In addition, the system menu bar now includes a Screen menu pad that contains a variety of options for designing your screen layout.

Note that the area in which you can lay out your screen form is displayed within the window. In the lower right-hand corner of the area you will find a size control. To display the Screen Builder window in full screen, maximize it by selecting the Maximize control. To change the size of the area, click on the size control and drag it until the desired size is achieved.

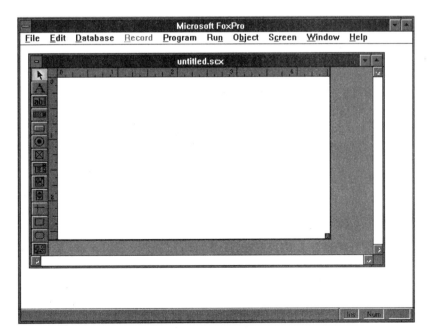

Figure 12.4 The Screen Builder window

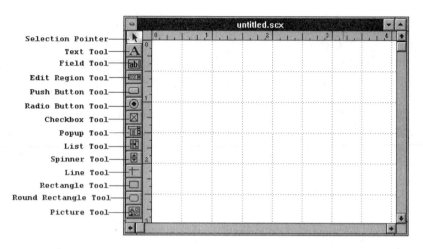

Figure 12.5 Screen design tools

Screen Design Tools

A set of tools is displayed at the left edge of the Screen Builder window (see Figure 12.5). By now, you should be familiar with many of these tools, such as the Selection Pointer, Text, and Field Tools, as well as those tools for drawing lines and rectangular boxes and for placing pictures on the screen. The procedures for using these tools are the same as discussed in the Report Writer.

In addition to these familiar tools, there are a number of new ones that you can use to place control buttons (push and radio buttons), popups, check boxes, drop-down lists, and spinner boxes. There also is an Edit Region tool that allows you to select an area in the screen form for editing and manipulation.

As an exercise, and to provide enough working space for designing the data screen, let's display the Screen Builder on the full screen by clicking on the Maximize control to enlarge it. Furthermore, enlarge the screen form by using the size control so that the form occupies almost the total (4 by 6 inches) area in the window.

Screen Layout Dialog

The first step in creating a custom data screen is to select the screen type. To do this, choose the Screen Layout option from the Screen menu popup, and the Screen Layout dialog shown in Figure 12.6 will appear.

Information in the Screen Layout dialog is divided into sections. An image of the screen form is displayed on the left of the dialog. It shows the relative location of the form on the screen. If necessary, you can use the size control in the lower

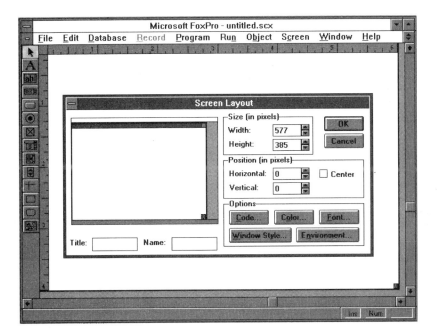

Figure 12.6 The Screen Layout dialog

left-hand corner of the form to resize the form. The size of the form (which is measured by number of pixels) also can be specified using the Width and Height spinner boxes in the Size section of the dialog. Similarly, you can reposition the screen form by clicking the mouse anywhere in the form image and then dragging it to a new position. Alternatively, you can use the Horizontal and Vertical spinner boxes in the Position section of the dialog. Values measured in pixels in the spinners determine the location of the screen form relative to the top left corner of the screen. For our example, we would like to position the screen form in the middle of the screen, so select the Center check box in the Position section. As a result, the screen form will appear in the middle of the window.

In the lower left-hand side of the Screen Layout dialog are two text boxes. The Name text box is used by the Screen Builder for identifying the window; it is optional. Unless you need to call the window by name in other FoxPro programs, do not assign a name to the window; FoxPro will automatically assign a unique name to the window upon creating the screen layout. In our example, we will leave it blank. In the Title text box, you can enter a title (e.g., Data Screen for SALES-MAN.DBF) that will appear in the title bar of a window if you choose to display your data form in a window format.

In the Options section are five push buttons. The Code button is used for defining the screen code; the Color button for specifying the background color of the screen form; the Font button for specifying the default type font; and the Environment button for saving, clearing, and restoring environment information; and the Window Style for selecting the screen type you will be designing.

Selecting Window Type

To use the Screen Builder to create a data screen that will appear in a window, first select the Window Style button. When the Window Style dialog appears (see Figure 12.7), select the window type and specify the attributes and border of the window.

In the Window Style dialog, the Type drop-down list allows you to select one of the five types of windows (Desktop, User, System, Dialog, and Alert) that the Screen Builder can create. Below the Type list are four check boxes for defining the window attributes and five radio buttons for specifying the window border. Most window types have default selections that you cannot change. For example, if you select a Dialog window from the Type list, the Double radio button will be selected, indicating that the window you create will have a double line as a border; in addition, the Close and Movable boxes will be checked automatically. As a result, the screen form that appears in the dialog will be movable and can be closed. Both the attribute and border options are grayed, indicating that they cannot be modified; those options that are selected will form the fixed attributes and border of the window. In the case of a User window, you have many choices for defining the attributes and the border of the window.

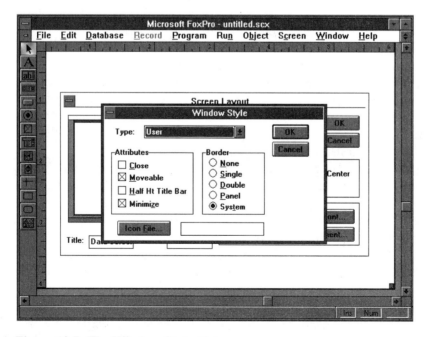

Figure 12.7 The Window Style dialog

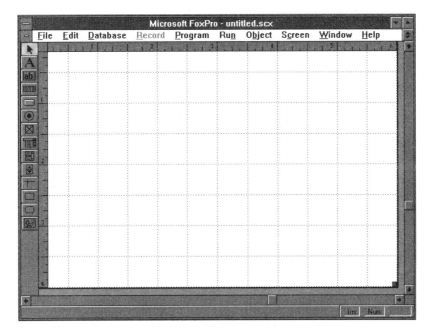

Figure 12.8 System window in the Screen Builder

To choose a System window, select System from the Type list before choosing the OK push button. Once you return to the Screen Layout dialog, select the Save button from the Environment dialog after you have selected the Environment button. Finally, select OK to exit from the Screen Layout dialog. When you return to the Screen Builder window, use the Ruler/Grid option in the Screen menu to display the grid. At this point, the System window that we defined should look like the one in Figure 12.8.

Note in this figure that the title of the data window we defined earlier is not displayed as part of the screen form layout in the Screen Builder window. Neither is the data window displayed in its relative location on the screen as defined in the screen layout dialog. But don't worry, all the attributes associated with the data window will be used to display the actual data screen.

Using the Quick Screen Layout

Having created the basic framework of the data screen, you can begin placing the screen objects on the screen panel. These screen objects can be placed individually or by using a quick screen layout as a shortcut, as mentioned before. To create a quick screen layout, select the Quick Screen option from the Screen menu popup to retrieve the Quick Screen dialog. If you have not selected the database to be used

526   Understanding FoxPro 2.5 for Windows

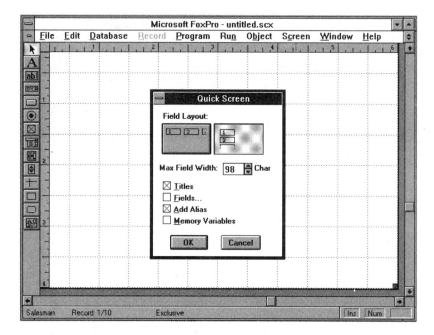

Figure 12.9 The Quick Screen dialog

for the screen, you will be asked to do so. Afterward, the Quick screen will appear (see Figure 12.9).

The Quick Screen dialog is very similar to the Report Writer's Quick Report dialog that was discussed in the previous chapter. In the Quick Screen dialog, the layout types (column or row) are selected by choosing the appropriate buttons. To select data fields to be placed on the screen layout, choose the Fields check box. If the Titles check box is selected (the default), data field names will be used as field titles; otherwise, no field titles will be placed on the screen layout. Select the Add Alias check box and all field names will include the names of their associated database files. The Memory Variables check box, when checked, creates memory variables for all the data fields.

You can adjust the width of the individual fields placed on the form in the screen form. The maximum width for any field, by default, is set to 98 characters as shown in the Max Field Width spinner box. You may change the maximum field width, but no field can exceed the default value.

After defining the Quick Screen settings, select the OK push button to return to the Screen Builder window, and all the data fields (or, if you chose the Fields option, all the fields that you selected) will be displayed in the screen panel as illustrated in Figure 12.10.

Using Custom Data Screens   527

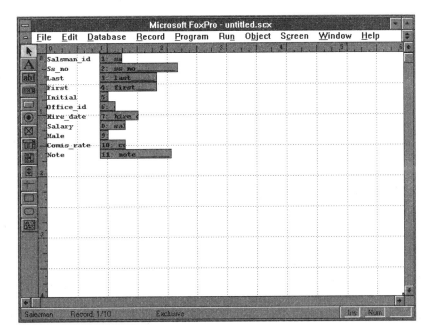

Figure 12.10 A Quick Screen layout

Saving the Screen Layout

The screen form now can be saved to a disk file with .SCX as its file extension. Select the Save option from the File menu popup, and then assign a name (e.g., SALESMAN.SCX) to the screen file. Be aware that if you did not select the Save push button in the Screen Layout dialog, you should now save the screen environment information by selecting the Yes push button in response to the "Save environment information?" prompt. This will allow you to execute the screen without having to prepare the FoxPro environment each time.

Generating a Screen Program File

After you have finished designing the screen layout, the final step in creating an executable screen is to convert the information about that layout into a set of FoxPro commands that are stored in a screen program file (a file with an .SPR file extension). This screen program file will then be used to display the custom data screen. To generate the screen program file, select the Generate option from the Program menu popup when the Screen Builder is the active window; the Generate Screen dialog shown in Figure 12.11 will appear.

528   Understanding FoxPro 2.5 for Windows

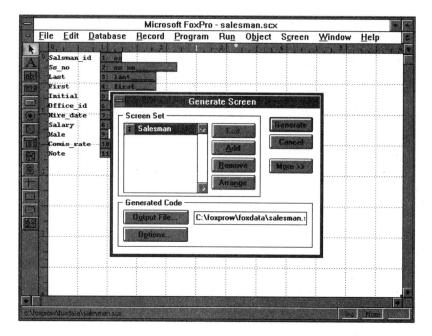

Figure 12.11 The Generate Screen dialog

Actually, FoxPro allows you to create screen programs that consist of one or multiple screen panels (each panel is a single .SCX file). This capability is reflected in the Screen Set box shown in Figure 12.11. The list box, which now contains Salesman (the name of the screen that we have just created), by default displays the name or names of all screen panels that are currently open in Screen Builder windows on the FoxPro desktop. The push buttons to the right of the Screen Set group box allow you to change the screen panels that will be used to create the screen program file. These four push buttons are:

- The Edit button, which allows you to open a Screen Builder window to edit screen panels that are not currently open on the FoxPro desktop. This means that you can make last minute changes to all your screens before generating the screen program file.

- The Add button, which allows you to add additional screen files that are not currently active in Screen Builder windows.

- The Remove button, which allows you to remove screen files that are visible in the Screens list box and will otherwise be included in the screen program file.

- The screen program file will display screens in the order in which their names appear in the list box. The Arrange button allows you to change the order of the screen panels when you are generating a screen program file that uses multiple screens.

Using Custom Data Screens 529

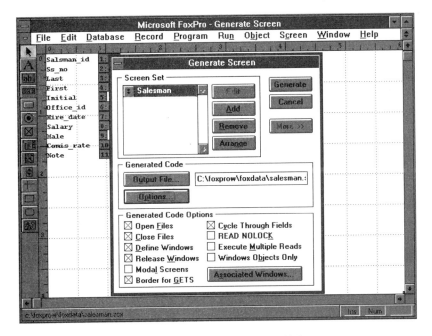

Figure 12.12 The Extended Generate Screen dialog

The Generated Code box shows two push buttons: Output File is used to specify the name of the generated screen program. By default, it assumes the same name as the screen file (e.g., SALESMAN.SPR). The Options button is used for bringing up the Options dialog in which you can record information about the developer and the location of the generated code. For most users, there is no need to select this button.

The More button in the Generate Screen dialog is used to bring up an extended version of the dialog in which you can specify a set of options governing the functions of the generated screen code. For most applications, use the default setting for these options. But, if you would like to see the list of options, select the More button, and the list of generated code options will be displayed in the lower portion of the extended Generate Screen dialog (see Figure 12.12).

As you can see in Figure 12.12, many of these options are selected by default. Most are advanced options that are of interest only to programmers who are designing screens as portions of a larger program. Two of these options, however, can be of use to nonprogrammers:

- *Open Files:* If environment information is saved with the .SCX file, this option instructs FoxPro to automatically open the necessary databases and indexes along with establishing any relations that existed among database files when the screen is executed. Because this option saves you from performing the same operations yourself, we recommend that you leave it

selected, except in those rare instances where multiple databases have identical formats and you are using the same screen for each of them.
- *Close Files:* This option automatically closes all files when you exit your custom screen. Again, we recommend that you leave this option selected.

Once you have specified the screens, code options, and output file, you can select the Generate push button to produce the screen program file. After the screen program file is generated, close the Screen Design window and exit from the Screen Builder.

Using the Data Screen

To use a screen file program that was generated from the Screen Builder, select the Screen option from the Run menu popup. Next select the screen program file that you would like to execute from the Screen To Run: list box. The screen program file will then execute and, if the Open Files option (a default setting) was selected when the file was created, it will automatically open the necessary database files. For example, after selecting SALESMAN.SPR from the list box, your screen should look something like Figure 12.13. The record pointer is positioned at the beginning of the database, and the first record of SALESMAN.DBF is displayed in the window that you have created.

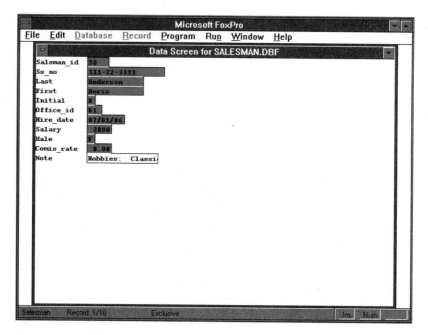

Figure 12.13 Displaying Data with the Quick Data screen

You can see in this figure that within the FoxPro system window the data screen is displayed in its own window with its own Close and Minimize controls. While the data window is displayed, many of the menu options in the FoxPro system window are disabled. The data window can be minimized and floated in the usual manner. However, as you will learn later, you cannot use the Control box to exit the data window. If you double click on the Control box, you would merely hide the data window from view. To bring it back to view, select it from the Window menu popup.

Be aware that there are two features peculiar to simple quick screens that are created in this way. First, as just stated, you cannot exit from the data screen by clicking your mouse on the Control box; this action merely hides the window, which continues to remain open. Instead, to exit the data screen window after viewing the data, you must press either the Esc key or the Ctrl+End key combination or choose the Cancel option from the Program menu, then couble click on the Control box. Second, the value of the screen for data entry or even for browsing the database is strictly limited by the fact that you cannot move beyond the current record to display another data record. The screen is capable of displaying *only* the current record. To display data in another record, it must first be made the current record. To do that, exit the window by pressing the Esc key; because the database is closed as soon as you exit the window, you must first reopen the database before selecting the next record to be displayed and rerunning the screen program file. As an exercise, use this procedure to display the record belonging to salesperson Jack Carter. Select the Locate option from the Record menu popup after reopening the SALESMAN database and define the search condition (e.g., LAST = 'Carter') in the For Clause. After the record is found, display the record by choosing the Screen option from the Run menu popup and selecting the SALESMAN.SPR screen program file.

These limitations all can be overcome by adding custom controls to the screen. The controls then may be used to move among the data records in the database, more easily close the screen window, and control the process of adding or editing information in the database. To add the control buttons, return to the Screen Builder window to modify the screen layout.

Modifying Existing Data Screens

To modify an existing screen layout, select the Open option from the File menu popup. (Although you are able to modify and save the screen with all your changes, unless you generate a new screen program file—using the Program menu—FoxPro will run the last—unmodified—saved version of the screen program.) When the File Open dialog appears, select the screen file (e.g., SALESMAN.SCX) that you want to modify. As a result, the screen layout will be shown in the Screen Builder window and you can begin making the necessary changes to it.

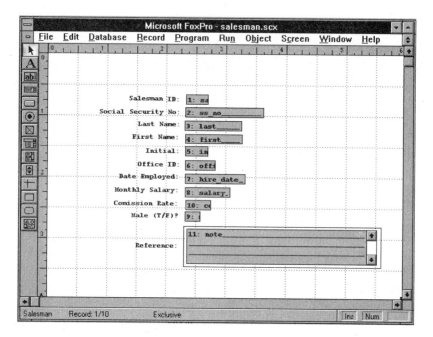

Figure 12.14 A custom data screen layout

The procedures for selecting and manipulating screen objects are the same as those you learned in the previous chapter for selecting and manipulating report objects. Follow those procedures to rearrange the data fields on the screen, edit the field titles, and add texts and graphics symbols to highlight certain objects on the screen. As an exercise, modify the screen layout to look like that shown in Figure 12.14.

The modified screen layout has been resized, the data fields have been rearranged, and field titles have been edited. In addition, a box has been placed around the contents of the memo field (NOTE) that is now titled "Reference:." If you were to use the modified screen to display a data record, it would look like the one in Figure 12.15.

You can see in this figure that field values are taken from the data record and displayed in the same format as that in the database. The monthly salary, for example, is displayed as 2800 without the dollar sign and commas. Note that the contents of the memo field also are displayed on the screen.

Formatting Fields

To format a data field in the screen layout, double click on the field to bring up the dialog for defining the field. When the dialog appears, begin specifying the field template in the text box next to the Format push button. To format the SALARY

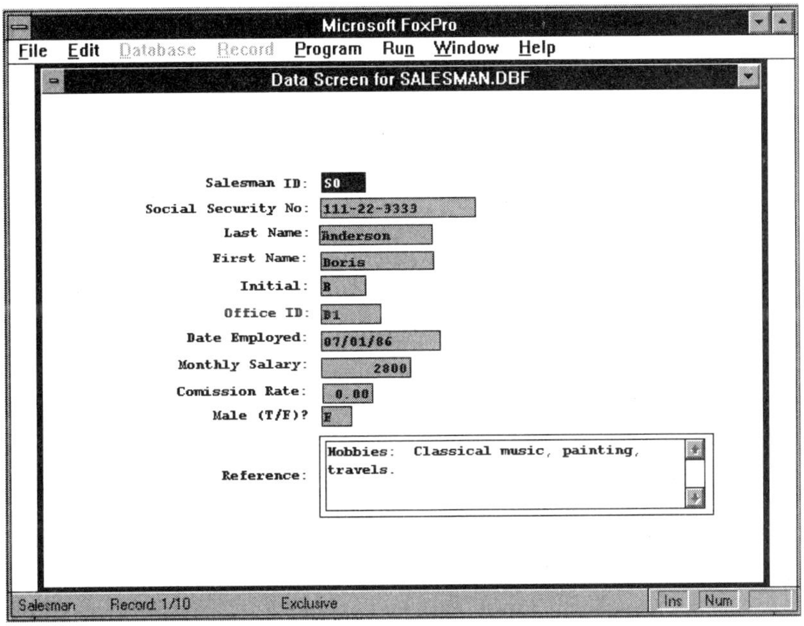

Figure 12.15 Displaying data on a custom screen

field, for example, double click on the field and then enter $$99,999 in the Format text box. When you return to the screen layout later, it may be necessary to adjust the field width to accommodate the field format.

A character field can be formatted in the same way. If, for instance, you would like to make sure that the first letter of all first names are in uppercase, format the FIRST field by using !AAAAAA as the field template. As a result, all first names will be displayed with their first letters capitalized. In addition, when you use the screen for data entry, the first letter you enter in that data field automatically will be converted to uppercase. Similarly, by using ! as the template to format the INITIAL field, all the middle initials will be displayed and entered as capital letters.

There are other buttons and check boxes in the Field dialog that you can use to define the type and value of a data field. We will discuss some of them later.

Setting Data Ranges for Data Fields

When you are in the Field dialog, you can specify a valid range for the values to be saved in a given data field. If you would like to restrict the valid range for the field value, enter the lower and upper limits in the Lower and Upper text boxes. As a result, only those values that fall within these limits will be accepted in the input process. For our example, let's set the lower and upper limits for the salary value to 0 and 9000, respectively. These values will be incorporated in the program

534   Understanding FoxPro 2.5 for Windows

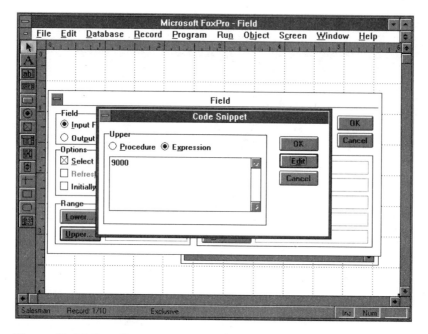

Figure 12.16 Specifying the upper limit for a field value

code for generating the screen. To set the upper limit, select the Upper Button. When the Code Snippet dialog appears, select the Expression radio button and then enter the value in the expression box (see Figure 12.16).

Using Display-Only Fields

In the Field text box located in the upper left of the Field dialog, you can specify whether the field is to be used for input (allowing you to enter a value to it) or for output (for displaying the field value only) by using one of the Field radio buttons. For our exercise, we will use the Input Field (Get) as the default field type. When data is displayed on a custom screen, it is also possible, by default, to view and edit the field values on the screen, a useful capability if you intend to modify the field values. But, if you intend to use the data screen only for viewing data, it is a good idea to ensure that users do not accidentally change the values. This "ounce of prevention" requires that you choose the Output Field (Say) radio button. Whereas the Input Field (Get) radio button, which is selected by default, both displays a record and notes any changes made to it by the user, the Output Field (Say) radio button only displays it. Therefore, to prevent a viewer from changing a social security number in the SS_NO data field, select the Output Field (Say) radio button when you bring up the Field dialog (see Figure 12.17). After making these changes, you can save the revised screen form to the screen file and then generate the screen program file.

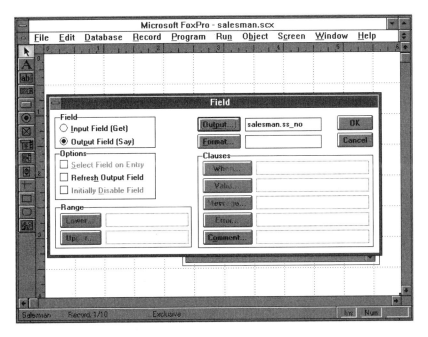

Figure 12.17 The Field dialog

It is important to recognize the implications of defining a field for display only. First, as you will see graphically when you create and execute the screen program file, display-only fields are shown in normal text; other input fields are displayed in reverse video and framed with rectangle boxes (see Figure 12.18). Second, besides being unable to modify the values of existing records, you also cannot enter values into the display-only fields of new records.

Adding Control Panels

Although the modifications that we have made so far to our custom screen have removed a number of its limitations, the screen at this point is still capable of displaying only the current database record. To be able to select and view another record without exiting the screen, you can add a set of push buttons that allows you to move around data records to view an individual record. Figure 12.19 shows a set of push buttons at the bottom of the data fields on the data screen.

Adding Push Buttons

You can place push buttons on the screen form by using the Push Button tool. Each time you use the tool, you can place one or more push buttons at a time on the

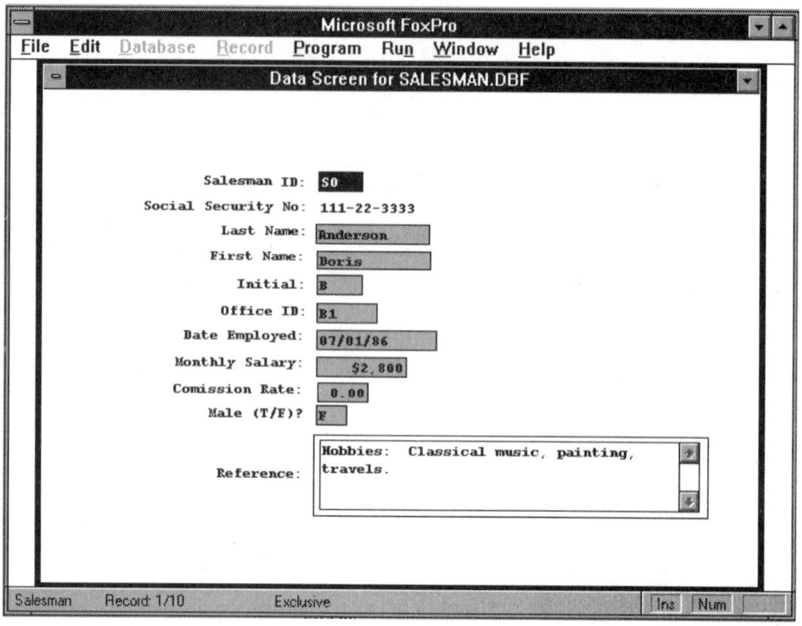

Figure 12.18 Output Field on the screen

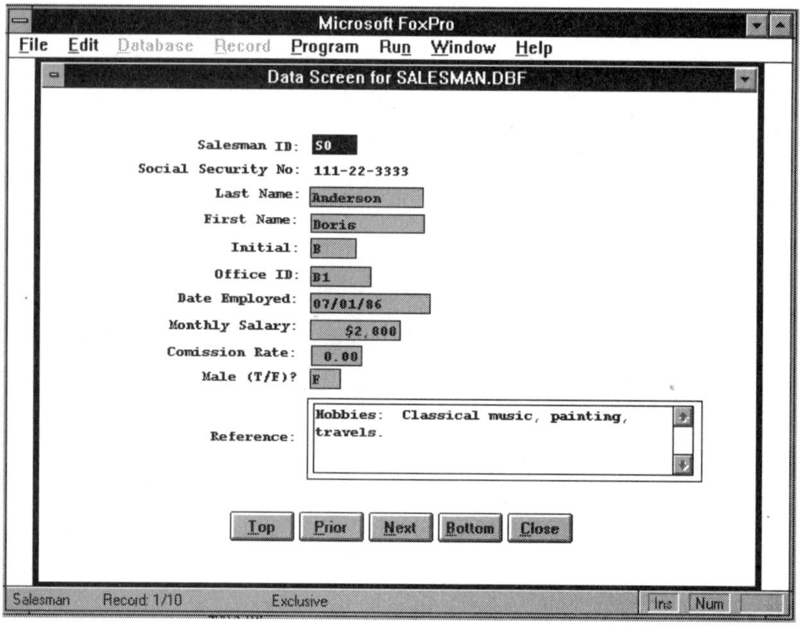

Figure 12.19 Sample push buttons on the data screen

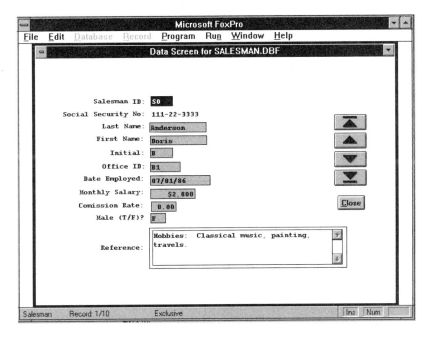

Figure 12.20 Sample graphics push buttons

screen form. If you place a set of push buttons, they can be arranged vertically or horizontally on the screen.

The process of placing push buttons involves defining the prompt and the functions of each button. A push button prompt can be represented by text (such as Top, Bottom, Next, Prior, and Close) or a graphic symbol (see Figure 12.20). The functions of the push buttons are defined with a set of FoxPro commands in a procedure as a code snippet.

As an exercise, we shall place the set of push buttons shown in Figure 12.19 on the SALESMAN.SCX screen form we have created. To do that, bring up the screen form in the Screen Builder window. To make room for the push buttons, move all the data fields and their labels up so that the push buttons can be placed at the bottom of the screen. Then select the Push Button tool and click the mouse where you would like the push buttons to appear. (The location does not have to be exact; you can reposition the buttons later.) As a result, the Push Button dialog will appear (see Figure 12.21).

Specifying Type of Push Buttons

In the Push Button dialog, select the type of push button you would like to place on the form. Most of the time, you will probably choose to create a push button with a text prompt (like that shown in Figure 12.19); the push buttons shown in

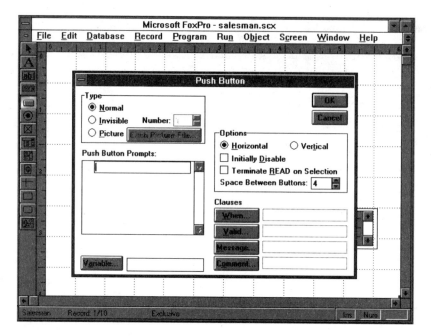

Figure 12.21 The Push Button dialog

Figure 12.20 are picture buttons. You also can create invisible buttons that function like normal or picture buttons when you select them, except they are invisible on the screen. For our example, we will create a normal push button, so select the Normal radio button in the Type box.

Arranging the Push Buttons

If you are placing more than one push button at a time, remember you must specify how you want them arranged on the screen: horizontally or vertically. To do that, select either the Horizontal or the Vertical radio buttons in the Options box of the Push Button dialog. The Spinner in the Options box allows you to define the space (measured in number of pixels) between buttons. You can ignore the two check boxes in the Options box because, in most cases, they should not be checked. For our example, accept the default setting: Select the Horizontal radio button and set 4 as the space between any two buttons.

Defining Push Button Prompts

The Push Button Prompts list is where you define the prompts to the buttons. Again, these prompts may be text or graphics symbols. For example, if you would like the first push button to be labeled as Top, enter Top as its prompt.

Defining Hotkeys for Push Buttons

Using a mouse to select a push button is simple: All you have to do is point at the one you would like to select and click on it. Using the keyboard to perform this same action, on the other hand, can be a much more cumbersome process. It requires that you tab through the available choices until the push button you want is highlighted. Only then can you press the Enter key to select it. FoxPro, in order to facilitate navigating with a keyboard, makes it possible to designate one letter of a push button's label as a hotkey that activates that push button. Pressing the designated hotkey then directly selects that push button. In our example, you might designate the letter "T" for the Top push button. Then pressing that letter on the keyboard activates the Top push button and positions the record pointer at the top of the database file.

To define a hotkey for a push button, place \< in front of the letter that you want to activate the push button. Continuing with the example above, to designate "T" as the hotkey for Top, type \<T. After entering the first prompt, press the down-arrow key (not the enter key) to enter the next button prompt. Enter \<Prior, \<Next, \<Bottom, and \<Close as the prompts for the next four push buttons (see Figure 12.22). Note that the hotkey symbols must immediately precede the keys to which they apply.

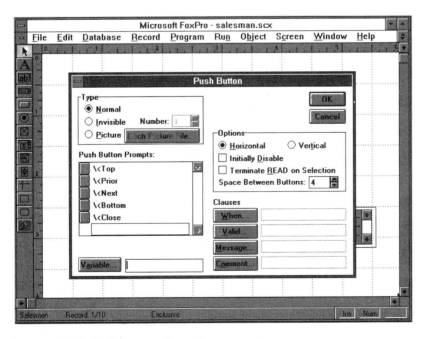

Figure 12.22 Defining push button prompts

Defining Functions of Push Buttons

After defining the push button prompts, you must tell FoxPro what their functions are. To do that, you need to assign a name to the variable that will be used to record the selection of a push button. Enter the name of the variable to the box that appears next to the Variables push button in the dialog. For our example, enter *act1* as the variable name.

Finally, we will write a short procedure to define the functions of these push buttons. The procedure consists of the following set of FoxPro commands:

```
DO CASE
    CASE act1 = 1
        GO TOP
    CASE act1 = 2
        IF EOF ( )
            GO TOP
        ELSE
            SKIP   -1
        ENDIF
    CASE act1 = 3
        IF EOF ( )
            GO BOTTOM
        ELSE
            SKIP +1
        ENDIF
    CASE act1   =4
            GO BOTTOM
    CASE act 1 = 5
        CLEAR   READ
ENDCASE
SHOW GETS
RETURN 0
```

The procedure instructs FoxPro what to do when a push button is pressed. If the first push button is pressed, the value of the variable *act1* becomes 1; the value of *act1* will be 3, for example, when the third push button is selected. The statements DO CASE and ENDCASE are used to enclose the commands that direct FoxPro in what to do if the *act1* variable takes on a different value. In the first case, when *act1* is 1, it will execute the command GO TOP and move the record pointer to the first record (top) of the database file. Similarly, when *act1* equals 4, the record pointer will be positioned at the last record (bottom) of the database file. When *act1* equals 2, the record pointer will be moved backwards one record (SKIP -1). However, if the record pointer is already at the top of the file, it remains at the top. Similar logic applies in the case when *act1* equals 4. When the fifth (Close) push

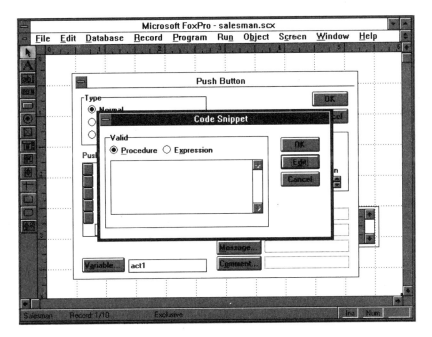

Figure 12.23 The Code Snippet dialog

button is selected, it instructs FoxPro to execute the command CLEAR READ, saving all the existing field values to the file. Finally, the commands SHOW GETS and RETURN 0 are used to exit the procedure and pass control back to FoxPro.

To enter the procedure, select the Valid push button in the dialog. When the Code Snippet dialog appears, note that the Procedure radio button is selected by default (see Figure 12.23). Accept the default selection to enter the set of commands as a procedure directly into the box that appears below the Procedure radio button. When you reach the bottom of the box, it will open automatically for more space.

Alternatively, you can enter the commands in the Edit window. In fact, let's use this approach because it enables us to see more commands on the screen. Select the Edit push button in the Code Snippet dialog. If the Screen Builder is in full-screen display in the FoxPro system window, you will not be able to see the editing window. To view other windows, click on the double-arrow control in the upper left-hand corner of the window to restore the Screen Builder window to its size prior to maximizing it. When you click on the double-arrow control, the editing window (labeled as salesman - act1 Valid) will appear behind the Push Button dialog (see Figure 12.24). To bring the editing window to the front, select the OK button in the Push Button dialog. When it appears, begin entering the set of commands (see Figure 12.25).

After entering the procedure, close the editing window to return to the Screen Builder window. To view the push button, use the scroll control to reveal the hidden

542 Understanding FoxPro 2.5 for Windows

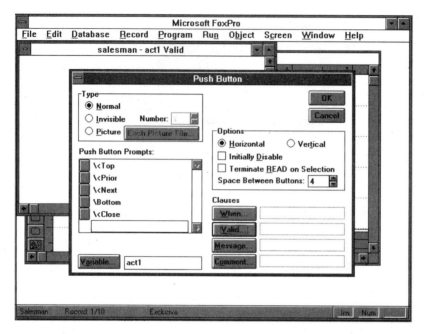

Figure 12.24 The Text Editor window

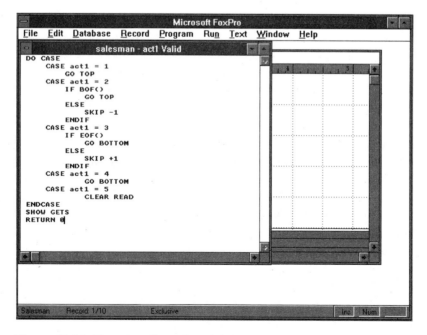

Figure 12.25 Entering the code snippet

Using Custom Data Screens   543

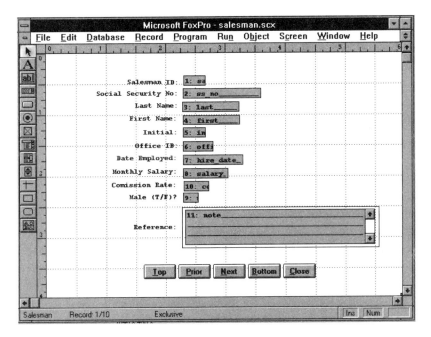

Figure 12.26 Showing push buttons on the screen form

part of the window, or maximize the Screen Builder window again. If you do that, the screen should look like Figure 12.26, in which you can see the set of push buttons displayed at the bottom of the data screen.

If you make a mistake and want to redefine a push button, double click on any button and the Push Button dialog will reappear. You can then revise the information in the dialog. You also can reposition the push buttons on the form. When you are satisfied with the functions and the layout of the button, save the changes to the SALESMAN.SCX screen file. Then, regenerate the screen program by selecting the Generate option from the Program menu.

When you display the data records with the revised data form, it will look like Figure 12.19. You can use the push buttons on the data form to move among the records in SALESMAN.DBF. When you are done viewing the records, select the Close button to close the database file and exit from the data screen and return to the FoxPro system window.

Rearranging Push Buttons

In Figure 12.19, the push buttons are arranged horizontally on the data form, but if you prefer, you can display them vertically simply by checking the Vertical radio button in the Push Button dialog. As an exercise, we will create a screen form

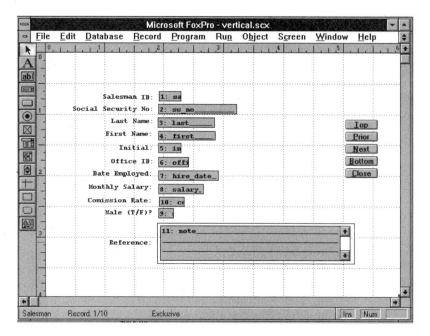

Figure 12.27 Arranging push buttons vertically

displaying a set of vertical push buttons. To do that, bring up the SALESMAN.SCX form in the Screen Builder window and then make a copy by saving it to a file named VERTICAL.SCX. We will then modify it by rearranging the push buttons.

To change the orientation of the push buttons, double click on any of the buttons to bring up the Push Button dialog. When the dialog appears, select the Vertical radio button. When you select the OK button to return to the screen form, the push buttons will be aligned vertically. You can then move them to the location of your choice. (see Figure 12.27).

Defining Graphic Push Button Prompts

So far, we have used text as the prompts for our push buttons, but you also can use a picture as a prompt. Before you can do that, however, you have to use a graphics program (such as the Paintbrush program in Windows) to create the picture and save it as a bit-map (.bmp) file. In Figure 12.20, the form uses a down arrow to label the push button for showing the next record. The graphic is saved as down.bmp, which is provided by FoxPro in the tutorial subdirectory. Similarly, the pictures for the other push buttons are saved in the top.bmp, bottom.bmp, and prior.bmp files. Since there is no picture file that we can use for the Close button, we will use the text for its prompt as before.

Using Custom Data Screens   545

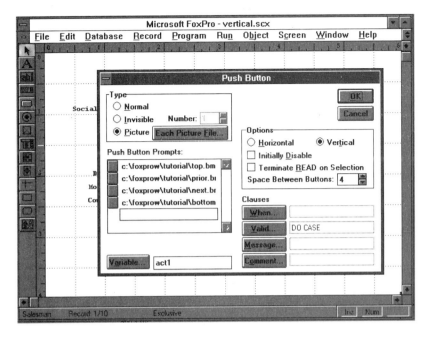

Figure 12.28 Defining picture push button prompts

To change the text prompts for the push buttons in the VERTICAL.SCX screen file, double click on any of the push buttons to bring up the Push Button dialog again. When the dialog appears, select the Picture radio button for defining picture push button prompts. Then, in the Push Button Prompts list, enter the name of the picture (.bmp) files. For example, enter c:\foxprow\tutorial\top.bmp as the prompt for the first push button. After entering all the picture button prompts, erase the Close text prompt and use the Valid push button to remove the statements that govern the Close button (see Figure 12.28). Next, select the OK button to return to the screen form. At this point, you will see that the push buttons are displayed with picture prompts. Since we do not have a picture file for the Close button, we will create a text prompt for that button. To do that, select the Push Button tool and use the same procedure discussed earlier. The push button prompt is \<Close. Use *act2* as the variable name and enter the following commands as the procedure:

```
DO CASE
    CASE act2 = 1
        CLEAR READ
ENDCASE
SHOW GETS
RETURN 0
```

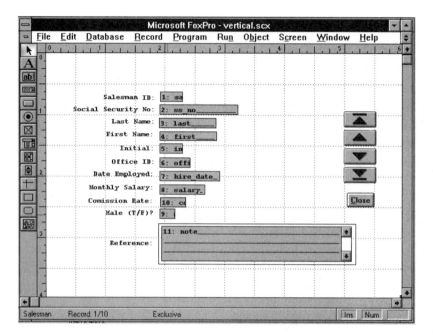

Figure 12.29 Picture push buttons on the screen form

When you look at the screen form after making the modifications to the push buttons, it should look like Figure 12.29. (The data form that is generated from this screen form was shown in Figure 12.20.)

Adding Graphics Objects

You can place different types of graphics objects on a screen form with the drawing and picture tools provided by the Screen Builder. For example, you can use the Line tool to draw lines for separating sections of the data form, or draw boxes with the Rectangle and Round Rectangle tools. You also can place a picture in a .bmp file on the form using the Picture tool. The procedures for placing graphics objects are identical to those discussed in the last chapter when we designed report forms. As an exercise, we will modify the existing screen form in the SALESMAN.SCX file to incorporate these graphics objects. After rearranging the data fields and adding lines, boxes, and a picture (the FoxPro logo) to the form, your screen layout should resemble Figure 12.30.

Ordering Data Fields

You can move freely from one data field to another on the data screen with the mouse. But, if you are using the Tab key to move around the data fields, the

Using Custom Data Screens 547

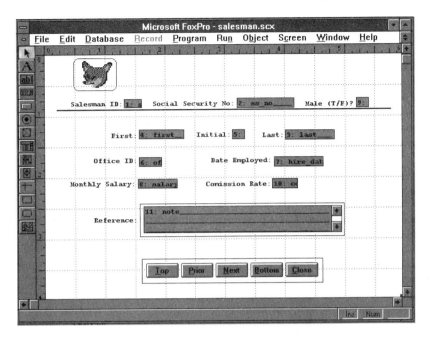

Figure 12.30 Adding graphics objects to the screen

sequence in which you can move from field to field is determined by a sequence number that the Screen Builder assigns to each field. This sequence number is displayed in front of the input field name in the Screen Builder window (see, for example, the input fields in Figure 12.30).

When you use the Quick Screen option to generate your screen layout, the input sequence is determined by the order of the data fields as defined in the database structure. If you then modify the position of the input fields in the screen layout, or if you define a custom layout from scratch, you often will find that the input order of individual fields is no longer sequential. You can, however, change the order of any one field displayed on the screen or the order of all fields simultaneously.

The first step, whether you are reordering one or all the fields, is to open the SALESMAN.SCX screen file in the Screen Builder window. Then, to change the order of a specific field, select the Object Order option from the Screen menu. When the Object Order dialog appears (see Figure 12.31), all the data fields will be displayed in their data structure order. You also can use this dialog to change the keyboard access order of the data fields on a screen.

The Object Order dialog contains two buttons—By Row and By Column—that you can use to order the data fields. If you choose the By Row push button, the data fields will be accessed by row, from left to right across the screen starting at the top. If you would like to move around data fields by column, from top to bottom down the screen starting at the left side, then select the By Column push button.

548 Understanding FoxPro 2.5 for Windows

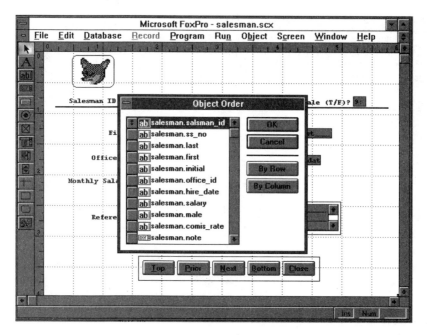

Figure 12.31 The Object Order dialog

You also can choose a specific order to move around the data fields by rearranging them in the drop-down list in the Object Order dialog. To move a data field up and down the list, click on the icon to the left of the field name and drag it up and down until the correct position is achieved. For our exercise, choose the By Row button so that when we edit data fields they will follow row sequence. (Note that when you set the order by row or column, the alignment of the fields on the screen is very important. Any field that is slightly taller or placed a little above other fields on the same row will result in incorrect order. Similarly, any field that appears slightly to the left of other data fields in the same column will result in that field being assigned a higher access order.) After ordering the data fields by row, your data screen should look something like Figure 12.32. When you use the data screen to display or edit data fields, the data fields will be accessed from left to right and top to bottom, as shown in the screen layout.

Adding Check Boxes

Check boxes in a data screen make it possible to display values in a logical data field. For example, instead of showing the value in the MALE field as .T. or .F., you can create a MALE check box and select it to indicate that a salesperson is a man.

Using Custom Data Screens 549

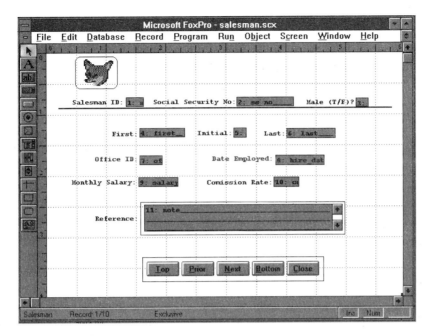

Figure 12.32 Ordering screen objects by row

To create such a check box, select the Check Box tool and then position the pointer on the location where the check box is to appear. To replace the MALE field on the current screen layout with a check box, for instance, delete the field and its field title by selecting them both and pressing the Del key. After selecting the Check Box tool, place the cursor on the location where the Male field was placed, and the Check Box dialog will appear. In the Check Box Prompt text box, enter the label (e.g., MALE) that describes the check box. Enter the logical field (i.e., Salesman.male) in the Variables text box that you intend to use for the check box. If you would like to set the value for the logical field to T by default, check the Initially Checked box (see Figure 12.33). If you would like to use your own picture for the check box, select the Picture Check Box and then specify the picture file.

When you return to the Screen Builder window after pressing the OK push button in the Check Box dialog, you will see the MALE check box displayed on the screen layout (see Figure 12.34). Note that you will need to reorder the fields after you have placed the check box on the screen layout.

Adding Radio Buttons

Radio buttons can be very useful for displaying a field that takes on a small set of predetermined values. For example, the OFFICE_ID field in the SALESMAN

550   Understanding FoxPro 2.5 for Windows

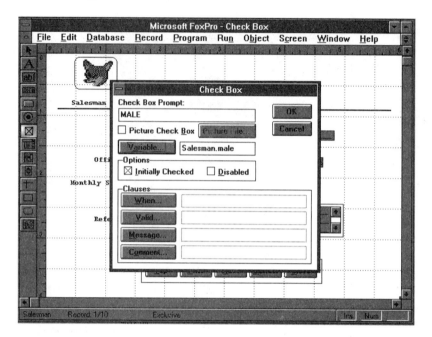

Figure 12.33 The Check Box dialog

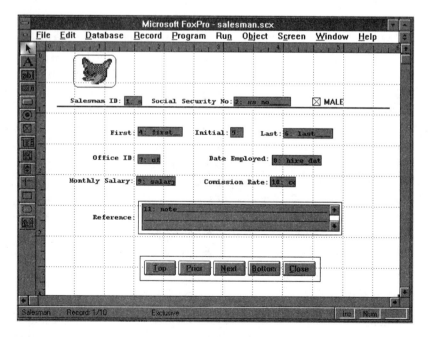

Figure 12.34 Check box on the screen form

Using Custom Data Screens 551

database can assume one of three values: B1, B2, and B3; and three radio buttons can be created to indicate those values in that field.

To place a set of radio buttons in the screen layout, select the Radio Button tool and then position the pointer on the location at which the radio buttons are to appear.

To replace the OFFICE_ID field in the current screen layout, for example, remove the existing field from the screen layout. Next select the Radio Button tool and then place the cursor on the previous location of the field. When the Radio Button dialog appears, choose the Horizontal radio button from the dialog so that the radio buttons to be created appear horizontally in the screen layout. Then enter the name of the data field (e.g., SALESMAN.OFFICE_ID) in the Variable text box. Finally, enter the possible values (e.g., B1, B2, B3) for the data field in the Radio Button Prompts list box. In return, the first value you entered will appear as the default initial value in the Initial popup window in the dialog (a different default value may be chosen from the popup window). When you are adding new data records to the database with this data screen, the default value will be used to fill the data field (see Figure 12.35).

When you return to the Screen Builder window, you will see that the three radio buttons are displayed horizontally on the screen layout next to the field title "Office ID:." Again, reorder the data fields after you have placed the radio buttons in the layout (see Figure 12.36).

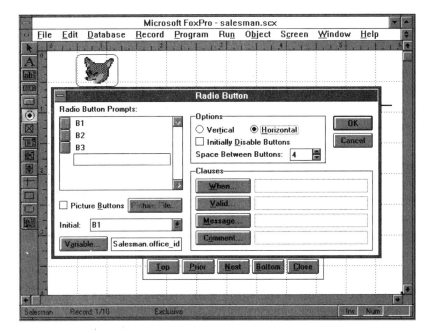

Figure 12.35 The Radio Button dialog

552   Understanding FoxPro 2.5 for Windows

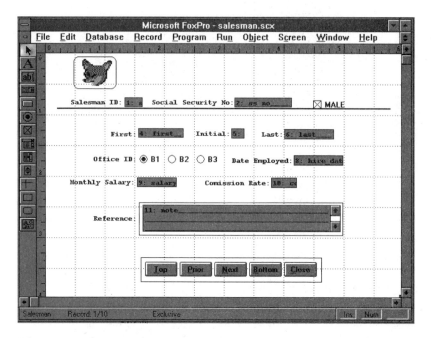

Figure 12.36 Radio buttons on the screen form

Adding Calculated Fields

When you are using a custom data screen to display data in a record, it is possible to create data fields that are computed from values in the existing data fields. The SALARY data field in the SALESMAN database, for example, contains monthly salaries for the sales staff. It is possible to use the values in the SALARY data field to create a calculated field that displays *annual* salaries on the screen layout. (Note: The calculated field can be used only for display; it cannot be edited.)

To create a calculated field, select the Field tool and then position the pointer on the intended location for the field. When the Field dialog appears, select the Output Field (Say) radio button to specify the field for display only. Then enter the expression for the calculated field in the Output text box and enter the field template in the Format text box. For example, to place the annual salary field on the existing screen layout, enter Salesman.salary*12 and $$999,999 as the field expression in the Output text box and field template respectively. In addition, select the Refresh Output Field check box so that the calculated field will be updated to display a different value when you move to another record (see Figure 12.37).

When you return to the Screen Builder window, you can add the appropriate label (e.g., "Annual Salary:") to the calculated field. After moving the Commission Rate popup to a different location and reordering the data fields, the modified screen layout might look like Figure 12.38. Note that the display-only field is shown dimmed, which differentiates it from those fields that you can edit. Now

Using Custom Data Screens 553

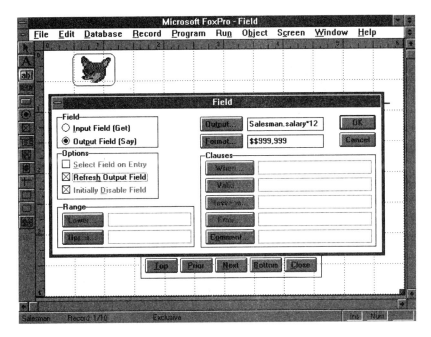

Figure 12.37 Defining a calculated field in the Field dialog

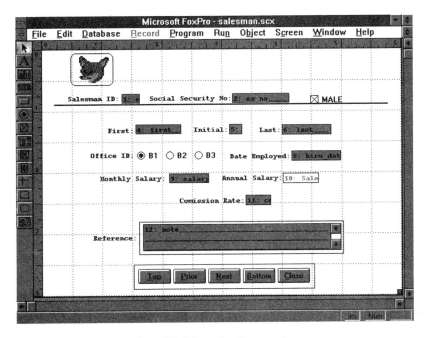

Figure 12.38 A calculated field on the Screen form

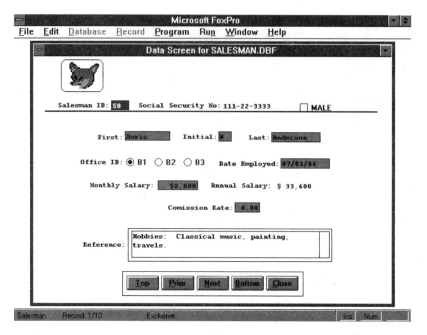

Figure 12.39 Displaying the value of a calculated field

when you display data records with the modified data screen, the annual salary for each salesperson will be calculated using the value in the SALARY data field in the record, as illustrated in Figure 12.39.

Figure 12.39 shows the calculated field as a display-only field (in normal text instead of in a highlighted text box.) When you move to a different record, the calculated field will be automatically updated using the value in the SALARY field for that record. However, when you are appending a new record to the database with the data screen, the calculated field will not be updated while you are still in the appended record. You will see the calculated value only when you return to the record after you have first moved to a different record.

As you can see in Figure 12.39, the first record of the SALESMAN database is shown in the data screen window. To view the next record, select the Next push button; to view the previous record, select the Prior push button; select the Top and Bottom push buttons to view the first and last records in the database, respectively. To exit from the data screen and save all the changes made to the database file, select the Close push button.

Adding a Data Maintenance Panel

When you use the screen form for data maintenance, you need to be able to add new records to the existing database. Similarly, you want to be able to delete those

Using Custom Data Screens   555

records that you no longer need. These procedures require that you add another set of push buttons. The operation for deleting records requires two steps: marking the record and then packing the database. Furthermore, you need to provide the means for recalling a record that has been marked for deletion by mistake. Therefore, the control panel for data maintenance should include four push buttons: Append, Delete, Recall, and Pack. The Append push button will execute the APPEND BLANK command that brings up a blank data form for entering new values to the record. When you select the Delete push button, it will mark the current record by executing the DELETE command. Selection of the Recall button will execute the RECALL command that will remove the deletion mark on the current record. Finally, the Pack push button, when chosen, permanently removes the records that have been marked for deletion from the database through the PACK command.

To add the set of push buttons for data maintenance, select the Push Button tool and position the pointer in the lower right-hand corner of the data screen. When the Push Button dialog appears, select Vertical in the Options box and enter the push button prompts, as shown in Figure 12.40.

To define the functions of the push buttons, assign *act2* as the variable name and select the Valid button to enter the commands for the Valid expression (see Figure 12.41). When you return to the screen form, you will see that the set of data maintenance buttons is displayed in the lower right-hand corner of the screen (see Figure 12.42).

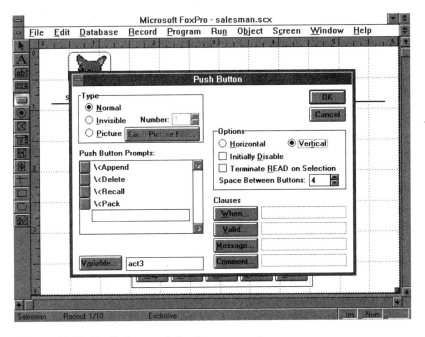

Figure 12.40 Defining push button prompts

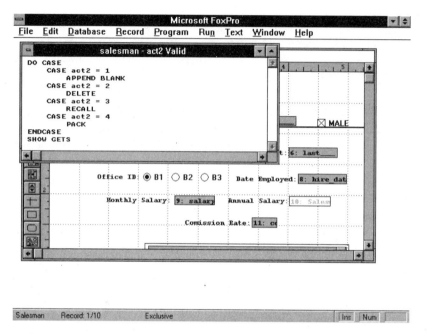

Figure 12.41 Defining a valid expression

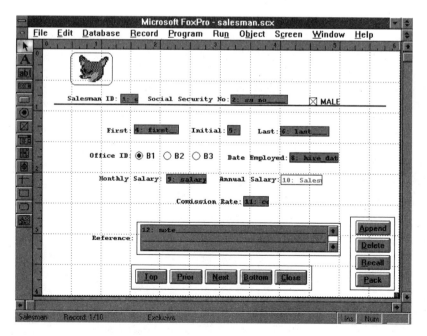

Figure 12.42 Data maintenance push buttons

Displaying Record Numbers

When viewing or editing database records in a Browse window, you may want to know which is the current record, and this can be determined easily if the number of the current record is displayed on the data screen. In addition, you can determine the total number of records in that database by looking at the record number for the last record in the database.

To display the current record number on a data screen, insert the FoxPro RECNO( ) function in the screen layout. A function is placed in a screen layout in a way similar to that for placing a data field in a display-only mode; that is, choose the Output Field (Say) radio button in the Field dialog. For example, if you would like to display the record number in the upper right-hand corner of the data screen, select the Field tool and then position the pointer in the upper right-hand corner of the screen. When the Field dialog appears, select the Output Field (Say) radio button. Then, define the function for showing the record number by entering the RECNO( ) function in the text box that appears next to the Output push button. Finally, select the Refresh Output Field check (see Figure 12.43) before selecting the OK push button to exit from the Field dialog.

When you return to the Screen Builder window, and after you have adjusted its position and field width, you can add the necessary text (e.g., "Record #") to describe the field (see Figure 12.44).

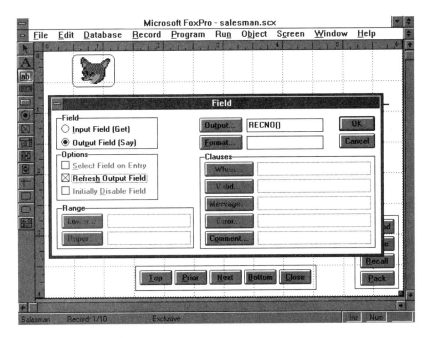

Figure 12.43 Defining the record number function

558 Understanding FoxPro 2.5 for Windows

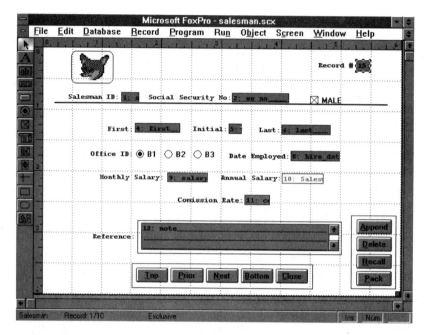

Figure 12.44 The Record Number field

Displaying Record Deletion Indicators

Similar to the preceding example, you can use the DELETED( ) function to indicate whether the current record has been marked for deletion. The DELETED( ) function displays either .T. or .F.

To display the record deletion indicator, select the Field tool before placing the cursor below the RECNO( ) field. Then, enter the DELETED( ) function in the Output text box after selecting the Output Field (Say) radio button. In addition, check the Refresh Output Field push button (see Figure 12.45).

When you return to the Screen Builder window, add the text (e.g., "Deleted?") to describe the field and adjust its width, position, etc. A modified screen layout is shown in Figure 12.46. When a record on display is marked for deletion, the record deletion indicator displays the value of T; otherwise, the value of F is shown.

Since we will use the form to enter new data records, we need to change the social security field, SS_NO from a display-only to an input field. To do that, modify the field definition by selecting the Input Field (Get) radio button in the Field dialog when you double click on the SS_NO field. After making all the changes, generate the revised screen and you will see how to use it to maintain the SALESMAN database. The generated data screen is shown in Figure 12.47.

Using Custom Data Screens   559

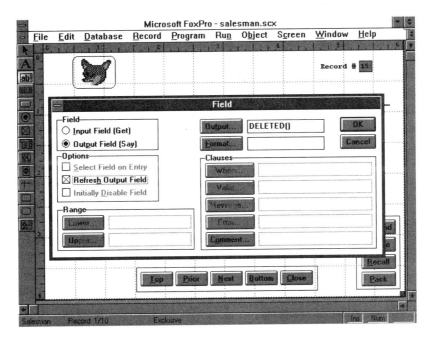

Figure 12.45 Defining the Record Deletion function

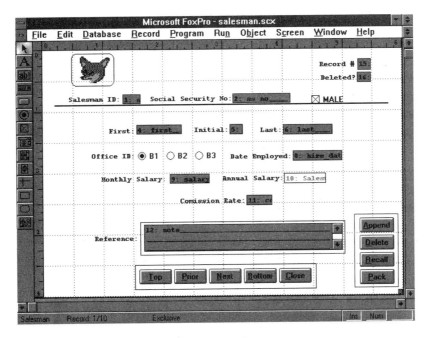

Figure 12.46 The Record Deletion mark

560 Understanding FoxPro 2.5 for Windows

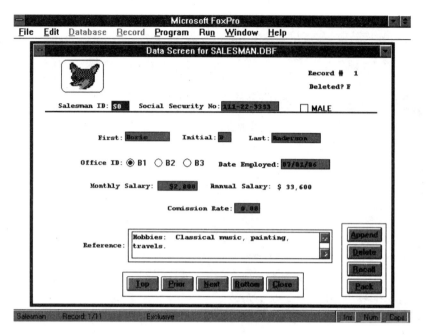

Figure 12.47 Displaying data in the revised data form

Figure 12.47 displays all the changes that were made on the screen form. In the upper right-hand corner of the screen, you can see the current record number. Since this record is not marked for deletion, the value of F is shown in the Deleted? field. This record belongs to a female salesperson, so the value in the MALE data field is .F., and the MALE check box is not checked. Also note that the Social Security No: field now is a normal field into which you can enter a value. In the lower right-hand corner of the screen, is the set of push buttons that we placed for performing the data maintenance operations.

Appending New Records

To add a new record to SALESMAN.DBF, select the Append push button in the screen form shown in Figure 12.47. As a result, a blank data form is displayed. At this point, we can enter values to the new record (as record #11). A sample new record is shown in Figure 12.48, in which you can see that the calculated field for the Annual Salary has not been calculated even though we entered a value for the monthly salary value. The calculated field will be updated only after you exit from the record and reenter it. To see that, click on the Prior button and the Next button, and then you will see the Annual Salary field updated accordingly.

Using Custom Data Screens   561

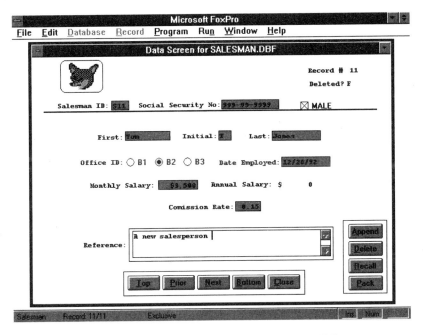

Figure 12.48 Adding a new record to SALESMAN.DBF

Deleting Records

Subsequently, if you would like to delete the new record (#11) we added to the database on the Bottom push button, then click on the Delete push button. As a result, the value of the Deleted? field will show the value of T, indicating that the current record has been marked for deletion. You can use the same procedure to mark other records to be deleted.

To permanently remove any records marked for deletion, select the Pack push button. As a result, all the records with deletion marks will be removed from the database, and the record pointer will be placed at the first record in the database file; to view the last record, select the Bottom push button. As an exercise, select the Pack push button to remove record #11 from SALESMAN.DBF. Afterward, select the Close push button to save the changes and close the data screen window.

Adding Popups

Radio buttons enable you to display a limited number of predetermined values for a character field on the screen. Similarly, a popup can be created for displaying these character strings. For example, a popup is a convenient way to enter a state

562 Understanding FoxPro 2.5 for Windows

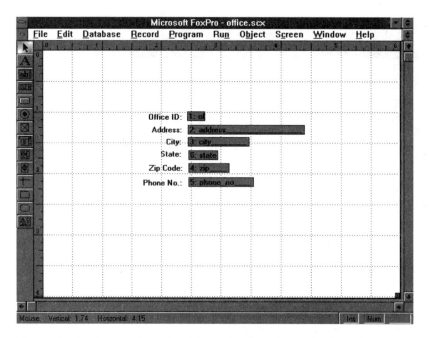

Figure 12.49 A data form for displaying data in OFFICE.DBF

code to the STATE data field. Then, during data entry, instead of typing in a state code, you can select one from the list of valid state codes in the popup. Another advantage to using a popup for data entry is that it ensures the validity of the data input. Because you are limited to choosing a character string from the popup, the possibility of typing errors is precluded.

To practice creating such a popup, first develop the custom data screen layout for OFFICE.SCX, as shown in Figure 12.49. In the current screen layout, the character string in the STATE data field is displayed in a normal text box, and to enter a state code into the data field during data entry, you would type the state code in the text box. To create a popup for achieving the same result, remove the current STATE field from the screen layout. Then select the Popup tool and place the cursor on the location of the removed data field. When the Popup dialog appears, specify the data field involved (e.g., OFFICE.STATE) in the Variable text box. Next enter the possible character strings for the specified data field in the dialog (see Figure 12.50).

Figure 12.50 shows a set of valid state codes (CA, IL, NY) available from the popup for the STATE field in the OFFICE database. When you return to the Screen Builder window, you can adjust the position of the popup so that it fits in the screen layout. After reordering the data fields and the push buttons, the modified screen layout might look like Figure 12.51.

Using Custom Data Screens 563

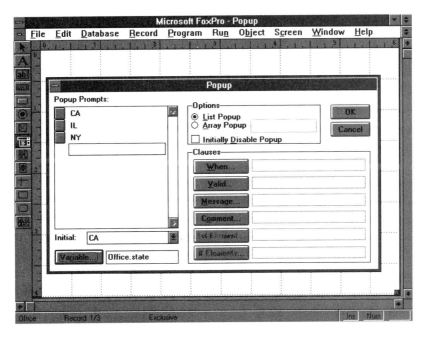

Figure 12.50 The Popup dialog

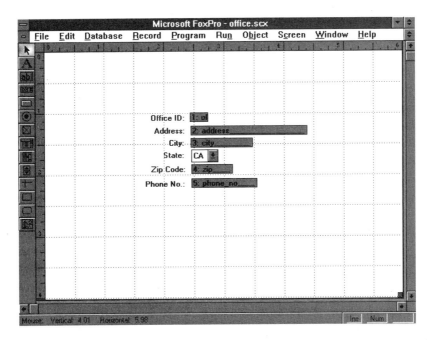

Figure 12.51 The popup on the screen form

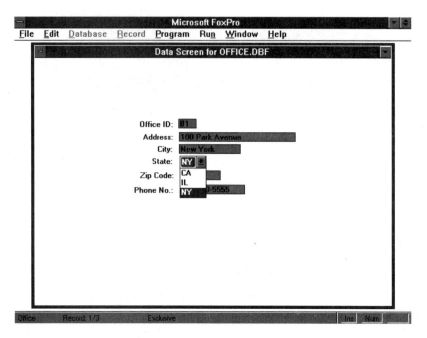

Figure 12.52 Displaying a value in the State field in a popup

When you use the custom data screen to display a record in the OFFICE database, the state code in the STATE data field will be displayed in the popup window. If you need to change the field value, simply open the popup and select another character string (see Figure 12.52).

Copying Screen Objects

In addition to creating a set of push buttons as a control panel, you also can use a shortcut to borrow a control panel that already has been created for other data screen forms. This is possible because FoxPro for Windows lets you open more than one screen form in the Screen Builder window at a time; hence, you can copy a control panel from one form to another. To do that, bring up the screen form that has the control panel you would like to borrow, make a copy of the panel, and then paste it onto another form.

For example, the screen form for OFFICE.DBF that we have created so far does not have any push buttons for moving between data records. Neither does it have a panel for performing the data maintenance operation. Instead of placing the push buttons on the form using the Push Button tool, you can borrow them from SALESMAN.DBF. To do that, first bring up SALESMAN.SCX in a Screen Builder window. Then select the set of push buttons to be copied by double clicking on any one of the buttons. As an exercise, double click on the Top push buttons.

Using Custom Data Screens   565

To make a copy of the set of push buttons, select the Copy option from the Edit menu. As a result, the set of push buttons is temporarily saved in a clipboard. Now, bring up OFFICE.SCX in another Screen Builder window. When the screen form appears, select the Paste option from the Edit menu. In return, the push buttons are added to the screen form. To copy another set of push buttons, bring SALESMAN.SCX into view and then repeat the same process. If you have maximized the OFFICE.SCX window, you can switch to the SALESMAN.SCX window by selecting that window after selecting the Window menu. Alternatively, you can minimize the current window and then move it around to reveal the other window and then bring it to the foreground by clicking on it.

You can copy more than one screen object at one time from one form to another by selecting more than one object form before selecting the Copy option from the Edit menu and then pasting both objects to another form. As an exercise, copy the data maintenance push buttons, the FoxPro logo, the record number, and the record deletion indicator from SALESMAN.SCX to OFFICE.SCX. Afterward, the data screen for OFFICE.DBF will look like Figure 12.53.

After you have borrowed the push buttons from SALESMAN.SCX, you need to close the screen file and keep only OFFICE.SCX open. *This step is very important:* If SALESMAN.SCX remains open and you save the revised OFFICE.SCX file, the environment information also will include SALESMAN.DBF. Therefore, close SALESMAN.SCX and then save the remaining screen form to

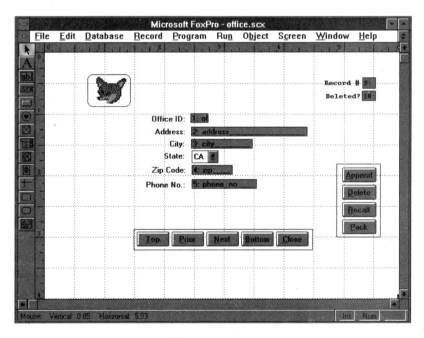

Figure 12.53 The custom data form for OFFICE.DBF

566   Understanding FoxPro 2.5 for Windows

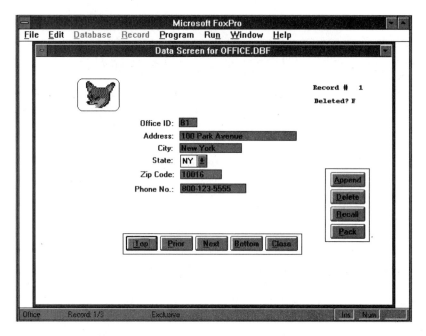

Figure 12.54 Displaying data with the custom data form

OFFICE.SCX before regenerating the screen program file. When you use the revised screen form for data display and maintenance, you will be able to use all the push buttons as if you had created them separately for OFFICE.SCX. (See Figure 12.54.)

Adding Lists

You can use a list to display a set of values for a given field on the screen form, and when you view the value of the field, you also can see other possible values for that field.

To place a list on the screen, select the List tool and then position the pointer on the location where you want the list to appear. As an exercise, bring up OFFICE.SCX in the Screen Builder window and then save it as TEST.SCX. We will use the screen form in TEST.SCX to experiment with adding a list to the screen without changing OFFICE.SCX.

For this example, we will use a list to display all the phone numbers that are saved in the PHONE_NO data field in OFFICE.DBF on the screen. To do that, remove the PHONE_NO field from the screen, select the List tool, and then place the pointer where the field was located. When the List dialog appears, select the From Field radio button and enter the field name in the Field and Variable text boxes (see Figure 12.55). Select the OK push button to return to the screen form.

Using Custom Data Screens 567

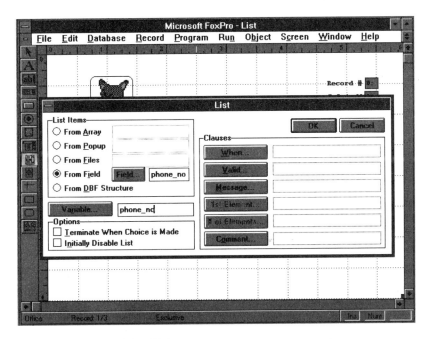

Figure 12.55 The List dialog

When you return to the screen form, you will see a list box on the form. You can adjust the size of the list box so that it can accommodate a typical phone number (see Figure 12.56). Notice that the height of the list box is set to accommodate up to three values because there are three values stored in PHONE_NO. You can make the list box taller, but not shorter.

When you use the screen form for displaying data, you will see that the values in PHONE_NO are given in the list box where the current value for the record is highlighted (see Figure 12.57). When you move to another record, it will highlight another phone number in the list.

A list is similar to the popup (or drop-down list) in which multiple values are displayed. However, a list can be used only for *viewing* data values in a field; you cannot select a value from the list to enter it into the field. As a result, a list is not as useful as the popup. A list does have more extensive uses, but a substantial knowledge of programming is required before you can incorporate them into your work. In any case, that information is beyond the scope of this book.

Adding Spinners

You have seen how a spinner can be used as a control, enabling you to "spin" through a set of numeric values displayed in a text box. When you were defining a data structure, for example, you used a spinner to set the field width.

568 Understanding FoxPro 2.5 for Windows

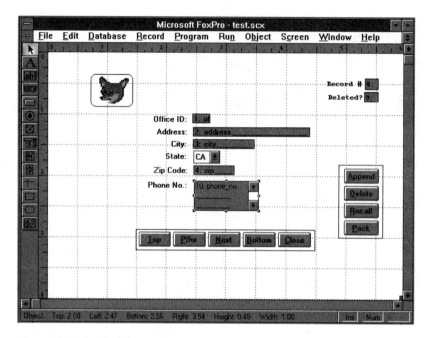

Figure 12.56 The list on the data form

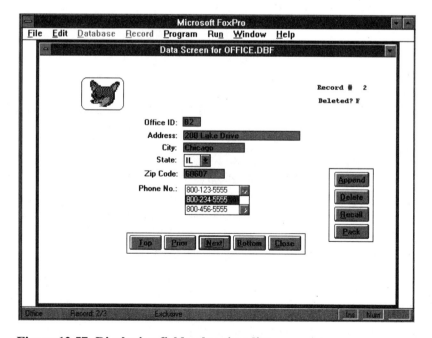

Figure 12.57 Displaying field values in a list

To enter a value to a field with the mouse and a spinner, click the mouse on the up or down arrow to increase or decrease a present value. For example, let's say you have a payroll database that contains a field named "dependent" in which you store the number of dependents for each employee (a salesperson). You can use a spinner to assign an integer to that field on the screen form.

Use the View window to open and modify the PAYROLL database so that we have a field named DEPENDENT (dependent, N,2,0). Exit, saving the changes to the PAYROLL database; then create a new screen form named PAYROLL.SCX. The window style is System and the title is Data Entry Screen for PAYROLL.DBF. Use the Quick Screen option from the Screen menu and copy the FoxPro logo and the RECNO( ) and DELETED( ) push buttons from SALESMAN.SCX to PAYROLL.SCX.

To place a spinner on the form, select the Spinner tool and then position the pointer where you would like it to appear. When the Spinner dialog appears, enter the name of the data field (in this case, DEPENDENT) in the Variable text box (do not include the database file name in the variable name). Then, enter the minimum and maximum values for the data field in the Minimum and Maximum text boxes in the dialog. These values determine the range that will be displayed in the spinner box. However, you may assign a range for the field value by specifying its lower and upper limits in the Lower and Upper text boxes in the dialog. Normally, the maximum and minimum display values are the same as the lower and upper limits for the value range. In our example, we will use the range between 0 to 10 for the DEPENDENT field. Finally, accept the default value for the increment value. Each time you click on the up or down arrow in the spinner, the field value will be increased or decreased, respectively, by that value (see Figure 12.58).

When you return to the screen form, you will see that the spinner box is displayed on the screen. The spinner shows a text box and up and down arrows (see Figure 12.59). When you use the form to display data in PAYROLL.DBF, you will see that the value in the DEPENDENT field is displayed in a spinner box (see Figure 12.60).

Adding Screen Background

A graphic image may be used to enhance the appearance of a data screen, but the image must be saved in a .bmp file before you can use it as the screen background.

As an exercise, let's add a screen background to the TEST.SCR screen form that we created earlier. We will use the image contained in the graphic file named region.bmp, which is provided by FoxPro and saved in the tutorial subdirectory. If you do not find the file in that subdirectory, it may be because you did not install the optional file during the installation process. In that case, create your own .bmp file and follow the same procedure to create a screen background.

570 Understanding FoxPro 2.5 for Windows

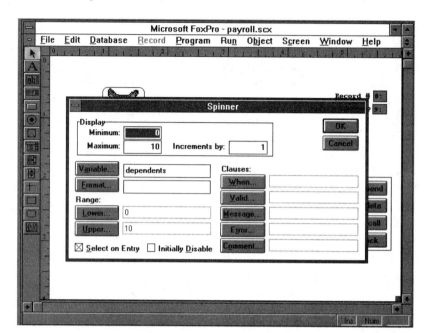

Figure 12.58 The Spinner dialog

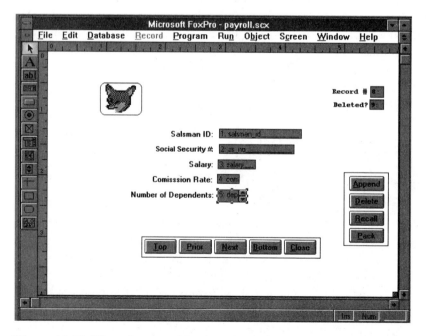

Figure 12.59 The spinner on the data form

Using Custom Data Screens 571

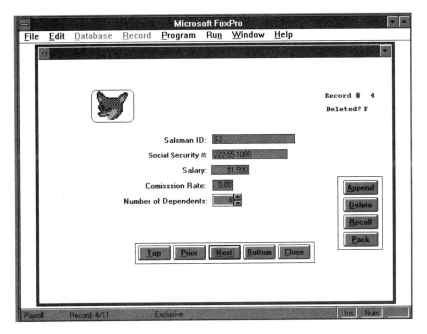

Figure 12.60 Displaying field values in a spinner

To add a screen background, choose the Layout option from the Screen menu. When the Screen Layout dialog appears, select the Color push button. After the Screen Color dialog appears, select the Wallpaper push button. You will be asked to specify the name of the .bmp file whose image you want to use as the screen background (wallpaper). At this point, select region.bmp in the c:\foxprow\tutorial subdirectory and select the Open button. In return, an image of the graphic file will be displayed in the Preview Picture box (see Figure 12.61).

When you return to the screen form, it will have the image of region.bmp as its background (see Figure 12.62). Subsequently, when you use the screen for displaying data in OFFICE.DBF, that image will be displayed accordingly on the screen (see Figure 12.63).

WORKING WITH MULTIPLE DATABASES

It is a relatively simple procedure to design a data screen for displaying and editing data in two databases at the same time—if there are one-to-one or many-to-one relations between them. For example, we can design a screen for displaying and modifying the data in the SALESMAN and OFFICE databases.

Before designing the screen form, you would link the two databases so that there are one-to-one or many-to-one relations between the parent file and the child file.

572   Understanding FoxPro 2.5 for Windows

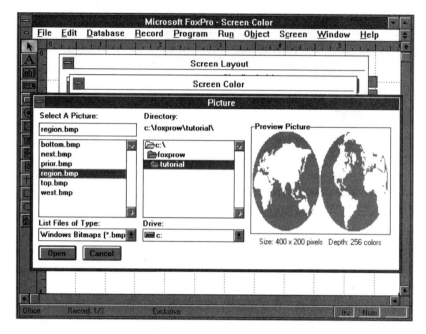

Figure 12.61 Previewing screen background in the Picture dialog

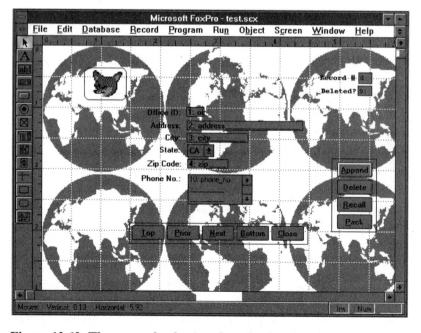

Figure 12.62 The screen background on the data form

Using Custom Data Screens 573

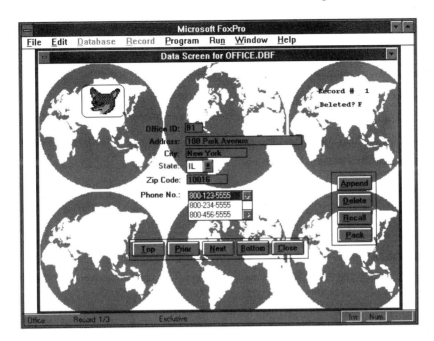

Figure 12.63 Displaying the screen background

Once the two databases are linked in this manner, each record displayed in the parent file will correspond to only one record in the child file. As an example, we will design a screen form for displaying the data in the SALESMAN and OFFICE databases.

You may want to review the procedure in Chapter 8 on how to link databases in the View window. As an exercise, link the SALESMAN and OFFICE databases in the View window, as shown in Figure 12.64. The two databases are related by using the OFFICE data field as the key field. Once you have linked the databases in the View window, you can then bring up a new screen form for displaying the data fields in the linked databases.

To do that, select the New option in the File menu to bring up the Screen Builder. In the Screen Builder window, design the form that includes all the data fields from the two databases that you would like to display. As a shortcut, you may choose the Quick Screen option from the Screen menu to place the data fields from the parent database (SALESMAN.DBF, which is highlighted in the View window). However, you need to place the data fields from the child database (the OFFICE.DBF) one at a time on the screen form. You can add the necessary control panels and other screen objects as you wish. An example of such a screen form (LINKSMOF.SCX) is shown in Figure 12.65.

In Figure 12.65 you can see that the data fields from both databases are displayed on the same screen. A control panel with the push buttons for navigating among

574   Understanding FoxPro 2.5 for Windows

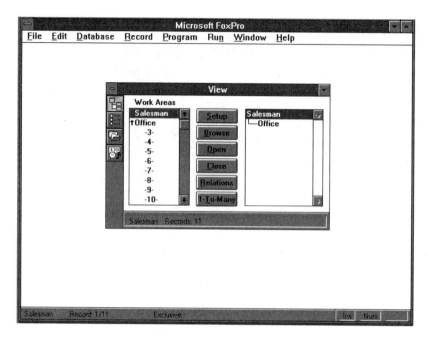

Figure 12.64 Linking two databases in the View window

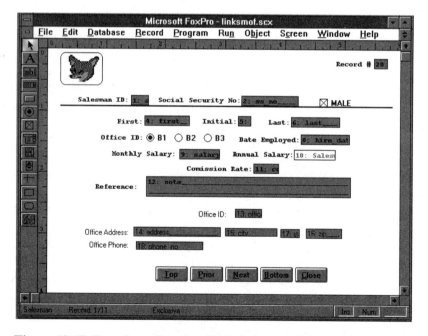

Figure 12.65 Data form showing fields from the linked databases

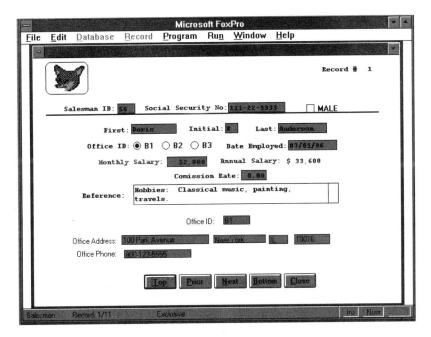

Figure 12.66 Displaying data from the linked databases

the records is shown at the bottom of the screen. When you use the screen form for displaying and editing data in two database, the screen will look similar to Figure 12.66. Note that each salesperson is linked to his or her office, and you also can edit the values in all the data fields in a normal manner.

As you can see, the screen can be useful for viewing and maintaining the existing data records in two database files simultaneously. You cannot, however, use the form to add new records to both databases; FoxPro allows you to add new records only to the parent file (in this case, SALESMAN.DBF) but not the child file (OFFICE.DBF). If you need to add new records to the OFFICE database, you must append them to the file individually on another data screen.

If you would like to use the screen for viewing data only, you can modify the screen form so that all the data fields are defined as output fields only. To do that, when you bring up the Field dialog for modifying the field definition, select the Output Field (Say) only radio button and check the Refresh Output Field box. The modified screen form (SHOWSMOF.SCX) will look something like Figure 12.67. Note that name of the salesperson is displayed with an expression that combines the first, initial, and last data fields in SALESMAN.DBF. The gender of the salesperson is displayed by using the IFF( ) function that displays the word "Male" when the value of the MALE logical field is true; otherwise, it displays the word "Female." An expression combining the address, city, state, and zip data fields is

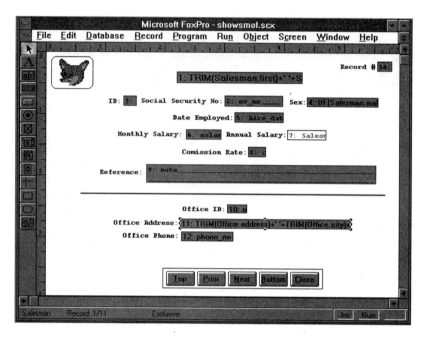

Figure 12.67 Data form for data display only

used to display the office address. The screen for displaying the information in the SALESMAN and OFFICE databases is shown in Figure 12.68.

In the preceding example, we linked two databases, and there are many-to-one relations between them. In relating the two databases, we specified the parent file (SALESMAN.DBF) so that multiple records are related to a single record in the child file (OFFICE.DBF). Since we can move between the records in the parent, we can view multiple records in the parent file in sequence. For each record in the parent file, you can view its related record in the child file.

If, however, many-to-many relations exist between the two databases, you would not be able to view multiple records in the child file that corresponds to each of the multiple records in the parent file. For example, there are many-to-many relations between SALESMAN.DBF and REGION.DBF. That is, each salesperson can have more than one sales region, and each sales region may be assigned to more than one salesperson. If you link the two databases by specifying SALESMAN.DBF as the parent and REGION.DBF as the child, you can show only one record from each file.

One solution to the problem is to link the two databases so that they have many-to-many relations via the third database. Recall that ASSIGN.DBF was used to link the records in SALESMAN.DBF and REGION.DBF. By specifying ASSIGN.DBF as the parent and SALESMAN.DBF and REGION.DBF as children in their relationship, we were able to view multiple records in the children files in

Using Custom Data Screens 577

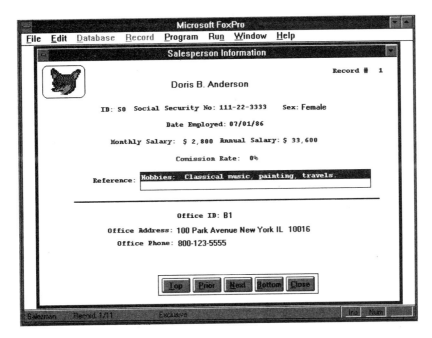

Figure 12.68 Viewing data from the two databases

sequence. The View window that relates the three databases is shown in Figure 12.69. ASSIGN.DBF is linked to REGION.DBF by using the REGION_ID field as the key field. Many-to-one relations exist between the parent and the child files; similarly, ASSIGN.DBF is linked to SALESMAN.DBF by using SALSMAN_ID, and there are also many-to-one relations between the parent and child files.

You can design a screen that displays all the data fields in the three databases. An example is SHOWREGN.SCX shown in Figure 12.70. The screen form is divided into three sections, each of which displays information taken from one database. Since the parent file is REGION.DBF, you can move around the records in that file. As a result, the control panel can be used to navigate the records in REGION.DBF. The other two sections on the screen are for displaying information taken from SALESMAN.DBF and OFFICE.DBF. Each time you display a record in the REGION file, one of the records in each of the SALESMAN.DBF and REGION files will be displayed on the screen. This can be seen in the data screen when it is used for displaying data in the three tables (see Figure 12.71).

You can see that the first record in ASSIGN.DBF shows R1 and S0 as the values for the REGION_ID and SALSMAN_ID fields. At the same time, the record corresponding to sales region R1 in REGION.DBF is shown at the lower right-hand side of the screen, displaying the name of the sales region and the regional manager. Information about salesperson S0, which is taken from SALESMAN.DBF, is also displayed on the screen. Since sales region R1 has more than one salesperson, you

578 Understanding FoxPro 2.5 for Windows

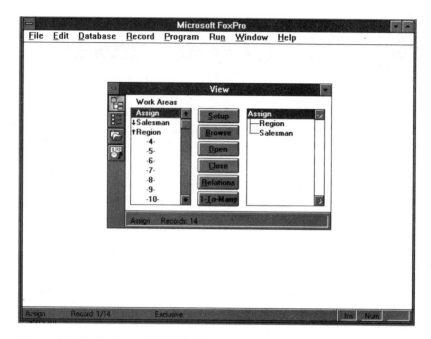

Figure 12.69 Linking SALESMAN.DBF and REGION.DBF through ASSIGN.DBF

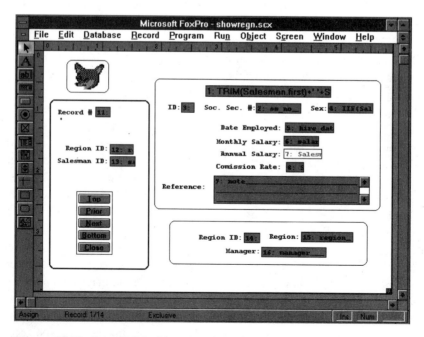

Figure 12.70 Data fields from the linked databases

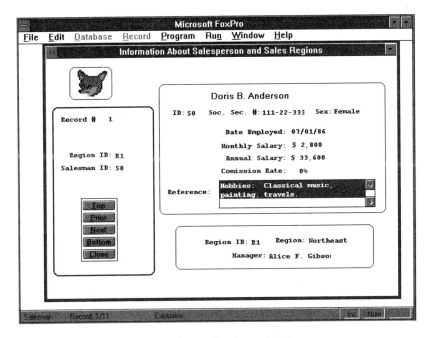

Figure 12.71 Viewing data from the three databases

can press the next push button to display another salesperson belonging to the same sales region. Keep pressing the next push button to view information about other sales regions and salespersons.

Using FoxPro Commands

The FoxPro command for invoking the Screen Builder is CREATE SCREEN or MODIFY SCREEN. To create a new screen layout, issue the CREATE SCREEN command in the following format:

```
CREATE SCREEN <screen filename>
```

In response, a blank screen is displayed in the Screen Builder window. Don't forget that it is necessary to open the database in the current work area before you issue the command. If you forget to take this step, you will be prompted to open the database when you attempt to place any data fields in the screen layout. For example, to create a new screen named TEST.SCX for the SALESMAN database with the Screen Builder, issue the following commands:

```
USE SALESMAN
CREATE SCREEN TEST
```

Likewise, if you are creating a screen and using more than one database, the databases must be linked before issuing the CREATE SCREEN command.

To modify an existing screen file, issue the MODIFY SCREEN command in the following format:

```
MODIFY SCREEN <screen filename>
```

To make changes to the screen file created earlier, for example, issue the following command:

```
MODIFY SCREEN TEST.SCX
```

After you have generated the screen program file that contains the screen code for the screen layout, execute the program by issuing the DO command:

```
DO <name of screen program file>
```

To execute TEST.SPR, for example, issue the following command:

```
DO TEST.SPR
```

Chapter Summary

This chapter detailed the steps for using the powerful Screen Builder to create custom data screens. It illustrated how these screens can be used to view and modify data, as well as to add new records to existing databases. These screens can be designed for one or more databases.

The two kinds of data screen layouts—desktop and window—were described. The type of screen you decide to create is determined in a window layout, but regardless of the type you choose, it is created by placing the screen objects in the Screen Builder window. These screen objects include data fields taken from one or more databases, text for describing the data, graphics objects (boxes and lines) and buttons (push buttons, radio buttons), check boxes, and scrollable lists.

The chapter also explained how to save a screen layout in an .SCX file. A screen program (.SPR) file is then generated from the screen file. To use the data screen, the screen program file is executed.

The preceding chapters specified all the components of a relational database system. The next chapter explains how to tie them together with a custom menu system.

13
Putting It All Together

An Overview

The early chapters of this book defined and described the principles for designing and developing a relational database system. Subsequent chapters detailed the procedures for creating and modifying databases with FoxPro. In addition, you learned how to use:

- The powerful RQBE Builder to extract meaningful information from databases.
- The Report Builder to produce professional reports.
- The Label Designer to design and output mailing labels.
- The Screen Builder to design custom data screens that enable you to view and modify data in existing databases, as well to aid in the data entry process.

This final chapter describes how to design and create a custom menu that integrates all of the above information.

A Custom Menu System

The only menu system that we have used up to this point is the System menu provided by FoxPro. The System menu bar contains a standard set of menu pads, each of which includes the standard set of menu options in the menu popup. Although many of these menu options are useful for certain applications, you may not need all of them in every database application. As a result, you may find it useful to create a customized menu system that includes only those menu options that are tailored for a specific application. This means that not only can you create a menu system that is more compact, but that you also can define a customized menu system that has options for specific operations you commonly perform.

For example, you ordinarily use the Open option in the System menu's File menu popup to open a file. This menu option has been deliberately designed to be so general that you can use it to open any type of file. Consequently, once you have selected this option, you must still specify a file type and a filename before you can actually open a file. A custom menu, on the other hand, allows you to create a menu option that is specifically designed to carry out a particular predefined operation. For example, you can define a menu option for opening a specific file. When you select that menu option, that file will be opened without FoxPro requiring any further information.

With a custom menu system, you can execute database management functions by selecting the menu options that are specifically defined for your application. You can, for instance, include a menu pad for viewing each of the existing databases on custom data screens. You also can use the menu options in another menu pad to make changes to your existing databases. And when producing custom reports, you may choose another set of menu options from the custom menu.

Besides custom menu options that you create, you also can include some standard options provided by the FoxPro System menu. You may, for example, want to include the Help, Filer, Calculator, and Calendar/Diary menu options that are provided in the FoxPro Help menu popup. Similarly, you can include the View option from the Window menu popup of the FoxPro System menu so that you can use it to open any existing databases. Or you may decide to include those menu options from the Window menu popup that clear the screen desktop area or manipulate the active window. Figure 13.1 shows an example of such a custom menu bar.

This menu bar has seven menu pads in the custom menu bar: File, ViewData, EditData, Report, Label, Window, and Help. The structure of the custom menu is depicted in Figure 13.2.

THE FILE MENU PAD

The custom system menu pad contains two menu options in its menu popup (see Figure 13.3). The first option, Print Setup provides a means for setting up your printer. With this option you can select the default printer or another installed printer. You also can specify the print orientation for the output. The Quit option, when selected, exits your application and returns you to the FoxPro System menu.

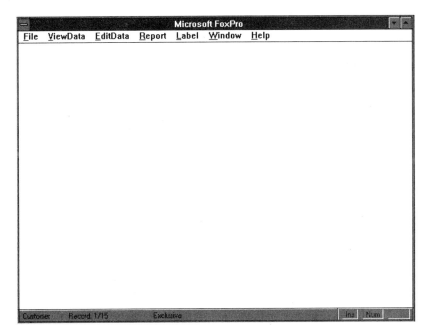

Figure 13.1 A custom menu bar

THE VIEWDATA MENU PAD

The second menu pad in the custom menu bar is for displaying data in various databases. The ViewData menu pad contains three menu options in its menu popup (see Figure 13.4), which you can use to view data in the SALESMAN, OFFICE, and REGION databases in different combinations.

Viewing the SALESMAN and OFFICE Databases

The Salesman/Office option allows you to view information about a salesperson and the sales office to which he or she is assigned. When this option is selected, data from the SALESMAN and OFFICE databases is presented on a custom data screen, as shown in Figure 13.5. This figure shows all the data in the SALESMAN and OFFICE databases for Doris B. Anderson. All the data fields in the SALESMAN database are displayed in the upper portion of the screen; the lower portion contains its related record from the OFFICE database. Note that all the field values are shown in the display-only mode, and their contents cannot be edited.

The two databases are linked according to the values in the OFFICE_ID data field. The SALESMAN database was designated as the parent and the OFFICE database was designated as the child. As a result, you can scan the data records in

584   Understanding FoxPro 2.5 for Windows

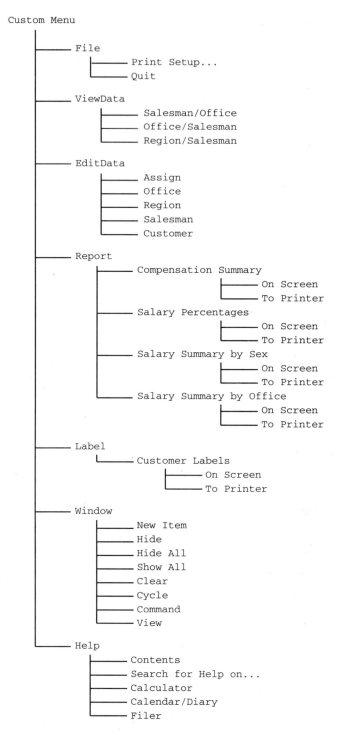

Figure 13.2 Structure of the customized menu system

Putting It All Together 585

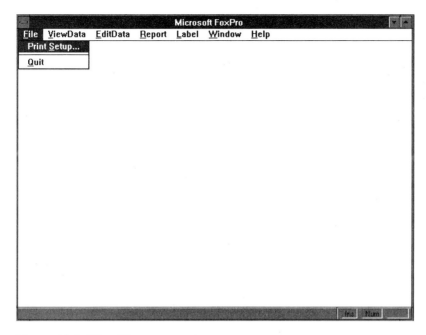

Figure 13.3 The File menu options

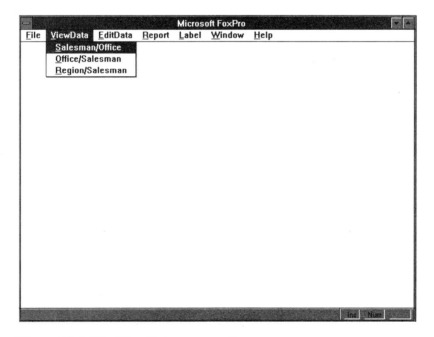

Figure 13.4 The ViewData menu options

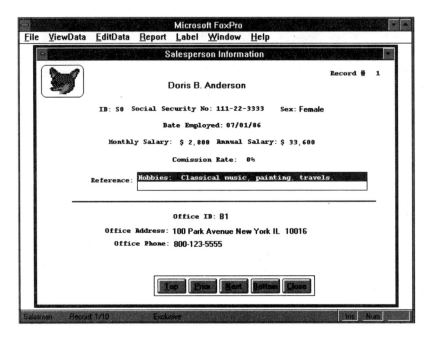

Figure 13.5 Viewing data in the SALESMAN and OFFICE databases

the SALESMAN database using the Top, Prior, Next, and Bottom push buttons provided in the custom data screen. When you do so, its related record in the OFFICE database is displayed on the screen as well.

In designing the menu option that displays this custom screen directly, we have had to do some preliminary work. First, we used the View window to open and link the two database files; in addition, we designated the last index tag as the master index for the SALESMAN database. Next, we used the Screen Builder to design the screen layout, which we have saved as a screen file named SHOWSMOF.SCX.

This custom menu system allows only one data window to be open at a time, so you must select the Close push button when you have finished viewing the data. When you do this, all work areas will be closed and the custom menu will again be displayed.

Viewing the OFFICE and SALESMAN Databases

Data viewed after selecting the second option (Office/Salesman) in the ViewData menu popup appears similar to that of the first menu option (Salesman/Office). When you select this option, however, the OFFICE and SALESMAN databases are linked using the OFFICE database as the parent and SALESMAN as the child.

Putting It All Together 587

Figure 13.6 Viewing data in the OFFICE and SALESMAN databases

Therefore, data fields of the OFFICE database are shown on the top of the screen, and the lower portion of the screen shows the data fields of the SALESMAN database (see Figure 13.6).

Since there is a one-to-many relationship between the OFFICE and SALESMAN databases, ordinarily we would want to show all the salespeople who are assigned to a given sales office. For example, Figure 13.6 shows information about sales office B1 and the first salesperson—Doris B. Anderson—who is assigned to it. To see the next salesperson assigned to the same office, if there is one, simply select the Next push button.

If, however, we simply create a custom screen modeled after our previous screen, SHOWSMOF.SCX, and continue to read the records in the two database files, our application will not work as we expect. Because OFFICE is the parent database, selecting the Top, Prior, Next, and Bottom push buttons will move the record pointer in the OFFICE database. Whenever the record pointer moves, our screen will display only the first record in the SALESMAN database for that particular office. Because moving the record pointer in the child database is automatically handled by FoxPro whenever the record pointer in the parent database moves, we cannot view information on other salespeople assigned to a particular sales office.

There are a number of ways to create the kind of data screen that we want. Perhaps the easiest, since it does not require a knowledge of programming or of

588 Understanding FoxPro 2.5 for Windows

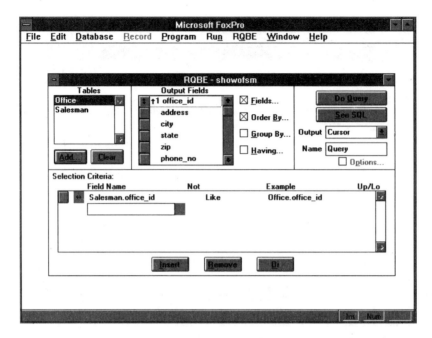

Figure 13.7 Linking OFFICE and SALESMAN with a RQBE query

FoxPro command syntax, is to create a query that generates a set of records that relate each sales office to all the salespeople who are assigned to it. Such an RQBE query (saved as SHOWOFSM.QPR) is shown in Figure 13.7.

The RQBE query shown in this figure links the two databases according to their values in each database's OFFICE_ID data field. All the data fields in both databases are selected to be included in the query's output, with the exception of the SALESMAN.OFFICE_ID field (since it is identical to the OFFICE.OFFICE_ID field). The resulting records are ordered by their values in the OFFICE_ID field. Because we have chosen Cursor as the output destination, output from the query will be stored in a temporary query table.

The records output by the query are shown in a Browse window in Figure 13.8. Notice that the query table has, in effect, joined the two databases together. Each record in the SALESMAN database has been matched with its corresponding information in the OFFICE database. As a result, we can use this table to easily view all the salespeople who are assigned to a given sales office.

Once you have developed and executed the query, you can create the screen (SHOWSMOF.SCX) shown in Figure 13.9 using the temporary database resulting from the query. This screen displays all the data fields from the temporary output database in display-only (Output File (SAY) mode) and contains a set of push buttons that allow you to navigate through the database.

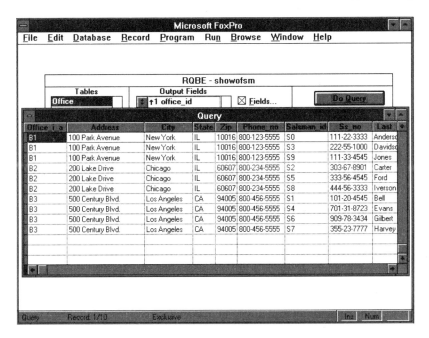

Figure 13.8 Records resulting from the RQBE

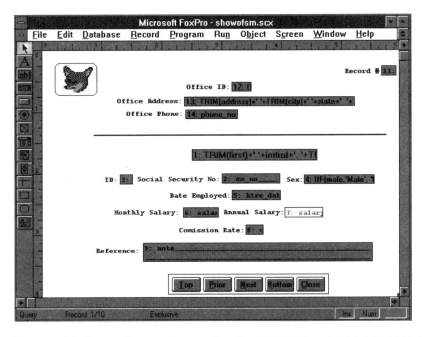

Figure 13.9 Screen layout for viewing the OFFICE and SALESMAN databases

Viewing the REGION and SALESMAN Databases

To view information about the sales regions and the salespeople assigned to them, select the Region/Salesman option from the ViewData menu popup. That information is displayed in the custom data screen, as shown in Figure 13.10.

Data records in the REGION database are linked to those in SALESMAN through the information in the ASSIGN database. Many-to-many relations exist between the REGION and SALESMAN databases, which, if you recall, means that each sales region may have more than one salesperson assigned to it and each salesperson may be assigned to more than one sales region. These relations are defined using the records in the ASSIGN database, whereby each record in the ASSIGN database file relates a sales region and a salesperson.

Information about the salesperson and sales region is shown on the screen in separate sections, as are the contents of the ASSIGN database that links the two files. Since ASSIGN.DBF is the parent in the database link, you can use the push buttons to move between its records. And because we have defined both the SALESMAN and REGION databases as children of ASSIGN, we can access all information from each relevant record in the child databases. For example, if you select the Next push button from the control panel on the data screen, the next record in ASSIGN.DBF will be displayed. At the same time, information on the

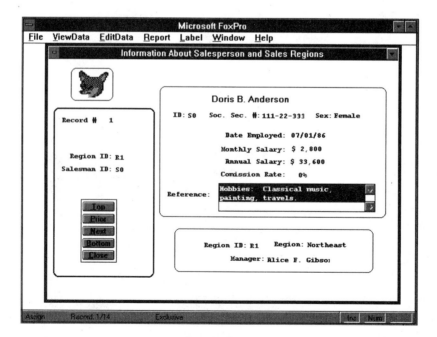

Figure 13.10 Viewing data in the REGION and SALESMAN databases

corresponding region and the salesperson will be displayed in their respective windows.

The data screen shown in Figure 13.10 was created by first linking the three databases in the View window. ASSIGN.DBF was linked with REGION.DBF according to values in the REGION_ID data field. ASSIGN.DBF also was linked with SALESMAN.DBF via the SALESMAN_ID data field.

After linking the three database files, the custom screen (named SHOW-REGN.SCX) was created with the Screen Builder by placing their data fields in the screen layout in Chapter 12. All the data fields are specified as display-only fields using Output File (Say) mode.

THE EDITDATA MENU PAD

The EditData menu pad on the custom menu bar is for editing data in each of the databases. It contains five options in its menu popup: Assign, Office, Region, Salesman, and Customer (see Figure 13.11).

These menu options can be used to modify the contents of existing database files or to add new records to the databases. Select, for instance, the Assign option from the EditData menu popup to edit the data records in the ASSIGN database; or choose the Office option to add new records to the OFFICE database.

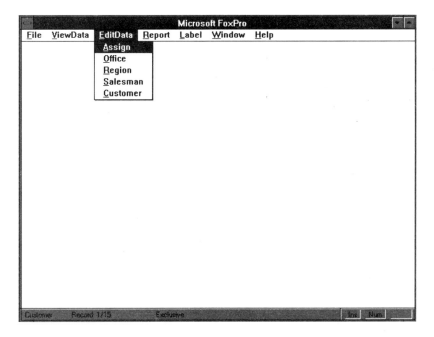

Figure 13.11 The EditData menu options

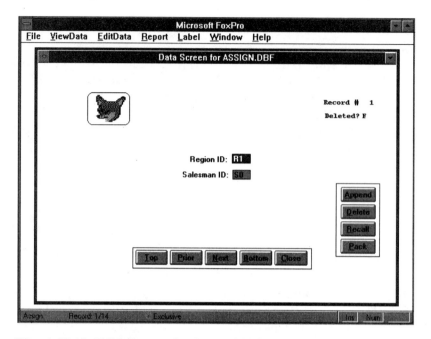

Figure 13.12 Editing records of the ASSIGN database

Editing the ASSIGN Database

When the Assign option is chosen from the EditData menu popup, data in the ASSIGN database is displayed on a custom screen, as illustrated in Figure 13.12. Each record in the database is used to relate a salesman to his/her sales region. The design and layout of this screen is very similar to the OFFICE.SCX screen that we built in Chapter 12.

Editing the OFFICE Database

The Office option in the EditData menu popup works like the Assign menu option. When it is selected, the contents of the current record in the OFFICE database are displayed for editing on a custom data screen, as shown in Figure 13.13. The screen form was created in Chapter 12 and saved in OFFICE.SCX.

Editing the REGION Database

The Region option in the EditData menu popup enables you to edit data in the REGION database. When this option is selected, the custom screen shown in Figure 13.14 appears. The design and layout of this screen is very similar to previous editing screens that we have built.

Putting It All Together 593

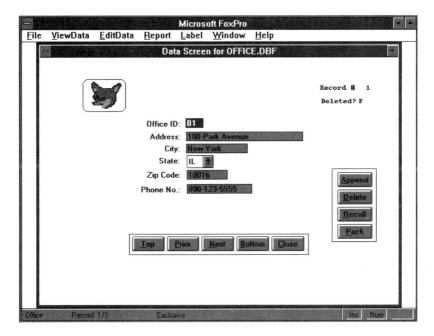

Figure 13.13 Editing records of the OFFICE database

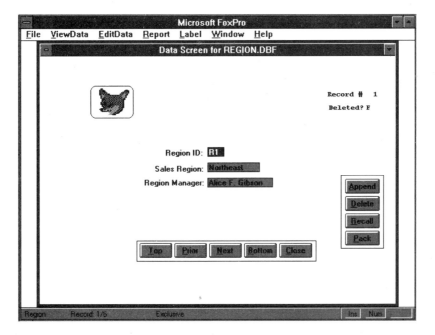

Figure 13.14 Editing records of the REGION database

Editing the SALESMAN Database

The Salesman option in the EditData menu popup allows for modification of the contents of the SALESMAN database. When it is selected, a custom data screen is displayed in Edit mode, and all the data fields in the current record of that database. Note in Figure 13.15 that some field values are displayed in text boxes while others are shown in check boxes, popups, and as radio buttons. The screen layout (saved as SALESMAN.SCX) is the same as that created in Chapter 12.

Editing the CUSTOMER Database

Like all the other editing screens, a custom data screen is created for making changes to the data in the records of the CUSTOMER database. To edit in this database, select the Customer option from the EditData menu popup for all the data fields in the CUSTOMER database to be displayed in Edit mode, together with the control push buttons (see Figure 13.16). The screen layout was created and saved as CUSTOMER.SCX in the usual manner with the Screen Builder.

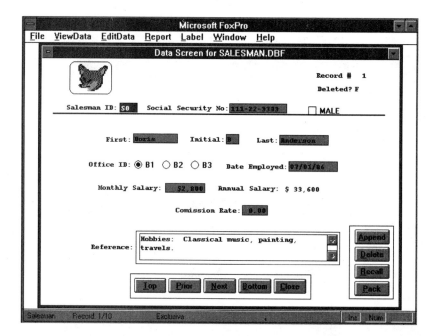

Figure 13.15 Editing records of the SALESMAN database

Putting It All Together 595

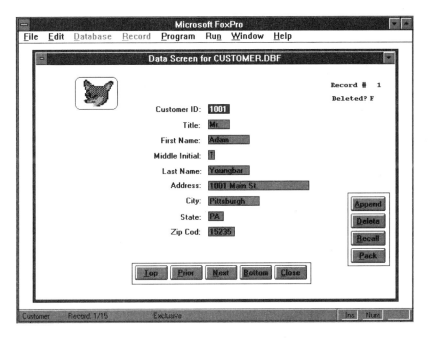

Figure 13.16 Editing records of the CUSTOMER database

THE REPORT MENU PAD

The Report menu pad is designed for producing custom reports that were created at an earlier time. In Chapter 11, we created four summary reports using the salary values in the SALESMAN database. One of the reports, saved as PAYREPT.FRX lists all the sales staff's salaries, while another one named PERCENT.FRX shows their salaries in percentages. The third report, which we saved as BYMALE.FRX, summarized the salaries of the sales staff delineated by sex; the fourth report, which we saved as BYOFFICE.FRX, listed the total salaries by sales office.

Figure 13.17 shows the four menu options that enable you to produce the salary summary reports. Further, each of these options has a set of two menu options. One is for displaying the report on the screen for preview purposes, and the other is for printing the report. Choose, for instance, the Compensation Summary, and another menu popup will appear. If you then select the On Screen option from the popup, the summary report will be displayed on screen, as displayed in Figure 13.18.

To print the report, select the To Printer option from the menu popup of the Compensation Summary.

Similarly, you can select the Salary Percentages option from the Report menu popup to preview and print the report. When you preview the report on the screen, it should look like Figure 13.19.

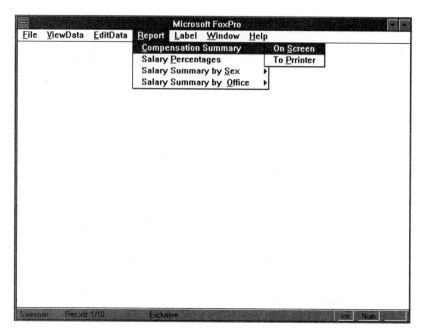

Figure 13.17 The Report menu options

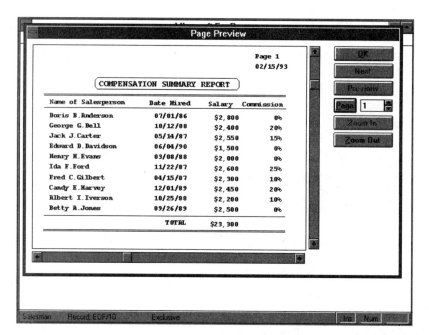

Figure 13.18 Previewing the Compensation Summary report

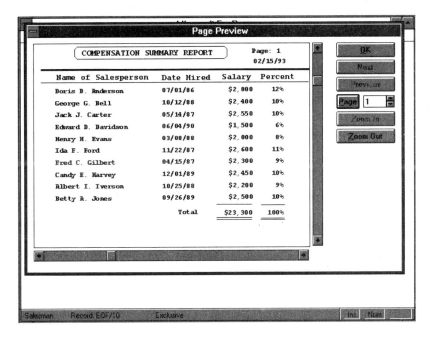

Figure 13.19 Previewing the Salary Percentages report

The Salary Summary by Sex and the Salary Summary by Office will be displayed for preview (see Figures 13.20 and 13.21) when their appropriate menu options are chosen.

THE LABEL MENU PAD

The Label menu pad includes a menu option that enables you to produce mailing labels from data in the CUSTOMER database. The Customer Labels menu popup, in turn, has two menu options, which you can see in Figure 13.22. As with reports described above, labels can be either previewed on-screen or printed, and the two menu options provide for these choices. The on-screen option is shown in Figure 13.23. The label design was created in Chapter 12 and saved as CUSTOMER.LBX.

THE WINDOW MENU PAD

The Window menu pad is included in the custom menu bar to provide the tools that enable you to manipulate the active window. Eight options are included in the Window menu popup and are shown in Figure 13.24.

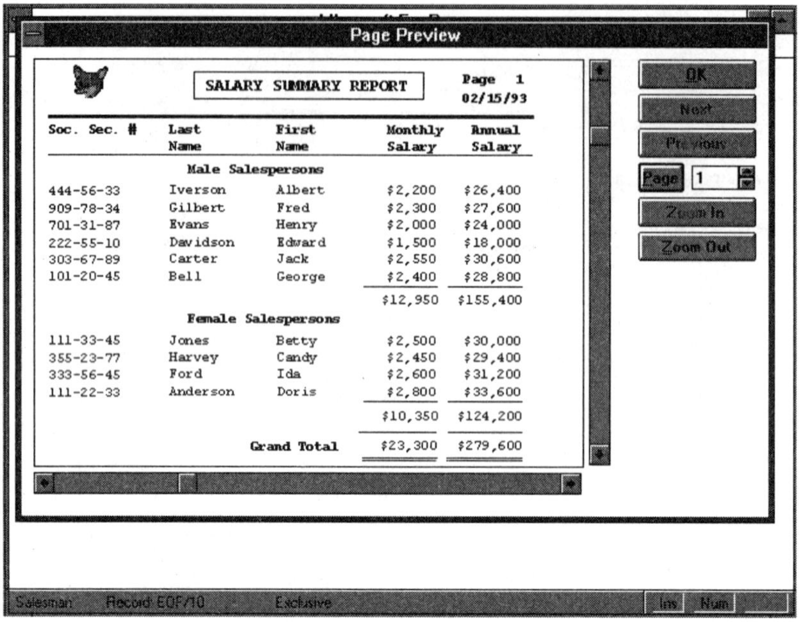

598 Understanding FoxPro 2.5 for Windows

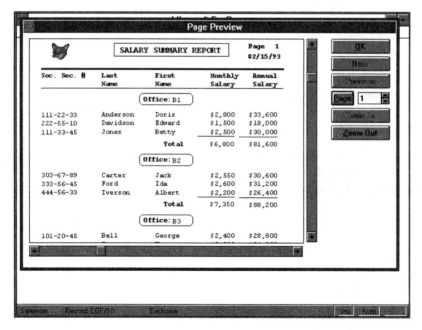

Figure 13.20 Previewing the Salary Summary by Sex report

Figure 13.21 Previewing the Salary Summary by Office report

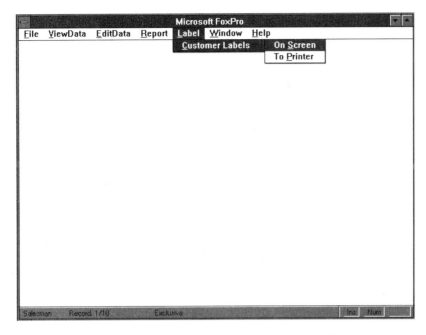

Figure 13.22 The Label menu options

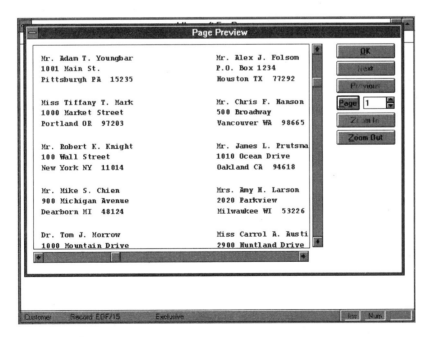

Figure 13.23 Previewing mailing labels

Figure 13.24 The Window menu options

All of these menu options are borrowed from the Window menu pad in the FoxPro System menu, and their functions are identical. Thus, you can use the View option to bring up the View window, select the Clear option to clear the desktop screen area, or choose Cycle to move between windows, etc. You also can bring up the Command window with the Command option.

THE HELP MENU PAD

The Help menu pad shows five options, all of which are borrowed from the FoxPro System menu (see Figure 13.25). The first two options, Contents and Search for Help on, enable you to access help by subject or keyword. The Calculator and Calendar/Diary are useful desktop accessories; the Filer option allows you to manage your disk files without leaving the program.

This completes our preview of the elements of the custom menu system. In the course of it, we also have created all of the elements—the editing screens, queries, and report and label forms—that our custom menu system will contain. What remains is to define the actual custom menu that will tie these various elements and procedures together.

Figure 13.25 The Help menu options

THE FOXPRO MENU BUILDER

FoxPro's Menu Builder is the tool that is used to design and create custom menu systems. It allows for broad flexibility in designing your own menus. With the Menu Builder, for example, you can:

- Define individual menu pads in a menu bar.

- Define a hotkey that allows the menu pad to be activated quickly with the keyboard by pressing Alt along with one other key.

- Define the operation of the menu pad. The menu pad itself can execute a single FoxPro command or a procedure (a set of FoxPro commands), or it can call a submenu (a menu popup) that contains a set of menu options.

- Define the operation of a submenu option. Like a menu pad, the submenu option can execute a single FoxPro command, a procedure (a set of commands), or it can call another submenu.

- Define a shortcut or accelerator key—a single key or key combination that, when pressed, will activate a submenu option. For example, pressing F1 activates the Help submenu option on the System menu pad.

The steps involved in creating a customized menu system are very similar to those described for creating a custom screen in the previous chapter. Once you have finished using the Menu Builder to design a custom menu, you can save it as a file with an .MNX extension; this is actually a special kind of database file that FoxPro uses exclusively for storing menu information. Then, when you select the Generate option from the Program menu pad, FoxPro generates a menu program file with a file extension of .MNX. The menu is executed by selecting the Run command from the Program menu pad and selecting the .MNX file.

Creating a Quick Menu

The first step in creating a custom menu is, of course, opening the Menu Builder. To do this, select the New option from the File menu popup. When the New dialog appears, select the Menu radio button followed by the New push button. FoxPro will open the Menu Builder's Menu Design window, which is shown in Figure 13.26, and add a Menu menu pad to the System menu bar.

In the same way that it lets you define a custom report or a custom screen, FoxPro allows you to adopt two approaches to build a custom menu system. You can design your menus completely from scratch, or you can copy FoxPro's default system menu and modify it until it suits the requirements of your application. We will once

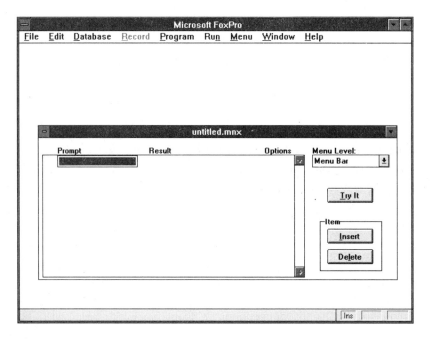

Figure 13.26 The Menu Designer window

Putting It All Together 603

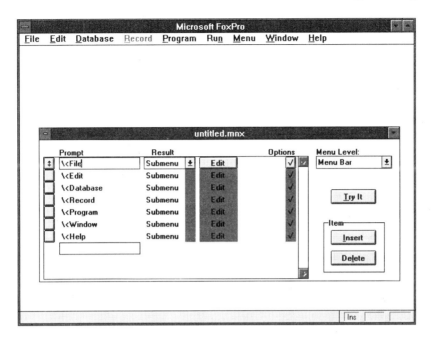

Figure 13.27 The Quick menu

again use this latter approach, in part because it will allow us to create our custom menu with far less effort and risk of error, but also because examining the structure of the FoxPro System menu is itself valuable in learning to use the Menu Builder.

To copy FoxPro's default system menu, select the Quick Menu option from the Menu menu popup. The result, which is shown in Figure 13.27, is a menu structure that is identical to the FoxPro System menu. Let's begin by exploring the System menu in the Menu Design window; from there, we can figure out how to build our own custom menu.

DEFINING THE MENU PAD PROMPTS

As you can see by comparing the contents of the Menu Design window's Prompt list box with the System menu bar, the Prompt list box is used to define the labels for each menu pad. When the menu program file is executed, each menu pad appears in the order in which it is listed in the Prompt list box. You can change the contents of the Prompt list box in any of several ways:

- You can delete unwanted menu pads by positioning the cursor on the unwanted menu prompt and pressing the DEL key, selecting the Delete push button in the Item group box, or selecting the Delete Item command from the Menu menu popup; or by pressing Ctrl+E, which is a shortcut key for the Delete Item command.

- You can insert a blank menu prompt by positioning the cursor on the prompt that you would like to have appear immediately after the new menu pad. Then you can select either the Insert push button in the Item group box or the Insert Item command from the Menu menu popup; or press Ctrl+I, the shortcut key combination for the Item Delete command. As a result, the Menu Builder will insert a new prompt and give it the default label "New Title."

- You can rearrange existing menu prompts by clicking the mouse on the button to the left of the prompt and dragging the prompt to its new location. With the keyboard, simply select the item you would like to move and then press the Ctrl key along with the up- or down-arrow key to move the item to its new location.

In addition, any single character in a prompt can be designated as a hotkey. A hotkey is defined by placing the \< symbol before the letter in the prompt that you want to designate as the hotkey. The hotkey is normally displayed underlined in the menu bar. For example, the prompt for the first menu pad is:

```
\<File
```

Although for the purpose of demonstration we designated 'F' as the hotkey, it is important to note that FoxPro, by default, automatically selects the first letter of the prompt as the hotkey if one is not designated.

DEFINING THE MENU PAD RESULTS

The result area of the window allows you to determine what happens when a particular menu pad is selected. In Figure 13.27, for example, each of the menu pads in the FoxPro system menu "results" in a submenu—that is, a submenu pops up when the menu pad is selected. So, for example, when you select the File menu pad, the File submenu or File menu popup is displayed. Submenu is the default result when a new menu pad is created; notice also that it is accompanied by the Edit push button to the right of the popup.

However, as Figure 13.28 shows, Submenu is just one option in a popup that contains four choices. The other three possible results are:

- *Command.* If the result of a menu pad is designated as a command, FoxPro will execute a single command when that menu option is selected. When Command is selected from the Result popup, the Edit push button that ordinarily appears beside the Submenu option in the result popup is replaced with a text box in which you can enter the command that is to be executed. If a command already has been entered, it will be displayed in the text box.

Putting It All Together   605

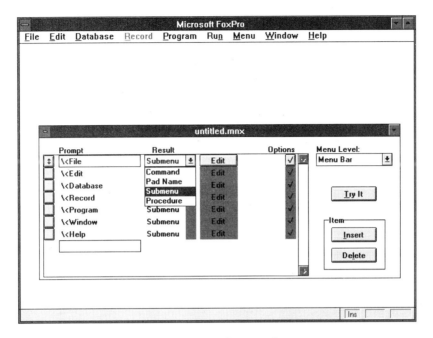

Figure 13.28 Defining the menu option result

- *Pad Name.* Selecting this option allows you to incorporate a menu pad from another menu system. This is an advanced feature, however, that requires some programming knowledge.
- *Procedure.* Designating the result of a menu pad as a procedure causes FoxPro to execute a set of commands (a procedure) that is stored along with the menu. Selecting the Edit push button will open an editing window where a new procedure can be entered or an existing procedure can be examined or edited.

DEFINING PROMPT OPTIONS

In Figure 13.27, note that the Options check boxes for each of the menu pads are all checked. Selecting the Options check box for a particular prompt opens the Prompt Options dialog shown in Figure 13.29. This dialog allows you to add a number of enhancements and fine points to your menu pad, although normally you will probably want to use only the Shortcut option. For example:

- The Comment text box allows you to enter notes to yourself or internal documentation about the menu item. Whatever you enter in the text box has absolutely no effect on the menu pad or on the operation of the menu; it serves

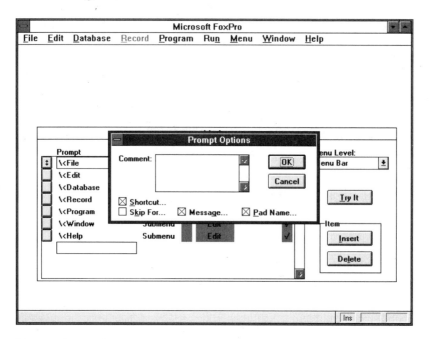

Figure 13.29 The Prompt Options dialog

only to store comments that might be useful for you or for someone else using the Menu Builder to examine your menu system.

- The Shortcut push button, if selected, opens the Key Definition dialog, which allows you to define a shortcut key combination (sometimes called an accelerator key) that provides a quicker method for selecting a particular menu item with the keyboard. If you examine the Key Definition dialog for the prompts that appear on the FoxPro System menu bar, note that their shortcut keys are the same as their hotkeys; this is required for menu pads if they are to be activated by the use of the ALT key. Figure 13.30, for example, shows that the shortcut key sequence to select the File menu pad is the Alt+F key combination. Return to the Prompt Options dialog by selecting the OK button.

- Selecting the Skip For push button from the Prompt Options dialog opens the Expression Builder, where you can enter an expression that returns a logical result. The result of this expression then determines whether or not that menu option will be available at any particular time. These options will still appear on a menu, but their text will appear in a light color and they will be disabled. For example, if you were to look at the FoxPro System menu bar inside the Edit drop-down list, you'd notice that only the Undo Paste and Select All options are enabled. This option is primarily of use to FoxPro programmers and developers.

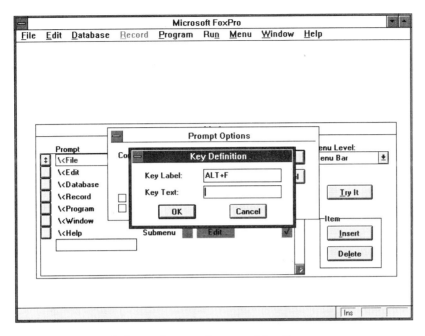

Figure 13.30 Defining a shortcut key combination

- The Message push button displays the Expression Builder so that you can specify a message to be displayed in the status bar when the menu pad is selected.
- The Pad Name push button allows you to give the menu pad a name, which in turn allows you to use it both in other menus that you may build and to refer to it by name in FoxPro menuing commands. This, however, is an advanced feature that requires a knowledge of programming.

OTHER FEATURES OF THE MENU DESIGN WINDOW

The upper right-hand corner of the Menu Design window contains a popup that shows the menu object you are currently defining. As you begin to define your menu, you can move it to navigate between submenus and from a submenu to the menu bar. Right now, however, because we are at the topmost level of our menu—the menu bar—the popup contains only one item. Therefore, it merely reports that you are working with the menu bar; you cannot select any lower-level menus with it. Later, we will see how it can be used to help us maneuver through the menu system that we are building.

Right beneath this popup, the Try It push button allows you to preview your menu system as you are creating it. When you select this push button, FoxPro replaces the current menu with the menu that you are in the process of building

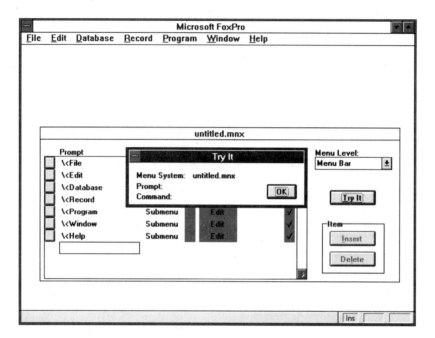

Figure 13.31 The Try It dialog

and opens the Try It dialog shown in Figure 13.31. You then can test your menu by selecting individual menu pads, checking your menu popups, selecting individual menu options, and trying out shortcut key and hotkey combinations. FoxPro will display the name of the menu prompt that is selected in the Prompt text box. Note, however, that while the menu itself will operate normally, the commands or procedures attached to menu options will not execute.

DEFINING THE SYSTEM MENU POPUP

We have, thus far, used the Menu Builder to explore only the topmost level of the FoxPro System menu. Before we continue our exploration by examining a particular menu popup, let us review menu terminology as it applies to FoxPro menus, in order to avoid ambiguity or confusion. The topmost level of a menu system is known as the **menu bar**; it is located along the top of the FoxPro window. Each option or label on the menu bar is called a **menu pad**. Ordinarily, although not always, selecting a menu pad opens a second menu known as a **menu popup**. This menu popup in turn contains additional items, known as **menu options**. Selecting one of these usually leads to some action (a program executes, a dialog box opens, etc.), although it can also open another menu.

To this point, we have been examining the FoxPro menu bar. Each item in the Prompt list box corresponds to a menu pad. If we select one of these menu pads from the system menu, we open a menu popup. For example, selecting the Help menu pad from the menu bar opens the Help menu popup, which consists of eight menu options (Contents, Search for Help on..., How to Use Help, About FoxPro..., Calculator, Calendar/Diary, Filer, Puzzle). In the FoxPro Menu Builder, these menu popups are known as submenus. Note that, in Figure 13.27, Submenu is the result of each of the prompts that represent pads on the FoxPro System menu bar.

To define a submenu or view an existing submenu, select the Edit push button that corresponds to a particular prompt whose result is a submenu. For example, if we click on the Help's Edit push button, the Menu Design window will now look like Figure 13.32, as FoxPro shows the Help submenu.

Although the general appearance of the Menu Level: popup is virtually identical whether a menu bar or a submenu is displayed, several differences are worth noting. First, along with text to describe particular menu options, FoxPro allows you to include lines that separate groups of options in a menu popup. For example, the FoxPro Help menu popup contains one such line to separate the Help options from the FoxPro desktop accessories (Calculator, Calendar/Diary, Filer, etc.). To include a line in a menu popup instead of text, enter \- in the Prompt text box; when your menu popup is executed, FoxPro will include a line across the width of the popup. Although the Menu Level: popup in Figure 13.32 shows that a result (a Bar # named _mst_sp100) is specified for the line, in fact, lines are not executable menu items; therefore, you can ignore their accompanying results when you define them.

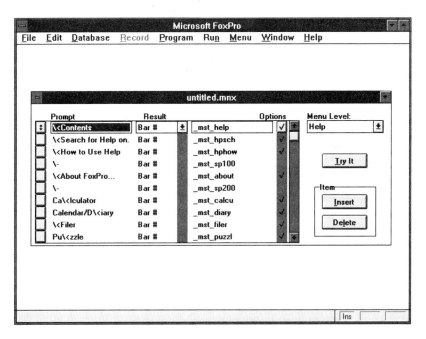

Figure 13.32 The Help menu option prompts

A second notable difference is that each Result popup now displays Bar # instead of Submenu. This is a new option that did not appear in the Result popup when we were working with the menu bar. And if we examine the options available in the Result popup, we would see that, although three options (Command, Procedure, and Submenu) are common to both popups, the Pad Name option in our previous Result popup has been replaced by the Bar # option.

Briefly, the Bar # option allows you to execute the same procedures in your own menus that are available from the FoxPro System menu. To do this, enter the bar name for the proper procedure in the Result text box. For example, a Bar # of _mfi_open will open the File Open dialog, while _mst_help will open FoxPro's Help window.

The third notable difference is the popup in the upper right-hand corner of the Menu Level: popup, which now reads Help instead of Menu Bar. This is the name that FoxPro assigns to the menu popup; usually, it corresponds closely to the menu pad prompt or, if a menu popup is called by another menu popup, to the menu item prompt. If you examine this popup, you will notice that it now contains two elements: Menu Bar and Help. If you select Menu Bar, FoxPro will update the Menu Level: popup to display the menu pads on the menu bar. So, while the Menu Builder provides an Edit push button to allow you to move from a higher- to a lower-level menu, this popup allows you to navigate from lower-level menus back to higher-level menus, from submenus to menu bars, or from submenus to their submenus to their menu bars.

MODIFYING THE QUICK MENU

With our admittedly hasty exploration of the Menu Builder complete, you have learned enough about how menus are constructed with the Menu Builder to move from observation to creation. As you may recall, one of our purposes in creating a quick menu was to make a copy of the default FoxPro System menu that we could examine. Our larger goal, however, was to "borrow" the FoxPro System menu so that we could retain some parts of it while modifying it by deleting those parts that we no longer need, and adding some other parts required by the custom menu system that was discussed at the very beginning of this chapter. In the remainder of this chapter, we will finally create and implement our customized menu system.

Deleting Existing Menu Pads

If you have not already done so, return to the menu bar from one of the submenus (make sure that Menu Bar is shown in the popup in the upper right-hand corner of the Menu Level: popup). Then we can begin by deleting unwanted menu pads. To

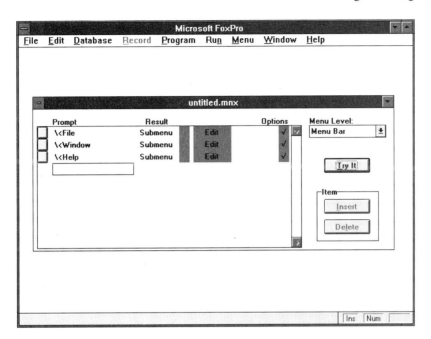

Figure 13.33 The Menu Designer window after deleting menu pads

do this, select the File menu pad and click on the Delete push button or press Ctrl+E. When you confirm that you want to delete the submenu, FoxPro will delete the File menu pad and its associated submenu. Since our custom menu will include only the File, Window, and menu pads, you also can delete other menu pads. When you are finished, your screen should look something like Figure 13.33.

Deleting Existing Menu Options

The next step is to delete unwanted menu options from the Window and Help menu pads. To delete a menu option from the menu pad, its submenu must be displayed in the Menu Level: popup and the menu option must be selected. The menu option then can be deleted in the manner discussed above—pressing the Delete push button or typing Ctrl+E.

For example, to delete unwanted menu options from the Help menu pad, select the Edit push button that corresponds to the Help menu pad. When the submenu is displayed in the Menu Level: popup, use the Delete push button or the Delete Item option from the Menu menu popup to delete the first unwanted menu option, About FoxPro.... Continue deleting menu options in this way until the Help menu options resemble Figure 13.34.

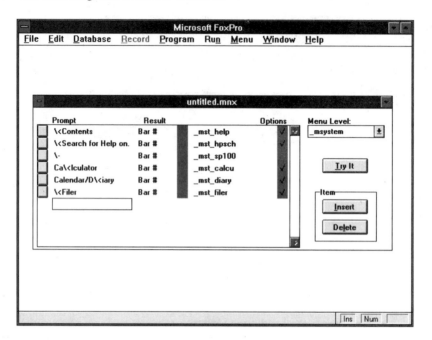

Figure 13.34 Deleting Help menu options

Adding New Menu Options

As mentioned earlier, you can add a new menu option to an existing menu pad by positioning the cursor on the location at which you want to insert the menu option and using the Insert push button or selecting the Insert Item option from the Menu popup. As an example, we will add the Quit menu option in the File menu pad after deleting other unwanted options. In addition, we will add a dividing line between the Print Setup and the Quit options.

For the dividing line, we will use Bar # named _mfi_sp100 as the result. To insert the dividing line like a menu option, first bring up the File submenu. Then position the cursor below the prompt for the dividing line and select the Insert push button or press Ctrl+I (or select the Insert Item option from the Menu popup). As a result, a new menu option entitled "New Item" appears in the menu option prompt. At this point, you can rename the prompt to \-. Select Bar # as the result and enter _mfi_sp100 as the bar name. Use the same procedure to add the Quit menu option below the dividing line so that your screen looks like Figure 13.35. Notice that the Submenu is selected as the Result by default.

Defining the Results of Menu Options

After we have created and named a menu option, the next step is to define its result, which determines what happens when the menu option is selected. The four options

Putting It All Together 613

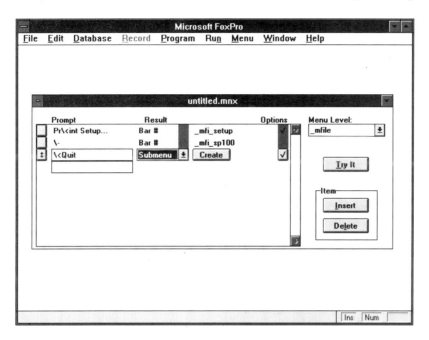

Figure 13.35 Adding the Quit option to the File menu

available from the result popup are discussed above. In our case, we want the Quit menu option to close our custom menu and return control to the default FoxPro System menu. The following sequence of two commands accomplishes this:

```
CLEAR
SET SYSMENU TO DEFAULT
```

The CLEAR command clears the desktop area of the screen, erasing anything displayed there. The SET SYSMENU command restores the FoxPro System menu bar. Since they are a set of two commands, they form a procedure; you should select Procedure as the result of the Quit prompt. The Quit prompt's text box now displays a Create push button. To define the procedure, select the push button and, when the Text Editor window opens, enter the two commands. Your screen should look like Figure 13.36. Close the Text Editor window by double clicking on the Control box or by pressing Ctrl+W. When you return to the Menu Design window, note that the Quit prompt's Create push button has been replaced by an Edit push button.

Rearranging Menu Options

Menu options can be reordered by moving an existing prompt up or down with the mouse or the keyboard. To change the order of a menu option with the mouse, click on the button at the left of the menu prompt. When a double-headed arrow appears,

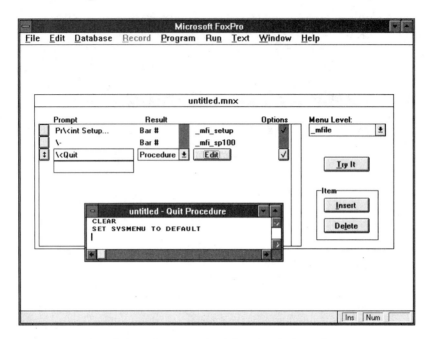

Figure 13.36 Defining the procedure for the Quit option

drag the menu option to the desired location. With the keyboard, position the cursor anywhere on the line associated with the prompt to be moved, then press the Ctrl key in conjunction with the up- or down-arrow key to move the prompt to the desired location.

TESTING THE MENU

During the design of the menu system, it is convenient to be able to make sure that the menu looks and is likely to behave in the way you expect. Selecting the Try It push button in the Menu Design window allows you to do just that—it causes the menu that you are designing to be displayed temporarily in place of FoxPro's default menu. Since we have just completed our first menu popup, this is a good time to preview our new menu system. When you select the Try It push button, the entire menu that you have created so far is displayed, and individual pads and menu options can be selected, as in Figure 13.37. Note, however, that the menu is display-only; none of the options are actually functional at this point. When you have finished previewing the menu, select the OK push button to return to the Menu Design window.

Putting It All Together 615

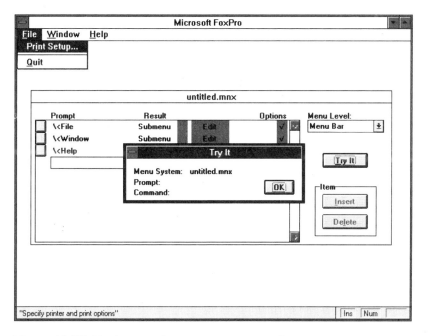

Figure 13.37 Trying out the custom menu options

ADDING NEW MENU PADS

So far, we have completed the definition of two menu pads and their associated popups. However, we still must add a number of other new menu pads—ViewData, EditData, Report, and Label—and their associated menu popups before our custom menu is complete. To add these menu pads, the Menu Design screen must display the menu bar. If your Menu Design screen currently shows one of the submenus, select the Menu Bar option from the Menu Level: popup.

You can insert a menu pad in the same way that you insert a menu option. So, to insert the ViewData menu pad between the existing File and Window menu pads, move the cursor to the Window prompt and either select the Insert push button, press Ctrl+I, or select the Insert Item option from the Menu popup. The Menu Builder adds a line for a new menu pad and labels it "New Item." Now you can type in the name of the new menu pad, ViewData. Since selecting the ViewData menu pad should open the Result menu popup with three menu options, you can accept the default result of Submenu. The Menu Design window should now appear like Figure 13.38.

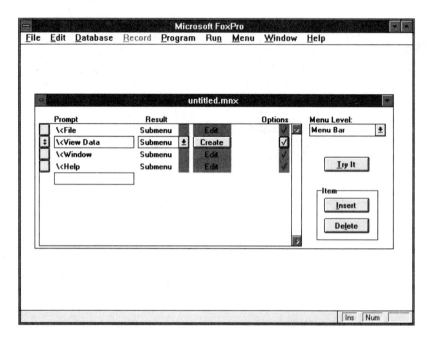

Figure 13.38 Inserting the ViewData menu option

Creating Menu Popups

To create the individual menu options in the ViewData menu popup, select the ViewData prompt's Create push button. When the Menu Builder opens a new ViewData submenu, you can begin defining its three menu options, which will allow you to view data in linked databases. These three options are:

- *Salesman/Office.* Displays data in the SALESMAN and OFFICE databases on the custom screen named SHOWSMOF.SCX. Displaying this screen requires only a single command:

  ```
  DO SHOWSMOF.SPR
  ```

  Consequently, select Command from the Result popup and enter the command in its adjacent text box.

- *Office/Salesman.* Displays data from the linked OFFICE and SALESMAN databases. Since the databases were linked using the SHOWOFSM.QPR RQBE query, we must have our menu system perform the query before it executes the screen program SHOWOFSM.SPR. Therefore, the result of the Office/Salesman prompt is a procedure that contains the following three commands:

  ```
  DO SHOWOFSM.QPR
  CLEAR
  DO SHOWOFSM.SPR
  ```

The CLEAR command is needed to erase the message that results from executing the query.

- *Region/Salesman.* Uses the SHOWREGN.SCX screen to display data from the linked REGION, ASSIGN, and SALESMAN databases. Like the Salesman/Office menu option, its result is a single command:

```
DO SHOWREGN.SPR
```

When you finish entering the three menu option prompts and defining the results, your Menu Design window should appear like Figure 13.39, in which you also can see the procedure for defining the function of the Office/Salesman menu option.

To complete the custom menu, now add the EditData, Report, and Label menu pads to the menu bar. Each of them results in a submenu, and each uses the first letter of its prompt as a hotkey. This enables that key to be used along with the Alt key to select the menu pad. Along with defining the hotkey by including the \< string in the prompt's text box, however, you must also enter this keystroke combination in the Key Definition dialog; otherwise, the first letter of the menu pad will be highlighted, but pressing it along with the Alt key will have no effect. To do this, select the Options check box and then select the Shortcut check box. The Menu Builder will then open the Key Definition dialog, which simply records your keystrokes as the shortcut key for that menu item. Simply press Alt+V for the ViewData menu pad, Alt+E for the EditData menu pad, Alt+R for the Report menu pad, and Alt+L for the Label menu pad.

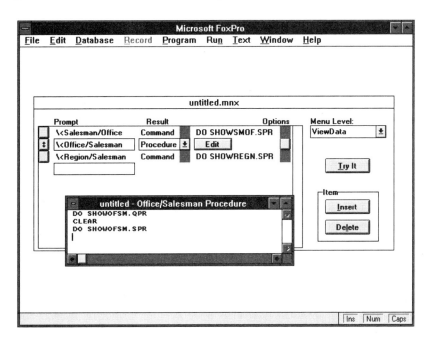

Figure 13.39 The ViewData menu options

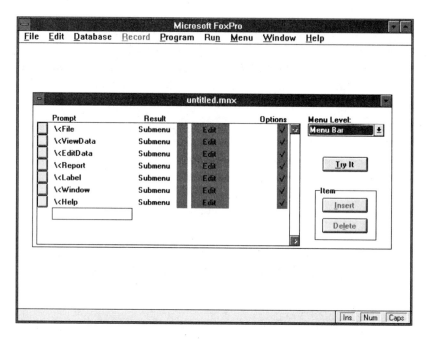

Figure 13.40 The custom menu pads

Once you have finished defining the additional menu pads for the custom menu, the contents of the Menu Design window should look like Figure 13.40. After defining the menu pads, you can continue to define their associated submenus. Figures 13.41, 13.42, and 13.43 show the submenus of the EditData, Report, and Label menu popups, respectively. Note that the Prompt text box truncates the full menu pad labels as well as the hotkeys in Figure 13.42. The first menu pad should read Compensation Summary (activated by Alt+C), the second should read Salary Percentages (activated by Alt+P). The third submenu should read Salary Summary by Sex (activated by Alt+S), while the fourth should read Salary Summary by Office (activated by Alt+O).

USING NESTED SUBMENUS

In designing custom menu systems with the Menu Builder, it is possible to have multiple levels of submenus. For example, on the menu bar, a menu pad can open a submenu that contains a number of menu options. One or more of these menu options, in turn, can have its own submenu with another set of menu options. This use of a submenu to call another submenu, which is referred to as nesting submenus, can continue for any number of levels.

Putting It All Together 619

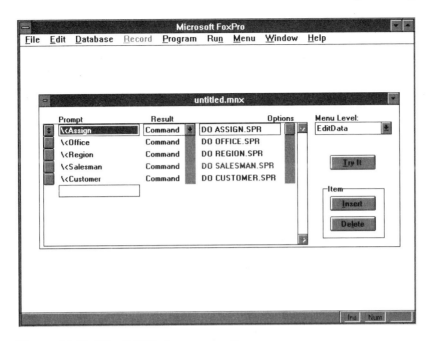

Figure 13.41 The EditData menu options

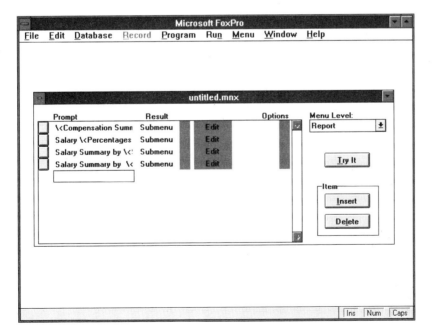

Figure 13.42 The Report menu options

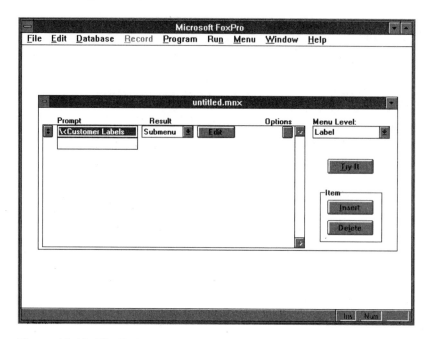

Figure 13.43 The Label menu option

The custom menu system that we have been building in the course of this chapter makes use of nested submenus. As you can see by referring back to Figure 13.17, the Report menu pad opens a submenu that contains four options: Compensation Summary, Salary Percentages, Salary Summary by Sex, and Salary Summary by Office. Selecting one of these four menu options, in turn, opens another submenu. So, if you select the Compensation Summary, for example, another menu popup with two options—On Screen and To Printer—opens.

The final step in designing our custom menu system, then, is to define these nested submenus. Let's begin with the submenu that is activated by selecting the Compensation Summary option. To create that submenu, navigate through the menu system until you return to the Report submenu, which should be displayed in the Menu Level: popup. Then select the Create push button that corresponds to the first menu option, Compensation Summary. FoxPro will create the new submenu in the Menu Design window. This can be filled in as shown in Figure 13.44.

Note that this is the final level of submenu. In each case, selecting a menu option will actually cause a report to be run as FoxPro executes either one or a series of commands. The commands are entered as a procedure for defining the function of a submenu option. For the On Screen submenu option, the following commands can be used to define its function:

```
USE C:\FOXPROW\FOXDATA\SALESMAN
SET ORDER TO LAST
REPORT FORM PAYREPRT PREVIEW
```

The first command opens the database file in the current work area, while the second command indexes the file by the last names (using the LAST index tag created earlier). The third command uses the PAYREPRT report layout that we designed earlier to display the report on the screen for preview.

To enter these commands in the procedure for the On Screen option, first select the Create push button and enter the code shown in the Text Editing window in Figure 13.44. When you are finished, close the Text Editor window.

The procedure for defining the To Print submenu option can be specified as follows:

```
USE C:\FOXPROW\FOXDATA\SALESMAN
SET ORDER TO LAST
REPORT FORM PAYREPRT TO PRINT
CLEAR
```

The TO PRINT clause in the third command sends the report to the printer instead of displaying it on the screen. Since FoxPro echoes on the screen reports that are being printed, it is best to clear the screen once a report has finished printing. This

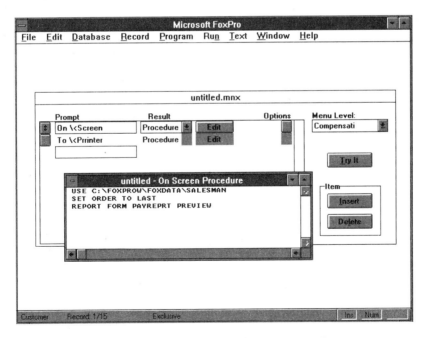

Figure 13.44 The Compensation Summary report submenu

is why we added the CLEAR command at the end of the procedure. On the other hand, because FoxPro will clear the screen when you finish previewing a report, you don't need to include the CLEAR command in the procedure for the On Screen submenu option.

The report menu contains three other reports—Salary Percentage Report, Salary Summary by Sex, and Salary Summary by Office—that have identical On Screen and To Printer options. Use the same procedure to complete these submenus. Figures 13.45, 13.46, and 13.47, respectively, show the submenus for the Salary Percentages, Salary by Sex, and Salary by Office menu options.

In Figure 13.45, notice that the procedure for the Salary Percentages submenu includes the following two commands:

```
SUM SALARY TO Total_Pay
RELEASE Total_Pay
```

The value of the memory variable that is used by the percentages report is created with the first command. The RELEASE command deletes the memory variable after the report is produced.

In the Menu Level: popup of Figure 13.47, notice, incidentally, that FoxPro has assigned a rather unusual name (_qd90z5qee) to the menu popup. This is because FoxPro ordinarily uses or concatenates the popup's menu prompt to form a

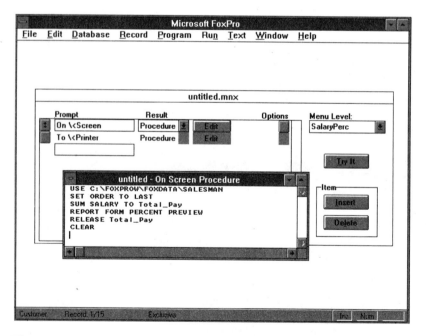

Figure 13.45 The Salary Percentages report submenu

Putting It All Together 623

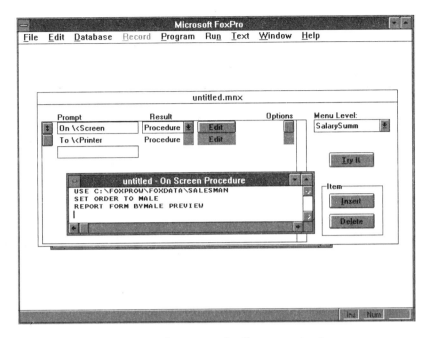

Figure 13.46 The Salary Summary by Sex report submenu

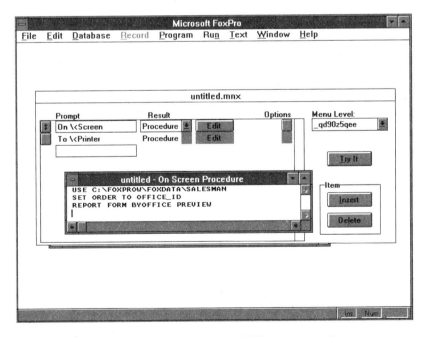

Figure 13.47 The Salary Summary by Office report submenu

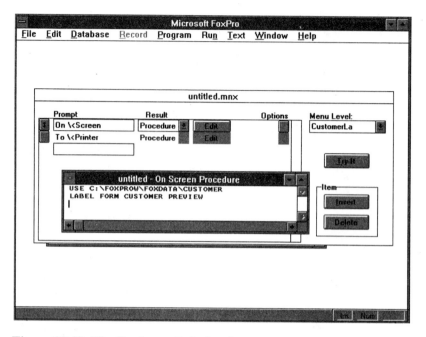

Figure 13.48 The Customer Labels submenu

10-character menu name. In this case, however, that would result in a duplicate submenu name, since the first 10 characters of the two menu options—Salary Summary by Sex and Salary Summary by Office—are identical. To avoid confusing itself, FoxPro assigns the name shown in the popup.

The submenu for the Customer Labels menu option of the Label menu pad is shown in Figure 13.48.

SAVING THE CUSTOM MENU FILE

Now that our nested submenus are defined, we have successfully used the Menu Builder to design a complete custom menu system. If you have not already done so, you should now save it as a menu file (a file with an .MNX file extension, which FoxPro assigns automatically) by selecting the Save As... option from the File menu popup and then entering the filename (MAINMENU.MNX).

GENERATING THE MENU PROGRAM FILE

As mentioned before, FoxPro actually stores a menu (.MNX) file as a special kind of database file that contains menu information. It cannot be used directly to display a menu. Instead, FoxPro uses the menu file to generate a menu program file (a program file with an extension of .MPR). It is this file that can be executed to display a menu system.

To generate a menu program file from the Menu Design window, select the Generate... option from the Program menu popup. FoxPro first checks to make sure that the menu system in the Menu Design window is identical to the menu system stored on disk. If there is a difference, FoxPro will respond with a prompt asking whether you want to save the changes to your file; selecting either No or Cancel will return you to the Menu Design window without generating the menu program file. If you select Yes, or if FoxPro can detect no difference between the two versions of the menu system, FoxPro will display the Generate Menu dialog shown in Figure 13.49. Here, FoxPro simply asks you to confirm the path and filename of the menu program file that it is about to create. By default, the path and root filename are the same as that of the menu file; the only difference is the .MPR file extension that FoxPro automatically uses for menu program files. You can, of course, change the path and filename of the menu program file that FoxPro is about to create, although we suggest that you do not modify FoxPro's default file extension. Once you select the Generate option, FoxPro will open a dialog box that graphically displays its progress in creating the menu program file. When it is finished and the file has been created, you can close the Menu Design window to exit the Menu Builder and return to the System menu bar.

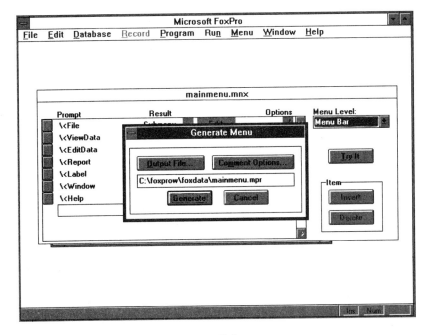

Figure 13.49 The Generate menu dialog

Using the Custom Menu

After you have generated the menu program file, you can bring up the custom menu by selecting the Do option from the Program menu popup. When the Do dialog appears, select the menu program filename. For example, to use the custom menu that you have created in the course of this chapter, select MAINMENU.MPR. As a result, the custom menu bar shown earlier in Figure 13.1 should replace FoxPro's default System menu bar.

Using FoxPro Commands

Although it is easiest to open and close the Menu Builder and select the menu files you would like to work with using FoxPro's menu driven interface, you also can open the Menu Design window by issuing either of the following commands:

```
CREATE MENU <menu filename>
```

or

```
MODIFY MENU <menu filename>
```

Normally, the first command is used to create a new menu, while the second is used to modify an existing menu. In practice, however, the operation of the two commands is virtually identical. As a result, you can issue either of the following commands to create a new custom menu named NEWMENU.MNX:

```
CREATE MENU NEWMENU

MODIFY MENU NEWMENU
```

In both cases, if FoxPro is unable to find a menu file named NEWMENU.MNX, it opens an empty Menu Design window and assigns the window the name NEWMENU.MNX. On the other hand, if FoxPro finds a menu file named NEWMENU.MNX, both commands will load the Menu Builder and open the file. The only practical difference between the commands occurs when the two commands are issued without any parameters. The command CREATE MENU will open a blank Menu Design window, which will be named UNTITLED.MNX. The command MODIFY MENU with no parameters, on the other hand, will cause FoxPro to prompt you with the File Open dialog.

To execute a menu program file, use the DO command. For example, to execute the MAINMENU.MPR menu program file, issue the following command:

```
DO MAINMENU.MPR
```

It is important to include the .MPR file extension. Otherwise, FoxPro will search for an ordinary program file with an extension of .PRG; if it is unable to find it, FoxPro will respond with a File Not Found error message.

Chapter Summary

In line with this book's premise that FoxPro places enormous power in the hands of the user without requiring a knowledge of programming, this concluding chapter focused on showing you how to integrate FoxPro's various components by building a customized menu system that lets you mold FoxPro to reflect the way you work and the projects you are working on.

The default menu system provided by FoxPro, as we saw, has been designed for flexibility so that it can meet the needs of all users, from the most inexperienced to the most advanced. However, if you intend to use FoxPro repeatedly to execute the same basic operations, developing a custom menu can enhance enormously the productivity of your FoxPro sessions.

In this chapter, we used the Quick Menu option, which opens a copy of the FoxPro default menu, to introduce you to the Menu Builder and to explore how it can be used to design a menu system. We then significantly modified the quick menu provided by FoxPro in order to develop a custom menu system that integrated the various procedures and applications that we developed in the course of this book. Although this menu system is a highly specific one that is geared to our sample applications, you can use it as a model or a starting point for your own menu system.

A customized menu system represents the culmination of FoxPro's interactive power, and provides a fitting conclusion to this book. Knowing just a few FoxPro programming commands, you can create an attractive, powerful menu system that is geared to the way that you work with FoxPro, and that can further increase your productivity while using FoxPro.

Appendix A
ASCII Table

0	NUL	1 ☺	SOH	2 ☻	STX	3 ♥	ETX	4 ♦	EOT	5 ♣ ENQ
6 ♠	ACK	7 •	BEL	8 ◘	BS	9 ○	HT	10 ◙	LF	11 ♂ VT
12 ♀	FF	13 ♪	CR	14 ♫	SO	15 ☼	SI	16 ►	DLE	17 ◄ DC1
18 ↕	DC2	19 ‼	DC3	20 ¶	DC4	21 §	NAK	22 ▬	SYN	23 ↨ ETB
24 ↑	CAN	25 ↓	EM	26 →	SUB	27 ←	ESC	28 ∟	FS	29 ↔ GS
30 ▲	RS	31 ▼	US	32		33 !		34 "		35 #
36 $		37 %		38 &		39 '		40 (		41)
42 *		43 +		44 ,		45 -		46 .		47 /
48 0		49 1		50 2		51 3		52 4		53 5
54 6		55 7		56 8		57 9		58 :		59 ;
60 <		61 =		62 >		63 ?		64 @		65 A
66 B		67 C		68 D		69 E		70 F		71 G
72 H		73 I		74 J		75 K		76 L		77 M
78 N		79 O		80 P		81 Q		82 R		83 S
84 T		85 U		86 V		87 W		88 X		89 Y
90 Z		91 [		92 \		93]		94 ^		95 _
96 à		97 a		98 b		99 c		100 d		101 e
102 f		103 g		104 h		105 i		106 j		107 k
108 l		109 m		110 n		111 o		112 p		113 q
114 r		115 s		116 t		117 u		118 v		119 w
120 x		121 y		122 z		123 {		124 |		125 }
126 ~		127 ⌂		128 Ç		129 ü		130 é		131 â
132 ä		133 à		134 å		135 ç		136 ê		137 ë
138 è		139 ï		140 î		141 ì		142 Ä		143 Å
144 É		145 æ		146 Æ		147 ô		148 ö		149 ò
150 û		151 ù		152 ÿ		153 Ö		154 Ü		155 ¢
156 £		157 ¥		158 ₧		159 ƒ		160 á		161 í
162 ó		163 ú		164 ñ		165 Ñ		166 ª		167 º
168 ¿		169 ⌐		170 ¬		171 ½		172 ¼		173 ¡
174 «		176 ░		177 ▒		178 ▓		179 │		180 ┤
181 ╡		182 ╢		183 ╖		184 ╕		185 ╣		186 ║

(continued)

187	╗	188	╝	189	╜	190	╛	191	┐
192	└	193	┴	194	┬	195	├	196	─
197	┼	198	╞	199	╟	200	╚	201	╔
202	╩	203	╦	204	╠	205	═	206	╬
207	╧	208	╨	209	╤	210	╥	211	╙
212	╘	213	╒	214	╓	215	╫	216	╪
217	┘	218	┌	219	█	220	▄	221	▌
222	▐	223	▀	224	α	225	β	226	Γ
227	π	228	Σ	229	σ	230	μ	231	
232		233		234	Ω	235	δ	236	∞
237		238	∈	239	∩	240	≡	241	±
242	≥	243	≤	244	⌠	245	⌡	246	÷
247	≈	248	°	249	·	250	•	251	√
252	^{n}	253	^{2}	254	■	255	NULL		

Index

ABS() function, 418
Accelerator keys, 601
   defining, 606
Active window, 85–86, 145
Add Alias check box, 446, 526
Add button, 90, 338
ADDITIVE clause, 397
Add to Index List button, 204
Alerts, 36
Alert windows, 518
All Fields list box, 149
All Files check box, 33
All radio button, 323
ALLTRIM() function, 403
Alt+C key combination, 235
Alt key, 77
Alt+S key combination, 247
Alt+Tab key combination, 87, 89
AND connector, 153, 331–332
APPEND BLANK command, 555
APPEND command, 289–290
Append From option, 281
Append option, 264–267, 516
Append push button, 560
.APP file extension, 61
ASC() function, 414–415
Ascending radio button, 183
Ascending sort order, 182, 195

ASCII (American Standard Code for
   Information Interchange), 182
Associated files, copying, 236
AT() function, 413–414
AVG() function, 371–373, 421–422

.BAK files, 60, 257
Bar # option, 610
Batch command processing, xix
Batch mode, 30
BETWEEN function, 153
Between operator, 355
   using, 358–359
Blank cells, 17
Boxes, drawing in reports, 473–474
Browse button, 38, 124–125
Browse columns, sizing, 134–135
BROWSE command, 169–170
BROWSE FIELDS command, 170
Browse menu option, 78
Browse menu pad, 31
Browse mode, 49, 80
   displaying data records in, 133–141
   editing of records in, 260–261
   entering data in, 113–114
   switching to, 132
Browse view, 131–132, 133, 136
BROWSE WINDOW command, 172

632 Index

Browse windows, 36, 38–39
  maximizing, 137–138
  minimizing, 138–139
  partitioning, 139–141
  switching between, 144–146
Browsing data, commands for, 169–171
Built-in functions, 397–431
By Column push button, 547
By Row push button, 547, 548

CALCULATE command, 419–423
Calculated fields
  adding to custom data screens, 552–554
  displaying, 370–371
Calculate dialog, 465
Calculate Field dialog box, 479–480, 484
Calculator tool, 46, 59
Calendar/Diary option, 59–60
Cancel option, 103
Case, in search strings, 327–328, 349
CDOW() function, 430
.CDX file extension, 61, 199–200
.CDX files, 216, 218, 223, 224–225
CDX radio button, 204, 206
Change mode, 39, 49, 80
  displaying data records in, 132
  editing records in, 259–260
  entering data in, 112–113
Change option, 146
Character fields, 100
  sorting, 182–184
Character string functions, 400–417
Character strings, searching for, 324–328
Check Box dialog, 549, 550
Check boxes, 33–34
  adding to data screens, 548–549
Check Box tool, 549
Child files, 294–301
CHR() function, 415–416
Clear button, 338
CLEAR command, 122, 613, 616–617, 622
Clear option, 73, 517
Clicking, 72–73
Clipboard, 459
Clock option, 126

Close button, 90, 125–126, 131
Close control button, 85
CLOSE DATABASE command, 160
Close option, 38, 114
Close window attribute, 518
CMONTH() function, 430
CNT() function, 419–420
Code Snippet dialog, 534, 541
Color dialog, 87, 88
Color icon, 87
Color Palette button, 89
Color Schemes drop-down list, 87, 89
Column grids, removing, 136
Column headings, in column reports, 437
Column reports, 52, 434–435
  components of, 438
  creating, 443–494
Columns, sizing, 134–135
Command keywords, abbreviating, 175
Commands. *See also* FoxPro commands
  for browsing data, 169–171
  for closing database files, 160
  for defining custom windows, 171–175
  for directing displayed data to printers, 168–169
  for displaying the data structure, 165–167
  for invoking Filer, 121–123
  for listing data records, 160–163
  for listing memo fields, 163–165
  for listing selected fields, 161–163
  for listing selected records, 163
  for opening database files, 159–160
  for setting filter conditions, 167–168
  using, 114–117
Command window, 44, 115
  moving, 73–74
Comment dialog, 465
Compact Index Structure check box, 221
Comparison operators, 344–345, 349–354
Complete Installation option, 67
Compound index files
  creating, 201–218
  modifying, 211
  nonstructural, 223, 230–231

saving in a structural format, 200–201
saving index tags to, 206–208
Confirmation messages, 35
Connect button, 90
Continue option, 328, 329
Control box, 37
Control Panel icon, 87
Control panels, adding to custom data screens, 535
Control Panel window, 87, 88
Copy dialog, 235, 237
COPY FILE command, 284–285
Copying
   of associated files, 236–237
   of database files using FoxPro commands, 284–285
   of multiple files, 237–239
   of selected data fields and records, 241–244
Copy option, 565
Copy Tagged Files As text box, 235
COPY TO command, 285, 291–292
Copy To dialog, 239–241, 242
Copy To menu option, using, 239–244
Copy To operation, 264, 282
COUNT() function, 373
CREATE command, 115
CREATE LABEL command, 510
CREATE MENU command, 626
Create push button, 613, 616, 620, 621
CREATE QUERY command, 378
CREATE REPORT command, 507–508
CREATE SCREEN command, 579
CREATE VIEW command, 302–303
CTOD() function, 400, 426
Ctrl+End key combination, 114, 264, 266, 287
Ctrl+F1 key combination, 85, 86, 143, 145
Ctrl+F2 key combination, 121
Ctrl+F4 key combination, 87
Ctrl+F5 key combination, 82, 84
Ctrl+F7 key combination, 81, 85
Ctrl+F8 key combination, 82
Ctrl+F9 key combination, 84, 138
Ctrl+F10 key combination, 82, 138

Ctrl+H key combination, 140
Ctrl+Home key combination, 111, 143
Ctrl key, 77
Ctrl+Tab key combination, 90
Ctrl+W key combination, 111, 143
Cursor keys, 76
Cursor option, 342
Custom color scheme, defining, 89
Custom data screens, 515–580
   adding a data maintenance panel to, 554–558
   adding check boxes to, 548–549
   adding graphic objects to, 546–549
   adding lists to, 566–567
   adding popups to, 561–564
   adding radio buttons to, 549–554
   adding spinners to, 567–569
   appending new records using, 560
   copying screen objects to, 564–566
   creating, 515–516
   deleting records using, 561
   displaying record deletion indicators on, 558–560
   displaying record numbers on, 557–558
   layouts for, 520–571
   multiple databases and, 571–579
   types of, 516–520
   using FoxPro commands with, 579–580
Custom form reports, creating, 491–494
Custom Installation option, 67
Custom menu bar, 583
Custom menu file, saving, 624
Custom menus, using, 626
Custom menu system
   creating, 581–627
   structure of, 584
Custom reports, creating, 457–487
Custom screens, 50–51
Custom setup, selecting desk accessories during, 57
Custom windows
   browsing data in, 172
   browsing memo fields in, 172–174
   closing, 173–174
   commands for defining, 171–175

634   Index

Cut option, 458
Cycle option, 145

Data
 displaying, 119–176
 editing, 233–292
 entering in Browse mode, 113–114
 entering in Change mode, 112–113
 grouping in reports, 482–487
 indexing, 198–232
 logical indexing of, 20–21
 printing, 159
 relating, 21–28
 sorting, 177–198
 storing in memory variables, 387–389
 versus information, 3–4
Database files, 12. See also Multiple
  database files
 adding new data records to, 264–267
 closing, 131
 command for closing, 160
 command for opening, 159–160
 copying, 233–244
 copying using FoxPro commands, 284–285
 deleting, 245–246
 deleting using FoxPro commands, 291
 modifying using FoxPro commands,
  284–292
 naming, 108
 opening, 128–130
 renaming, 244–245
 renaming using FoxPro commands, 286
 splitting, 282–283
 viewing, 123–159
Database management, xix
Database management system (DBMS), 3
Database menu pad, 31
Databases. See also Linked databases;
  Multiple databases; Relational databases
 creating, 97–117
 defined, 2
 linking, 293–319
Database structures
 displaying, 131
 modifying, 246–258

Data cells, 16–18
Data conversion functions, 425–428
Data directory, creating, 70–71
Data elements
 defined, 2
 identifying, 14–15
Data entities, 4–5
Data field attributes, defining, 98–102
Data fields. See also Selected data fields
 adding new, 247–251
 assigning to memory variables, 389–390
 deleting existing, 251–252
 hiding, 136
 identifying, 98
 moving, 136–137
 naming, 99
 rearranging existing, 251
 redefining existing, 252–254
 renaming, 252–253
 resetting, 151–152
 scrolling, 136
 selecting for display, 149–151
 selecting for quick reports, 447
 types of, 100–102
 versus memory variables, 384–385
Data Grouping dialog, 482, 483
Data Grouping option, 442, 482
Data models, 7–14
Data querying, 321–336. See also Queries;
  RQBE queries
 with RQBE (Relational Query By
  Example), 337–378
Data records. See also Marked data records;
  Selected data records
 adding to a database file, 264–267
 adding using FoxPro commands, 289–290
 command for listing, 160–163
 deleting existing, 268–274
 deleting using FoxPro commands,
  290–291
 editing using FoxPro commands, 286–289
 locating, 321–336
 marking for deletion, 268–269
 modifying, 259–281
 saving, 114

Index 635

saving edited, 264
sorting, 180–194
viewing, 131–141
Data relations, 4–7
types of, 5–7
Data screens. *See also* Custom data screens
adding check boxes to, 548–549
modifying existing, 531–546
using, 530–531
Data structures. *See also* Modified data structures
borrowing using FoxPro commands, 291–292
canceling changes in, 257
command for displaying, 165–167
creating index tags in, 216–218
defining, 97–102
flexibility in, 19–20
modifying using FoxPro commands, 286
saving, 108–109
Data tables, 10–14
creating, 102–114
eliminating redundancies in, 23, 27
entering data values in, 110–114
DATE() function, 362, 398, 478, 494
Date drop-down list, 155
Date fields, 101
sorting, 185–187, 188
Date manipulation functions, 398, 428–430
Dates
in reports, 437, 478
searching for, 328–330, 353
DAY() function, 429
dBASE, 10
dBASE files, compatibility with FoxPro files, 29
.DBF file extension, 60, 122
.DBF files, 47
Default buttons, 33
Default data directory, setting, 92–93
Default Drive drop-down list box, 126
Define Custom Colors button, 90
DEFINE WINDOW command, 172
Delete All button, 246
Delete button, 224, 245–246, 251–252, 561

DELETE command, 290, 555
DELETED() function, 558
Delete Item command, 603
Delete Item option, 611
Delete option, 269
DELETE TAG command, 229
DESCENDING keyword, 226
Descending radio button, 183
Descending sort order, 182, 195
Desk accessories, 57–60
Desktop screens, 516–517
Detail band, 43, 52, 444–445
Detail section, of a column report, 437
Dialog popups, 32–33
Dialogs, 32–35
nested, 34–35
Dialog windows, 518
DIFFERENCE() function, 409–410
Dimensions radio buttons, 450
DIR command, 122
Directories drop-down list box, 121
Directory list box, 33, 78
DIR SAMPLE.MEM command, 394, 395
Disk files, subdirectory for saving, 70–71
DISPLAY ALL command, 166
DISPLAY command, 307, 381
using, 165–167
Displayed data, commands for directing to printers, 168–169
DISPLAY MEMORY command, 391–392
DISPLAY STATUS command, 226–228, 229, 230
DISPLAY STRUCTURE command, 165
DISTINCT argument, 372–373
DO CASE statement, 540, 545
DO command, 580, 616–617, 626
Do dialog, 626
Do option, 626
Do Query button, 339, 346, 368, 502
DOS COPY command, 284
DOS DELETE command, 291
DOS ERASE command, 291
DOS prompt, accessing, 70
DOS RENAME command, 286
DOS-Style keystrokes option, 67

Double clicking, 74
DOW() function, 430
Down arrow, 39
Dragging, 73–74
Drive drop-down list, 108
Drive popup, 32
Drives drop-down list box, 121
Drop-down lists, 32
DTOC() function, 398, 400, 426
DTOS() function, 426–427
Duplicated records, identifying and removing, 277–281

EDIT command, 286–288
EditData menu options, 619
EditData menu pad, 55, 56, 591–595
Edited data records, saving, 264
Editing
   of data, 233–292
   of data records using FoxPro commands, 286–289
   of record contents, 259–264
   of records in Browse mode, 260–261
   of records in Change mode, 259–260
   of report text, 461
   of selected data fields, 261–262
   of selected data records, 262–264
Editing Options check boxes, 467
Edit keys, 260, 261
Edit mode, 211
Edit push button, 609
Edit Region tool, 522
ENDCASE statement, 540, 545
End key, 76
Enter key, 76
Environment check box, 33
Environment dialog, 499
Environment push button, 451, 452
Equals (=) command, 389
ERASE command, 231–232, 291
Esc key, 75
Exactly Like operator, 344, 345, 349, 352–353
Exact setting, 326–327

Example text box, 345
EXCEPT qualifier, 395, 396
Exclusive check box, 33, 34
.EXE file extension, 61, 62
Exit option, 117
Exit Windows option, 70
Expression Builder, 154–156, 192, 205, 212, 214, 242, 264, 270, 275, 305, 324
Express setup, 57

F1 function key, 45–46, 93–94
Field attributes, specifying, 103–107
Field dialog, 533, 534, 535, 552, 553, 557
Field labels, in form letters, 439
Field Name drop-down list, 343, 360, 361
Field Picker dialog, 34, 35, 149–150, 151, 152, 191, 242, 262, 447
Fields. *See* Data fields; Memo fields
Fields button, 149
Fields check box, 191, 192, 193
FIELDS clause, 196, 197, 285
Field Selection dialog, 368, 369
Fields Option box, 187
Field templates, defining, 467–469
Field tool, 442, 464, 479, 497, 552
Field types
   changing, 253–254
   specifying, 100–102
Field widths, resetting, 253
File alias, 298
File directories, displaying, 119–123
File extensions, 60–62
File menu pad, 582
File Open dialog, 32, 129, 180
File organization, 71
Filer, 57–59, 223–224
   using, 120–123, 234–239
FILER command, 121
File recovery, 246
Filer window, 120, 121
Files. *See* Database files; Index files
File Selection panel, 92, 93, 126, 127
File Selection push button, 126
Files Like text box, 120–121, 237

File system, 47
File Type drop-down list, 241
Fill Color option, 474
Fill option, 474
Filter conditions, 153–159
  commands for setting, 167–168
  defining, 154–155
  defining to save selected records, 191–194
  for marking groups of records for deletion, 270–271
Filter Data button, 149, 154, 264
Filter expressions
  entering, 155–156
  modifying existing, 156–159
Financial functions, 423–425
.FKY file extension, 62
Float data field, 100
Float window attribute, 518
Font dialog, 146, 147, 462, 463
Font option, 146
Footers
  in column reports, 437
  placing on reports, 478
For check box, 192, 193
FOR clause, 170, 197, 285, 333
For conditions, 323–324
Foreign field, 305
Foreign keys, 24, 25
Format dialog, 466–467
Form letters
  components of, 439
  created in Report Writer, 53
  layout of, 494
  producing, 52–53
Form reports, 435–436
  creating, 488–494
  custom, 491–494
Forms
  mailing label, 499
  office memo, 436
  quick report, 504
FoxBase, 10
FoxBASE+, 200
Foxdata subdirectory, 70–71, 119

FoxPro command language, xix
FoxPro commands. *See also* Commands
  creating mailing labels with, 510–512
  creating queries with, 378–381
  creating reports with, 507–510
  custom data screens and, 579–580
  indexing with, 225–232
  for invoking Filer, 121–123
  menu design using, 626–627
  modifying database files using, 284–292
  sorting with, 194–198
  using, 114–117, 159–175
FoxPro files, types of, 60–62
FoxPro for Windows, 29–30
  exiting, 94
  getting help in, 93–94
  installing, 65–70
  major components of, 46–62
  starting, 71–92
FoxPro for Windows icon, 71
FoxPro index files, 199–201
FoxPro reports. *See* Reports
FoxPro user interface, 30–46
Foxprow directory, 66
  creating a foxdata subdirectory within, 70–71, 119
FoxPro windows, components of, 36–37. *See also* Windows
.FPT file extension, 60
.FPT files, 47
FREEZE clause, 286, 289
.FRT file extension, 61
.FRX file extension, 61
Function arguments, 327–328
Function keys, 75
Functions
  built-in, 397–431
  character string, 400–417
  data conversion, 425–428
  date manipulation, 428–430
  financial, 423–425
  numeric, 417–419
  statistical, 419–423
Functions drop-down list, 372

Functions/Expressions text box, 370, 371, 372
FV() function, 424–425
.FXP file extension, 61

Generated Code box, 529
Generate Menu dialog, 625
Generate option, 625
Generate Screen dialog, 527, 528–529
GO BOTTOM command, 166
GOMONTH() function, 430
GOTO command, 287
GOTO 2 command, 285
GO TOP command, 166, 540
Graphical user interface (GUI), 29
Graphic objects
   adding to reports, 472
   adding to screens, 546–549
   in column reports, 437–438
Graphic push button prompts, defining, 544–546
Graphics features, 42
Graphics programs, 544
Grid option, 136
Group band, adding to a report form, 482–483
Group Footer band, 446
Group Header band, 445–446
Group headings, in column reports, 437
Group Info dialog, 483
Groups of records, marking for deletion, 269–271
Group statistics, in column reports, 437
Group summary statistics, producing, 375–378

Having check box, 376, 378
Help, obtaining, 93–94
Help key, 46
Help menu pad, 57, 600–601
Help menu popup, 609
   options in, 72–73
Help windows, 45–46
   scroll controls in, 94
Hidden windows, 80
Hide option, 144
Hierarchical data model, 7–9

Home key, 76
Hotkeys, 32
   defining, 604
   defining for pushbuttons, 539

.IDX file extension, 61, 199–200
.IDX files, 218–225, 229
IDX radio button, 204
Ignore Case check box, 181, 183
IIF() function, 486
Index Description text box, 209, 210
Index dialog, 202, 203, 211, 212
Indexes
   master, 209–211, 228–229
   rebuilding, 258
Indexes list box, 208
Index File Name dialog, 221
Index files. *See also* Compound index files
   deleting, 223–225
   deleting using FoxPro commands, 231–232
   FoxPro, 199–201
   removing, 223
   saving in a compact format, 200
   standard, 218–223, 229
Indexing
   of data, 198–232
   of data records, 20–21
   with FoxPro commands, 225–232
   versus sorting, 178–179
Index Key button, 212, 214
Index keys, 199
Index Key text box, 204, 206
INDEX ON command, 225–226, 228, 229, 230
Index status, displaying, 226, 227
Index tags, 200, 201–202
   adding new, 212
   adding with a FoxPro command, 228
   creating, 202–205
   creating in a data structure, 216–218
   modifying existing, 213–216
   modifying with a FoxPro command, 229
   removing existing, 213
   removing with a FoxPro command, 229

saving to a compound index file, 206–208
   using multiple data fields in, 205–206
Information, versus data, 3–4
In operator, using, 359
Input Field (Get) radio button, 558
Insert button, 247–248
Insert Item command, 604
Insert Item option, 612, 615
Installation types, selecting, 67
INT() function, 418
INT(x) function, 398
Interactive mode, 30
Interactive processing, xix

Joint search conditions
   defining, 363, 364
   multiple, 365

Keyboard
   basics of using, 74–77
   moving data fields with, 137
   resizing columns with, 135
Keyboard cursor, 76
Key combinations, 77
Key Definition dialog, 606, 617

Label Designer, 42, 47, 54–55, 433
Label Designer window, 494, 495–497
Label Design screen, 54
Label dialog, 499
LABEL FORM command, 512
Label Layout window, 42–43
Label menu options, 620
Label menu pad, 597
Labels. *See* Mailing labels
Landscape radio button, 92
.LBT file extension, 61
.LBX file extension, 61
LEFT() function, 410–411
Left arrow, 39
LEN() function, 416–417
Less Than operator, 356–358
Letters. *See* Form letters
Like comparison operator, 349–354
LIKE operator, 392

Lines, drawing in reports, 474–475
Line tool, 442, 474–475, 497, 546
Linked databases, 293–319
   many-to-many relations in, 311–318
   many-to-one relations in, 309–310
   one-to-many relations in, 304–309
   one-to-one relations in, 294–304
Linking keys, 24–25
Link Partitions option, 141
List boxes, 33
LIST command, 160–164, 194, 301,
   307–309, 317–318
List dialog, 566, 567
List Files of Type drop-down list, 180, 348
List Files of Type popup, 32–33
List tool, 566
Local area networks (LANs), 29
LOCATE commands, 333, 379
Locate dialog, 322, 323
Locate operation, 379–381, 390
   using, 322–333
Locate Record For text box, 379, 380
LOG() function, 419
LOG10() function, 418
Logical connectors, 153, 331–333
Logical drop-down list, 155
Logical fields, 101
   sorting, 187, 189
Logical operators, 157
Logical values
   grouping report data by, 484–487
   searching for, 330, 353–354
LOWER() function, 405–406
LOWER(LAST), 327
LTRIM() function, 401–402

Mailing label forms, 499
Mailing labels, 494–499
   creating with FoxPro commands, 510–512
   defining the dimensions of, 497–498
   designing, 54–55, 495–498
   previewing, 599
   producing from multiple databases,
      506–507
   viewing on the screen, 498

640   Index

Many-to-many data relations, 6–7
  handling, 25–28
  linking databases having, 311–318
Many-to-one data relations, linking
  databases having, 309–310
Marked data records
  recalling, 271–274
  removing, 274
Master index
  designating, 209–211
  designating with a FoxPro command,
    228–229
Master table, primary key in, 25
Math drop-down list, 155
MAX() function, 373, 422–423
Maximize button, 84, 86, 114, 138
MDY() function, 429
.MEM file extension, 61, 393–394
Memo fields, 40, 102
  browsing in a custom window,
    172–174
  commands for listing, 163–165
  querying, 379–381
  viewing, 142–143
Memo field width, changing, 164–165
Memory files, saving memory variables to,
  393–395
Memory variables, 383–397
  assigning data fields to, 389–390
  deleting, 395–396
  deleting from a memory file, 397
  displaying, 390–393
  naming, 386–387
  restoring, 396–397
  saving to memory files, 393–395
  storing data in, 387–389
  types of, 385–386
  using in reports, 487–488, 509–510
Memory Variables check box, 526
Memo window, 40–41, 143
Menu bar, 30–31, 608
Menu Builder, 47, 55–56, 601–602
  opening, 602
Menu design, using FoxPro commands,
  626–627

Menu Design window, 43, 44, 55, 602, 603
  features of, 607–608
Menu Level: popup, 609–611, 615, 622
Menu options, 55, 608
  adding new, 612
  defining the results of, 612–613
  deleting existing, 611–612
  rearranging, 613–614
Menu pad prompts, defining, 603–604
Menu pad results, defining, 604–605
Menu pads, 31, 55–56, 608
  adding new, 615–618
  deleting existing, 610–611
  deleting unwanted, 603
Menu popups, 608
  creating, 616–618
Menu program file, generating, 624–626
Menu system, 30–32
Menu testing, 614–615
Message push button, 607
Microsoft Word icon, 65
MIN() function, 373, 422–423
Minimize button, 84, 86, 138–139
Minimize window attribute, 518
Minimum Installation option, 67
MLINE function, 164, 381
.MNT file extension, 61
.MNX file extension, 61, 602, 624
Mode option, 474
Modified data structures
  saving, 254–255
  viewing records in, 255–256
Modify button, 211, 213, 247
MODIFY LABEL command, 512
MODIFY MENU command, 626
MODIFY QUERY command, 378
MODIFY REPORT command, 508
MODIFY SCREEN command, 580
MODIFY STRUCTURE command, 286
Modify Structure dialog, 255
MONTH() function, 429
More Than/Less Than operator, using, 356–358
Mouse
  basics of using, 71–74
  installing, 71

Index 641

moving data fields with, 137
moving report objects using, 460
resizing Browse columns with, 135
using to select a push button, 539
Mouse pointer, 71–72
Move button, 181
Move Field option, 137
.MPR file extension, 61, 627
.MPR files, 625
.MPX file extension, 61
MS-DOS Prompt icon, 70
Multiple database files
  browsing, 174–175
  using in RQBE queries, 366–370
  viewing data records in, 143–148
Multiple databases
  custom data screens and, 571–579
  producing mailing labels from, 506–507
  producing reports from, 500–502
Multiple data fields
  sorting, 190, 196
  using in index tags, 205–206
Multiple files, copying, 237–239
Multiple records, replacing data for, 275–277

Nested dialogs, 34–35
Nested submenus, using, 618–624
Network data model, 9–10
New database files, creating, 103
New Key button, 205, 212
New Label dialog, 495, 496
New option, 103, 220
New text button, 33
No Duplicates check box, 340–341
No Initial Form Feed check box, 454
Nonstructural compound index files, 223
  creating using FoxPro commands, 230–231
NOTE memo field, 40, 47, 106, 165, 173
NOT operator, using, 355
Numeric fields, 101
  sorting, 185
Numeric field templates, defining, 469
Numeric functions, 398, 417–419
Numeric values, searching for, 328, 352–353

Object Order dialog, 547–548
Objects
  graphic, 437–438, 472, 546–549
  moving and resizing, 73–74
  report, 458–460
  screen, 564–566
Office memorandum form, 436
OFF keyword, 407
OK button, 254–255
One-to-many data relations, 5–6
  handling, 22–25
  linking databases having, 304–309
One-to-one data relations, 5
  handling, 22
  linking databases having, 294–299
ON keyword, 196
On Screen option, 595
On Screen submenu option, defining, 620–621
Open option, 32
Open button, 125
Open dialog, 78, 79
Open File dialog, 32, 124, 128–129, 202, 203
Operators
  comparison, 344–345, 349–354
  logical, 157
Ordering Criteria list box, 342
OR logical connector, 153, 331, 332–333
  using, 363–366
Output box, 181, 184, 185
Output data fields, selecting, 339–341
Output destinations, identifying, 341–342
Output Field (Say) radio button, 552, 557, 558
Output Fields list box, 338
Output File box, 204
Output Location options, 454
.OVL file extension, 62

PACK command, 290, 555
Pack operation, 268, 274, 278
Pack push button, 561
Pad Name push button, 607
Page Footer band, 52, 445

Page Header band, 52, 444
  resizing, 461–462
Page headings, in form letters, 439
Page Layout dialog, 450
Page Layout option, 441, 484, 497–498
Page layouts, specifying for quick reports, 450–451
Page numbers, in column reports, 437
Page Preview dialog, 448
Page Preview option, 441, 498
Page spinner, 448
Paintbrush program, 544
Panel buttons, 92, 125
Paradox, 10
Parent files, 294–301
Partitions option, 139–140
Paste command, 459
Paste option, 565
Pattern symbols, use in searching, 351–352
PAYMENT() function, 423–424
Payout Layout dialog, 499
Pen Color option, 474, 475
Pen option, 474, 475
PgDn key, 76, 260
PgUp key, 76, 260
Picture buttons, 125
Picture dialog, 572
Picture fields, 100
Picture radio button, 545
Pictures, adding to reports, 475–487
Picture tool, 442, 475, 497, 546
.PJT file extension, 61
.PJX file extension, 61
Point-and-click action, 72–73
Pointing, 71–72
Popup dialog, 562, 563
Portrait radio button, 92
Preserve directories box, 236
PREVIEW keyword, 509, 512
Preview Picture box, 571, 572
.PRG file extension, 61
Primary field, 305
Primary key, in master tables, 25
Print dialog, 455
Printer control commands, 416

Printers
  commands for directing displayed data to, 168–169
  selecting for quick reports, 451–452
  setting up, 90–92
Printers dialog, 90, 91
Printers icon, 90
Printing
  of data, 159
  of mailing labels, 499
  of quick reports, 449–452, 453–456
Print menu option, 159
Print Order buttons, 451
Print Report dialog, 456
Print Setup dialog, 91, 92, 451
Print Setup option, 90, 582
Print When dialog, 465
Private memory variables, 391
Program Manager window, 65, 66
Project Builder, 56–57
Project Manager, 43, 47
Project windows, 43, 44
Prompt list box, 603, 608
Prompt options, defining, 605–607
Prompt Options dialog, 605–606
PROPER() function, 412–413
Public memory variables, 391
Push Button dialog, 537–538, 541, 542, 555
Push button prompts, defining, 538
Push buttons, 33
  adding to custom data screens, 535–546
  in the Help window, 94
Push Button tool, 535–537, 545, 555

.QPR file extension, 61, 348
.QPX file extension, 61
Queries. *See also* RQBE queries
  creating with FoxPro commands, 378–381
  modifying existing, 348
  repeating existing, 348
  saving to a file, 346–348
Query results, ordering, 342–343
Question mark (?) command, 392–393
Quick Data screen, displaying data with, 530

Quick menu
  creating, 602–626
  modifying, 610–614
Quick Menu option, 603
Quick Report dialog, 446, 447
Quick Report form, viewing, 504
Quick report layouts, using, 490–491
Quick Report option, 442, 446
Quick Report push button, 453–454
Quick reports
  creating, 446–456
  default form layout of, 491
  printing, 449–452
Quick Screen layout, using, 525–527
Quick Screen option, 547, 569, 573
Quit menu option, 612, 613
Quit option, 94

Radio Button dialog, 551
Radio buttons, 34
  adding to screens, 549–554
Radio Button tool, 551
RBase, 10
Read Only check box, 33, 34
RECALL command, 290, 555
Recall option, 273
RECNO() function, 557
Record contents, editing, 259–264
Record groups, marking for deletion, 269–271
Record menu popup, 152
Record pointer, 321–322
Records. *See also* Data records
  deleting groups of, 269–271
  editing in Browse mode, 260–261
  editing in Change mode, 259–260
  removing duplicate, 277–281
  scrolling, 136
Record scope, defining, 269–270
Record view, 131–132
Rectangle tool, 442, 473, 497, 546
Redundant data, avoiding, 20
Related data records, viewing, 299–301
Related files, saving to View files, 301–303
Relational database management system
  (RDBMS), 29

Relational databases
  designing, 14–28
  properties of, 15–18
  requirements for designing, 18–21
Relational data model, 10–14
  data table in, 11
Relational tables, 13–14, 25
  structuring, 16
Relations operation, 294–295, 312
RELEASE ALL LIKE command, 396
RELEASE command, 396, 397, 622
Remove button, 181, 223
Remove From List button, 204, 213
RENAME command, 286
Rename operation, 244–245
Replace operation, 275–277
Report bands, 443–446
  inserting text into, 462–464
  placing data fields into, 464–465
  resizing, 461–475
Report column widths, changing, 470–471
Report dates
  in column reports, 437
  placing, 478
Report Design Tool Palette, 442–443
Report Design window, 36, 440
Report dialog, 453–455
Report environment, saving, 452–453
Report Expression Builder, 466
Report Expression dialog, 464–465, 466, 477
Report field expressions, defining, 466
Report fields
  formatting, 466–467
  reformatting, 469–470
REPORT FORM command, 508
Report form file, changing the name of,
  505–506
Report forms, revising, 502–505
Report/Label option, 342
Report layout, 53
Report Layout window, 42, 43, 52, 434, 440,
  457, 490
Report menu, 440–443
Report menu options, 619
Report menu pad, 31, 595–597

Report objects
 deleting, 458
 moving, 460
 restoring deleted, 458–459
 selecting, 457–458
Report Picture dialog, 475, 476
Reports, 433–494. *See also* Column reports; Custom reports; Form reports; Quick reports
 components of, 436–439
 creating, 439–443
 creating with FoxPro commands, 507–510
 modifying existing, 457–461
 numbering the pages of, 477
 printing, 453–456
 producing from multiple databases, 500–502
 saving, 452–453
 types of, 434–436
 using memory variables in, 487–488
Report summary, adding to a report, 479–482
Report title, 437
 adding, 472
Report Variables dialog, 488, 489
Report Writer, xx, 30, 42, 46, 52–54, 433, 439, 443
Resize Partitions option, 142
RESTORE command, 397, 510
Restore Environment check box, 453
RESTORE FROM command, 396–397
Result popup, 604, 610
Return key, 76
Revert option, 459
RIGHT() function, 410–411
Right arrow, 39
ROUND() function, 418
Round Rectangle tool, 442, 474, 497, 546
RQBE (Relational Query By Example), xx, 46, 321. *See also* RQBE queries
RQBE Builder, 41, 47–49
RQBE Display Options dialog, 500, 502
RQBE Group By dialog, 375
RQBE queries, 337–378, 588, 589
 creating, 337–346
 defining selection criteria for, 343–346, 348

 executing, 346
 extracting report data with, 500–502
 specifying compound selection criteria for, 363
 using formulas in selection criteria for, 359–362
 using functions in selection criteria for, 362
 using multiple database files in, 366–370
RQBE Quick Report dialog, 500–502
RQBE Select Fields dialog, 339, 340–341, 372, 500, 501
RQBE window, 41, 47–49, 337–339
RTRIM() function, 400–401
Ruler/Grid option, 441–442, 443, 471, 525
RUN command, 284–285
Run option, 66

SAVE ALL command, 394–395
Save As dialog, 108, 184, 239
Save As option, 484, 499
Save As text box, 241
SAVE TO command, 393–394
Save View dialog, 302
Scope button, 322–323
Scope dialog, 270, 271
Screen background, adding, 569–571
Screen Builder, xx, 42, 46, 49–51, 515, 516, 520, 573
 System window in, 525
Screen Builder window, 521
Screen Color dialog, 571
Screen colors, setting, 87–90
Screen design tools, 522
Screen Design window, 41–42
Screen layout
 formatting data fields in, 532–533
 saving, 527–531
 setting data ranges for data fields in, 533–534
 using data-only fields in, 534–535
Screen Layout dialog, 522–524, 571
Screen menu pad, 521
Screen objects, copying to custom data screens, 564–566
Screen program file, generating, 527–530

Screens. *See* Custom data screens; Data screens
Screen Set box, 528
Scrollable list boxes, 33
Scroll control, 39, 132
Scroll Down button, 33
Scrolling, of data fields and records, 136
Scroll Up button, 33
.SCT file extension, 61
.SCX file extension, 60, 61, 516, 527, 528, 529
Search conditions, defining, 323–324
SEEK commands, 335–336
Seek operations, 332
   using, 333–336
See SQL button, 339
Select a Table list box, 80, 366, 367
Select Directory dialog, 93, 94, 126
Selected data fields
   command for browsing, 170
   command for listing, 161–163
   copying using Copy To, 241–244
   editing, 261–262
   saving, 191
   saving with the SORT command, 196–198
   viewing, 148–152
Selected data records
   command for browsing, 170–171
   command for listing, 163
   copying using Copy To, 241–244
   defining filter conditions to save, 191–194
   editing, 262–264
   saving with the SORT command, 196–198
   viewing, 152–159
Selected Fields list box, 149, 150
Selection Criteria text box, 363
Selection Pointer button, 442
Selection Pointer tool, 457, 471
Set As Default Printer button, 90
Set Fields operation, 261–262
SET FILTER command, 167–168
SET FILTER TO command, 171
SET HEADING ON command, 410
Set Index Order dialog, 295
SET MEMOWIDTH command, 164, 416

Set Miscellaneous Values panel, 92, 128
Set Option panel button, 326
Set Options On/Off panel, 92, 126, 127
Set Order button, 218, 281
SET ORDER command, 228–229, 336, 509
Set Order operation, 209
SET PRINT commands, 169
SET RELATION command, 298–299
SET RELATION Expression Builder, 295
SET RELATION TO command, 308
SETSYSMENU command, 613
Setup button, 124, 131
Setup dialog, 34, 35, 124, 131, 132, 148–149, 484
   defining index tags in, 202
Setup option, 31
SET VIEW TO command, 304
SET WINDOW OF MEMO TO command, 173
Shadow window attribute, 518
Shift key, 77
Shift+Tab key combination, 106
Shortcut keys, 601
   defining, 606
Shortcut option, 605, 606
Show Position option, 441, 444
Single Index File radio button, 220, 221
Single-value data cells, using, 16–18
Size control, 39, 81
Size Field option, 135
Skip For push button, 606
Snap to Grid option, 442, 471, 480
SORT command, 194–196
Sort Destination File box, 184
Sort dialog, 180, 181
Sorted records, viewing, 184–185
Sorting
   of data, 177–198
   of data records, 180–194
   with FoxPro commands, 194–198
   versus indexing, 178–179
Sort option, 180
Sort order
   defining, 182–191
   specifying, 195

646 Index

Sort Order box, 183, 187
SOUNDEX() function, 407–409
SPACE() function, 406–407
Space key, 34
Specific Printer radio button, 90
Spinner dialog, 569, 570
Spinners, adding to custom data screens, 567–569
Spinner tool, 569
.SPR file extension, 60, 61, 516, 527, 529
.SPX file extension, 61, 516
SQRT() function, 417
Standard index files
    creating, 218–223
    creating using FoxPro commands, 229
Statistical functions, 398, 419–423. *See also* Summary statistics
STD() function, 422
STORE command, 387–389
STR() function, 428
String drop-down list, 155
String functions, 398
Structural compound index files
    creating, 201–218
    creating with a FoxPro command, 225–228
Structural index file, 179
Structural Index Structure check box, 223
Structured Query Language (SQL), 339
STUFF() function, 407
Subdirectories, highlighting database files in, 80
Submenus, nested, 618–624
SUBSTR() function, 398, 411–412
SUM() function, 373, 398, 420–421
Summary band, 52, 446
    adding to a report form, 479
Summary Information Only check box, 455
Summary statistics
    in column reports, 437
    displaying, 371–375
System capacities, 62
System menu, 581–582
System menu pads, 43
System menu popup, defining, 608–610
System variables, 392

System window, 518, 519
    in Screen Builder, 525
System window screens, 520–521

Tab key, 76–77
Table/DBF option, 342
Table/DBF radio button, 34
Tables. *See also* Data tables
    creating, 102–114
    organizing data in, 15–16
    relational, 13–14, 16
    simplicity in, 21
Table Structure dialog, 103, 104, 109, 117, 216–218, 247, 248
Tag All button, 237
Tag box, 218
Tag Name text box, 204, 206
Tag None button, 235
TALK setting, 388
.TBK file extension, 60
Templates, field, 467–469
Text
    editing in reports, 461
    inserting into Report bands, 462–464
Text editing windows, 44–45, 621
Text editor, 111
Text Editor window, 613
Text tool, 442, 461, 462–464, 497
Thumb button, 33
Thumb control, 39
TIME() function, 398, 399
Title band, 444
Title bars, 36–37
Title Summary dialog, 479
Title/Summary option, 442, 472, 479
.TMP file extension, 62
Tool Palette, 442–443
TO PRINT clause, 168, 509, 512
To Printer option, 595
To Print submenu option, defining, 621–622
TRIM() function, 400–401, 491–493, 505
Try It dialog, 608
Try It push button, 607–608, 614
.TXT file extension, 62

Index 647

Type drop-down list, 106
Type fonts, setting, 146–148

Undo operation, 459
Undo option, 473
Undo Paste option, 606
Unique check box, 204
UNIQUE keyword, 226
Unique option, 278
Up arrow, 39
Up/Lo check box, 349
UPPER() function, 403–404
UPPER(LAST), 327–328
USE command, 159–160, 194, 225, 231, 509
Use Fields list box, 150–151, 262
User windows, 518, 519, 520, 524

VAL() function, 427–428
Variable Definition dialog, 488, 489
Variables option, 442, 488
Verify button, 154, 155, 192
Vertical radio button, 543–544
ViewData menu options, 617
ViewData menu pad, 583–591
View files
    saving related files to, 301–303
    using existing, 303–304
Viewing
    of database files, 123–159
    of data records, 131–141
    of mailing labels, 498
    of memo fields, 142–143
    of multiple database files, 143–148
    of the Quick Report form, 504
    of quick reports, 448–449
    of records in modified data structures, 255–256
    of related data records, 299–301
    of selective fields, 148–152
    of selective records, 152–159
    of sorted records, 184–185
View menu option, 78, 123
View panel, 126

View window, 37–38, 78, 79
    invoking, 123–128
    linking databases in, 573, 574
    Panel buttons in, 92
.VUE file extension, 61

Warning dialogs, 35
While condition, 323–324
Wildcard characters, 237, 284, 351, 394, 396
Window attributes, 518
Window frame patterns, 518–519
Window icons, arranging, 84–85
Window menu options, 600
Window menu pad, 78, 597–600
Windows, 36–46, 77–78. *See also* Browse windows; Custom windows
    activating, 85–86
    closing, 86–87
    installing, 65
    maximizing, 37, 82–83
    minimizing, 37, 84
    moving, 80–81
    opening, 78–80
    sizing, 78, 81–83
    types of, 518
Window screens, 517–520
    creating, 520–527
Window Splitter, 39–40
Window Splitter button, 139, 142
Windows-Style Keystrokes option, 67
Window Style dialog, 524
Window type, selecting in Screen Builder, 524–525
.WIN file extension, 62
Word for Windows window, 65
Word Setup program icon, 65
Working Directory button, 93

YEAR() function, 429

ZAP command, 291, 292
Zoom control, 38
Zoom control button, 85
Zoom In button, 448–449